THE
INSIDERS'®
GUIDE
TO

The Lake
Superior Region

THE INSIDERS' GUIDE TO
The Lake Superior Region

by
Susan Stanich
&
Janet Blixt

The Insiders' Guides Inc.

Co-published and marketed by:
Duluth News-Tribune
424 W. First St.
P.O. Box 169000
Duluth, MN 55816-9000
(218)723-5281

Co-published and distributed by:
The Insiders' Guides Inc.
The Waterfront • Suite 12
P.O. Box 2057
Manteo, NC 27954
(919) 473-6100

•

FIRST EDITION
1st printing

•

Copyright ©1996
by Duluth News-Tribune

•

Printed in the United States
of America

•

Publications from The Insiders'
Guides® series are available at special
discounts for bulk purchases for sales
promotions, premiums or
fundraisings. Special editions,
including personalized covers, can be
created in large quantities for special
needs. For more information, please
write to The Insiders' Guides Inc.,
P.O. Box 2057, Manteo, NC 27954
or call (919) 473-6100 x 233.

ISBN 0-912367-92-X

Duluth News-Tribune

Specialty Publications Director
Sharon Almirall

Editor
Cindy Finch

Sales Manager
Jan Zigich

Artists
M. Jill Bugbee
Ted Heinonen
Diane Schafer

The Insiders' Guides Inc.

Publisher/Editor-in-Chief
Beth P. Storie

President/General Manager
Michael McOwen

Affiliate Sales and Marketing Director
Rosanne Cheeseman

Partner Services Director
Giles MacMillan

Sales and Marketing Director
Julie Ross

Creative Services Director
Mike Lay

Online Services Director
David Haynes

Managing Editor
Theresa Shea Chavez

Fulfillment Director
Gina Twiford

Project Editor
Dan DeGregory

Project Artist
Stephanie Myers

Preface

Can you imagine the daunting task of planning, pulling together and writing about food, festivals, fishing and more in a three-state, two-country area all united in commonality only by the wet boundary of Lake Superior? To paraphrase the late Jerry Garcia, it's been a long, strange trip. But in writing this preface, we feel we've returned home after completing a whirlwind tour replete with discoveries and surprises about our beloved Lake Superior region. We pulled in the driveway a little more savvy about assumptions we'd set out with and refreshed by our confirmed belief that we continue to be both students and teachers throughout our lifetimes.

The Insiders' Guide® to the Lake Superior Region is for anyone who is drawn to the mystery and power of Lake Superior, the world's largest freshwater lake. We can offer you some prime spots to simply stare at the Lake — or paint it, photograph it, fish it, boat it or watch it at a distance from the shore in all its fury during a November storm.

This guide is for anyone who finds solace and rejuvenation in the outdoors. We can recommend city and state parks, national forests and wilderness areas in which to camp, hike, bike, hunt, fish, canoe and kayak. We concur with Henry David Thoreau who wrote more than 100 years ago: "In wildness is the preservation of the world."

This guide is for anyone who lives in or is relocating to the area. We hope to help you deal with some practical but pressing everyday matters: finding child care for your son or daughter, a medical specialist for your partner, housing options for a parent or the right school for your children or yourself.

This guide is for anyone who finds pleasure and intrigue in historic places and the stories they tell. We believe, as American architect Frank Lloyd Wright once said, "architecture is the truest record of life as it was lived"; so, we have picked some of our favorite buildings and places for you to explore and admire.

This guide is for anyone who believes in the power of the performing and visual arts to transform the mind and soul. Lake Superior and its constantly changing landscape inspire many visual artists, musicians and writers. We've included a compendium of galleries, theaters, museums, presentation venues and other arts resources.

Lastly, *The Insiders' Guide® to the Lake Superior Region* is for anyone seeking adventure. Chart your own path, of course, but consult with us frequently. We expect this book to be dog-eared, well-thumbed, scribbled upon, underlined and passed around. And let us know what you like and don't like about the book. We'll revise it annually to always keep you up-to-date about what's best and brightest around Lake Superior. Please share your comments with us by writing:

Editor, Insiders' Guides Inc.
P.O. Box 2057
Manteo, North Carolina 27954

How To Use This Book

When we agreed to write *The Insiders' Guide® to the Lake Superior Region*, we wondered just how to go about it. Should we do the whole Lake? Just the main cities? How far inland should we go?

We finally decided to write about the western, most populous end of Lake Superior in some detail — from Thunder Bay, Ontario, in the north; to Duluth, Minnesota, and Superior, Wisconsin, in the southwest; and to Ironwood, Michigan, in the east. These are arbitrary cutoffs and not intended to diminish the beauty or importance of the rest of magnificent Lake Superior (hereupon also referred to as simply "the Lake"). We try to cover the "rest" of the Lake (eastward from Thunder Bay along Canada's North Shore around to Sault Ste. Marie, and Michigan's Upper Peninsula) in our Circle Tour chapter.

When considering how far inland we should go, we decided to stick pretty close to the Lake. After all, that's what the book is about. A few events or places inland 20 or 30 miles were just too significant not to mention, so those are included. And two popular inland areas get their own collective chapter entitled Beyond the Ports and Shores.

Except for those two chapters, our focus is from Thunder Bay to Ironwood: the land, people, water, buildings, history, institutions, services and events. Each chapter describes a particular aspect of life here, and most are divided into geographical segments: "Twin Ports Area"; "Along the North Shore"; "Along the South Shore" and "Thunder Bay Area." History and Annual Events (both chronological) and Media (type of outlet) are exceptions. For example, if you're wondering what's happening on the Fourth of July, check out the "July" section of our Annual Events chapter and scan the entries for an event near you. On the other hand, if you're looking for the nearest campground in Thunder Bay, turn to our Camping and Campgrounds chapter and then check the "Thunder Bay Area" classification. Previous exceptions noted, we've done the same geographic organization with all our chapters, whether the subject is real estate or recreation, architecture or accommodations. Some chapters, such as Recreation, also are arranged alphabetically; others are arranged by proximity — such as Shopping, so you can move from store to store like a true-blue shopper.

We hope you'll enjoy our area, and we think *The Insiders' Guide® to the Lake Superior Region* can enhance your time here, however long you stay. Remember, it's not intended to be read cover-to-cover — just take it along for reference. But use this guide until it's ragged! You don't want to learn about some special offering here only after you've left.

About the Authors

Susan Stanich moved to the North Shore of Lake Superior in the early 1970s, where she raised two children, Shoshana and Ben, in view of the Lake, with its wind, fog and crashing waves. She worked as a commercial fish dealer on both North and South shores and as a construction worker at both a taconite facility and a grain elevator before becoming a reporter for the *Duluth News-Tribune*. She left the newspaper to pursue a freelance career in 1995.

Stanich grew up on a farm in rural central Minnesota and in St. Paul, attended Macalester College and the University of Minnesota and loves good literature, music, horses, cleaning barns, baking and being outdoors. She lives in a cabin on the St. Louis River, next door to her daughter, son-in-law and two young granddaughters who toddle next door to rescue her from her computer. Her freelance feature stories have appeared in *The Washington Post*, Native papers and other journals around the country and national magazines. She's working currently on a biography of a prominent Ojibwe leader. She dislikes looking at her computer, so you can't reach her via e-mail.

"Up to the lake" always meant the big lake for **Janet Blixt,** who spent summers camping and hiking with her family at Gooseberry Falls State Park on Minnesota's North Shore of Lake Superior. All the kids wore bright red sweatshirts, a clothing tactic Mom employed to keep track of the kids playing on the rocky shores of the big, cold lake. When Janet was 10 years old, she traveled around the entire lake, camping with her family and following the route that later became the now-popular Lake Superior Circle Tour.

Originally from Bloomington, Minnesota, Janet emigrated from the Twin Cities to the international freshwater port of Duluth, Minnesota, in 1990. She lives in a historic Italian immigrant house nestled into a hillside and overlooking Lake Superior on the steepest street in Duluth (with a 26 percent grade). Aware that she would find endless distractions if her office overlooked Lake Superior, Janet took heed of Gertrude Stein's observation, "I like a view but I like to sit with my back turned to it," and set up her desk and computer looking out at her hillside gardens instead of Lake Superior.

An outdoor enthusiast, Janet has helped lead river-rafting trips and has taught white-water paddling, sharing her firsthand experience in surviving a few breath-gasping swims. She enjoys canoeing, cross-country skiing, hiking and camping. Passionate about the performing arts and historic architecture, Janet is actively involved in the transformation of Duluth's landmark 100-year-old former cathedral, with its stunning acoustics and 19th-century Felgemaker tracker pipe organ, into Sacred Heart Music Center, a nonprofit regional performing arts space.

Janet's public relations career with Twin Cities agencies includes 10 years of award-winning marketing communications writing, product promotion and special events work for high technology and public affairs clients as well as Fortune 500 companies Federal Express, 3M and Data Card Corporation.

She runs her own freelance writing and marketing consulting business, with a focus on environmental and performing arts organizations. Janet is currently involved in a capital campaign to build a wildlife education center for the Crex Meadows Wildlife Area near Grantsburg, Wisconsin. Her feature writing and poetry have appeared in regional publications, including the *Northern Reader* and *Minnesota Volunteer* magazine.

Acknowledgments

Susan Stanich would like to thank the Helpers for sending helpers: Paul Ojanen for historical perspective, many tips and (with Caleb Bond) computer disentanglements; Cheryl Walsh Bellville for letting Insiders' Guides Inc. use her photo of the writer; Shoshana and Renan Cruz for great meals, cigarettes and patience; Diane and Paul Shea for feedback and good ideas; Jim Northrup for humor; Ixmucane and Susanita for joy; Georgiana Podulke, Roger Jourdain and Media Mike Hazard for encouragement; Marilyn Walters and June Rudd for research help; Pat Northrup, Ifiemi Ombu, Ben Sjoberg and Bob Stanich for being themselves; Paulie and Jeremy Shea for fun (and help from Paulie); Star Ames and Thor Nielsen for family hospitality; Clara Wu for beauty; Esther Nahgahnub and Walter Bresette for winning; Ann Glumac, Bruce Bennett, Irv Mossberger and Terry Hill for allowing her to pick their brains; Carl Gawboy, Larry Sundberg and Bob Baldwin for taking time; and Frederick.

Janet Blixt thanks her parents, Bob and Marion Blixt, for camping trips around the Lake and on the North Shore; her sister, Pam Blixt, and brother, Paul Blixt, for putting up with her; her friend, Bruce Peura, for his steadfast nature; her fellow writer and friend, Mike Savage, for his hard-earned freelance wisdom and willingness to always help; her friends, Maggie Boyle and Dan Theis and Ian and Alec Boyle Theis; her Twin Cities friends, Kim Crooks, Rick Korinek, Micah, Bones, Gabe, Bob Hicks and Annette Toews, Bob Booker and Brad Trabing, and Kathryn Rosebear and Steve Parsons, for their support during this long project; Sandy Peterson in Cloquet, for sharing her computer know-how on the coldest night of winter; her boat-watching friend, John Desautel; John Donahue, who knows West Duluth so well; Jill Fisher and Maryanne Norton, for their love and knowledge of historic architecture; all the incredibly helpful people at the Duluth and Superior public libraries; Barbara Fraser and Pat LeCocq of Tourism Thunder Bay; her Thunder Bay friends, Joe and Connie Miranda and Bev Werbowy, who know their city and want to share it; Rachel Martin at Superior's Fairlawn Museum; Pat Labadie at the Canal Park Marine Museum; all the great people at the state and provincial parks and national forests; Jay Andersen, Suellen Kruse and Darcy Pete of Grand Marais; Dan Byrnes, for his real estate knowledge; and Mary Somnis of the Lutsen-Tofte Tourism Association.

Duluth and Superior

Lake Superior Region

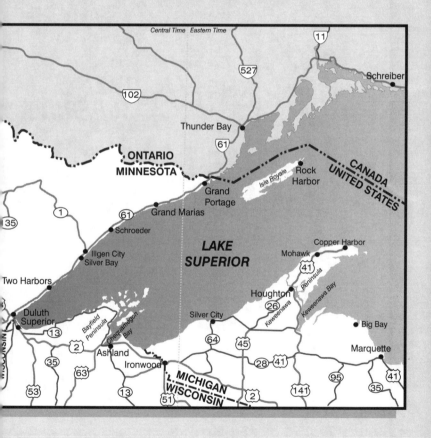

Central Time | Eastern Time

11

527

102

Schreiber

Thunder Bay

61

ONTARIO

MINNESOTA

CANADA

UNITED STATES

Isle Royale

Rock Harbor

Grand Portage

35

1

61 Grand Marias

Schroeder

LAKE SUPERIOR

Copper Harbor

Mohawk

Illgen City

Silver Bay

41

Keweenaw Peninsula

Two Harbors

Houghton

26

Keweenaw Bay

Duluth Superior

13

Bayfield Peninsula

Chequamegon Bay

Silver City

Big Bay

WISCONSIN

2

Ashland

64

45

Marquette

35

63

Ironwood

28

41

141

95

35

41

53

13

MICHIGAN

WISCONSIN

51

2

Thunder Bay

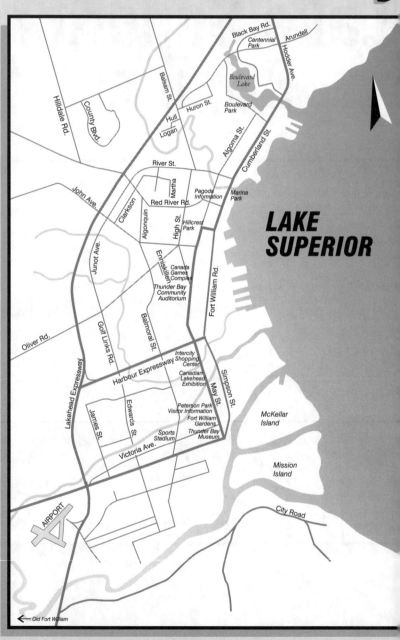

Black Bay Rd.
Centennial Park
Arundell
Hodder Ave.
Boulevard Lake
Balsam St.
Huron St.
Boulevard Park
Hull
Logan
Algoma St.
Cumberland St.
Hilldale Rd.
County Blvd.
River St.
Martha
Pagoda Information
Marina Park
John Ave.
Clarkson
Red River Rd.
Algonquin
High St.
Hillcrest Park
LAKE SUPERIOR
Junot Ave.
Enniskillen
Canada Games Complex
Fort William Rd.
Thunder Bay Community Auditorium
Golf Links Rd.
Balmoral St.
Oliver Rd.
Intercity Shopping Center
Canadian Lakehead Exhibition
Harbour Expressway
Simpson St.
May St.
McKellar Island
Lakehead Expressway
Edwards St.
Peterson Park Visitor Information
Fort William Gardens
James St.
Sports Stadium
Thunder Bay Museum
Victoria Ave.
Mission Island
AIRPORT
City Road
← Old Fort William

Duluth's Skywalk

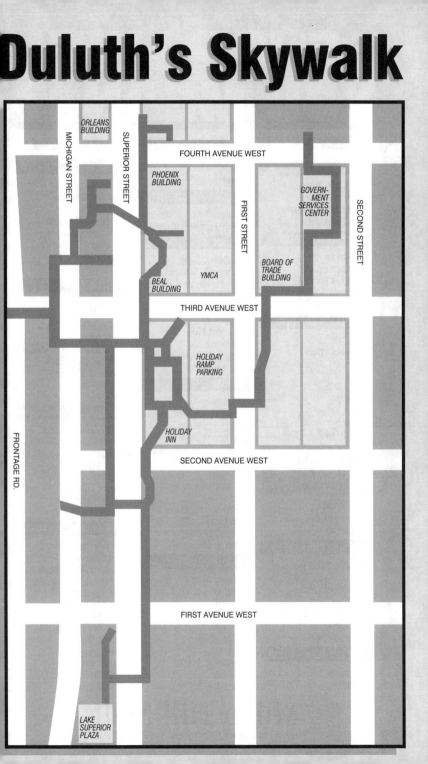

Table of Contents

Directory of Maps

Duluth is named after French explorer Daniel Greysolon, Sieur du Lhut, who left a prestigious position in the Royal Guard of Louis XIV to adventure in New France. Superior is named after the Lake, which in Ojibwe is called Kitchi Gami, meaning "big lake."

Inside
In the Ports and
Along the Shores

In the Ports

Duluth

You're about to drop into another world.

It's August and you've reached the crest of the Thompson Hill above Duluth on Interstate 35. Whether a first-time visitor or a fourth-generation Duluthian, you're bound to be struck by the deep, wide river valley, the lush green islands and the silver-blue water of the miles-wide St. Louis River, which leads into the natural harbor and bay of Lake Superior.

As you pick up speed, your attention is drawn to the shimmer of the St. Louis River and, on the horizon, Lake Superior. Toward the bottom of the hill, your eyes fix on the Aerial Lift Bridge, a 225-foot-high, elegant steel structure. This beloved landmark arches over the Duluth Ship Canal where it greets lakers (domestic ships) and salties (foreign vessels), calling a welcome or good-bye with a master salute of its horn. Working like a giant gate, the bridge raises and lowers its 900-ton central span to let the ships pass. As you approach the bottom of Thompson Hill, your ears pop from the rapid decrease in elevation, and you open your window in some strange ritual to clear your head and ears. Wow! . . . The air is perceptibly cooler, fresher, cleaner.

WELCOME TO DULUTH

The Aerial Lift Bridge and the Duluth Ship Canal on the waterfront in Canal Park are emblematic of Duluth's past and present economies and the city's collective mind-set. Each year, more than 1,000 domestic and foreign ships arrive in the international port of Duluth-Superior to load grain, taconite and low-sulphur coal shipped *to* this port via railway and *from* here via waterway. In 1995, about 40 million metric tons of cargo were shipped, making the Duluth-Superior port the busiest on the Great Lakes and 17th-largest in the United States.

A thriving tourism economy works hand-in-hand with this bustling harbor industry. In 1995, 3.3 million people visited Duluth. The main reason? To see Lake Superior. In the last 10 years, Canal Park, a lively waterfront area near the Aerial Lift Bridge, has undergone a metamorphosis. Warehouses, factories and industrial services have been replaced by coffeehouses, restaurants, hotels, gift shops and antiques malls, giving new life to many of these sturdy, red-brick buildings. The new Lakewalk, an award-winning 3-mile landscaped pathway, starts in Canal Park and follows the lakeshore past pockets of little parks, sculpture and flower gardens. The nationally renowned 26.2-mile Grandma's Marathon road race (see our Spectator Sports and Annual Events chapters) starts in Two Harbors (north of the city on Lake

Superior's North Shore) and ends in Duluth's Canal Park.

During the summer, Canal Park and Bayfront Park, with a nearby outdoor music stage, host all sorts of food, music and ethnic festivals. (See our Annual Events chapter for additional information on these venues.) And, of course, the quintessential thing to do in Canal Park is to stand along the piers and watch the ships move up-bound (headed to Duluth) or down-bound (leaving Duluth) through the shipping canal and under the Aerial Lift Bridge. It's a perfect symbiosis of tourist leisure time and Great Lakes tradition.

DULUTH'S BEGINNINGS

What did French explorers Sieur de Radisson, Pierre d'Espirit, Medard Chouart and Sieur des Groseilliers see when they traveled the Great Lakes from Montreal in the mid-17th century and came to what is now Duluth? Immense forests of tall white pine, densely covering the rocky hills above the Lake, along the rivers and on the 7-mile spit of land now called Park Point. Those vast pineries were logged out by the early 1920s. Duluth sawmills peaked in production in 1902 when more than 435 million board feet were cut. But the natural resources of the area — ore deposits on the Mesabi, Cuyuna and Vermilion iron ranges; hardwood and conifer forests; and the teeming coldwater fishery of Lake Superior — provided the economic base for the development and sustenance of Duluth and Superior that continues today.

Upstream about 14 miles from the Twin Ports on the St. Louis River is the sleepy little neighborhood of **Fond du Lac**. Once its own town, Fond du Lac is one of the oldest sections of Duluth. Dakota and Ojibwe villages thrived here. Later, a fur-trading post was built here by John Jacob Astor in 1817.

The first railway, the Lake Superior and Mississippi line, linked Duluth with St. Paul, Minnesota, in 1870. This railway link was the transportation impetus that spawned Duluth's development.

Duluth lies at the far western end of Lake Superior, a healthy 2,342 freshwater miles from the Atlantic Ocean. In 1959, Duluth became the farthest inland port on the Great Lakes following the opening of St. Lawrence Seaway.

If you view Lake Superior as shaped like a wolf's profile facing west, Duluth and Superior sit at the tip of the wolf's nose. Duluth is approximately 165 miles from the Canadian border and 187 miles from Thunder Bay, Ontario. From downtown Duluth, the metropolitan Twin Cities area is 155 miles (about a three-hour drive) southward. The port city of Superior, Wisconsin, is a five-minute drive across either the Bong Bridge or Blatnik Bridge, which span the St. Louis River.

The economy of Duluth and its environs is a curious and thriving mix based on extractive industries of paper and wood products and taconite processing. (Taconite is pellets made from low-grade iron ore and used in steel production.) Manufacturing and railway and waterway ship-

Insiders' Tips

For speedsters who cruise through Superior on Belknap Street and U.S. Highway 2/53: Remember, the speed limit in town is 25 mph, and a patrol car may be lurking around any corner.

ping are the other parts of the equation. Since the early 1980s, Duluth has been a burgeoning tourism mecca, a retail market, an expanding regional healthcare center for northern Minnesota and northwestern Wisconsin, and a growing nucleus for higher education and specialized vocational training.

DULUTHIANS

Pick up the *Duluth News-Tribune*. The daily obituary page is a snapshot of Duluth's people. Finnish, Italian and Slavic names jump out at you. Some of these folk were born across the sea. The ways in which they earned a living — as steelworkers and shipbuilders, longshoremen and loggers, cooks, waitresses, sailors and teachers — paint a vivid picture of the hard-working nature of the area's people and their lifestyles.

Notice how long people live around here. The median age in Duluth and Superior is 34, although both cities have significant older-adult populations. (Twenty-five percent of Duluth's population, for instance, will be older than 65 by the year 2000.) Maybe it's sauna-worship, the cold and lengthy winters . . . or just plain stubbornness. We don't know the answer, but there's a certain elixir in the air.

Today, Duluth and the surrounding area are home to the descendants of immigrants from England, Scotland, Finland, Sweden, Norway, Denmark, Ireland, Italy, Yugoslavia, Russia, Germany, the Ukraine and Poland — relative newcomers who arrived in the past 125 years to start a new life. This area also is home to the descendants of the people who have been here all along — the Ojibwes of the western Great Lakes. Duluth is the urban hub for American Indian people living on or near about six Ojibwe reservations in Minnesota and Wisconsin.

In a population of about 86,000 residents, Duluth has about 28,000 inhabitants claiming German ancestry, 17,300 Swedes, 14,700 Norwegians and about 10,500 Irish. And let's not forget the 7,200 Finns and 4,400 Italians. You can find a lot more Finns in the rural areas of St. Louis and Carlton counties, because of their farming heritage.

As you can probably gather from the immigrant influence, Duluth is largely a white city. Newcomers, particularly those who have lived in more diverse metropolitan areas, notice this immediately. Duluth's population is 96 percent Caucasian, a little more than 2 percent American Indian and less than 1 percent African American.

INDUSTRY AND ECONOMY

In the last decade, Duluth has successfully courted a variety of new industries and with them — jobs. The new emphasis is on supporting the start-up and expansion of small entrepreneurial businesses, such as **Thomson Berry Farms**, **Husky Rustic Siding Company** and **Schott Power Systems**, which manufactures rechargeable batteries. This success has somewhat made up for the loss of well-paying, blue-collar jobs when the taconite industry downsized to become more globally competitive and several major employers either closed down or relocated. After major layoffs and a series of changes in ownership, the leaner and meaner taconite facilities on the Iron Range and along the North Shore now compete in boom times. They enjoy more efficient production and provide taconite for the modern steel minimills on the Great Lakes.

Want high-tech? There's the U.S. Postal Service's **Remote Encoding Center** where employees use computers to decipher illegible addresses on mail. (We never imagined people with poor handwriting would be the impetus for job growth!) **US West Communications** invested $52 million in a fiber optic transmission and digital switching system. **Fingerhut Corporation** opened a telemarketing center here in 1992. **Cirrus Design**, a designer and manufacturer of premier, lightweight personal aircraft, moved its headquarters here in the early 1990s. **Northwest Airlines** is building an airline maintenance base here to service its fleet of jumbo jets and opened an airline reservation center on the Iron Range. **Superior Recycled Fiber Industries**, built in 1994, recycles office paper to create new paper products. **United Healthcare** has recently expanded their insurance claims processing division in Duluth.

Duluth is home to Jeno Paulucci's frozen food empire, including a factory where his latest success story, Michelina's pasta entrees, are produced. And let's not forget the line of wild rice dishes Jeno produces in partnership with **Louis Kemp**. . . .

New services and facilities for the tourism industry also are springing up. The Duluth Entertainment Convention Center has added an **Omnimax Theater** to its convention facilities. A planned $30 million **Lake Superior Center** will anchor the west end of the Canal Park area. The center will emphasize the Lake Superior region as a connected set of ecosystems and will feature a freshwater aquarium and hands-on, interactive exhibits. Duluth has seen a number of new hotels and restaurants spring up in the last five years to serve sleepy and hungry visitors. We locals rejoice when new restaurants such as **Green Mill Pizza, Applebee's** and **Little Angie's** come to town.

Duluth's economy continues to expand. Since 1985, more than $1.5 billion in private and public funds have been invested in the city, including more than $185 million has been invested in the downtown and waterfront areas, including a **skywalk** system and the **Lakewalk**.

Some major shopping areas have benefited from a total $40 million worth of expansions. These include **ShopKo, TOYS-R-US, Kohl's** and the **Miller Hill Mall**, the major mall in Duluth.

Duluth's medical community has invested $120 million in major capital improvements. Professional employment is currently strongest in the medical and healthcare fields. The Duluth healthcare community, including **St. Mary's Medical Center, St. Luke's Hospital, Miller-Dwan Hospital** and **The Duluth Clinic**, is the third-largest in Minnesota, ranking behind the Twin Cities and Rochester's Mayo Clinic. (See our Hospitals and Healthcare chapter for details.)

Education also plays an important role in Duluth's economy. More than 60

Insiders' Tips

Public holidays in Ontario include Victoria Day (May 24 or the preceding Monday); Canada Day (July 1); Civic Holiday (first Monday in August); Labour Day (first Monday in September); Thanksgiving (second Monday in October); Boxing Day (December 26); Christmas; New Year's; and Good Friday. Banks, government offices, schools and most businesses close for those days.

percent of the city's high school students go on to college or a post-secondary education. Twenty percent of high school graduates receive scholarship awards each year. Duluth is home to one of four campuses of the University of Minnesota. The **University of Minnesota Duluth** (or UMD) employs 1,300 faculty and staff and has an enrollment of 7,500 students. The **College of St. Scholastica**, ranked by *US News and World Report* as one of the country's "best buys" among private liberal arts colleges, enjoys an enrollment of 1,850 students and employs 418 faculty and staff. The **Fond du Lac Community College** in Cloquet is both a tribal college and a member of the Arrowhead Community College region. **Lake Superior College** is part of Minnesota's community college system and includes a new, specialized vocational center in western Duluth trains students in fire-fighting techniques.

Duluth is also a regional center for legal, architectural, engineering and advertising and marketing services. The city and county governments also employ a major white-collar and service-worker base.

The city's largest private employers include the **Duluth Clinic**, **St. Mary's Medical Center**, **St. Luke's Hospital**, **Miller-Dwan Medical Center**, retail clothier **Maurice's**, retail grocers **Miners Inc.**, school supply distributor **Beckley-Cardy Inc.**, publisher **Advanstar Communications**, and utility company **Minnesota Power**.

Adding the public sector, the four largest employers are the **City of Duluth**, the **Duluth School District**, **St. Louis County** and the **University of Minnesota Duluth**.

GEOGRAPHY AND GREEN SPACES

If biology is destiny, so seems geography. Duluth is squeezed into an approximately 30-mile-long, 2-mile-wide strip of land flanked by Lake Superior and the bays of the St. Louis River. The city's west side runs into rugged basalt and granite cliffs and hills. Duluth covers more than 66 square miles in St. Louis County, Minnesota's largest county. Intersecting Duluth and creating green corridors are more than 20 creeks and rivers that make their way to Lake Superior.

Duluth is both wild and industrial. It's home to strange but not impossible bedfellows: its industrial past and present, and the natural resources of its extensive river, stream and lake ecosystems. Depending on which way the wind is blowing and where you stand, Duluth can look and smell industrial: Some say the odor from the paper mills of Cloquet is the smell of money; the sulphur smell of rotten eggs fills the air from the Western Lake Sanitary System on some days; and the toasty, though not entirely unpleasant, smell from the Superwood plant is distinctive.

Perhaps it depends on how you look at it. A little boy, riding with his mother past one of the paper mills, observed the white puffs of steam coming from the stacks and said, "Look, Mom, that's where the clouds are made."

Early tourism literature pegged Duluth as the air-conditioned city. And it's true: We've had frost in June. For the cool summers in the Twin Ports, carry a lightweight jacket, especially if you plan activities near the Lake.

Insiders' Tips

is much more desirable than a harbor view, which reveals the clutter of the train yards, rusting ships and piles of taconite and coal. We, however, happen to enjoy the industrial architecture of the train yards and the rows of grain elevators and ore docks.

Ask any wildlife biologist about the St. Louis River, and invariably you'll hear about the number of wildlife habitats within whistling distance of old smokestacks, paper mills and giant iron-ore loading docks. For instance, a favorite birding spot is the turnoff at 40th Avenue W. near a heavy industrial area near Rice's Point, snowy owls and hawks hang out by the train tracks, waiting for grain-feeding pigeons.

The water quality of St. Louis River in Duluth has benefited from the reduction of effluent from upstream paper mills and other industries over the last 15 years, although leaking landfills and chemical by-products from the pulp-making process still pose significant discharge problems.

A thorough, grass-roots Remedial Action Plan for the river system is in constant play through cooperating industries, governments, schools, private citizens and environmental groups that have been and remain interested in cleaning up and protecting the river. Accumulations of heavy metals, such as mercury, and toxins, such as PCBs, in the bottom sediment of the riverbed pose serious risks to aquatic life and the entire food chain. For that reason, you'll notice fish consumption warnings posted at public boat landings.

Not unlike the rest of the country, Duluth remains vulnerable to the degradation of wildlife habitat, primarily due to nonpoint-source pollution, runoff from parking lots and sewer systems and continuing development — all of which impact wetlands in particular.

Duluthians are fiercely protective about their green spaces and actively vocal about conservation and cleaning things up. The Twin Ports' wake-up call to protect and clean up the area's natural resources rang in the early 1970s. Citizens brought a federal class-action lawsuit against Reserve Mining that challenged the company's discharge of tons of asbestos-like taconite tailings directly into Lake Superior over decades of production. The citizens won the lawsuit, and now tailings are processed in controlled holding ponds. Duluth built a new water treatment filtration system because of this pollution.

We think you'll be pleasantly surprised by the lack of garbage on the white sand beaches of **Park Point**, the 7-mile natural breakwater in the Duluth harbor. A beach sweep takes place every year, and people are pretty careful about carrying out litter. But, sadly, it seems folks don't hesitate to throw things into the Lake or its tributaries.

A friend who lived on Park Point walked the beach every morning for years. He cataloged the repeat garbage that would wash in on the shoreline: fishing line, lost lures, pieces of net, cigarette butts and plastic housings from spent shotgun shells — some of it carried down the St. Louis River after a rainstorm or washed in from the Lake.

On a larger scale, arguments still arise over the merits of locating, recovering and inspecting more of the approximately 1,400 sealed barrels of possibly hazardous refuse dumped into Lake Superior in the 1960s. Fewer than two dozen barrels have been brought to the surface for testing thus far; the contents were benign. Barrels from a dumping area in the Lake that has registered radioactivity, however, have not yet been tested.

Photo: Duluth News-Tribune

Duluth's hills and proximity to Lake Superior are why many call it the "San Francisco of the North."

RECREATION AND
THE GREAT OUTDOORS

You don't need to leave Duluth in order to play. We've got a limited warm season, and we like to get outside to enjoy it. But we like to play outside in winter too. Duluth has 105 municipal parks and playgrounds and 22 recreation centers. There are two 27-hole golf courses, 41 tennis courts, 29 baseball and softball fields, 45 miles of snowmobile trails, the Spirit Mountain downhill ski area, 44 kilometers of cross-country ski trails and eight designated hiking trails. Each of Duluth's 21 neighborhoods enjoys the convenience of a nearby park and recreation center. And many neighborhoods have creeks tumbling though deep gorges filled with red and white pines and lined with hiking paths.

For whitewater kayakers, canoeists, birders, hikers and campers, Duluth is a great home base and jumping-off point for some of the largest wilderness areas in the country. Minnesota is home to the largest population of timber wolves in the lower 48 states, and it hosts one of the largest populations of nesting bald eagles. A short drive up the North Shore will take you to the immense **Superior National Forest**, 11 state parks and forests, and numerous points between Duluth and the Canadian border where you can access the 200-mile-long **Superior Hiking Trail**. It's less than a half-day's drive to **Ely**, the **Sawbill Trail** or the **Gunflint Trail** — access points to the non-motorized **Boundary Waters Canoe Area Wilderness**, a canoeist's paradise. The trout fishing in many of the North Shore streams is incredible; trolling Lake Superior for lake trout is another angling option.

HEART AND SOUL OF DULUTH

Duluth's downtown and its waterfront are really its heart and soul. These areas are filled with significant historic architectural landmarks, embodied in the striking brownstone clock tower of the 1891 **Central High School** building on Second Street. Other landmarks include the **Civic Center** on Fourth Avenue W. that includes the city hall, county courthouse and Federal building on First Street. Dropping down the hill from the Civic Center, you can walk to the magnificent, restored 1892 **Union Depot** on Michigan Street, now in its second life as the city's cultural center. It's home to the **Duluth-Superior Symphony Orchestra**, the **Minnesota Ballet**, the **Duluth Playhouse**, **Arrowhead Chorale**, **Matinee Musicale**, the **Duluth Art Institute**, the **Children's Museum**, the **Lake Superior Museum of Transportation** and the **St. Louis County Historical Society**. (See our Attractions, Architecture and Historic Places, and Arts and Culture chapters for details.) Across from the Depot is the **Duluth Public Library**, enjoying one of the busiest circulations for a library of its size in the country.

Heading east on Superior Street, the main drag, you'll find restaurants, clothing and antiques shops, record and book shops, all housed in late 1800s brownstone and brick storefronts. In winter, people stroll the **skywalk**, a multi-block system of second-story, enclosed heated walkways (with the exception of the underground section of the Skywalk near the Radisson Hotel). The downtown Skywalk stretches from Lake Avenue and Superior Street west to the **Duluth Entertainment Convention Center** (see our Arts and Culture chapter). The Skywalk is so pervasive, there's even a weekly downtown newspaper called *Skyworld News*.

In **Canal Park** (see our Parks and Forests chapter), you'll find more window-shopping and browsing possibilities and more restaurants. In colder months, Duluthians are pleased to have Canal Park pretty much to themselves; but be prepared for crowds in summer, particularly during big events, such as **Grandma's Marathon** in mid-June (see our Spectator Sports and Annual Events and Festivals chapters) and the **Bayfront Blues Festival** in early August (see Annual Events and Festivals).

Ship-watching in Canal Park is a classic (and free) thing to do. The ships generally run from mid-March (depending on when the Soo Locks open up) to early January. The Canal Park Marine Museum draws ship-lovers to observe its constantly updated big screen of ship schedules (listed in military time) and its historic exhibits.

Canal Park also provides a front-row seat for storm-watching. It draws people in late fall and early spring when the big rollers surge and crest over the protective walls of the piers and the waves crash over the Lakewalk, sometimes throwing boulders on the path.

The **Lakewalk** is Duluth's promenade. On a warm summer night, early fall evening or glorious first warm day of spring, you'll find people everywhere along this 3-mile pathway, which hugs Lake Superior's shoreline. It begins in Canal Park and provides both a wooden walking path and an asphalt path for bikers and in-line skaters. Numerous access points to the Lakewalk include **Fitger's Brewery Complex**, **Superior Street**, the **Rose Gardens** and up the shore at 21st Street. (See our Attractions chapters for details.)

DULUTH'S FUTURE

In 1994, Duluth embarked on a "community visioning" process, meant to get input from the grass-roots level rather than from only the mountain top. Named 2001 and Beyond, the two-year planning exercise was designed to get citizens involved and talking — through cracker-barrel chats held in neighborhoods all over town, surveys, committee work and a televised town hall meeting — to decide what was important for the future direction of the city. As a result of this city-wide participation, Duluthians reached common ground on three guiding principals: preserving and enhancing the environment; investing in people, neighborhoods and communities; building a strong economic base.

New development in Duluth is limited by the city's geographical boundaries. Most new commercial building is occurring over the hill. Other issues on the public's agenda that the city has had to grapple with involve Duluth's growing tourist economy. Proposed tourists attractions, such as a factory outlet mall on the waterfront and a retired Navy warship, have been advocated and debated. Duluth's head is spinning a little. The city is successfully making the transition from an industrial-based (especially manufacturing and transportation) cyclical economy to a wider mix of healthcare, retail, education, tourism and service-based companies and a variety of start-up businesses. There are certain to be some headaches with this success. Let's hope Duluth can keep its head above water.

Superior

Ask Superiorites to describe their town of 27,000 people and, invariably, the answer is as low-key and down-to-earth as the city they live in: "Friendly"; "easy to talk to people"; "folks will help you if your car breaks down"; "unpretentious"; "trustworthy — I never lock my doors"; and "we're not a trendy town" are some of the answers you'll hear.

Superior and Duluth enjoy and sometimes disdain their close relationship as port towns. Indeed, their historic rivalry dates back to the 1870s when Superior was platted to become "the Chicago of Northwest." Speculators banked on its booming commercial shipping industry facilitated by its protected harbor and the natural channel of the St. Louis River from Wisconsin Point to Lake Superior. Duluthians, to avoid the deadline of a federal injunction, worked night and day to dig a competitive shipping channel through Minnesota Point in 1871. Today, that channel is known as the Duluth Ship Canal.

Despite the competition, Superior today accounts for more than half the total annual tonnage shipped from the Duluth-Superior Port (or, as they say in Wisconsin, the Port of Superior-Duluth). Superior boasts tremendous grain storage capacity at the **Harvest States Elevators**, the largest in the United States; the **Burlington Northern Railroad** taconite loading facilities, the largest in the world;

and the state-of-the-art coal loading facility at the **Midwest Energy Terminal**, the largest of its kind in the country.

Besides sharing shipping facilities and a common port, Superior and Duluth share other resources too. Recently, Superior's former mayor moved to Duluth, his boyhood home, to run for mayor; Superior's **Memorial Hospital** became part of the St. Mary's Medical Complex; and the Duluth Clinic has several affiliates in Superior. A new **U.S. Veterans Administration Clinic** for the region has been built in Superior.

The port towns share performing arts resources, including the **Duluth-Superior Symphony Orchestra**, which performs its summer season at Lucius Woods Park's outdoor theater in Solon Springs, south of Superior. And other arts organizations, such as the Duluth Art Institute and the Children's Museum in Duluth, offer programs in Superior and Douglas County as well as their home city.

The Twin Ports of Duluth and Superior once were connected only by ferry boat; later, by a toll-bridge. In winter, people crossed back and forth on the ice. Now, on any given workday, the **Bong and Blatnik bridges** carry commuters who live in Superior to their jobs in Duluth (and vice versa). According to the Superior-Douglas County (Wis.) Development Association, nearly 4,000 people commute to Minnesota daily, and approximately 2,300 people come from St. Louis County, Minnesota, to Douglas County, Wisconsin, to work.

Duluth and Superior share common ground on issues affecting both cities. Environmental concerns about the health of St. Louis River have prompted citizen advisory committees from both sides of the river, resulting in a formal **Remedial Action Plan** to protect, clean up and restore this ecosystem. Other concerns involving port and shipping topics and infrastructure issues (highways and bridges) bring Minnesotans and Wisconsinites together.

SUPERIOR'S PEOPLE

To understand Superior's first inhabitants, you must first understand a tidbit of geographic history. **Wisconsin Point**, a narrow strip of land in easternmost Superior that juts out to create the natural mouth of the St. Louis River, once was home and sacred ground to the **Ojibwe** people. According to Ojibwe folklore, the point was formed as follows: An Ojibwe youth was being pursued by hostile Sioux, the mortal enemy. Trapped on the shore of Lake Superior, he had no where to escape but to jump into the icy waters. He called out, and the Great Spirit created an island around him, saving him from his enemies.

Today, Wisconsin Point, at the end of Moccasin Mike Road, is a wild, windswept place. It's lined with red and white

Insiders' Tips

About 220 centimeters (86.6 inches) of snow fall yearly in Thunder Bay, and another 53 centimeters (20.87 inches) of rain. The average summer temperature is 15.9 Celsius (60.6 Fahrenheit); the average winter temperature is -12.8 C (9 F). The hottest time on record was in August 1993, when it reached 40.3 C (104.5 F). The coldest was in January 1951, with -41.1 C (-42 F).

pine forest, and at its end sit several Coast Guard keeper homes and the Wisconsin Point lighthouse. This is a wonderful spot to picnic, walk and bird-watch.

Heading west on U.S. Highway 2/53 from Wisconsin Point back into the east end of town, you'll cross the **Nemadji River** where Superior started as a village of trappers and traders in 1888. This East End was the original "downtown" area. As you drive along the old main street (E. Fifth Street), note the historic architecture, including a charming Victorian fire house, now the **Old Fire House and Police Museum**, at 23rd Avenue E. (see our Attractions chapter for details).

Like Duluth, Superior was built and settled by European immigrants. Distinctive neighborhoods sprang up for Finns, Poles, German and Russian Jews, Swedes and other ethnic groups. You can still see some of the social halls that served as important meeting places for those who spoke the same language: the **Belgian Club** in eastern Superior on U.S. Highway 2, the **Polish Club** off Tower Avenue on Banks Avenue and Broadway Street, and the now-closed Agudas Achim synagogue on Hammond Avenue and Sixth Street, to your right as you come off the Blatnik Bridge. The active **Finnish-American Bookstore**, remains at 1720 Tower Avenue where a the *Finnish-American Reporter* is published.

INDUSTRY AND ECONOMY

According to the Superior/Douglas County Chamber of Commerce, Superior's and Douglas County's largest employers include the following: **Burlington Northern Railroad**; the **City of Superior**; **Douglas County**; the **Superior School District**; and the **University of Wisconsin/Superior**, **St. Mary's Hospital**, **St. Francis Home, Inc.**, a nursing home; **Flemming Foods**, a wholesale grocery company, **Barko Hydraulics**, a hoist and crane manufacturer; **Field View Manor**, a nursing home; **Aquila**, a knitted apparel manufacturer; **Superior Water, Light and Power**; **Wisconsin Indianhead Technical College**; **Lakehead Pipeline**; **Superior Fiber**, a hardboard manufacturer; **Murphy Oil Corporation**, an oil refinery; and the **Wisconsin Department of Transportation**. Despite its economic diversity, general perception remains that Superior's mainstay industries are manufacturing and transportation. Understandably, this perception is borne from what is readily seen and heard around town. And, in fairness, this perception constitutes a valid assessment.

Anywhere you drive in Superior, you'll find railroad lines crisscrossing the city like a giant grid. Close your eyes and listen. The grinding and creaking sounds of trains being loaded, hooked up and moved permeate the city. The railroad yards dominate downtown Superior near Tower Avenue and Belknap Street.

East Coast investors developed Superior in the 1800s, spurred by the prospect of profitable shipping and iron ore industries. Later, the railroad expanded commerce with the East and West coasts

---

In 1995, tourism in Duluth generated $120 million in direct spending and had a $240 million economic impact.

through the inception of the Northern Pacific line. Today, Superior and Douglas County are major transportation hubs for the region. Douglas County is served by six railroads. (Don't miss the double-decker railroad bridge that crosses the St. Louis River from the town of Oliver, Wisconsin, to the Gary-New Duluth neighborhood.) And at the eastern edge of town on U.S. Highway 2, look up at the intersection of U.S. Highway 2 and 38th Avenue E. You'll see the conveyor belt that links the iron ore docks to the train cars carrying taconite and other products.

As a shipping port, Superior is home to grain-, ore- and coal-storage facilities. **Fraser Shipyards** on Clough Avenue near the Blatnik Bridge and Connors Point is one of the oldest working shipyards in the United States. In winter, you might see a laker getting a fresh coat of paint. Sometimes nearly a dozen ships are laid up; it takes a skillful parking job to squeeze these ships into such a constricted area.

A number of major manufacturers call Superior home. **Superior Wood Systems** makes hardboard for the automotive and construction industries. **Murphy Oil** operates a giant refinery that can produce as many as 35,000 barrels of crude oil per day. The refinery covers several acres near Stinson Avenue, and when you stumble upon it, as we have after trying to cut across town, you'll be awestruck by its alien hugeness.

Railroad equipment; railroad ties; marine, bakery and heavy construction machinery; and insulation are produced in Superior. There's a lime plant, a creosote plant and a company that makes synthetic lubricants. Despite the town's industrial facade, Superior's and Douglas County's largest employers include a mix of government, education, healthcare and transportation agencies, manufacturers, utility companies and wholesale grocers.

Superior may be a railroad town, but it's also a university town. Established in 1896, the **University of Wisconsin-Superior** (UWS) is northwest Wisconsin's only university. This institution provides 36 major fields of study and is renowned for its music department's curriculum and faculty. Its main campus is bordered by Caitlin Avenue and Belknap Street; it sprawls onto a second campus that includes student housing and athletic facilities on Caitlin Avenue and 28th Avenue. Student enrollment totals approximately 2,700. Wisconsin Indianhead Technical College, which offers vocational training, occupies the edge of the UWS campus.

GEOGRAPHY, ENVIRONMENT AND RECREATION

Superior's 45 square miles are nearly surrounded by water. The city is part of Douglas County, Wisconsin's fourth-largest county. Its limits are defined by Lake Superior, three bays (St. Louis, Superior and Allouez) and two rivers (St. Louis and Nemadji). Acres of federally protected wetlands comprise these areas. This protected land limits Superior's ability to sprawl with development — in one instance, the cause of controversy when several new retailers built near and on sensitive wetlands.

The Twin Ports received a rude wake-up call one early June morning in 1992 when a Burlington Northern railroad car derailed from a bridge and fell into the Nemadji River on the south end of Superior. The car broke open, spilling benzene, a toxic chemical, into the water and air, creating a blue cloud that crept down the river, along the Lake and up Park Point.

Songbirds near the river were killed instantly. Superior and Duluth were evacuated without incident, making the national news.

Four years later, the long-term health and environmental affects of the spill are still being assessed. If nothing else, this industrial accident increased awareness of the area's vulnerability and spurred evaluation and planning by city and county authorities to prevent future accidents.

While this incident is a salient example of Superior's recent history, in fairness we must stress that it and related occurrences are overwhelming exceptions — not the norm. Similarly, we would be unfair to overlook the myriad positive aspects of what this port town has to offer — especially its recreational opportunities (see our Recreation, Winter Sports, Camping and Campgrounds and Parks and Forests chapters for additional related information).

Superior is a flat town and, as such, is great for biking. For some strange reason, we frequently get lost in this town. (Perhaps our sense of direction is thrown off by the magnetic pull from all the iron ore at the docks.) Our skewed sense of direction tells us north is west and south is east. Perhaps this is partly explained by Superior's layout. The town is tilted at an angle and influenced by its waterways, flanked by the St. Louis River and the Lake. (St. Paul, Minnesota, and Boston, Massachusetts, are similarly influenced by their waterways; their street layouts radiate from the Mississippi River and Boston harbor, respectively.) Of course, locals have no problem finding their way around town.

Superior enjoys one of the largest municipal forests in the country. The 4,500 acres of the **Superior Municipal Forest**, near 28th Street on the west end of town, border the St. Louis River and include the mouth of the Pokegama River. This winter and summer playground is a quick trip from Duluth over the Bong Bridge. Winter brings well-groomed cross-country ski and snowmobile trails. In summer, this is

Photo: Duluth News-Tribune

The grain elevators in Thunder Bay bustle with activity.

Information Resources

Call the following centers or chambers of commerce for up-to-date tourism and business information.

Chambers of Commerce

Ashland, Wis.	(800) 284-9484
Bayfield, Wis.	(800) 447-4094
Cloquet, Minn.	(218) 879-1551
Duluth, Minn.	(218) 722-5501
Grand Marais, Minn.	(218) 387-2387
Hurley, Wis.	(715) 561-4334
Ironwood, Mich.	(906) 932-1122
Silver Bay, Minn.	(218) 226-4870
Superior, Wis.	(715) 394-7716
Thunder Bay, Ont.	(807) 622-9642
Two Harbors, Minn.	(218) 834-2600

Tourism Centers

Apostle Islands	(800) 284-9484 ext. 9
Ashland (Wis.) area	(715) 682-2500
Beaver Bay (Minn.) Tourism Information Center	(218) 226-3317
Superior-Douglas County (Wis.) Tourism	(715) 394-7716
Duluth (Minn.) Visitors and Convention Bureau	(218) 722-4011
Grand Portage (Minn.) Tourist Association	(218) 475-2401
Gunflint Trail (Minn.) Association	(800) 338-6932
Ironwood (Mich.) Tourism Council	(906) 932-1000
Iron Trail Convention and Visitors Bureau	(800) 777-8497
Lake County (Minn.) Visitor Information	(218) 834-4005
Lutsen-Tofte (Minn.) Tourism Association	(218) 663-7804
Northern Lights Tourism Alliance	(800) 664-WILD
Red Cliff (Wis.) Visitors Bureau	(715) 779-5225
Thunder Bay (Ont.) Hotline	(807) 343-2790
Tip of the Arrowhead (Minn.) Association	(218) 387-2524

Thunder Bay (Ont.) Visitors and Convention Bureau	(807) 625-2149
Thunder Bay North of Superior Tourism	(807) 626-9420
Western Upper Peninsula (Mich.) Visitors Bureau	(906) 932-4850

a great place to put in a canoe and explore the bays of the St. Louis River and the slow-moving Pokegama River. Hikers will find plenty of trails, and anglers, a number of launch spots.

Superior has 21 city parks, including the attractive **Billings Park** near the St. Louis River. The city enjoys close proximity to several top-notch state parks too: **Pattison State Park**, just a few miles southeast of town boasts the tallest waterfall in the state on the Black River, and **Amnicon Falls State Park** to the east on U.S Highway 2 offers great hiking, picnicking and camping opportunities as well as beautiful waterfalls. The Brule River, a nationally renown trout stream, flows through **Brule River State Forest** east of town. And on Superior's shoreline, you'll find the protected Superior Harbor and Allouez Bay, both of which offer excellent opportunities for boating, sailing and fishing.

Winter sports are big in Superior. The city maintains 12 supervised and four non-supervised outdoor ice-skating rinks. It operates an indoor municipal curling rink with artificial ice. Figure-skating lessons and ice hockey are preferred activities, and the city maintains nine outdoor lighted hockey rinks.

ESTABLISHING AN IDENTITY

A recent billboard campaign produced by the Superior Chamber of Commerce proclaimed in 4-foot-tall black letters, "Next to Duluth, we're Superior." Although the pun is somewhat lame, we've gotta give Superior points for chutzpah.

While Duluth may be a more assertive and glamorous neighbor, Superiorites seem pretty happy with the city's neighborhoods and the accessibility of things in town. There's pride in the strong work ethic and the town's general friendliness. (Not to say Duluth doesn't enjoy the same assets and values; we're generally cut of the same cloth.)

While Superior may seem a little tougher, even a little more defensive at times than its Minnesota neighbor, it will surprise you. Superior might take more time to get to know; you must first scratch the surface. Anyone lucky enough to make friends with locals finds that Superiorites will do what they can to show off the town they love.

Along the Shores

Lake Superior: The biggest expanse of fresh water in the world, it rules the lives of those who live around it. Covering 31,280 square miles (the size of New Hampshire, Massachusetts, Connecticut, Vermont and Rhode Island combined), it brings us cool air in the summer and warmth in the winter, breathes banks of fog and whips up winds and waves and stark beauty.

Although Lake Superior doesn't have the most fresh water of any lake in the world (Lake Baikal in Siberia, five times as deep, holds that honor), it does contain 10 percent of the world's fresh water and holds the record for largest circumference: 1,826 miles. From one end to the other is 383 miles; its widest point is 160 miles.

When it's still the sleepy first light of dawn on the western end, the sun already is shining brightly in Sault Ste. Marie, Michigan, in the east. Waves of up to 30 feet have been recorded on this inland sea. Its chop, as opposed to the oceans' swells, makes it hard to navigate in stormy weather, and it has claimed more than 300 ships. Lake Superior is big, moody, dangerous, beautiful — and still relatively clean.

The Lake's Development

After 20 million years of lava flows that accumulated to 3,000 feet, a great fracture in the Earth rent the land from here to Oklahoma. Rock on either side heaved upward at a tilt. That was followed by four ice ages (the first, a million years ago), during which glaciers covered all of northern Minnesota and much of Canada. The glaciers were heavy — thousands of feet thick — and shoved land along as they advanced, making craters, gouges and mountains and weighing down the land. As you walk along Lake Superior's shores, you'll climb over rock outcrops scored with grooves from this glacial period. Lake Superior has the oldest and hardest rock of any of the Great Lakes.

The last glacier melted about 11,000 years ago. As its waters receded, it left Glacial Lake Duluth, with a shoreline about 500 feet higher than that which now edges Lake Superior. You can see that old shoreline in the distance beyond the South Shore. Relieved of the ice-weight, the land began to rise, and most of the

As a young boy, President Franklin Delano Roosevelt fell into the icy waters of Lake Superior at a Superior shipyard when visiting with his father who was looking to invest in the city.

Lake's present shoreline is comprised of the hills caused by this lift. The lift is still happening, at a few feet per century.

Today, Lake Superior's cold water is not full of life like the oceans; you'll see no plankton soup or floating seaweed, smell no ebb and flow of life and death. If you're used to the ocean, the Lake may appear sterile to you, and you're almost right. Superior's water is a cold, clear liquid rolling over dense stones and sand. Not enough nutrients are released into the water to sustain plants, so a relatively small amount of life makes it home. Away from population centers, you can drink the water, and most old-timers do. Some homes pipe their water directly out of the Lake. There certainly is a lot of it — about 3 quadrillion gallons (that's a "3" followed by 15 zeros) — enough to flood all of North and South America to a foot in depth.

Feeling Territorial

We love our Lake, and most of us feel protective about it. From state and provincial officials to jobless youths, we are offended by a never-quite-dead proposition that our beautiful water be transferred via pipeline to the arid southwest to make up for that region's wasteful depredation of the underground Ogallala Aquifer.

"Tell them to quit throwing their water away on lawns and air conditioning and golf courses," the person-on-the-street growls. "They all crowded down there for the sunshine — if they wanted water, they could have moved here."

There's always the implication that life is a balance of joy and suffering, and people who try to escape the latter will get their comeuppance. You want cold clean water and lots of it? Then you'd better be prepared to put up with dense cold fog in June,

frost in August and mountains of snow much of the rest of the year.

We do. So we get the Lake.

Defining the Shores

What do we mean by "the shores?" For most of this book, we'll use the perspective of the Twin Ports: The South Shore reaches into Michigan's Upper Peninsula, and the North Shore extends to Thunder Bay, Ontario. You can imagine the shoreline as a leaning "V" with twin towns at each point. On the left (northeast) point is Thunder Bay, consolidated from Port Arthur and Fort William, which until 1970 were known as the Twin Cities (not to be confused with the bigger metropolis in southern Minnesota). Down the "north" side, at the foot of the "V," are the Twin Ports of Duluth and Superior, separated by the St. Louis Bay. Going east along the southern side of the "V" we come to the point of Hurley, Wisconsin, and Ironwood, Michigan, separated only by the Montreal River and a state line.

In reality, of course, both the North Shore and the South Shore extend all the way around the Lake to Sault Ste. Marie. We'll discuss those regions of Lake Superior in our Circle Tour chapter.

Ethnicity and Economy

THE PEOPLE

The ethnic pattern here is tied to historic economic activity. The Ojibwes settled in the region primarily because of the shallow inland lakes full of wild rice and the wonderful Lake Superior fishery. French voyageurs, in search of beaver and other skins and furs, linked themselves to Indian communities where they married and raised children. Scottish, English and Yankee fur traders set up shop at intersections of ancient tribal trading routes near the "big lake." Norwegians settled along the Lake, lured by familiar rocks and pines and commercial fishing. Swedes settled where they could farm, both near the Lake and inland. Finns settled in remote wooded areas where they could follow their Ojibwe-like life of hunting, gathering and farming. Eastern and southern Europeans as well as experienced miners from England settled where they could find work in the copper and iron mines. Everyone worked in the logging industry. Thus, we have odd pockets of leftover heritage: Italian bocce ball in Ironwood, Michigan, and Minnesota's Iron Range; Cornish "pasties" in Duluth and Ironwood, Michigan; wild rice and cranberries (which grow wild and abundantly in some areas here) on restaurant menus; Ojibwe dream-catchers hanging from rearview mirrors; lutefisk (fish) showing up at supermarkets at holiday time; curling clubs all the way around the Lake; and Scottish bagpipe bands in Duluth and Thunder Bay. French names are common in Indian communities, and a few older Ojibwes still know the French songs their ancestors learned several centuries ago, which researchers recently showed are virtually the same as those still sung in France.

THE RESOURCES
(NATURAL AND MAN-MADE)

The economic story here is the same as anywhere on the continent: Industrial capitalism transformed a country unbelievably rich in natural resources into personal fortunes, jobs, universities, hospitals, service industries, a lifeline to Europe and a denuded landscape. The great white pine forests were swept away in a shockingly short time (in the first decade of this century, 3.3 billion board feet of white pine were milled in Duluth alone), leaving a wasteland that was soon pocked with copper and iron mines. Michigan led the country in iron production until Minnesota took over, where, also in the first decade of this century, 200 million tons of iron ore were extracted. Copper production in Michigan reached its peak during World War I, with 266 million pounds; fisheries boomed too, reaching 25 million pounds in 1941. The big trees were gone, the fishery went into sharp decline — partly because of the abuse to the Lake from logging and mining industries — and the mines gave out.

What does a region do when it has all but used up its natural resources? Find more or get into service industries. Both have happened here. New technology to extract low-grade ore gave a second, less exuberant (but still beating) life to the mining industry. You'll see some mining activities on the North Shore (at Silver Bay and Taconite Harbor, where facilities process or ship taconite pellets made from low-grade iron ore), and in Michigan's Upper Peninsula, where White Pine Copper Mine is still in operation. Northshore Mining at Silver Bay (population 1,900) has a capacity of 10 million tons of taconite pellets a year. White Pine smelts more than 4 million tons of copper ore a year, producing 100 million pounds of copper. The commercial fishery is being replaced with a sports fishery that's supported with fish planting programs. Nature and tree-planting programs have restored greenery and provide pulpwood for paper companies.

But the phrase "when the forest was dark" — a phrase that octogenarian Finns and Ojibwes sometimes use to begin stories about their childhoods — isn't likely to be heard in future generations; there are plans to double timber harvest on public lands throughout the area. Proponents say the forests can tolerate the increased pressure, which is needed for the paper and pulp industry. Opponents say the pressure will leave us with an aspen ("popple") monoculture not diverse enough to sustain a lively community of native plants and animals. A few pockets of 300-year-old trees remain, such as hemlocks in Wisconsin's Apostle Islands and white pines near Two Harbors on the North Shore. In early 1996, a legislative effort was under way to protect such stands from the increased logging.

A second part of the economic retrenchment has been to diversify, and the biggest piece of that diversification is tourism. As you drive along the Lake on either shore, you'll see that the area's transition from logging/fishing/mining to tourism is at an ideal point for the tourist. There's still enough of the former to maintain an authentic flavor and authentic activity; there's enough of the latter to support a feeling that you really are on vacation and people around you are having fun. You'll see more wild shore land than development, and you won't be inundated with the overwhelming commercialism that has descended on other tourist regions and obliterated the reason tourists wanted to come. Almost anywhere along either shore, you can find a secluded place to go rock-hunting or skinny-dipping (make it quick if you're in the cold waters of the North Shore!).

There's a nonstop "progress-versus-environment" argument in our area, even over such a seemingly innocuous proposition as building a marina somewhere between Duluth and Knife River, 15 miles up the North Shore. Some Insiders — particularly the newcomer refugees from overdeveloped cities — strive to keep the shores from becoming "another Door County." (Door County, on Wisconsin's Lake Michigan shore, is cited over and over around here as an example of a beautiful place that is suffocating under unregulated tourism growth.) Other Insiders — particularly those who are "from here," meaning they're descendants of the settlers — strive for a livelier economy so neither they nor their children will have to move away to find jobs.

Both shores are slowly but surely undergoing tourism development. Summers are colder and foggier, and the land is more rugged along the North Shore, which means farmers are few. The forested rock-and-clay coastline has a wild, occasionally desolate feel to it. The South Shore is a mellower place; Lake Superior is more shallow here, meaning the summertime air is warmer; the hills aren't so rugged; and, in many places, sand overlays the clay, making it easier to farm.

Both shores have their municipal jewels: Grand Marais on the North Shore;

Bayfield on the South. Each of these villages is a must-see for visitors to the region. They're rich in beauty and history and sustain lively artist colonies and still-functioning commercial fisheries.

As you explore along the creeks (pronounced "cricks" here) and rivers on the North Shore, you'll notice that the water is tea-colored. It's a natural phenomenon. Some say it's caused by the iron in the water, but experts say it's tannin — from tamarack, sphagnum moss and marsh plants in the inland wetlands that are the source of the streams.

GOVERNMENT'S HAND

Much of the economic life of the region is from government dollars — such as a recent highway project that sunk $38 million into two tunnels on the North Shore's Minn. Highway 61. Opened in 1994, the two are the only mined tunnels in the Midwest (others are cut open and then covered). The road at Silver Creek Cliff used to go up and around the cliff, for a spectacular view of the Lake that a few people saw from the air as their cars sailed over the edge. The 1,340-foot-long tunnel was built not because of poor drivers, how-ever, but because the road was eroding so badly, and highway officials feared there would be a major failure. Sure enough, six months after the tunnel was opened, the road caved in — fortunately, nobody was on it. The 852-foot-long Lafayette tunnel a few miles farther up the shore is 60 feet wide, making it (as of 1996) the widest mined tunnel in the world.

Erosion is a problem along much of the shoreline and has been ever since people cut a road and began artificially manipulating Lake Superior's level at Sault Ste. Marie to accommodate shipping and control water levels on the more populous lower lakes. After a "nor'easter," you'll notice a red cloud welling out into the Lake — that's the red clay of the lakeshore.

Two Harbors and Grand Marais are the county seats of Lake and Cook counties, respectively. Both counties have far more public land (in forests, parks and wilderness areas) than private, making government the biggest employer in many communities. Duluth and Superior are the political centers of St. Louis and Douglas counties. On the South Shore, Washburn, Ashland, Hurley and Iron-

In Duluth, we have two temperatures: "over the hill" and "downtown." Over the hill is usually much hotter in the summer and colder in the winter than it is downtown where the waters of Lake Superior moderate the air. An 85-degree day on the hill might be 48 degrees downtown. A 20-below day over the hill might be 15 above downtown. We've noticed that broadcasters in the Twin Cities and elsewhere consistently choose inconsistency when reporting our temperatures. But who can blame them? There's shock value in using the downtown temperature in the summer and the over-the-hill temperature in the winter!

Insiders' Tips

wood are the respective county seats of Bayfield, Ashland, Iron and Gogebic counties.

Wisconsin counties are governed by elected supervisors; Minnesota's and Michigan's by elected commissioners. In additional to county, provincial and state government, there are five tribal governments here — one near Thunder Bay and four in the United States.

TRIBAL GOVERNMENTS

The Lake Superior Ojibwes reserved beautiful homelands when they ceded the rest of their territory to the United States in the 1854 Treaty of LaPointe. Grand Portage near the Canadian border has the least population and the most rugged, forested land, along with a lodge/casino, a logging operation and a fishery. Fond du Lac, inland from Duluth about 25 miles, overlaps with the city of Cloquet and has a community college, lodge/casino and beautiful wild rice lakes.

Red Cliff, a few miles north of Bayfield on the Wisconsin shoreline, has a lively commercial fishery, a fish hatchery and a casino. Its sister-band is at Bad River, east of Ashland. In treaty times, the two were known as the LaPointe band, but now they're independent, each with its own reservation. Included on Bad River's are 16,000 acres of pristine wetlands known as the Kakagon and Bad River sloughs. Besides the wildlife-rich sloughs, the reservation has an abundance of wild rice, a fish hatchery and a casino. Bad River is also the site of the Great Lakes Indian Fish & Wildlife Commission, an inter-tribal group that co-manages natural resources in the ceded territories.

The band governments are run by elected councilors. Fond du Lac and Grand Portage, while governing most of their own affairs, are also part of the six-reservation Minnesota Chippewa Tribe, which is based far inland in Cass Lake, Minnesota, and has a governing committee made up of members of the band governments. The other reservations in the region are politically independent.

Fort William First Nations has a reserve on the outskirts of Thunder Bay at Mount McKay. The band maintains the

---

Photo: Duluth News-Tribune

The Oliver Bridge crosses the St. Louis River and connects New Duluth, Minnesota, and Oliver, Wisconsin.

road to the 1,000-foot-high mountain lookout and offers camping and an authentic historic village, complete with native artisans in traditional dress.

Thunder Bay Area

The world's largest freshwater port and "mile zero" of the St. Lawrence Seaway, Thunder Bay, population 115,000, is on a beautiful natural harbor and is a major shipping center of Canada. It handles 20 million tons of cargo yearly — grain, coal, potash, steel, wood products — in 1,000 annual ships' visits (some ships return over and over again).

It's busy here and apparently has been for thousands of years. Ancient Indians dug 30-foot-deep copper mines and crafted fine copper tools more than 5,000 years ago; 3,000 years later, their descendents were trading their metal and pottery for goods from Wyoming to the Atlantic coast, making the area a major trade crossroads long before French and English fur traders entered the scene in the 17th and 18th centuries. In the 19th century, Fort William became a thriving fur trading center, and Port Arthur became the shipping center for the growing mining and forestry product industries.

Although this two-part city has been one since 1970, it still retains a feeling of separateness. It has two downtowns and two voting districts with two provincial courthouses. Thunder Bay/Atikokan votes for provincial and federal members of parliament; Thunder Bay/Nipigon votes for a different pair. There's a federal government building on the south side and another beautiful new federal building on the north.

Terms such as Thunder Bay North and Thunder Bay South are mostly used by officials and by outsiders; Insiders stick to Port Arthur and Fort William. The feeling of separateness is deep-rooted, both because of historic rivalry (a Thunder Bay publication described them as "side-by-side, cheek-by-jowel (sic) and fang-to-fang"), and the way in which consolidation came about — painfully. Even the choice of the name was the result of controversy. Voters had three choices: Thunder Bay; Lakehead; and The Lakehead. Voters obviously liked the "Lakehead" term best, because the two versions together got 8,000 more votes than "Thunder Bay" — but neither version had enough votes alone to win.

The city is about halfway between the Atlantic and Pacific, and 430 land miles from the other end of the lake at Sault Ste. Marie. It's about the same number of miles west to Winnipeg, Manitoba. There are no counties in the Northwest Region of Ontario; the geographic equivalent is a district, but that isn't a political entity and there are no elected officials. Thunder Bay is in the Thunder Bay District; the city's residents vote for a 12-person city council.

Thunder Bay has a healthy French minority as well as a smaller Oji-Cree-speaking minority, and French is taught in the schools. However, the city is officially an English-speaking town; city council reports, telephone bills and water bills are only in English.

Tourism accounts for more than 4,000 jobs here, with about 1.3 million tourists making an annual impact of $300 million on the economy. In addition, there are three major pulp and paper mills; eight sawmills; and 10 operating grain elevators.

The lovely Lakehead University is a four-year liberal arts college, and the city also has a two-year-technical school — Confederation College. Their combined enrollment is 10,000. (See our Child Care and Education chapter for details.)

Thunder Bay loves sports. It has two pro teams (hockey and baseball) and a training-for-the-pros team (hockey), supports many annual sporting events and is the site of regular national sports competitions. In 1996 alone, the city hosted the Canadian national women's curling bonspiel and the Canadian Olympic wrestling trials. The Canada Games Complex is a giant indoor playland for the athletically minded, with an Olympic-size pool, diving, racquetball, squash, a 73-meter

curving "thunderslide" that drops you into the pool and weight and fitness rooms. Annual Thunder Bay-Duluth summer games competitions died in 1995 — not because of lack of enthusiasm on the part of this sports-minded town, but because Duluth had a hard time finding enough people who shared that enthusiasm. Parks, arenas and curling rinks pepper the city, and cross-country and downhill skiing ring it.

Thunder Bay is also rich culturally, with a giant annual music festival (three weeks of string, piano, brass, woodwind, vocal, band and dance competitions), an orchestra, art galleries, live theater and museums. The Centennial Conservatory is a haven of serenity and beauty, with footpaths winding through glass-enclosed rooms of exotic trees, cacti and flowers.

Ashland

Entering Ashland from either direction on U.S. Highway 2, you'll suddenly realize you're getting some wide-open views reminiscent of the plains. This South Shore Wisconsin city, with a population of 8,600, is mostly flat and stretches along Chequamegon Bay. It has rich wetlands nearby where waterfowl nest, with woodlands nearby and Chequamegon National Forest only minutes away. What a perfect place, the visitor might think, to study environmental issues. That's what academicians thought too, and that's why the four-year Northland College is here. It was named the best environmental college in the United States in 1994. The Wisconsin Indianhead Technical Institute, also in Ashland, offers five associate degree programs. (See our Child Care and Education chapter.)

Historically, transportation and manufacturing dominated Ashland's economy, and most of Michigan's iron ore was shipped from six docks here. One remains — an imposing structure 1,800 feet long and 80 feet high. Another reminder of the busy transportation days is the lovely brownstone Soo Line Depot, which has been restored and now houses a fine restaurant and lounge.

These days, service dominates the city's economy, with manufacturing and retail trade almost as strong. About 500 people work in public schools and post-secondary education. Memorial Medical Center is the largest employer, with more than 400 workers, and Bretting Manufacturing (paper machines) is a close second. Several hundred people work for the city, the county or the federal Bureau of Indian Affairs, which has an agency office here. This is a town that still has its busy main street, with beautiful government buildings, stores, and the original, still used, movie theater. The Vaughn Municipal Library is not only a lovely building but well-used and administered; it includes the Ashland Museum.

Hurley/Ironwood

The twin towns of Hurley, Wisconsin (population 1,780), and Ironwood, Michigan (population 6,800), share an economy over the state border. It's been a struggling economy for years but apparently has bottomed out and is on the rise again. The largest single employer in the area is the White Pine Copper Mine, with 1,075 workers, followed by White Cap Mountain Ski Corporation in Montreal,

Wisconsin (730 people). Forest and fiber industries are next, employing a total of about 1,000 workers at nine companies. Five sewing firms and other manufacturers employ about 575 people in the twin towns and surrounding communities.

The attractive Gogebic Community College in Ironwood has its own ski hill within snowball distance of classrooms where students can get on-hands experience in one of the college's specialties: ski hill management. The students do a lot of skiing too. (See the Child Care and Education chapter for more information.)

The Old Ironwood Theatre brings symphony orchestras, string quartets, Broadway shows and concerts to town, and Ironwood's own Gogebic Range Players offer stage productions here throughout the year.

The Iron County Historical Museum is a beautiful three-story building in Hurley that features exhibits on logging and mining. Also, a busy group of retired people makes rugs and demonstrates rug-making on several looms here.

The twin towns are surrounded by high hills and rock outcrops and are transformed in the wintertime into skiing/snowmobile heaven. They're within what Insiders call the "snow belt," receiving more than 200 inches of the white stuff a year. Four popular ski hills, with a total of 24 chair lifts, draw skiers from all over the Midwest. See our Winter Sports chapter for details about skiing opportunities here and elsewhere in the region.

The Aerial Lift Bridge was built in 1905 with a ferry car and later modified in 1929 to include the lifting central span. In winter, weight is added to the 500-pound counterweights at each end to account for ice and dirt the central span picks up from the roadway that traverses it.

Insiders' Tips

Commercial fisheries were established at Bayfield, Wisconsin, and in the St. Louis River as early as the late 1850s.

Inside
History

In the Beginning…

Before the Egyptians were making pyramids, ancient Indian people were living in the Lake Superior region. They mined the copper that was abundant in the Thunder Bay area, on Isle Royale and on Michigan's Upper Peninsula. Using smelting techniques lost in time, they crafted fine implements: awls, spear heads and fish and gaff hooks — the latter probably to haul big fish from the Lake. Their descendants developed pottery. And 500 years before the birth of Christ, they were trading pottery and metalwork all over North America.

People valued the riches of Lake Superior long before the first European dipped his paddle in its waters. The European was Frenchman Etienne Brulé, and he paddled into Chequamegon Bay — at the present city of Ashland, Wisconsin — around the time the Pilgrims landed at Plymouth Rock. Like Columbus, he was searching for a passage to the Orient. Instead, he came to another passage, a river that connects with inland water routes to the Mississippi and now bears his name. The route would be used for the next 200 years in a lively fur trade, as would others: Pigeon River at Grand Portage and the St. Louis River at Duluth.

Furs, copper and religion were the thrusts of the early European penetrations into this region. Jesuit missionaries and French entrepreneurs arrived in a heavily wooded, watery world controlled mostly by Ojibwes, an Algonquian people who earlier had migrated from the East.

The Dakotas were in this region long before the Ojibwes. Their central community, however, was inland at Lake Mille Lacs in Minnesota. The Dakotas were strong fighters, having relinquished their Lake Superior territory to the better-equipped advancing Ojibwes only after strong resistance. (Some Hurons traveling with the explorer Radisson were loathe to enter Dakota territory because of the Dakotas' fighting reputation.)

Fur Trade Dominates

For much of the 18th and well into the 19th centuries, the economy of our region was dominated by the fur trade. It involved all tribes, an army of French voyageurs, trading posts, a fleet of canoes, and the French, British and (later) American governments. The War of the Spanish Succession, Queen Anne's War, the Seven Years' (French and Indian) War, the War of 1812 — all these affected and were affected by the fur trade. But despite wars and warlike competition between trading companies, the furs poured out of the vast interior of North America. Europe and the growing cities of the east wanted beaver and other fine furs for hats, robes and coats.

For three decades, Grand Portage in northeastern Minnesota was the primary Lake Superior hub of this fur trade and was run by the North West Company. Bales of pelts (beaver, bear, mink, fox, raccoon, muskrat, fisher and wolverine) arrived from inland and left via canoe for the East. Cargoes of trade goods (blankets, kettles, hatchets, knives, wine, ammunition and guns) arrived from the East, destined for inland. After the Jay Treaty of 1794, which established a boundary between the United States and Canada and set up trading rules, the company moved the trading post across the border to avoid U.S. taxes. And Fort William was built, the first of the settlements that would become Thunder Bay.

The American Fur Company established another post at Fond du Lac. But by the 1830s, populations of beaver and other fur-bearing animals had gone into sharp decline. The glory days of the fur trade were over.

A Changing World

Meanwhile, none of the countries owned any of the land they were surveying, delineating and ceding to one another in treaties made in Europe. The land around Lake Superior was Indian land. A growing number of non-Indian speculators, farmers and loggers wanted clear title to it. So began a series of treaties in which Ojibwes in both countries ceded all their Lake Superior lands, with the exception of small parcels the bands reserved as homelands.

The Ojibwes also reserved rights to hunt, fish and gather on the ceded lands, never dreaming that those lands would be transformed utterly. Within years (sometimes months) of each cession, from 1836 in the Upper Peninsula to 1854 on Minnesota's North Shore, an army of loggers descended and literally wiped out the great primeval forests. Caribou and other wildlife disappeared. Rivers and bays were often solid with floating logs being boomed to sawmills. Development companies, dams, railroads, bridges and brownstone quarries combined to create cities — cities with no trees but with room to accommodate new immigrants recruited in Europe by North American industrialists who needed laborers. By 1900, half the people on Minnesota's Iron Range were foreign-born; in 1930, a quarter of Duluthians were born outside the country. Some of those laborers brought "foreign" ideas and were persecuted. Greeks and Italians rebelled against inhuman working conditions in labor camps in Thunder Bay and staged the first walkouts; newspapers condemned them and other "aliens" with ugly epithets;

During the great fire of 1918, a Swedish immigrant-farmer in Duluth Township was about to flee the area when he remembered that his neighbor's 11 children were alone, the parents having gone on an errand. So he hurried through the woods to that farm, placed the youngsters end-to-end in the depression along the edge of a plowed field, and plowed a second furrow to cover them. He fashioned breathing holes for each and then covered himself; the fire rushed across the open field so rapidly that all survived.

Insiders' Tips

Southern Europeans, non-whites and Jews were kept out of the loop of Anglo-Saxon power in Thunder Bay, Ontario, and Duluth, Minnesota.

Finnish people, too, were subject to harassment. Coming from a communal culture that put high value on education, Finnish immigrants quickly organized cooperatives and workers associations, and met to discuss political issues. They were reviled as Bolsheviks who were attempting to overthrow the government. In time, the efforts of these immigrants resulted in a strong labor movement and a liberal political viewpoint throughout much the region.

Soo Lock Links Lake Superior

The year after the final Lake Superior treaty was signed in 1854, the locks at Sault Ste. Marie (French for St. Mary's Falls) opened, allowing the first big ships onto the Lake. That meant more goods could be exported from the shores of Lake Superior, and supplies could be imported; economic activity swung into even higher gear. Dozens of sawmills opened — in Ashland, Washburn, Bayfield and Superior, Wisconsin, as well as in Duluth, along the North Shore and in Thunder Bay. The amount of lumber milled was staggering. In Duluth alone during the three decades from 1890, 7.7 billion board feet were milled. The "Soo" ("Sault" Ste. Marie locks) meant that all this lumber could be shipped down through the Great Lakes to eastern cities. Likewise, the boats could carry copper and iron from the mines being opened on Michigan's Upper Peninsula and Minnesota's Iron Range.

Excavating and Extracting

Copper was abundant, even legendary, around Lake Superior — such as the 6,000-pound copper boulder on the Up-

Father Baraga's cross can be seen on the North Shore, near Schroeder, Minnesota.

Photo: Duluth News-Tribune

per Peninsula, which was taken to the Smithsonian in 1843 and triggered a copper rush. Prospectors with picks, dynamite and camping gear descended on the Upper Peninsula (UP). By 1860, 33 companies were mining there; 25 million pounds of copper were produced in 1872; and the annual yield was even 10 times greater during World War I. Copper wasn't mined out in Michigan; it simply became less lucrative to mine it there than elsewhere, and the industry moved west to Montana. White Pine Mine continues its operation on the UP, as do a few mines on the Ontario side where copper mining never reached the heights it did in Michigan.

Iron soon dominated the landscape. Within a few years of the signing of the 1836 treaty, the Upper Peninsula was opened for iron mining. Shipments from the UP grew from 1,500 tons in 1855 to

Lake Superior's Ojibwe People

According to legend, the Anishinaabe people lived in the Lake Superior region in the dim reaches of time past, many thousands of years ago. A long migration took them east to the Atlantic Coast where they remained for hundreds of years and were given their religion — the Midewiwin.

That brings us to "recent" history — perhaps 1,000 years ago. The vibrant culture of the Anishinaabe (which means "spontaneously created people" in

Photo: Northeast Minnesota Historical Center

This 1870s photo for a stereoscope shows a group of Ojibwe men from Bemidji, Minnesota, who came to Duluth to sell furs. When viewed through a stereoscope, the double image gave a three-dimensional effect.

their Algonquin-family language) had gone into decline, possibly because of war with the Iroquois, and the people began another great migration — this time back westward. They settled by the St. Lawrence River (near present-day Montreal, Quebec) and once again became a strong people centered on their religion.

Another long period of time passed, and the people once again moved westward, this time settling near Lake Huron. According to some accounts, the Anishinaabes gradually separated into three groups around this time. The people who would become known as the Ojibwe people ("those who roast until a thing is puckered up") continued on to Bow-e-ting, which French immigrants would later dub Sault Ste. Marie.

The Ojibwes' Anishinaabe relatives who settled in Michigan and eastern Wisconsin became known as the Potawatomis (firekeepers) and Ottawas (traders); the three still share a closely similar language and are considered the "Three Fires."

The Ojibwe city at Bow-e-ting went into decline, and the people moved again — some around the north side of Lake Superior, others around the south. The southern division came to Moning-wuna-kauning (now known as Madeline Island) in western Lake Superior. Madeline Island became the political, cultural and religious center of the Ojibwe. A 6-square-mile city (population 6,000) is said to have been established there.

As the Ojibwe prospered, they gradually thrust farther westward and southward, displacing the Fox and Dakota people who had inhabited Wisconsin and northeastern Minnesota. The city at Moning-wuna-

The picture, taken about 1918, shows a woman identified only as Mrs. Grasshopper standing beside a wigwam made of birch bark. Her daughter (at right) is unidentified.

Photo: Northeast Minnesota Historical Center

kauning was in decline by the time French missionaries arrived in the area, but the Ojibwe people were still at the height of their expansion; the two divisions had circled the Lake and by the late 1600s had penetrated long-held Dakota country in Minnesota's Upper Mississippi region. Today, Ojibwe people remain in their pre-European homelands in Michigan, northern Wisconsin and northern Minnesota as a result of treaties signed between 1837 and 1866 in which they ceded most of their land but reserved many of the best spots for themselves.

Consequently, although Ojibwe reservations underwent considerable plundering since treaty times, they remain some of the prettiest places in the region. Visitors are welcomed, particularly at powwows (see our Annual Events chapter) and casinos (see our Nightlife and Casinos chapter). Ojibwes also reserved the right to use much of the ceded land for hunting, fishing and gathering. That's why the Lake Superior bands today co-manage, with the states, the natural resources in the ceded territories (see our Fishing and Hunting chapter).

There are various ways of spelling the name of this branch of the Anishinaabe people: Ojibwe, Ojibway, Otjippeway, Odjibbiwa, Ojibwa, Chippeway, Chippewa and others. "Chippewa" has been the most common and is used on treaties, by most Ojibwe band governments and by older people. Younger people tend to prefer "Ojibwe" or "Anishinaabe."

Incidentally, many Indian people in the region still prefer the word "Indian" to Native American, Native person or indigenous person, although all of the latter terms are coming into wider use, as is the Canadian term "First Nations person." Officials of the Minnesota Chippewa Tribe, which with six member-bands is the largest tribe in the region and one of the largest in the United States, decided in 1995 that they would use the term "American Indian."

114,000 tons five years later. By 1900, Michigan led the country in producing iron ore. Until the "Soo" opened, there was difficulty transporting the ore, so more than 25 blast furnaces were installed — all fueled by locally made hardwood charcoal. After the locks were built, ore docks were built, and the ore was taken by ship to the big smelters farther east.

Iron mining in Minnesota began several decades behind Michigan's, but soon surpassed it. Using the open-pit method instead of shafts, the ore was extracted by immigrants and people who had come from mining country in the eastern United States. In the 1890s, Minnesota produced 43 million tons. By the time World War II rolled around, output was boosted to 338 million tons to meet the wartime steel demand.

The cities on the Lake had no mines; their mother-lode was the shipping connected to the inland operations. Ashland, Wisconsin; Duluth-Superior; Two Harbors, Minnesota; and Port Arthur, Ontario, all were beneficiaries of this trade. Ashland already was a thriving sawmill town and port for Lake Superior brownstone quarried nearby. But after the pines were gone and brownstone went out of fashion, ore gave the city a second breath, and 1886 and '87 were boom years.

From 1885, the year the "Soo" opened, until 1935, 1.5 billion tons of iron ore and 24 billion board feet of lumber were shipped from the lakeside communities. Also passing through their ports, coming from the Great Plains, were buffalo hides — and, after the buffalo were gone, 260 million tons of grain.

Canadian Reunification

The Civil War had some unexpected effects in our region. Duluth's still-tiny population — about 500 — was reduced when some men joined the Union cause and others went to Canada to avoid the draft. In what is now Thunder Bay, change came with the close of the war. Britain had been openly sympathetic to the South, and after Gen. Robert E. Lee's surrender, it was feared that the Union army was poised to take over Canada. The British North American Act was a defensive move that united Ontario and the eastern provinces into the Dominion of Canada. Efforts immediately began to bring the rest of Canada into the Dominion. A unified Canada could best fight American aspirations. This alarmed the Metis of the Red River country in Manitoba, who feared their property and traditional way of life would vanish with an invasion of Canadians. Led by Louis Riel, they revolted. What is now Thunder Bay became the base of operations for a thrust against Riel.

Col. (later General and Field-Marshall Viscount) Garnet Wolseley, veteran of British operations in India, Burma, China and the Crimea, arrived on the scene in May, 1870. His mission was to lead two battal-

Photo: Duluth News-Tribune

Commercial fishermen still operate on Lake Superior, although on a small scale.

ions, fully equipped and battle-ready, through hundreds of miles of swamp, forest and rivers to confront Riel. Apparently he thought Riel would wait for him as he accomplished this daunting and historic task. It included building a 37-mile road inland, which became part of the Red River-Dawson Road that cuts through Thunder Bay today. Wolseley did get his soldiers through; they arrived at Riel's base in late August. Riel, naturally, wasn't there; he escaped into the United States and much later was captured — though not by Wolseley — and executed.

The place Wolseley landed when he arrived in Thunder Bay he dubbed "Prince Arthur's Landing" — after the third son of Queen Victoria, Prince Arthur William Patrick Albert, a name it retained until it was incorporated in 1884 as Port Arthur. A few years later, amid much fanfare, the prince visited his namesake port — for an hour.

The Riel Rebellion prompted the building of a British lock at Sault Ste. Marie. The Americans had allowed Wolseley's upbound ships to use their locks, but only if the ships were empty; it was with much difficulty that the soldiers and military equipment were portaged on the Canadian side. The Canadian lock was completed in 1895.

Dry Land — Hot Fires

Wolseley had written that Thunder Bay in 1870 was a "desolate" sight, having been ravaged by one fire after another. Fires were common throughout the post-

French Voyageurs:
On the Long Haul

French voyageurs were the over-the-road truckers of the 18th century, but their highways were made of water. They hauled trade goods and provisions inland to Indian trappers and bales of pelts back out. The packs they toted, with the help of a tump strap across their foreheads, weighed up to 400 pounds. For their inland work, they used smaller canoes that could go up rivers and be portaged around rocks and waterfalls. For plying the waters of Lake Superior, they used "Montreal" canoes that could hold up to 12 people plus cargo. Pea soup was the staple fare for these sturdy, colorful and often rowdy people. An old-timer greeting on the North Shore has survived the voyageur era: "Bonjour, Pea Soup! How're things on the tote road?"

logging region; they fed on slash and sun-dried undergrowth left by the loggers. A 1918 fire that burned Cloquet south of Duluth killed hundreds and reached communities far up the North Shore. People took refuge in their wells and root cellars where many smothered. Duluthians and refugees gathered at the Lake, preparing to swim or row out if the fire poured over the brow of the hill; the firestorm created an updraft from the Lake, however, and the blaze fell back on itself and died. Other serious fires in the 1920s blackened much of the North Shore along what is now the scenic drive.

Plying the Waters

Commercial fishing, too, boomed after the treaty signing period, from the mid-1800s through the first half of this century — especially once the heavy logging ended at the turn of the century. Fisheries were established at Bayfield, Wisconsin, and in the St. Louis River in the late 1850s. By 1879 there were 130 commercial fishermen in Bayfield, and a year later there were 250. Most of their harvest (310,000 pounds of whitefish, trout, herring and walleye in 1879) went to Buffalo, Chicago and other points east, and to the Twin Cities. An-

other 140 fishermen worked out of the Upper Peninsula. Most of their harvest (410,000 pounds in 1879) went to the copper and iron mines in the region, with the rest shipped to Detroit, Cleveland and Milwaukee. Whitefish already were on the decline, partly because of sawdust from lumber mills being dumped into the Lake. The catch on the North Shore the same year was about 300,000 pounds. Peak total catches in Lake Superior's U.S. waters were 5 million pounds of whitefish in 1885, an equal number of trout in 1903, and 17 million pounds of herring in 1940. The trout harvest in Canadian waters peaked with 4 million pounds in 1910 and has been unmatched since.

As the fishermen and gear increased, the catches decreased. In 1939 there were 1,800 Americans fishing, using 1,200 boats and 3 million square yards of gill net mesh. Eventually, overfishing and exotic species added their destructive pressures to logging, mining and navigation pollution, and fish populations went into decline.

Moving into High Gear

After the Civil War, American financier Jay Cooke visited the Twin Ports, which then had a total population of 300. He was enthusiastic about their economic future and sank much of his wealth into building railroads that would have Duluth as their terminus. He also promoted the construction of railroad docks, wharves, grain elevators, stores and a bank. Superior residents called Duluthians "Jay Cooke's people" and "cliff-dwellers" (Duluth's epithet for them was "swamp-jumpers"). By 1870, Duluth had 3,000 people and had become a city, taking the modified name of the French explorer, Daniel Greysolon Sieur du Lhut, who visited its shores in the 17th century. The following year, backed by Cooke, Duluthians began digging a canal across Minnesota Point to give access to a harbor and accommodate increasing shipping. Superiorites requested and were granted a federal injunction to stop the dredging, but the order was coming by army courier who would take five days for the trip. Duluth companies, helped by residents who brought shovels and coffee and sandwiches, dug night and day and beat the courier. The canal was opened, the St. Louis River current soon widened it, and floating islands in the bay (some with houses) sailed out on the Lake. The golden age of sailing schooners (from 1864 to '68 there were 1,875 on the Lake) was over, and steel ships began replacing wooden.

The first recorded commercial watercraft enterprise in our region had been run by Osagi, a headman of the Lake Superior Ojibwe who set up a canoe yard in what is now Douglas County in the early 1800s. His business is believed to have been up the Nemadji River a few miles from where U.S. Highway 2 now crosses it in Superior. Osagi and his workers supplied large lake canoes and smaller river canoes to paddlers in the fur trade, mostly at the old Fort St. Louis on the bay in Superior.

A couple of miles away and a few decades later — in 1889, the same year Superior became a city — a colorful Scot named Alexander Dougall built the first steel ship — a whaleback freighter. By the next year, he had 2,000 people working for him, building ships. The shipyard would make 46 whalebacks in the next nine years, a precursor to its high-gear shipbuilding for World War II.

Canada's first cross-continental railway, the Canadian Pacific, was completed in 1886, and Port Arthur and its twin town, Fort William, were on the line. Grain from the Great Plains poured into the ports that year. During the next year, more grain than dreamed of arrived on trains. The elevators bulged, the trains continued coming, and old sheds were filled. The trains kept coming. A giant shed that would hold 800,000 pounds was hastily erected, and 20 four-man crews worked night and day with shovels to move the ever-flowing grain. They managed to get all of it under cover, but the twin towns realized they needed much more storage room than anticipated.

A million-bushel elevator was built in 1889 and another, larger one, the next. By 1891 the twin towns were handling 12 million bushels a year and had become the biggest grain port in the world.

Settling Down

The communities around the Lake had become settled, rooted. Most churches, school systems, hospitals, colleges, universities, arts groups and social societies were established in the 1880s and '90s.

Two communities were yet to be built, however — they were planned towns, and both served the iron industry. In 1916, U.S. Steel built a smelting plant in western Duluth and then developed a model village for the employees. It was called Morgan Park, after the company's founder and owner, J. Pierpont Morgan. The attractive community remains, but the plant, which had become Duluth's largest employer, closed shop in 1975.

In 1955, Reserve Mining Company built a taconite plant at Silver Bay, and a town to go with it. This was Minnesota's first large-scale taconite operation, taking low-grade iron ore, crushing it, extracting the ore from it and rolling it into little balls called taconite pellets. But by the 1970s, the plant became the focus of one of the most bitter controversies ever in these parts. During the previous 15 years, the plant had poured 274 million tons of taconite "tailings" back into the Lake; the cloud of floating asbestos-like threads settled on trout spawning beds, wandered with the current around to Duluth and the South Shore and got into the drinking water. The state took Reserve to court, and a federal judge threatened to shut down the plant unless an onshore disposal site was built. Tailings are now piped inland into a settlement pond. Now the plant is operated by Northshore Mining, which can produce almost 10 million tons of pellets a year.

Ojibwe-white relations in our area historically have been relatively good — spectacularly good when compared with some other areas of the country. In the mid-1800s, Wisconsin whites blocked a move from the White House to push their good neighbors, the Wisconsin Ojibwes, west to Indian Ter-

Col. Wolseley, who led a fighting force from Thunder Bay into Manitoba to quell the Louis Riel Rebellion, left a diary and some unflattering remarks about the area. He described mosquitoes so prevalent his eyes were swollen shut from their bites, and "immense quantities of lake trout, many of them weighing 10 or 12 pounds. They are without exception the most tasteless of the finny tribe. We know of nothing which is less palatable without being positively nauseous." He also was revolted by the French; the Irish; Catholics in general; and Indians, even those who weren't Catholic.

ritory; Ojibwes were voting in Duluth elections as early as the late 1800s; and, throughout the region, intermarriage long has been common and widely accepted.

There's a nasty blot, however, on Duluth's history regarding African Americans. Blacks had settled in Duluth to work in the lumber and steel industries early in the 1900s. But in 1920, three young traveling circus workers, all African Americans, were lynched here on a downtown street, after a young white Duluth woman claimed someone had raped her. In the aftermath of the only recorded race lynching in the upper Midwest was an exodus of black Duluthians and Superiorites. The black population of St. Paul immediately grew — both with people fleeing the Twin Ports and with migrating Southerners who decided to stop well south of the Twin Ports. As a result, St. Paul became a center of civil-rights activity and Duluth got a reputation as a place to avoid. Today, its African-American population remains small — about 900, fewer than either Asians or Hispanics.

Rivals No More

In 1970, a man named Saul Laskin rang two ships' bells and a new era began. Laskin was the new mayor of a new-old town: Thunder Bay. The bells were from the HMCS *Fort William* and HMCS *Port Arthur*. The two old rivals had finally got together. United, they could draw industry and business as a single strong city instead of competing for development as two smaller towns; hold more political clout in the province and nation; and stanch a population drain.

Two Views of the Interstate

The beginning and end of the era of Interstate highway building happened in

Duluth, and the difference is plain to see. The western end was begun on the heels of federal legislation enacting the system in 1956 — before there was a lot of experience with such freeways. It wiped out entire neighborhoods and was stopped dead at Mesaba Avenue by community controversy. It's an unattractive piece of work, with dirty, unadorned concrete, gloomy recesses of column-forests and a tangle of entrances and exits, all cutting through neighborhoods. In the words of one highway department spokesperson, "It's a classic example of why you've got to put a lot of lipstick on a pig." The second piece, which continued the freeway through Duluth and is remarkably attractive for a freeway, opened in 1992 as the last piece in the national system. The project got a lot of community input and was chosen as the least jarring route for neighborhoods. That 3-mile strip cost $275 million — $74 million for landscaping alone, which included much of the downtown renovation: the skywalks, brickwork and lighting on downtown streets and the Lakewalk.

What a Long, Strange Trip It's Been

From the days of a lively Ojibwe economy in the vast, damp forests where woodland caribou and bison roamed, until today, our region has waxed and waned many times over — economically, ethnically, environmentally, visually, politically. The coming of the Europeans, followed by industrial capitalism, made the fastest and most obvious changes; but change, of course, has continued. Since our industrial peak in the mid-1900s, we've become less industrial, less rural and more yuppified. Where bleak warehouses, industrial docks and sailor saloons once crowded the waterfront, shops, parks and restaurants now cater to tourists. We produce less, and play and serve more: We catch-and-release fish for fun instead of netting fish for others' tables; we garner grants to interpret wolves and hawks to urban visitors; we offer tourists Jacuzzis and espresso in upscale motels, rather than a little cabin by a fishing dock or a six-room motel along the highway. We've learned that winter can be a moneymaker and, with that knowledge, peddle our region to outsiders as a skiing, snowshoeing and snowmobiling heaven (which it is). Very often, "we" are not even "we," but outsiders who recently have arrived after fleeing failed urban centers.

Our own urban centers have had their share of failure, too. Duluth's population peaked at more than 100,000 early in the century, maintained that level for decades, and began dropping in the 1970s. It appears to have leveled out at about 85,000. Likewise Ashland, Superior and other South Shore communities have seen population declines. In the 1960s, it appeared Port Arthur and Fort William would go the same way; their consolidation in 1970 reversed that trend, and the city now has 25,000 more people than it did then.

During the late 1980s and early 1990s, Shore communities (Grand Marais and Tofte, Minnesota, and Bayfield, Wisconsin) have boomed. People have been pouring into the Bayfield area to buy up old farmsteads and lakeshore property; the North Shore is a little behind, but land there, too, has become prized for retirement, tourism businesses and summer homes.

We still can't decide how to balance "development" with the environment, but we're trying. For example, in 1996, two companies wanted to develop further the malled area of Duluth on U.S. Highway 53. Some citizens blocked the move, arguing that there already was too much store space, too many paved lots and too much damage to the environment. Others argued for the jobs and tax dollars more stores would bring. The issue went to referendum; voters allowed one development and disallowed the other.

A blot on Duluth's history was addressed in 1991 when some Duluthians decided it was time to look hard at the lynching of the three circus workers. They located the unidentified graves of the slain young men, prompted a community discussion of the tragedy and held a public memorial healing ceremony at the graveside where the mayor spoke. New

Defeated" were put up over the graves of Isaac McGhee and Elias Clayton, hometowns unknown, and Elmer Jackson of Topeka, Kansas; another joint memorial was held later in Topeka. The graves are at Park Hill Cemetery, 2500 Vermilion Road.

A significant development during the past several decades in our region has been the reclamation of tribal rights and governmental authority by the Lake Superior Ojibwes. These rights had been pinched increasingly as the newer states developed and began enforcing state codes and regulations indiscriminately, disregarding the preexisting governmental status of the tribes. (One longtime Minnesota game warden said after his retirement in the early 1990s that he and his colleagues knew that under the treaties they had no authority to arrest Indians who were hunting and fishing out of state season; but wardens were directed "by St. Paul" to do it anyway. In some cases, state judges, cognizant of the rights, threw out the complaints; in most, tribal members lost game, wild rice, guns and vehicles, and were fined or jailed as well.) After lengthy court battles over land, jurisdictional and hunting/fishing rights, and after sometimes nasty confrontations with anti-treaty white citizens, Ojibwe tribes have re-established their status as separate government entities. They're reclaiming land, assuming jurisdiction over issues like licensing, taxation and land use, asserting sovereign governmental rights (to allow gambling on tribal lands, for example) and co-managing natural resources with the states in much of the ceded territories. Some Ojibwes argue that the treaties can be used by both Indians and non-Indians as a constitutional lever to protect the environment. The idea is that pollution effectively erases the right to hunt, fish and gather guaranteed in the treaties, and the U.S. Constitution identifies treaties as the "highest law of the land."

Through all this, Lake Superior remains — huge, cold, powerfully beautiful, a bit dirtier but still largely unchanged, attracting a continuing stream of us tiny, variegated humans who hope, somehow, to make its shores home.

Most of the western Lake Superior region is in the Central time zone. However, when you cross the border into Canada or go 25 miles into Michigan's Upper Peninsula, you'll be in the eastern zone. Set your watch ahead (later) an hour.

Inside
Getting Here,
Getting Around

You know the old joke: A tourist gets lost on a country road and asks a local for directions to the nearest city; the local ponders the question and finally responds, "You can't get there from here."

That joke must have originated in our neck of the woods, where lifelong Insiders often exhibit a combination of dry humor and resentment toward too-inquisitive strangers. But ask anyway; a lot of newcomer-Insiders are eager to show off their knowledge about this beautiful part of the world. And if you get an old-timer, the worst that will happen is that you'll get joshed or ignored.

Some means of "getting there" are really simple in our region. You can get out of Duluth or Thunder Bay on foot, if need be; these cities are not so big and sprawling that lack of transportation means you must languish in an urban center. You can get from Ashland, Wisconsin, to Thunder Bay, Ontario, by canoe, and from Duluth, Minnesota, to Sault Ste. Marie, Michigan, by sailboat; and you can get virtually anywhere by snowmobile when the ground is covered. You can get to the rural casinos for free simply by showing up at regular pickup places (see our Nightlife and Casinos chapter). But there are other choices too, such as planes, trains and automobiles — and huskies, catamarans and Clydesdales.

Transportation Services

Before venturing out on a journey in these parts, call the following numbers to find out about travel and weather conditions throughout the Lake Superior region.

ROAD CONDITIONS INFORMATION
Duluth, Minn.	(218) 723-4866
Minnesota (statewide)	(800) 542-0220
Thunder Bay, Ont.	(807) 473-2100

WEATHER INFORMATION
National Weather Service
Duluth, Minn.	(218) 729-6697
Environment Canada	
Thunder Bay, Ont.	(807) 345-9111

By Automobile

With a car under you, travel is downright easy. The roads range from OK to excellent, and signage is good everywhere. Expect to run into road work, however — particularly after a deep-frost winter like that of 1995-96. The frost does major damage to roads, and summertime is when they get repaired.

Four national highways cut through this region: **Interstate 35** begins in Superior, crosses the Blatnik Bridge to Duluth and continues south through Minnesota, ultimately winding up in Laredo, Texas.

U.S. Highway 2 goes east-west from the Straits of Mackinac connecting Lakes

Huron and Michigan, through Michigan's Upper Peninsula and northern Wisconsin, across the Bong Bridge to Duluth and west through Bemidji, Minnesota; then on through northern tier states to Washington's Puget Sound. It's mostly a two-lane roadway in our area, with some stretches of four lanes and several points of three lanes for passing. "Two" is known as a dangerous road — truckers, whitetail deer and late-night tavern patrons use it — so exercise caution.

U.S. Highway 53 heads north-south from International Falls, Minnesota, to Duluth, across the Blatnik Bridge into Superior and into southern Wisconsin. The **Trans-Canada Highway 11/17** runs from Ottawa in the east, through Thunder Bay and on to Regina, where it divides and winds its way to the Pacific Coast at Prince Rupert and Vancouver via Edmonton and Calgary, respectively. **Minn. Highway 61**, which ran "right by [Bob Dylan's] baby's door," no longer has a federal designation because it mostly follows I-35. Nevertheless, it still reigns supreme on the North Shore as a state highway and continues into Thunder Bay, Ontario, as a provincial highway. Plan on some construction delays between Two Harbors and Grand Marais in the summer of 1996 and 1997. The delays are likely to be minor, because although the highway is being completely reconstructed, the work will happen in small increments. A major construction project at Gooseberry Falls, where a new bridge and information center are going up, probably will add some confusion to an area that in good weather during the summer is already crowded. There will be no detours, either at Gooseberry or elsewhere during road work. The highway will remain a two-laner but will gain wider lanes and 10-foot paved shoulders to accommodate walkers and bicyclists. From the border into Thunder Bay, the highway is in good shape and is a four-lane. If you're traveling through the night on either shore, make sure you gas up before leaving a city. There are long stretches on both shores where you won't find an all-night filling station.

Snowmobiling!
Rules and Regulations for Cruising the White Stuff

The enormously popular snowmobile is used primarily for recreation, except after particularly severe snowstorms when the roads are impassable; then it becomes a serious mode of transportation. But just because snowmobiles are for fun doesn't mean you can take them anywhere, or that just anyone can drive them. Here are a few regulations and recommendations, which are generally uniform throughout our area (where they're not, they will be; snowmobile clubs all around the Lake are trying to achieve some uniformity between jurisdictions).

• Keep to the marked trails. Most streets and highways are off-limits to snowmobiles. If there's no trail near a highway, you're allowed to drive on the far slope of the ditch, with the traffic.

• Children aren't allowed to drive snowmobiles. Youngsters ages 12 to 16 who have had a safety certification course can drive them, but 12- to 14-year-olds can't drive across a highway (they must get off and let an adult drive the machine). Information on certification courses is available at snowmobile dealerships and departments of natural resources.

HISTORIC
TWO HARBORS

We're just 30 minutes up the North Shore from Duluth, so take some time to step back in time!

The Two Harbors Light Station, constructed to improve safety in the Harbor, began 24 hour operation in 1892. The Lighthouse is the oldest, operating Minnesota light station on the North Shore and is listed on the National Register of Historic places.

ATTRACTIONS

- Depot Museum*
- '3' Spot Mallet Engine
- North Shore Scenic Railroad Excursions Train
- Lighthouse Point and Harbor Museum*
- Two Harbors Light Station
- Golfing/Winter Curling

- 3M/Dwan Museum* Minnesota Mining & Manufacturing (3M) was founded in Two Harbors in 1902.
- Hotels• Shopping
- Liquor Store

- Breakwater/Boat Launch
- Paul Gauche Bandshell
- Thomas Owens Park
- Anchor Park with ore boat schedule
- Tugboat Edna G.*
- Ore Docks
- Restaurants

THE Wild NORTH

Two Harbors Chamber of Commerce   1-800-777-7384
R.J. Houle , Visitor Center   1-800-554-2116
Municipal Campground   834-2021
Golf Course & Curling Club   834-2664

•Any licensed automobile driver older than 16 can drive a snowmobile, without certification.

•Everyone should wear a snowmobile helmet, although it's not required by law everywhere.

•There's a speed limit; usually 50 or 55 mph, depending on the jurisdiction. That applies everywhere — trails, lakes, rivers and open spaces — except where marked differently.

•If you've never driven a snowmobile, learn something about the machine and how to read weather conditions and terrain before you jump on and drive off. Several-hour classes for about $5 are available for novices; ask a snowmobile dealer or conservation officer where to find them.

•Don't drink and drive.

Twin Ports Area

Our twin towns are separated by the waters of St. Louis Bay but connected by three bridges: the Blatnik Bridge, stretching from I-35 and 21st Avenue W. in Duluth to Hammond Street in Superior; the Bong Bridge, which connects 46th Avenue W. and I-35 in Duluth with Belknap Street in Superior; and the Oliver Bridge, which connects Duluth's western Gary-New Duluth neighborhood and the tiny Superior-suburb community of Oliver.

The **Blatnik Bridge** has a colorful history. Throughout the 1950s, traffic passed between the towns on a privately owned railroad toll bridge — a swing bridge that had to move every time an ore boat came through. On two occasions, ore boats smashed right into and broke it. Officials began talking about replacing it. Congressman Alvin O'Konski of Wisconsin wanted a tunnel; in those cold-war days, he argued it could double as a bomb shelter. Congressman John Blatnik of Minnesota wanted a bridge high enough that boats could pass under it. There were hot arguments over the issue, which to some extent was moot because there was no money for either project — unless some manipulating was done.

It was. Blatnik had been an author of the 1956 law that established the interstate system, which built 42,000 miles of superhighways connecting every major city and strategic defense area in the country (did you know that its formal title is still the U.S. System of Defense and Interstate Highways?). Interstate 35 was slated to end in Duluth. Blatnik argued that Superior should be connected to that system, because the twin inland ports were a strategic defense site, and because there was no other interstate in northwestern Wisconsin. Congress agreed. Oh, by the way, Blatnik said, we'll need a way to get I-35 across the bay....

The Blatnik Bridge was opened in 1961. A major renovation in the early 1990s closed the bridge for nine months. It was the largest and quickest major bridge reconstruction in the country's history.

The **Bong Bridge** was named for World War II flying ace Richard Ira Bong of Poplar, Wisconsin, and opened in 1984, replacing the old Arrowhead Bridge. Its long,

graceful S-curve was necessitated by currents and boat traffic. The Bong is a handy access for Superiorites who want to get to the Twin Cities via I-35 and have no reason to linger in Duluth.

Both bridges are high and unprotected during serious gales from the lake, so if there's a storm and you're driving an RV or pulling a trailer, you might wait until the wind abates. Or you could drive around to the scenic little **Oliver Bridge**, which is low and better protected from the elements but worth the trip in any case. The bridge accommodates freight trains overhead; automobiles cross on the lower wood-plank deck, which is not enclosed except for wooden rails. Your car rattles pleasantly over the planks, slowly enough and low enough to the water to get an intimate look at the reeds and marsh grasses of this section of the St. Louis River, which is a nesting site for heron and other aquatic birds. It's narrow but will accommodate two-way traffic — not that it matters, because you're likely to be alone on the bridge.

DULUTH

Superior Street is the main street of Duluth, with its busiest commercial and business intersection at **Second Avenue W.** In late 1995, the City Council decided to end metered parking downtown and turn two of the four lanes into nose-in parking areas. There is surprisingly little disturbance in the traffic flow as drivers pull in and out, and it's much easier finding parking places now. The downtown has a busier, more intimate feel.

The Civic Center, at the top of Fifth Avenue W. at First Street, is the home of the St. Louis County building (you pay your parking tickets here; if you forget to do so, you'll find the state courtrooms and judges here too). It's flanked by City Hall and the federal building (with congressional representatives, immigration, customs, Superior National Forest, U.S. Fish & Wildlife and federal judges and courtrooms). Most state offices and the county welfare department are in the Government Center behind City Hall on Second Street and Fourth Avenue W. There's metered parking in the Civic Center circle and more pay parking in the ramp behind the county building. And there's always lots of pay parking down at the Duluth Entertainment Convention Center along the waterfront.

The wind from the lake often funnels down Superior Street, battering pedestrians and forcing them into a leaning walk — unless they use the skywalk system, that is. This heated system comprises walkways in the buildings and glassed-in overhead bridges that cross streets. It reaches from the Duluth Entertainment Convention Center nine blocks to Second Street, and from Fourth Avenue W. to First Avenue W. It accesses a dozen buildings, many longstanding businesses and new retailers that opened right on the skywalk. Many people use the well-marked system for noontime race-walking; others use it for a stroll to the nearest steakhouse.

The streets of long, narrow Duluth are laid out so orderly that even if it weren't for the Lake and hills, which always orient you, you'd have a hard time getting lost. Most downtown streets are numbered, with "point zero" being Superior Street and Lake Avenue and numbers going upward to all directions. The directions are somewhat disorienting, however; the "north-south" avenues actually run northwest-southeast; the east-west streets actually run northeast-southwest.

Most visitors think of going "north" to Canada, a direction Insiders refer to as "east." Interstate 35 S., in the Duluth context, goes west. The town reaches from 134th Avenue W. in the Fond du Lac neighborhood, to 80th Avenue E. at Lakewood Road on the North Shore.

The "can of worms" at I-35 and 21st Avenue W. is a tangle of curving pairs of freeway entrances and exits that connects with Lincoln Park, Piedmont, I-35 and the Blatnik Bridge. A major road con-

Although many Canadians still measure distances in miles, those numbers on the speed limit and mileage signs are always in kilometers. (Perhaps we should call them kilometerage signs!) A kilometer is five-eighths of a mile. To convert miles to kilometers, multiply the miles by 1.6. If you see a sign that says a town is 160 km away, you'll know it's 100 miles distant. To convert kilometers to miles, multiply the number of kilometers by .6 (100 km=60 miles).

Insiders' Tips

struction project on Piedmont Avenue from I-35 onto the hill won't be done until after the turn of the century. You should pay a lot of attention to yields, lights and traffic here; in wet or icy weather, take it especially slow on the curves.

A word about winter driving in Duluth. It's a very hilly city, and driving should be treacherous — and would be, were it not for an astoundingly efficient snow-removal and sanding crew. The city puts a lot of money into keeping the roads clear, and the effort pays off. In fact, we're spoiled; if a little side street in an outlying neighborhood isn't plowed within hours of a snowstorm, we complain. Needless to say, you should nevertheless exercise special caution on our steep hills and curving roads in wet or snowy weather.

SUPERIOR

Superior has a couple of city hubs; one is the "government" intersection at **Belknap Street** and **Hammond Avenue**. The city-county building, with city offices, police department and county jail, is on one corner; the Douglas County courthouse is on the other. Another hub is at **Belknap Street** and **Tower Avenue**, with the new Superior Public Library, a couple of popular stores and access to the Bong Bridge. Other busy spots in town are east on Belknap at the University of Wisconsin-Superior and south on Tower along the newer commercial corridor.

The city is relatively flat, and the streets aren't crowded. Unlike Duluth, the downtown streets actually do go north-south and east-west (they're set on the angle in the east end of town). Police pay attention to the 25 mph speed limit, so you probably should too. There are two main problem driving areas — one for

drivers, the other for law enforcement officials. The first is at the base of the Blatnik Bridge. As you make the big circle under the bridge and come to the intersection with U.S. Highway 2, you'll note a great big stop sign and feel your car go over a washboard reminder in the pavement. The warnings are there for a reason; this is not a four-way stop, folks. There's something about the layout that must subliminally inform some motorists to the contrary; they stop and then drive right into the path of an oncoming grain truck, with many near misses and several casualties. So remember: Just sit tight until the way is clear before you head for Barkers Island or the South Shore.

The other spot is on the long approach on Belknap Street to the Bong Bridge. The road goes over the railroad yard and eventually climbs up onto the airy bridge. There's a wide-open feeling about the road that directly affects the foot on the gas pedal, seemingly unbeknownst to the driver. Superior's police are remarkably reasonable people, but dealing with the endless line of speeders there can make them irritable.

Superior still has an active railroad yard, and you can expect to be stopped at train crossings in several areas of town, including on busy Hammond Avenue near the approach to the Blatnik Bridge.

Thunder Bay Area

The sprawling city of Thunder Bay is crisscrossed with fleet roads that make it easy to get from one end of town to the other. There are no freeways, so you're not likely to find yourself going in the wrong direction. However, there are a couple of points of confusion in this lovely city; keeping them in mind should make your "getting around" much simpler. The first is

Winter Travel
Survival Tips

If you're from the Great Plains or other serious winter-cold areas, you already know that you should carry a survival kit in your car in winter. It should include:

- matches
- candles
- dry food (items that won't freeze, because you leave the kit there all winter, such as nuts, chocolate or other candy, tea, dry fruit, dry soups and jerky)

Photo: Duluth News-Tribune

This station wagon is nestled nicely into a snowbank behind
427 N. 57th Avenue W, apparently hibernating.

- a spoon
- a couple of quarters and dimes (for a phone call, if you're near a rest area in the wee hours).

Store all this in a large coffee can that has a carrying string through two holes punched near the top. In the event of trouble, you can hang the can from your rearview mirror and heat snow in it (for a body-warming beverage or soup) by holding the lighted candle underneath. In addition, you need to carry a small shovel, a blanket and some extra mittens (if you have room and really want to be on the safe side, include extra blankets, socks and scarves).

If it's very cold or snowing hard, you should stay in your car until help, daylight or better weather arrives. *Don't* allow your car engine to run in an effort to keep warm — sitting in a car buried in the snow, carbon monoxide poisoning is more likely than freezing.

that despite more than 25 years of unification, Thunder Bay retains a two-city persona. Thunder Bay North (Port Arthur) and Thunder Bay South (Fort William) are communities complete in themselves, with city centers, shops and provincial courthouses. The second, related point of confusion is that major roads have a way of changing their names as they meander through town. As **Arthur Street** moves east, passing through Thunder Bay South, it becomes **Simpson Street**; then it curves north and becomes **Fort William Road** in the intercity area; as it passes into Thunder Bay North it becomes **Water Street**, then **Cumberland Street** and finally **Hodder Avenue**. What northern city residents call **John Street** is called **Balmoral Street** in the south. **Red River Road** begins by Lake Superior in the east and is called **Dawson Road** by the time it crosses the Expressway into the northwest. **May Street** in the south becomes **Memorial Avenue** in the intercity area and **Algoma Street** in the north.

Most of the highways in the area are in good shape; **Ont. Highway 61**, between Thunder Bay and the U.S. border, is four lanes and particularly well kept. There was a project in the works to make the **Trans-Canada Highway** (Ont. Highway 11/17) a four lane, but a new provincial government put that and other highway projects on hold, where it remained as of early 1996.

Ont. Highway 11/17 enters the city from the west on Arthur Street; you can choose the downtown route (11/17B) that continues straight ahead and takes you into Fort William and eventually into Port Arthur; or turn north onto the **Thunder Bay Expressway**, which is also called 11/17 north of Arthur Street. The Expressway is a particularly handy road for the first-time visitor. Beginning in the south part of town, where it's known as Ont. Highway 61, this continuous route could take you right past the city into the northeast and on to Nipigon — if you didn't want to stop. But you do, right?

From the Expressway, you can easily access Old Fort William (on Broadway Avenue); the business section of Fort William (on Arthur Street); and Prince Arthur Marina and the business section of Port Arthur (on Red River Road). Don't make the mistake of taking the 61B turnoff south of town that looks as though it will put you into the downtown areas. It will, but only after a long drive through sometimes unpleasant scenery.

By Bus

Our own **Bay Area Rural Transit** (BART), 300 Industrial Park Road, Ashland, Wisconsin, (715) 682-9664, doesn't go as fast as San Francisco's system of the same acronym, but it does the job. It gets us around Chequamegon Bay from Odanah to Red Cliff and points in between and serves as a city bus in Washburn, Bayfield and Ashland, Wisconsin. Ticket prices depend on how far you go. For instance, Odanah to Ashland is 90¢; Barksdale to Ashland is 60¢; Red Cliff to Odanah is $3. Discount passes are available; otherwise, you must have the exact fare.

The **Duluth Transit Authority** (DTA), 2402 W. Michigan Street, Duluth, Minnesota, (218) 722-SAVE, operates 20 routes throughout the Twin Ports; fares are $1 during bust periods (7 to 9 AM and 2:30 to 6 PM weekdays) and 50¢ the rest of the time; you must have correct change. Monthly passes cost $28 for adults and $22 for folks 17 and

Insiders' Tips

You needn't hurry to get out of our downtowns when 4:30 PM rolls around; "rush hour" in the Twin Ports and Thunder Bay means it might take you five or 10 minutes longer to get where you want to go. Our rush hour looks like other cities' mid-morning traffic.

younger. The buses are wheelchair-accessible and include racks for transporting bicycles. The DTA also operates **STRIDE**, a curb-to-curb bus service in Duluth for people with mobility handicaps. The American Public Transit Association named the DTA America's Safest Bus System in 1992, and America's Best Transit Service in its class in 1990.

Gogebic County Transit, 100 E. Aurora Street, Ironwood, Michigan, (906) 932-2523, operates five buses on a daily weekday schedule (please call for details) throughout the county that will swing off their regular routes to pick up passengers. Passengers also may arrange in advance for the bus to return them home. Two buses have automatic wheelchair lifts. A "demand response" service also is available within a 3-mile radius of Ironwood, Monday through Friday.

Greyhound Lines (Duluth), 2122 W. Superior Street, Duluth, Minnesota, (218) 722-5591, has twice-daily runs to the Twin Cities, departing at 7:30 AM and 5:15 PM; on Friday and Sunday, an additional run leaves at 1 PM. Trips take about 3½ hours., and passengers connect to Chicago and Madison, Wisconsin,

among other cities. You can also buy tickets here via other bus companies to regions Greyhound doesn't serve, for example: up the North Shore to Thunder Bay, Ontario, on **Happy Times** lines of Thunder Bay; and along the South Shore to Ashland, Wisconsin, and Michigan's Upper Peninsula on **White Pines** lines (both listed below).

Greyhound Lines (Thunder Bay), 815 Fort William Road, Thunder Bay, Ontario, (807) 345-2194, departs Thunder Bay for Winnipeg, Manitoba, two or three times a day and for Toronto three times a day. Most of these runs are direct, without transfers. You can get connections with major cities in Canada and the United States from these urban centers. Schedules are subject to change.

Happy Times Lines, 1480 W. Walsh Street, Thunder Bay, Ontario, (807) 473-5955, makes a Duluth run four times a week and offers regular service for casino aficionados to Grand Portage on the U.S. side of the border. The company also arranges charters all over Canada and daytrips to Kakabeka Falls, Ouimet Canyon and some amethyst mines.

Port Town Trolley, run by the Duluth Transit Authority, 2402 W. Michigan Street, Duluth, Minnesota, (218) 722-SAVE, looks like a trolley, but no streetcar tracks or overhead trolley lines remain in Duluth. Actually, it's a bus — a pretty little vehicle in the style of the turn-of-the-century horse-drawn buses. For 50¢, you can catch a ride around the more attractive parts of downtown: Canal Park, Fitger's complex, the Lakewalk, Bayfront Park and downtown hotels. The little trolley bell tolls its arrival every half hour from 11 AM to 7 PM daily in the summertime.

Superior Shuttle, 960 Minn. Highway 61, Two Harbors, Minnesota, (218) 834-5511, provides transportation for people who want to go by foot. It allows you to take a one-way hike along the 200-mile Superior Hiking Trail and enjoy a slow tour of the cliffs, rivers, wilderness and lake views of the North Shore. Just park your car at the ending spot of your hike, catch the shuttle to a starting point and hike back to your car. You can choose short or long sections of the trail (4 and 11 miles, respectively) or, especially for backpackers, several sections. The 15-person van shuttles people along 20 trailheads Thursday through Sunday from late May to mid-October. Rates are $6 for adults and $3 for children younger than 16. Add $2 for each additional trailhead.

Thunder Bay Transit, 570 Fort William Road, Thunder Bay, Ontario, (807) 684-3744, operates a daily municipal bus with main crosstown routes and about 17 belt lines. Fees are $1.30 for adults, $1.10 for high schoolers and $1 for seniors and children. A rate hike to $1.50 was proposed early in 1996. Bus brochures and individual pocket schedules are available at the Brodie Street and Water Street bus terminals.

White Pine Bus Service Inc., 401 Florence Avenue, Ironwood, Michigan, (906) 932-4731, serves South Shore communities, with a daily route along U.S. Highway 2 from Michigan's Upper Peninsula through Ironwood, Hurley, Ashland, Poplar and Iron River, into Superior and Duluth's Greyhound depot.

By Air

Charters, scenic flights and flight instruction are all available at **Ashland Airport**, Sanborn Avenue S., Ashland, Wis-

Photo: Duluth News-Tribune

Sleigh rides are a great way to see Lake Superior country.

consin, (715) 682-7070. The site has 5,200-foot and 3,600-foot runways, jet fuel and 100-octane low-lead fuel. A courtesy car can take you the 3 miles to town. The Unicom frequency is 122.8.

Cloquet Airport, 1660 Airport Road, Cloquet, Minnesota, (218) 879-4911, about 25 miles inland from Duluth, has a 4,000-foot paved runway and a 2,500-foot grass strip. It has 100-octane low-lead and jet fuel available. The Unicom frequency is 122.8. You can call **Woodland Aviation** here for charters, instruction and scenic flights.

The **Sawtooth Air Service** at **Cook County Airport**, Devil's Track Lake, Grand Marais, Minnesota, (218) 387-2721 or 387-2008, provides scenic rides into the Boundary Waters Canoe Area Wilderness and along the Lake, by wheel plane and sea plane. The fee is $25 per person for a 20-minute ride. You can fly out of the airport or out of the harbor in Grand Marais; the service also flies into the area's resorts and has a flight school. (See our Attractions chapter for information about this and other aero-tours.)

The airport has a 4,200-foot blacktop runway and an arrival-departure building that is open 24 hours. You can get 100-octane low-lead fuel any time, day or night, from the self-serve pump. At the time of publication, the service was planning to carry jet fuel beginning in spring 1996. The Unicom frequency is 122.8.

Duluth International Airport, 4701 Airport Drive, Duluth, Minnesota, (218) 727-2968, is quieter than it was 20 years ago, having lost the service of some airlines in the wake of industry downsizing. Nevertheless, it has the feel of a city airport, without the attending crowds and chaos of most city terminals. You can relax in the attractive lounge, restaurant or cafe and watch planes come and go. It has the longest runway of any airport in the state — 11,000 feet, capable of handling the Concorde and Boeing 747 (neither of which comes to Duluth, although the Concorde stopped for a visit in the mid-1980s). Military planes at the nearby Duluth Air National Guard base use it, as do standard-size planes of **Express One Northwest Airlink** and **Northwest Airlines**, (800) 225-2525 (both), and **United**

Express, (800) 241-6522. You can get flights to Chicago and the Twin Cities on these lines, making connections there for your national or international flights. Take U.S. Highway 53 (Miller Trunk), go 6 miles to Airport Road and turn right. You can load and unload in front of the building, but parking is available only in the lot below.

United Express offers daily flights to Minneapolis and Chicago from **Gogebic County Airport**, E5560 Airport Road, Ironwood, Michigan, (906) 932-5808 or (800) 241-6522. The runway is 6,501 feet long, Unicom frequency is 122.8, and 100-octane low-lead and jet fuel are available. The airport is about 2 miles northeast of downtown Ironwood.

Madeline Island Airport, LaPointe, Wisconsin, (715) 747-6855/6913, a small airport, is 1.5 miles east of the island town. It has an uncontrolled, 3,000-foot paved runway.

Sky Harbor Airport, 5000 Minnesota Avenue, Duluth, Minnesota, (218) 722-6410, at the end of Park Point has a 3,051-foot hard-surface runway, float-equipped airplanes and aircraft parking ramps and hangars. The Unicom frequency is 122.8, and 100-octane low-lead fuel is available. You also can rent and charter aircraft and receive flying instruction from Foster Aviation here. Twenty-minute scenic flights are $20 per person and are offered year round. (See our Attractions chapter for details.)

Situated by Head Of The Lakes Fairgrounds, **Superior Municipal/Bong Airport** (named, like the bridge, for World War II flying ace Richard I. Bong), 4804 Hammond Avenue, Superior, Wisconsin, (715) 394-0282, has a 4,000-foot hard-surface lighted runway. You'll find 100-octane low-lead and jet fuel here. The Unicom frequency is 122.7. Additional services include a restaurant, aircraft rental and maintenance, charters through **Sailboats Inc. Air Charter**, (715) 392-7131, and flight instruction through **Twin Ports Flying Service**, (715) 394-6444. You can charter a plane for up to three passengers for $59 an hour.

Thunder Bay Airport, Ont. Highway 61 and Neebing Avenue, Thunder Bay, Ontario, (807) 473-2600, is a very busy

---

Insiders' Tips

In the wintertime in Bayfield, Wisconsin, you'll notice a line of little evergreen trees stuck in the snow on the Lake, reaching over to Madeline Island. They're put out there to mark the first car route of the season, after the ice thickens sufficiently. But it isn't long before the route changes, as ice thickness fluctuates with the currents and weather. The trees remain where they are, but the cars find better routes, and you should follow those tracks. (For a few days at each end of the ice season, neither ferry nor car can navigate the thin-ice route. That's when a local takes out his wind sled — a boat with a big fan sticking up in the air — and hauls island high-schoolers over to Bayfield in the morning and mainland workers back.)

airport — the third busiest airport in Canada, after Toronto and Montreal (and before Ottawa!). The reason is that Thunder Bay is the jumping-off place for so many small planes heading into the wilds of northwest Ontario. A new terminal building offers full services, and the 6,200- and 5,300-foot runways serve commercial airlines, with direct flights to Toronto, Winnipeg and Minneapolis. Carriers include **Air Canada, Air Ontario** and **NorOntario**, (807) 623-3313 (all three); **Canadian Airlines International**, (807) 577-6461; **Mesaba Northwest Link**, (807) 475-7822; and **Thunder Air**, 807) 475-4211. Call the **Thunder Bay Flying Club** (see our Attractions chapter), (807) 577-1118, for charters, sightseeing flights and flying lessons. The charter charge is $138 per hour or $1.65 per nautical mile for up to three passengers.

Scenic North Shore air tours, flight instruction and aircraft maintenance are available from **Lake Region Aviation Inc.** at **Two Harbors Airport**, Two Harbors, Minnesota, (218) 834-2162. Tours include 15-minute flights over the ore docks and bays of Two Harbors for $15 per person; a Gooseberry Falls-Split Rock Lighthouse tour for $35; a Two Harbors-Duluth tour for $45; and a Split Rock-Duluth one-hour tour for $55. The all-weather airport has a 4,400-foot paved runway and 80- and 100-octane low-lead fuel. The Unicom frequency is 122.9. The airport is 3 miles northwest of Two Harbors.

By Train

Train travel in our region means freight or excursion, unless you're willing to travel by other means to the nearest passenger line. There never was a rail route from the Twin Ports to Thunder Bay, and Amtrak and Via Rail Canada no longer serve the region elsewhere. If you're determined to travel by rail — and you don't want to jump a freight — you can get passenger connections in Ontario at Armstrong (near Lake Nipigon), Longlac (300 kilometers to the east) and Winnipeg, Manitoba (680 kilometers to the west); call **Via Rail Canada**, (800) 561-3949 for schedules and rates. In the United States, rail connections via **Amtrak** are available out of the Twin Cities; call (800) 872-7245.

The classic train of the **Lake Superior & Mississippi Railroad**, 506 W. Michigan Street, Duluth, (218) 624-7539 (weekends) and 727-0687 (weekdays), leaves from the Western Waterfront Trail parking lot across from the Lake Superior Zoo. It travels 12 miles along the St. Louis River where you can watch river, reeds and waterfowl. Typically, the train departs in the late morning and early afternoon Saturday and Sunday from early July through Labor Day. In 1995, prices were $6 for adults, $5 for seniors and $4 for children. Call for 1996 hours and prices.

You can travel the **North Shore Scenic Railroad**, 506 W. Michigan Street, Duluth, (800) 423-1273 or (218) 722-1273, for 56 miles from Duluth to Two

Ontario and the three states of our Lake Superior region require the use of seat belts. You can turn right on a red light following a complete stop, except where otherwise designated. A driver's license (from any country) is valid in Ontario for three months.

Insiders' Tips

Harbors; the journey takes about six hours. Departing from the Depot, the new DECC station and Fitger's, the route cuts through the woods of the North Shore where travelers have frequent views of Lake Superior. The trip includes a two-hour layover in Two Harbors, near historic sites and restaurants. The railroad also offers a shorter "pizza" route. This two-hour daily trip has lots of pizza and some narrative; the sun sets on the return trip from Palmer's Siding, partway up the shore. Other choices include a shorter narrated round trip to Lester River and dining runs with hors d'oeuvres.

By Watercraft

Water, water everywhere . . . so much, in fact, that getting around the Lake Superior region by watercraft is a legitimate transportation option (and, in some cases, a necessity to reach certain islands) as well as a recreational endeavor (see our Watersports and our Nightlife and Casinos chapters for additional watercraft-related activities).

At **Apostle Islands Cruise Service**, City Dock, Bayfield, Wisconsin, (715) 779-3925, you can visit all 22 Apostle Islands or only a few favorites aboard the *Island Princess*, a fully fitted cruise boat that has soft drinks and snacks, indoor and outdoor seating and restrooms. Narrated cruises include stopovers, so you can

climb into a historic island lighthouse, visit a historic fish camp, beachcomb or explore. You also can catch a ride on the sailboat *ZEETO*, a 54-foot three-masted schooner, or get yourself and your camping equipment hauled by powerboat to a remote island. Prices in 1995 for most cruises were $20 for adults and $9 for children (the Sunday brunch cruise cost $6.50 more). Call for current rates.

Charter a sailboat and travel throughout the Apostle Islands from the deck of a classic sailing yacht — a restored 1969 Morgan craft — at **Catchun-Sun Charter Co.**, City Dock, Bayfield, Wisconsin, (715) 779-3111. Licensed captains will take you on the 3½-hour ride for $40 per person. The yacht sets sail at 9 AM and 1 PM.

Madeline Island is accessible in the summertime only by water or air. The **Madeline Island Ferry Boat**, City Dock, Bayfield, Wisconsin, (715) 747-2051, takes cars, trucks, supplies and passengers back and forth from ice-out in the spring to freeze-up in the winter. The 2.6-mile trip takes 20 minutes; you can ride inside the heated cabins or out on the deck. During the busy season from late June until early September, fees are $3 for passengers 12 and older, $1.75 for children ages 6 through 11 and free for kids 5 and younger. For vehicles (driver not included): auto, $6.75; bicycle, $1.50; motorcycle, $4.25; pickup camper and motorhomes, $8. Fees are slightly less in

Photo: Duluth News-Tribune

*An affordable and fun way to tour downtown Duluth is aboard
the Port Town Trolley.*

off-seasons. No reservations are accepted. Passengers who need special assistance should notify boat personnel before boarding. The ferry leaves City Dock every half-hour to hour, depending on the time of day and season.

You can rent a sloop, ketch, catamaran or cutter at **Superior Charters Inc.**, Port Superior, Route 1, Box 719, Bayfield, Wisconsin, (800) 772-5124, just 3 miles south of Bayfield. Prices range from $175 to $550 for two days, depending on the type of watercraft. You can stay out longer for an additional fee.

Renters must demonstrate their ability to handle the craft. The two- to six-sail crafts are fully equipped, with inboard engines, depth sounders and knot meters, dinghies and even barbecue grills. Superior Charters also has a sailing school and charter certification program.

You can travel for days to Rossport, Ontario, or Isle Royale, Michigan, or go out on the Lake for a few hours near Thunder Bay with **Sailboats Ontario**, 108 Robinson Drive, (807) 767-1972. This company is affiliated with Sailboats

Inc. of Superior, Wisconsin, and offers bareboat (sail yourself) or captained charters. Most people take bareboats out from four to seven days; the four-day rate ranges from $975 to $1,800, depending on the length of boat (27 to 33 feet, which will carry four to six people). The boats are fully equipped, with berths and galleys, and sailors bring only personal gear, food and bedding. You must prove sailing competency. If you'd rather have Capt. Rich Clarke and his son David take you around the bay from two to eight hours, the cost ranges from $150 to $550, depending on the length of boat — up to 37 feet long. Four to eight people can ride for that price. Sailboats Ontario will cater food — steaks, barbecue, hamburgers, snacks — for the charters.

You can get a good look at the Duluth-Superior harbor aboard the boats of the **Vista Fleet**, (218) 722-6218. Trips depart from the Duluth Entertainment Convention Center Dock on Harbor Drive in Duluth, Minnesota, or Barkers Island Dock in Superior, Wisconsin and range from two-hour sightseeing trips to lunch and dinner cruises. Weather permitting, the ship also takes you under the Aerial Lift Bridge and out onto Lake Superior. The season is mid-May to mid-October. Fees range from $8.50 for the sightseeing tour to $25 to $30 for the dinner cruise (prime rib, lake trout or Texas barbecue). Children are slightly less than half price.

By Critter

While you won't find any place to rent a sled-dog or horse team to shuttle you around the region, a few places offer sled-dog tours or horse-drawn sleigh rides over hill and dale, and we've listed a couple here. For similar travel-by-starlight options, see the "Something Different" section of our Nightlife and Casinos chapter.

Leaving from four Upper Michigan locations in Ironwood, Michigan, **Royal Palm Ranch**, (906) 943-0770, offers sleigh rides Tuesday through Sunday while the big snow of the Upper Peninsula lasts (usually from November through March). You can travel on a one-horse open sleigh; a Clydesdale-pulled big sleigh; or a sleigh fitted with fur robes, hot cider, champagne, hot chocolate and beer. Go in the daytime or go by moonlight; the fee is $6 each, and the setting is woods, snow, rustic lodges and hay-bale sofas near open fires.

Take a look at our region from dog sled, courtesy of **Norwest Sled Dog Adventures**, 7 Jarvis Bay Road, Thunder Bay, Ontario, (807) 964-2070. Friendly huskies pull you (sometimes with thrilling speed) along the North Shore where you'll catch spectacular views of the Lake. One choice is the two-hour trip ($20 for adults and $12 for children); you sit in the sled as you fly toward a destination of hot chocolate and a campfire. Another is a four-hour trip ($84 per person), in which you help hook up and drive a team.

Insiders' Tips

Most of our region is in the Central time zone. However, when you cross the border into Canada or go 25 miles into Michigan's Upper Peninsula, you'll be in the eastern zone. Set your watch ahead (later) an hour; for example, when it's 6 PM in Minnesota and Wisconsin, it's 7 PM in Thunder Bay, Ontario, and Ontonogan, Michigan.

Photo: Duluth News-Tribune

A ship passes under Duluth's Aerial Lift Bridge.

The two-day trip is $235 per person and includes hot meals and overnight accommodations.

By Foot

Trails abound in our region, throughout national forests and state parks and along the Lake (see our Parks and Forests chapter for more information). By far the most famous, however, is the rugged 200-mile-long **Superior Hiking Trail** along the North Shore from Castle Danger below Gooseberry Falls to the Cascade River past Lutsen. *Backpacker* magazine has named this trail one of the top 10 in the nation. It's too rugged for cross-country skis, and mountain biking isn't allowed, but people do use snowshoes in the wintertime. Stop in at the office of the **Superior Hiking Trail Association**, (218) 834-2700, in the basement of Mimi's Gift Shop, 731 Seventh Avenue, Two Harbors, Minnesota. You'll find maps, T-shirts, mugs and the *Guide to the Superior Hiking Trail*, a $15 book that gives a detailed mile-by-mile description of the trail. The association arranges group hikes and promotes and maintains the trail.

Psst...

Wanna know about a great place to eat that's not very far away and serves up some of the freshest fish, the most succulent seafood, the perfect prime rib, choice USDA steaks and other delicious entrees, all at prices that can't be beat?

Come to the **Hammond Steak House!**

It's just a short drive away and you'll find fast, friendly service and all your favorite beverages!

P.S. Don't forget dessert.

MasterCard   VISA
DISCOVER   DINERS CLUB

• BANQUETS
• LOUNGE • LIQUOR STORE

Hammond
STEAK HOUSE
At the Foot of the Blatnik Bridge, Superior, WI • 715-392-3269

Inside
Restaurants

W̶ho wouldn't enjoy researching this chapter? The main difficulty was pacing ourselves, as we tried to check out a stomach-full of restaurants within a day in some areas. (Yes, we have grown in girth as the book has grown in chapters.)

The good news is that the classic restaurants people grew up with — the Pickwick Restaurant in Duluth; Lutsen Resort on the North Shore; the Old Rittenhouse Inn in Bayfield, Wisconsin; the Branding Iron in Hurley, Wisconsin; the Shack Supper Club in Superior; and Harrington Court in Thunder Bay — are alive and well, still serving traditionally delicious foods.

On the other hand, we were excited to come across many new menus at restaurants in the Lake Superior region, such as Kamloops Restaurant at Superior Shores, the CoHo Cafe in Tofte, the Howling Wolf Saloon and Grill in Grand Marais — all on Minnesota's North Shore — and the Unicorn Inn in Thunder Bay. A similar treat was revisiting innovative restaurants that emphasize fresh ingredients: Bennett's Bar and Grill and the Lake Avenue Cafe in Duluth; Maggie's in Bayfield, Wisconsin; the Scenic Cafe, between Duluth and Two Harbors, Minnesota; and the Angry Trout in Grand Marais, Minnesota, are becoming new classics.

Then, there are the home-cooking places featuring blue-plate specials with mashed potatoes and gravy, such as the Miller's Cafe and Shari's Kitchen in Two Harbors; the Rustic Inn in Castle Danger, Minnesota; Sandie's in Washburn, Wisconsin; the Hoito in Thunder Bay; and Greunke's in Bayfield, Wisconsin. All continue to serve up big portions of good comfort food at reasonable prices.

We've tried to provide you with a wide selection of restaurants, based on ambience, price, menu variety and our own preferences. We haven't included any national franchise restaurants. We figured you already know what's on their menus, and we wanted to emphasize the diversity and richness that regional restaurants have to offer. Happy dining!

The Price-code Key (see gray box) indicates what you can expect to pay for a dinner for two, with some exclusions. Lunch at most restaurants costs less than dinner. Major credit cards are accepted unless otherwise noted.

The following key represents the average cost of dinner for two, including appetizer, non-alcoholic beverage, entree and dessert each. Expect to pay extra for alcoholic beverages, tax and gratuity.

PRICE-CODE KEY

$	Less than $20
$$	$21-$40
$$$	$41-$60
$$$$	$61 or more

Twin Ports Area

Restaurants in Duluth and Superior are veritable diners' delights. Whether your food preferences are regional, continental or international, ordinary or extraordinary, you'll find tempting cuisine in the Twin Ports. Try a Lake Superior fish specialty or sample a taste of immigrant influence, whether Scandinavian, Italian, German, Vietnamese . . . the key here is variety.

One thing is certain: It's nobody's fault but your own if you leave a Twin Ports restaurant hungry. Entrees are usually plentiful, and menu items range from the mild to the wild. So peruse this section with your appetite in tow. We think you find something to please virtually any palate.

In addition to our specified price-code amount, expect to pay 10.5 percent for taxes on your bill in Duluth and 5.5 percent in Superior. Also note that, by law, all Minnesota restaurants must provide a nonsmoking section.

Duluth

AUGUSTINO'S
600 E. Superior St., Duluth, Minn.(218) 722-2787
$$$

Tournedoes Rossini, perfectly prepared hard rolls and Death by Chocolate while relaxing in an elegant dining room with a wide, sun-filled view of Lake Superior or on the new patio with deck umbrellas — is this heaven or what? No surprise: Augustino's is known for doing it right. Tournedoes are twin filets mignons

and garlic rounds topped with a basil pesto and cognac pâté, accompanied by a burgundy-currant sauce.

Italian dishes are Augustino's specialty but by no means the only offerings at this gourmet restaurant where steaks are grilled over mesquite, and fresh- and saltwater fish are served daily. Ask to see the dessert tray and choose from rich cheesecakes, puddings and chocolate creations. The luncheon buffet, served weekdays, offers a very nice selection of pastas, soups, entrees and fresh fruits and vegetables.

Augustino's makes its own pasta, Italian sausage, baked goods and desserts and imports Italian cheeses. A full bar is available, which serves local microbrews. Augustino's is open for breakfast (tasty, attractive and relatively inexpensive), lunch and dinner seven days a week.

THE BELLOWS
2230 London Rd., Duluth, Minn. (218) 724-8531
$$-$$$

The Bellows is known for good food and for a couple of side dishes: fresh popovers with fresh strawberry preserves that are served with every dinner, and artichoke hearts mixed with various cheeses and served with garlic bread (this Bellows dish started an artichoke cheese craze in some Duluth restaurants).

The Bellows' circular building — large but cozy — offers a good view of the Lake, a bar and lounge. The menu includes both cold- and warmwater lobster tails; steaks (try the 8-ounce fillet stuffed with onions, mushrooms and bacon and topped with melted provolone, served

RESTAURANT & LOUNGE
Specializing in:
Steaks • Seafood
Authentic Hickory Smoked BBQ

LIQUOR STORE
"Largest Selection in the Northland"

Wide variety of fine wines, imported
& domestic beers & liquors

3301 Belknap St., Superior, WI 54880• 392-9836
Just "Right" Off the Bong Bridge

with whole sautéed mushrooms); and pastas, particularly the three alfredos — fettuccine, chicken and shrimp.

The Bellows is open every day for lunch and dinner.

BENNETT'S BAR & GRILL
319 W. Superior St.
Duluth, Minn.   (218) 722-2829
$$$

Kosher chicken, Arizona egg rolls, lamb, yellow squash sandwich — Bennett's is an upscale restaurant that serves an eclectic, health-conscious menu. The food isn't kosher, but owner Bob Bennett uses kosher chickens because they're chemical-free, corn-fed and tasty. The menu is flexible, coordinating as many fresh, seasonal products as possible (pheasant, rabbit, fresh fish, fresh produce and berries) with regional flavors (Southwestern, Asian, Mediterranean). The Arizona egg rolls, for example, include kosher chicken, summer squash, carrots, red onions and Southwestern seasonings and are accompanied by an anchovy-chile-honey-maple syrup dipping sauce. There are no-meat dishes like the vegetable club sandwich (eggplant, yellow squash, zucchini and tomato marinated with red wine vinegar and grilled) and big-

meat dishes such as steak or the pork chop with apple fritters.

A full bar is available, with a large variety of wines. Bennett's is open for lunch Monday through Friday and for dinner Tuesday through Saturday. It's closed Sunday. Reservations are recommended for weekend dinners.

BLACK BEAR CASINO
Fond du Lac Reservation
I-35 and Minn. Hwy. 210
Carlton, Minn.   (218) 878-2327
$$

The Friday buffet is your best deal at the Black Bear where your choice of fine foods includes poached walleye or salmon, prime rib, wild rice (the real stuff, gathered on Fond du Lac rice lakes by Fond du Lac members) and ultra-fresh fruits and vegetables. The breakfast menu is served all day, most dinner items are available at lunchtime, and the salad bar is excellent. Favorites are the filet mignon and pork chop dinners. If you haven't tried tasty but caloric fry bread (a now-traditional Native dish that was developed during impoverished post-treaty times), now's your chance.

Meal discounts are available for guests of the adjoining lodge. The restaurant is an attractive place, with displays of Ojibwe beadwork and basketry, and the wait staff is empathetic and carefully trained to help restore your serenity if you've had a tough day in the casino.

THE BLUE NOTE CAFE
357 Canal Park Dr.
Duluth, Minn.   (218) 727-6549
$-$$

A relaxing, attractive coffee house in Duluth's Canal Park area, the Blue Note has excellent sandwiches, soups and cheesecakes — and, of course, specialty coffees. It's open for lunch and dinner; outdoor seating is available during the summer.

CONEY ISLAND
112 W. First St., Duluth, Minn.   (218) 722-2772
$ No credit cards

An old downtown standby, the Coney Island has lots of hot dogs and old wooden booths to munch them in. It's open for light breakfasts, lunch and early dinner.

GRANDMA'S SALOON & GRILL
522 Lake Ave. S.
Duluth, Minn.   (218) 727-4192
2202 Maple Grove Rd.
Duluth, Minn.   (218) 722-9313
$$ (both locations)

Grandma's is filled with memorabilia from Duluth and a lively clientele that relishes its Italian food, fancy burgers and other tasty dishes. At the Lake Avenue (Canal Park) restaurant, an upstairs saloon-dance floor and an old-time bar in the restaurant downstairs keeps this a busy place in the evening. Outdoor seating is available in the summer, with a nice view of the Lake and the Aerial Bridge next door. The Maple Grove Road restaurant, near Miller Hill Mall, is smaller but also lively. Grandma's serves lunch and dinner daily.

HACIENDA DEL SOL
319 E. Superior St., Duluth, Minn.(218) 722-7296
$-$$ No credit cards

The Hacienda is a local favorite, with a full Mexican menu, imported beer, wine and a feisty wait staff. The owner-chef has made good use of the old building and existing trees out back to create the prettiest outdoor seating in the region. On warm summer evenings, people like to linger long after the quesadillas are gone. The Hacienda serves lunch and dinner every day except Sunday (when it's closed).

HANGING HORN VILLAGE
Little Hanging Horn Lake (Off Beaver Rd.)
Barnum, Minn.   (218) 389-6162
$$

The Hanging Horn is a bit distant from the Twin Ports area but is worth a visit if you're up for a beautiful drive, some English stout or ale, a casual meal and perhaps a row around a lake. The owners of the rustic cafe let customers take out the rowboats that are beached between the water and the restaurant windows. The atmosphere is relaxed, and the food — steaks, burgers and salads — is satisfying.

This is a good place to take kids; they can play darts or pool in an adjoining room or explore the safe outdoors while you linger over your coffee.

The Hanging Horn is open for dinner on weekdays and for lunch and dinner on weekends. To find it, drive into Barnum from I-35 and turn left on Carlton Road. Go 2.2 miles to Beaver Road, take a left and follow the signs for another 1.5 miles.

LAKE AVENUE CAFE
394 Lake Ave. S., Duluth, Minn. (218) 722-2355
$$

Some elegant food in a casual setting is served at this attractive cafe where homemade bread, spinach, cheeses, herbs, olive oil, yogurt and various meats, fruits

and vegetables are put together in delicious, mostly light, combinations. The servings are modest, but the food is truly delicious. Check out the art on the menus and the salt and pepper shakers — every table has a different collector set, and each menu a different painting. The cafe has lots of windows and is open for lunch and dinner. You'll find it in the back of the DeWitt-Seitz building in Canal Park.

LAKEVIEW COFFEE EMPORIUM

600 E. Superior St., Duluth, Minn. (218) 720-4464
$-$$

Big sandwiches, homemade soups, rich sweets and specialty coffees are served at this small but beautiful cafe overlooking Lake Superior. You can get a croissant/cafe au lait breakfast or a lunch or dinner sandwich here; if the Lake doesn't hold your interest, books at each table, conversation with other diners or the ever-changing art originals on the walls will.

LITTLE ANGIE'S CANTINA & GRILL

Canal Park Dr. and Buchanan St.
Duluth, Minn.   (218) 727-6117
$$

Margaritas and an array of authentic Mexican, Southwestern and North American dishes are the fare at Little Angie's, which has become a well-liked place since one of Duluth's most imaginative entrepreneurs opened it in 1994. Try the tacos de cazuela — black bean-pepper casserole covered with cheese, accompanied by a side of corn tortillas.

If you don't want anything that ends in a vowel, the steaks and burgers here are excellent too. All grilled foods are cooked over Duluth's only real wood fire restaurant grill. The mixed decor — Southwest, northern Native, cowboy and Mexican — makes it a fun place for kids and adults.

Little Angie's is open for lunch and dinner every day.

LOUIS' CAFE

1500 London Rd., Duluth, Minn. (218) 720-8370
$$

Everybody loves Louis' (pronounced "Louie's"). The original restaurant (see the subsequent "Superior" section) was founded in 1946 by the current owner's grandfather, Louis Letsos. This London Road restaurant, scheduled to open in mid-1996, was awaiting a wine and beer license at time of publication. Menu items include authentic Greek food (gyros and kebabs), big burgers and pancakes.

LOUIS' CAFE & RESTAURANT

3904 Grand Ave., Duluth, Minn. *(218) 624-3131*
$$

Most local people probably don't know it, but this Louis' is no longer affiliated with the previously mentioned Duluth cafe by the same name or the original Louis' in Superior (listed subsequently). It's a popular place nevertheless, serving great big delicious pancakes, fresher-than-fresh Athenian salads, gyros and delightful dolmades, along with Greek wines and a Greek beer. Daily American dinner specials are served, and outdoor seating is available. Breakfast, lunch and dinner are served.

From I-35, exit on 40th Avenue West, drive north to the semaphore and turn right.

NATCHIO'S GREEKTOWN

109 N. Second Ave. W.
Duluth , Minn. *(218) 722-6585*
$$

A favorite of downtowners for lunch, Natchio's offers an atmospheric place to enjoy a variety of excellent Greek food both at lunch and dinnertime. Belly dancers entertain diners Saturday evenings. The owner, a Macedonian, invented our favorite sandwich: "taxo," a thin flour tortilla wrapped around ground seasoned lamb/beef or beans, covered with divine Greek sauces and vegetables. Try the dolmades, lentil or chicken lemon rice soup, or the Greek caviar dip. Wines and beers are served.

Natchio's is open Monday through Saturday.

OLD COUNTRY BUFFET

Miller Hill Mall, 1600 Miller Trunk Hwy.
Duluth, Minn. *(218) 722-7013*
$

Buffet style is the only way you can eat here, and you have to do some walking to get to all the food. It's abundant, fresh and nicely prepared: fried and baked chicken, baked fish, ham, roast beef and salads. The early Sunday brunch is a hit, and lunches are served on other days. Old Country is also open daily for dinner.

THE PICKWICK

508 E. Superior St., Duluth, Minn. (218) 727-8901
$$$

The Pickwick. That's the only word a hungry visitor needs — unless he or she is looking for breakfast or a Sunday meal. For everything else — some of the finest lunches and dinners anywhere in the region; a great lake view; an absolutely lovely building; history; local people visiting so hard, the place sings with voices and coffee spoons; gracious ambiance; an English club-style bar; and top-notch wait staff — this is the place.

Charcoal grilled steaks, daily prime rib and seafood are the main fare here; and German food is a treat, especially served in the Dutch room, which like the lounge has a tasteful old-country decor. Try the homemade onion rings and a pepper cheeseburger for lunch.

The Wisocki family has owned the Pickwick since 1914; prior to that, the 115-year-old structure was part of the Fitger's Brewery complex, serving as the brewery sandwich room.

The Pickwick is closed Sunday and holidays.

PORTER'S

Holiday Center, 200 W. First St.
Duluth, Minn. *(218) 727-6746*
$$$

According to the chef, "Porter's sells more Caesar salads than McDonald's sells Big Ma—" . . . well, a lot, anyway. The chicken Caesar is the most oft-ordered meal with the downtown power-lunch crowd, and Porter's is packed full at lunchtime. Black Angus steaks and prime rib are the most selected dinnertime choices. A full

bar is augmented by 50 beers and 44 wines, including imports and microbrews.

Porter's is open for breakfast, lunch and dinner every day but is closed between 2:30 and 4:30 PM. Reservations are recommended.

SARA'S TABLE
728 E. Superior St., Duluth, Minn.(218) 723-8569
$ *No credit cards*

One of the newer coffee houses in Duluth, Sara's Table is also the most intimate, with only a few tables and a great view of the Lake. Books — mostly feminist and eco-conscious — are stacked everywhere for customers' perusal, service is friendly, and the lunch/dinner vegetarian chili and cookies are wonderful. You also can get excellent sandwiches, bagel with egg (great for breakfast), teas and, of course, specialty coffees.

SIR BENEDICT'S TAVERN ON THE LAKE
805 E. Superior St., Duluth, Minn.(218) 728-1192
$ *No credit cards*

"Sir Ben's" is a charming little restaurant with a fine Lake view that offers delightful soups; thick sandwiches made with healthy breads, sprouts and other veggies, meats and cheeses; and ales, stouts, non-alcoholic beers, wines and juices. The veggie melt is huge, messy and absolutely delicious. The interior atmosphere is English and intimate, with plenty of windows; you can sit outdoors in good weather. It's open for lunch and dinner every day except major holidays.

TASTE OF SAIGON
394 Lake Ave. S., Duluth, Minn. (218) 727-1598
$

Some of the best Asian food in the region is created here in the DeWitt-Seitz building where a Vietnamese family serves Chinese and Vietnamese dishes every day for lunch and dinner. The restaurant is small and pleasantly appointed, and it's easy to pick a dish: just close your eyes and point at the menu, because they're all excellent. Try the egg rolls, Moo Goo Gai Pan, Mocduck vegetables, lemon/curry chicken or at least one of the wonderful fried rices. The portions are large, and your cup will be kept filled with fresh-steeped jasmine tea. Although Taste of Saigon does not serve dessert, many Insiders go across the hall to Hepzibah's Sweet Shoppe for fancy chocolates or yogurt cones.

TOP OF THE HARBOR

Radisson-Duluth Hotel
Fifth Ave. W. and Superior St.
Duluth, Minn.   *(218) 727-8981*
$$$$

Even if the food weren't good, people probably would come here to enjoy the grand view, the circling dining platform, the crisp linen tablecloths and lemon ice water. But the food is very good for all three meals: omelettes, luncheon specials and a marvelous salad bar and swank dinner steaks. A delicious evening meal is the chicken Oscar — chicken breast with crabmeat, asparagus and Béarnaise sauce.

The restaurant is on the top floor of the cylindrical hotel, and the tables rest on a rotating outer floor that almost imperceptibly carries diners around the fixed center and past a continuous row of windows, affording the best view of the harbor and city of anyplace in town.

The restaurant is open every day, but is closed between 2 and 5 PM. It has a full-service bar.

TIMBER LODGE STEAKHOUSE

325 S. Lake Ave., Duluth, Minn. (218) 722-2624
$$

This restaurant, one of 10 Timber Houses run by the Minnesota-based company, is a relative newcomer to Duluth but has captured a following of hearty eaters. It offers a warm setting near the harbor when the cold winds blow (and a friendly setting when they don't), with a woodsy decor of turn-of-the-century memorabilia and mounted animals and fish. You'll get excellent steaks, chicken, seafood and ribs at the Timber Lodge, and a full bar is available. The restaurant is open for dinner only.

Superior

BARKERS ISLAND INN

300 Marina Dr., Superior, Wis. (715) 392-7152
$$

A beautiful harbor view with full sun all day long isn't the only reason to come to Barkers Island Inn. The restaurant locals call "the Pickwick of Superior" serves choice food. Chefs cut their own porterhouses, filets, T-bones and New York strips, and Lake Superior trout and whitefish are standbys. Both types of fish are served as Friday and Saturday night specials as well. The head chef's own favorite lunch is the seafood croissant, baked with hollandaise sauce and served with fries or fruit; and in the evening, chicken parmigiano. Easter, Mother's Day and Thanksgiving buffets are big hits, bringing more than 1,000 diners.

The recently renovated restaurant is open for breakfast, lunch and dinner every day. From U.S. Highway 2, turn toward the Lake at the Visitors and Convention Center and continue on Marina Drive to the Inn.

HAMMOND STEAKHOUSE

1402 N. Fifth St., Superior, Wis. (715) 392-3269
$$

The Hammond's specialty is slow-cooked prime rib, but the restaurant has been branching out with considerable success into Pacific Ocean fish that are rare in restaurants hereabouts: opha from Fiji, sea bass from Chile, rockfish, mahimahi and others — a different fish every week. They're boned, skinned and marinated in teriyaki, broiled or cooked in Jack Daniels butter. Fresh salmon is also offered once a month. The prime rib is always on the menu, as are steaks, walleye and other dishes. A full bar is available.

Enjoy Outdoor Seating with Spectacular View of Lake Superior

Sir Benedicts
On The Lake

- Unique Homemade Sandwiches & Soups
- Over 200 of the Best Imported & MicoBrewery Beers from around the World
- Wines and Gifts
- Live Contemporary & Traditional Folk & Bluegrass Music on Wednesday & Thursday Nights

805 East Superior Street • Duluth, MN • 728-1192

The Hammond is closed Tuesdays and otherwise is open for dinner only. It's at the foot of the Blatnik bridge on the Superior side.

LAN-CHI'S

1320 Belknap St., Superior, Wis. (715) 394-4496
$$ No credit cards

Asian restaurants that provide good soy sauce are a rarity in our area, but relative newcomer Lan-Chi's is an exception. The sparse decor (except for a wall painted with an idyllic Vietnamese lake scene) belies the abundant food — Chinese, Vietnamese, American and Greek. The restaurant is open for lunch and dinner.

THE LIBRARY/ZONA ROSA

1410 Tower Ave.   (715) 392-4821
Superior, Wis.   (715) 392-4161
$$ (both restaurants)

Two restaurants in one building, under one owner, draw diners from all over the region to Superior. The Library has an English-manor air and is a bit more expensive than its sister restaurant, serving lobster and steaks and a smashing Sunday brunch (crab legs, prime rib, omelettes, pastas and free champagne and vodka). Zona Rosa serves elegant Mexican foods — fajita and burrito dinners lead the way. Except for the Sunday brunch, the restaurants are open for lunch and dinner all week.

LOUIS' CAFE

1602 Tower Ave., Superior, Wis. (715) 392-3058
$$

Everybody loves Louis', which everybody pronounces "Louie's." Founded in 1946 by the owner's grandfather, Louis Letsos, Louis' in Superior (one block from Belknap next to the library) has long been an all-night favorite for authentic Greek food, big burgers and 24-hour pancakes. The Superior cafe has a full bar and spacious, pleasant seating.

THE SHACK SUPPER CLUB

3301 Belknap St., Superior, Wis. (715) 392-9836
$$

Caesar salads with homemade dressing tossed tableside are one of the attractions of the Shack, which recently was renovated but continues its standby menu of prime rib and barbecued beef ribs. The menu was expanded in 1996 to include smoked meats: barbecued beef brisket, chicken and pork ribs. Sunday specials are mainly of the home-cooking genre and draw a lot of locals.

The Shack is open for lunch and dinner Monday through Saturday and for dinner on Sunday, and is open every day except Christmas. For several weeks in the spring and fall, the Shack hosts a dinner theater; call for the production schedule.

Along the North Shore

Fresh raspberry pie. Wild blueberry muffins. Lake trout grilled with walnut butter. Pan-fried Lake Superior herring on a bun. Simmering bowls of homemade chicken soup, thick, spicy chiles and wild rice creamy chowders. Crusty, thick breads. Fish boils and Swedish meatballs. Cooking on the North Shore has historically played to its strengths, taking advantage of the wild bounty growing on the land and in the icy cold fisheries of Lake Superior.

These classic comfort foods are served up at many of the following restaurants — and done quite well. But you know something? We're seeing more adventuresome fare and more experimentation with menus at newer restaurants, such as the Scenic Cafe between Duluth and Two Harbors, Kamloops Restaurant at the Superior Shores Resort near Two Harbors, the Northern Lights Restaurant in Beaver Bay, the CoHo Cafe in Tofte and the Howling Wolf Saloon and Grill and the Angry Trout Cafe in Grand Marais. These places feature their own eclectic food and beverage menus, and all are worth a stop.

Please note that some restaurants are only open part of the year, generally from about Memorial Day through the peak fall colors season in early October. The restaurants that do stay open year round usually have shorter hours in winter than in summer; be sure to check with each.

In addition to our specified price-code amount, expect to pay 10.5 percent for taxes on your bill. And you may wish to note that Minnesota law requires restaurants to provide a nonsmoking section.

LAKEVIEW CASTLE DINING ROOM
5135 North Shore Dr.
Northeast of Duluth, Minn. (218) 525-1014

You can't miss Lakeview Castle as you drive along Scenic Highway 61 just 12 miles northeast of Duluth. This family-owned business is more than 50 years old. The dining room has views of the Lake and plenty of seating on several levels. House specialties are the dolmades, a Greek dish made of lamb, beef and rice wrapped in grape leaves. The Greek spanakopita — flaky pastry wrapped around spinach, seasonings and feta cheese — is another favorite. The broiled scallops are a oft-ordered menu choice as well. A full bar and wine list are available. Lakeview Castle also serves full breakfast and lunch seven days a week.

SCENIC CAFE
5461 North Shore Scenic Dr.
Northeast of Duluth, Minn. (218) 525-6274
$$

Imaginative, humorous, comfortable and eager to please. If Scenic Cafe were a human friend, that's how we would describe this place — one of our favorite haunts. The menu changes seasonally, and the cafe produces a monthly newsletter announcing special dinners, events and food tips. A low-key, casual atmosphere prevails here.

Scenic Cafe's menu features creative vegetarian entrees; it also offers a great sesame marinated steak and roasted pheasant with lingonberries on Valentine's Day. How about salmon cakes with cranberry relish? Or Jamaican vegetable rundown (an exotic stew filled with chayote and butternut squash, hot

peppers and mushrooms and seasoned with fresh lime and ginger root)? Scenic's soups are always fresh, and sandwiches include a tempeh Reuben, a grilled salmon cake sandwich, a Philly beef and Swiss and burgers.

The always-changing beer list includes only microbrews. We've enjoyed some marvelous bottles of wine here from the list of 10 selections — a small but carefully chosen offering. Press-pot coffee and marvelous pies and tortes are real treats. Check the blackboard for specials.

Scenic Cafe is open for lunch and dinner year round and is a totally smoke-free environment.

The Scenic Cafe is halfway between Duluth and Two Harbors. It's about a 13-mile drive from Duluth; take Minn. Highway 61.

EMILY'S GENERAL STORE AND DELI
Scenic Hwy. 61
Knife River, Minn.   (218) 834-5922
$ No credit cards

Creak, creak, creak. The worn, narrow strips of the hardwood floor tell you you've come into a well-loved place. Emily's has been run by the same Norwegian family since 1929. A dark wood counter runs one length of the little grocery room and in the back of the deli, and antique wood tables and chairs are clustered to take advantage of the view of the Knife River. If you walk through the doorway to your left, you'll end up in the Knife River Post Office.

Emily's has deli lunches and light supper choices. Feast on huge, stacked sandwiches; homemade wild rice, cheese and Lake Superior fish chowder; Emily's home-baked beans; and ice cream sundaes inside or out — or take your order to go. A seasonal summer favorite is the smoked trout salad, served on greens with a vinaigrette dressing. Don't miss the Friday night fish boil from February to October, with whitefish, Swedish meatballs, coleslaw, beans and bread.

Emily's is open daily year round.

SHARI'S KITCHEN
812 Seventh Ave. (Minn. Hwy. 61)
Two Harbors, Minn.   (218) 834-3714
$

If heaven could be rooms of antiques to browse and "homemade everything" to eat, Shari's Kitchen is it. Let's start with the antiques — Carousel Antiques is connected to the restaurant; two dining rooms are filled with furniture, prints and decorative plates, graniteware, tins, cookie jars and other collectibles for sale.

The restaurant is managed by Shari's sister, Joan, who told us she wouldn't serve anything here that she wouldn't eat herself. We like the dining area lined with old wood booths, antique schoolhouse light fixtures and an ornate soda fountain. It's a sunny, relaxed room.

Now, the food. Breakfast is served until late afternoon. Besides the traditional eggs, pancakes and omelettes, Shari's specialties are Aebleskivers (Danish pancakes made from a buttermilk batter, fried in a special iron skillet and served with powdered sugar and strawberry sauce) and Swedish pancakes (thin crepes served with fruit and whipped cream). Many folks stop by to pick up boxes of Swedish toast, made with sour cream and cardamom seed.

Lunch sandwiches are served on homemade bread that's baked on the premises. We were lucky to come the day after Joan had roasted a turkey, meaning hot turkey sandwiches with real made-from-scratch gravy, and real mashed potatoes. Pasties — meat and vegetable fold-overs in a flaky crust — served with gravy, soup and coleslaw, are favorites, as are pastrami and Reuben sandwiches.

The dinner menu reflects the sisters' Iron Range Italian heritage, with homemade ravioli, gnocchi pastas and pepperoni/mozzarella bread leading the way. Wine is available with dinner. Desserts run from simple homemade pies, cookies and fresh rice pudding to the pecan praline crepes smothered with sauce and ice cream.

Shari's Kitchen is open daily year round for breakfast, lunch and dinner.

BLACKWOOD'S GRILL & BAR
612 Seventh Ave. (Minn. Hwy. 61)
Two Harbors, Minn.   (218) 834-3846
$$

If you've got a carload of finicky eaters, Blackwood's may be your best bet. This family restaurant has a huge menu, including kids selections and smaller portions for seniors. Prime rib is the house specialty. Dinner choices include seafood, pasta and combinations of steak, seafood and chicken. The shore lunches of either trout or walleye are local favorites.

Blackwood's is a big place, seating 160 amid newly done modern decor. The full bar offers many call liquors, slush cocktails and ice-cream drinks, and the house wine is decent. You can also choose from a number of nonalcoholic beverages.

This is a hotspot in winter for snowmobilers, with sled parking out back. Blackwood's is open daily for breakfast, lunch and dinner.

MILLER'S CAFE
605 Seventh Ave. (Minn. Hwy. 61)
Two Harbors, Minn.   (218) 834-2452
$ No credit cards

Looking for filling, blue-plate specials with mashed potatoes, gravy, rolls and an occasional side of corn, carrots or peas?

NORTHERN LIGHTS RESTAURANT
"A North Shore Dining Experience"

SERVING LUNCH • DINNER • SAT. & SUN. BRUNCH

Featuring: The North Shore's Best Soup & Salad Bar
"All You Can Eat • Over 70 Items"
Fresh Lake Superior Fish
Wide Array of Fantastic Gourmet Specialties
Handcrafted Micro Brews & Wine

BEAVER BAY, MN • (218) 226-3012   **OPEN YEAR**
"On The Beautiful North Shore"   **'ROUND**

Miller's Cafe features turkey dinners, roasted chicken, meat loaf and, on occasion, fresh herring and lutefisk. This is definitely a locals place where the waitresses know the customers. It's smoky in here at times and a bit crowded, but we like the specials and the friendly, chatty staff.

Miller's Cafe is open for breakfast, lunch and dinner year round except Christmas and New Year's days.

KAMLOOPS RESTAURANT

At Superior Shores Lodge
Minn. Hwy. 61   *(218) 834-5671*
Two Harbors, Minn.   *(800) 242-1988*
$$$

Superior Shores, a deluxe resort set on a beautiful bay a mile north of Two Harbors, has recently come under new ownership, and the main lodge has been remodeled. Here, you'll find the new Kamloops Restaurant.

Kamloops' innovative menu was created by chef Glenn D'Amour. A native Duluthian, D'Amour trained at the Culinary Institute of America and went on to work with some of the best chefs in Italian, Mexican and Cajun cooking in Bologna, Italy, various sites in Mexico and New Orleans, respectively. His international experience and tastes are reflected on the menu; his local restaurant roots, in the fresh fish and premier steak entrees.

While there are six salad choices for the light eater, we suggest you dine at Kamloops with a *carpe diem* attitude and forget counting your fat grams for the day. Appetizer choices range from an antipasto plate to fried walleye cheeks served with fresh basil, lemon, mayonnaise and salsa. We stuffed our faces with the baked brie wrapped in puff pastry, served with a currant fruit sauce and herb-garlic toast rounds. Heavenly.

The extensive menu features wood-grilled selections, including five that feature certified dry-aged steaks. More exotic grilled fare includes roasted pork loin stuffed with corn bread and served with black mole sauce and grilled medallion of tenderloin topped with jumbo shrimp and ancho chile wine sauce. Pasta specialties include a recipe from Hotel Royale Carlton in Bologna, Italy: fresh pasta tossed with garlic, prosciutto ham, bacon, Parmesan, egg and black pepper. Rice specialties include a New Orleans barbecue shrimp and camarones de mole verde — grilled shrimp in a spicy sauce of fresh green tomatillos and cilantro in saffron rice.

• **69**

The fish menu includes lake and rainbow trout, walleye, whitefish and salmon, all cooked to order. We enjoy the lake trout — grilled, topped with bacon, onions, roma tomatoes and herbs, then baked. For dessert, bread pudding with brandy butter sauce, fresh strawberries with sabayon wine custard and chocolate Grand Marnier truffle cheese cake are a few of the choices. The fresh-ground house coffee — a custom blend of five beans including Sumatra, Mundeling, Kenya AA, Mexican Antiqua and Selawsi — is excellent.

An extensive wine list and full bar service are available. Kamloops is open for breakfast, lunch and dinner year round. Reservations are taken only for parties of eight or more.

RUSTIC INN CAFE AND GIFTS

Minn. Hwy. 61
Castle Danger, Minn.   (218) 834-2488
$

Red-topped tables and chairs set in a cozy log dining room, combined with home-cooked meals, make this one of our favorite stops on our way up the North Shore. A chef friend of ours proclaimed that Rustic Cafe served the best apple pie he'd ever tasted. We recommend the pumpkin, blackberry and lemon pies too. Fresh herring and lake trout are served here, and there's a children's menu for the little ones.

The Rustic Inn Cafe is open daily in summer for breakfast, lunch and dinner.

NORTHERN LIGHTS RESTAURANT

Minn. Hwy. 61
Beaver Bay, Minn.   (218) 226-3012
$

Northern Lights, a newly remodeled and expanded casual restaurant, is perched lakeside of the highway with close-up views of Lake Superior. Patio dining is available when the weather cooperates. We recommend the 70-item soup and salad bar. This extravaganza features homemade wild rice soup as well as homemade pasta salads, such as smoked trout with pasta, wild rice and fruit salad, and tomato-basil pasta with pepperoni. Rather than the standard iceberg lettuce, the salad bar features a mix of baby lettuces and spicy lettuces, such as arugula.

Another house specialty is the fresh fish. It's literally caught before your eyes from the Lake each morning. Try the walleye with raspberry sauce, the lake trout in a lemon -butter-sherry sauce or the grilled blue fin. Work by local artists — paintings, photography, and sculpture — cover the antique pine walls. Minnesota microbrews are featured, and house wines are available by the glass. Northern Lights offers a five-item children's menu. The restaurant is open year round for lunch and dinner, Monday through Sunday, and brunch is served on Saturday and Sunday.

BETTY'S PIES

Minn. Hwy 61
Ilgen City, Minn.   (218) 834-3367
$

"Did you stop at Betty's Pies?" is frequently asked of travelers coming up the North Shore. This restaurant is known for its fruit pies, summer berry pies and rye bread, but the menu also includes trout, hamburgers, fries and short-order breakfasts. It's open daily for breakfast, lunch and dinner from mid-May to mid-October and is closed in winter.

CROSS RIVER CAFE

Minn. Hwy. 61
Schroeder, Minn.   (218) 663-7208
$ No credit cards

Stop here to admire the waterfalls on the Cross River and then enjoy one of

Cross River Cafe's huge omelettes and the fresh-baked goodies. The cafe is open daily year round for breakfast, lunch and dinner. Beer and wine are served. (Don't miss the dozens of varieties of sausage made next door at the Cross River Store.)

BLUEFIN BAY RESTAURANT

Bluefin Bay Resort
Minn. Hwy. 61
Tofte, Minn.   *(218) 663-7297*
$$$

This is a romantic setting for a dining room, even if you're by yourself. The Bluefin Bay Restaurant is on a corner overlooking the Tofte harbor. Nice touches here include the brass and glass candles on the tables, the brass oil lamps on the walls, hand-woven placemats, real linens and blue-and-white striped window treatments and wall paper.

For dinner, check the appetizer, entree and wine specials. We recommend the artichokes, Parmesan bruschetta and any fresh fish or pasta. The wine list is impressive. And don't miss the desserts — try the carrot cake.

Although the place was busy while we were there, the service was top-notch. The restaurant is open every day for dinner.

THE BRIDGE RESTAURANT

Bluefin Bay Resort
Minn. Hwy. 61
Tofte, Minn.   *(218) 663-7296*
$$

The Bridge is upstairs in the same building as the Bluefin Bay Restaurant. It also enjoys great views of the harbor in a more casual and noisy setting. This place is a good choice for families with kids seeking pizza and sandwiches.

The Bridge is open daily in summer but may be closed during weekdays in winter.

COHO CAFE BAKERY AND DELI

Bluefin Bay Resort
Minn. Hwy. 61
Tofte, Minn.   *(218) 663-8032*
$

Soups or bread? Onion-dill. Cheddar-onion. Tomato-basil. Roasted pepper. Wild rice-herb. Potato. In fact, these are a sampling of the breads made at the CoHo Cafe under the instruction of head chef Tracy Jakobsen (who also designs the menus for the other Bluefin Bay Resort restaurants).

Check the blackboards for daily specials. Soups and salads, sandwiches, pizza, pasta and sweets are the basis for the cafe. Try the fisherman's chowder, which is full of seafood and a cream stock. The wild rice artichoke marinated salad is a worthwhile choice for something different. You can build your own sandwich, picking any of these fancy breads, deli meats and cheeses, such as Danish havarti and provolone. Cheesecakes, tortes and pies are the featured Sawtooth Sweets, and there's a freezer-full of eight Häagen-Daz flavors and fancy ice-cream cones.

The cafe, bedecked in blond wood, terra cotta-tile floors and teal upholstery, seats about 40 people — plus there's an outside deck. It's a laid-back atmosphere, and lots of skiing and hiking folks come in for lunches to go.

The CoHo is open year round Friday through Monday and on holidays.

LUTSEN RESORT & SEA VILLAS

Minn. Hwy. 61   *(218) 663-7212*
Lutsen, Minn.   *(800) 258-8736*
$$$

The Lutsen Resort has been feeding hungry travelers for more than 100 years since the Nelson family settled here from Sweden to fish, log and make a new life. The main lodge, designed by noted St. Paul architect Edward Lundie in the

1950s, is one of our favorite places to have lunch or dinner. Inspired by Scandinavian architecture, the place has a quiet, understated feel, with its huge, white pine beams and hand-hewn timbers. The lodge flanks the Poplar River, down low on the cove, and the views through the big picture windows in the dining room and lobby are at lake level — quite exciting during fall and spring storms.

For breakfast, try the made-from-scratch buttermilk pancakes. For lunch, we enjoy the fresh herring sandwich and a nice glass of white wine. Don't miss the raisin-rye bread (another family recipe). Our favorite regular dinner features include the Scandinavian meal of Swedish meatballs and herring or fresh fish (salmon or lake trout) with raspberry hollandaise sauce. And for dessert, the bread pudding is a tried-and-true family recipe.

The dining room in the main lodge is open daily for breakfast, lunch and dinner. Special meals are offered on holidays, notably the substantial Thanksgiving buffet.

VILLAGE INN RESTAURANT
Village Inn Resort
Ski Hill Rd.
Lutsen, Minn.   (218) 663-7316
$$

Moose Mountain looms large and impressive through the two-story windows in the Village Inn Restaurant. This is a perfect spot to kick back and watch the buzz of outdoor activity.

Set in the valley by the Lutsen Ski Hill, this busy resort and restaurant cater to the skiing and snowmobiling crowd, including families. It's casual dining here, with homemade soups, burgers, salads, pizza and sandwiches, free refills on pop and a kids menu. We like the walleye sandwich and

the turkey noodle soup. There's a full bar here too.

The restaurant is open daily for breakfast, lunch and dinner and features a well-attended Thursday night Mexican buffet.

ANGRY TROUT CAFE
Minn. Hwy. 61
Grand Marais, Minn.   (218) 387-1265
$$

We don't know if the trout is wont to act out its anger, but who cares? This is the best place in Grand Marais to sit outside by the harbor in the summer. Wonderful salads, fish and desserts are featured here as well as beers from regional microbreweries and exclusive wines from small California vineyards.

The hallmark of this unpretentious restaurant is simple and elegant food made with organically grown regional produce. The signature dinner is char-grilled lake trout served with a lemon pasta and a mixed green salad with Dijon-maple or tomato-basil vinaigrette dressing.

The Angry Trout is open for lunch and dinner Wednesday through Monday from early May to mid-October.

SVEN & OLE'S PIZZA
9 W. Wisconsin St.
Grand Marais, Minn.   (218) 387-1713
$

An informal get-your-own pop and silverware pizza joint, Sven & Ole's is a local institution that's known for dopey commercials and its sponsorship of the annual Fisherman's Picnic pickled herring and pizza-eating contest. But Sven & Ole's also makes a darn good pizza, served by the slice or as an entire pie. You'll also find hot and cold subs, salads and pastas. You can get pickled herring and crackers here too.

Sven & Ole's is open daily for lunch

and dinner and is a great place to bring kids. Sven & Ole's Pickle Herring Club meets upstairs in the small full-service bar, which features imported and domestic beers and wine coolers.

INGA AND LENA'S

7 N. Broadway
Grand Marais, Minn.   (218) 387-9111
$$

"Mexico meets the North Woods" is how one of the owners described this new restaurant. Inga and Lena's is run by the Backlund brothers who started Sven & Ole's. The menu features traditional Mexican fare and some spins, including a wild rice burrito. Steak and shrimp dinners also are available, and there's a children's menu.

Inga and Lena's is open daily for lunch and dinner in the summer and on weekdays for dinner in the winter.

HOWLING WOLF SALOON AND GRILL

Minn. Hwy. 61
Grand Marais, Minn.   (218) 387-1236
$$

Buffalo burgers and a pork steak with cranberry barbecue sauce are two of the adventuresome menu items featured at the new Howling Wolf Saloon and Grill. On the lakeside right before you come into Grand Marais driving up the shore, Howling Wolf is where a bowling alley and Chinese restaurant existed in another life. The owners have done a fine job of remodeling and redecorating. We prefer sitting in the lounge area where it's more open than in the smaller dining room.

The owners wanted to provide different food than the usual standard fare, so they researched other restaurants on the North Shore. The results? The aforementioned buffalo burger and sandwiches with a twist, such as a seafood salad pita and a veggie burger; lots of fresh fish, including bluefin and trout; and a turkey steak with

dill mushroom sauce. Local favorites include the spinach salad and the teriyaki chicken salad, with dressings made from scratch and freshly baked bread sticks.

Howling Wolf is open daily for lunch and dinner and features a variety of live music on the weekends.

BIRCH TERRACE AND TERRACE LOUNGE

Minn. Hwy. 61
Grand Marais, Minn.   (218) 387-2215
$$$

It's hard to believe Birch Terrace was originally a 19th-century log house. One of the North Shore's oldest restaurants, Birch Terrace features steaks, ribs and seafood served in a quiet and elegant setting. The Terrace Lounge (open daily) has comfy swivel chairs to sink into, with drink in hand, and gaze at Lake Superior. Birch Terrace restaurant is open daily for dinner.

LOAFER BAKERY & DELI

Minn. Hwy. 61
Grand Marais, Minn.   (218) 387-1747
$ No credit cards

The Loafer is known for its soups and sandwiches as well as its giant soft chocolate chip cookies, lemon bars and blueberry and raspberry muffins. It's open for breakfast rolls and lunch fare Tuesday through Saturday in the winter and daily in the summer. Grab a sack lunch here and hang out on the porch — and take some bread and rolls home with you.

NANIBOUJOU LODGE

Minn. Hwy. 61
About 15 miles north
of Grand Marais, Minn.   (218) 387-2688
$$$

The 1928 Naniboujou Lodge, listed on the National Register of Historic Places, features a colorful and airy Great Hall that's used as the central dining room. It holds the largest stone fireplace in Minnesota and vivid painted ceilings

The Hammond Restaurant in Superior offers fine dining and fantastic service.

Photo: Duluth-News Tribune

featuring Cree Indian designs. Breakfast, lunch and dinner are served here, with brunch on Sundays and tea from 3 to 5 PM daily in the summer. Check winter hours; they're much more restricted to weekends.

Along the South Shore

In any community on Wisconsin's South Shore, you can find restaurants with views of Lake Superior and menus that include lake fish. In most towns you can find elegant dining as well — don't forget Madeline Island, which in summertime has everything from sandwich shops to lakeside screened-porch fine dining. We advise you to start driving and when your stomach tells you to stop, check this guide to find a match between your geographical position, your taste buds, your aesthetic inclinations and your wallet.

Remember, 5.5 percent sales tax in Wis-

consin and the 6 percent tax in Michigan will be added to your overall meal tab.

Cornucopia

THE VILLAGE INN
Wis. Hwy. 13, Cornucopia, Wis. (715) 742-3941
$$$

A sunny room in a chalet-style building is the site of fine lunches and dinners during the summer (and, in winter, on Friday and Saturday evenings and Sunday afternoons). Diners enjoy whitefish and lake trout, deep-fried beer-battered shrimp, broiled lobster and the Saturday night prime rib special. Cheese and crackers are included with each dinner. If you're lucky, you'll happen by the Village Inn during one of the unscheduled fish boils. The adjoining bar is open for lunch (fish sandwiches, burgers, appetizers) all day, every day except Christmas.

FISH LIPPS

Off Wis. Hwy. 13
Cornucopia, Wis.   (715) 742-3378
$$

Fish livers, not lips, give this restaurant its tasty reputation. Whitefish livers are on the menu for breakfast, lunch and dinner most days in season (early May through October). You won't find any fish lips on the menu, but you will find some strolling around — namely owner Tom "Fish Lipps" Lovick, who was saddled with that moniker in his previous life as a fishing guide in northern Minnesota. The restaurant serves whitefish and lake trout, steaks, burgers, pasta and chicken. It's open every day for three meals during the summer; in wintertime, breakfast is served on weekends and lunch and dinner on weekdays.

Fish Lipps is in "downtown Corny," a block up the hill from Wis. Highway 13 just east of the Siskuit River.

Bayfield and LaPointe

BAYFIELD INN

20 Rittenhouse Ave.
Bayfield, Wis.   (715) 779-3363
$$

Upscale dining with views of the Bayfield marina, the bay and the charming town park mark this attractive inn. It's open every day for lunch and dinner during the busy season, and in July and August breakfast is served as well. During the off season, the inn is open for lunch and dinner on Thursday, Friday and Saturday. A bar and lounge adjoin the nonsmoking dining area.

Trout and whitefish are the most asked-for dishes here, followed by the increasingly popular barbecued rib special. Also offered are a salad bar, steaks, Saturday night prime rib, homemade pies and a Friday night fish fry. A bar and grill (burgers and hot dogs) is on the outside deck.

The Inn is usually closed in April.

GREUNKE'S

17 N. First St., Bayfield, Wis. (715) 779-5480
$$

This Bayfield landmark is probably the oldest continuous food-and-lodging place in the entire region. Built in the 1860s as a boarding house, Greunke's hasn't changed much: People still eat in the old dining room and sleep upstairs, and its homey, nostalgic hospitality still draws crowds.

The menu includes homemade raspberry pies and other home cooking. Greunke's made *The New York Times* in 1990 for its whitefish liver appetizer, described in that paper by owner Judith Lokken-Strom as "Once you get a taste for them it stays with you," which Insiders know to be true.

Greunke's is open for breakfast, lunch and dinner and serves beer and wine. If you'd rather dine outdoors, Greunke's also has a hamburger-and-ice cream kiosk out front and a nightly fish boil (summer through Labor Day) out back. The fish boil meal includes rye bread, fresh berry shortcake, coleslaw and iced tea. Greunke's planned to add in 1996 broasted chicken to the "out back" dinner, for folk who haven't yet developed a taste for fish boil.

MAGGIE'S

257 Manypenny Ave.
Bayfield, Wis.   (715) 779-5641
$$

Possibly the most frequented place in Bayfield, Maggie's is small but rustically attractive, with a menu that has far outgrown its dining space. Dinner entrees include whitefish livers, fresh Lake Superior trout and whitefish, chicken fajitas and champagne-basil grilled chicken breasts. Grilled duck sausage and black bean dishes are among the appetizers, and Maggie's salads and burgers are top-notch. A full bar is available, as is dining outside on a deck.

Maggie's is open every day for lunch and dinner.

OLD RITTENHOUSE INN
301 Rittenhouse Ave.
Bayfield, Wis.   (715) 779-5111
$$$$

Without a doubt the most elegant dining in the region takes place in this beautiful Victorian home on a hill in Bayfield. You'll get no menu; instead, the maître d' will tell you what gourmet courses will be presented on this particular day. Depending on the season, it could include fresh berries from nearby farms, wild leeks local kids bring in or whitefish livers fresh off the fishing boats down the hill.

The five-course meal always includes a choice from three soups, three salads, a sorbet and a choice from three or more entrees that always include fresh fish, poultry and a couple of steaks. Depending on the chef's inclinations and meat availability, additional entrees could include leg of lamb; venison; pheasant; 2.5-inch thick pork chops slowly roasted in fruit glazes; roulade with lamb, spinach and fontina; or other delicacies. Also served are side dishes of vegetables, pasta, potatoes and wild rice; homemade breads and muffins and homemade jams and preserves; fruits; and fantastic desserts, including tortes, cakes and chocolate creations.

It takes about two hours to eat this meal, although you're welcome to linger longer over coffee. Wine is extra, and you can select from the respectable wine list; beer and mixed drinks also are available.

You dine here by reservation only. The Rittenhouse is open seven days a week in the summer for dinner, late breakfasts and Sunday brunch. In the winter, it's open weekends for dinner and late breakfasts.

THE PIER-PLAZA
13 Front St., Bayfield, Wis. (715) 779-3330
$$

The Pier is usually jammed during the summer and, often, off-season as well. A hotspot with locals, it also attracts tourists for its tasty fish platters and fish sandwiches — fresh Lake Superior fish, naturally. A salad bar, excellent baked goods and hearty homemade soups make this a good all-round cafe. It has lots of windows and is a good place to wait for the ferry — you can watch it coming from distant Madeline Is-

Insiders' Tips

Fish boil is both an event and a meal in our region (as in "We're having a fish boil" or "I ate fish boil"). It usually involves combining water, potatoes, onions and seasoning in a cauldron that hangs outside over a wood fire; chunks of Lake Superior fish — sometimes herring, often trout, but most often whitefish or a combination — are dropped in and gently boiled. The meal usually includes a bowlful of this delectable mixture with bread, salad, coffee and dessert. As cooked fish and vegetables are removed from the broth, more raw ones are added, and the broth gets tastier as time passes.

land. When you can see the faces of the people on board it's time to pay your check and stroll down to the ferry dock.

The Pier serves breakfast, lunch and dinner all year long, except some winters when it closes in January and early February (just be sure to call ahead if you plan to stop by in winter).

PORTSIDE RESTAURANT
Wis. Hwy. 13, Bayfield, Wis. (715) 779-5380
$$$

A lovely restaurant with an airy view of Lake Superior, the Portside sports a nautical theme (it's tucked in a marina, protected from the highway by a hill and forest) and an upscale menu — fine dining in a casual atmosphere. A trained-in-France certified chef prepares gourmet sauces and lots of fresh fish and seafood, such as the shrimp-clam-angel hair pasta in a tomato-basil sauce. Usually five or six special entrees are prepared in addition to the everyday menu. Whitefish livers are available here. Diners can choose to take their meals on the outside deck.

Portside is open for lunch, dinner and Sunday brunch from June 15 through Labor Day. It's open shorter hours in May from Wednesday through Sunday for dinner only.

Washburn

IT'S A SMALL WORLD
114 W. Bayfield (Wis. Hwy. 13)
Washburn, Wis.   (715) 373-5177
$$ *No credit cards*

This small cafe in a small town has a large perspective — the entire world. You might not guess it from the generic cafe decor, but every week the owners/cooks offer a different ethnic specialty, along with occasional travelogues and guest speakers. Some weeks are tied to ethnic

holidays. Around St. Patrick's Day, for example, you can count on dishes such as Irish stew and boxty (grilled potato pancake) or cock-a-leekie soup. Amish week (there's a large Amish settlement in southern Wisconsin) includes onion rivvel soup and ham baked in milk and brown sugar; Colombian week offers plantanos and skewered barbecued beef; and Cajun, Czech, Polynesian, Jewish, Chinese and another two dozen cuisines are among the yearly offerings. Appropriate wines and beers are also served.

For everyday American fare, you're in the right place. You'll find excellent breakfasts (you can get croissants, bagels and granola if not morning sunshine) and a large selection of sandwiches and burgers for lunch. Dinners include steaks, pastas and seafood (Lake Superior fish and southern-fried catfish as well as fish 'n' chips).

SANDIE'S LOG CABIN
905 W. Bayfield (Wis. Hwy. 13)
Washburn, Wis.   (715) 373-5728
$$

Sandie's has been a favorite cafe for decades here, even before it moved next door to a beautiful new airy log building. The lumberjack breakfasts are huge, delicious and inexpensive, and the sun shines in; the lunchtime burgers, soups and salads are plentiful. Dinner specialties include walleye; Superior's lake trout and whitefish; ribs, steaks, chops, and chicken; and an Italian sausage-pasta dish.

Sandie's is open seven days a week all day.

STEAK PIT
125 Harbor View Dr.
Washburn, Wis.   (715) 373-5492
$$$

Overlooking Lake Superior at Washburn's marina, the Steak Pit, with aged black Angus beef, giant porterhouse steaks and weekend prime rib, is an old local standby for irredeemable red-meat eaters. For those who aren't, the Steak Pit offers seafood platters, fresh trout and whitefish, Friday night fish fry, crab legs and other foods. The homemade salad dressings are so sought after, local people buy them by the bottle. A full bar is available, along with inexpensive but good-quality wines.

The Steak Pit is open for dinner seven days a week, except for Thanksgiving, Christmas Eve day and Christmas Day.

Ashland

BLACK CAT COFFEEHOUSE
211 Chapple Ave., Ashland, Wis. (715) 682-3680
$

Sandwiches of hummus, whitefish, vegetables or specialty cheeses; coffees; home-baked muffins and pies; homemade soups and nachos are all part of the scene at this long, narrow and lively cafe, which has quickly become a favorite for Ashland's young literati.

The Black Cat is open for morning coffee, lunch and dinner, seven days a week. Customers lounge over chess or magazines in the back room or listen to evening poetry readings. You serve yourself here.

THE CORNERSTONE
316 W. Main St., Ashland, Wis. (715) 682-3232
$

Thick soups, healthy sandwiches, specialty coffees, plenty of seating and a play area for children define this cafe, known locally as the "Christian coffeehouse" because it's owned by the folks who run the Christian-oriented book shop next door. The food is good, the atmosphere relaxed, and photos of historic churches of Ashland adorn the walls. This serve-yourself cafe is open for lunch and dinner.

THE DEPOT
400 Third Ave. W., Ashland, Wis. (715) 682-4200
$$

This upscale restaurant and the Railyard Pub (listed subsequently) are in the beautifully renovated former Union Depot of the Wisconsin Central Railroad. For dinner, the restaurant offers appetizers such as wild rice and ham soup and aged baked brie with fresh raspberry sauce, French bread and fresh fruit. Fresh Lake Superior trout and whitefish are offered broiled in butter, baked in wine or crusted with a potato creation; pork loins are sautéed with apples and chopped walnuts and topped with apple cider cream sauce. The adjoining lounge has the original wainscoting, flooring and arches from the 1888 depot.

The Depot is open for lunch (sandwiches, salads and burgers) and dinner. From Lake Shore Drive (U.S. Highway 2), turn south on Third Avenue W. and continue three blocks to the depot.

FIFIELD'S AND MOLLY COOPER'S
Hotel Chequamegon, 101 Lake Shore Dr.
Ashland, Wis.   *(715) 682-9095*
$$$ and $$, respectively

One of the best things about dining at these sister restaurants is that you must first go into the lovely, gracious Hotel Chequamegon. The aroma of food wafts up the staircase into the lobby; follow your nose downstairs to Molly Cooper's if you want casual dining with a bar or next door to Fifield's if you want elegance. Both places overlook Lake Superior through plentiful windows, and both have excellent wait staffs. (Wait staff manager Missy Nabozny can't stay away; when she and her husband, Bill, got married in 1995, they chose one of the gazebos along the breakwater out front. Bill had coordinated Wisconsin Conservation Corps young people who built the boardwalk and the gazebos.) Fifield's offers fine breakfasts (the vegetable omelette is oh-so fresh and colorful) and dinners (try the spinach-wild mushroom-herb-cheese baked chicken served with apple marney sauce).

Molly Cooper's serves substantial but inexpensive lunches and dinners, including a no-fat whitefish dish and eggplant parmigiana. This restaurant's specialty, though, is a made-from-scratch Bloody Mary. If you're having trouble navigating after one of these monsters, check out the Great Lakes and Chequamegon Bay navigational charts on the walls. Lunches are served on the outside deck in the summer.

GOLDEN GLOW
CAFE AND ICE CREAM PARLOR
519 W. Main St., Ashland, Wis. (715) 682-2838
$

A plain, straightforward cafe frequented by local people, the Golden Glow has a large all-day menu of homecooked favorites and real ice cream desserts, including malts, milk shakes, sundaes, banana splits, floats, sodas, cones and sherbets. Half-orders for small appetites; inexpensive breakfasts with free coffee; roast beef, roast pork and fresh Lake Superior fish dinners; and Mexican cuisine on Tuesdays are among the offerings.

PAISANO'S FAMILY RESTAURANT
111 W. Main St., Ashland, Wis. (715) 682-5577
$$

Raphael and Renoir prints adorn the walls, and philodendrons grow lustrous at Paisano's, which is an Italian and Mexican restaurant in the front and a coffeehouse (serving espressos, cappuccinos and lattes) in the rear. Paisano's makes homemade Italian sauce from an old family recipe, and also bread; both can be purchased to take home. The restaurant is open for lunch and dinner.

THE RAILYARD PUB
400 Third Ave. W., Ashland, Wis. (715) 682-9199
$$

A charming pub adjoining a microbrewery, the Railyard is appointed like the old depot that houses it and is a patron magnet. Besides locally brewed beers, the pub has a full-service bar. Menu items include burgers, pita and other sandwiches and vegetarian dishes and entrees. Favorites are the smoked pepper turkey lefse sandwich and South Shore stew (beef tips sautéed in nut brown ale with potatoes, carrots and onions). You can watch the glassed-in brewery operate as you dine. From the Lake Shore Drive (U.S. Highway 2), turn south on Third Avenue W. and continue three blocks to the depot.

Ironwood-Hurley Area

If you're looking for fast foods with familiar logos, try the strip on U.S. Highway 2 in Michigan. For homey little cafes frequented by locals, head to downtown Ironwood to such places as the **Uptown Cafe**, at the corner of E. McLeod and S. Curry streets, a friendly corner cafe with the usual cafe food and coffee; or **Rigoni's Bakery**, 110 S. Suffolk Street, featuring an unbelievably inexpensive hot potato-onion-beef pasty that's big enough for two. But if you're looking for something a bit more special, try the following:

THE ALPEN INN
Big Powderhorn Ski Resort, Powderhorn Rd.
Bessemer, Mich. (906) 667-0211
$$

Burgers, pasta, seafood and steaks, ribs and chops draw hungry skiers into the Alpen for lunch and dinner. The food is good, and it's OK to tramp in here in your ski boots. Unfortunately, the Alpen is open only during ski season.

Big Powderhorn is 2 miles north of U.S. Highway 2 between Ironwood and Bessemer.

THE BRANDING IRON
214 Silver St., Hurley, Wis. (715) 561-4562
$$

The best prime rib in snow country and Margaritas on tap are featured at this watering hole, which has been gaining renown since opening in 1977. The Branding Iron, naturally, has a western decor and a lot of beef plus ribs, seafood, chicken and a salad bar that's included in dinner prices. Because the servings are so big, the restaurant allows two guests to order one dinner, visit the salad bar and get extra potatoes and bread at a reduced price for the second person.

Nothing is deep-fried — the steaks are charbroiled, and the seafood is steamed, except for swordfish steak, which is grilled. You can order side dishes of corn-on-the-cob, mushrooms in wine and butter and salsa and chips. The prime rib, voted by *SnoGoer Magazine* as the best of 1995, is served Friday and Saturday. Imported and domestic beers and ales, wines and wine coolers are served.

Kids don't have to take a back seat here. Their menu offers charbroiled steakburger and chicken as well as a salad bar.

CARIBOU LODGE
Big Powderhorn Ski Resort, Powderhorn Rd.
Bessemer, Mich. (906) 932-4714
$$$

Ski boots may be OK at the Caribou's sister-restaurant (the Alpen, listed previously), but the Caribou is for fine dining and finely shod diners. From specialty appetizers, such as baked scallops with lobster sauce, to cappuccinos and cheesecakes, the Caribou serves a variegated menu. Try the New Orleans vermicelli, with shrimp, crayfish, tomatoes, wild mushrooms, vermouth and herbs; or the saltimbocca alla Romana — a boneless chicken breast rolled around prosciutto, fontinella and spinach and seasoned with garlic, wild mushrooms and pinot noir. A Saturday all-you-can-eat buffet includes prime rib and a much reduced rate for children.

Like the Alpen, the Caribou is open only during ski season. Big Powderhorn is 2 miles north of U.S. Highway 2 between Ironwood and Bessemer.

COPPER HEARTH POWDERMILL INN
Powderhorn Rd., Bessemer, Mich. (906) 932-0800
$$$

One of the newer restaurants in the area, the Copper Hearth is part of a Best Western motel complex adjoining Big

Photo: Duluth News-Tribune

The Shack Supper Club in Superior.

Powderhorn Ski Complex. A "land and sea buffet" on Friday and Saturday includes crab legs, shrimp and roast beef, and there are nightly chef's specials. The daily menu includes lake trout, walleye, roast duck, wiener schnitzel, steaks and pastas. This very attractive restaurant — wood paneling, a working fireplace and floor-to-ceiling windows for great views of the outdoors — also features homemade soups, a full bar, hot and ice cream drinks and an economical children's menu.

The Powdermill Inn, closed during April, is 1.5 miles north of U.S. Highway 2 between Ironwood and Bessemer.

DON & GG'S

1300 E. Cloverland Dr. (U.S. Hwy. 2)
Ironwood, Mich.   (906) 932-2312
$$

An attractive, intimate restaurant-bar that catches the sunshine, Don & GG's serves up specialty salads and sandwiches, burgers and fine dinners, including fresh Lake Superior whitefish grilled with mayonnaise and Parmesan, served with garlic linguine and garden salad; and chicken breast stuffed with pro-sciutto and fontina, served with artichoke cream sauce. Like most restaurants in the twin towns, both help and clientele are chatty and friendly. Outdoor seating is available in warm weather. GG (Goldene Johnson) and her late husband, Don, opened the restaurant in 1952 and sold it in 1979 to the current owners. The restaurant is open for lunch and dinner.

ELK & HOUND

N-10233 Country Club Rd.   (906) 932-4545
Ironwood, Mich.   (906) 932-2515
Prices not established at press time

The lovely rock-and-tile building that houses the Elk & Hound was built in 1922 by the Civilian Conservation Corps up on a hill. Diners can gaze through tall windows at an expanse of golf course and woods or stroll over to outdoor seating beneath an overhang. A new restaurateur was taking over the business at the time this book went to press, so we can't tell you what the food is like; but if you're in the area, the building is worth a visit, and while you're there, check out the menu. As of mid-June 1996, the restaurant was to be open for lunch on Wednesday and dinner on Thursday, Friday and Saturday, with plans to expand hours as the season rolled on.

From U.S. Highway 2 a mile east of the Ironwood mall, turn south on Country Club road and continue a few blocks until you see the lodge on the left.

FONTECCHIO'S BELL CHALET
109 Fifth Ave. S., Hurley, Wis.   (715) 561-3753
$$

The pizza is fantastic, but this is no mere pizza house. "The Bell" serves some of the same Italian foods, using the same recipes, that Bernardino and Carmella Fontecchio used to cook here in the early 1900s.

Bernardino (a.k.a. "Fred") was a full-time miner, but the couple had bought a bar next to a bocce ball court. They began sharing their food with the loggers and miners who gathered there — and finally they were cooking it on the court and handing it out for free. Their neighbors begged them to open a restaurant, which they did in 1923. Their children handled a 1962 expansion (into the bocce ball courtyard), using materials that included beams from the dismantled Ashland, Wisconsin, ore docks, and copper for the bar and fireplace from nearby White Pine mine. Gradually, old books, old mining and logging equipment and other local historical mementos found their way onto the walls and shelves as decorations.

Now, the Fontecchios' grandchildren and great-grandchildren cook Fontecchio specialties, including homemade noodles, veal Parmesan and linguine with clam sauce. But Great-Grandma Fontecchio's pizza remains the big favorite, along with her granddaughter's Caesar salad. A salad bar, wine and beer fill out the menu.

Lunch is served Monday through Thursday, and dinner is offered seven nights a week. The only exception is a common one in skiing country: The business closes for several days in April for housekeeping.

MAMA GET'S
U.S. Hwy. 2, Ironwood, Mich. (906) 932-1322
$$

Here's a place that delights everyone: the singles skiing crowd, couples, children and grandparents. "Mama 'get" was the name the owner's child gave to grandma, whose last name the little one found difficult to pronounce.

The log building is primarily circular, with pine beams, bannisters and newel posts carved with considerable artistry into the shapes of animals. Antlers, beaver skins and other woodsy hangings decorate the place. Other amenities are a half-loft for dining, plenty of windows with a southern exposure, a full bar, working fireplace, video room for kids, dance floor and live music on Wednesdays (also Fridays and Saturdays during

Insiders' Tips

Seeking pizza and burger fast-food chains? Try cruising along the Red River Road in Thunder Bay North and along Arthur Street in Thunder Bay South. In the Twin Ports, try cruising Grand Avenue in West Duluth, London Road in East Duluth or near Miller Hill Mall (U.S. Highway 53); U.S. Highway 2 and Tower Avenue in Superior have a number of burger, pizza and taco stops.

ski season), featuring mostly folk singers and groups.

Burgers, Mexican food and dinner entrees featuring beef, pork and chicken are the fare. Meals are served in very large portions. Weekly specials include the quesadilla-Margarita special on Wednesday.

Mama Get's is small and does not accept reservations, so line up early. The restaurant is 2 miles east of Ironwood and is open for dinner only.

MANNY'S
316 E. Houk St., Ironwood, Mich. (906) 932-0999
$$

Manny's isn't fancy, but if you're in the mood for great Italian food, take Suffolk Street up the hill to the statue of Hiawatha and turn north on Houk Street. Manny's does it all: homemade pasta, including spaghetti; four Italian buffet menus; polenta; noodle omelette; and baked Parmesan. The menu also includes seafood, "American" food and sandwiches.

Other attractions are wintertime skating at the rink just outside (with hot chocolate) and a full bar. Manny's is owned and run by the offspring of Italian-born parents still living in Ironwood and uses old family recipes.

MIKE'S
106 E. Cloverland Dr. (U.S. Hwy. 2)
Ironwood, Mich.   (906) 932-0555
$$

The best reason for going to Mike's for breakfast isn't the food, although it's excellent; it's that you get plenty of morning sunshine. Mike's also serves Italian sandwiches and salads plus pizza, steaks and seafood for lunch and dinner — all of which give this restaurant a solid reputation in the twin towns (Hurley, Wisconsin, and Ironwood, Michigan).

You'll find the roomy establishment on the north side of Cloverland Drive.

PETRUSHA'S
Wis. Hwy. 51, Hurley, Wis. (715) 561-9888
$$$

If you like lamb, you'd better stop here; restaurants that serve lamb are scarce throughout our region. Besides broiled lamb chops, Petrusha's serves roast duckling, garlic-stuffed filet mignon, Austrian beefsteak (a large filet in a sauce of mushrooms, chicken livers and giblets, and cognac) and a variety of Italian foods. Daily specials include six fish dishes on Friday, such as shrimp linguine and lemon-pepper cod, several pork dishes on Wednesday and prime rib on weekends.

The restaurant is closed Monday and open for dinner the rest of the week, and it stocks an extensive bar. Petrusha's, established by the current owners in 1946, is a mile south of Hurley.

SILVER DRAGON
403 Silver St., Hurley, Wis. (715) 561-9807
$$$

The decor leaves something to be desired, but the menu is astonishing considering this area's small population. More than 100 Chinese entrees — Mandarin seafood, hot Szechuan chicken and Hunan beef dishes, Shanghai and Mandarin shrimp dishes, tofu and soups, foo youngs and rices — are augmented by two dozen American, Italian and Mexican entrees. The prices might cause you to double-take, but the servings are generous. Also, the family dinners, including soup, egg rolls and as many Chinese entrees as there are people in your party, are more economical. You can get sake, plum wine, Chinese beer and a "Singapore sling maitai" from the bar, along with other wines, beers and mixed drinks.

The restaurant is open for lunch, with an abbreviated menu, and dinner Sunday through Friday and for dinner only on Saturday. There's a minimum charge per person of $2.50. MSG is used in most Chinese dishes here.

VILLA ROMANO

Olson St., Ironwood, Mich.   (906) 932-5461
$$

An unassuming little restaurant high on a hill in an ash-maple forest, the Villa Romano has acquired a devoted clientele since opening here in 1994 — and for good reason: The all-Italian menu is excellent and inexpensive. Included are chicken in white wine, butter and garlic; Italian sandwiches; pizzas that some say are the best in town; and a homemade spaghetti sauce that the Romanos have been perfecting for many years. (The couple's first restaurant was in copper-mining country in South Range, Michigan, where Signor Romano's grandfather immigrated from the Primonte area of northern Italy.) Wednesday is all-you-can-eat spaghetti night, a deal that includes salad, homemade garlic bread and dessert, and regularly draws 130 diners to the small restaurant.

Villa Romana also offers reduced-price children's portions of pasta dinners, views of the woods where deer and birds visit and a full bar. It's open for lunch and dinner every day but Monday. From U.S. Highway 2 a mile east of the Ironwood mall, turn south on Country Club Road, go a few blocks up the hill and turn right at the sign.

Thunder Bay Area

Thunder Bay's immigrant history certainly influences some of the fine food in the area. The Scots, English, Finns, Swedes, Germans, Chinese, Poles, Italians, Ukrainians and Greeks are some of the ethnic groups who make up Thunder Bay's colorful past.

In particular, you'll discover wonderful Finnish cooking and fine Italian food in Thunder Bay's restaurants. Incidentally, Thunder Bay is home to the largest population of Finns outside Finland.

For starters, try some delectable Finnish pancakes for a must-eat experience. Typically razor-thin, these rich pancakes spread out like a map to cover your plate and are served with syrup, real butter and traditional blueberry, raspberry or strawberry sauce. We've mentioned subsequently some of our favorite Finnish pancake breakfast spots. Generally, the reasonably priced pie and soup served in these places is homemade and delicious.

The Italian halls, social and recreational gathering spots, feature luncheon buffets with mountains of food for reasonable prices. There are dozens of small local Italian eateries and deli/bakeries; check out the breads, sausages, and olives, and don't miss the panzarotti (a huge stuffed Italian-style sandwich.)

The following suggestions run the gamut from some of Ontario's top gourmet experiences to neighborhood deli/bakery places where you can pick up the fixings for a great picnic or a quick lunch.

Something fishy here? Pickerel is Thunder Bay-speak for walleye.

(Check out the Parks and Forests chapter for ideal picnicking spots.) We're confident there are many more tucked-away neighborhood places just waiting to be discovered; for instance, a local born-and-bred Italian friend told us he's still stumbling upon new places with great Italian meatball sandwiches.

You may notice the prevalent French-Canadian influence here, especially in the names of menu items and ingredients. You're bound to come across creme (cream) and terrine (tureen), among other examples.

We've included some expensive but worthwhile places to enjoy a wonderful dinner. Acclaimed area gourmet restaurants include the Unicorn Inn, Harrington Court, the Castillo Dining Room at the Airlane Hotel and the White Fox Inn. Each one of these restaurants has the food, decor, service and setting that create a special dining experience.

We've also included some restaurants for family dining — places that are reasonably priced and have children's menus and where parents won't be too embarrassed if their children are noisier than usual because there are other little noisemakers in the room.

For practicality's sake, we've organized the restaurants by location under three categories: "Thunder Bay North," which is the old Port Arthur area; "Thunder Bay South," which is the old Fort William area; and "Outside Town." Thunder Bay became one city in 1970, combining the towns of Port Arthur and Fort William. Most local people still refer to their part of Thunder Bay by its original city name.

Remember that our price code is based on a general idea of a dinner for two. What's not included are cocktails, gratuity and taxes — expect to add 15 percent for taxes on your bill in Canada. Although there are no laws restricting smoking in Ontario's restaurants, most eateries provide separate smoking and nonsmoking sections.

Thunder Bay North

ARMANDO FINE ITALIAN CUISINE
28 N. Cumberland St.
Thunder Bay, Ont.   (807) 344-5833
$$$

In downtown Thunder Bay (old Port Arthur) across from the Prince Arthur Hotel, this is one of the best places to go in town for true fine Italian dining. Armando himself is the gregarious and charming host. The decor is attractively done in burgundy and gray, with soft lighting. The service is top-notch, and the place fills up fast. Tables of Italian families patronizing Armando's tell you it's the genuine article. While the atmosphere is relaxed, people tend to dress up, as many come here before the theater or symphony.

The bread basket is always full of crusty, chewy Italian bread served with a garlic herb butter. The pastas are made fresh. We feasted on the manicotti, ravioli and gnocchi, all served with rich and well-flavored sauces. The house wines include quality reds, and there's full bar service.

Ethnic traditions run strong in Thunder Bay, especially the Italian wine-making tradition. Each fall, people make pilgrimages to neighborhood delis and large supermarkets to buy crates of trucked-in California grapes for home wine-making.

Insiders' Tips

For dessert, the strong coffee goes well with homemade tiramisu, which is layers of coffee liqueur and chocolate, marscapone and ladyfingers, served in a wine goblet.

Armando's is open Wednesday through Friday for lunch and Tuesday through Saturday for dinner.

ITALIAN CENTENNIAL HALL
132 Algoma St. S.
Thunder Bay, Ont.   (807) 345-5511
$ No credit cards

Want bulk for your buck? Try either of the Italian halls (also see Da Vinci Centre's listing in this chapter's "Thunder Bay South" section) for total fulfillment at a reasonable price. As a local buffet habitue put it, "you're gasping for air when you get out." The luncheon buffet attracts loyal folks who stand in line for this cafeteria-style smorgasbord of Italian cooking. The menu changes daily, but expect lots of pasta, meatballs, chicken and good bread as well as roast beef, mashed potatoes and Jell-O salads.

The Italian Hall is in old Port Arthur's Italian neighborhood (appropriately enough). The lunch buffet is offered from Monday through Friday.

MALTESE GROCERY
301 Pearl St.
Thunder Bay, Ont.   (807) 344-5911
$

This is a great place to go for picnic stuff. It's on the edge of the old Italian neighborhood in old Port Arthur. There's an expansive meat and deli section in back, with smiling helpers behind the counters. You'll find lots of exotic marinated stuff

here, such as squid and antipastos, a great olive selection, good cheeses and sausages. Check out the wall of fresh-baked breads from the renowned Roma Bakery (see the "Thunder Bay South" section), including baguettes (regular and sandwich-size) and rounds displayed on red and white checkered napkins in wicker baskets.

It's open seven days a week from 10 AM to 10 PM.

HOITO RESTAURANT
314 Bay St.
Thunder Bay, Ont.   (807) 345-6323
$ No credit cards

This is one of our favorite spots in Thunder Bay for breakfast (Finnish pancakes, sausage, coffee and sometimes pie). Bay Street runs through the heart of the old Finnish neighborhood. Although there's usually a line on weekends and the little lobby is tiny, it's worth the wait — and no one seems to mind.

In the basement of the old Finnish hall (a local landmark), the Hoito Restaurant is decorated with blond wood tables, chairs and paneling accented with travel posters of the homeland. The bustle of the place, and the fact that you're elbow to elbow with folks at the next table, is more charming than annoying. This is a great place to take kids.

Hoito Restaurant is open daily for breakfast, lunch and dinner.

KESTITUPA CAFETERIA
309 Bay St.
Thunder Bay, Ont.   (807) 345-9381
$ No credit cards

Kestitupa Cafeteria is another option

for Finnish pancakes and pie, especially when the line at the Hoito across the street is long. It's more low-key than its bustling neighbor, but the food is good, inexpensive and available for take-out. Try the homemade soups, cabbage rolls and perogies (rich stuffed dumplings).

Kestitupa is open daily for breakfast, lunch and dinner.

SCANDINAVIAN DELICATESSEN
307 Bay St.
Thunder Bay, Ont.   (807) 344-3632
$

Across the street from the Hoito in the old Finnish neighborhood is the Scandinavian Delicatessen, another great picnic supply possibility. It's a small shop packed with all sorts of goodies, including rye, wheat and cardamom breads, cheeses, baking supplies, mustards, jams, syrups, coffee, juices and chocolates.

The deli is open Monday through Friday from 9 AM to 6 PM and on Saturday from 9 AM to 5 PM.

HARRI BAKERY
223 Algoma St.
Thunder Bay, Ont.   (807) 344-8588
$ No credit cards

Around the corner from the Hoito Restaurant is Harri, a Finnish bakery. Try the wonderful rye and cardamom breads and pastries. Harri Bakery is reputed to have the best jellyroll cake in the city.

It's open Tuesday through Friday from 9 AM to 5:30 PM and Saturday from 9 AM to 5 PM.

KANGAS SAUNA
379 Oliver Rd.
Thunder Bay, Ont.   (807) 344-6761
$ No credit cards

Food at a sauna? Kangas, a bright and modern place filled with pine paneling and skylights, houses public sauna facilities and a small restaurant. A community tradition, it's a local gathering place where you can rent individual saunas or a communal sauna room.

This is one of the best places in town to sit at the counter and eat those famous Finnish pancakes. Other menu specialties include soups, homemade pies (try the rhubarb), tortes and tarts (try the strawberry short cake) and sandwiches.

Kangas is open daily for breakfast, lunch and dinner.

HARRINGTON COURT DINING ROOM
170 N. Algoma St.
Thunder Bay, Ont.   (807) 345-2600
$$$$

Harrington Court is an elegantly restored mansion owned by a Swiss-born proprietor who has furnished this formal place with antiques, linens, crystal and candles. The seating is cozy and intimate, and the dining experience is more appropriate for adults than families with children.

Harrington Court's highly recommended menu specialities include Swiss-

If you have just an hour for lunch and no wristwatch, go to the Top of the Harbor in Duluth's Radisson Hotel. When your table on the revolving platform comes around to where you started, your hour is up. (On the other hand, if you want a table in the sunshine, you'll have to keep moving to the one behind you!)

Insiders' Tips

influenced veal dishes, fresh fish, lamb, Châteaubriand and steaks. Don't miss tasting the white chocolate terrine and the crème brûlée for dessert. Fresh sorbet and tortes are other house specialties worth succumbing to. Because Harrington Court is big with the downtown business crowd for lunch and a romantic spot for dinner, reservations are essential.

Harrington Court is open for lunch and dinner Tuesday through Saturday.

BISTRO DANUBE
109 Regina Ave.
Thunder Bay, Ont.   (807) 767-8878
$$

Off the beaten track in a little mall, Bistro Danube is a tasty dumpling of a restaurant offering German-Austrian cuisine. This family-run bistro (the owning family cooks, bakes and serves) offers simple, country German meat-and-potatoes dishes, such as goulash, schnitzel and beef medallions with made-from-scratch gravy and fresh green salads with homemade dressing. While seated in this long and narrow space with tables on one side, patrons can watch the food being prepared in the kitchen. The dessert menu carries on the German-Austrian tradition of rich, creme-filled pastries and cakes; try it with a cappuccino, espresso or Vienna coffee. Wine and liquor are available.

Bistro Danube is open every day for breakfast, lunch, dinner and late-night desserts.

Thunder Bay South

MERLINS BISTRO
127 S. May St.
Thunder Bay, Ont.   (807) 622-3445
$$

Merlins Bistro is in former downtown

Fort William. This mellow nightspot features an open stage where music and poetry readings happen regularly. You're bound to see local characters here. Original art for sale on the restaurant walls, Magical Mystery Tour decor, Merlins' location (on a downtown block that has seen better days) and its tarot card or tea leaf readings make for a quasi-bohemian feel.

Merlins is known for its cheesecakes and tortes, made by a variety of home bakers throughout the city. There's a full bar with wine and beer as well as a selection of specialty coffee and tea. Service staff are friendly and accommodating. Our waiter (an oboe player with the symphony) brought us several flavors of cheesecake to test. The menu includes simple, fresh lunches and dinners, with excellent homemade soups and breads.

Merlins is open daily for lunch, afternoon tea, dinner and late-night desserts.

BLUE PARROT RESTAURANT
376 Lisgar St.
Thunder Bay, Ont.   (807) 345-5345
$$

Blue Parrot, a family-owned Greek restaurant, is near several public facilities, including the Canada Games Complex, a huge health club and the Thunder Bay Community Auditorium (the main venue for symphony concerts, Broadway shows and pop music). The lighting is low, Greek art and posters adorn the walls, and Greek music wafts in the background. But, no belly dancers. . . .

Locals rave about the Greek and Caesar salads; dressings are made from scratch with lots of garlic. House specialties include Greek mousaka (an eggplant casserole with tomato and beef and a cheese custard topping), Greek souvlaki (a baby shish kebab, marinated and braised with pita bread and sauces) and chicken reganato (a chicken fillet in a seasoned sauce served with a garlic spread). Specialty desserts include homemade cheesecakes and pies — hits with the after-concert crowd. The full bar includes varieties of Greek wine.

Blue Parrot's children's menu includes Canadian-American food.

This casual eatery is open daily for breakfast, lunch and dinner.

CASTILLA DINING ROOM

In the Airlane Motor Hotel
698 W. Arthur St.   (807) 577-1181
Thunder Bay, Ont.   (800) 465-5003
$$$$

The Airlane Motor Hotel won the Thunder Bay Chamber of Commerce's 1995 Best Hospitality Award for northwestern Ontario. Staff members are justifiably proud of this recognition.

Locals recommend the Castilla Dining Room for its consistently superb food. House specialties include Châteaubriand, steak Diane, panfried walleye, trout and salmon (in the summer) and the New Zealand rack of lamb with red-wine sauce. The grilled medallions of ostrich entree, served with mushroom sauce and shallots, is a surprisingly big draw. Soups are made daily, including lobster bisque, Naniboujou chicken consommé, three-onion soup and Louisiana gumbo.

Castilla Dining Room offers specials every night, including Wild Bill's Prime Rib on Sunday and Monday, Pasta, Pasta and More Pasta (always fresh and made from scratch) on Tuesday and Wednesday and Seafood Festival Thursday, Friday and Saturday (with selections such as baked swordfish and mussels marinara).

All breads, muffins, pies and pastries are baked on the premises. The restaurant is known for its Castillo cheesecake — a light, fluffy, unbaked dessert topped with raspberry or strawberry puree.

A lunch buffet is offered Monday through Friday, including five hot items, a seafood bar (shrimp, herring and crab), a huge salad bar and various breads.

Sunday brunch is a pricey but well-organized extravaganza if you want to pig out. There's so much food you have to go to another room to browse the selections and order your custom-cooked waffles and omelettes.

ENSENADA RESTAURANT

In the Airlane Motor Hotel
698 W. Arthur St.   (807) 577-1181
Thunder Bay, Ont.   (800) 465-5003
$$

This is a family-dining restaurant in the award-winning Airlane Hotel. For adults, the menu features "Old Faithfuls" from the fancy Castilla Dining Room; for children, anything on the menu (you'll find the basics, such as chicken fingers and grilled cheese sandwiches) is discounted 50 percent. Try the homemade ice cream.

Wondering why Italian food dominates in Michigan's Upper Peninsula, even though the UP received equally large numbers of Finnish and Slavic immigrants? According to a Finnish cook here, it's because the cuisine of non-Italians was too darn uninteresting to survive the competition!

Insiders' Tips

Ensenada is a casual atmosphere, open seven days a week for breakfast, lunch and dinner.

NORDIC DINING ROOM

In the Valhalla Inn
1 Valhalla Inn Rd.   (807) 577-1121
Thunder Bay, Ont.   (800) 964-1121
$$$

The Nordic Dining Room features handsome, Scandinavian-influenced decor, with cathedral ceilings and richly colored wood appointments in a low-light setting. This is an elegant hotel restaurant targeted for adult clientele, with a wine list and full bar service.

Open for dinner only from Monday through Saturday and for brunch on Sunday, the dining room features prix fixes (select appetizer, entree, dessert and beverage choices for one set charge).

TIMBERS RESTAURANT

In the Valhalla Inn
1 Valhalla Inn Rd.   (807) 577-1121
Thunder Bay, Ont.   (800) 964-1121
$$

Timbers Restaurant in the Valhalla Inn is a casual place, serving sandwiches, soups, pastas, burgers and an excellent spinach salad. Check out the weekly international buffet specials. They're presented with a twist on the usual steam-table fare. The excellent Chinese buffet on Friday and Saturday nights features an appetizer table and a main buffet table where you pick fresh ingredients that are cooked on the spot. The Italian buffet on Wednesday and Thursday nights offers the same custom approach but with different flavors.

Timbers Restaurant is open seven days a week for breakfast, lunch and dinner. A wine list and full bar selections are available.

GIORG RISTORANTE

114 N. Syndicate Ave.
Thunder Bay, Ont.   (807) 623-8052
$$$

Giorg's is frequently mentioned by locals as a great place to go for dramatic Northern Italian cooking. The menu items are listed in Italian, spoken in Italian and featured on chalkboards. It's a light, open, airy space where you can watch the cooks prepare the food. This restaurant is usually hopping (and seatings are few), so reservations are advised. This is a wonderful place for fine Italian dining, and pastas are made fresh daily on the premises. The red sauce has a spicy kick.

The atmosphere is casual and geared toward adults. Wine and liquor are available, and the desserts are Italian-oriented, sometimes Amaretto-based.

Giorg Ristorante is open for dinner Tuesday through Saturday.

DA VINCI CENTRE

340 Waterloo St.
Thunder Bay, Ont.   (807) 623-2415
$ No credit cards

Da Vinci Centre is Fort William's Italian hall. The luncheon buffet attracts a midday crowd for cafeteria-style Italian fare. The menu changes daily but always includes the standard pasta, meatballs, chicken, bread, roast beef and mashed potatoes and Jell-O salads.

Da Vinci Centre is open for lunch Monday through Friday.

ROMA BAKERY

401 Frederica St. W.
Thunder Bay, Ont.   (807) 475- 5313
$ No credit cards

Select Italian delis and restaurants around town get their bread from Roma Bakery. Hearth-baked and preservative-free, it's crusty, chewy, wonderful stuff made in small quantities to retain qual-

The 3M Company was born at this plant near Two Harbors.

ity. Try the Italian rounds and the French-style baguettes.

The Pedulla family has been making bread and sausages for 30 years. They stock an extensive deli with meats, cheeses and wine-making supplies.

Roma Bakery is open every day except Tuesday from 7 AM to 6 PM.

Outside Town

WHITE FOX INN

1345 Mountain Rd.   (807) 577-3699
South of Thunder Bay, Ont.   (800) 603-3699
$$$$

White Fox Inn is just minutes south of Thunder Bay in a historic house renovated to serve as a restaurant and inn. The 60-seat restaurant serves breakfast, lunch and dinner — as well as views of the country. In a wooded setting, the inn is known for its classic and stunning decor and feels, as one local put it, like Colonial Williamsburg, Virginia.

The New World-cuisine menu is known for putting a spin on standard classics. For breakfast, indulge in the signature French toast stuffed with creme cheese and fresh strawberries. The dinner menu features 15 to 20 changing entrees, including fresh salmon, walleye and hand-cut steaks, all cooked with fresh herbs. Desserts feature French pastries and seasonal items such as fruit tarts. The zebra cake — chocolate cake with vanilla creme filling — is a house specialty.

The chef is known for adhering to freshness, and he may change menu listings if the quality of available ingredients does not meet his standards. A full bar and wine cellar complement the menu. Reservations are advised.

To find White Fox Inn coming from Duluth, take Ont. Highway 61 north to the end of the 15th Sideroad, then take a left on Mountain Road and continue just past the Fort William Golf and Country Club.

UNICORN INN

RR #1, South Gillies, Ont.   (807) 475-4200
$$$$

An astounding place, we don't know of anything quite like Unicorn Inn. In the middle of the stunning wild country of South Gillies, Unicorn Inn is nestled in a wide-open river valley surrounded by ancient cliffs and woods. It's not much to look at from the outside, but inside, this unassuming little farmhouse is a warm and unpretentious place.

Run by David and Arlan Nobel, the inn features evening dining from Thursday through Sunday, with a single seating for a prix fixe dinner. The cost of the meal includes an appetizer, breads, soup, a main entree, side dishes, a surprise dessert creation and coffee and tea. Everything is prepared on site with the freshest ingredients, many of which are grown in the gardens.

We had the privilege of watching David Nobel, the head chef, prepare bread from scratch for an evening dinner as he explained his approach to cooking. (The well-organized, professionally appointed kitchen is not much larger than a yacht's galley!) Nobel is passionate about using fresh ingredients — and the best ingredients — down to the salt from England, the special malt syrup used to "wake up" the yeast and the select milled spring wheat flour used to make his French-style peasant bread.

Whoever calls first each day for reservations selects the menu. Fifteen entrees comprise the house specialities, many of them Nobel's original creations, including seafood raviolini with pink shrimp sauce, Caribbean shrimp in va-nilla butter sauce, roast pintelle with brandy and wild mushroom sauce, roast marinated rack of Colorado lamb and chicken amandine with Alsatian Gewurztraminer sauce. The first Thursday of every month is India Night when David cooks up authentic East Indian dinner fare, including namkeen, shorva, roti, tandoori-style roasts, dal and raita.

Many people opt to eat dinner and spend the night. You can dine on incredible cuisine, perhaps hear David Nobel sing and play the guitar and then spend the night in one of the freshly decorated rooms. (See our Accommodations chapter.) Breakfast is another adventure, with fresh-baked scones, homemade preserves, a German pan souffle and fresh orange juice and coffee.

Dinner is served by reservation only, although space occasionally is available on short notice. No smoking is allowed, and there's no liquor on site. We advise you call for directions. Depending on from where you're coming, finding Unicorn Inn can be complicated (although there are signs for the inn along the way).

NEEBING ROAD HOUSE
2121 Ont. Hwy. 61
Thunder Bay, Ont.   (807) 475-0792
$$$

The Neebing Road House, called "casual gourmet," is just south of Thun-

---

der Bay. This informal restaurant offers great views of Mount McKay and the Nor'Wester Mountains. Ask for a window seat in the lower section when you make a reservation — there are 12 good-view spots. The decor is patterned cedar and antique stained glass. The staff is known for attentive service. Because the Neebing House is right outside Thunder Bay proper, many people driving the Lake Superior Circle Tour (see our Circle Tour chapter) stop here.

House specialties include prime rib (usually a weekend special) and highly acclaimed steaks. The seafood, Greek and chicken curry salads are popular lunch items. Another house specialty is the Swedish chowder with scallops, shrimp and fresh dill. In the summer, try the fresh trout or walleye. The extensive wine list features French, German, Canadian, Australian and California wines. There's a full bar and lounge too. Reservations are suggested.

Dinner is served seven days a week, and lunch is available Monday through Friday.

To get to Neebing Road House, drive 9.2 kilometers southwest of the junction of Can. highways 11 and 17 and Ont. Highway 61 to Loch Lomond Road.

Cash ♦ Food ♦ Lodging

The Northland's Only 24-Hour Entertainment Center!

- 28 Blackjack Tables
- Bingo Emporium
- Video Keno
- Over 1,000 Slots
- Live Weekend Entertainment
- All-You-Can-Eat Buffets
- Fine Dining
- Sports Bar & Lounge

- Convention Center
- Cub' Den Child Care Center
- Video Arcade
- Incredible Pool Atrium
- Luxurious Jacuzzi Rooms
- On-Command Pay Movies
- Exercise Room
- In-Room Nintendo

Black Bear Casino
Carlton, Minnesota
(218) 878-2327

Black Bear Hotel
Carlton, Minnesota
1-800-553-0022

20 minutes south of Duluth at I-35 and Hwy. 210

Owned and Operated by the Fond du Lac Band of Lake Superior Chippewa

Inside
Nightlife and Casinos

Nightlife

People wouldn't live in our region if big-city entertainment were necessary to our existence. For many of us, the outdoors is the main source of our fun; we think a perfect evening is skiing or snowmobiling in the dark and winding up at the neighborhood tavern for a beer and maybe a pool game. We like to build a bonfire on a Lake Superior beach, fish by a starlit river, camp.

Visitors from other parts of the country and the world remark that our cities are relatively quiet places — even boring. During summertime street dances, you won't see much uninhibited dancing unless there's been considerable drinking first.

Nevertheless, we do have indoor nightlife opportunities sprinkled among the ubiquitous neighborhood taverns. A relatively new one is spending an evening at one of the five casinos hereabouts. They don't have roulette or live poker and aren't as glitzy or grandiose as those in Las Vegas; some are downright homey. But they offer some head-spinning jackpots, lots of slots, high-stakes bingo and live blackjack with betting limits high enough to make most people nervous. All except Fond-du-Luth in Duluth are in rural areas and offer the only late- or all-night bright-light gathering places to be found.

We haven't listed here the lounges at most ski hills throughout the region — see our Winter Sports chapter for those.

In this chapter we've tried to give you a wide sampling of the other nightlife possibilities, ranging from cheesecake (with bump-music and alcohol) to cheesecake (with coffee and blues).

Twin Ports Area

DULUTH

There's almost more music than bakery at **Amazing Grace Bakery**, (218) 723-0075, in the basement of DeWitt Seitz Marketplace in Canal Park. Musicians play folk, blues and jazz beginning at 7:30 PM Thursday through Saturday. On Monday nights, there's an open stage; you're welcome to get up and perform music or read poetry. On Tuesdays, an old-time folk band comes to jam. There's no cover charge, unless the performer is a big-name artist. Keep an eye out for late-night (until 3 AM) jazz and alternative music in the summer of 1996. Amazing Grace is a smoke-free place (no smoking allowed inside).

A half-block away, **Grandma's Sports Garden**, (218) 722-4722, 425 Lake Avenue S., has indoor and outdoor sports and entertainment. The "college dry night" every Thursday gives the younger-than-21 crowd a chance to dance too. The cover charge for that night is $4. There's line dancing from 7:30 to 10 PM Mondays, for a $2 cover charge.

The Blue Note Cafe, (218) 727-6549, 357 Canal Park Drive, is a coffeehouse that features live music (mostly folk, blues and jazz) every weekend from 7:30 to 10:30 PM. On most Thursdays, there's also an informal jazz jam session. There is no cover charge. The Blue Note is a smoke-free cafe — no smoking allowed.

Down the block at 331 Canal Park Drive, the **Saratoga Night Club**, (218) 722-5577, also has a jazz jam session — but that's not what gives the Saratoga its notoriety. The club is better known for its exotic dancers who wiggle across the stage nonstop every day, except Saturday, from 4:30 PM to 1 AM; dancing starts later on Saturday, after the 3 PM jam session concludes. There's a $2 cover after 8:30 PM.

In the western part of town is a hotspot with the over-the-road trucker and country-western crowd: **The Western**, (218) 624-7742, 2801 W. Superior Street, has live music Tuesday through Sunday. There is no cover charge.

Charlie's Club, (218) 624-3150, 5527 Grand Avenue, has been serving the dancing needs of western Duluth for decades. Dancing to old and new rock 'n' roll happens every Thursday (karaoke), and Friday and Saturday (live bands), drawing a mixture of generations to the bar and dance floor. There is no cover charge.

The Rustic Bar, (218) 624-7463, 401 N. Central Avenue, is a sports bar, with seven televisions, two big screens and an enthusiastic clientele.

If you need line-dance lessons, go early to **Roby's Bar & Lounge**, (218) 722-1825, 2023 W. Superior Street. The lessons are from 7 to 9 PM, then a variety of live bands take over. Live bands also play Friday and Saturday. There usually is no cover charge.

A big favorite with snowmobilers and summertime Munger State Trail bicyclists is the **Buffalo House**, (218) 624-9901, 2590 Guss Road. It's a rural place to have a drink or a meal and visit in an attractive family setting. Take the Exit 245 south of Duluth on I-35.

The downtown **Pioneer Bar**, (218) 727-4452, 323 W. First Street, has long been a favorite after-work hangout of reporters and police officers. The narrow place is near police headquarters, the *Duluth News-Tribune*, KDAL radio and KDLH television, so it's often packed with these high-spirited schmoozers.

Sneaker's Sports Bar & Grill, (218) 727-7494, 207 W. Superior Street, is on the second floor of the Holiday Center. It's a busy spot both after work and on weekends, when sports aficionados gather. Downstairs, at **Porter's** lounge, (218) 727-6746, local and imported comics stand up and do their routines at an open mike on Monday and Tuesday beginning at 8 PM.

Wednesday is blues/R & B night across the street at **RT Quinlan's Saloon**, (218) 722-3573, 220 W. Superior Street. You can hear alternative music on weekends, with a $2 to $4 cover charge.

The **Lakeview Coffee Emporium**, (218) 720-4464, in Fitger's Brewery Complex, 600 E. Superior Street, has live folk or jazz from 8 to 10 PM Saturdays. There is no cover charge. This place is renowned for its coffee, the ever-changing art gallery on the walls and intimate tables with a great view of the Lake. **The Brewhouse**, (218) 726-1392, also in Fitger's Complex, is an increasingly popular place, particularly among young professionals. It sells "100 percent pure" locally made beers from the nearby Lake Superior Brewery, and you can get a six-beer sampler for $5. It features live music — acoustic blues, jazz, folk, New Age and rock — every Tuesday and Thursday. Wednesday night is "Adventure Night," when local explorers share their exploits, and big-name groups perform on weekends, at which time there's a

Photo: Duluth New-Tribune

The 20-and-younger crowd wears what it pleases at Recycla-bell in Duluth.

$4 cover charge. The mezzanine floor is a good spot to visit with friends or play checkers or cribbage. You might stop for a drink first in **The Tap Room**, also in the complex, because it's fun to walk through the whitewashed stone tunnel into this lower-level hangout.

Every Wednesday and Thursday evening, bluegrass musicians gather at **Sir Benedict's Tavern on the Lake**, (218) 728-1192, 805 E. Superior Street. There's usually a fiddler, banjoist, guitarist, mandolin player and often several more instrumentalists. Bring your instrument, your voice or just your ears, buy an imported beer and one of Sir Ben's famous jumbo sandwiches and enjoy yourself.

The Reef Bar, (218) 724-9845, 2002 London Road, features blues, rock or jazz every Friday and Saturday. This roomy place along the Lake has no cover charge.

Recycla-bell, 1804 E. First Street, is a quirky place that used to be a Northwestern Bell company building. On Saturdays beginning at 7 PM, it's a coffeehouse with an open mike where patrons can read poetry or play music. Other nights — and this is a "whenever" type of thing — it becomes a dance place for the younger-than-21 crowd. Dress as you please: dredlocks, fluorescent mops, Marine-spiffy, Shirley Temple nice — both people and music are all-inclusive. Local high school and college bands play reggae, punk, alternative, rock and New Age music from 6:30 to 11 PM. There's a $3 cover charge. It's not easy finding out about these events, because Recycla-bell doesn't have a phone. Watch the bulletin boards at coffee shops and alternative shops in the area.

For those who would rather relax in a dark movie theater, a trip up to the Miller Hill corridor is necessary — none of the city's neighborhood theaters is still in operation. **Cinema 8 Theaters**, (218) 727-5554, has eight screens at 4191 Haines Road and Miller Trunk just beyond Miller Hill Mall. Nighttime admission price is $5.50. Farther up Miller Trunk, at Stebner Road, is **Lakes 8**, (218) 729-0335. This theater has four screens for first-run movies ($5) and four for second-run movies ($1.75). Back toward Duluth on Miller Trunk, you'll find **Movies at Miller Hill Mall** (inside the mall), (218) 727-7893, where there are four screens. Admission is $5 unless you're a student, in which case you pay $4.

SUPERIOR

Some of Superior's busiest nightspots are in an area of town that is better not seen in the daylight — the tattered northern end of Tower Avenue. **Shooters**, (218) 392-6660, at 624 Tower Avenue, has line dancing from 9:30 PM to 1:30 AM Wednesday through Sunday. There is no cover charge.

Female exotic dancers perform from 4 PM to 2 AM every day at the **Lamplighter**, (218) 394-5149, 628 Tower Avenue. There's a $2 cover charge after 8:30 PM.

If you like heavy metal, you'll find it at the **Pacific Club**, (218) 394-9226, 702 Tower Avenue, where heavy metal bands perform seven nights a week. There is no cover charge, unless a big-name band is on stage.

Country music is the specialty at **Johnny's Honkytonk**, (218) 394-3373, 1506 N. Third Street. Live bands perform on weekends, and karaoke happens on weekdays. There's no cover charge anytime.

The Cove, across the street at 701 Tower, is the loudest, most crowded and (among younger people) the most hip dance place in the Twin Ports — so hip it doesn't even need a phone. It's open seven nights a week. There is no cover charge.

The main gay bar in the Twin Ports is the **Main Club**, (218) 392-1756, 1813 N. Third Street. There's no live music at this gathering place of gays and lesbians, but dancers enjoy the jukebox, and there's no cover charge.

Farther south is **Popeye's**, (218) 392-3200, 1217 Tower Avenue, where customers dance to a DJ. Popeye's has no cover charge.

Across the street is **Le Petit**, (218) 392-5515, 1220 Tower Avenue, an espresso coffee shop that has music on weekends. Alternative rock is usually on Fridays; folk, blues or jazz on Saturdays. Performances are from 7 to 10 PM, and you should expect a $2 to $3 cover charge.

Down in South Superior is **Les Bird's**, (218) 394-9995, 5801 Tower Avenue. Locals hang out and cheer on the Brewers

Insiders' Tips

In Minnesota, Wisconsin and Michigan, you must be 21 or older to drink alcohol. Ontario serves customers 19 and older. Bars close at 1 AM in Ontario and Minnesota; 2 AM in Michigan; and, in Wisconsin, at 2 AM on weeknights and at 2:30 AM on Fridays and Saturdays.

Thrill-seekers will find gaming action at the Grand Portage Casino.

and Packers. If you're a Dallas Cowboys fan, better keep it to yourself.

Superior's moviegoers do visit Duluth, but Duluthians frequently zip over to Superior to the **Mariner Four Theatres**, (218) 392-7145. This is another four-screen movie house in a mall (the Mariner Mall, 28th Street and Hill Avenue), but it somehow manages to emanate a more relaxed neighborhood atmosphere. The main entrance is around back. Tickets are $5.50.

Along the North Shore

About 5 miles out of Duluth on Scenic Highway 61 is the **Lakeview Castle**, (218) 525-1014, where the attractive lounge is a draw for locals as well as for tourists staying in the motel. A DJ makes music every weekend, and occasionally a live band performs. There's no cover charge.

Farther up Minn. Highway 61 is the town of **Two Harbors** where the **American Legion Club**, (218) 834-4141, 614 First Avenue, features live entertainment on some Fridays and Saturdays. Anyone may attend for free, but you must sign in

as a guest. Call first to make sure something's happening.

Just outside town on Minn. Highway 61 is **Superior Shores Lodge**, (218) 834-5671. The restaurant and lounge were being moved to the second floor in mid-1996 so that customers could have a high clear view of the Lake. Live entertainment is likely to accompany this change.

Up in the **Lutsen** ski area is the **Chalet Bar**, (218) 663-7283, which has live music on Friday and Saturday nights and occasionally on Sunday. Quality acts "from the Cities" play rock 'n' roll, blues and R&B. The cover charge is $3, and the place closes with skiing season. Take Ski Hill Road inland from Minn. Highway 61 to the chalet.

In **Grand Marais**, you'll see the **Birch Terrace Lounge**, (218) 387-2215, on the upper side of Minn. Highway 61 as you roll into town. Besides fine dining in an 1800s log mansion with a fireplace, the complex has live music every weekend all summer and on some weekends in the wintertime. There's no dance floor, but people dance anyway. There's no cover charge.

On the other side of town, also on Minn. Highway 61, is **Harbor Light**, (218) 387-1142, with music, cocktails and dancing but no cover charge.

The Howling Wolf, (218) 387-1236, about 2 miles farther north on Minn. Highway 61, has bands on two or three Saturdays a month. They play country, classic rock and enough of a variety to keep all ages dancing on the large dance floor. There's no cover charge.

Along the South Shore

Nightlife along the South Shore is largely a matter of hanging out at local taverns — perhaps as part of a bowling, pool or dart league — or staying home and renting a lot of movies, unless you head for the movie theaters in downtown Ashland or suburban Ironwood. But there are some notable exceptions: Two bars in **Bayfield** draw enormous crowds. They don't have live music, but they do have a lot of live talk.

Morty's Pub, 108 Rittenhouse Avenue, has the largest selection of imported and domestic beers, fine liquors and fine wines in the area.

Isle Vista Casino (see the subsequent Casinos section in this chapter) has a bar and weekend entertainment.

If you have a dog along, you don't have to leave it in the car when you go into the **Brokedown Palace**, (715) 373-5578, 142 W. Bayfield in **Washburn**. The dogs just walk around while their owners visit — some nights, there are more dogs than customers, but not often, because this is a favorite human hangout. The music is mainly R & B, but reggae bands occasionally perform here too. There are bands every Saturday, with cover charges between $3 and $6. Fridays are reserved for open stage. The Pal-

ace is open Wednesday through Saturday.

Also in Washburn, **Patsy's Bar**, (715) 373-5792, 328 W. Bayfield, is a favorite hangout and a good place to talk to local folks.

In **Ashland**, the **Black Cat Coffeehouse**, (715) 682-3680, 211 Chapple Avenue, is a place people visit, read poetry and listen to live music: folk collective jams; drumming; acoustic guitar. There's an open stage for poetry and student readings. Every Sunday is backroom game day, with chess and Scrabble tournaments. Occasionally there's a cover charge of $3 or $4, depending on the band. The Black Cat is open 7 to 11 PM daily and until midnight on weekends.

The busy **Railyard Pub in the Depot**, (715) 682-9199, 400 Third Avenue W., serves locally brewed beers and intense chatter in a charming renovated depot. On Fridays during the tourist season, it also features entertainment: classical, folk, jazz and rock 'n' roll.

Also in Ashland, the **Office Bar**, (715) 682-8583, 407 W. Main Street, draws a sporting events crowd as well as a weekend dance crowd, with DJ music to keep 'em hoppin'.

Hurley taverns are legendary as landmarks from the days when it was a raw mining boomtown. **The Horse's Corral**, (715) 561-9945, 318 Silver Street, has two bars and a large dance floor. **The Krash Inn**, nearby on Silver Street, has great live music, Foosball, pool and darts. Another 17 saloons on Silver Street (in the high old days, they numbered more than 100!) will help you forget where you left your car.

The **Ironwood Sports Bowl**, (906) 932-4132, 213 E. Cloverland Drive, is a locals haunt, with a game room, pool table, bowling and three screens to watch the games.

Films? **Ashland** maintains its old movie theater right downtown, but **Bay Theatre**, (715) 682-3555, 420 W. Main Street, has been enlarged to three screens and features first-run movies. Admission is $3.50. **Ironwood** has the two-screen **Cloverland Cinema**, (715) 932-4424. Tickets are $4 unless you're a student ($2). The theater is on U.S. Highway 2 on the strip outside town.

Thunder Bay Area

The intercity area has the newest, hottest nightlife in town. If you like heavy metal and alternative music, try **Crocks & Rolls**, (807) 344-3123, 24 S. Cumberland Street.

Across the street is the busy **Stages**, (807) 345-5199, 37 Cumberland Street S., with live music six nights a week, mainly rock 'n' roll. There's a cover charge of $3 Thursday through Saturday.

The Office, (807) 345-3203, 215 Red River Road, is the only blues bar in Thunder Bay; performers take the stage from 9:30 PM to 1 AM Friday through Sunday. There is no cover charge unless there's a big band from Chicago.

Country western is the menu at a new bar in town: **Coyotes**, (807) 344-2929, 439 Memorial Avenue, which has live bands six days a week. Wednesday is student night, with a $3 cover charge; Thursday is ladies' night, when women get in free and men pay $2; on weekends, the cover is $2 until 9 PM and $4 until closing.

Centerfolds Ltd., (807) 344-7795, 802 Memorial Avenue, features exotic female dancers from 1 PM to 1 AM; there's no cover charge.

A popular coffee shop in town has been talking about getting live entertainment. By the time you read this, the **Seattle Coffeehouse**, (807) 622-3003, 1100B Memorial Avenue, might have small bands and live poetry in addition to bagels, books, buns, magazines, yards of desserts and fancy coffee.

The Orpheum, (807) 346-4373, 28 S. Court Street, is another new nightspot. It's the biggest club in northwest Ontario, in the renovated Odeon Theatre. The old theater lobby has become a restaurant, a bar is on the balcony, and what was the theater section now is the site of concerts, fundraisers (Thunder Bay native Paul Shaffer donated his piano talents in a 1996 fundraiser for the Thunder Bay Cancer Treatment and Research Foundation), a bikini contest every Thursday (for a purse of $4,000) and dancing on weekends.

Over at Lakehead University, the **Outpost Bar & Grill** (also known as The Pub), (807) 343-8561, 955 Oliver Road, has live music, an open stage, special dances and concerts. On Saturdays, the music is psychedelic '80s rock. The cover charge varies from $2 to $6, depending on the band. For special events, call 343-8260.

In the southern (**Fort William**) end of town, beverages, entertainment and three pool tables are the fare at **Arthur's Nightclub**, (807) 577-1181, at the corner of W. Arthur Street and the Expressway. Hours are 4 PM to 1 AM Monday through Saturday.

Spotlights, (807) 623-5442, 201 Syndicate Avenue S., has DJ music daily, but call if you're looking for something special on a weekend; comedians, hypnotists, reggae bands and Top-40 bands perform occasionally. There is no cover charge.

The large dance floor at the **Inntowner Palace**, (807) 623-1565, 301 S. Brodie at Arthur Street, is busy on weekends when live rock 'n' roll bands play. The weekend cover charge is $2.

Nearby is the **Golden Nugget**, (807) 475-6977, 555 Arthur Street, with live

Ramble to Gamble

Outside the
Lake Superior Region

A few casinos outside our region are a regular draw for local gamblers who are looking for variety. One is the Bois Forte band's **Fortune Bay Casino**, (800) 992-PLAY. It's on the Iron Range at Tower, Minnesota, along the eastern shore of sprawling Lake Vermilion. Like Fond-du-Luth, this casino, too, has a unique history: Whereas most states in the country have been wary, sometimes belligerent, about tribes developing gambling, the state of Minnesota helped Bois Forte get Fortune Bay off the ground in the mid-1980s. Bois Forte was the most impoverished and remote tribe in the state and was surrounded by communities in economic decline. The Iron Range Resources and Rehabilitation Board (IRRRB), a state agency whose mission is to restore economic vitality to the Iron Range, helped the band finance and develop the casino. Because Fortune Bay is off the beaten path (and because it lost considerable money to some unethical managers, now gone), it hasn't become as flush as other casinos; so the tribe is in the process of developing a destination resort at the beautiful site. The 24-hour casino has 360 slots, 14 blackjack tables, a full-service bar, a gift shop and a restaurant with a first-rate buffet. Fortune Bay is about a two-hour drive from Duluth.

At the other end of the spectrum is **Mystic Lake Casino** at Prior Lake, near Minneapolis, which belongs to the small Shakopee Mdewakanton Dakota Community. It was the largest tribal casino in the country until 1992 when the Mashantucket Pequot Tribe opened its giant gambling establishment — Foxwoods — at Ledyard, Connecticut. But Mystic Lake, (800) 262-7799, needn't take a back seat; it's a dazzling Las Vegas-style spread with 2,200 slots, 130 blackjack tables, more than 200 deluxe hotel rooms, four restaurants, nightly live entertainment and a mall with 10 retail stores. It generates enough income to cover housing, healthcare and full college scholarships for every tribal member plus about $35,000 a month in dividends — each. Mystic Lake is about a 3½-hour drive from Duluth.

Also outside our area, but nearer than Mystic Lake, is **Grand Casino Hinckley**, (800) GRAND-21, which belongs to the Mille Lacs Band of Ojibwes. Off I-35 about 70 miles south of Duluth, this place is a draw not only for gamblers but for diners, with big but inexpensive country breakfasts, spectacular buffets (50 hot entrees, dozens of desserts and fresh-baked bread) and a 24-hour fine dining restaurant. This casino has 51 blackjack tables, 1,600 slot machines, bingo and several offbeat games: live video roulette, blackjack and craps (same rules and payouts as traditional games) and "horse race" betting — miniature doll horses and jockeys racing on an in-house track, broadcast on a big screen. Grand Casino also has an RV park and a 175-room hotel with Jacuzzi suites.

country entertainment seven days a week. Two-step and line-dance sessions are on Tuesday and Wednesday, and country rock Friday and Saturday. The cover charge is $3.

Merlin's Bistro and Tea House, (807) 622-3445, 127 S. May Street, is a pleasant combination of delicious cheesecake with tea or cappuccino and live weekend music (folk and folk rock). There usually is no cover charge. With a name like Merlin's, there's got to be magic; you can get tarot card consultations here too.

The other kind of cheesecake is at the **St. Louis Hotel**, (807) 622-0657, 401 Victoria Avenue E., where women strippers perform daily from 1 PM to 1 AM. There is no cover charge.

The **5-55 Club**, (807) 625-5559, on the corner of Simpson and Miles streets, features live entertainment Wednesday through Saturday. The dance floor often is packed, as bands play rock 'n' roll, Top-40 and occasionally country and blues.

Armani's Nightclub, (807) 626-8002, 513 E. Victoria Avenue, is divided into two sections until 10:30 PM when the wall between them opens. On one side, you'll find 11 billiard tables, three of them coin-operated and the others costing $6.50 an hour. On the other side is dancing: classic rock on Thursday and retro-rock, classic rock and other dance music on weekends. The cover charge is $3.

If you want to sample neighborhood flavor, stop in at the **Wayland**, (807) 577-9123, 11016 W. Gore Street, near the airport. It hosts live bands Fridays and Saturdays — country rock, blues rock, Top-40 and plain old rock. There are two big-screen and 10 smaller TVs for the sports crowd, and games, such as shuffleboard and a Daytona Race screen. There is no cover charge.

Want to catch a flick? No problem in Thunder Bay. On the south side of town, **Capitol 1 & 2**, (807) 623-8612, 111 Brodie Street S.; **Cineplex Odeon Theatre**, (807) 623-3035, 125 S. Syndicate Avenue in the Victoriaville Mall; and **Cineplex 8**, (807) 622-1923, with eight screens, 320 E. Victoria Avenue. On the north side of town are the **Cineplex Odeon**, (807) 344-3451, 115 N. Cumberland Street; and **Paramount 1 & 2**, (807) 345-1780, 24 Court Street. The price of admission at these theaters is $6.

Casinos

Minnesota tribes were the first in the nation to develop high-stakes tribal casinos, and now the 11 tribes have 17 casinos on reservation land throughout the state. The casinos in our part of Minnesota and Wisconsin are too far from large urban centers to bring in spectacular revenues, although all are making money. Tribes are using the proceeds to build housing, schools, clinics and sewer systems; provide jobs (for Indians and non-Indians); invest in other economic development (against the time when the gambling pendulum swings the other way); and, in a few cases, to give modest yearly dividends to tribal members, who are casino stockholders. Since tribes can't be taxed by the state, most tribes kick money

Insiders' Tips

Who would have believed it? It is possible to enjoy jazz in a smoke-free environment. Just stop in at The Blue Note or Amazing Grace (both in Duluth) and check it out. These establishments do not permit smoking inside.

into counties in lieu of taxes (to cover the increased pressures on nearby law enforcement and emergency personnel); they also contribute to programs to combat gambling addiction. Under federal law, tribes can't offer casino-style games without an agreement with the respective states regarding bet limits, types of games and oversight responsibilities.

Twin Ports Area

BLACK BEAR CASINO
Fond du Lac Reservation
1789 Minn. Hwy. 210
Carlton, Minn.   *(218) 878-2327*

Black Bear is the second casino built by the Fond du Lac Ojibwe band (see the subsequent Fond-du-Luth listing). It's much bigger and has a more luxurious look, and its restaurant is becoming a local favorite.

The casino paid for itself within a couple of years; as soon as that happened, the band built a new luxury hotel alongside, which opened in 1995. The casino has more than 1,000 slot machines, including video keno and video craps; dozens of blackjack tables; a bingo emporium; and live entertainment every weekend in the Lady Slipper Lounge.

The Cub's Den Child Care Center is an extravagant place, with a computer center, play and climbing area, games and Nintendo and Sega machines (some call them casino-training games), all coordinated by licensed elementary teachers. The center is open seven days a week from 7 AM to midnight and accommodates kids ages 16 months through 12 years.

Black Bear is open 24 hours. Take I-35 south of Duluth to the Cromwell exit; you'll see the complex there. The casino runs a free daily shuttle service from hotels, motels and other pickup points in Duluth, Superior, Carlton and Cloquet. You can either catch one on the regular route or call for special service. There is no charge.

FOND-DU-LUTH CASINO
129 E. Superior St.
Duluth, Minn.   *(218) 722-0280*

This casino has a unique history: It's the nation's first and only cooperative gambling enterprise between a city and a tribe. The deal was struck by officials of the Fond du Lac Ojibwe band and the city of Duluth in the mid-1980s; a piece of downtown Duluth became tribal trust land and an abandoned Sears building was turned into a casino. The partnership was not a happy marriage, and the business had a rocky start. Despite continuing disagreements and a lawsuit or two, the business landed on steady ground and has been growing. The tribe

A little neighborhood tavern on the outskirts of Duluth bears a pre-Garrison Keillor name: Wabegon. Keillor, who grew up in Ojibwe-Dakota border country in central Minnesota, altered its meaning ("clay") with his punchy pronunciation when he applied it to his imaginary hometown — Lake Wobegon. "The Wab," as locals know the tavern, is just across the St. Louis River from Duluth on Minn. Highway 23 and features delicious $1 burgers Thursday evenings.

Insiders' Tips

now runs the operation, paying the city 25 percent of the profits.

Since Fond-du-Luth is right in downtown, it's the only casino in the region that is easy to get to on foot; but parking is available in an attached parking ramp. The casino has 340 nickel, quarter and dollar slot machines, including video poker and video keno; 16 blackjack tables, with up to $1,000 maximum betting limit; and a 1950s-era full-service lounge. You can't come in unless you're 21 or older. Hours are 10 to 2 AM Monday through Thursday and 10 AM Friday through 2 AM Monday, continuously.

Along the North Shore

GRAND PORTAGE CASINO
Grand Portage Reservation
Minn. Hwy. 61   (218) 475-2441
Grand Portage, Minn.   (800) 543-1384

The 24-hour casino moved into a beautiful new building in 1996, where there's a lounge, eight blackjack tables and about 400 slot machines, along with a lodge and fine dining. Still more beautiful is the setting: the northeasternmost, rugged corner of the state where the forested Sawtooth Mountains contain 167 nearby kilometers of hiking and cross-country ski trails. The casino is near the Grand Portage National Monument (a restored trading post) and Grand Portage State Park, with Minnesota's highest waterfall. The picturesque setting is making this casino a tourist destination.

Along the South Shore

BAD RIVER CASINO
Bad River Reservation
U.S. Hwy. 2
New Odanah, Wis.   (715) 682-7121

The Bad River Ojibwe band once had a woodworking and log-building train-

ing enterprise in a beautiful log structure along the highway. When the band converted the building into a casino, it kept the beautiful lines and rustic ambiance; and in mid-1996, it was expanding into a new building next door but continuing some operations in the older building.

The casino has 223 slots, eight blackjack tables, bingo, a smoke shop and a restaurant. Hours are 10 AM to 2 AM daily. The casino has a shuttle service from Michigan's Upper Peninsula and Ashland, Wisconsin. The round-trip ride is included free in a package: You buy a $10 or $20 coupon booklet and get at least double your money in tokens, and (with the $20 booklet) 25 percent off at the cafe.

ISLE VISTA CASINO
Red Cliff Reservation
Wis. Hwy. 13   (715) 779-3712
Red Cliff, Wis.   (800) 226-8478

Isle Vista has 175 slots, including video poker and keno; reel slots; and progressives. It also has blackjack and two-deck pitch, a lounge, live weekend entertainment, bowling and bingo. Go 3 miles north on Wis. Highway 13; the casino is at left on the curve. Check out the 84-foot mural inside, created by a local artist; it depicts the life and culture of Lake Superior Ojibwe people in the context of the seasons.

This place has the best travel deal in the region. For a purchase of $5 in tokens, you get $15 more, the buffet at half-price and a free round trip from the Twin Ports, Ashland, Wisconsin, or the Upper Peninsula of Michigan. Call for the regular pickup times.

Something Different

How about a starlit sleigh ride or a moonlight cruise? Or a solitary stroll under the dark skies of our rural world?

The **Royal Palm Ranch** at Ironwood,

Michigan, (906) 932-0770, offers nighttime trips in a one-horse open sleigh or a Clydesdale-pulled big sleigh, along with hot cider, hot chocolate, champagne and beer. You'll head through the snow to hay-bale sofas near open fires. The $6 trips are offered Tuesday through Sunday, as long as the snow lasts.

Winter or summer, you can have a nighttime hay/sleigh ride behind the Belgian draft horses of **Carol's Horse Drawn Rides**, (218) 384-4825. You'll travel through the woods near Wrenshall, Minnesota (just south of Duluth), back to a log cabin warming house. Rides are $5 for people 13 and older and $3 for those younger. Call for directions and reservations.

Sundown summertime cruises aboard the *Catchun-Sun* sailboat, (715) 779-3111, are available out of the Bayfield, Wisconsin, city dock through **Catchun-Sun Charter Company**. You'll sail in the lovely waters of the Apostle Islands, watching the sun sink behind the high hills of Bayfield. The fee is $20 per person per hour. Food and beverages can be arranged.

Starlight-moonlight cruises are offered every Friday and Saturday in the Duluth harbor through **Vista Fleet**, (218) 722-6218. Its two cruise ships, the *Vista King* and *Vista Star*, offer indoor and outdoor seating and nighttime views of the passing lights of Duluth's hills, ships, Barkers Island in Superior, the Aerial Bridge and ore docks. The cruise is family-oriented and relaxing. Boarding time is 9:30 PM, and the cruise ends at 11:30 PM. The fee is $8.50 for adults, $4 for children 11 and younger and free for little ones. In the fall, the cruise is on Saturday only.

How about flying through the snowy night toward a destination of hot chocolate and a campfire — behind a team of friendly huskies? **Norwest Sled Dog Adventures** of Thunder Bay, (807) 964-2070, offers this two-hour ride for $20 for adults and $12 for children. The trip is along the North Shore, with spectacular views of the Lake.

Winter or summer, you shouldn't leave our area until experiencing — at least once — a solitary late-night stop on the rural North or South shore. It won't cost you a penny; you don't need anyone to train you or sell you instructions on how to do it.

On a quiet, clear night, take a blanket down to the Lake in some totally secluded spot, wrap up and just linger for an hour or more — why not all night? Listen to the summertime lap of waves or creak of wintertime drifting ice and sink your eyes into the starry heavens (the skies are still dark enough to see the stars in most of our region).

Or, when the moon is at least half-full (so you can find your way), take any one of many trails up to a lookout point on a high hill and linger there in the silence, watching the moonlight play on the water below.

The only wildlife you'll have to worry about are mosquitoes (black bears, wolves, moose and the rare cougar go the other way when people approach). And this quiet stopover, in which you can allow yourself to shed your ego, worries and aspirations, is likely to be among the most lasting and rewarding memories of your visit here.

Inside
Accommodations

Our area has come a long way in the past few decades, since the days tourists were satisfied with humbly appointed little cabins where they slept and cooked and then went outdoors to find their own fun.

Now, visitors want to be entertained and served, and to sleep in style. We've adjusted to those desires, and visitors to our shores now enjoy indoor pools and Jacuzzis, HBO and Nintendo, lavish rooms and charming, pricey bed and breakfast inns.

You still can see remnants of the old cabins here and there on both shores; a few are in service, but most are sinking into the soil like the old commercial fishing skiffs that sometimes are beached near them. Nowadays, visitors who want rustic simplicity — and there are plenty who do — go camping.

You'll never be far from lodging in our region, but you might be too late for lodging. Our places fill up fast in both winter and summer, so make sure you call early for reservations.

The accommodations we list here, unless otherwise indicated, have cable TV and telephones in the rooms and don't allow pets. If any pose problems for mobility-impaired people, we've tried to mention them; but make sure you ask for an appropriate unit when you make your reservation. Bed and breakfast inns tend not to have wheelchair access, and they also tend not to accept children.

Be aware of any additional taxes for lodging or special services, which vary by state and country and are not factored into the following price code; inquire when you make your reservation. See our "Price-code Key" gray box for room-rate information.

The following key denotes the average cost of a one-night stay for two people (double occupancy) during peak season.

PRICE-CODE KEY

$	$50 or less
$$	$51 to $75
$$$	$76 to $100
$$$$	$101 or more

Unless otherwise noted, all lodging options in this chapter accept major credit cards.

Enjoy your stay, and pleasant dreams.

Twin Ports Area

We've included hotels, motels and bed and breakfast inns in Duluth and Superior here; but we also have included in the Duluth section motels in Cloquet and Carlton, Minnesota, 25 miles from town. They're a good backup when the Twin Ports lodgings fill up — which they very often do during summer weekends. On really big weekends — for Grandma's Marathon the second weekend in June, the Beargrease in mid-January and the Bayfront Blues Festival the second weekend in August — most Twin Ports bed and breakfast inns and many motels are reserved for months in advance.

Duluth and Environs

AMERICINN
Minn. Hwy. 210 and I-35
Carlton, Minn.   (218) 384-3535
$-$$

This and Cloquet's Americinn (listed subsequently) are only a few miles from one another. The motel offers free continental breakfast, a fireplace lobby, HBO and ESPN on the cable TV, refrigerators in all rooms and access to four restaurants. Snacks are provided in the lobby Sunday through Thursday. This inn is near the Black Bear Casino (see our Nightlife and Casinos chapter) and offers free gambling coupons and shuttle to the casino. Managment was planning to have an indoor pool ready for use by fall 1996 as well as another dozen rooms added to its existing 27. Call first if you're thinking of bringing a pet.

AMERICINN
Minn. Hwy. 33 and Big Lake Rd.
Cloquet, Minn.   (218) 879-1231
$$

Right in the heart of the malled shopping area of Cloquet, this motel has an indoor pool, whirlpool and sauna as well as a fireplace lobby, continental breakfast, 24-hour coffee in the lobby, HBO and The Disney Channel on the cable TV, and access to restaurants and shopping. Two of its 51 rooms are suites: one, at poolside, sleeps six; the other sleeps four. Pets are allowed as long as they're not left in the room alone or brought into the pool area.

BLACK BEAR HOTEL
Fond du Lac Reservation
Minn. Hwy. 210 and I-35
Carlton, Minn.   (218) 878-7400
$$

This new hotel is connected by skywalk to the Black Bear Casino and offers a $20 casino book as part of the room rate. The hotel features a decorative pool atrium; in-room Nintendo, HBO, ESPN and TNT on cable; on-command pay movies; luxurious Jacuzzi rooms; a workout room; a gift shop featuring Indian artwork and crafts; a game room; and, for children, day care and an arcade. Restaurants are in the casino and at two other nearby locations.

COMFORT INN
3900 W. Superior St.
(Off I-35 at 40th Ave. W. exit)   (218) 628-1464
Duluth, Minn.   (800) 4-CHOICE
$$-$$$

This 81-room inn has an indoor pool and whirlpool, Jacuzzi suites, a sauna, Showtime and Disney on the cable, free 24-hour coffee, USA Today in the lobby and free continental breakfast. It's walking distance from a Perkins Restaurant and a longer walk from the popular Louis' Cafe (see our Restaurants chapter). You'll need your car, however, to get to downtown Duluth and the Lake.

COMFORT SUITES
408 Canal Park Dr.   (218) 727-1378
Duluth, Minn.   (800) 4-CHOICE
$$$$

This newer inn at Canal Park has a glorious view of the Lake — or rather, half of its 82 rooms do. Guests also can enjoy an indoor pool and whirlpool, Jacuzzi suites, a sauna, free continental breakfast, HBO on cable and refrigerators in rooms. The "cityside" rooms have a pleasant view as well — of the hills of

Cloquet Area Motel Association

AMERICINN
Hwy. #33 & Big Lake Rd.
Cloquet, MN 55720
1-218-879-1231 / 1-800-634-3444

DRIFTWOOD
1413 Hwy. #33 South
Cloquet, MN 55720
1-218-879-4638

GOLDEN GATE
I-35, Exit 239, Jct. Hwy. 45 & 61
Scanlon, MN 55720
1-218-879-6752 / 1-800-732-4241

SUNNYSIDE
Hwy. #33 North
Cloquet, MN 55720
1-218-879-4655

SUPER 8
Hwy. #33 & Big Lake Rd.
Cloquet, MN 55720
1-218-879-1250 / 1-800-800-8000

For additional community information, please call or write the Chamber.
The Chamber is the community clearinghouse and will be happy to
supply you with maps & brochures for a variety of things to do & see.

The Cloquet Area Chamber of Commerce
P.O. Box 426 - 225 Sunnyside Dr., Cloquet, MN 55720
1-218-879-1551 / 1-800-554-4350
FAX 1-218-878-0223

Duluth and charming Canal Park, with its interesting shops and excellent restaurants. The hotel is on the lakeside boardwalk and just a block from the Canal Park Marine Museum and the Aerial Lift Bridge.

DAYS INN
909 Cottonwood Ave.
Duluth, Minn.   (218) 727-3110
$$

Just across from Miller Hill Mall, the 86-room Days Inn is walking distance from the largest shopping area in the region and a movie theater. Standard accommodations include HBO, continental breakfast and 24-hour coffee. The largest room sleeps up to four adults. Pets are allowed.

ECONO LODGE AIRPORT
U.S. Hwy. 53 and Haines Rd. (218) 722-5522
Duluth, Minn.   (800) 922-0569
$$

Just a mile from the airport and from Miller Hill Mall, this Econo Lodge has lots of clean and spacious rooms, cable TV and coffee and doughnuts. Be sure to inquire about discounts for AARP members and other affiliations.

EDGEWATER BEST WESTERN
2211 and 2400 London Rd.
Duluth, Minn.   (218) 728-3601
$$-$$$

The two Edgewaters, east and west, are across London Road from one another. Each has an indoor pool, saunas, a whirlpool, Jacuzzi suites and free breakfast. The rooms have refrigerators, and some suites also have microwaves. HBO, Showtime and ESPN are augmented by pay-per-movie television. Pets are allowed in two sections, in smoking rooms only (even if your pet doesn't smoke). The eastern side of this conference-convention center is on the Lakewalk, from

which guests can stroll past rose gardens, shops and beautiful scenery all the way into Canal Park.

THE ELLERY HOUSE
28 S. 21st Ave. E.   (218) 724-7639
Duluth, Minn.   (800) ELLERY-H
$$-$$$$

Near the Lakewalk, the 1890-built Ellery House has four elegant rooms with antiques, fireplaces, a heated sleeping porch, balconies and private baths. A full three-course gourmet breakfast is served in the bedroom or dining room. The rooms are named after past owners (Ellery is the name of the man who built the home), and some rooms have Lake views. It's a bright, airy Victorian house.

FITGER'S INN
600 E. Superior St.   (218) 722-8826
Duluth, Minn.   (800) 726-2982
$$$-$$$$

The highly acclaimed Fitger's is truly elegant, with a lovely lobby and 60 beautifully appointed rooms — although you can find reasonably priced rooms here. Some whirlpool suites have balconies overlooking the Lake on which you can lounge in luxurious cotton robes and enjoy a tasty breakfast — not included in the room rate. A less elegant retreat in an outside wall was purposely left alone during a recent renovation/addition on behalf of the pair of pigeons that nests there every year.

Fitger's is in a renovated 1857 brewery and is on the National Register of Historic Places. The hotel is right above the Lakewalk and near some fine shopping and restaurants, including its own Augustino's (see our Restaurants chapter). Make reservations far in advance if you need weekend accommodations.

In 1995, Fitger's was named 18th of city-category hotels by the national *Lodging and Hospitality Magazine*.

Old Rittenhouse Inn
Elegant Victorian Lodging and Dining

Antique, wood-burning fireplace, jacuzzis, flower filled porches overlooking Lake Superior.

Gourmet dining featuring regional specialties.

Ideal setting for group luncheons, weddings and business retreats.

Open all year
715-779-5111
301 Rittenhouse Avenue
Bayfield, WI 54814

"Best Inn in Wisconsin"
Wisconsin Trail Magazine - Reader's Choice

HOLIDAY INN

200 W. First St.   *(218) 722-1202*
Duluth, Minn.   *(800) 477-7089*
$$$-$$$$

Probably the primary convention and conference center in Duluth, the downtown Holiday Inn has more than 350 deluxe rooms and two-room suites in its 16 stories. Guests in the top five stories have an excellent view of the Lake. The inn also has two pools as well as saunas and whirlpools; most rooms are fitted with data ports for personal computers, and rooms have pay-per-view movies. Frequent guests get free newspapers delivered to their rooms. The hotel is part of the 40-store Holiday Center shopping complex, which has fine dining, a bar and grill and a French sandwich shop. Parking is available in back of the Holiday, in a lot accessible from First Street (which is a one-way running west).

MANOR ON THE CREEK INN

2215 E. Second St.   *(218) 728-3189*
Duluth, Minn.   *(800) 428-3189*
$$$$

An elegant mansion with more than 55 rooms, the manor was built in 1907 in the heart of historic Duluth, overlooking 2 acres of wooded Oregon Creek. The inn is near the Lakewalk, and rooms include whirlpools, private baths and fireplaces. A full breakfast is included. Overnight guests can opt for a three- to seven-course dinner, served at the inn by reservation only.

THE MANSION

3600 London Rd., Duluth, Minn. (218) 724-0739
$$$$

Built by Duluth heiress Marjorie Congdon and her husband, Harry Dudley, in 1929, this stone-exterior English Tudor home sits on 7 acres along 500 feet of Lake Superior beachfront. The 10 rooms, all no-smoking, are furnished with antiques and queen- or king-size beds. The property includes formal gardens, woods and manicured lawn and is accessible to guests. A full country breakfast is included in the stay. The Mansion is open every day from May to early October and on weekends the rest of the year.

MATHEW S. BURROWS 1890 INN

1632 E. First St.   *(218) 724-4991*
Duluth, Minn.   *(800) 789-1890*
$$$$

Mathew Burrows was an early Duluth clothing store owner who built this mostly Victorian (with hints of Gothic) home for his family. Now, Alan and Kathy Fink run it as a bed and breakfast inn, with about a 90 percent guest return rate. Five smoke-free rooms have gas fireplaces, queen-size beds and private baths. Common areas are two outside porches (one with a fine view of Lake Superior), a library with new and old books flanking the fireplace, and a music room with a player piano and woodburning fireplace. Stained glass is throughout the house. Breakfast includes fresh muffins or bread, fresh fruit, juice, coffee and a main entree — maybe a fancy egg dish or stuffed French toast and sausage. It's served in the dining room, where a stained-glass window fills most of one wall. The Burrows is open year round.

MOUNTAIN VILLAS

9525 W. Skyline Pkwy.   (218) 624-5784
Duluth, Minn.   (800) 642-6377
$$$-$$$$

Fourteen furnished rustic villas are nestled in the forest of Spirit Mountain near the ski hill. Each has a full kitchen, a free-standing woodburning fireplace, two bathrooms, two bedrooms and a pullout couch in the living room, decks and grills.

OLCOTT HOUSE

2316 E. First St., Duluth, Minn. (218) 728-1339
$$$$

Situated in the historic East End of Duluth, close to downtown and the Lakewalk, this bed and breakfast inn is the former home of William Olcott (president of Oliver Mining and one of the first railroads in Duluth). From the mid-1930s to the mid-1950s, it served as the Olcott Hall School of Music — part of what is now the University of Minnesota Duluth. Now, the Georgia Colonial 1904 mansion is run as a bed and breakfast inn by Barb and Don Truman. The spacious suites, both in the home and the romantic carriage house, have private baths and comfortable beds.

The full breakfast is always what Barb Truman calls "hot and hearty" — coffee, rolls, fruit, juice and an entree, such as stuffed French toast and potatoes. Guests often relax in Adirondack chairs on the grand porch with coffee or lemonade.

PARK INN INTERNATIONAL

250 Canal Park Dr.   (218) 727-8821
Duluth, Minn.   (800) 777-8560
$$$

The Park Inn has one of the best motel sites in Duluth — just off the freeway at the entrance to Canal Park on the Lake and the lakewalk. It was undergoing renovation in mid-1996, which could accompany a name change (same telephone, however). All of the 143 rooms have coffee pots, data ports for personal computers, HBO and Cinemax and pay-per-view movies with Nintendo. Some rooms have refrigerators and microwaves, and there's a Jacuzzi suite. About 54 of the rooms have a view of the Lake, and smoking and non-smoking rooms both cityside and lakeside have king, double and single beds. Pets are allowed. An easy, short stroll gets you to fine restaurants and shopping, unless you want to stay right in the hotel to dine or hang out in the lounge.

RADISSON HOTEL
DULUTH-HARBORVIEW

505 W. Superior St.
Duluth, Minn.   (218) 727-8981
$$$-$$$$

The cylindrical Radisson greets drivers coming into Duluth from the south. Its 268 rooms offer views of the harbor, hillside or downtown area; those near the top of the 14-story hotel overlook the Lake, harbor or hillside. The rotating Top of the Harbor Restaurant (on the top floor) serves fine breakfasts, lunches and dinners and gives the best view in Duluth (see our Restaurants chapter). A lounge with live en-

Cove Point Lodge — quiet charm with only 45 rooms on a private 150 acre preserve. Each room has a spectacular view of Lake Superior and our secluded rocky cove. The rustic Scandinavian style lodge is done in warm pine and cedar. Deluxe rooms offer a Jacuzzi and/or fireplace. Split Rock Lighthouse, Tettegouche State Park, the Superior National Forest and Superior Hiking Trail are nearby. Bring your sea kayak, climbing gear, diving mask, mountain bike or canoe and explore the best places on the North Shore. Honeymooners and nature lovers have all this plus our full service lodge featuring great hall with fireplace, dining room, lounge, pool, hot tub, sauna and more.

Call 800-598-3221
218-226-3221
COVE POINT LODGE
Beaver Bay, MN 55601

Prices $55 to $159 – Located 50 minutes north of Duluth

Professionally Managed By Central Group Management Co., St. Cloud

tertainment serves sandwiches and soups at lunchtime. This is one of Duluth's premier convention centers.

The Radisson is across the street from the spacious Duluth Public Library, a half-block from the government center and just two blocks from downtown shopping. A tunnel that connects the hotel with the downtown skywalk system was scheduled for completion in 1996. (Why a tunnel? Because a skywalk would have blocked the sweep of trees, fountain, statue and county building as viewed from Superior and Michigan streets.)

ROYAL PINES MOTEL

Minn. Hwy. 210 and I-35   (218) 384-4242
Carlton, Minn.   (800) 788-9622
$

The best thing about Royal Pines is that it's nestled in some magnificent pines, softening the setting at this busy intersection. The largest suite of its 20 rooms, which open directly outside, sleeps eight. Rooms have cable TVs with HBO, and a continental breakfast is available in the office. Pets are allowed in the smoking rooms for $10 extra. The motel is near the Black Bear Casino and 24-hour restaurants.

SELECT INN

200 27th Ave. W. (off I-35)   (218) 723-1123
Duluth, Minn.   (800) 641-1000
$$

Relatively new, clean and inexpensive, Select Inn has cable TV and a free continental breakfast, and pets are welcome. It's just a few minutes from downtown.

SPIRIT MOUNTAIN LODGE

9315 Westgate Blvd.
Duluth, Minn.   (218) 628-3691
$$$

A swimming pool, sauna and whirlpool and continental breakfast in a rustic setting are notable amenities at this lodge, near Duluth's municipal ski hill. During ski season, packages are available.

SUPER 8

Minn. Hwy. 33 and Big Lake Rd.   (218) 879-1250
Cloquet, Minn.   (800) 800-8000
$

You'll find plenty of clean, comfortable rooms at this Super 8. Amenities include cable TV with HBO and continental breakfast each morning. Suites with whirlpools are available. Pets are allowed. Cribs are provided by request at no cost. A restaurant is nearby.

SUPER 8

4100 W. Superior St.
(off I-35, 40th Ave. W. exit) (218) 628-2241
Duluth, Minn.   (800) 800-8000
$$

In keeping with this national chain's standards, this Super 8 offers clean, safe rooms in which to sleep and wash up. Rooms include cable TVs with Showtime. You'll find a whirlpool and sauna on-site, and free cribs are available upon request for the wee ones. A decent restaurant is close by.

VIKING MOTEL

2511 London Rd.   (218) 728-3691
Duluth, Minn.   (800) 345-6912
$-$$

Inexpensive but neat, the Viking gives easy access to both downtown and the North Shore. Its 30 rooms have basic cable, and the lakeview rooms have a bath as well as a shower. Continental breakfast is served.

VOYAGEUR LAKEWALK INN

333 E. Superior St.   (218) 722-3911
Duluth, Minn.   (800) 258-3911
$$

The Voyageur is handy to a couple of wonderful restaurants, the Lakewalk, hospitals and the downtown casino. Some of its 40 units have refrigerators, and all have coffee makers and Showtime on cable. Five suites have VCRs. The Voyageur has been undergoing renovation. Pets are allowed — if they're kept quiet.

THE A. CHARLES WEISS INN

1615 E. Superior St.   (218) 724-7016
Duluth, Minn.   (800) 525-5243
$$$$

A bed and breakfast inn with five smoke-free rooms furnished with antiques, the Charles Weiss is just a couple of blocks up the hill from the Lakewalk. Guests can relax in the parlor, library, dining and music rooms, all of which have fireplaces. Rooms include a suite with a woodburning fireplace and a room with a gas fireplace and double Jacuzzi. Weiss was the owner-editor of the Duluth newspaper at the turn of the century.

WILLARD MUNGER INN

7408 Grand Ave., Duluth, Minn. (218) 624-4814
$$

Kitchenette apartments, fireplace suites, a Jacuzzi suite, nonsmoking rooms, a cafe, and rentals of bicycles, snowmobiles, Rollerblades and canoes are all available here in this modest but attractive inn near Spirit Mountain. The Lake Superior Zoo is across the street, so if you hear a lion roar or hyenas cackle, don't be surprised. The inn's namesake, a state legislator, hangs around the coffee shop on weekend mornings to chat with constituents. (See our sidebar on Willard Munger in our Winter Sports chapter.)

Insiders' Tips

Should you decide to stay on Madeline Island, catch the ferry at City Dock in Bayfield. You can go with or without your car; if you're planning to lodge in LaPointe, you can do without the vehicle (which is about $13 more round trip), because restaurants, stores, golf, the museum, pubs and beaches are in walking distance. You can rent bicycles in LaPointe for island-touring — an easy ride on the mostly flat terrain.

Superior

BARKERS ISLAND INN

300 Marina Dr.	(715) 392-7152
Superior, Wis.	(800) 344-7515

$$-$$$$

On a beautiful spit of land in the harbor, this inn has 115 rooms, some poolside, all of which face either the Lake or the marina. The inn is a notable convention center, and some rooms have data ports for personal computers. Cable TV with Showtime is in all rooms, and a couple of suites — twice the size of other rooms — have refrigerators, coffee makers and microwaves. Besides the indoor pool, whirlpool and sauna, the inn offers a game room, fine dining, a lounge with a big-screen TV and tennis courts. No pets, please.

BAY WALK INN BEST WESTERN

1405 Susquehanna Ave.	(715) 392-7600
Superior, Wis.	(800) 528-1234

$$$

An indoor pool, whirlpool and sauna plus whirlpool and family suites are part of this motel. A deluxe continental breakfast is included. The Bay Walk Inn is just off the Bong Bridge, next to the Shack Restaurant.

CRAWFORD HOUSE
BED AND BREAKFAST

2016 Hughitt Ave., Superior, Wis.   (715) 394-5271

$$$

Opened in 1995, Crawford House is a turn-of-the-century Colonial-revival mansion. A master suite has a large sitting room and fireplace and a private bath. Two other rooms share a bath with a whirlpool tub. A billiard room has a walkout porch, and the inn is fitted out with antiques and offers a full breakfast. No smoking or pets, please.

DAYS INN

110 E. Second St. (U.S. Hwy. 2)	(715) 392-4783
Superior, Wis.	(800) 325-2525

$$$

At this Days Inn, you don't get continental breakfast or special cable channels, but you do get an indoor pool, whirlpool, sauna and game area. A restaurant and lounge are also part of this complex, which has 110 rooms. Rooms sleep a maximum of five. Many of the rooms have a good view of the bay across U.S. Highway 2.

SUPERIOR INN

525 Hammond Ave.	(715) 394-7706
Superior, Wis.	(800) 777-8599

$$

Handy to both downtowns, Superior Inn has a pool, sauna and whirlpool and offers continental breakfast. It's near the foot of the Blatnik Bridge.

SUPER 8

4901 E. Second St. (U.S. Hwy. 2)	(715) 398-7686
Superior, Wis.	(800) 800-8000

$

This Super 8 offers cable TV with Showtime and free cribs. Continental breakfast is served, and a restaurant is nearby for larger meals. Children 12 and younger stay for free. The motel is a short distance from Lake Superior.

Along the North Shore

The North Shore has been a vacation destination since the late 1800s when fishing families opened their homes to veterans recovering from the Spanish-American war and to hay fever and tuberculosis patients seeking the healing power of clean, fresh air. Water travel was the main transportation. Steamers, such as the *America*, made weekly runs up and down the shore from Duluth to Isle Royale and points in between. The North Shore Scenic Highway from Duluth to Canada was completed in 1925, opening a new world to travelers. Because the highway was a rough, winding road, and because of vehicles' low engine power at that time, cars traveled at about 30 mph. So going up the shore to Grand Marais or farther was a two-day proposition; an overnight stay at a cabin or lodge midway up the shore was an expected part of the trip.

In the past 10 years, the complexion of overnight housing on the North Shore has changed, allowing for more choices to accommodate different needs. Classic pine-beam lodges, small 1950s-style motels and mom-and-pop cabin resorts have been the traditional lodging choices. Now, in addition to those accommodations, options include bed and breakfast inns in both historic and modern homes; commercial chain motels, ranging from the basic to the luxurious and chock-laden with services and amenities; new lodges featuring classic designs; and fancy condominiums. Of course, camping remains a popular option; if you're seeking camping information, check out our Camping and Campgrounds chapter.

Not everyone is happy with the commercialization and development of the North Shore. Some argue that the area's rugged character, the spirit of Lake Superior and the proximity of great tracts of national and state forests and parks are what attract people — and that increased commercial and residential development place undue demands on the land and create visual clutter. Others, however, observe that the tourism market is changing and contend that the expansion of lodging and food services accommodate these market needs.

Well, back to the practical — a room or cabin with a view or a whirlpool or both. For your best deals, its important to

understand the basis of the pricing framework of North Shore accommodations. A number of factors influence room cost and availability. And while each accommodation has its own specific pricing structure, certain general factors influence the cost of a North Shore room.

First of all, expect seasonal rates. You'll find winter versus summer variations and, within those seasons, quiet — read slow — periods: November through early December and late March through early May. For example, winter variations include a slow period before Christmas and a rush during peak skiing and snowmobiling time in February and March. Annual community events, such as Grand Marais Fisherman's Picnic in August and Duluth's Grandma's Marathon in mid-June, cause room prices to peak, as do holidays such as the Fourth of July and Labor Day.

With that in mind, the following is an overview of the North Shore calendar year and specific times when you can expect fluctuations in lodging rates:

•The week from Christmas to New Year's Day is a busy time; expect peak holiday rates.

•January is a quiet time, and you can find economical packages. January can be a bitterly cold month, with lots of below-zero days and intense wind chills, but the deep snow cover makes for excellent cross-country skiing.

•February and March are peak times for downhill and cross-county skiing and snowmobiling. Try midweek pricing — Sunday through Thursday — for the best room rates.

•April, called the "mud season" by locals, can be a marvelous time to visit the North Shore. The leaves are not yet on the trees, so you can glimpse some wonderful lake vistas and river canyon

Photo: Prince Arthur Hotel

The historic Prince Arthur Hotel in Thunder Bay, Ontario.

views. This is an in-between time. People seeking quiet and privacy as well as folks willing to bring both mud and snow gear for hiking will find April a worthwhile month to visit. Expect great bargains on lodging.

• May sees an increase in visitors. Fishing season opens mid-month, and things start to pick up as the summer season get going in late May. (Lilacs bloom in early June on the North Shore.)

• From mid-June through Labor Day (the summer season), premium rates apply, particularly during special events and holidays.

• After Labor Day, the fall color season brings peak room rates from mid-September to the first or second week in October, depending on the color change.

• From late October through Christmas, things slow down. The leaves have fallen, the air is crisp (OK, sometimes nippy), and the skies are deep blue. This is

a great time for hiking and birding the North Shore — and a great time to take advantage of inexpensive room rates.

A quick reminder: Our price code does not include local taxes (which can add 10 percent to the final bill) or charges for optional amenities and services. A housekeeping cabin or suite means you'll find a kitchen with stove, sink and refrigerator as well as dishes, utensils, pots and pans.

Once again, keep the price variations in mind. Many places will require a two- or three-night minimum stay, particularly during peak seasonal times, but most have package deals. We've indicated if an accommodation is open only in summer; otherwise, you can assume our lodging suggestions are open year round.

The following accommodations are listed as you'd encounter them traveling northward along the North Shore between Duluth and Thunder Bay.

THE INN ON GITCHEE GUMMEE

North Shore Dr.   *(218) 525-4979*
Northeast of Duluth, Minn.   (800) 317-4979
$$

You'll be struck by this inn's handsome pine log front, which faces Lake Superior. It's hard to believe that this seven-suite, two-story inn was created by raising two cabins, remodeling them and adding a new first floor. The handy and talented owners, Julie and Butch Sievert, did the work themselves, with stunning results.

This is a family business where friendly Mr. Spock, the resident cat, may be the first to greet you in the antique-filled office. Kids' bicycles lean against the office door. If the kids aren't on the bikes, you might find them at the play area, which includes a tower. And beach access is available just across the road.

Some of the sunlight-filled suites feature the woodworking skills of Butch Sievert, who crafted the black walnut kitchen cabinets and birch branch bed frames. Each suite features antiques, fresh flowers and plants and handmade quilts; some have kitchens. Ample windows and a full-length glass door provide an unobstructed Lake view.

LAKE BREEZE MOTEL RESORT

North Shore Dr.   *(218) 525-6808*
Northeast of Duluth, Minn.   (800) 738-5884
$$

This classic motel resort, on 5 acres overlooking Lake Superior, has 17 units, including suites (some with kitchenettes), and offers many recreational bells and whistles. Guests can play horseshoes, basketball, volleyball or badminton on the outdoor courts or hike the trails nearby. Picnic tables with grills and a campfire circle make for easy summer living. A sauna compliments the outdoor pool. Owner Bob Kirchmaier's 33-foot cutter, *Lake Breeze,* is available for sailing charters.

LAKEVIEW CASTLE MOTEL

5135 North Shore Dr.
Northeast of Duluth, Minn.   (218) 525-1014
$-$$

The Lakeview Castle Motel offers 15 units. All of them face the Lake. Some units have full kitchens, some have refrigerators, some have stoves and refrigerators, and some are basic motel rooms. The motel will accommodate small dogs, but they must be caged if the owners leave the premises. A horseshoe pit is available in the back yard. The Lakeview Castle Dining Room is next door (see our Restaurants chapter). The motel is about 12 miles from downtown Duluth and is open year round.

JOHN'S BREEZY POINT RESORT

West Star Rte.
Two Harbors, Minn.   *(218) 834-4496*
$$

Seeking privacy and a Lake view? This cabin resort is tucked away on the shore with its own playground and beach. The cabins are fresh and up-to-date, with picture windows, decks, refinished wood floors and fireplaces, but they retain a classic feel. Units accommodate two to six people, depending on their size.

Insiders' Tips

For information about events and activities in Thunder Bay, call the helpful and polite people at Tourism Thunder Bay, (800) 667-8386.

EMILY'S KNIFE RIVER INN AND GENERAL STORE

North Shore Scenic Dr.
Knife River, Minn. (218) 834-5922
$$ no credit cards

Emily's has been a fixture in the village of Knife River since 1929 when it served as the general store. The granddaughter of the original owner still runs the place, and she's added a deli and a small dining room. An upstairs suite, with a large picture window overlooking the Knife River, is furnished with wicker and lace and plump comforters. It has a private bath and two bedrooms that sleep four people. A continental breakfast of sticky buns, muffins, a fresh fruit plate, coffee, tea and juice is included in the room rate.

BRYAN HOUSE BED AND BREAKFAST

123 Third Ave. (218) 834-2950
Two Harbors, Minn. (800) 950-4797
$$

This 1905 Mission-style bungalow was built by Henry S. Bryan, the first president of 3M, the corporate giant that had its industrial beginnings on the North Shore (don't miss the sandpaper museum in Two Harbors). Bryan House is right in town, within walking distance of many historic attractions and shops and the working harbor where you can see iron ore being loaded on the big ships.

This bed and breakfast inn is run by Karl and Alene Aho, who cook up rich, light Finnish pancakes for breakfast. Three large bedrooms feature antique decorations, and you'll be welcomed with a taste of homemade fudge in every room.

SUPERIOR SHORES RESORT

10 Superior Shores Dr.   *(218) 834-5671*
Two Harbors, Minn.   *(800) 242-1988*
$$$

This sprawling, fairly new resort is just east of Two Harbors, set on a bay and affording expansive views of the Lake. It features indoor and outdoor pools, hot tubs (sit outside on an early September evening and watch the hawks fly overhead) and tennis courts. The recently remodeled lodge features a bar (check out the mosaic tile trout table) with fireplace and frequent live entertainment and a restaurant; both are on the second floor. A huge deck (the width of the two rooms) capitalizes on the sublime view of the harbor.

The resort offers several lodging options. Rooms and suites in the main lodge are decorated in tasteful Boundary Waters modern, with blond wood, wicker and willow furniture, fresh geometric textiles and modern lighting. One- to three-bedroom lake homes with fireplaces, Jacuzzis and decks are available in a more private setting along the arm of the peninsula.

This is a popular winter spot for snowmobilers who enjoy the direct access to trails. The parking lot can be a challenge in winter — watch out for sleds buzzing by.

CLIFF 'N SHORE RESORT

436B Minn. Hwy. 61 E.
Northeast of Two Harbors, Minn. (218) 834-4675
$

The hunkered-down Cliff 'n Shore Resort is front and center on the Lake, facing right into nor'easters. It's below the windy, narrow, closed-to-traffic Silver Cliff highway road, now routed through the Silver Cliff tunnel. According to resort owner Anna Mae Peterson,

the old road makes a darn good hiking trail, with plenty of quiet and a great view.

The resort is made up of a seven-unit motel. Each room features knotty pine paneling and large picture windows facing the lake. Two units have kitchenettes.

The motel common room has a fireplace, a telescope and a table for cards and games.

Three cabins also are available, and pets are welcome in each of them.

HALCYON HARBOR

524 Minn. Hwy. 61
northeast of Two Harbors, Minn. (218) 834-2030
$$$

Down a steep hill you'll find five large, pine log cabins, painted in bright colors and perched on high bluffs above Lake Superior in a very private setting. Four of the five cabins — Cliff House, Guest House, Beach House and Lake House — have fireplaces and banks of windows affording views of the Lake. All cabins are completely furnished and include full kitchens.

True of many historic resorts along the North Shore, Halcyon Harbor's past is a colorful one. The resort was originally a private residence, built in the 1930s by a steel mill manager. Later, it was the summer home for a well-to-do Duluth family who entertained such luminaries as Sinclair Lewis, Dorothy Thompson and Milton Berle here. One of the cabins was originally the cook's house and kitchen.

It is best known nowadays for its Cliff House, built around an outdoor stone fireplace on the shore and later expanded into complete living quarters. The cabin extends over the cliff, 30 feet above Lake Superior.

Reservations often are needed more

than a year in advance for this captivating place. None of the cabins has a telephone, making all popular destinations for writers and others seeking peace and quiet.

COUNTRY INN

1204 Seventh Ave.	*(218) 834-5557*
Two Harbors, Minn.	*(800) 456-4000*
$$	

The Country Inn, a new Carlson Companies property, is a great winter spot for snowmobilers, with access to nearby state and public trails and a parking lot with room for trailers. Unlike many strip motels, the inn has a real lobby, a cozy area with antiques and a plump sofa and chairs by the fireplace.

This is a good family place, with an indoor pool, whirlpool and sauna — and reasonable rates. Kids 18 and younger stay free with an adult. A free continental breakfast and newspaper is included in the room price. For an additional $5 charge, pets can stay on the main floor.

The rooms are nicely decorated, with brass beds and upholstered easy chairs. Some Jacuzzi suites are available.

COVE POINT LODGE

Minn. Hwy. 61	*(218) 226-3221*
Beaver Bay, Minn.	*(800) 598-3221*
$$-$$$	

You can't see Cove Point Lodge from the highway. It's tucked down the hill on the lakeshore on 150 heavily wooded acres about 4 miles east of Split Rock Lighthouse; look for the blinking sign on the lakeside. The newly built lodge is nestled on a lovely cove on Lake Superior. The lodge was designed and constructed in the Scandinavian tradition of classic North Shore lodges, with liberal use of pine and cedar throughout the building. For a lodge on this scale, it fits the site well. All 45 rooms have Lake views

through a wide bank of windows and are furnished with rustic, Adirondack-style furniture and dark green and tartan coverings. Every room has a refrigerator.

The sunny common areas in the lodge are ample, with a lobby seating area for reading and another reading area by the huge two-story flagstone fireplace. Pull up a chair at one of the glossy pine tables tucked on two levels in the common area. Enjoy the view, play games or graze on the continental breakfast buffet, including toast-your-own bagels and muffins and plenty of cereal choices — a hit with the kids. Kids also seem to enjoy the pool, hot tub and sauna.

The modest-size menu at the on-site dining room features walleye, steak and chicken.

FENSTAD'S RESORT

1190 Minn. Hwy. 61	
Little Marais, Minn.	*(218) 226-4724*
$$$	*No credit cards*

Fenstad's 17 lakeshore cabins dot the curve of Little Marais Harbor, spaced well apart for plenty of elbow room. Operated since 1936, most cabins at this resort are newly built, with a few older ones mixed in. Kitchens are fully equipped, and linens and towels are furnished.

This is an impeccably maintained, family-run cabin resort. Fenstad's caters to anglers seeking salmon and trout and maintains a boat ramp and dock area in the protected cove. Boats and motors are available for rent. In winter, the resort has its own cross-country ski trails; you'll find summer and fall hiking trails too.

BLUEFIN BAY

Minn. Hwy. 61	
Tofte, Minn.	*(800) 258-3346*
$$-$$$$	

Bluefin Bay, a fairly new resort perched on the edge of Lake Superior, was built on the site where fishing houses of Norwegian immigrants once stood. According to promotional literature, Bluefin Bay was designed to be reminiscent of a coastal fishing village. Well, it's a village, but the fish for the restaurants comes from Grand Portage (up the shore), and a room in the village costs more than you'll earn from a week's catch.

The rows of blue and white luxury townhomes flank the shore. These units offer handsome, airy interiors with plenty of windows, high ceilings, fireplaces and balconies. Bluefin draws clientele from the Twin Cities. In fact, Bluefin Bay was called "New England close to home," by the *Twin Cities Reader*. Lodging choices range from a no-frills hotel room with queen-size bed to the aforementioned two-story townhome with balcony, Jacuzzi, fireplace and kitchen.

This well-designed resort offers three terrific places to eat: the Bluefin Bay Dining Room for seafood; the CoHo Cafe with take-out soups, sandwiches and breads; and the Bridge for pizza and burgers. (See our Restaurants chapter for details.) Recreational amenities include an indoor pool, two saunas, an indoor whirlpool/spa, an outdoor pool and hot tub and a workout room.

Chateau Laveaux

Minn. Hwy. 61   (218) 663-7223
Tofte, Minn.   (800) 445-5773
$$-$$$$$

Chateau Laveaux offers furnished, full housekeeping condominiums with fireplaces and balconies overlooking the Lake. Motel rooms also are available. Amenities include an indoor pool, whirlpool, sauna, game room and in-room movies. A newly remodeled lobby with plenty of comfortable couches and chairs overlooks the Lake. Pets are allowed for an additional $10 per night and must be leashed at all times.

Holiday Inn Express

Minn. Hwy. 61
Tofte, Minn.   (218) 663-7899
$$-$$$

The Holiday Inn Express is a great choice for a family vacation. Kids can have a good time in the pool room and the lobby; reasonable amounts of noise are not frowned upon.

This 52-unit hotel features a large indoor pool area, complete with the latest in skid-free flooring, a whirlpool and sauna. The pool room, with its high-beamed pine ceilings, sunny exposure and chairs and tables, is a comfortable place to hang out. The main lobby features a hand-built stone fireplace, plenty of tables for playing games and enjoying snacks and sofas for relaxing.

Insiders' Tips

When traveling in Canada, keep in mind that some national holidays are different from those in the States. This may affect lodging prices and room availability as well as banking services and public transportation. Canada's independence day is July 1, Thanksgiving is the second Monday in October, and Victoria Day is the third Monday in May. The three-day Memorial Day weekend is not a Canadian holiday, but September's Labor Day weekend is celebrated in Canada.

Adults enjoy the 24-hour coffee and juice bar, and kids love the big selection of cereal and pastries at the continental breakfast offered each morning.

BEST WESTERN CLIFF DWELLER MOTEL

Minn. Hwy. 61   *(218) 663-7273*
Lutsen, Minn.   *(800) 223-2048*
$-$$$

The Cliff Dweller is perched on the lakeside of Minn. Highway 61. Its 22 units are outfitted with wonderful private balconies overlooking the Lake. The motel is near the Lutsen Mountain downhill ski area and the Superior National Golf Course. Cross-country skiing and hiking trails are nearby. The Cliff Dweller has a low-key feel that suits people looking for a little quiet time. The Primrose Restaurant is within the motel complex and serves breakfast basics, such as eggs and pancakes, and dinner selections, including fish, steak and pasta. Cocktails are available.

EAGLE RIDGE AT LUTSEN MOUNTAINS

Mountain Rd. (County Rd. 36)(218) 663-7284
Lutsen, Minn.   *(800) 360-7666*
$$-$$$$$

Eagle Ridge is a 41-unit condominium development. It's next to the Lutsen downhill ski area, with "ski-in and ski-out" access. Most of the condominiums are one-bedroom units, but two- and three-bedrooms units and studios also are available. All units have kitchens except the studios. Woodburning or gas fireplaces are featured in all units, and double Jacuzzis are offered in most. The decor is light and airy, with locally made log beds and tables. There's great views of Moose Mountain from the year-round indoor and outdoor pools, with sauna and whirlpool nearby. This is a popular place

for downhill skiers. Expect the highest rates in the winter.

LUTSEN MOUNTAIN INN

Mountain Rd. (County Rd. 36)(218) 663-7244
Lutsen, Minn.   *(800) 686-4669*
$$-$$$

The local owner and manager at the Lutsen Mountain Inn takes pride in running a friendly, locally owned place. The 30-unit inn is near the Superior National Golf Course and the Lutsen Mountain downhill ski area. You can access the Lutsen Snowmobile Trail right from the inn's parking lot. There's plenty of trailer parking too. In summer, access to the Lutsen Park mountain biking trails are nearby.

Each rooms features a wet bar, refrigerator and microwave oven. The contemporary decor includes lots of birch wood and regional photography by wildlife photographer Craig Blacklock. A continental breakfast of juices, coffee, tea, hot chocolate, muffins and Danish rolls comes with the room. Two rooms are designated for people who travel with pets.

LINDGREN'S BED AND BREAKFAST

Cook County Rd. 35
Lutsen, Minn.   *(218) 663-7450*
$$$

Housed in a 1920s log home on the Lake, Lindgren's Bed and Breakfast has Lake views from all the rooms. The easily accessible shoreline offers hiking, fishing and rock-collecting possibilities, and if the weather turns bad, try making your own entertainment on the baby grand piano — or just sit in front of the fireplace. All rooms have private baths. There's a Finnish sauna and whirlpool for guests, and a hearty full breakfast is served each morning.

LUTSEN RESORT AND SEA VILLAS

Minn. Hwy. 61   (218) 663-7212
Lutsen, Minn.   (800) 258-8736
$$-$$$

The Nelson family opened Lutsen, Minnesota's first resort, in the late 1880s. Today, the main lodge, known for its Scandinavian-influenced architecture, endures as one of the classic North Shore fixtures. It offers 32 guest rooms in the main lodge, many with Lake views. On the main floor, you'll find the dining room, which overlooks Lake Superior, and the inviting lobby, with its massive stone fireplace, hand-hewn white pine beams and deep leather couches and chairs. Amenities include a lounge, game room, large indoor pool, whirlpool and sauna. Don't miss a walk over the covered bridge that crosses the Poplar River.

Lutsen has expanded since it first opened. The Cliff House, perched above the main lodge, offers 13 standard guest rooms and four two-bedroom units; the new, smoke-free Lakeside Log Cabins feature full kitchens, decks, and Lake views; and guests at Sea Villa Townhomes, modern housekeeping cabins 3 miles south of Lutsen's main lodge, have full use of the lodge's amenities.

Lutsen Lodge also offers conference facilities at the 100-person capacity Main Hall and three meeting rooms, each of which seats 10 to 20 people. Audiovisual equipment and group catering are available.

VILLAGE INN RESORT AT LUTSEN MOUNTAIN

Mountain Rd. (County Rd. 26)(218) 663-7241
Lutsen, Minn.   (800) 642-6036
$$-$$$$$

The Village Inn Resort enjoys a prime location for downhill and cross-country skiers, snowmobilers and golfers. The resort is situated in the valley of the Sawtooth Mountains near the Superior National Golf Course and the Lutsen Mountain ski resort, with access to plenty of summer and winter trails for both motorized and non-motorized recreation. The Village Inn buzzes with activity in the winter, with folks coming and going; this place is more for the mover and shaker than the solitude-seeker.

Accommodations are broad-based, including lodge rooms, condominiums, townhouses and executive lodges available. The main lodge rooms are tastefully decorated in Northwoods country style, with plenty of pine appointments and fresh prints. Besides the standard television, a selection of private reading material is provided in the rooms. There's a restaurant, lounge, pool, sauna and whirlpool in the lodge.

The condominiums are adjacent to the main lodge. All units have microwave ovens, decks, one or two full baths, queen-size sleeper sofas in the living room, kitchens, TVs and VCRs, fireplaces and, of course, mountain views. The condo courtyard has a indoor pool and spa area.

Insiders' Tips

As you drive eastward into Duluth on Interstate 35 and reach Spirit Mountain, don't forget to force a yawn, chew gum or sing to the radio to make your ears pop. You'll descend 501 vertical feet in about 10 minutes as you approach town, and your ears probably will plug.

The three-story townhomes overlook the Poplar River valley. The main floor includes a fireplace, balcony deck, TV/VCR, queen-size sleeper sofa and a full kitchen with microwave; most units have half-baths. All units have lofts with queen beds and full baths and a walkout level with full bath.

Executive lodges are three-story units, each with two master bedrooms, 3½ baths, a four-person whirlpool, stone fireplace, balcony and deck, a dining area seating 10 to 12, TV/VCR and stereo.

THE WOODS BED AND BREAKFAST

Caribou Tr. (County Rd. 4)
Lutsen, Minn.   (218) 663-7144
$$

A short drive up the Caribou Trail leads to a beautiful hillside spot where you'll find the Woods Bed and Breakfast. This simple, wood-sided, modern home takes advantage of its views; a full deck on the main level and a baby deck on the second floor face Lake Superior. Three separate bedrooms and a lower-level suite (with private entrance and bath, television and VCR) are available year round. Breakfast features quiche, muffins and pancakes. This is an ideal place to access cross-country ski trails, snowmobile trails, Lutsen's golf and downhill skiing, and Grand Marais' arts, restaurants and shopping.

SOLBAKKEN RESORT

Minn. Hwy. 61   (218) 663-7566
Lutsen, Minn.   (800) 435-3950
$$-$$$

Solbakken, Norwegian for "sunny hills," is a warm, relaxed place. The main lodge is the former Sawbill Lodge, moved from the Boundary Waters and painstakingly restored for its present use. The common space has a stone fireplace and is filled with comfortable chairs and sofas, reading lamps and lots of reading material. A humorous and fascinating collection of framed vintage magazine and catalog covers, revolving around a ski theme, decorates the log walls. Careful when you sit down; Goldie, the resident cat, favors the chairs saved from the old lodge. The gift shop here is thoughtfully stocked, with lots of books, jewelry and tasteful items.

Solbakken is known for its focus and passion for cross-country skiing. This touring center rents skis and snowshoes, offers skiing lessons and maintains a ski shop. Just hop across the road to access an extensive trail system.

Lodging options include deluxe suites on the lower level of the lodge, fully furnished cabins on the lakeshore and motel-style kitchenettes. The suites were added after the historic lodge was relocated and furnished in modern Scandinavian decor. All afford great views of the Lake and include amenities such as fireplaces, televisions and fully-equipped kitchens.

KAH-NEE-TAH GALLERY AND COTTAGES

Minn. Hwy. 61
Lutsen, Minn.   (218) 387-2585
$$

You can see the art gallery from the highway, but you can't see these three blue and white cabins tucked away in the woods. The owners' artistic sensibilities are reflected in the care (and decor) they've given these cabins — one was rescued from a closed-down resort and restored. For the individual seeking privacy and quiet, these cottages are a tasteful blend of contemporary bathrooms and kitchens and the traditional family cabin we all seek, with cobblestone fireplaces, built-in bookshelves and comfy sofas and reading chairs. All cottages have outdoor decks, and furnishings include towels, linens, kitchen utensils, dishes and firewood. Modern conveniences include appliances, microwaves, cassette tape players and baths with showers.

CASCADE LODGE

Minn. Hwy. 61   (218) 387-1112
Lutsen, Minn.   (800) 322- 9543
$$-$$$

Cascade Lodge, on the upper side of Highway 61, has been a fixture of the North Shore since the 1930s. Typical of older lodges, the rooms are small, but all have been redecorated. Lakeside rooms have great views. The living room and fireside room on the main floor feel well-worn and cozy, like an old pair of slippers, with a grand piano, banks of multi-pane windows, old wicker, couches and chairs. We like the cabins tucked on the hillside, particularly Cabin No. 11 — you have to cross the creek by bridge to get to it. Many cabins have porches with rockers. There's also a four-unit motel. Breakfast, lunch and dinner are served at the Cascade Restaurant next door.

THOMSONSITE BEACH MOTEL

Minn. Hwy. 61, In Cascade River State Park
Southeast of Grand Marais, Minn. (218) 387-1532
$$-$$$

The Thomsonite Beach Motel is a North Shore fixture, its low-key neon sign a landmark signaling travelers coming from points south that Grand Marais is just ahead. The wooded complex offers a guest house, suites and motel rooms, and no two units are exactly alike. Kitchen facilities are available in some units and include microwave ovens, stoves, refrigerators and dishwashers.

Decor in the motel rooms is fresh knotty pine, with lots of Lake-blue fabric. The furniture is all custom-made hardwood.

Thomsonite Beach is right on the Lake. There's nearby access to the hiking and skiing trails at Cascade River State Park — the motel is within the park boundaries.

This is a well-kept, laid-back place. Owner Tania Feigal is an experienced jeweler who works with the Thomsonite gemstone mined on the property. You can admire her original creations at the jewelry shop on site and watch the intensive, time-consuming process of mining, polishing, shaping and creating pendants, bracelets, cuff links and rings made of Thomsonite gemstone.

LUND'S MOTEL AND COTTAGES

919 W. Minn. Hwy. 61   (218) 387-2155
Grand Marais, Minn.   (218) 387-1704
$$

These Cape Cod-style cottages, with red doors and gray trim to contrast well-kept white exteriors, are traditional winter and summer getaways for many folks (some of our friends spend the New Year's holiday here). The housekeeping cottages, with bay windows, flower boxes and fireplaces, feel more like little houses than cabins. Family-owned since 1937, Lund's cottages are right in town within walking distance of everything, including the municipal pool and sauna, restaurants and shopping. Pets are allowed in the cottages. Each room at the modern six-unit motel includes a refrigerator, coffee maker with coffee and cable TV. You can see the bustling harbor from the motel rooms.

THE SHORELINE

20 S. Broadway   (218) 387-2633
Grand Marais, Minn.   (800) 247-6020
$-$$

The Shoreline, a quiet, small-scale, concierge-style hotel, is on the edge of downtown Grand Marais, overlooking Artist's Point on Lake Superior. The large corner rooms, with windows facing two directions, are your best bet. Walk out the door for a quick morning stroll to the Coast Guard station and lighthouse.

Built in the 1950s, The Shoreline has been extensively updated but retains its classic feel. Many families stay here year after year. The lobby has a well-appointed fireside common area, with plump sofa and chairs, a television and view of the Lake.

SUPER 8 MOTEL

Minn. Hwy. 61	(218) 387-2448
Grand Marais, Minn.	(800) 247-6020
$-$$	

Don't turn up your nose. This Super 8 has special features that make it a whole lot different from most budget chain motels. It's set on an extensively landscaped site surrounded by aspen and spruce. There's a whirlpool-sauna with a sun deck, a guest laundry, refrigerators in each room and a continental breakfast each morning. Pets are allowed with permission.

NELSON'S TRAVELERS REST CABINS AND MOTEL

Minn. Hwy. 61	(218) 387-1464
Grand Marais, Minn.	(800) 249-1285
$-$$	

Nelson's is another in-town resort, with well-kept log cabins set amid tall pines. Although this resort is in Grand Marais, it feels like the country. There's lots to do here for kids and adults, with a playground, hiking trails to the Lake and miniature golf next door. The resort provides free firewood and an outdoor fire pit, barbecue grills, picnic tables and lawn chairs, so you can enjoy a cookout or an evening campfire.

All cabins have fireplaces, some have a view of the Lake, and cable TVs in both the cabins and motel rooms include free HBO.

Nelson's is open from May through October only.

PINCUSHION MOUNTAIN BED & BREAKFAST

220 Gunflint Tr.	(218) 387-1276
Grand Marais, Minn.	(800) 542-1226
$$	

About 3 miles up the Gunflint Trail from Grand Marais, the Pincushion Mountain Bed & Breakfast is a consistent choice of hikers, mountain bikers and cross-country skiers. The reason? The Superior Hiking Trail and the Pincushion Mountain Trail — for summertime mountain-biking, hiking and wintertime snowshoeing and cross-country skiing — are a stone's throw away.

The bed and breakfast inn is set amid 44 acres on the Sawtooth Mountain ridge and includes a grand view of Lake Superior 1,000 feet below. In addition to four bedrooms, each with private bath, there's a sauna, fireplace and sun deck.

NANIBOUJOU LODGE & RESTAURANT

Minn. Hwy 61	
East of Grand Marais, Minn.	(218) 387-2688
$$$	

Fifteen miles east of Grand Marais, the Naniboujou Lodge, like Lutsen Resort, is another classic fixture on the North Shore. It was built in 1928 as a private club for the wealthy and famous, including Babe Ruth, Jack Dempsey and several Chicago gangsters. It is renowned for its dramatic and striking interior design, specifically in the Great Hall; note the huge stone fireplace and colorful, Cree Indian-inspired ceiling murals and fabrics.

The lodge is near the Brule River (a blue-ribbon trout stream) and Judge C.R. Magney State Park. There are plenty of hiking trails in the vicinity, but if you want peace and quiet, grab one of the Adirondack chairs on the lawn and enjoy the view of Lake Superior. The dining room is known for its exquisite food prepared with fresh

The Lutsen Resort has been a stopping point for travelers for more than a century.

ingredients. The Sunday brunch is top-drawer, and the afternoon teas are fun.

The lodge includes 24 rooms and a solarium/library in the modern addition that overlooks Lake Superior.

Naniboujou Lodge has limited weekend winter hours but is open all summer.

GRAND PORTAGE LODGE & CASINO

Minn. Hwy. 61   *(218) 475-2401*
Grand Portage, Minn.   *(800) 543-1384*
$$

The Grand Portage Lodge & Casino is set on the edge of a wide Lake Superior bay. Be sure to request a lakeside hotel room. The view of the moon on the water at night and the sunny east light in the morning makes these standard hotel rooms extra special.

The hotel is connected to the casino where you'll always find plenty of action (see our Nightlife and Casinos chapter). This is a bustling, noisy place, with lots of families and bus tour groups. There's an indoor pool and sauna and a full-service restaurant and lounge. Check out weekend package deals for bargain room prices.

Along the South Shore

Accommodations along the South Shore range from rustic to quaint to swanky. Bed and breakfast inns abound. Pick your pleasure and enjoy the lovely countryside flanking Lake Superior. Don't forget the myriad recreational opportunities — fishing, swimming, hiking, biking, snowmobiling, sailing — regardless of the season.

Iron River, Herbster and Cornucopia

IRON RIVER TROUT HAUS

205 W. Drummond Rd.
Iron River, Wis.   *(800) 262-1453*
$$

It's a way from the shore, but if fishing is your thing, you might want to stop at this bed and breakfast inn where you can get a regional gourmet breakfast or, if you stay two nights, a fresh trout breakfast from the spring-fed pond (which you can fish the night before). Four rooms in the renovated 1892 home have themes: railroads, logging, birds and fish. The Trout Haus caters to outdoors enthusiasts.

Take Lea Street north from U.S. Highway 2 for 2½ blocks, pass over the Tri-County Corridor and turn left on Drummond Road.

THE BEACH RESORT
Bark Point Rd., Herbster, Wis.   (715) 774-3826
$

Looking for something secluded — not fancy but with a great view? Try these cabins and motel in out-of-the-way Herbster. The Beach Resort is near the beach, just across the road from a wide sandy area that continues on the flatland into the Lake. You should be able to hear the Lake's waves from your bed. Don't expect many amenities; this is an old-fashioned cabin-motel setup.

From Wis. Highway 13, turn toward the Lake at the Cardinal Lumber Co., just east of Herbster, onto Old School Road. Continue a few blocks to the water; the Beach Resort is on the left.

DEERING TOURIST HOMES
Wis. Hwy. 13, Cornucopia, Wis. (715) 742-3994
$$

With large cabins facing the highway, marina and Lake beyond, the Deering has been around for a long time and is usually occupied. The cabins have baths, living rooms, kitchens, showers and basements. These accommodations are open all year.

THE VILLAGE INN
Wis. Hwy. 13, Cornucopia, Wis. (715) 742-3941
$

Upstairs from the dining room and cafe/lounge are four rooms rented out by the owners of this rustic complex. The rooms have the intimate feel of a bed and breakfast inn and are decorated attractively for each season of the year. They look over the forested area to the west. A commons parlor area with a fireplace and outdoor balcony overlooks the eastern wooded area.

SOUTH SHORE MOTEL
Wis. Hwy. 13, Cornucopia, Wis. (715) 742-3244
$

Just across the road from Lake Superior, but still with a great view, this well-kept motel has 10 rooms and offers complimentary coffee and doughnuts. Rooms have TVs but no cable hookup. Two good restaurants are within walking distance. In the summertime, the nearby waterfront comes alive with gift shop patrons. You can see that activity and the sunset across the Lake in Minnesota from your room; all have Lake views.

Bayfield and LaPointe

Over on Madeline Island, homes and cottages are available year round at daily and weekly rates. Contact Island Management Services at (715) 747-6085 for additional options.

APOSTLE VIEW INN
Wis. Hwy. 13, Bayfield, Wis.(715) 779-3385
$$

A charming country inn a few miles south of Bayfield, Apostle View has a wonderful Lake view and six smoke-free units. It's like a bed and breakfast inn — cozy, with quilts, rocking chairs, teddy bears, coffee and herbal teas in each room — but without the breakfast. All rooms have queen beds and picture windows that look over the Lake, big thick towels and cable TVs with HBO. The large yards have cedar lawn furniture and swings. No children, please.

BAY FRONT INN
City Dock, Bayfield, Wis.   (715) 779-3880
$$$

This motel overlooking the attractive

waterfront offers private decks and continental breakfast. Rooms have double and queen-size beds and, in some, Jacuzzis in the corner. Guests relaxing on the deck can watch the ferryboat come and go as well as the visitors and shoppers who stroll leisurely by the inn's small, flowered front yard. Five excellent restaurants are within a few blocks of the lodging, as are many gift and art shops.

BAYFIELD INN

20 Rittenhouse Ave.
Bayfield, Wis.   (715) 779-3363
$$

Twenty-one rooms, 13 with an uncluttered view of the Lake, are featured at this inn near the water. Most rooms have two double beds and basic cable, a tub and shower. One room has a fireplace. Complimentary coffee and blueberry muffins are served in the morning; VCR rentals, a sauna, lounge, restaurant for fine dining, bar and grill also are available.

BAYWOOD PLACE BED & BREAKFAST

20 N. Third St., Bayfield, Wis. (715) 779-3690
$$ No credit cards

Look past the big yard with lots of perennials and raspberry bushes; there, tucked beneath 100-year-old white pines, is this river town-style 1924 house. It has decks and porches that all look out on Lake Superior. The four bedrooms have private bathrooms. Limited smoking is available. Please call to inquire about the policy for children. Pets are allowed. A full gourmet, multi-course breakfast is served daily. Baywood Place is open year round.

COOPER HILL HOUSE

33 S. Sixth St., Bayfield, Wis. (715) 779-5060
$$$

Larry and Julie McDonald live in this house and provide bed-and-breakfast ac-

commodations. Three of the four rooms have queen-size beds; the fourth has an antique double bed, but with a new mattress. All rooms have private baths. Common areas are furnished with antiques. This 1888 home is up on a hill, a few blocks from the water, and guests relaxing in the evening on the front porch can watch the lighthouse blink on distant Long Island. No smoking is allowed; inquire about children.

BROOKSIDE MOTEL AND PORT SUPERIOR CONDOMINIUMS

Wis. Hwy. 13, Bayfield, Wis.(715) 779-5123
$$$-$$$$

Just south of Bayfield is the Port Superior Marina, clustered with lodging options, a restaurant and place to charter sailboats. The condos are on the waterfront and have private boat slips, decks and fireplaces. The motel is secluded in the woods, not far from the water, and offers suites with full kitchen facilities.

DREAMCATCHER LODGING

Wis. Hwy. 13, Bayfield, Wis.(715) 779-5538
$$

You'd be hard put to find a more attractive set of rooms in a lovelier setting than these; the problem is, they're usually full. The second-story rooms and common balcony face the Lake; each room has its own entrance and a full private bath. Nearby are a sun room, breakfast room (continental breakfast is included), sauna and gift shop (with Native American-oriented gifts — the inn is the only Ojibwe-owned lodging in the area). Each room has a mural depicting Ojibwe and northern woods scenes, painted by a local Ojibwe artist. You can walk to Bayfield along a lakeside hiking trail in about 10 minutes.

Dreamcatcher is just south of Bayfield on the lake side.

GREUNKE'S FIRST STREET INN
17 N. First St., Bayfield, Wis.(715) 779-5480
$$

This Bayfield landmark is probably the oldest continuous food-and-lodging place in the entire region. Built in the 1860s as a boarding house, Greunke's hasn't changed much: People still eat in the old dining room downstairs and sleep upstairs, and its homey, nostalgic hospitality still draws locals and visitors. One guest was John Kennedy Jr. who in 1995 dropped in from a backpacking-kayaking trip and chose one of the humble shared-bathroom rooms. You can get private bathrooms, however, and the lodging rate includes a fisherman's breakfast, complete with blueberry pancakes, fries and sausage.

HARBOR'S EDGE MOTEL
33 N. Front St., Bayfield, Wis.   (715) 779-3962
$$

If you're newly married or celebrating a wedding anniversary, you'll get champagne and snacks with a two-night stay at this 20-room motel. It's down by the ferry dock, with lots of flowers in the little yard out front, and an easy walk from five excellent restaurants and many gift shops. The units are standard, but some are two-bedroom suites that accommodate six. Harbor's Edge also has its own antiques/gift shop.

THE INN ON MADELINE ISLAND
LaPointe, Wis. (715) 747-6315, (800) 822-6315
$$$-$$$$

This resort on Lake Superior has 50 units, a condo, rental cottages, a heated swimming pool, a beach and tennis courts. A popular restaurant also is housed here. The Inn is four blocks from the ferry landing, next to the Yacht Club.

MADELINE ISLAND HOME RENTALS
LaPointe, Wis. (715) 747-5135, (800) 977-2624
$$$$

Three homes — all with fully equipped kitchens and decks with gas grills — are available May to October for nightly, weekly or monthly rentals. Treasure House is in LaPointe, across the street from Lake Superior and near a public beach, village stores and a museum. It has two bedrooms, the owner's rare book collection, a fireplace and a hot tub on the deck.

Hideaway is a cabin on the north side of the island in a secluded part of the woods but with a view of Basswood Island. The cabin has a living room, bedroom and a large screened porch with hammock and bed. A walk down steep steps takes you to the Lake.

Carriage House is on the south side of the island and has a private beach and dock. The owner lives next door but out of sight! The living and dining rooms are bright and airy with vaulted ceilings, loft, a fireplace and old rare books. Carriage House has two full bathrooms, two bedrooms and a hot tub on the deck.

MADELINE ISLAND MOTEL
LaPointe, Wis.   (715) 747-3000
$$

Just two blocks from the ferry dock,

this 11-unit motel has handicap access and offers guests a free continental breakfast. It's near the quaint shops of LaPointe and, like everywhere in the village, is not far from the water. Children younger than 18 stay free in the same room.

OLD RITTENHOUSE INN
301 Rittenhouse Ave.
Bayfield, Wis.   *(715) 779-5111*
$$$$

Guests in the 20 units in three nearby historic buildings (the Rittenhouse, Chateau Boutin and Grey Oak Guest House) enjoy a continental breakfast with fresh fruit, or have a reduced-rate full breakfast — both served at the famed Rittenhouse dining room. The handicapped-accessible rooms have working fireplaces, private baths and Jacuzzis and are furnished with antiques. All three buildings are in easy walking distance of Bayfield shopping, the marina and the harbor.

MORNING GLORY B & B
119 S. Sixth St., Bayfield, Wis.   *(715) 779-5621*
$$

Three rooms in this 1905 settlement-style home are available to guests. One has a private bathroom, and the other two rooms share a bathroom. The inn offers guests sunny Lake views, antiques, a library, a parlor with a piano and a continental breakfast. Outdoors, enjoy the flowered yard where you can play croquet and badminton. Children are allowed. Inquire about pets.

PINEHURST INN AT PIKE'S CREEK
Wis. Hwy. 13, Bayfield, Wis.(715) 779-3676
$$

Offering country charm overlooking Lake Superior, Pinehurst is a bed and breakfast inn with a full gourmet breakfast and four cozy rooms with private baths. It's on 5 acres of private grounds, with Victorian pond gardens, tall pines and nature trails. Common areas include an antiques-furnished library, a fireplace and a sauna. Massage is available. Children and pets are allowed. Smoking is limited on the premises.

SEAGULL BAY MOTEL
325 S. Seventh St.
Bayfield, Wis.   *(715) 779-5558*
$$

This attractive hillside motel is right in town where you can walk to all the shops and restaurants. Large groups are welcome; one of the 25 units sleeps 10, and another sleeps eight. Another has two rooms with adjoining interior doors. Six are kitchenette units, with pots, pans and dishes. All units have in-room coffee and a terrific view of the Lake. Although this lodge is on a steep hill, you can drive right to the door of nine of the units. If you have mobility problems, request one of these. Pets are allowed.

THIMBLEBERRY INN
BED AND BREAKFAST/
BERTH AND BREAKFAST
Bayfield, Wis.   *(715) 779-5757*
$$$$ *No credit cards*

On 40 secluded acres on Lake Supe-

Photo: Duluth News-Tribune

Canal Park in Duluth is a popular spot for a summertime stroll.

rior with a view of five of the Apostle Islands, Thimbleberry offers lodging with private entrances, working wood fireplaces, private baths and gourmet full breakfasts — and a gently rocking bed. Beginning in 1996, the inn also provides lodging in the Sandpiper, a 35-foot classic wooden ketch that's moored at the Thimbleberry dock. This is no rough boat berth; you'll get ultra-fine linens and breakfast prepared by one of the owners who wrote *Cooking at Thimbleberry Inn with Sharon Locey*. No children, please. No smoking either.

From Wis. Highway 13 at the Isle Vista Casino (about 3 miles north of Bayfield), turn north on Blueberry Road, go 1.3 miles, turn right on Pageant Road and continue for a half-mile until you see Fire Number 15021.

WINFIELD INN

Wis. Hwy. 13, Bayfield, Wis. (715) 779-3252
$$$

The largest lodging in Bayfield, the very attractive Winfield Inn nevertheless has an intimate feel to it. Its 31 rooms are situated for a spectacular view of the Apostle Islands, as is the outdoor deck. Rooms have air-conditioning and coffee. Some units are kitchenettes, with fully equipped kitchens. Pets are allowed. The inn is just four blocks north of the ferryboat landing, right on the Lake.

WOODS MANOR

LaPointe, Wis. (715) 747-3102
$$$$

A bed and breakfast inn, Woods Manor offers rooms with fireplaces and whirlpools as well as a boat dock, canoes,

• *135*

a sauna, bikes, tennis courts and a beach. It's open May to December.

Washburn

BODIN'S BAYFIELD RESORT

Washburn, Wis.   (715) 373-2359
$$

Several miles south of Bayfield and about 9 miles north of Washburn is this homey resort, with housekeeping cottages, lots of trees and the sound of waves lapping a secluded sandy beach along Lake Superior. You furnish the linens; pets are welcome. Bodin's is open May to October.

SUPER 8

Harbor View Dr.   (715) 373-5671
Washburn, Wis.   (800) 800-8000
$$

This national chain motel has 35 rooms about a block from Lake Superior and nearby to restaurants. A whirlpool, sauna, games and continental breakfasts are included. All rooms have cable TVs with ESPN. A copy machine also is available. Children 12 and younger stay for free.

Ashland

ASHLAND MOTEL

2300 Lake Shore Dr.
Ashland, Wis.   (715) 682-5503
$

An attractive, locally owned motel with 34 rooms, the Ashland has a good view of Lake Superior across the road. The largest room has two double beds and a fold-out sofa, and sleeps six; all rooms have cable TVs with HBO. Restaurants are nearby. Pets are allowed.

BEST WESTERN HOLIDAY HOUSE

U.S. Hwy. 2   (715) 682-5235
Ashland, Wis.   (800) 528-1234
$$

This Best Western has 65 rooms,

many of them with fine, wide-open views of the Lake — and the others have pleasant views too. It's right along the water and has an indoor pool, whirlpool, sauna, cocktail lounge and two restaurants.

CREST MOTEL

U.S. Hwy. 2 and Sanborn Ave.
Ashland, Wis.   (715) 682-6603
$

The family-owned Crest has 22 rooms (two rooms sleep up to five) and a lot of yard area for such a busy part of town (the main drag through Ashland). Guests enjoy picnicking, playing badminton or just lounging on the lawn furniture on more than an acre of yard space by the motel. Rooms have lap-top computer hookups and in-room coffee. Pets are allowed.

HOTEL CHEQUAMEGON

101 W. Lake Shore Dr.   (715) 682-9095
Ashland, Wis.   (800) 946-5555
$$$

This gracious Victorian-style hotel by Lake Superior has established itself as a real landmark since it was built in 1985 as a $2.5 million replacement for an 1877 beauty that burned in 1958. The Chequamegon has real wood clapboard siding, which lends an authentic external air that is repeated indoors as soon as you enter the welcoming Victorian lobby, with lovely rooms for writing, reading or visiting. The hotel has beautifully appointed rooms, a spa with a pool and whirlpool. Two excellent restaurants (one with a bar) also are part of the Chequamegon's charm.

LAKE AIRE MOTOR INN

104 Ellis Ave. N., Ashland, Wis. (715) 682-4551
$

This family-run attractive motel is right next to Hotel Chequamegon. It has access to the Lake, the breakwater and boardwalk. A whirlpool, sauna, a spacious and sunny lobby with lots of plants and fitness and game rooms are some of the amenities. Places for fine or casual dining and an attractive lounge are close by, and the Ashland movie theater is within walking distance.

LAKESIDE MOTEL

1706 Lake Shore Dr. W. (U.S. Hwy. 2)
Ashland, Wis.   (715) 682-4575
$-$$

The 10 rooms at family-owned Lakeside recently were remodeled. The largest has three double beds. Coffee is provided in all rooms, and some have VCRs. You can also rent videos here. Guests have a good view of the Lake.

SUPER 8

1610 W. Lake Shore Dr.   (715) 682-9377
Ashland, Wis.   (800) 800-8000
$$

The 70 rooms of this Super 8 are near Lake Superior and downtown Ashland, walking distance from fast-food chains and other restaurants. Movies are available for rent, and a continental breakfast is served. This is the largest Super 8 in the Lake Superior region. Rooms include cable TVs with HBO and ESPN. An indoor pool rounds out the amenities.

TOWN MOTEL

920 W. Lake Shore Dr.
Ashland, Wis.   (715) 682-5555
$

Although the 12 rooms here don't have much of a Lake view, the big water is right across the road; you can stroll over or walk downtown for shopping or dining. The locally owned motel has courtesy coffee and a fax machine available. The largest room has two double beds. This is an easy choice for people driving large RVs or pulling trailers; there's plenty of swing-wide parking close to the rooms. Discounts for seniors, groups and longer stays are available.

Ironwood-Hurley Area

This is "Big Snow Country" (22 feet fell in winter 1995-96), and all the hotels listed here are near ski hills, snowmobile and cross-country ski trails. In the summertime, the remote area is a draw for anglers, camping enthusiasts, ATV users and others who relish the outdoors. Busy seasons, consequently, are when the ski hills are open (usually November to March) and summertime; you're most likely to get off-season rates in April and October.

Locals call it the "tourist zone." Canal Park on Duluth's waterfront is a fun place to go, but summer traffic can be heavy and parking scarce. Park in the huge, cheap lots near the Duluth Entertainment Convention Center and follow Waterfront Drive to the Minnesota Slip bridge and Canal Park. Or take the Port Town Trolley shuttle for 50¢ from the DECC to Canal Park and other attractions, such as Fitger's Brewery Complex and the Depot. Children 2 and younger ride free. You can catch the Port Town Trolley at many downtown hotels too.

Insiders' Tips

ADVANCE MOTEL

663 E. Cloverland Dr. (U.S. Hwy. 2)
Ironwood, Mich.   (906) 932-4511
$

The businesslike name belies the clean rusticity of this woodsy cluster of cabins on the Ironwood motel strip. Recently renovated, the Advance has kitchenettes, housekeeping cabins, a three-bedroom house and a five-bedroom house. It's near restaurants and a convenience store.

AMERICAN BUDGET INN

U.S. Hwy. 2 and Wis. Hwy. 51 (906) 561-3500
Hurley, Wis.   (800) 356-8018
$-$$

Although it is a budget motel, this American has a small but especially lovely indoor pool and whirlpool — open 24 hours a day — and a lounge. Some of the 70 rooms have a microwaves and refrigerators, and the larger rooms will sleep five (two queen-size beds and a rollaway). Cats and dogs less than 25 pounds are allowed. A continental breakfast is served mornings in the lobby.

BEST WESTERN POWDERMILL INN

N-11330 Powderhorn Rd.   (906) 932-0800
Bessemer, Mich.   (800) 528-1234
$$

One of the newer hotels in the area, the Powdermill offers fine lodging in deluxe rooms, an indoor pool, spa and sauna, a playground and a restaurant. Rooms in this attractive building include wet bars, microwaves and queen-size beds, with views of woods on one side and Big Powderhorn Ski Hill on the other.

BIG POWDERHORN LODGING ASSOCIATION

N-11360 Powderhorn Rd.
Ironwood, Mich.   (906) 932-3100
$$$-$$$$

Swiss-style chalets are scattered around the hills of Big Powderhorn Ski Hill and are available for rent by the night (a two-night minimum, the total price reflected above) or by the week year round — except there's no summertime maid service. There's room for 3,000 lodgers here. A swimming pool, sauna, whirlpool, gift shops and restaurants are part of the complex, and ski packages are available. The association will help you put together skiing packages as well as summer recreation: mountain biking, fishing, golfing, kayaking, fall color tours, hiking and waterfall tours.

BLACK RIVER LODGE

N-12390 Black River Rd.
Ironwood, Mich.   (906) 932-3857
$-$$$$

A small family resort complex on 150 wooded acres along the Black River, this lodge has an assortment of accommodations options: 1,200-square-feet condos with full kitchens and dishwashers; suites with whirlpools and wet bars; and motel rooms. All lodgings have cable TVS with HBO, and pets are allowed if you call first. Fine dining, a lounge, a pool and miniature golf also are available.

BLUE CLOUD

105 W. Cloverland Dr. (U.S. Hwy. 2)
Ironwood, Mich.   *(906) 932-0920*
$-$$

A nicely kept motel along the highway near Ironwood, the Blue Cloud is on a snowmobile trail, rents VCRs and videos and offers a continental breakfast. The owner is a motorcycle aficionado who, with another local businessman, organizes the yearly Big Bike and Trike International Gathering (see our Annual Events chapter).

BUDGET HOST INN/ CLOVERLAND MOTEL

U.S. Hwy. 2, Ironwood, Mich. (906) 932-1260
$

Your basic lodging needs are served here — clean queen-size beds, coffee and proximity to restaurants. Besides economy, the thing that makes the Cloverland a standout on this highway of motels is its fine grove of pine trees.

CEDARS

U.S. Hwy. 2, Ironwood, Mich. (906) 932-4376
$ *No credit cards*

The family-owned Cedars has a down-home friendliness that accompanies basic lodging needs. It's one of the first motels on the western side of the Ironwood motel strip and has a wide western view of hills, forests and highways.

THE COACHLIGHT OF IRONWOOD

101 N. Lowell St.
Ironwood, Mich.   *(906) 932-3650*
$

Across from the historic depot in downtown Ironwood, the Coachlight was formerly a brewery, built in 1892, and then a creamery; in the 1920s, it was converted to an apartment house. The house has since been restored, and apartments are available with period furniture, cold and "sometimes hot" running water, fully equipped kitchens, steam heat and extra "Murphy" beds — the kind that swing up and fit behind a door. It's a homey, cozy and clean place, and out back there's a rose garden, arbor and play area where people can picnic. No pets, please.

COMFORT INN

210 E. Cloverland Dr.
(U.S. Hwy. 2)   *(906) 932-2224*
Ironwood, Mich.   *(800) 572-9412*
$$

Free continental breakfast, 63 spacious rooms, an indoor heated pool and whirlpool, and computer-compatible phones (equipped for hearing-impaired folks) are all available here. Some rooms have microwaves and refrigerators, and all rooms have cable TVs with HBO. Restaurants are nearby.

EAGLE BLUFF CONDOMINIUMS

990 10th Ave. N.   *(715) 561-2787*
Hurley, Wis.   *(800) 336-0973*
$$-$$$

On Lake Michelle at the intersection of Wis. Highway 51 and U.S. Highway 2 in Hurley, these condos have fully equipped kitchens, fireplaces (wood is supplied) and one to three bedrooms. Like other lodging in this area, they're near four ski areas; cross-country skiing, snowmobiling and hiking trails; and beautiful waterfalls.

HOLIDAY INN

U.S. Hwy. 2 and Wis. Hwy. 51 (715) 561-3030
Hurley, Wis.   *(800) HOLIDAY*
$$

The first hotel as you come into the

Ironwood-Hurley area from the west, the Holiday Inn has 100 deluxe rooms, an indoor pool, men's and women's saunas, a whirlpool, exercise equipment, electronic amusement game room and fireplace lobby. A fine restaurant and lounge are in the building, which is handy because the Holiday is some distance from the city centers. A snowmobile trail at the door leads to thousands of miles of groomed trails in both states.

THE INN BED AND BREAKFAST

104 Wisconsin Ave.
Montreal, Wis.   *(715) 561-5180*
$$

Six guest rooms, a family loft, a fitness exercise room and a Finnish sauna are available at this traditional bed and breakfast inn in out-of-the-way Montreal, just west of Hurley. Cross-country ski trails are right outside the door.

MONTREAL HAUS RENTALS

Historic District, Montreal, Wis.   *(414) 733-5766*
$$$$

Several homes in the historic mining district of Montreal are available for rent. You'll find neither tourist attraction nor glitz here, but rather some of the prettiest little homes around — identical mining-town clapboard houses, attractive and freshly painted. Montreal Haus has made available some of them — two- to four-bedroom homes that include fireplaces, fully equipped kitchens, linens and towels; some have washers and dryers too. An Appleton, Wisconsin, firm rents these homes.

RIVER FALLS OUTDOORS

N-10675 Junet Rd.
Ironwood, Mich.   *(906) 932-5638*
$-$$$

An A-frame, a bunkhouse and a cottage are available for rent in the Ironwood area through this firm. All are nestled in a hardwood forest overlooking Peterson Falls on the Montreal River. The A-frame has a full kitchen, artist's loft and large wood stove and sleeps up to 10 people. The bunkhouse and cottage have kitchenettes and woodstoves. All three units have access to a Finnish wood-fired sauna and lounge. A swimming pool, sand volleyball court and expeditions (mountain biking, canoeing and cross-country skiing) are available, along with equipment, instruction and guide services.

ROYAL MOTEL

715 W. Cloverland Dr. (U.S. Hwy. 2)
Ironwood, Mich.   *(906) 932-4230*
$

A family-run, single-story motel on the main highway outside Ironwood, the Royal offers 16 clean rooms with comfortable beds, full baths, in-room phones and self-controlled heat. A snowmobile trail begins here.

SUPER 8

160 E. Cloverland Dr.
(U.S. Hwy. 2)   *(906) 932-3395*
Ironwood, Mich.   *(800) 800-8000*
$-$$

Inexpensive, clean and near snowmobile trails, Super 8 offers free coffee, cable TV with HBO and proximity to restaurants. Other amenities include a whirlpool and sauna. Children 12 and younger stay for free, and cribs are available upon request.

TRAVELER'S
E. U.S. Hwy. 2, Bessemer, Mich. (906) 667-0243
$

A 12-unit "ma and pa" business, Traveler's has knotty pine appointed rooms and proximity to ski hills. The units are clean and economically furnished.

TWILIGHT TIME MOTEL
930 E. U.S. Hwy. 2
Ironwood, Mich.   (906) 932-3010
$

This very nice motel is locally owned, walking distance from restaurants and a movie theater and right on a snowmobile trail. Among the 20 units are family rooms that easily can sleep six.

WHITECAP MOUNTAIN RESORT
Wis. Hwy. 77   (715) 561-2776
Montreal, Wis.   (800) 933-SNOW
$-$$$$

Whitecap, an enormously popular place in the wintertime, is trying to develop its summer business by establishing a golf course and offering destination options such as boating, horseback riding and fishing. It's out in the woods, all by itself, west of Montreal; the hills have a lot of iron in them, and the only television the slope picks up on its satellite are three stations from Denver (one is The Disney Channel). Whitecap has a lively restaurant during snow season, but in summer — in 1996, anyway — you'll have to bring your own food or drive into Hurley (11 miles east) or Ironwood to eat. Lodging includes basic motel rooms with two queen-size beds and bath/shower; three- and four-bedroom condos right against the slopes with three bathrooms, sauna and hot tub; and chalets, tucked in the woods, with several bedrooms and two bathrooms. Condos and chalets have fully equipped kitchens, living rooms and dining rooms. Pets are allowed in some units.

Thunder Bay Area

Thunder Bay offers a full range of accommodations, from economy chain motels to luxurious, amenity-filled hotels and small-scale bed and breakfast inns.

According to the city's tourism department, Thunder Bay is home to more than 30 hotels and motels, with a total room capacity of approximately 1,700. Of course, if an urban experience is not your cup of tea, you'll find plenty of places to stay outside of the city. If you're seeking camping options specifically, check out our Camping and Campgrounds chapter.

A great number of lodging options exist in two main areas of Thunder Bay proper. It's helpful to know that Thunder Bay used to be two separate cities: Port Arthur in the northern end of town and Fort William in the southern. The two cities became one in 1970. So, you'll still hear and see references to both.

Old downtown Port Arthur near the waterfront and Marina Park is one of our favorite lodging areas. It's within walking distance of eclectic antique and gift shops, ethnic and continental fine restaurants, nightclubs and a shopping mall. It's also within short driving distance of several city parks, including Boulevard Lake, Centennial Park and Hillcrest Gardens.

The other area to find accommodations is near the Thunder Bay airport where Highway 61 enters the city and turns into the Lakehead Expressway and the Trans-Canada Highway 11/17 intersects with Ont. Highway 61. While this traffic-thick area is not a great place for foot travel, it does offer a number of conveniences. Several major attractions, including the Big Thunder Ski Area, Old Fort William (the world's largest reconstructed fur-trading post) and Kakabeka Falls Provincial Park, are nearby.

Expect an additional 12 percent lodging tax on your bill at Thunder Bay area accommodations. Many places offer weekend packages, and in the winter, some hotels offer packages which include either cross-country or downhill ski passes.

PRINCE ARTHUR HOTEL

17 N. Cumberland St.	(807) 345-5411
Thunder Bay, Ont.	(800) 267-2675
$$	

Smack-dab in downtown Port Arthur, this venerable 1911 hotel anchors a city block and overlooks the harbor. While the guest rooms are small and the decor rather modest, we love the views of the harbor and Sleeping Giant (see our Attractions chapter).

The Prince Arthur is a busy full-service convention hotel with banquet and meeting facilities for 200 people. Amenities include an indoor pool, sauna and whirlpool. The hotel also has its own restaurant (serving breakfast, lunch and dinner) and lounge. To walk or jog in Marina Park adjacent to the harbor, just stroll over the pedestrian crosswalk near the hotel.

OLD COUNTRY MOTEL

500 N. Cumberland St.	
Thunder Bay, Ont.	(807) 344- 2511
$	

A small, quiet motel near Boulevard Lake, the Old Country Motel has cable TV and laundry facilities and accepts small pets. Kitchenette units are available, and there's a picnic area with a gas barbecue. Old Country Motel is within walking distance of popular Boulevard Lake, a huge park area with running and in-line skating paths, picnic and playground areas, a sandy swimming beach with concessions and a miniature golf course. Downtown Port Arthur is just a few minutes drive away.

VALHALLA INN

1 Valhalla Rd.	(807) 577-1121
Thunder Bay, Ont.	(800) 964-1121
$-$$	

The Valhalla Inn is one of the more luxurious places to stay in town. It's Thunder Bay's largest conference and convention hotel, with 275 guest rooms and meeting and banquet facilities for 10 to 1,000 guests. The spacious rooms look out onto an inner garden courtyard filled with trees, flowers, walking paths and terraced sitting areas. Guest rooms include thick towels, ceramic coffee mugs and a coffee maker and breakfast brought to your room if you so desire.

The Old Rittenhouse Inn in Bayfield is an elegant bed-and-breakfast establishment.

The Valhalla Inn has two restaurants: the Nordic Dining Room for fine dining and the Timbers Restaurant for more casual fare. (Check out the Restaurants chapter for more details.) Hotel amenities include a sports and fitness center with tennis and basketball courts, a swimming pool, sauna, whirlpool and exercise equipment.

The Valhalla Inn offers competitive weekend rate packages and complimentary limousine service to the airport.

AIRLANE HOTEL

698 W. Arthur St.	(807) 577-1181
Thunder Bay, Ont.	(800) 465-5003
$$	

The award-winning Airlane Hotel features 140 guest rooms and 10 suites, full banquet services, a pool and fitness complex with sauna and whirlpool, a gift shop and the 698 Arthur's Night Club, featuring live music.

The guest rooms have in-room coffee service and plenty of shampoo and body lotion. Ask for a room facing south; you'll get a grand view of the Nor'Wester Moun-

tains. Suites include a double Jacuzzi, gas fireplace, two televisions, a VCR and a shower/steam room.

You'll also find two restaurants: the acclaimed gourmet Castillo Dining Room and the casual Ensenada Dining Room. (See our Restaurants chapter for more details.) The staff here is friendly and eager to please. Small pets are allowed in the smoking rooms.

BEST WESTERN
CROSSROADS MOTOR INN

655 Arthur St.	(807) 577-4241
Thunder Bay, Ont.	(800) 265-3253
$$	

This is your basic clean, safe room at a chain-motel kind of place, with cable TV and free coffee. The Best Western Crossroads Motor Inn offers special discounts for sports groups, senior citizens and corporate travelers. The inn was recently recognized by the Commercial Travelers Association for quality service. Sixty rooms have individual climate-control systems and parking outside each door.

COMFORT INN BY JOURNEY'S END
660 W. Arthur St.
Thunder Bay, Ont.   *(807) 475-3155*
$$

Near the airport, this two-story Comfort Inn has garnered high-quality ratings. The inn's 80 rooms include comfy recliners in which to kick back and play with the remote-control TV; hookups for your personal computer; message alert service; full-length mirror; and a free daily newspaper. Ground floor rooms feature patio doors that lead to the parking area. Pets are accepted.

Although the Comfort Inn has no restaurant on site, a continental breakfast is available for $2. You also will find dozens of places to eat along Arthur Street, many within walking distance.

BEST WESTERN NORWESTER RESORT HOTEL
2080 Ont. Hwy. 61
Thunder Bay, Ont.   *(807) 473-9123*
$$-$$$

If you're seeking a resort hotel near the city but desire rural quiet, try this Best Western. A luxurious resort hotel, the NorWester is south of Thunder Bay, with views of the striking Nor'Wester Mountains. The guest rooms are spacious and well-appointed with coffee makers and cable TVs. Second-story rooms have balconies to enjoy the view of the mountains. Five suites with fireplaces also are available. Fitness amenities include a heated indoor pool, sauna, whirlpool and exercise room.

The stunning two-story amethyst fireplace in the lounge is a famous attraction, and an on-site restaurant offers breakfast, lunch and dinner.

To get here, drive 9.2 kilometers southwest of the junction of Trans-Canada Highways 11/17 and Ont. Highway 61 at Loch Lomond Road.

UNICORN INN
R.R. #1
South Gillies, Ont.   *(807) 475- 4200*
$-$$

In a splendid valley south of Thunder Bay surrounded by the Nor'Wester Mountains, this little farmhouse and separate guest house offer an idyllic base for hiking, cross-country skiing, birding, and fishing. And for an urban fix, Thunder Bay is about a half-hour drive.

What's particularly significant about the Unicorn Inn is its gastronomic claim to fame. Innkeepers David and Arlan Nobel run a restaurant that is considered one of the top gourmet experiences in Canada. (See the Restaurants chapter for more delectable details.) Breakfast at the Unicorn Inn typically features freshly squeezed orange juice, hot scones with homemade preserves, German pan souffle with Grand Marnier (served with strawberry and honey sauce) and freshly ground Colombian coffee and a selection of teas. (Are you gasping?)

The guest rooms are cozy and bright, with pine paneling, unicorn prints, oak floors and knotty-pine beds, bunks, desks and armoires. A deluxe furnished cottage

Insiders' Tips

Looking for accommodation bargains? Midweek (Sunday through Thursday nights) is typically slow on the North Shore, resulting in more competitive prices for rooms.

is also available, with a kitchenette, king-size bed, private bath and a 10-foot bay window overlooking the fields and the mountains.

This is a no-smoking bed and breakfast inn. Call for directions to find the Unicorn Inn — they can be tricky.

WHITE FOX INN

1345 Mountain Rd. *(807) 577-3699*
Thunder Bay, Ont. *(800) 603-3699*
$$$

Just south of Thunder Bay, the White Fox Inn is renowned for its gourmet dining experience (see our Restaurants chapter). Its nine Jacuzzi suites overlook the Nor'Wester Mountains and rolling, wooded hills. The suites all have different color schemes and names, such as the Athenaise and Elise suites. The furniture is hand-carved reproductions of antiques, and most rooms have gas fireplaces, VCRs with free movies, and plush bath robes. A full breakfast is served daily.

White Fox Inn is a relatively new accommodation but has received rave reviews from many local people who consider it a great place to stay for an anniversary celebration or a honeymoon. The Frisky Fox package features an overnight stay, with champagne and a fruit tray in the room, a four course dinner the evening of check-in and a full breakfast the following morning. (See our Restaurants chapter for more food details.) Be sure to call for reservations far in advance for summer weekends.

The 4,500-acre Superior Municipal Forest, one of the largest municipal forests in the United States, is one of the best examples of a boreal and hardwood mix forest in Wisconsin. Its warm-weather hiking and biking trails become wonderful winter cross-country ski trails.

Inside
Recreation

Locals may be somewhat smug about living here. And who could blame us? After all, the fresh water of Lake Superior is some of the most beautiful in the world; the Boundary Waters Canoe Area Wilderness and the Apostle Islands National Lakeshore are a hop, skip and a jump away; and great state parks and mammoth national forests are practically in our backyards.

For that matter, we don't need to leave our backyards. Duluth has its own incredible greenways and parks, and Superior is the site of one of the largest municipal forests in the country. As in the television show "Northern Exposure," moose and black bear do occasionally wander through the Twin Ports. In fact, they've been spotted on downtown streets, in city parks and near backyard apple trees.

We're no slouches when it comes to trails either. The Superior Hiking Trail is one of the top-rated hiking trails in the country; the popular paved Willard Munger State Trail starts in West Duluth and runs through Jay Cooke State Park to Carlton; and Duluth's nationally recognized Lakewalk is a boardwalk and paved trail that hugs the shore of Lake Superior from the Canal Park district to 21st Avenue E. Thunder Bay, Ontario; Superior and Ashland, Wisconsin; and Two Harbors, Minnesota, recognizing the beauty of their lakefronts, are developing waterfront trails and parks too.

Folks around here are an active bunch. Pick up the Sunday paper. You'll notice the outdoor section is filled with club activities, reports and feature stories covering fishing, hunting, hiking, canoeing, camping and travel adventures. Because there is so much to do in the area (Duluth has become a national travel destination for many folks, attracting 3.3 million visitors in 1995), we've dedicated separate chapters to Fishing and Hunting, Winter Sports, Watersports, Camping and Campgrounds, and Parks and Forests.

Step outside and breathe deeply. Grab a picnic lunch. Put air in those bike tires. Stretch a little. Call a friend for a walk. Study those maps. Grab the binoculars. Take a drive up the shore. Try something new. Just get out and do it. Lake Superior country is wilderness country. Take advantage of it.

ATV Trails

With plenty of "snow highways" developed for snowmobiles (see our Winter Sports chapter for details), many counties are transforming their winter trails for summer use by All-Terrain Vehicles (ATVs). For information about trails along Minnesota's North Shore, contact the Superior National Forest headquarters, 515 W. First Street, Room 354, Duluth, (218) 720-5324, for trail maps and user guidelines.

Wisconsin's South Shore has an extensive ATV trail system, including the 60-mile **Tri-County Recreational Corridor Trail**, connecting Superior and Ashland. For trail maps, call (715) 372-8200. The most extensive ATV system in Wisconsin lies in Iron County near Hurley: Approximately 100 miles of trail are available as ATV routes. Hurley is also a nationally recognized snowmobile paradise. For trail maps of the Hurley area, call (715) 561-2922.

Birding

For birders working on life lists, western Lake Superior offers the strong possibility of adding quite a few rare species. More than 330 bird species have been counted within Duluth's city limits, considered the premier birding location in Minnesota. The elusive gyrfalcon has been sighted at Hawk Ridge in Duluth, and magnificent snowy owls are common winter residents near the Twin Ports' grain elevators and train yards and along the South Shore. We recommend Kim Eckert's *A Birder's Guide to Minnesota* as a reference; the book includes a county-by-county guide to more than 800 birding locations.

For more information, contact one or more of the following birding organizations: **Minnesota Ornithological Union Birding Hotline**, (218) 525-5952; **Duluth Audubon Club**, (218) 721-3065; or **North Shore Bird Club**, (218) 726-0840.

Twin Ports Area

Hawk Ridge Nature Reserve on Skyline Parkway, a mile east of Glenwood Avenue in east Duluth, is a nationally recognized area for the spring and fall migration of hawks, eagles, owls and songbirds. A well-marked series of trails leads you to great overlooks, or you can

simply drive along Skyline Parkway and pull over to watch the birds soar by. (Check out this chapter's sidebar for more Hawk Ridge information.)

Another great area for birding is Park Point, a 7-mile-long sandbar in the Duluth harbor lined with beaches. From Lake Avenue in Canal Park, cross the Aerial Lift Bridge on Minnesota Avenue and drive until the road dead-ends; park near Sky Harbor Airport. Walk the road past the airport to the trails in the wildlife preserve, which is filled with red and white pine. Migratory shorebirds, songbirds and waterfowl are common in the spring and fall. Hawks are also seen cruising along the Point.

At the end of Park Point is the natural mouth of the St. Louis River — the Superior, Wisconsin, entry for ships; across the channel lies Wisconsin Point. A combination of marsh, lake and woodland habitat makes this one of the most prominent migrant bird areas in Wisconsin. At the west end of Superior on U.S. Highway 2, take the Moccasin Mike Road. When the road splits, keep to the left on Wisconsin Point Road.

Along the South Shore

The broad marshes and estuaries of the South Shore rivers, the ample vegetation and the protected islands of the Apostle Island National Lakeshore provide habitat for a variety of species. More than 240 bird species breed and/or migrate throughout this archipelago of 22 unspoiled islands at the tip of the Bayfield Peninsula.

The Chequamegon Bay, on the South Shore of Lake Superior near Ashland, Wisconsin, has a wide variety of waterfowl habitat concentrated in a compact area. Arctic-dwelling scoters and other waterfowl migrate through here. Warblers and shorebirds can be seen in the spring and fall,

and snowy owls and bohemian waxwings in winter. A recommended reference book is *Wisconsin's Favorite Bird Haunts* by Darryl Tessen.

For additional information about birding opportunities along the South Shore, contact the **Wisconsin Society of Ornithology Birding Hotline**, (414) 352-3857; the **Chequamegon Bay Birder's Club**, (715) 373-2289; or the **Apostle Islands National Lakeshore**, (715) 779-3397.

Thunder Bay Area

The place to see birds in the Thunder Bay area is the **Thunder Cape Bird Observatory**, (807) 473-6169, in Sleeping Giant Provincial Park. The observatory conducts migratory spring and fall bird counts and bird-banding. Many of the sharp-shinned hawks and saw-whet owls banded at Thunder Cape are caught again at the Hawk Ridge banding station in Duluth. This observatory, at the tip of the Sibley Peninsula on Lake Superior, is open to the public in spring and fall.

Take Trans-Canada Highway 11/17 for 25 miles north of Thunder Bay. Turn east on Highway 587 and follow it into the park. It's an arduous 16-mile round-trip hike to the observatory, or you can get there by boat. Call ahead to make sure someone is going to be there (unless, of course, you're in the mood for a hike anyway).

There are several easily accessible birding spots in Thunder Bay. **Mission Island Marsh Conservation Area** is a wetlands restoration project with newly created islands on the waterfront in Thunder Bay. Formerly a garbage dump, it now attracts thousands of birds during spring and fall migration, including shorebirds and ducks. Viewing platforms and a boardwalk are provided. To access this area, cross the Jacknife Bridge off S. Syndicate Avenue and follow the signs.

Another popular spot for local birders is **Chippewa Park** at the south end of Thunder Bay near Mount McKay. From Canada Highway 61 take Exit 61B (City Road) and proceed to the park. Walk through the campground to the still-operative landfill near the park for bird watching (a potentially odoriferous proposition, we know, but the fowl abound).

Call or write **Thunder Bay Field Naturalists**, P.O. Box 1073, Thunder Bay, Ontario P7C4X8, (807) 345-7122, for more information about birding sites around Thunder Bay.

Duluth's Hawk Ridge: A Midwest Mecca for Bird Lovers

It starts in daylight in mid-August. Look up in the sky above Duluth. Everywhere the naked eye can see, swooping and soaring with pointed wings, are the nighthawks. Like clockwork, thousands pass, heralding the start of the fall migration. This North Shore bird highway is created when the winds meet the ridges of the Sawtooth Mountains, producing thermal air currents. Birds are funneled down Lake Superior's shoreline on these "thermals," thus avoiding the strenuous big-lake crossing.

One of the best places to see and learn about the migratory birds, particularly hawks, is at **Hawk Ridge Nature Reserve** on Skyline Parkway in east Duluth. This 300-acre preserve, owned by the city of Duluth and managed by the Duluth Audubon Club, is a wonderful area for hiking among red and white pine, birch and poplar forests as well as the winding, narrow Amity Creek and Lester River. Several miles of trails bring you to spectacular overlooks on rocky outcrops.

The fall migration has been counted and recorded since 1972. A banding station — closed to the public except by prior arrangement — traps, bands and releases owls and hawks. Hawk Ridge offers fall programs with an on-site naturalist who gives talks — often accompanied by a recently banded hawk. It's an unforgettable experience to be arms-length from the brilliant eyes, striking colors and strong talons of a northern goshawk.

It's good news that the number of bald eagles, ospreys and merlins officially counted has steadily increased over the past five years. In 1994, a record-breaking 42,000 broad-winged hawks were recorded. The number of people coming to the ridge has steadily increased too. Hawk Ridge is busiest in mid-September when bus loads of birders from the Twin Cities make their pilgrimage. After the fall colors peak in late September, you often can have the trails to yourself during the week. October is the best time to

Hawk watchers gaze skyward at Hawk Ridge.

see golden and bald eagles, kettles of red-tailed hawks and northern goshawks passing through. So grab a pair of binoculars and go to the ridge.

Weather and the time of day make a big difference in what you see. Look for birds from about 10 AM to 4 PM during the day. Listen to the National Weather Service. A sunny fall day doesn't necessarily mean great flying weather. West and northwest winds are best for thermal ridge-riding; fog, rain and east winds are the poorest conditions for bird travel. Birds hole up in bad weather, although they will precede a cold front, trying to get the heck out of Dodge — or Duluth.

You can support Hawk Ridge by becoming a member of the Friends of Hawk Ridge and adopt a saw-whet owl, a hawk, a falcon or a bald eagle through the Hawk Ridge banding program. For information, write the Hawk Ridge Nature Reserve, c/o Biology Department, University of Minnesota-Duluth, Duluth, Minn. 55812, or call (218) 525-6930.

Bocce Ball

Bocce ball, an Italian bowling game played indoors or outdoors, has gained popularity with folks who like to haul their bags of balls around, seeking appropriate terrain for a challenging game. The late former Governor of Minnesota Rudy Perpich, an Iron Range native, helped popularize bocce ball in this region. You may see people playing on Minnesota Point or in Duluth's city parks — and, of course, on the Iron Range.

Twin Ports Area

Duluth's comprehensive parks and recreation department organizes leagues for many team sports, including adult bocce ball. Call Duluth Parks and Recreation at (218) 723-3852 for a list of leagues and contacts. The **Wheeler Building**, 35th Avenue W. and Grand Avenue, West Duluth, is the site of six outdoor lighted bocce ball courts open 24 hours. League play begins in late May and continues throughout the summer.

Thunder Bay Area

In addition to boasting the largest Finnish population outside of Finland, Thunder Bay also has had a large Italian immigrant population for several generations. League bocce ball is played at the **Da Vinci Centre**, 340 Waterloo Street S., (807) 623-2415, which houses the Principe Di Piemonte, an Italian service organization. Four indoor courts are open to the public. Call to reserve a court; leagues and tournaments take precedence. The Da Vinci Centre is open daily from 9 to 1 AM.

Bowling

Twin Ports Area

The Twin Ports area has many active bowling leagues. We've highlighted a few of the bowling facilities here; call for league information and schedules. Most lanes have league bowling during weeknights and on the weekends. Generally, open bowling is available after league time and during the day.

INCLINE STATION BOWLING CENTER
601 W. Superior
Duluth, Minn.   *(218) 722-0671*
This popular downtown bowling spot has 24 lanes with automatic scoring and an on-site service bar. Next door you'll find a restaurant with full-service bar and live music. (During the Bayfront Blues Festival in August, be sure to catch one of the acts here.) The bowling center is named after the long-gone incline station where folks caught the elevated car ride to the top of Skyline Parkway.

Incline Station is open from 9 AM until midnight Monday through Friday and 9 to 1 AM Saturday and Sunday.

LANDMARK LANES
1914 Broadway
Superior, Wis.   *(218) 394-4422*
Landmark, in downtown Superior, offers 12 lanes and the latest in automated scoring. Every lane has a television monitor to watch a ball game (or whatever) while you bowl. A full bar with snack food is provided. Saturday night is the time for moonlight bowling; for the kids, there's bumper bowling. Landmark also offers a full-service trophy and pro shop on the premises.

Landmark's hours are 9 to 2 AM Monday through Friday, 8:30 to 2 AM Saturday and 11 to 2 AM Sunday.

SKYLINE BOWLING LANES
4894 Miller Trunk Hwy.
Hermantown, Minn.   *(218) 727-8555*
Over the hill past the Miller Hill Mall you'll find Skyline Bowling Lanes. Skyline offers 28 lanes with conventional scoring, a full bar and lounge and a 15-seat restaurant that serves pizza, subs and burgers. Birthday party packages and bumper bowling are available for the kids. Friday night from 11 PM to 2 AM is the time for late-night discount bowling. And volleyball is a fun alternative here in the summer.

Skyline is open from 8 AM to 11 PM Monday, Tuesday and Thursday; 8 AM to midnight Wednesday, Friday and Saturday; and noon to 11 PM Sunday.

STADIUM LANES
34th Ave. W. and Grand Ave.
Duluth   *(218) 628-1071*
Near the historic open-air Wade Stadium, home of the Duluth-Superior Dukes minor league baseball team, this west-end bowling alley was recently rebuilt after a fire. Stadium has 32 lanes and automatic scoring with televisions. There's also a bar and restaurant on the premises. Spe-

cialities include bumper bowling for the kids and midnight bowling.

Stadium Lanes is open from 11 AM to midnight Monday through Thursday, noon to 2 AM Friday and Saturday and noon to 10 PM Sunday.

VILLAGE LANES

6419 Tower Ave.
Superior *(218) 394-4436*

Village Lanes, at the south end of Superior near the city limits, has 12 lanes with automatic scoring as well as a grill and bar. Kids ages 5 to 18 can participate in the extensive Juniors bowling program here.

Village Lanes is open daily from 10 to 2 AM.

Along the North Shore

CURT'S HARBOR BOWL AND PRO SHOP

514 First Ave.
Two Harbors, Minn. *(218) 834-3630*

Curt's Harbor Bowl is one of two bowling alleys on the North Shore. Curt's offers a pro shop where you can get balls drilled. There are six lanes with manual scoring, a snack area and kid's bumper bowling. Curt's holds a 3.2 (percent alcohol) beer license.

In winter, the Harbor Bowl is open on Monday from noon to 10 PM; Tuesday from 2 to 11 PM; Wednesday, noon to 10 PM; Thursday, noon to 10 PM; Friday, noon to 10 PM; Saturday, 1 to 10 PM and Sunday, noon to midnight. In summer, it's open Monday from 3 to 6 PM; Tuesday, 5 to 9 PM; Friday from 6 to 10 PM,

Saturday from 1 to 10 PM; and Sunday from noon to 6 PM.

SILVER BOWL

97 Outer Dr.
Silver Bay, Minn. *(218) 226-4479*

Besides Curt's Harbor Bowl in Two Harbors, the Silver Bowl is the only other bowling alley on the North Shore. People travel down the shore from Grand Marais to bowl. The place is set up with six lanes and manual scoring. It's open every day from 9 AM to midnight and features a teen room with a pool table. There's bumper bowling for children. Soda pop, 3.2 beer, pizza and sandwiches are available.

Along the South Shore

RED CLIFF BOWLING LANES

Wis. Hwy. 13
Bayfield, Wis. *(715) 779-3737*

Eight lanes with manual scoring are the setup here at this lively bowling alley. It's connected to the Isle Vista Casino, so when you tire of bowling, you can gamble on something else. The full-bar lounge features live music on the weekends, and you can get snacks to full meals here, including hamburgers, pizza and steaks. Red Cliff Bowling Lanes is open morning to late night Monday through Saturday from 10 to 2 AM and Sunday from 10 AM to midnight.

SUPER BOWL LANES AND LOUNGE

532 W. Bayfield
Washburn, Wis. *(715) 373-2162*

On the main drag in Washburn, the

Traveling up the North Shore on Minn. Highway 61? If you're a Bob Dylan fan (his boyhood town is Hibbing, Minnesota), you're on the road that inspired his "Highway 61 Revisited" tune.

Insiders' Tips

Super Bowl Lanes has eight lanes with automatic scoring and bumper bowling with small 6-pound balls for kids. Pizza is available for snacking, and there's a full bar in the lounge. Friday night is karaoke night in the lounge. Super Bowl is open Monday through Thursday from 4 to 11 PM, Friday from 4 PM to midnight, Saturday from noon to 2:30 AM and Sunday from noon to 11 PM.

Curling

To an outsider, curling may appear to be a bunch of people with scruffy-looking brooms chasing an oversized hockey puck on ice. This sport is a tradition here in the North Country as well as in St. Paul.

In fact, there are several world-champion curlers in the Twin Ports, and Duluth, a curling hot spot, has hosted the Silver Broom, the international curling championship, several times.

To the uninitiated: You'll find curling wherever Scottish immigrants lived, including the Twin Ports, Thunder Bay and St. Paul, Minnesota. Scotsmen brought the sport with them from the Old Country. Evidence of this legacy is found in the actual curling stones — a special kind of granite that slides well. You can only get the genuine article from Scotland. Curling is a team sport played by folks of all ages on an indoor ice rink. It's a great spectator sport too.

To join a curling club or to learn more about curling opportunities in Minnesota's western Lake Superior region, contact any or all of the following organizations: **Duluth Curling Club**, Duluth, (218) 727-1851; **Superior Curling Club**, Superior, (715) 392-2022; **Two Harbors Curling Club**, Two Harbors, (218) 834-2664; and the **Cook County Curling Club**, Grand Marais, (218) 387-9031.

Thunder Bay is another veritable curling hot spot. Like Duluth and Superior, Thunder Bay is home to world-champion curling teams. The city has four excellent curling rink facilities: **Fort William Curling and Athletic Club**, 218 N. Vickers Street, (807) 622-5377; **Kakabeka Falls Curling Club**, R.R. 5, Highway 17, Kakabeka Falls, (807) 939-1391; **Port Arthur Curling Club**, 214 Egan Street, (807) 345-9552; and **Thunder Bay Country Club Limited**, R.R. 17, 1055 Oliver Road, (807) 345-8225.

Mountain Biking

The North and South shores of Lake Superior host some glorious off-road mountain biking trails. Make sure the trails you ride are open to mountain biking. Access is a hot issue and many areas around the United States are being closed to mountain biking. Problems — genuine or perceived — with trail erosion, on-trail conflicts with hikers and equestrians and a few bad apples ignoring trail etiquette have prompted restricted access by bikers.

Remember the Rules of the Road (as outlined by the International Mountain Biking Association):

1) Ride on open trails only.

2) Leave no trace and stay on the trail.

3) Control your bicycle.

4) Always yield the trail and make your presence known in advance; don't startle others.

5) Never spook animals. Give animals, such as horses, extra room and time to adjust to you.

6) Plan ahead by knowing your equipment, your ability and the area in which you're riding. Wear a helmet, keep your machine in good condition and carry necessary supplies for changes in weather or other conditions.

For a comprehensive look at mountain biking trails in northern Minnesota and Wisconsin, we recommend *The North Country Guide to Mountain Biking*, published by White Pines Press.

For the latest news on local mountain biking trails and races, call the following Twin Ports sports equipment stores: **Ski Hut**, Duluth, (218) 724-8525; **Twin Ports Cyclery**, Duluth, (218) 722-0106; or any of **Trek & Trail's** three locations — in Duluth, (218) 722-1027, the headquarters in Bayfield, Wisconsin, and in Ironwood, Michigan, (800) 354-8735. On the North Shore, in Grand Marais, contact **Pincushion Mountain Bed and Breakfast**, (218) 387-1276 or (800) 542-1226, or **Superior North Outdoor Center**, (218) 387-2186. In Thunder Bay, contact **Fresh Air Experience**, (807) 623-9393.

Twin Ports Area

While people ride mountain bikes on many of Duluth's city trails along the creeks, these trails can be rather crowded with runners and hikers during nice weather. But some of the trails in east Duluth, including the **Amity Creek Trail** on Skyline Parkway and the trails by the ski area at Chester Bowl Park on Chester Parkway, are worth checking out.

To reach the challenging **Mission Creek Trail**, in the Fond du Lac neighborhood in western, take Minn. Highway 23 to 131st Avenue W. Turn right at Fond du Lac and follow the road until it dead-ends. Mission Creek can be a wet, slippery trail.

We like the trails at Jay Cooke State Park on Minn. Highway 110 south of Duluth. Choose from the **Triangle Trail**, **Four Bay Lake Trail** and the **Oak Trail**, with ridge-top views of the St. Louis River. Use the paved **Willard Munger**

State Trail east of Carlton as an artery to these state park trails. These trails are also used by horseback riders and hikers, so be aware of the traffic.

Across the St. Louis River, the **Superior Municipal Forest**, south of Superior on 28th Street, offers some challenging mountain biking on cross-country ski trails. Check out the advanced yellow loop of the ski trail system. This sometimes soggy trail travels out and back on a heavily wooded peninsula into a bay of the St. Louis River, offering great river scenery with a few ups and downs.

The new **Lutsen Mountain Bike Park**, part of the Lutsen Ski Resort complex on Minn. Highway 61, offers 18 miles of trails with great views of Lake Superior. Access this area via Lutsen Mountain's gondola ski lift. A fee is charged to use the trails and the gondola lift. The **Lutsen Mountain Bike Festival**, a three-division race, and the **Moose Mountain Bike Classic** are held here in the summer. Call (218) 663-7281 for more information.

The Pincushion Mountain Ski Area, near Grand Marais, has moderate to challenging trails, all with great views. To get here, drive 2 miles north of Grand Marais on the **Gunflint Trail**. Be alert for hikers. The **Superior Hiking Trail** passes through here on a section of the **Pincushion Trail**.

Along the South Shore

Two major South Shore trail systems, the **Mines and Pines Mountain Bike Trail System** that originates in the Ironwood/Hurley area and the Chequamegon Area Mountain Biking Association's (CAMBA) trails, provide comprehensive mountain biking opportunities in northern Wisconsin and western Upper Peninsula Michigan. These trail systems are rated for difficulty based on steepness, length and trail surface. Trails are marked and, of course, afford some great scenery.

The CAMBA trails are actually south of the official South Shore near Drummond, Cable, Hayward and Seeley. Many are in the Chequamegon National Forest. For a complete set of maps, write to CAMBA, P.O. Box 141, Cable, Wisconsin 54821.

The CAMBA **Rock Lake Trail** is our personal favorite: a continuous roller coaster ride on a narrow, challenging track. It winds through the Chequamegon National Forest (7.5 miles east of Cable on County Road M). The Rock Lake Trail is a wonderful cross-country ski route in the winter. Ample parking and U.S. Forest Service maps are available at the trailhead.

The **Mines and Pines Trail** wanders through the forests of Michigan's Upper Peninsula and northeastern Wisconsin, including the Ottawa National Forest. Three main trail systems — Iron County Trails, the Pomeroy/Henry Lake Mountain Bike Complex and Ehlco Tract Bike Complex — offer varying degrees of difficulty and solitude. For map information, call (715) 561-2922.

Thunder Bay Area

Many people combine hiking and mountain biking at **Sleeping Giant Provincial Park**, on the 24-mile-long, 6-mile-wide Sibley Peninsula. A common routine is to bike the easy but long hiking trail to the base of the Sleeping Giant — a huge rock mesa — and then hike and climb up. Take Trans-Canada Highway 11/17 for 25 miles north of Thunder Bay. Turn east on Highway 587 and proceed into the park.

A popular in-town mountain biking area is at the **Big Thunder Sports Park**, (807) 475-4402, south of Thunder Bay on Canada Highway 61. The 1995 Nordic World Ski Championships were held at this challenging cross-country ski area. You can bike up the hills or take the chairlift. The park is open weekends for mountain biking and hiking; call ahead about hours. Helmets are required. You must furnish your own gear.

Health and Fitness Clubs

While the Twin Ports (Duluth and Superior) and Thunder Bay don't have the scores of franchise health clubs found in bigger cities, we are fortunate to have major sports and health complexes as well as a number of locally owned fitness clubs. These indoor steamy-warm sanctuaries are essential for cabin-fever relief during our long, cold winters — and even on one of our cooler-by-the-Lake summer days. Buy an inexpensive day pass, ranging from $3 to $7, at one of these centers and check out the ambiance and amenities.

Twin Ports Area

CENTER
FOR PERSONAL FITNESS

Fifth Ave. E. and Second St.
Duluth, Minn.   *(218) 725-5400*

This is the premier health and fitness center in the Twin Ports. It's part of the Miller-Dwan Medical Center complex and includes a rehabilitation center. Designed on two stories, you can walk or jog around the indoor track on a balcony overlooking the swimming pool. Expansive windows afford a view of Lake Superior and the downtown skyline. The latest in equipment includes NordicTrack equipment, rowing and bicycling machines, a weight room, coed whirlpool, men's and women's saunas and an aerobics studio with a wooden floor. Day passes are available.

A mixed crowd works out here, ranging from weekend and once-in-a-while warriors to serious weightlifters and fitness buffs. Hours are Monday through Friday from 5:30 AM to 10 PM and Saturday and Sunday from 7 AM to 6:30 PM. Child day care is available Tuesdays and Thursdays from 4:30 to 7:30 PM and Saturdays from 9 AM to noon.

PHASE II

404 W. Superior St.
Duluth, Minn.   *(218) 727-4644*

This downtown club attracts a twenty-something and early thirty-something crowd. You won't find a pool but you can enjoy the coed whirlpool and sauna. Amenities include various exercise machines, free weights, Nautilus, tanning booths and a giant exercise studio for a variety of classes, including step aerobics, Jazzercize and karate. Day care is provided with advance reservations. Day passes are available. Hours are Monday

through Friday from 6 AM to 9 PM, Saturday from 9 AM to 6 PM and Sunday from noon to 6 PM.

LINCOLN PARK ATHLETIC CLUB

2215 W. Superior
Duluth, Minn.   *(218) 727-5039*

Your first visit is free at Duluth's newest health and fitness center. A mix of 18-and-older folks take advantage of the new amenities here. Nearly 20 stations of excercise equipment (including new Trotter Galileo stations) provide a full-body workout, and the cardiovascular area has simulating stairs, treadmills and stationary and recument bikes. You can opt between a whirlpool, cold plunge or swimming pool as well as a sauna, steam room or an inhalatin room. Lincoln Park Athletic Club also has tanning beds, aerobic and aquatic classes for adults, family activities and personal training programs. Memberships can be arranged for a month, quarter, half-year or year, and there also is a couple's rate. The club is easily accessed from I-35 and features plenty of free parking. Lincoln Park Athletic Club is open from 6 AM to 10 PM Monday through Saturday and noon to 6 PM Sunday.

YMCA

302 W. First St.
Duluth, Minn.   *(218) 722-4745*

Here at the Y, aerobics are taught and volleyball and basketball are played in what is still called "the gym." The Y is known for its swimming programs, including water aerobics, and offers men's and women's saunas and a coed whirlpool. The Cardiovascular Center has free weights, Nautilus, treadmills and the standard lineup of exercise machines simulating stairs, skiing, biking and rowing. An indoor running track, racquetball and squash courts are popular with the downtown professional crowd. Day passes are available, and day care is provided. The Y is open Monday through Friday from 5 AM to 9:20 PM, Saturday from 7 AM to 6:20 PM and Sunday from 1 to 4:20 PM.

BODYWORKS

5324 E. Superior St.
Duluth, Minn.   *(218) 525-2073*

Bodyworks is in eastern Duluth near the Lakeside neighborhood. So if you live in eastern Duluth and use distance as a reason not to workout, Bodyworks forces you to look for other excuses.

This fitness center attracts a mixed crowd with a lot of neighborhood folks. Facilities include an aerobics solarium with one of the widest selections of Nautilus equipment in town (including lower-back strengthening machines), free weights, a StairMaster, NordicTrack, treadmills, rowing machines and Lifecycles. A coed sauna and four tanning beds are notable amenities. No day care available. Day passes are available.

Bodyworks is open Monday, Wednesday and Friday from 6 AM to 9 PM; Tuesday and Thursday from 9 AM to 9 PM; Saturday from 10 AM to 5 PM; and Sunday from noon to 5 PM.

SUPREME COURTS AND HEALTH SPA

1420 Oakes
Superior, Wis.   *(715) 392-9860*

Supreme Courts has four racquetball courts and a pro shop. This facility maintains a separate aerobics studio with a wooden floor as well as a free-weights room. The cardiovascular training area has Nautilus equipment, stair climbers and aerobics cycles. Men's and women's separate saunas, whirlpool, and tanning beds round out the amenities. An informal sweats-and-T-shirt crowd is typical here. Supreme Courts is open Monday through Friday from 6 AM to 10 PM, Saturday from 8 AM to 9 PM and Sunday from 9 AM to 9 PM.

Along the North Shore

GRAND MARAIS MUNICIPAL POOL

Eighth Ave. W.
Grand Marais   *(218) 387-1275*

After a day of cross-country skiing, the Grand Marais Municipal Pool is a pleasant and inexpensive place to warm up, suds down and steam out. The pool is open daily and is a regular gathering place for local folk. Call for specific hours. Amenities include a sauna, whirlpool, a swimming pool and a wading pool for the kids. One admission is good for all day. Day passes are available.

TWO HARBORS HIGH SCHOOL

Fourth Ave. and Fifth Street
Two Harbors, Minn.   *(218) 834-8201*

The swimming pool at the Two Harbors High School is available for public swimming from 6:30 to about 8 AM. Schedules and availability change depending on school meet schedules and the season, so check with the high school.

ation facility vary greatly and are subject to change, so please call in advance.

Along the South Shore

CHEQUAMEGON COURT CLUB
419 Chapple Ave.
Ashland, Wis.   *(715) 682-8590*

Visitors and travelers are welcome to the locally owned Chequamegon Court Club in the historic former Chicago Northwestern Railroad Depot. The club has two racquetball courts and two sand volleyball courts and hosts wallyball (volleyball played on a racquetball court — the walls are in play), volleyball and racquetball leagues and tournaments. Other amenities include two tanning beds, a free-weight room, Cybex weight-training equipment and cardiovascular workout machines, including treadmills, three Stairmasters, a Lifestep, three NordicTracks, a LifeRower, two Lifecycles, a VersaClimber and four Panasonic stationary bikes. Aerobics classes are taught here. Day passes are available. Day care is occasionally offered — call first.

Hours are Monday through Friday from 5:30 AM to 11 PM, Saturday from 8 AM to 10 PM and Sunday from 10 AM to 9 PM.

BAYFIELD POOL
AND RECREATION FACILITY
Broad and Wilson
Bayfield, Wis.   *(715) 779-5408*

Nestled in the picturesque downtown area, this modern community center has an Olympic-size pool, a coed whirlpool, a lounge and kitchenette for group activities and spacious locker-room facilities with showers. Two racquetball courts and a fitness room with NordicTrack, rowing and biking equipment are also available. The Bayfield Pool is open year round. You can buy daily punch cards or a membership. Hours and rates for the pool and the recre-

Thunder Bay Area

CANADA GAMES SPORTS COMPLEX
420 Winnipeg Ave.
Thunder Bay, Ont.   *(807) 625-3311*

The Canada Games Sports Complex is the place to go in Thunder Bay for swimming or working out. It's also a popular place for parents with young children. Parents like the extensive day-care services, and kids love the Thunderslide in the swimming pool.

Built in 1981 for the Canada Summer Games, the complex has become a year-round community center for aquatics and other fitness and recreation activities. The Olympic-size swimming pool is one of Canada's largest. Swimming lessons are offered by qualified instructors.

Four squash and two racquetball courts are available for year-round action. A spectators lounge allows fans to enjoy a bird's-eye view of the tournaments held here in the winter. The complex offers drop-in fitness classes and a variety of aerobics classes.

The comprehensive fitness center has a fully equipped weight room with Cybex weight-training equipment. The Multi Training Area has more than 20 aerobic stations, including Stairmasters, Windrace Bikes, rowing machines and a skating machine.

Day passes are available. Hours are Monday through Thursday from 6:30 AM to 9 PM, Friday from 6:30 AM to 9 PM and Saturday and Sunday from 8 AM to 9 PM.

CONFEDERATION
COLLEGE FITNESS CENTRE
1480 Nakina Dr.   *(807) 475-6398*

Open daily, the Confederation College Fitness Centre is another top-notch public facility in Thunder Bay. The Fitness Centre is the place to go for indoor and outdoor tennis. You'll find plenty of other on-court action here too, including squash, basketball, volleyball and badminton. A Nautilus strength training center and an exercise room with Stairmasters, Lifecycles, rowers and NordicTrack Ski Trainers round out the calorie-burning options. The center has separate saunas for men and women, and the men get a steam room too. Day care is provided, and day passes are available. The Fitness Centre's hours are Monday through Thursday from 7 AM to 11 PM, Friday from 7 AM to 10 PM, Saturday from 7:30 AM to 7 PM and Sunday from 9 AM to 9 PM.

Hiking and Walking

So many trails, so little time. We've just scratched the surface of hiking and walking possibilities here. If you like to explore trails on day hikes, backpack rugged trails for adventure and solitude, or enjoy an evening walk next to Lake Superior, watching the ships as well as the people watching the ships, you've come to the right place.

Twin Ports Area

In **Duluth**, you'll find moderate to challenging hiking along the many rivers and creeks that feed Lake Superior. Running through deep, rocky gorges lined with giant red and white pine and hardwoods, these greenways are part of what makes living in Duluth so wonderful.

In eastern Duluth, the **Lester Park Trail** winds along Amity Creek and the Lester River, crossing many footbridges. An easy trail of less than a mile long, start your hike from the west side of Lester

River Road, about one block north of Superior Street.

The **Congdon Park Trail** meanders for 1.5 miles along Tischer Creek, with its many waterfalls and lovely cascades. You can park on Superior Street at 32nd Avenue E. to start this easy trail.

Another popular hiking route is the **Chester Park Trail**, running from Fourth Street and 14th Avenue E. to beyond Skyline Parkway. Access the Chester Park Trail from the east at 19th Avenue E. and Kent Road, or from the west from Chester Parkway to Skyline Parkway. This can be a challenging trail, as it's prone to washouts.

In western Duluth, the **Western Waterfront Trail** winds along the marshes and bluffs of the St. Louis River for 5 miles. It's a great trail for birding, and you may spot a bald eagle or osprey winging by. It's also an easy trail — designed for walking and biking. Access the trailhead directly across from the Duluth Zoo on Grand Avenue. Plenty of parking is available in a designated lot.

The **Willard Munger State Trail** (see our Willard Munger sidebar in the Winter Sports chapter) parallels Grand Avenue and crosses near the designated parking lot for the Western Waterfront Trail. It runs all the way to Hinckley, but many people start in West Duluth and walk, run, bike or in-line skate up the paved trail to catch a glimpse of the great vistas of the St. Louis River valley. If you turn around and come back to West Duluth, your reward is the gentle but continuous downhill ride along this former railroad bed. If you keep going, the trail continues to climb, winding away from the St. Louis River Valley and running through Jay Cooke State Park to Carlton. It's about a 15-mile journey from West Duluth to Carlton.

Mission Creek Trail, in the Fond du Lac neighborhood of western Duluth, follows the original western end of Skyline Parkway. Take Minn. Highway 23 south to 131st Avenue W. Turn right at the Fond du Lac and follow the road until it dead-ends. Mission Creek is a steep trail and can be challenging when wet. It's about 3.2 miles long and generally takes about four hours to complete.

At the end of Minnesota Point, the **Park Point Trail** runs through a nature preserve of red and white pine forest and along a sandy path to the ship canal, passing the Minnesota Point lighthouse, a local landmark, on the way. The sand makes walking difficult, so plan on three to four hours to hike this 4-mile trail. The trail begins just past the Sky Harbor Airport. To get there, take Lake Avenue to Canal Park, then follow Minnesota Avenue over the Aerial Lift Bridge until it dead-ends at the airport.

For ship-watching and strolling, the handicapped-accessible **Lakewalk** is a popular promenade for Duluthians and visitors. Walk, jog, bike or skate the 6-mile round trip on a boardwalk and paved trail that hugs the curve of the lakeshore from the Canal Park district to 26th Avenue E.

You can access the Lakewalk from a number of places. Most folks start at Canal Park, but you can cross the pedestrian bridges (marked by signs) from various points along Superior Street in downtown Duluth to reach Lake Place Park and the Lakewalk. The Fitger's Brewery Complex on Superior Street has several sets of stairs to the shore, and the Rose Garden near Leif Erikson Park has bridges that connect with the trail. Parking and bathrooms are available at 21st Avenue E and near the Rose Garden.

The beautifully landscaped, winding path is dotted with wooden benches and picnic tables, pine and birch trees, hardy black-eyed Susans, rugosa roses and aza-leas. The Lakewalk will take you past two parks and a formal garden: Lake Place Park, with its picnic area, wind shelters for lake-watching in stormy weather, and sculpture; and Leif Erikson Park where a replica of a historic Viking ship was restored. If you're lucky enough to be here during Duluth's short but glorious summer, you'll notice lots of people bending to sniff the flowers in the lovely formal rose garden. Many of the rose beds are grouped by color — a true visual feast. (See our Parks and Forests chapter for additional information.)

Be on the lookout for tiny paths and stone steps dropping down to cozy, private beaches on the lake. You'll see people letting go of their work ethic for awhile — sitting and reading a book, staring at the lake or playing with rocks along the shores.

Check out the series of commissioned international sculpture, fountains and murals in **Canal Park**, **Lake Place Park** and along the **Lakewalk**. Kids love to cross the stepping stones of the "Fountain of the Wind" in Canal Park, featuring a giant fish blowing streams of water. One of our favorites is a bronze sculpture called "Green Bear" in Lake Place Park, a gift from Duluth's sister city of Petrozavodsk, Russia. A self-guided walking-tour brochure for Duluth's waterfront art is available at Endion Station.

Superior is home to one of the largest municipal forests in the United States, the 4,500-acre **Superior Municipal Forest**. Called one of the best examples of a boreal and hardwood mix forest in Wisconsin, the forest borders the bays of the St. Louis River and mouth of the Pokegama River. Hiking and biking trails in the warm weather months become wonderful winter cross-country ski trails, running through woodlands and wet-

Superior Hiking Trail

Called one of the nation's "ten prime trails that leave all the others in the dust," by *Backpacker* magazine, the Superior Hiking Trail is a foot traveler's delight. The 200-mile trail begins just above Two Harbors, Minnesota, and ends near Hovland, Minnesota, at Jackson Lake close to the Canadian border. The trail, divided into 36 sections, has access points via county roads, parks and towns, and is well-marked by trailhead signs with maps. The gradient is remarkable; within 100 miles, the trail climbs up and down 14,000 feet.

The Superior Hiking Trail offers something for everybody: day hikes with easy access from North Shore towns and campgrounds; overnight trips for the weekend backpacker; month-long odysseys covering the entire trail; and the luxurious option of hiking during the day and riding a shuttle back to a lodge or bed and breakfast inn at day's end.

The trail was originally developed in 1987 with funding from the Minnesota Department of Natural Resources. In partnership with the DNR, the nonprofit Superior Hiking Trail Association was created to build and maintain the trail. Today, the trail association is 1,570 members strong, with approximately half of its members hailing from the Twin Cities and others from as far away as Alaska.

Trail maintenance and bridge-building is handled by a core group of 100 volunteers and recreation groups — the North Shore Rotary Club, the Sierra Club, the Voyageur Outbound School, the Women's Outdoor Network and others — who adopt and take care of specific trail sections and campsites. According to Nancy Odden, president of the Association, "It's easy to get money to build trails. But to get money to maintain trails is difficult. We rely on members to keep the trails in shape." Part-time seasonal staff also work on trail maintenance.

Photo: Sam Cook

A hiker pauses to gaze out over the headwaters of the Poplar River from the Superior Hiking Trail. The trail winds through the Sawtooth Mountains along the North Shore of Lake Superior and will eventually extend from Duluth to the Canadian border.

The trail runs through private, state and federal land. The cooperation of 23 land owners in providing access for the trail was critical in the trail's creation. Seven state parks including Gooseberry Falls, Split Rock, Tettegouche, Crosby Manitou, Temperance River, Cascade River and Judge Magney (see our Parks and Forests chapter for details about these parks) help link the trail up and down the North Shore. The Superior National Forest, Finland State Forest and Pat Bayle State Forest also host sections of the trail.

Trail features include 39 designated campsites, with 18 more planned for 1996. There are 36 major bridges, including a single-cable suspension bridge over the Baptism River. Dozens of split-log bridges provide a dry path for every water crossing.

The indispensable *Guide to the Superior Hiking Trail* is edited and compiled by the Superior Hiking Trail Association. It's available by mail and at bookstores, North Shore retailers and the association office. The Superior Hiking Trail Association offers, among other things, annual group hikes, backpacking trips and winter snowshoe outings.

The Superior Hiking Trail Association Office on Minn. Highway 61 in Two Harbors is open to the public for information, gift-shop items and the latest news on the trail. Peak-season (May 1 through November 1) hours are Monday through Friday, 9 AM to 5 PM, Saturday from 10 AM to 4 PM and Sunday from noon to 4 PM. Off-peak hours are Monday through Friday from 9 AM to 5 PM. Call the Association at (218) 834-2700 or write Superior Hiking Trail Association, P.O. Box 4, Two Harbors, Minnesota 55616.

lands. The main trailhead access is on 28th Street south of downtown Superior.

Along the North and South Shores

SUPERIOR HIKING TRAIL

The North Shore is home to the **Superior Hiking Trail**, one of the top 10 hiking trails in the country, according to *Backpacker* magazine. Beginning east of Two Harbors, the Superior Hiking Trail loosely follows the spine of the Sawtooth Mountains up the shore of Lake Superior for 200 miles. When complete, it will reach the Minnesota-Ontario border. (See this chapter's sidebar for more information.)

Day hikes are a popular way to explore sections of the trail. Don't worry about getting lost. The Superior Hiking Trail is consistently well-marked and well-maintained. But do wear sturdy shoes, carry water and snacks, and bring warm clothing and rain gear.

Here's a sampling of the day hikes recommended by the *Superior Hiking Trail Association Guide* as an introduction to the trail. The **Mount Trudee** hike begins at the Tettegouche State Park Trail Center near the park campground. This is a challenging hike, approximately 6 miles round trip, to Mount Trudee where rugged cliff tops overlook the Palisade Creek Valley, alpine lakes and Lake Superior.

Another hike with breathtaking views is the **Carlton Peak** hike, which begins at the Britton Peak trailhead and parking area at the crest of the hill on the Sawbill Trail (County Road 2) above Tofte. Hike 2 miles to the summit of Carlton Peak (4 miles round trip), a granite rock dome affording panoramic views. This high point was the site of a fire tower until the 1950s.

If you desire more remote and mysterious surroundings, try the **Devil Track River Canyon** hike. It starts northeast of Grand Marais at Wood's Creek, crossing about a mile uphill from Minn. Highway 61. It's about a half-mile walk to the deepest canyon in Minnesota. You can walk from 2 to 6 miles along the canyon rim before returning.

For shore-level lake views, the **Lake Superior Walk** is the only section of the Superior Hiking Trail that follows the shoreline of Lake Superior. The trail crosses Minn. Highway 61 just southwest of Judge C.R. Magney State Park and follows a cobblestone beach for 1.5 miles.

STATE PARKS

All of the Minnesota and Wisconsin state parks have terrific, well-marked hiking trails, most of which follow the river gorges featured in the parks. The Superior Hiking Trail runs through all of the Minnesota state parks on the North Shore, except Grand Portage, sharing trails and bridges with paths within these parks.

The **Porcupine Mountains State Wilderness Area** in western Upper Peninsula Michigan has miles of trails that are popular with backpackers who set out to explore the interior of this pristine, old-growth mountainous forest. Check with the ranger station or visitors center at each of these parks for maps and directions, or see our Parks and Forests and Camping and Campgrounds chapters or more information.

NATIONAL FORESTS

Three national forests — Superior National Forest on Minnesota's North Shore, the Chequamegon National Forest on the South Shore of Wisconsin and the Ottawa

National Forest in Upper Peninsula Michigan — offer miles of hiking trails. Keep in mind that trail access in national forests is open to a multitude of users — including ATVers, horseback riders and mountain bikers — so it's likely your hiking trail may be used for more than just pedestrian traffic. Guides to U.S. Forest trail systems are available at district ranger stations or U.S. Forest Service headquarters, including **Superior National Forest District Headquarters**, 515 W. First Street, Room 354, Duluth, (218) 720-5324; **Chequamegon National Forest - Washburn Ranger District**, 113 E. Bayfield Street (Wis. Highway 13), Washburn, Wisconsin, (715) 373-2667; and **Ottawa National Forest District Headquarters**, 2100 E. Cloverland Drive, Ironwood, Michigan, (906) 932-1330.

Thunder Bay Area

In town, local folks enjoy walking the trails in Boulevard Lake Park, in the north end of Thunder Bay. The lovely **Boulevard Lake**, created by a dam across the Current River, is the jewel setting for 182 acres of forest and maintained parkland. You can get to the park from N. Algoma or N. Cumberland streets.

Another favorite local spot is **Centennial Park** (and its **Trowbridge Falls**), also near the Current River and about 15 minutes from anywhere in town. This city park features 12 miles of nature trails for hiking that lead through the woods and along the river. You can get to Centennial Park by exiting from Trans-Canada Highway 11/17 via Hodder Avenue to Arundel Street.

For wilderness hiking, the trails of **Sleeping Giant Provincial Park** on the Sibley Peninsula are incredible. The 38 miles of trails are a backpacker's paradise.

A sailor tends to a spinnaker. Duluth's Aerial Lift Bridge is in the background.

Sleeping Giant features diverse terrain, including the steepest cliffs in Ontario, as well as alpine lakes, northern boreal forests and wetlands; all are accessible by the well-developed trail system. Take Trans-Canada Highway 11/17 north of Thunder Bay for 25 miles. Turn east on Ont. Highway 587, which leads into the park.

The **Thunder Bay Hiking Association** produces a comprehensive trail guide to the entire Thunder Bay area. You can buy one at **Fresh Air Experience**, 311 Victoria Avenue, (807) 623-9393.

Horseback Riding

Twin Ports Area

Jay Cooke State Park on Minn. Highway 210 near Carlton, south of Duluth, allows horses on 10 miles of trails, including the scenic **Oak Trail**. Contact the park at (218) 384-4610.

Along the North Shore

The **North Shore State Trail**, managed by the Minnesota Department of Natural Resources, covers 170 miles from Duluth to Grand Marais. Built on an old railroad grade (c. 1898), the trail is used by snowmobilers in the winter and for the **John Beargrease Dog Sled** race in January (see our Annual Events chapter for details). Fifty miles of this trail, from Finland to Grand Marais, are open to horseback riders. Contact the Minnesota Department of Natural Resources, (800) 766-6000, for guides and maps.

Guided horseback trips for all skill levels are offered by the **Village Homestead Stables**, (218) 663-7241, on Mountain Road near Lutsen, Minnesota, on the North Shore. The horse trails wander through the forests near Moose Mountain and the Poplar River Valley. Overnight backpacking trips can be scheduled as well as breakfast and lunch trips of two to three hours.

Along the South Shore

On the South Shore, the **Smith Rapids Horse Campground**, in the Chequamegon National Forest near Fifield in Price County, offers horseback riding on 80 miles of trail. Contact the **Chequamegon National Forest** at (715) 762-2461.

In-line Skating

Twin Ports Area

In Duluth, you can rent Rollerblades at **Twin Ports Cyclery**, (218) 722-0106, on Lake Avenue in Canal Park and take off from there. Though frenetic in peak summer months, Canal Park is point of departure for in-line skaters. Wheel out and back 5 miles along Minnesota Avenue on Park Point and connect with the Lakewalk for a round-trip of 6 miles, including one action-filled, cliffside hill near Leif Erikson Park.

The **Willard Munger State Trail** in West Duluth is *the* trail for challenging in-line skating. This former railroad grade — now converted to multiuse asphalt-paved path for bikers, walkers and in-line skaters — climbs the St. Louis River Valley to afford views of wide vistas of the river and Lake Superior and continues on for 15 miles to Carlton. You can rent Rollerblades (and bikes) at the **Willard Munger Inn and Coffee Shop**, 624-4814, on Grand Avenue.

Along the South Shore

On Wisconsin's South Shore, please note that in-line skating is not allowed in Ashland, but you can roll around on the streets of Bayfield where several rather daunting hills lead down to the lake. There,

you can roll onto the Madeline Island Ferry and skate the back roads of old LaPointe on Madeline Island.

Thunder Bay Area

In Thunder Bay, a popular place for in-line skating is around Boulevard Lake on the Current River. You can get to the park from N. Algoma or N. Cumberland streets.

Sports Leagues

A few towns in the Lake Superior region have well-developed and organized league systems for both kids and adults. Departments with extensive league programs include the **Duluth Parks and Recreation Department**, 330 City Hall, (218) 723-3852; **Superior Parks and Recreation Department**, 1409 Hammond Avenue, (715) 394-0270; **Grand Marais Recreation Area**, Eighth Avenue W., (218) 387-1712; and **Thunder Bay Community Services Department — Recreation**, 500 Donald Street E., (807) 625-2351. For league events — including baseball, softball, basketball, football, volleyball, soccer, bocce, horseshoes, hockey, tennis and a host of other activities — contact the respective city recreation department in your area.

Outdoor-Recreation Resources, Programs and Outfitters

Twin Ports Area

UNIVERSITY OF MINNESOTA-DULUTH OUTDOOR PROGRAM
University of Minnesota-Duluth
121 Sports and Health Center
10 University Dr.
Duluth, Minn. (218) 726-6533

The well-established UMD Outdoor Program offers reasonably priced classes, trips and workshops for community members as well as students. The **Canoe and Kayak Institute** teaches sea kayaking, whitewater kayaking and canoeing, and flatwater canoeing, using the St. Louis River as a base. The **Vertical Pursuits Climbing School** offers an indoor climbing wall and rock-climbing classes at North Shore locations. Extended adventure trips, day trips and skill workshops — including map and compass basics, survival skills and situational leadership — are available.

Along the North Shore

WOLF RIDGE
ENVIRONMENTAL LEARNING CENTER
230 Cranberry Rd.
Finland, Minn.   (218) 353-7414

Wolf Ridge is a nationally recognized environmental education center that works with 4th through 7th graders. Adult workshops and related trips focus on activities such as dog sledding, snowshoe making, winter camping, photography and fly fishing. A family camping program and Elderhostel classes for grandparents with their grandchildren are also part of the center's programming.

Along the South Shore

TREK & TRAIL
222 Rittenhouse Ave.
Bayfield, Wis.   (800) 354-8735

Trek & Trail is a well-established outfitter and outdoor retailer. A comprehensive catalog of outdoor learning adventures is offered, including a range of activities from sea kayaking to dog sledding — all taught by experienced and certified guides and instructors. Trek & Trail is headquartered in Bayfield near the Apostle Islands and has additional retail stores in Duluth, 824 Minnesota Avenue, (218) 722-1027,

and Ironwood, Michigan, at 174 E. Michigan Avenue, (800) 354-8735.

Thunder Bay Area

FRESH AIR EXPERIENCE
311 Victoria Ave.   (807) 623-9393

This outdoor retailer is a good local source of information about mountain biking, hiking, cross-country skiing and camping in the Thunder Bay area. Also ask about various cycling, hiking and skiing club activities.

WILD WATERS NATURE TOURS
AND EXPEDITIONS LIMITED
R.R. 14, Dog Lake Rd.   (807) 767-2022

This place is a great source for canoes, kayaks and information about regional excursions. Owner Bruce Hyer knows the flatwater and whitewater of western Ontario well and can advise and guide you accordingly. Wild Waters is about 15 miles from Thunder Bay off Dawson Road. Call before you drop by.

Outdoor Adventures for Women

WOODSWOMEN
25 W. Diamond Lake Rd.
Minneapolis, Minn. 55419   (612) 822-3809

The Twin Cities-based, nonprofit Woodswomen organization offers summer and winter adventure travel around the world as well as outdoor leadership and skill-building programs for women of all ages. Programs include winter camping in the Boundary Waters Canoe Area, dogsledding in the Superior National Forest and whitewater canoeing on the Brule River in Wisconsin.

TREK & TRAIL
222 Rittenhouse Ave.
Bayfield, Wis.   (800) 334-8735

This commercial outfitter and adven-

Photo: Duluth News-Tribune

A walk through Lake Place Park in downtown Duluth is an ideal way to experience summer.

ture-travel company includes a women's program that focuses on sea-kayaking and hiking trips in the beautiful Apostle Islands.

WOMEN'S OUTDOOR NETWORK

c/o University of Minnesota Duluth Outdoor Program
10 University Dr.
Duluth, Minn.   *(218) 726-6533*

This active women's group coordinates winter and summer sports programs in the Twin Ports area, including skiing, hiking, camping and outdoor skills programs.

Rock Climbing

Rock climbing is a highly skilled, technical sport. Although not risk-free, it can be a relatively safe sport with the proper equipment and training. The sheer rock cliffs of Minnesota's North Shore and Ontario's Thunder Bay area make for challenging climbing opportunities. Hot places to climb are Palisade Head and Shovel Point in Tettegouche State Park on the North Shore, the Sibley Peninsula in Thunder Bay and Ely's Peak in Duluth off the Midway Road.

If you're interested in learning to climb, the **Vertical Pursuits School of Climbing,**

(218) 726-6553, provided by the Outdoor Program at the University of Minnesota in Duluth, offers classes and an indoor climbing wall for the public. The school holds open houses throughout the year, with free trial climbs on the indoor wall. Climbing instructors are present to assist.

Rowing

Twin Ports Area

The **Duluth Rowing Club,** founded in 1889, holds a legacy of national championships. In 1916, the Duluth Rowing Club won eight out of nine national championship races. In the 1920s and '30s, the club remained a national powerhouse. Former Duluthian and Duluth Rowing Club member Dave Krmpotich earned a silver medal in the 1988 Olympic Games.

An active, competitive organization, the Duluth Rowing Club, 3900 Minnesota Avenue, (218) 727-8689 or 628-1657, is a member of Northwestern International Rowing Association. Facilities are on Park

Point where, depending on the wind, rowers take advantage of the sheltered waters on the harbor or lakeside. Youth programs for young men and women ages 14 through 19 are offered by professional coaches.

Thunder Bay Area

The **Thunder Bay Rowing Club**, One Dock Street, (807) 622-1044, is also a member of the Northwestern International Rowing Association. This active club's facilities are upstream from Lake Superior on the Kaministiquia River in downtown Thunder Bay.

Skinny-tire Biking

Twin Ports Area

Skinny-tire biking in Duluth can be an all-day proposition, considering the number of trails available coupled with the 22 miles of city roads running along the St. Louis River and Lake Superior.

The **Willard Munger State Trail** on Grand Avenue in West Duluth is a popular route with long-distance bikers en route from Hinckley. A new biking loop follows this trail to Carlton. From Carlton, follow the trails signs to Wrenshall, then enjoy a ride down the little-used Evergreen Memorial State Highway linking back into Minn. Highway 23 in Fond du Lac. You'll find wonderful views of the St. Louis River Valley along this route.

The **Western Waterfront Trail**, also on Grand Avenue, covers nearly 6 miles of shared-use trail that borders the bays of the St. Louis River. **Skyline Parkway**, running from West Duluth to the Lester River Road near Hawk Ridge, offers great vistas but has the bumpy road surfaces typical of this city.

Along the North Shore

Leaving Duluth and heading up the shore, **Scenic Highway 61** has designated bike lanes all the way to Two Harbors. Traffic is generally slow along here because people tend to look at the lake as they drive. (Folks in a hurry take the expressway to Two Harbors.)

Thunder Bay Area

Boulevard Lake Park's biking trails, in north Thunder Bay, are popular with locals. Check out the recreational walking trail system at Confederation College between Balmoral Street and Golf Links Road. These paved trails link up with different parts of city and allow in-line skaters and bikers. Call **Thunder Bay Community Services**, (807) 625-2351, for a trail map.

Skydiving

Twin Ports Area

SKYDIVE SUPERIOR

1106 Ogden Ave.
Superior, Wis.   (218) 392-8811

Yes, the Twin Ports has its own Elvis jumpers who floated into the open-air Wade Stadium preceding a Duluth-Superior Dukes baseball game. Skydive Superior, at the Superior Richard I. Bong Airport, offers skydiving lessons and popular tandem rides where you're literally hooked up to a professional skydiver. Costs and hours vary, so please ask when you call for reservations.

Minnesota, Wisconsin and Michigan each rank in the top 10 states nationally in sheer numbers of golfers.

Inside
Golf

The glacier might have had golf in mind when it slid into the region; it left behind delightful hills, valleys, watercourses, bumps, potholes, ponds and rolling terrain that the sport's followers have carved into a golfer's dreamland.

The season is barely six months long and modified by many wet, cold days, but nevertheless golf is booming. Most established courses doubled their activity in the past decade, so new courses have been opened and existing ones expanded. Much of the increased activity comes from within a few hundred miles. Residents of southern Wisconsin and Minnesota flock north to Lake Country in the summertime, and these folks are golfers. The National Golf Foundation in 1994 listed Minnesota and Wisconsin as having the highest percentage of golfers in the nation (almost 20 percent); Michigan was ranked seventh. And in sheer numbers of golfers, all three states rank in the top 10 (1.2 million in Michigan; around 750,000 each in Minnesota and Wisconsin).

Although clubhouses are closed in the winter, you sometimes can see intrepid golfers out on the "whites," batting around an orange ball. (Mainly, however, the wintertime courses are used by cross-country skiers and kids with sleds.)

We've listed here only the courses that don't require membership to play. Four courses in the region — the AAA Minnesota, Northland and Ridgeview country clubs in Duluth, and the Cloquet Country Club in Cloquet — are exclusively for members and their guests.

Golf Courses

Twin Ports Area

BIG LAKE GOLF COURSE
18 Cary Rd.
Cloquet, Minn.   *(218) 879-4221*

Once rated as the toughest Par 3 course in the Upper Midwest, this nine-hole, 2000-yard, par 27 course offers bunkers on every hole and a water hole. Greens fees are $8 for nine holes and $12 for 18 holes or all-day play. Pull carts, clubs and motorized carts are available for rent. A full-service restaurant is on site.

Take County Road 7 west from Cloquet.

GRANDVIEW GOLF CLUB
5665 Grandview Rd.
Duluth, Minn.   *(218) 624-3452*

A wide-open course of rolling terrain, this 2700-yard, par 36 nine-hole course boasts a spectacular view of the great Wisconsin hills that define the southern edge of Glacial Lake Duluth, Lake Superior's ice-age predecessor. One of the few courses in the region that's excellent for beginners, you can rent carts and clubs here. Greens fees are $8.75 for nine holes and $12.75 for all-day play.

The club offers season passes as well as rates for juniors and seniors.

From I-35 just southwest of Duluth, take the Midway exit west; Grandview is a quarter-mile down the road.

ENGER PARK GOLF COURSE
1801 W. Skyline Blvd.
Duluth, Minn.   (218) 723-3451

A municipal 27-hole course (three nine-hole, par 36 courses) built atop hills overlooking Duluth and the Lake, Enger Park is 6434 yards long on the front 18 and 3195 yards long on the back nine, with difficult rolling terrain and numerous water hazards. An upgrade and expansion in 1990 added a new nine-hole layout that's one of the more challenging courses around.

The greens fee is $18, but there are twilight and off-season discounts; carts are $15. Call ahead to book tee times or to inquire about season passes for city residents.

HIDDEN GREENS
County Rd. A   (715) 378-2300
N. Solon Springs, Wis.   (800) 933-6105

This new (opened in summer of 1995) 18-hole course features considerable seclusion, rolling terrain, tall trees and water. It's built with the average golfer in mind — not terribly long but fairly narrow and with plenty of trees and roughs. The course measures 6100 yards from the back tees and 5540 yards from the front.

Greens fees are $10 for nine holes and $16 for 18 holes Monday through Thursday; add $1 for Friday through Sunday and holiday play. Riding carts and clubs are available.

Go south from Superior on Wis. Highway 53 to Solon Springs; turn left on County Road A. About 5.5 miles down, on the right, you'll find the course.

LESTER PARK GOLF CLUB
Lester River Rd.
Duluth, Minn.   (218) 525-1400

A municipal 27-hole course (three courses of nine holes each) along the lovely Lester River, this course was upgraded and expanded in 1990 with the addition of a difficult, demanding new nine-hole course (called the Lake Nine) that overlooks Lake Superior. Few sub-par rounds are shot on this course. The length is 6371 yards (front 18) and 3417 yards (back nine). A driving range is available.

The greens fee is $18, but there are twilight and off-season discounts; carts are available for $15. City residents should inquire about season passes. Call ahead to book tee times.

NEMADJI GOLF COURSE
5 N. 58th St. E.
Superior, Wis.   (715) 394-0388

This popular, beautiful 36-hole championship course includes four par 36 nine-hole courses. The first two nines measure 6683 yards; the second nines, 6337 yards. It's a municipal course but has the look and feel of a country club, with its fine grounds, new clubhouse and lounge and excellent instruction program. The course has sections of steep terrain and difficult hazards to challenge the scratch player, but it appeals to beginners and old-timers as well because it's mostly flat.

The greens fee is $18, but there is a fall discount; carts are $18. Call ahead to book tee times.

Pattison Park Golf Course
County Rd. B
Superior, Wis.   *(715) 399-2489*

Here's a good beginners' course; Pattison is mostly flat and open, with not many trees or obstacles. The short executive course is par 31 (2035 yards) for nine holes. Dress is casual, carts and clubs are available for rent, and greens fees are $8 for nine holes and $12 for 18. You can get drinks (hard and soft), pizzas and sandwiches on site.

Go south from Superior on Wis. Highway 35, turn left on County Road B and go east 2 miles.

Pine Hill Golf Club
215 Minn. Hwy. 61
Carlton, Minn.   *(218) 384-3727*

Pine Hill Golf Club is a little hard to find, but it's worth the trip for a quick and fun round. The par 30 course plays 1850 yards. Greens fees are $7.50 for nine holes and $10.50 for as many holes as you care to play.

Take the Carlton exit east from I-35 and get on the frontage road on the south side. It curves around to Minn. Highway 61. Take Minn. Highway 61 south about 1.5 miles; Pine Hill is on the right. This is a good course for beginners.

Poplar Golf Course
U.S. Hwy. 2
Poplar, Wis.   *(715) 364-2689*

This busy course added nine holes in 1995. Its original nine holes — a par 31, 3100-yard executive course — are on hilly terrain, mostly in the open, with a serious water hazard along the Middle River. The new nine-hole course is par 35, 3300 yards and carved out of the woods. The greens fee is $7.

Poplar, the home of World War II flying ace Richard Ira Bong, is about 15 miles east of Superior on U.S. Highway 2.

Proctor Golf and Clubhouse
U.S. Hwy. 2
Proctor, Minn.   *(218) 624-2255*

Snuggled in the hills above Duluth, this municipal nine-hole course is a hilly, pretty place dotted with trees. It's par 34 (three par 3s and six par 4s) and 2281 yards long.

Clubs are available for rent; the greens fee is $8.

Enter Proctor from I-35 on U.S. Highway 2; you can't miss the airplane and train exhibits that mark the entrance to the golf course.

Twenty Nine Pines Country Club
2871 Sundberg Rd.
Mahtowa, Minn.   *(218) 389-3136*

This nine-hole, par 34 executive course (1995 yards) is fairly difficult. It has four ponds, and owner Virgil LaFond (a professional club-maker whom you can watch at work on the site) says the last five holes "get everybody."

Greens fees on weekdays are $7.50 for nine holes, $10 for 18 holes and $7 for players 17 and younger and 60 and older. On weekends, add $1 to those fees. Memberships are available, as are clubs and carts for rent.

From I-35 south of Duluth at the Mahtowa exit, take County Road 4 west 2 miles; turn left just past the Lutheran church; go to the stop sign and turn left again. A half-mile down is the course and the club's food service that includes beer.

Along the North Shore

GUNFLINT HILLS
MUNICIPAL GOLF COURSE

Gunflint Trail
Grand Marais, Minn.   (218) 387-9988

A hilly, challenging nine-hole course, Gunflint Hills offers great views of Lake Superior. The course is augmented by a driving range and merchandise shop. Rentals are available. You'll find the course 4 miles up the Gunflint Trail above Grand Marais.

The greens fee is $11.

SILVER BAY COUNTRY CLUB

Golf Course Rd.
Silver Way, Minn.   (218) 226-3111

A nine-hole, par 36 course that golfers of all abilities enjoy, Silver Bay is a municipal course of rolling hills and plentiful trees. A large pond and the east branch of the Beaver River add interest to this 3170-yard layout.

Greens fees are $12 for nine holes and $18 for 18 holes. Riding carts are available for $10 for nine holes and $18 for 18 holes. Clubs also are available to rent.

From Minn. Highway 61, turn inland at the semaphore; follow Outer Drive two blocks. Just beyond the high school, turn left onto Golf Course Road and continue for 2 miles.

SUPERIOR NATIONAL AT LUTSEN

Minn. Hwy. 61
Lutsen, Minn.   (218) 663-7195

This championship public course

was completed in 1991. Along the rocky Poplar River, close by several resorts, the 18-hole par 72 layout is arguably the most scenic anywhere in the upper Midwest. Cart paths along this 6323-yard course are paved, but wildlife sightings — bear, moose, deer, eagles — are common. The signature hole is the 17th, where the tee perches on a hill 135 feet above the green, with the Poplar River wrapping behind it and Lake Superior as the backdrop.

Lessons, a fully equipped pro shop, a restaurant and clubhouse are part of the complex. Green fees are $35; carts are $25.

TWO HARBORS
MUNICIPAL GOLF COURSE

Minn. Hwy. 61
Two Harbors, Minn.   (218) 834-2664

A good course for a player of any proficiency, Two Harbors is undergoing a major renovation that isn't scheduled for completion until 1997. Its existing nine holes covering 3300 yards are being wrapped into an expansion that will total 18 holes, so all nine won't be playable in 1996.

Greens fees will be adjusted during 1996 to accommodate the number of playable holes. Be sure to call ahead to find out the course's status and fee. Lessons and a driving range are available.

The course is just a few blocks northeast of town on the "upper" (inland) side of the main highway.

Along the South Shore

APOSTLE HIGHLANDS GOLF COURSE

1433 Apostle Highlands Blvd.
Bayfield, Wis.   (715) 779-5960

Tee off over a miniature Lake Superior here, where nine holes were added to its existing nine in 1995. The 6332-yard course

Photo: Duluth News-Tribune

A golfer concentrates on her shot at Nemadji Golf Course in Superior, Wisconsin.

(3249 yards on the front nine, 3083 on the back) is 500 feet high, offering a spectacular view of Chequamegon Bay and the islands.

Greens fees are $15 for nine holes and $25 for 18. Other amenities include a driving range, complete rental equipment and a shop where you can get snacks, soft drinks and beer.

From Wis. Highway 13 north of Bayfield, take County Road J inland a half-mile.

ELKS COUNTRY CLUB
Wis. Hwy. 137
Ashland, Wis.   *(715) 682-5215*

Although the lodge is closed to non-members, the nine-hole, par 36 course is open. The course of 3150 (back tees) and 3001 yards (front tees) overlooks Lake Superior. It's within the city limits of Ashland.

You can get there on Highway 137 from either Wis. Highway 13 or U.S. Highway 2, just west of town. Rentals and a driving range are available. Greens fees for non-members are $12 for nine holes and $17 for 18.

MADELINE ISLAND GOLF CLUB
LaPointe, Wis.   *(715) 747-3212*

This beautiful 18-hole, par 71 course takes an extra effort to get to, but the effort itself is half the fun. Take a boat (the Madeline Island Ferry will carry your car too) from Bayfield to LaPointe.

The 20-minute ride gives a good view of the mainland shore. Once you dock on the island, follow the road to the right; it will take you to the golf course, which offers pine forests and glorious views of the lake. The course is 6366, 6069 and 5506 yards long from the back, middle and front tees, respectively. This semi-private course is used mostly (but not exclusively) by club members.

Amenities include a pro shop, club rentals and refreshments. Greens fees for the 1996 season were not established as this book went to press.

Thunder Bay Area

CHAPPLES MEMORIAL GOLF COURSE
Chapples Park Dr.
Thunder Bay, Ont.   (807) 623-7070

This 18-hole, 6198-yard, par 71 course takes up most of Chapples Park. It's relatively flat and without sand traps, but it does feature several water hazards, beautiful scenery and some challenging holes along its 6148 yards.

The club offers a concession, lockers, club storage, shower rooms, merchandise shop and a driving range. The course is open to the public for a greens fee of $18.20. Carts are $20. You should book your tee time in advance.

FORT WILLIAM COUNTRY CLUB
1350 Mountain Rd.
Thunder Bay, Ont.   (807) 475-8925

A beautiful, semiprivate course nestled up against the mountain range,

this 6500-yard, par 72 course offers 18 holes of difficult play — the most challenging course in the city. The greens have been completely rebuilt since 1994.

Power carts and golf clubs are available to rent. The greens fee is $35 for nonmembers.

Take Ont. Highway 61 south from Thunder Bay; Mountain Road is about 5 miles from the city center.

THUNDER BAY GOLF AND COUNTRY CLUB
1055 Oliver Rd.
Thunder Bay, Ont.   (807) 345-8225

A semiprivate golf course right in the middle of the city, this course has nine holes and two sets of tee boxes to accommodate 18 holes of play. This par 72 course plays 5300 yards from the front tees and 6134 from the back. It's a challenging course, hilly in places and with difficult undulations in the greens; about half the tees are on the river.

Fees are $25 if you are with a member, $35 without. Amenities include a full clubhouse, restaurant, bar, pro shops and rentals.

STRATHCONA GOLF COURSE
500 Hodder Ave.
Thunder Bay, Ont.   (807) 683-8251

In the Current River area in Thunder Bay N., Strathcona is the most challenging and the best-maintained of the three municipal courses here. Many sand bunkers protect the greens, and you'll find beautiful hardwoods amid hilly terrain on this 18-hole, 6667-yard course (3340 yards

Insiders' Tips

Particularly on the North Shore, bring along your windbreaker and gloves. You'll be all set for that sudden switch of wind that in a matter of moments can turn a sweltering pursuit of the ball into a much-too-refreshing reminder of a wintertime sprint for the nearest shelter.

from the front tees and 3327 yards from the back).

Strathcona offers a concession, lockers, club storage, showers and a sales shop. The greens fee is $18.20, and carts are $20.

THUNDER BAY
MUNICIPAL GOLF COURSE
Twin City Crossroads
Thunder Bay, Ont.   *(807) 939-1331*

A simple nine-hole, par 36 course is excellent for seniors or beginners, the Mu-nicipal is a flat 2862-yard course, easy to walk, and is dry enough to play after a week's rain. Play this course for an ego booster! It offers a concession, lockers, club storage and sales shop.

You should book tee times in advance. The greens fee is $18.20; carts are $20.

Reservations are
strongly recommended,
though not required,
for campers in the
Lake Superior region
during the peak
summer months.

Inside
Camping and Campgrounds

Camping has come a long way since the days when you'd set up a heavy canvas tent (a tedious process using countless ropes and stakes) and pray the rain wouldn't completely soak the floor and your sleeping bag. And that moose rumbling through the camp at midnight? You'd hope it wouldn't get tangled in your tarp and tent lines . . . but that was part of the excitement of camping near Lake Superior.

Today, while the moose may still be on the loose, camping styles have changed due to the advent of high-tech equipment and fabrics as well as the burgeoning retirement market that loves the RV lifestyle. Whether you like to camp with a body-size backpack tent and gaze at the stars or "rough it" in a pop-up trailer big enough to set up a table and play gin rummy or in a RV with shower, compact disc player and microwave, we offer you this chapter dedicated to camping and campgrounds.

Just as camping styles range from the primitive to the luxurious, there are camping spots to fit your comfort and privacy needs. The following is a selection of our top campground choices.

The North and South shores of, and inland from, Lake Superior boast numerous campgrounds, including municipal, private, state park and U.S. Forest Service facilities. We've included camping options for the Twin Ports of Duluth, Minnesota, and Superior, Wisconsin; Minnesota's North Shore to Thunder Bay, Ontario; and

Wisconsin's South Shore to Ironwood, Michigan. (For more information on these natural areas, check out our Parks and Forests chapter; for information about the eastern portion of Lake Superior, see our Circle Tour chapter.)

Campsite Reservations

Have you ever driven all day in your car, packed with outdoor gear, fleeing the city, only to be disappointed by a "Campground Full" sign? You're not alone. Reservations are strongly recommended, though not required, for campers during the peak summer months. Minnesota state parks hold 30 percent of their campsites on a first-come, first-served basis. Wisconsin state parks and Canada's provincial parks block 50 percent or more of their sites, depending on the park, for first-come, first-served. And Michigan state parks apportion 20 to 40 percent of their campsites for first-come, first-served campers. The remainder of the parks' campsites are held by reservation throughout the entire season.

Permits

State Parks

Whether you're camping, hiking or picnicking, Minnesota, Wisconsin and Michigan state parks require a vehicle permit for entry. Permits are sold at the entrance to each park, and fees help support the respective state's park system.

If you're in the park for one day or an overnight stay, you'll need a daily vehicle permit. Permits cost $4 in Minnesota and Michigan; in Wisconsin, daily permits cost $7 for nonresidents, $5 for all residents except seniors ($3).

If you plan to stay more than a day, buy an annual park sticker: $18 in Minnesota, $20 in Michigan and $18 and $25 in Wisconsin (for residents and nonresidents, respectively). In Canada's provincial parks, the vehicle fee is included in the campsite fee.

National Forests

Don't forget that our national forests are considered truly public land; they're yours, and you can camp anywhere within their boundaries without a permit. Camping fees apply only in established campgrounds; elsewhere, it's free. Note that this applies to national forests only, not to national parks or wilderness areas.

Campsite Reservations

All it takes is a phone call and a major credit card to reserve a campsite in national and state parks as well as Canadian provincial parks in the Lake Superior region.

For state parks in **Minnesota**, call (800) 246-CAMP; in **Wisconsin**, call the individual park; and, in **Michigan**, call (800) 543-2YES.

U.S. Forest Service campgrounds differ. A few take reservations through (800) 280-CAMP; most don't, but a few campgrounds on Minnesota's North Shore also take reservations through private lodges and outfitters. Check the individual campground's listing in this chapter for specifics.

To reserve a campsite in **Canada's provincial parks**, call the individual park.

Campgrounds

Unless otherwise noted, all campgrounds accept major credit cards.

Twin Ports Area

JAY COOKE STATE PARK
500 E. Minn. Hwy. 210
Carlton, Minn.   *(218) 384-4610*
Daily camping fee:
Summer $12, electric hookup $14.50, backpack sites $7
Winter $8, electric hookup $10.50

Amid the rugged St. Louis River Valley, about 20 minutes south of Duluth via Interstate 35 (watch for brown exit signs along I-35 at Highway 210), Jay Cooke's camping facilities include a campground with 83 drive-in sites, 21 with electric hookup, and four remote backpacking campsites at Silver Creek, High Landing, Ash Ridge and Lost Lake.

Flush toilets, showers and a dump station are available from mid-May through early October. Ten camp sites, five with electrical hookup, are available in the winter. The park also has two primitive group camps to accommodate larger groups. A popular park for campers, hikers and picnickers, reservations are strongly recommended.

Established in 1915, Jay Cooke is one of Minnesota's oldest state parks. It lays in the area of the Grand Portage of the St. Louis River — the historic fur-trading route between the Mississippi River and Lake Superior. Part of this portage is now a hiking trail in the park. For a cheap thrill, cross the swinging bridge — a 221-foot cable steel suspension bridge spanning the river gorge near the park headquarters — and feel your footsteps shake the bridge.

INDIAN POINT CAMPGROUND
902 S. 69th Ave. W.
Duluth, Minn.   *(218) 624-5637*
Daily camping fee $10, electric hookup $13, full hookup $15

Expansive views of the wide St. Louis River, its islands and bluffs make this 50-site city campground a special spot. The park's 27-acre tract, on a narrow point of land flanked by bays of the St. Louis River, was originally used in World War II by troops guarding the harbor to protect the boat-building industry.

Open mid-May to October 1, Indian Point has six full-hookup sites, 32 electric hookups and 12 primitive sites. All the full-hookup sites and two with electric hookup are pull-throughs. Plumbing services include a dump station, showers and flush toilets. Firewood, ice, a few groceries and RV supplies are sold at the office. RV repair services are available on site. Besides a playground for kids, you can access the Western Waterfront Trail, a biking and hiking route that wraps around Indian Point. It's a good spot for birding, and you may see bald eagles and osprey.

Indian Point is only one of two campgrounds in Duluth proper (the other is Spirit Mountain; see subsequent listing). Summer weekends and holidays fill up quickly. Reservations are accepted by phone starting May 1.

To find this campground, ignore the confusing street address. If you're driving north on Interstate 35 into Duluth, take the Cody Street exit at the bottom of the big hill to 63rd Avenue. Turn right and take 63rd Avenue to Grand Avenue. Turn right on Grand going southwest, drive for .2 miles to 75th Avenue. Turn left and look for signs. If you're driving south on Interstate 35 through Duluth, take the Grand Avenue exit. Drive .3 miles to 75th Avenue. Turn left and look for signs.

SPIRIT MOUNTAIN CAMPGROUND
9500 Spirit Mountain Pl.   *(218) 628-2891*
Duluth, Minn.   *(800) 642-6377*
Daily camping fee (tent site) $12, electric hookup $15, electric and water hookup $17, more than five people per site $2.50 per person per night

Spirit Mountain Campground is set amidst the rolling hills above the St. Louis River valley. Campers enjoy the privacy of the sites among the oak, maple and birch forests. In late May and early June (springtime for this area), large-flowered trilliums — gorgeous wild lilies — blanket this campground. You'll find 100 wooded sites here: 49 with water and electric hookup, 26 with electric hookup only and a dozen pull-throughs for large RVs. A dump station is available. Sites have picnic tables, fire rings and grills. This well-maintained campground also provides showers and flush toilets.

Spirit Valley is near Magney Snively City Park where you'll find hiking trails with great views of the river valley. Jay Cooke State Park, with its own extensive trail system, is also nearby. The western end of the original Skyline Parkway passes by the campground and is the least-traveled section of that route, boasting some splendid vistas; it's also a great biking route, ending at Beck's Road.

You'll need reservations here for the big summer weekends in Duluth: Grandma's Marathon in mid-June (call by April), Fourth of July weekend and the Blues Festival in early August. (See our Annual Events chapter for details about these and other happenings.) Reservations are accepted year round. The campground is part of the Spirit Recreation Area, which includes a ski hill and is open from Memorial Day to Labor Day.

To get here, exit I-35 at Boundary Avenue (Exit 249). Follow the signs for the Spirit Mountain ski area; it's about 1.5 miles from Exit 249 to the campground.

PATTISON STATE PARK
6294 S. Wis. Hwy. 35
Superior, Wis.   *(715) 399-8073*
Daily camping fees $8 to $12

This lovely state park 10 miles south of Superior's city limits on Wis. Highway 35 is close to an urban area yet quite wild. It is home to Wisconsin's highest waterfall, the 165-foot Big Manitou Falls on the Black River, which makes its way to Lake Superior. The park offers 59 campsites, 18 with electric hookup. Some sites are pull-through. A popular place, the campground at Pattison enjoys a 98 percent occupancy rate in late June, July and August, so campsite reservations are essential. Generators can be used only during daylight hours to ensure quiet in the campground at night; all Wisconsin state parks have this quiet-time rule.

The park is open year round and offers cross-country skiing in the winter. Hiking trails, a 300-foot sand swimming beach and a nature center offering interpretative programs attract throngs of visitors to this full-service state park.

Along the North Shore

BURLINGTON BAY CAMPGROUND
Minn. Hwy. 61
Two Harbors   *(218) 834-2021*
RV sites:
Electric and water hookup $15 daily, $90 weekly, $300 monthly
Full hookup $17 daily, $102 weekly, $340 monthly

Smack-dab on the lakeshore, this city RV campground, open May 10 to October 10, offers great views of Lake Superior with the convenience and comfort of home. You can motor out to fish for lake trout from the Burlington Bay boat landing, an ideal spot to launch even in the winter when local diehards fish for salmon. Later, hit a few rounds at Two Harbors Municipal Golf Course directly across Minn. Highway 61.

Burlington Bay gives you a choice of 66 sites with water and electric and 25 sites with full hookup. Plumbing amenities include flush toilets, showers and a dump station. June through the Labor Day weekend in September is peak season; reservations are strongly recommended.

GOOSEBERRY FALLS STATE PARK
1300 Minn. Hwy. 61 E.
Northeast of Two Harbors   *(218) 834-3855*
Daily camping fee: Summer $12, Winter $8

Gooseberry State Park, 13 miles east of Two Harbors, offers easy access and boasts stunning scenery. For these and other reasons it's one of the most visited sites in Minnesota — and, in peak season, it can be a zoo on Minn. Highway 61. Our suggestion: Get off the road and into the park. Once you're away from the crowds rubbernecking the falls at the main bridge, set up your campsite and walk down to Lake Superior or find the 15 miles of well-marked hiking trails that traverse the park's 1,662 acres to see the five waterfalls on the Gooseberry River. Inquire about a trail map at the brand-new visitors center. If you're feeling social, there's always a naturalist program going on in the summer. For rock hounds and agate hunters, Lake Superior is always bringing in new merchandise at the mouth of the Gooseberry River.

Gooseberry has 70 sites with a RV length limit of 40 feet. Three of the sites are pull-through. Handicapped-accessible

Photo: Duluth News-Tribune

Campfire cooking is to be savored!

flush toilets and showers are available at the campground.

For true solitude, try one of the four backpack sites. Gooseberry is open year round and offers cross-country ski trails in the winter.

To reach Gooseberry Falls State Park, take Minn. Highway 61 east for 14 miles from Two Harbors.

SPLIT ROCK LIGHTHOUSE STATE PARK
2010A Minn. Hwy. 61 E.
Northeast of Two Harbors   (218) 226-3065
Daily camping fee: Summer $10, Winter $8

The 21 little gems of cart-in campsites at Split Rock are lusted after and waited for like a special vintage of Cabernet Sauvignon or a new Harley-Davidson. Everyone has a favorite campsite, and reservations are made decades in advance (OK, actually in late January when cabin fever hits).

Get ready to get down to your basic camping gear and chuck your worldly goods. You haul your stuff in a big, brown cart with sturdy bicycle wheels. Two of the cart-in sites are handicapped-accessible. Split Rock has no drive-in sites, but it does have showers and flush toilets, both of which are handicapped-accessible. Four wonderful backpack sites add to spells of winter daydreaming.

Split Rock State Park is home to the celebrity Split Rock Lighthouse, recently featured in color on a U.S. postage stamp. This marvelous historic landmark can be viewed from the shores of Lake Superior and the cliffs above, or you can tour the tower by climbing up the lighthouse stairwell.

There's also a great trail system for outdoor hiking, including the Day Hill Trail that climbs to overlook Lake Superior, the lighthouse and the Apostle Islands. Trails are well-marked, and maps are available at the park headquarters if you need them. You may cross paths with hikers following the Superior Hiking Trail — a 200-mile pathway running along the North Shore of Lake Superior from Two Harbors, Minnesota to Canada, ending at the Border Route Trail — as they walk through the park on shared trails.

To access the park, drive 19 miles east from Two Harbors on Minn. Highway 61.

TETTEGOUCHE STATE PARK

474 Minn. Hwy. 61 E.
Silver Bay   (218) 226-3539
Daily camping fee: Summer $10, Winter $8

Tettegouche is known for the spectacular vistas from Shovel Point and Palisade Head, the falls of the Baptism River and the views of Lake Superior and the interior alpine lakes of the Sawtooth Mountains. Covering 9,346 acres, it's the largest state park on the North Shore. It's a favorite spot for locals who daytrip to hike and ski the park's extensive trail system and diverse terrain of deep valleys, high ridges and mature northern hardwood forests.

Plan to camp here for several days and take time to explore. Early fall is a wonderful, bug-free time for hiking, with glowing oak and maple stands complementing the deep-green conifers. Visitors sometimes see black bears fattening up for their winter snooze, feasting on the oak acorns in the Palisade Valley.

The campground has 28 drive-in sites with a RV limit of 60 feet and six walk-in sites. There is no dump station or hookups, but handicapped-accessible showers and flush toilets are available.

Walk from the campground to the High Falls on the Baptism River. It's a half-mile hike to the highest falls in Minnesota. We also suggest a hike into the Tettegouche Camp on Mic Mac Lake. The rustic log retreat here was built in 1910 by a group of wealthy businessmen as a fishing and hunting camp. The four charming log cabins in the camp are available year round for overnight rental.

Access the park 5 miles east of Silver Bay on Minn. Highway 61.

GEORGE H. CROSBY MANITOU STATE PARK

Lake Co. Rd. 7
Finland   (218) 226-3539
Daily camping fee: Summer $10, Winter $8

It's worth driving the 10 miles off the beaten path of Minn. Highway 61 to revel in the solitude of Crosby-Manitou. This backpacker's paradise includes an extensive trail system and the cascading Manitou River amid its 5,259 acres. Camping is limited to 21 backpack sites, most of them situated along the Manitou River, a magnificent setting edged with towering pines and yellow birch. Campsites are usually available on weekdays and many weekends. The farther into the park you hike, the more likely you'll have the place to yourself. Hiking distances range from a three-block walk to five sites on Lake Benson to a 4-mile trek to the most remote sites along the Manitou River.

From Minn. Highway 61 at Illgen City, take Lake County Highway 1 to Finland; then follow Lake County Road 7 east for 8 miles to the park entrance.

TEMPERANCE RIVER STATE PARK

Minn. Hwy. 61
Schroeder   (218) 663-7476
Daily camping fee: Summer $12, Winter $8
Electric hookup (both seasons) $14.50

Temperance River State Park is halfway between Duluth and the Canadian border near the Sawbill Trail in Tofte — one of the entry points into the Boundary Waters Canoe Area Wilderness. The Temperance River got its name because it has no bar across its mouth (pardon the pun).

The park has two campgrounds on each side of the river, with 55 drive-in sites, including four pull-throughs, 18 sites with electric hookups and three cart-in sites. Choose a bluffside spot to view Lake Superior or enjoy a site on the lake shore. Temperance, with a mile of shoreline, is the only North Shore state campground with sites on the lake. Handicapped-accessible showers and toilets are available.

Typical of North Shore state parks, Temperance River offers great hiking trails — part of a secret master plan to get you outside and moving. Eight miles of trails run along the Temperance River and its waterfalls. Stop at and catch your breath at any of the seven overlooks, marvel at the scenery, snap some photos and wish you could stay here forever.

From Schroeder, drive a mile east on Minn. Highway 61.

CASCADE RIVER STATE PARK
Minn. Hwy. 61
Lutsen   (218) 387-1543
Daily camping fee: Summer $10, Winter $8

Aptly named for the series of stair-stepping waterfalls on the Cascade River, Cascade State Park provides 40 drive-in sites with an RV limit of 35 feet. Three pull-through sites, five backpack sites and two group camps make this a versatile camp-

ground. Showers, flush toilets and a dump station are available.

Cascade's trail system for summer hiking and winter cross-country skiing brings you along and across the Cascade River, with its lush cedars and balsams (check out the gorge from the footbridge). Or, explore the trail to the great vistas of Lookout and Moose mountains. The Superior Hiking Trail continues to work its way up the North Shore, passing through the park on shared trails.

Cascade River fishing is plentiful and diverse. The steelhead salmon pass during their spawning run in the spring and fall. Brook and rainbow trout are found in the upper stretches of the river. Fish at the mouth of the river and in Lake Superior for lake trout. A Minnesota fishing license and state trout stamp are required to fish North Shore trout streams.

Cascade River State Park is 9 miles west of Grand Marais.

JUDGE C. R. MAGNEY STATE PARK
Minn. Hwy. 61
Hovland   (218) 387-2929
Daily camping fee: Summer $10, Winter $8

Called Magney by locals, this state park, with 4,514 acres in the pristine Brule River Valley, enjoys relative quiet in the height of the summer season. That's because many of the summer visitors from the Twin Cities tend not stray farther up the shore than the bustling town of Grand Marais.

Magney is renowned for the mystery of the Devil's Kettle Falls on the Brule

Worried about Minnesota's other state bird, the mosquito? A campsite close to Lake Superior and its cool winds will bug you less than camping back in the woods. But don't forget your non-toxic bug dope for the silent and sneaky black flies; they are arguably worse to deal with than the noisy and shameless mosquitoes.

Insiders' Tips

River. Above the drop, a jutting rock divides the river into two falls. The eastern falls drops 50 feet into a deep gorge and pool. The western falls plunges into a huge pothole and, according to local legend, disappears. Folklore has it that gallons of colored ink were dropped into the western falls to see if the colored water would show up at the mouth of the river. No luck — no sign of the ink flowing into Lake Superior.

The small, quiet campground has 33 drive-in sites with an RV limit of 45 feet and one backpack site. Handicapped-accessible showers and flush toilets are available, but there is no dump station. Picnic grounds along the river offer a beautiful spot for lunch on your way up or down the North Shore.

Brook and rainbow trout inhabit the Brule River and its tributary — Gauthier Creek. The Brule River is stocked with trout each year by the Minnesota Department of Natural Resources. A Minnesota fishing license and state trout stamp are required to fish North Shore trout streams.

Judge C.R. Magney State Park is 14 east of Grand Marais.

GRAND MARAIS RECREATION AREA/RV PARK AND CAMPGROUND
Minn. Hwy. 61
Grand Marais   *(218) 387-1712*
Daily camping fee $13.50, waterfront $16, electric and water hookup $17, complete hookup $18

This popular city campground on the lakeside of Minn. Highway 61 (right in town) is open from May to mid-October. It's a big place: Nearly 300 sites — 40 primitive, 104 with electric and water hookup and 147 with complete hookup. The 120 sites on the east side of the campground are held for first-come, first-served business, but reservations are strongly recommended for July and August, particularly during the famous annual Fisherman's Picnic celebration held in early August.

This park offers urban camping at its best. You can walk anywhere in town from the campground. The Sweethearts Bluff Trail is a nice hike west. There's a great pebble and stone beach for the kids and a playground with new play-safe equipment. Across from the campground is an indoor municipal facility with a big open-swim and lap pool, wading pool, sauna and whirlpool; it's open every day.

SUPERIOR NATIONAL FOREST
District Headquarters
515 W. First St., Room 354
Duluth   *(218) 720-5324*
Daily camping fees $6 to $10

Established in 1909, the Superior National Forest is known for its northern boreal forests, more than 2,000 sparkling-clean lakes and colorful human history. It's the largest U.S. Forest east of the Rocky Mountains, covering roughly 3.8 million acres. One million acres of the forest comprise the Boundary Waters Canoe Area Wilderness. The wild, remote country of Superior National Forest is home to the endangered timber wolf. Chances are you'll hear wolves calling to each other in the night, but to actually see wolves in the wild is a rare and fortunate thing.

Generally, camping in the Superior National Forest is primitive, but the spacious sites and quietude are your compensation. Facilities include hand-operated pumps for water and pit toilets. Pets are welcome but must be leashed. Most of the campgrounds are handicapped-accessible, including some with fishing docks. A few campgrounds have electric hookups. Check with each ranger district office for maps and directions.

Keep in mind national forest service roads are gravel-surfaced. If you're coming up the North Shore through Duluth, you can stop at the Superior National Forest district headquarters in the city for information and maps, Monday through Friday from 8 AM to 4:30 PM.

Superior National Forest has a total of 27 campgrounds. We've selected a few campgrounds in the Tofte and Gunflint districts that are the closest to the North Shore and Minn. Highway 61 for easy access. Many of these campgrounds are at the edge of the Boundary Waters Canoe Area Wilderness.

The Tofte Ranger District Office is on Minn. Highway 61, Tofte, (218) 663-7981. **Tofte Ranger District** campgrounds include:

Poplar River Campground's four sites on National Forest Service Road 164; Crescent Lake Campground's 33 sites on National Forest Service Road 170; and Sawbill Lake Campground's 50 sites on Cook County Road 2.

The Gunflint Ranger District Office is on Minn. Highway 61 in Grand Marais, (218) 387-1750. **Gunflint Ranger District** campgrounds include:

Devil Track Lake Campground, with 16 sites on Cook County Road 57; Kimball Lake Campground's 10 sites on National Forest Road 140; Cascade River Campground's four sites on National Forest Road 158; and Two Island Lake Campground, with 38 sites on Cook County Road 27.

Along the South Shore

AMNICON FALLS STATE PARK
County Rd. U
Superior, Wis.
Summer   *(715) 398-3000*
Winter   *(715) 399-8073*
Daily camping fees $7 to $11

Looking for privacy and your own waterfall with whirlpool? You'll find it at Amnicon State Park. This 825-acre park includes 36 primitive campsites and features waterfalls and rapids on the Amnicon River — complete with covered bridge. Though the park has no showers, swimming is allowed in the river. Sit under the waterfalls in gentle whirlpools and pretend you're in a northern tropical paradise. Primitive means no hookups, no pull-throughs for big rigs and pit toilets for everybody. Sites fill up on weekends from Memorial Day to Labor Day, so call for reservations. (Waterfalls are first-come, first-served.)

Take U.S. Highway 2 east for 12 miles from Superior or U.S. Highway 2 west from Ashland, Wisconsin, for 55 miles to County Road U. Drive north a quarter-mile to the park entrance. If you're on Wis. Highway 13 following the Lake Superior Circle Tour, turn south on County Road U and drive 4 miles to the park entrance.

TOWN OF CLOVER PARK
Bark Point Rd.
Herbster, Wis.   *No phone listing*
Daily summer camping fees $5 to $8

It's tiny and sometimes a little crowded, but, hey, you're on the wonderful sandy South Shore beach of Lake Superior, and the swimming is great. This city campground has 60 sites and 24 electric hookups. Flush toilets, water and free firewood are available. It's first-come, first-served here.

Take Bark Point Road off Wis. Highway 13 and follow the lakeshore.

BRULE RIVER STATE FOREST
South of U.S. Hwy. 2
Brule, Wis.   *(715) 372-4866*
Daily summer camping fee $7

People come to the Brule River to fish this nationally renowned trout stream — brimming with brown, rainbow and brook trout. People canoe, kayak and float in inner tubes on the gently moving flatwater and exciting whitewater in spring and early summer before the water gets too low. Brule River State Forest is also a popular fall hunting area.

The two state forest campgrounds, the Bois Brule and Copper Range, flank the river and have designated canoe landing spots. Because the Brule River is protected, you must launch or land at designated sites and camp in designated areas. You'll need a Wisconsin fishing license and river trout stamp to fish the Brule.

Bois Brule Campground, south of U.S. Highway 2 near the State Forest headquarters, is a primitive campground with pit toilets, hand-pumped water and 23 sites (one is handicapped-accessible). No electric hookups are available. It's a heavily wooded site with huge red and white pine. No reservations are accepted here — it's first-come, first-served. The campground is open from the opening day of trout season in April until December 1.

Copper Range Campground is 4 miles north of U.S. Highway 2 on County Road H, then west on Park Road. You'll find 17 sites here, one of which is handicapped-accessible. Pit toilets and hand-pumped water are standard. Sites are available on a first-come, first-served basis. The campground is open from the first day of trout season in early April until December 1. Chose a campsite next to the Brule River and doze off to its soothing sounds as it flows to Lake Superior.

KREHER PARK
End of Prentice Ave.
Ashland, Wis.   *No phone listing*
Daily camping fee $10

Kreher Park is a 23-site RV campground on the shores of Lake Superior's Chequamegon Bay. Though lacking in seclusion, this city-owned campground offers great views of the historic Soo Line ore dock (see our Architecture and Historic Places chapter), a sandy swimming beach and boat launch and access to the waterfront trail that runs west to the marina and the Hotel Chequamegon. You can see remnants of old sawmills along the shore.

Kreher Park has full hookups, a dump station, showers and a playground. The campground is open from mid-May to mid-October; it's first-come, first-served here.

Take U.S. Highway 2 to Prentice Avenue on the east end of Ashland. Turn toward the Lake; the road ends at the park.

Insiders' Tips

Camping in January? Minnesota state parks, as well as many in Wisconsin and Michigan, stay open year round. But don't expect hot showers; plumbing is shut off from October until May to keep the pipes from freezing.

CHEQUAMEGON NATIONAL FOREST

Washburn Ranger District
Washburn, Wis.   *(715) 373-2667*
Daily camping fee $6
Lakeside sites at Two Lakes Campground $9

Chequamegon (insiders' pronounce it shi-WAH-me-gun) National Forest's campgrounds offer privacy, boat launches, good river and lake fishing and a variety of hiking, biking, backpacking and horseback-riding trails. The pit toilets, hand pumps for water and lack of electrical hookups are characteristic of U.S. Forest Service camping facilities.

Campgrounds open May 1. Two Lakes closes on October 15; Birch Grove, Perch Lake and Wanoka Lake close November 1. All facilities except Birch Grove have campground hosts.

The 90-site Two Lakes Campground on Lake Owen is the busiest of the lot. Call the U.S. Forest Service at (800) 280-CAMP for reservations. Take U.S. Highway 2 to U.S. Highway 63 S. Follow to U.S. Forest Road 213 southeast of Drummond. It's about 5.5 miles to the campground.

Perch Lake Campground, with its 16 sites and backpacking opportunities, is the most remote campground here. It's part of the Rainbow Lake Wilderness Area. Take U.S. Highway 2 to U.S. Highway 63 S. At Drummond, Wisconsin, take U.S. Forest Road 223 N. The campground is 5 miles north of Drummond.

Birch Grove Campground has two boat launches as well as horseback riding, mountain biking, hiking and motorized ATV trails. Five of the 16 campsites are handicapped-accessible. Follow Wis. Highway 13 for a mile south of Washburn and turn right onto Long Lake Road heading west. Long Lake Road becomes U.S. Forest Road 251. Af-

ter 7.5 miles, turn north on U.S. Forest Road 252 and proceed 2 miles, then turn onto U.S. Forest Road 435 for a half-mile.

Wanoka Lake Campground, with its 20 sites, offers trout fishing in the Wanoka River and biking trails. It's the easiest campground to find, right off U.S. Highway 2 east of Iron River, Wisconsin. Drive 7 miles east of Iron River on U.S. Highway 2. Look for campground signs on the south side of the road.

WASHBURN MEMORIAL PARK

Wis. Hwy. 13
Washburn, Wis.   *No phone listing*
Daily camping fee $10, electric hookup $14

At the north end of town (if you're leaving Washburn towards Bayfield) is Washburn Memorial Park. True to the curse of most city campgrounds, sites are so close to one another that you'll feel like you're double parked. But the park has its charms. Huge red and white pines fill the air with their fragrant presence, and the great little sand swimming beach, playground, free firewood and showers should persuade you to stay at least one night. Electric hookups are available at some of the 51 sites from May to October, as is a dump station. No reservations are accepted; it's first-come, first-served here.

DALRYMPLE PARK

Wis. Hwy. 13
Bayfield, Wis.
Daily camping fee $7, electric hookup $8

If you're lucky, you can grab a site on the lakeshore looking out at Basswood Island, one of the Apostle Islands. It's first-come, first-served here. The benefits of location prevail over privacy at this heavily wooded, close-to-town city campground. You can walk into Bayfield to enjoy its historic Victorian cottages and handsome

Solitude and scenery await winter campers in the Porcupine Mountains.

brownstone buildings as well as the many shops, galleries and restaurants.

The campground has 30 sites, half of them with electric hookup, and is open from mid-May to mid-October. Amenities are limited to pit toilets and drinking water (strange bedfellows indeed). If you need a shower, check out the Bayfield pool and recreation facility — open year round.

Take Wis. Highway 13 north from Bayfield. The park is on the lakeside about a half-mile from town.

BIG BAY STATE PARK
Ferry access at Wis. Hwy. 13 in Bayfield
Madeline Island, Wis.

Summer	*(715) 747-6425*
Winter	*(715) 779-3346*
Madeline Island Ferry	*(715) 747-2051*
	(715) 747-6801

Daily camping fees $8 to $12

On Madeline Island in the Apostle Islands, Big Bay State Park has sandstone bluffs dotted with caves created by Lake Superior's powerful wind and waves. The 1.5 miles of glorious sandy beach attracts campers, as do the hiking and nature trails leading to wonderful vistas. The campground has 60 drive-in sites, showers and a dump station. For campers seeking more privacy, walk-in sites are available.

Drive about a mile west from Ashland, Wisconsin, on U.S. Highway 2. Turn north on Wis. Highway 13 to Bayfield. At Bayfield, take the 20-minute ferry ride to Madeline Island. The park is 7 miles from the ferry landing once on the island.

APOSTLE ISLAND VIEW CAMPGROUND
Star Rte., Box 8
Bayfield, Wis. 54814   (715) 779-5524
Daily camping fee $12 (tent), electric/water hookup $15, full hookup $17 or $19 (depending on location)

Great views of Lake Superior and the Apostle Islands make this operator-owned campground a popular spot for RV campers. Close to town, it's about a mile south of historic Bayfield's charming Victorian homes, great restaurants, shops and galleries. A shuttle bus takes campers to the Big Top Chautauqua, a summer tent theater where you'll find music and other live entertainment.

Run by friendly locals, this clean and safe campground caters to RV campers. The camping season opens in early May, weather permitting, and closes in mid-

October. The 56 sites include 11 with full hookup and cable TV (and the best views of Lake Superior and the Apostle Islands). Thirty-four sites offer water and electric hookup. Tent sites, some with views, are also available. Showers and a game room round out the amenities. Reservations (mail a check) are recommended during the summer and are essential to secure a spot during the famous Apple Festival Weekend — the first full weekend in October.

Take Wis. Highway 13 to County Road J. Drive west and follow the campground signs.

LITTLE SAND BAY CAMPGROUND
Apostle Islands National Lakeshore
County Rd. K
Red Cliff, Wis.   *No phone listing*
Daily camping fee $5, electric hookup $6

Little Sand Bay Campground is a great place to watch the swirl of activity at this bustling harbor. Generally not too crowded during the week, the campground is operated by the town of Russell, although it's officially on the Apostle Islands National Lakeshore. This is an active harbor and contact station for Lakeshore patrol boats, excursion boats and pleasure craft. Twenty sites, half with electric hookup, are just a short walk from the wonderful white-sand beach and sea kayak launching spot on Lake Superior. The historic Hokenson's Fishery, now a commercial fishing museum with docks and quaint buildings, adds to the beauty of the place. It's first-come, first-served here, so hurry.... It's worth the drive.

Take Wis. Highway 13 north for 5 miles from Bayfield to County Road K. Turn right and drive 13 miles to Little Sand Bay.

COPPER FALLS STATE PARK
Wis. Hwy. 169
Mellen, Wis.   *(715) 274-5123*
Daily camping fees $8 to $12

The 2,483 acres of river canyons, mixed hardwood and conifer forests and waterfalls of Copper Falls State Park are worth the short trip from Lake Superior's South Shore. From the gregarious socialite to the solitude seeker, camping at Copper Falls offers something for everybody. The 55 drive-in sites are divided into north and south campgrounds. Pit toilets are provided at both campgrounds, and flush toilets are available in the picnic area.

The north campground accommodates RVs. The 13 sites include electrical hookup and a dump station. No pull-throughs are available, but you will find large sites for big rigs.

The south campground is designed for tent camping and includes showers. For more privacy, check out the four walk-in sites; for the ultimate in privacy, a 2-mile hike brings you to a pair of backpack sites near the Sandstone Cliffs along the Bad River.

From either campground, the magic of the Bad River is just a short hike away. Take the loop trail for 1.7 miles from the concessions stand. This trail takes you to Copper Falls on the Bad River, the Brownstone Falls and the Cascade on the Tyler's Fork of the Bad River and Devil's Gate in the Bad River Gorge.

From U.S. Highway 2 in Ashland, turn south on Wis. Highway 13 and proceed 24 miles to Mellen. From Mellen, drive 2 miles on Wis. Highway 169 to the park entrance.

BLACK RIVER HARBOR CAMPGROUND
Bessemer Ranger District/Ottawa National Forest
500 N. Moore St.
Bessemer, Mich.   *(906) 667-0261*
Daily summer camping fee $6

On the lovely Black River Harbor, off Gogebic County Road 513, this national forest service campground and recreation complex has 40 drive-in sites open from

May 15 to October 15 (10 are available by reservation). You won't find hookups or showers here, but flush toilets and a dump station are provided. A campground manager is on-site 24 hours.

The North Country Hiking Trail, a well-marked route extending from New York to North Dakota, crosses through the park and may be accessed at the harbor and upstream in the Copper Peak Ski Complex. The hiking trails along the Black River highlight the Rainbow, Sandstone, Gorge, Potawatomi and Great Conglomerate waterfalls. The harbor has beautiful beaches, docking facilities and a native stone picnic pavilion and playground.

PRESQUE ISLE RIVER
UNIT CAMPGROUND

Porcupine Mountains Wilderness State Park
Gogebic County Rd. 519   (906) 885-5275
Daily summer camping fee $8

The Presque Isle River Campground is near the park's western border in an old-growth forest of mainly sugar maples. Wander the rocky beach where the Presque Isle River joins Lake Superior; it's a great place to discover small and large pieces of driftwood. On a bluff overlooking Lake Superior, the campground has 88 drive-in sites but no electric hookup or pull-throughs.

Flush toilets, showers and a dump station are available. The campground is open mid-May to mid-September and fills up in July and August. For reservations, call (800) 543-2937.

From Wakefield, take Gogebic County Road 519 north about 15 miles or until you reach the Lake.

PORCUPINE MOUNTAINS
WILDERNESS STATE PARK

412 S. Boundary Rd.
Ontonagon, Mich.   (906) 885-5275
Backpacking permit $6

Called the Porkies by locals,

Michigan's largest wilderness state park boasts the highest mountains between Pennsylvania's Allegheny Mountains and the Black Hills in the Great Plains. It's a backpacker's paradise, with great vistas, alpine lakes (including the renowned Lake in the Clouds) and old-growth forest — still intact because of the rugged terrain. This park includes one of the most significant remaining old-growth stands of hardwoods and conifers in the Midwest.

Backpackers must purchase a permit. Instead of designated backpack sites, hikers can pitch a tent wherever they want for trailside camping. Sixteen primitive trailside cabins with bunks, wood stoves and cooking utensils are available for rent. For reservations, call the park.

For an introduction to the Porkies, stop at the park's visitors center to see the multimedia show and exhibits and chat with the helpful park staff members; they love this area and want to share it. From the visitors center, hike to the incredible overlook above Lake in the Clouds, a pristine blue alpine lake rimmed with ancient forest.

From Ontonagon, take Mich. Highway 107 for 17 miles west to S. Boundary Road. Take a left and proceed south for a quarter-mile to the visitors center.

UNION BAY CAMPGROUND

Porcupine Mountains Wilderness State Park
Mich. Hwy. 107
West of Silver City   (906) 885-5275
Daily summer camping fee $12, winter $10

Union Bay is a popular campground for trailer campers and RVs. It's right on the shores of Lake Superior on the site of an old shipping dock from the mining days. Each of the 100 sites (two of which are handicapped-accessible) has electric hookup. Some sites are right on the lakeshore. Facilities include handicapped-accessible toilets and showers.

Photo: Duluth News-Tribune

Camping accommodations range from primitive to modern at parks and resorts along Lake Superior's shores.

You can access 25 miles of mountain biking trails from Union Bay as well as 90 miles of hiking trails. For reservations, call (800) 543-2937.

From Silver City, head west 3 miles on Mich. Highway 107 to reach Union Bay Campground.

OTTAWA NATIONAL FOREST
District Headquarters
2100 E. Cloverland Dr.
Ironwood, Mich.   *(906) 932-1330*
No fees or permits for access

In the western upper peninsula of Michigan, the Ottawa National Forest spreads out across 954,000 acres and includes the Sylvania, Sturgeon River Gorge and McCormick wilderness areas. Seven major river systems within the forest offer more than 1,000 miles of watery playland for kayaking and canoeing. There are 27 national forest campgrounds with available fees.

A notable area of great natural beauty in the Ottawa National Forest, particularly in the fall, is the Black River National Forest Scenic Byway. From U.S. Highway 2 east of Ironwood, take the Powderhorn Road (a.k.a. Gogebic County Road 513) north to Black River Road. This scenic route takes you along the Black River to Lake Superior, with overlooks at Rainbow, Sandstone, Gorge, Potawatomi and Great Conglomerate falls. The overlook at Potawatomi Falls is handicapped-accessible.

Thunder Bay Area

MIDDLE FALLS PROVINCIAL PARK
Canadian Hwy. 593   *(807) 964-2097*
Daily camping fee $15.25

Just across the border from Minnesota is Middle Falls Provincial Park, next to the Pigeon River, with its major waterfalls, deep gorges and impressive cliffs that once challenged fur-trading voyageurs and loggers. You'll find 25 campsites, half of which are big enough for trailers and RVs; however, there are no hookups. Flush toilets and hot and cold water are available. The park also has a wonderful sheltered picnic area and hiking trails to the falls.

TROWBRIDGE FALLS CAMPGROUND
Trowbridge Falls Regional Park
Copenhagen Rd.
Thunder Bay, Ont.   *(807) 683-6661*
Daily camping fee $14, electric hookup $17.50

It's hard to believe you're in a city of 120,000 people while camping near the rush of the Current River. At the north end of town, Trowbridge Falls Campground flanks a stretch of rapids in a thick conifer forest. A network of hiking trails run near the river and make for great cross-country skiing in winter.

This full-service campground is operated by the city from mid-May to Labor Day and includes 145 sites — 25 pull-throughs (note the 35-foot maximum RV length restriction) and 75 with electric hookup. Amenities include flush toilets, showers and laundry facilities. Just a five-minute drive away, you'll find Centennial Park — a great place for kids — which includes an animal farm, a 1910 logging camp replica, a playground and train rides; also check out Boulevard Lake where you'll find paved pedestrian trails and a swimming beach.

Take the Hodder-Copenhagen exit off Trans-Canada Highway 11/17 and proceed 300 yards on Copenhagen Avenue to the campground.

CHIPPEWA PARK CAMPGROUND
City Rd., Thunder Bay, Ont.   (807) 622-9777
Daily camping fee $14, electric hookup $17.50

Open from May 15 to Labor Day, this city park and campground is at the southern edge of Thunder Bay. It's a full-service campground with 104 sites — 40 pull-throughs, 60 with electric hookup and 40 with water hookup. Facilities include a dump station and showers. You won't find any swimming here, but you will find great diversions for the kids, including a playground, an amusement park with rides and a wildlife exhibit. You'll also find some wonderful historic log buildings here, including a pavilion and picnic booths.

From the junction of highways 11/17, 11B/17B and 61, follow Trans-Canada Highway 61 for 5 miles to Highway 61B. Proceed east on Highway 61B for 6 miles and follow signs to the park.

SLEEPING GIANT PROVINCIAL PARK
Canadian Hwy. 587
Pass Lake, Ont.   *(807) 977-2526*
Off-season   *(807) 475-1506*
Daily camping fee $15.25

Sleeping Giant Provincial Park is on the 24-mile-long, 6-mile-wide Sibley Peninsula. At the south end of the park, the legendary Sleeping Giant dominates the scenery. Thrusting southward into Lake Superior, Sleeping Giant's eastern lowlands rise gently from the lake, while the western shore is dominated by huge cliffs — the highest in Ontario. Deep valleys, sheer cliffs, fast-running clear streams and alpine lakes characterize the terrain. Hiking, backpacking and cross-country skiing are the best ways to see the landscape and take in the incredible views of Lake Superior, Thunder Bay, Marie Louise Lake, Black Bay and Edward Island.

The campground on Marie Louise Lake has 168 drive-in sites, some of which are pull-through. Showers and flush toilets and a dump station are available. Sixteen backpack sites are scattered throughout the park. No hookups are provided, and visitors are not permitted to use generators.

The park's hiking and cross-country trails are open year round. Camping is permitted seasonally from the third weekend in May to October 9. Reservations are recommended for July and August.

Take Trans-Canada Highway 11/17 north from Thunder Bay for 25 miles. Turn east on Highway 587 and follow it into the park.

KAKABEKA FALLS PROVINCIAL PARK
Trans-Canada Hwy. 11/17
Thunder Bay, Ont.   (807) 473-9231
Daily camping fee $15.25, electric hookup
$18.25

Some campers are lulled to sleep by the roar of Kakabeka Falls (the "Niagara of the North") on the Kaministiquia River. Other campers prefer to stay in the upper campground where there's a little less whitewater power. A big campground, Kakabeka Falls has 166 sites, including 50 with electric hookup and numerous pull-through sites. The park is divided into the upper campground with electric hookups, a dump station and a water filling station and the lower campground with tent sites. Amenities include showers and flush toilets.

Family campers will enjoy the guided hikes in summer, naturalist campfire talks and a children's playground. The park's hiking and cross-country trails are open year round; camping is seasonal from the third weekend in May to October 9.

Take Trans-Canada Highway 11/17 west from Thunder Bay for 18 miles.

When you're hunting or fishing in the Lake Superior region, don't be surprised if you cross paths with a game warden wearing a non-state insignia. Tribal ceded territory wardens and state wardens are cross-deputized, and enforcement officers of both jurisdictions have the authority to nab any errant hunters and anglers.

Inside
Fishing and Hunting

Fishing

Winter or summer, head for our inland lakes and rivers for walleye, northern pike, bullhead, bass, bluegill, catfish, sunfish and crappies. Or wade up our lovely streams for brookies, steelhead, brown trout, rainbow and splake (a hybrid trout). Wade out into the mouths of rivers flowing into Lake Superior to make those long casts that haul in a trout or salmon (coho, chinook, pink and Atlantic), or get out on the big lake in a launch. You'll have to go inland a way for muskellunge, but if you're looking for an inland monster fish experience, a trip to the Hayward, Wisconsin, area will be worth it (muskies are so popular there, at least six men in the area make muskie lures that are distributed throughout the region).

This is fishing country. For as far back as anyone can remember, people here always have relied on fish as a mainstay. Ojibwe people established fish camps to harvest the seasonal surges of fish in the bays and tributaries of Lake Superior. The wonderful fishery attracted Norwegian immigrants; their seafaring ways adapted easily to this inland sea, and they bestowed an old country saltwater name on a local whitefish subspecies: herring. Commercial fishing boomed. The huge harvest of lake trout, herring, chubs (also called ciscoes) and whitefish reached its

height in the early 1900s. Commercial fishermen from that era who are alive today can still remember those "gangs" of gill nets teeming with fish. Lake sturgeon, too, were abundant until the demand for their caviar triggered a buffalo-like slaughter of the slow-breeding giants.

But by the 1950s, the Lake Superior fishery was in trouble. Foreign species invaded the Great Lakes along the newly opened St. Lawrence Seaway, which connected the interior to the Atlantic Ocean. One invader was the smelt — an innocuous, tasty little fish that allegedly devoured herring eggs and trout eggs and soon dominated the underwater scene. Another was the sea lamprey — an eel-like creature that attaches itself bloodsucker-style to its prey and almost wiped out whitefish and trout throughout the Great Lakes. Both lamprey and smelt are now permanent residents; smelt are fished both commercially and for sport (with dip nets during spring spawning), and sea lamprey populations are held barely at bay with intense control programs.

Two more recent immigrants — zebra mussels and the Eurasian ruffe — arrived in ocean-going ships' ballast and are multiplying rapidly and spreading inland; it's unclear what their ultimate impact will be. Also finding a foothold in our inland lakes is Eurasian milfoil, which already is well-established in southern Minnesota and Wisconsin. The attractive plant grows so fast it eventually chokes out most native plants and fish, turning a waterway into a salad bowl. (See this chapter's Insiders' Tip on your responsibilities in regard to these invaders.)

And yes, pollution is a problem even here. It's a problem for the fish and a problem for us fish-eaters. The effluent from human activity, particularly the pulp, paper and taconite (iron) industries, has ruined some prime spawning habitat. And toxins dangerous to humans — PCBs, dioxins, toxaphene, mercury — are present in Lake Superior and inland waters. (See this chapter's sidebar about the fish consumption advisories that have been issued by Ontario, Minnesota, Wisconsin and Michigan.)

Nevertheless, we love our fish.

After the lamprey invasion, public restocking programs got under way, and now the states and the fishing tribes maintain hatcheries and stock both Lake Superior and inland lakes. "Catch-and-release" fishing is widely accepted and likely is responsible for a muskellunge comeback in Wisconsin (more than 90 percent of the 1,600 muskies caught in Wisconsin in 1994 were released).

The sportfishing industry has almost eclipsed commercial activity in U.S. waters, but in Ontario, commercial fishing remains lively. In 1994 in the Great Lakes, Ontario fishermen harvested 18.6 million kilos of yellow perch, walleye, whitefish and smelt. The fish had a value at the landings of $42 billion.

Angling has become big business in the region. In each of the Lake Superior states, it brings in between $1 billion and $1.5 billion a year. In Ontario, 2 million anglers in 1990 invested $1.2 billion directly into fishing equipment and activities and another $1.3 billion for related

services such as lodging and transportation.

Fishing Licenses

Anyone 16 or older, except tribal treaty anglers or folks fishing in private waters (fish farm), must purchase a state or provincial license. They're available at most bait and tackle shops as well as at county and natural resources offices.

Also, pick up a booklet of fishing regulations. Besides giving you essential information you'll need to fish legally, the booklets are full of handy tips and sketches of native fish species.

For more information, contact the respective state (or provincial) department (or ministry) of natural resources. (See this chapter's "Fishing and Hunting Licenses" gray box for information about these agencies.)

Fishing and Hunting Licenses
(Fees and Regulations)

MICHIGAN
DEPARTMENT OF NATURAL RESOURCES
Region 1 Headquarters
710 Chippewa Sq.
Marquette, Mich.   (906) 249-1161

A nonresident can fish, and hunt birds, small game, bear, deer and turkey in Michigan. Nonresident licenses range from $20.85 for three days of small-game hunting to $150.85 for bear for the season. Only residents can hunt elk. Resident licenses range from $1.50 for older-than-60 turkey hunters to

$100.85 for elk. See the regulations for other licenses and additional stamp fees.

MINNESOTA
DEPARTMENT OF NATURAL
RESOURCES

Northeast Region
1201 U.S. Hwy. 2 E.
Grand Rapids, Minn.   (218) 327-4413

A nonresident can hunt deer, bear, small game, wild turkey, pheasant, grouse, waterfowl, woodcock and fur-bearers (bobcat, grey fox, coyote). Only residents can get a moose license. Non-resident licenses range from $61 for small game to $166 for bear. Resident licenses are $23 for deer, $34 for bear, $15 for small game and $22.50 for a combination small game/angling li-cense. A nonresident angling license is $27.50 for a year; there are rates for one, three and seven days. A resident fishing license is $13. See the regulations for other licenses and additional stamp fees. Write for a copy of *A Guide to Lakes Managed for Stream Trout.*

ONTARIO
MINISTRY OF NATURAL RESOURCES

435 James St. S.
Thunder Bay, Ont.   (807) 475-1471

Nonresidents can hunt moose and bear in Ontario. However, you must be staying at a lodge whose owner has the right to issue a license for his or her management area. Other licenses are available the conventional way — through equipment outlets and at the natural resource offices. For nonresi-dents, a moose license is $272; a bear or deer license is $123; a small game li-cense is $59; and fishing licenses range from $10 for one day to $45 for the sea-son. Ontario residents get a three-year "outdoors card" for $6 plus the license

they want: moose, $31; deer, $24; small game, $10; fish, $15.

WISCONSIN
DEPARTMENT OF NATURAL
RESOURCES

Box 7921
Madison, Wis. 53707   (608) 266-2621

For residents, a deer license is $18; for nonresidents, $120. The fee is the same for firearms and archery, although they're separate licenses. Small game li-censes (includes ruffed grouse) are $12 for residents and $70 for nonresidents. A resident fishing license is $12; non-resident fees range from $13 for an in-dividual for four days to $28 for 15 days for a family, or $28 for all year for an individual.

Ice Fishing

Don't forget winter ice fishing. Places like Island Lake north of Duluth, Lake Gogebic in Michigan's western Upper Peninsula, Lax Lake on Minnesota's North Shore, the pristine lakes along the Gunflint Trail and dozens of ponds and rivers in between abound with fish houses above the ice and fish below. Fish houses also dot Lake Superior on the South Shore — close to shore — and near the Twin Ports; but anglers must poke their heads out of the fish house every so often to see which way the wind is blowing and whether the ice is moving, or they may find themselves out at sea on an ice floe. (A fine is levied on anyone who must be rescued, the amount of which depends upon the magnitude of the procedure.)

Generally speaking, ice houses are not available for rent. People build their own privy-like wooden houses or buy collaps-ible houses, using them year after year.

You don't really need an ice house — just bring along something to sit on and dress warmly. But you probably should buy a short fishing pole (available in season at discount stores, service stations and tackle shops) or contrive one yourself, so you can sit close to the hole. An ice auger is handy too; you won't get splashed as you would chopping through ice into water with an axe. Better yet, find an abandoned hole. The ice won't be so thick there.

Walleyes, northerns (pike), crappies and trout are all caught through the ice.

Fishing in Public Waters

Fishing opportunities are many on public lands. Chequamegon National Forest on Wisconsin's South Shore has boat launches and excellent river and lake fishing. The 954,000 acres of Ottawa National Forest on Michigan's Upper Peninsula have seven major river systems. Brule River State Forest in Wisconsin boasts a nationally renowned trout stream. (President Calvin Coolidge established a "summer White House" on the Brule River in 1928 so he could fish for trout. One day, he exceeded the catch limit — with 25 — but he wasn't arrested!) Handicapped-accessible fishing piers dot the 3 million acres of Superior National Forest on the North Shore.

For more information about public fishing access in a specific area, contact the respective local chamber of commerce or tribal government.

Bait and Tackle Shops

Twin Ports Area

CHALSTROM BAIT & TACKLE
5067 Rudy Perpich Memorial Dr.
Duluth, Minn.   *(218) 726-0094*

You'll find plenty of bait, fishing gear and archery equipment here. Chalstrom's also has an archery range and serves as a deer and bear registration station. Locals hang out here, exchanging information about the latest fishing hotspots.

The shop is open seven days a week all year long. In summer, hours are 5 AM to 10 PM; in winter, 6 AM to 8 PM.

From Central Entrance in Duluth, take Arlington Avenue (County Road 4) north. In 1995, the extension of Arlington formerly known as Rice Lake Road was given a new name. Insiders are getting used to the new name, bestowed in honor of the late Gov. Rudy Perpich.

FISHERMAN'S CORNER
5675 Miller Trunk Hwy., Pike Lake
Duluth, Minn.   *(218) 729-5369*

Live bait, rods, reels, tackle, licenses, fly-tying and rod-building supplies are all found aplenty at Fisherman's Corner. The store is 7 miles past Miller Hill Mall on U.S. Highway 53, not far from a couple of nice walleye lakes.

Fisherman's Corner is open from 7 AM to 7 PM every day except summer Sundays when it closes early depending on business.

Insiders' Tips

Lake Superior is no place to be if you don't know the lake. Take along an experienced person; get the weather forecast before departing; and pay attention to signs of wind and weather changes.

JIM'S BAIT SERVICE

319 E. 14th St.
Duluth, Minn.   *(218) 722-1279*

He wasn't so ancient that you could call him the Grandfather of Fishing, nor so formidable that you could call him the Godfather of Fishing, but Insiders know that the late Jim Keuten knew about all there is to know about angling. He always was willing to share what he knew — and sell you a leech or two from the 5,000 pounds he had on hand for the fishing season opener. He stocked them for 30 years, during which time he convinced walleye anglers in the region that a leech is something more than just a big bloodsucker. Jim's wife will carry on the business.

Jim's is open every day from 8 AM to 5 PM in winter and 6 AM to 7 PM in summer.

GANDER MOUNTAIN

1307 Miller Trunk Hwy.
Duluth, Minn.   *(218) 726-1100*

Imagine a scruffy little bait shop tucked into a neighborhood near a river. Then imagine the other end of the spectrum — and you've got Gander Mountain. This huge sporting goods and outdoor retail store has everything in reels, rods, lures and marine accessories you could hope for. Gander doesn't carry live bait, but it offers lots of seminars: ice fishing, firearms certification, gun loading and others.

Hours are 9 AM to 9 PM Monday through Friday; 9 AM to 6 PM Saturday; and 10 AM to 5 PM Sunday.

MARINE GENERAL SPORTS

1501 London Rd.   *(218) 724-8833*
Duluth, Minn.   *(800) 777-8557*

Marine General has one of the largest selections of fishing tackle, life jackets, rods and reels, rain gear, fly fishing supplies, life jackets and boat accessories of any place in the region. It has a 40-foot wall just plumb full of unpackaged gear (if it were in the package, it would require an 100-foot wall). Marine General also has live bait and fishing tips.

The shop is open year round from 8 AM to 6 PM Monday through Thursday and Saturday; 8 AM to 8 PM Friday.

NORTHWEST OUTLET

1814 Belknap
Superior, Wis.   *(715) 392-9838*

Most outdoors-minded insiders on this side of the lake have visited this landmark at some time. It's chock-full of canoes, waders, rods and reels, rod-building equipment, guns, rackets, sporting goods — just about anything you could wish for. The shop has a good assortment of lures, but no live bait.

You can count on the advice of the salespeople: They'd rather be fishing, too, which is why the store closes early on summer Saturdays. Otherwise, you'll find doors open from 9 AM to 6:30 PM weekdays, except Thursdays when the shop closes at 8 PM.

The 1996 deer hunt is not expected to be as productive as usual. Unusually deep snow and unusually cold weather (48 below in some areas) took a heavy toll on the region's deer herd.

Insiders' Tips

SPORTSMAN'S CHOICE
ARCHERY & FISHING
721 Belknap
Superior, Wis.   (715) 394-6077

Archery and fishing are the specialties here. You can get lures, live bait, and fishing and archery equipment. And the staff is happy to pass on the latest gossip about fishing hotspots.

Summer hours are 7 AM to 6 PM every day. Winter hours are 8 AM to 5 PM Monday through Saturday and 8 AM to 1 PM Sunday.

Along the North Shore

BEAR TRACK OUTFITTERS
Minn. Hwy. 61
Grand Marais, Minn.   (218) 387-1162

You can rent boats for Lake Superior and inland lakes, get fishing licenses, buy gear and find a fishing guide at Bear Track. This full retail shop also stocks a complete line of camping gear.

Hours are 8 AM to 8 PM seven days a week from May through the fall.

BUCK'S HARDWARE HANK
First Ave. W. and First St.
Grand Marais, Minn.   (218) 387-2280

It looks like a gas station and hardware store, but Buck's is the place to come for licenses, maps, fishing information and equipment. Here you can get flyfishing gear, deepwater gear for Lake Superior and tips on where to get those fish.

The store is open 6 AM to 8 PM in the winter and until 9 PM in the summer, every day.

SAWBILL CANOE OUTFITTERS
Minn. Hwy. 61
Tofte, Minn.   (218) 387-1360

Fishing gear, tips and licenses are available here from 7 AM to 9 PM seven days a week from early May through October. Sawbill also outfits canoe and camping trips into the Boundary Waters Canoe Area Wilderness.

SAWTOOTH OUTFITTERS
Minn. Hwy. 61
Tofte, Minn.   (218) 663-7643

You can get live bait, tackle, fishing advice and canoe rentals here. Like other area outfitters, the main business is getting people organized for the BWCA.

Hours are 7 AM to 7 PM daily from early May through September.

VOYAGEURS MARINA
Hat Point
Grand Portage, Minn.   (218) 475-2412

Everyone calls the place "Melby's," because that's the name of the old-time family that runs it. You can rent canoes and pick up books, maps, charts, marine equipment, information and Michigan fishing licenses (for Isle Royale).

Along the South Shore

ANGLERS ALL
2803 E. Lakeshore Dr. (U.S. Hwy. 2)
Ashland, Wis.   (715) 682-5754

You can walk up to Anglers All with-

Photo: Duluth News-Tribune

The hunt is successful for this pair in Ontario.

out a license or piece of equipment to your name, and folks here will handle the rest — including guiding you to the fish you want, either inland or on Lake Superior, winter or summer. The shop has a full line of fly and conventional fishing tackle, ice fishing, archery and hunting equipment.

Hours are 6 AM to 6 PM Monday to Saturday and 6 AM to 4 PM Sunday.

FLAG RIVER OUTFITTERS
(FORMERLY FISHERMAN'S COVE)
500 Washington Ave.
Port Wing, Wis.   *(715) 774-3886*
Here's a bait and tackle shop with flair. The Hanson family runs a guide service

(son Josh), a charter boat service (dad Gary and son Jeremiah) and the shop, where mom Barb sells bait and tackle and, with Josh, builds custom rods, ties flies and teaches flyfishing. She'll also send you to the fishing spot where you can reasonably expect to find fish. Or Josh will guide your flyfishing trips.

From Wis. Highway 13 in Port Wing, turn toward the lake at Don's service station; the shop is three blocks up on the right.

The shop opens March 15 to get ready for steelhead fishing in the nearby streams, and closes in late November so the family can go deer hunting. Hours are 9 AM to 5

Deer Ticks

Our region, particularly on the South Shore and lower North Shore, is home to the tiny deer tick, which carries Lyme disease. We don't stop enjoying the outdoors because of it, but it does make us more watchful.

Check yourself and your kids from head to toe once a day after you've been out in the woods or in tall grass. (The ticks wander around on you for more than a day before attaching themselves.) Should you notice the telltale "bull's eye" reddish patch on your skin, showing a Lyme-carrying tick has bitten you, see a doctor. The disease can be debilitating unless caught immediately.

If all this sounds troublesome, remember we don't have poisonous snakes, scorpions, fire ants, killer bees, earthquakes, typhoons or (well, almost never, anyway) tornados!

PM Monday through Friday; 7 AM to 5 PM Saturday; and 7 AM to noon Sunday.

Thunder Bay Area

BLACKFOOT MINNOW AND BAIT
274 N. Cumberland St.
Thunder Bay, Ont.   (807) 345-5965

Owner Hartley Cannon and son Jeff will be happy to give you lots of fishing tips along with your live bait. The shop also sells tackle and fishing licenses and is planning on expanding into other equipment in 1997. It's open 7 AM to 7 PM seven days a week.

DOG LAKE RESORT
Dog Lake Rd. (Hwy. 589)
RR 14, Box 30, Site 12
Thunder Bay, Ont.
Summer   (807) 933-4407
Winter   (807) 767-1809

Fish here or within a 100-mile radius with Brian Cashman as your guide. Likely catches are walleye, northern pike and

smallmouth bass. Brian and wife Susan also run a lodge, with cabins, a bar, restaurant, camping area, bait shop (you can get licenses here) and boat and motor rentals.

KAMPHERM GUIDE SERVICE
235 Munro St.
Thunder Bay, Ont.   (807) 626-4964

Harold Kampherm would rather have just a few happy customers than a lot of half-satisfied anglers, and emphasizes his one-to-one guiding service. He'll take you to trophy walleye, pike and trout lakes within an hour of his place at Hick's Lake. You can also get lodgings and rent a motorboat from him.

P & S WILDERNESS BOOKINGS LTD.
607 Strand Ave.
Thunder Bay, Ont.   (807) 767-8468

This company will clue you in to great fishing spots — lodges and camps — back in the Ontario bush. You'll be going in after northern, walleye and trout. Group rates are available.

SLEEPING GIANT TAXIDERMY
337 S. May St.
Thunder Bay, Ont.   *(807) 622-9989*

Live bait, tackle and guides are all available here. If you don't know where to fish, just ask; they'll tell you where the hotspots are.

WILD WATERS
EXPEDITIONS AND NATURE TOURS
R.R. 14, Dog Lake Rd.
Thunder Bay, Ont.   *(807) 767-2022*

Wild Waters arranges fly-in fishing trips, outfitting for your own trout runs and plenty of gear. Its specialty, however, is adventure-and eco-tourism, and canoeing.

Trolling on Lake Superior

Lake Superior is big, the water is cold, and the fish are nomads of the first order. When you're out on Superior, expect to do some traveling. The direction to head and the depth to fish vary yearly, depending on weather and other factors. In a "normal" season, however, lake trout and salmon (chinook and coho) roam along the South Shore or Minnesota Point early in the year. From early May through June, they tend to remain shallow; most of the action is on the surface, and minnow imitations (Rapalas and Rebels) are good for trolling. July and August are good months to go after the lake trout in the deep water off the Minnesota shoreline. Downriggers are needed to get baits down to 50, 100 or 150 feet. In late August and September, trollers head for the shallow water along the North Shore, especially at river mouths. They're after chinook salmon. Lake trout also can be caught through September in the shallows, where they move in before spawning.

Charter Fishing

Charter fishing opportunities are abundant all around the lake. The few listed here are only a sample of a large number of reputable services. Half-day (five or six hours) trips for four passengers run from $225 to $300. Full-day (eight or nine hours) trips range from $350 to $500. It costs more for additional anglers. Most captains are licensed to carry up to six passengers. The bigger boats also have fishing licenses (resident and nonresident) and trout stamps on board, for their customers' convenience. And most captains will book reduced-rate hotel rooms for customers (or provide tents for those camping on Isle Royale or in the Apostles).

For free brochures, contact the **North Shore Charter Captains Association** at P.O. Box 292, Duluth, Minnesota 55801; the **Isle Royale Charter Captains Association** at 5101 Lester Street, Duluth, Minnesota 55804; or the **Superior Charter Dock Association** c/o the Superior-Douglas Chamber of Commerce, 305 Harborview Parkway, Superior, Wisconsin 54880.

APOSTLE ISLANDS CHARTER SERVICES
P.O. Box 1331
Bayfield, Wis. 54814   *(715) 779-5555*

Capt. Steve Prevost and his 31-foot *Driftwood* will take you out among the islands for a half-day or several days, anchoring and camping there. Gear is supplied; bring food and beverages unless otherwise arranged. The *Driftwood* is moored at Bayfield City Dock.

BILL'S TIME OUT CHARTERS
1643 Wildwood Rd.
Duluth, Minn.   *(218) 525-4598*

Capt. Bill Miller and his first mate

will take up to six people on the 32-foot *Time Out*. The luxury Trojan boat has a sedan flybridge. It docks at the Grand Portage Marina near the casino at Grand Portage from the last weekend of July through the third week in August; the rest of the time, from May until late September, it docks at the Waterfront Plaza Marina in downtown Duluth. All gear is supplied; bring your own food and beverages.

BJ's Charter Service
Rt. 3, Harborview Dr.
Washburn, Wis. 54891   (715) 373-5200

The 38-foot *Crusader* puts out from Bayfield City Dock under Capt. Ralph Brzezinski and his first mate, son Joshua. The *Crusader* stays mostly in the Apostle Islands. If you charter a two-day trip you'll sleep in a berth on board as the ship moors at an island. Bring your own food, beverages and sleeping bags. The captain supplies breakfast and a steak dinner on overnight trips. Write or call to make a reservation.

Flag River Outfitters (formerly Fisherman's Cove)
500 Washington Ave.
Port Wing, Wis.   (715) 774-3886

Capt. Gary Johnson and his first mate, son Jeremiah, ply the waters along the South Shore between Brule Point and Bark Point, in the Port Wing-Herbster area. The 34-foot *Reel E-Z* also takes overnight charters to the Apostle Islands. Johnson has been a leader in promoting catch-and-release in charter fishing. Bring your own beverages and snacks, unless you arrange for Hanson to provide lunches or full meals.

Captain Charlie Haslerud's Dr. Juice Charters
5101 Lester St.   (218) 525-3418
Duluth, Minn.   (800) 777-8590

For those who want a luxury experience, Capt. Charlie and his first mate offer fishing for up to six people on the 40-foot *Nordic Venture*. The *Venture* has two full staterooms, a stand-up head (bathroom-shower), a salon (common area) and a full galley. Charters are from the *Venture's* Duluth dock (Waterfront Plaza Marina in

Fishing enthusiasts are rewarded with views of Barkers Island and the Meteor *at the Superior, Wisconsin pier.*

downtown) in May and June. In July, the boat moves up the shore to the Grand Portage Marina (near the casino), where it takes people fishing near Isle Royale in July and August. The *Venture* returns to Duluth for September fishing. ("Dr. Juice" refers to a local physician, Greg Bambanek, who developed a fish lure scent that users say is a sure thing.) All gear is supplied; bring your own food and beverages.

LAKE SUPERIOR
SPORTSFISHING CHARTERS
1315 E. Eighth St.
Duluth, Minn. 55805   *(218) 724-9104*

You can be fishing within 15 minutes of leaving Duluth with Capt. Steve Johnson and his first mate. The 31-foot luxury *Hard Times* will accommodate up to six people and stays within 10 miles of the Twin Ports, pursuing not only trout and salmon but trophy walleye as well. All gear is provided; bring your own food and beverages.

LOU'S CHARTER SERVICE
2914 E. Lake Shore Dr. (U.S. Hwy. 2)
Ashland, Wis.   *(715) 682-2646/5710*

The *Athena* is a 32-foot Trojan craft with a flybridge that's out on the lake a little longer than most charters — until October 15. Capt. Louis Bickel offers half-day, all-day and overnight trips in pursuit of trout, salmon and northern. All equipment is supplied; bring your own snacks and beverage.

NOURSE'S SPORT FISHING
HC 64, Box 6
Bayfield, Wis. 54814   *(800) 779-3257*

Capt. Ken Nourse and his dad, Capt. Laurie Nourse, handle their two charter boats in the tradition of Laurie's uncle, Capt. Lyman Nourse, who started a charter business here in the early 1940s. They also continued the boat-naming tradition: their 36-footer is called *Black Hawk II* and their 39-footer is *Black Hawk III*. You can fish half-day, full day or for two days. The latter includes a full day of fishing, an onboard steak dinner, an all-night rest in the boat or on Rocky Island (in the building where Ken's grandma once had a restaurant) and another day's fishing.

Nourse boats stay in the Apostle Islands, fishing mostly trout. All gear is supplied, as is fish-cleaning and packaging, and a lounge area at the boathouse is provided. Bring your own snacks and beverages.

From Wis. Highway 13 in Bayfield, turn east on Manypenny, go down the hill to Maggie's, turn right and continue to Black Hawk Dock.

PRINCE ARTHUR'S LANDING MARINA
Marina Park
Thunder Bay, Ont.   *(807) 345-2344*

You can find fishing charters and visitor information at this city-owned marina on Lake Superior. The marina is open May 15 to October 15.

Commercial and subsistence fishermen set nets throughout much of Lake Superior. The nets hang from floating buoys or jugs, which are clearly marked. The fishermen are licensed by a state, province or tribe, and it is against the law to interfere with these nets. It's also bad for the fish; a severed net floats unattended for years, sunken but still fishing.

Insiders' Tips

SUPERIOR CHARTER FISHING SERVICE
2719 N. 28th St.
Superior, Wis.   *(715) 394-7289*

The *Hound Dog* follows the fish from near the Amnicon River on the South Shore (where walleye are found in addition to the usual trout and salmon) to the Talmadge River on the North Shore, guided by Capt. Alex Kotter. The 29-foot cruiser has a sedan flybridge. All gear is provided; bring your own food and beverages.

VOYAGEURS MARINA
Hat Point
Grand Portage, Minn.   *(218) 475-2412*

Charter boats head out from this marina, where you also can buy books, maps, charts, marine equipment rentals and Michigan fishing licenses (for Isle Royale).

Suit Yourself . . .

What if you want to troll in your own skiff, or fish in the wintertime? You'll be able to catch fish, but you must know what you're doing whenever you're out on this inland sea, which is capricious and often dangerous. Lake Superior has frozen over completely only once in many decades, and the North Shore is usually accessible by boat, unless the wind has blown the floating ice up against the shore. You have to keep a close watch on the wind and the wandering ice floes, so you don't get cut off from shore. (The shallower South Shore is usually frozen, particularly among the Apostle Islands.) You can put your skiff in at Agate or Burlington Bay in Two Harbors, Minnesota; take a compass and an extra engine, even though you won't be going more than 2 miles out.

Kamloops rainbow trout can be trolled from Duluth up the shore, almost to Knife River, from October through December.

Come January, trollers go farther up the shore to Two Harbors to fish coho salmon. In February and March they move back down to Knife River and troll toward Duluth; and in April they move toward the river mouths to go after rainbow, which is also where shorecasters fish.

Fish Retailers

Maybe you like fish, but you don't care to harvest them. No problem; you still can get a taste of our fishing heritage at one of the fish shops in the region. You'll find fresh fish — slabs of yellow, orange and pink fillets of trout, salmon and whitefish; headless, scaled herring; whole whitefish, scales and heads still on. All are great fried, but try poaching the fillets, baking the whole trout and whitefish (peel away cooked whitefish skin and scales in one easy motion), or boiling the herring with potatoes and onions. These shops also sell smoked fish — mounds of shiny golden ciscoes (chubs), which are small, oily fish that when freshly smoked are truly delectable; the larger herring, which are drier, leaner and have a strong flavor; soft, delicate whitefish, the largest of this fish family. All of these usually are smoked whole, so you'll be buying heads — sunken, smoked eyeballs and all — which is a good way to wake up travel-weary kids. (Few Insiders eat the eyeballs, although many will dig into the jowls for the delicious cheek meat.)

In the trout family, smoked-fish shops sell fillets and chunks of lake trout, siskowet ("fat trout") and salmon. Siskowets are very heavy, deepwater trout that have delicious meat, but the bigger ones absolutely drip with oil. This characteristic has two edges: The oil is rich in heart-healthy Omega-3 fatty acids; but it probably is laden with toxic PCBs too (from industrial waste). Pregnant women

A Few Words About Fish Consumption

Don't let the abundance of happy anglers and happy angling businesses mislead you: The toxins in our area's fish are no light matter. Get the health department fish advisory booklets before eating fish caught in our region, which give specifics about which fish in which waters contain which poisons.

A good general rule of thumb is: Pregnant women should eat no fish from our area; children and women of childbearing age should eat only small amounts of fish; and everyone should avoid eating the skin and fat of larger fish.

The booklets are free; you can get them at local health departments (see our Hospitals and Healthcare chapter), Department of Natural Resources offices and state park headquarters. The Michigan Department of Health's fishing advisories are listed right in the fishing regulations pamphlet. Or, you can write or call: Fish Advisory, Minnesota Department of Health, P.O. Box 64975, St. Paul, Minnesota 55164, (612) 215-0880; Fish Advisory, c/o Wisconsin Department of Natural Resources, Box 7921, Madison, Wisconsin 53707, (608) 267-7610; Guide to Eating Sports Fish #590, Ontario Ministry of the Environment, 135 St. Clair Ave. W., Main Floor Public Information Center, Toronto, Ontario M4V 1P5, (416) 323-4321.

and small children should not eat siskowets (see this chapter's sidebar on fish consumption). The more common trout in fish shops is the ever-popular "lean" lake trout, which is a meaty, flavorful fish. Salmon, also meaty, usually is smoked with brown sugar or maple sugar, for a mellow, slightly sweet flavor.

Some shops also sell quirky items dear to the hearts of many old-time residents: whitefish livers (they're milder and richer than chicken livers); fish cake (chopped fish mixed with onion, egg, crumbs and occasionally cream, which you take home and fry); fish heads (for soup); whitefish-family roe (the eggs are in the skein, which you fry as is, or smush with salt into caviar). You usually have to ask for these items.

Twin Ports Area

SIVERTSON FISHERIES
1507 N. First St.
Superior, Wis.   (715) 392-5551

The oldest fish business in the Twin Ports, Sivertson boats often are seen out on the lake as they go after smelt and herring. (Sivertson also owns the long-established ferry from Grand Portage to Isle Royale.) The company got its start in the 1890s, when a pair of Sivertson brothers established a mail-order business. A second generation of brothers established the direct-sales business in 1941; the widow of one, Clara Sivertson (who grew up in the fishing village of Grand Marais, herself the daughter of a commercial fisherman), continues to run the business.

You can buy all kinds of smoked fish, frozen ocean fish and, depending on the season, fresh Lake Superior fish. Even better, you can get Clara to talk about the fishing history of the area. If you visit in late April, early May, September or October, you'll see a working commercial boat unloading its harvest.

Take the U.S. Highway 53 turnoff at the foot of the Blatnik Bridge on the Superior side; instead of circling under the bridge, go straight toward the waterfront.

SMOKIE'S FRESH & SMOKED FISH
109 Ave. D
Cloquet, Minn.   (218) 879-3710

Salt- and cholesterol-conscious snackers might try this shop for low-salt smoked fish and low-fat sausage. The shop's main business is service (smoking other people's fish and turning other people's venison into sausage) but about 10 years ago branched out into retail sales. Smokie's sausage contains no vital organs and is all lean meat. The shop is open year round but closed on Sundays.

From I-35, take the Minn. Highway 33 exit into Cloquet. Turn left at the third semaphore (Cloquet Avenue); Smokie's is on the right. On your way back, take a look at the building a long kitty-corner from Smokie's. The odd-shaped Best Service station is said to be the only gas station the renowned architect Frank Lloyd Wright ever designed.

Along the North Shore

RUSS KENDALL'S SMOKE HOUSE
Minn. Hwy. 61
Knife River, Minn.   (218) 834-5995

Fishing was long the tradition in the tiny village of Knife River, and the Kendalls are an old-time fishing family. Russ' specialties are brown sugar trout and

Clean your watercraft's hull and discard water from bait containers, livewells and engine cooling systems on shore (not in the water!) before you get back on the road. Harmful exotic species are carried stuck to the bottoms of boats and in containers of lakewater. A small, dry bit of milfoil, the egg of a zebra mussel or spiny water flea, or a small Eurasian ruffe can seed an unspoiled lake — with sometimes disastrous results. You'll find sketches of these species in fishing regulation booklets and at some boat landings. It is illegal to transport these species.

Insiders' Tips

salmon and homemade beef jerky. The shop is open every day, all year. If you're driving along Scenic Highway 61, you can't miss it.

Lou's Fish House

331 Seventh Ave.
Two Harbors, Minn.   *(218) 834-5254*

This shop's specialty is sugar-cured salmon and jerky (beef and turkey) smoked with a secret recipe. A wide variety of cheeses is also sold here. The shop is open from May through Labor Day.

Eckel Fish House

Grand Marais Harbor, Dock A
Grand Marais, Minn.   *No phone*

Brothers Dick and Tom own adjoining fish houses here. Both commercial fishermen sell fresh fish — but only when they're in from the lake, so don't bother going down to the fish house unless you see swooping gulls or open doors.

Along the South Shore

Bodin Fisheries

208 Wilson
Bayfield, Wis.   *(715) 779-3301*

This retail shop is right on the dock; fishermen bring their haul in the back, and the cleaned or smoked fish are sold out the front. Bodin's is open 8 AM to 4:30 PM weekdays (except at lunchtime, noon to 1 PM) and from 8 AM to 1 PM Saturdays.

From Rittenhouse Avenue, turn south on Bayfield Street. Go two blocks to the waterfront and turn left on Wilson.

Buffalo Bay Fish Co.

Wis. Hwy. 13
Red Cliff Reservation
North of Bayfield, Wis.   *(715) 779-3753*

You can watch several fishing boats come and go at this tribally owned fishery, which has a retail shop near its dock. Fresh, frozen and smoked Lake Superior fish as well as walleye, perch and smoked salmon are sold here. Buffalo Bay (named for a 19th-century principal chief of the Lake Superior Ojibwe bands, whose descendants still live here) is open 8 AM to 5 PM Monday through Saturday in the summer and 8:30 AM to 3 PM weekdays in the winter. The fishery is visible from Wis. Highway 13 just north of Bayfield.

Everett's Fish/Johnson's Store

Wis. Hwy. 13
Port Wing, Wis.   *(715) 774-3511*

The fish smoked here is arguably the best-known in the region, for this smokehouse supplies many retail stores with its fine fare. You can buy both smoked and fresh fish here when the owner (son of the late Everett) is fishing. The town is famous for its annual fish boil (an outside cauldron holding boiling water, several kinds of lake fish, onions and potatoes). The shop is open seven days a week all year, except Christmas.

Peterson Fishery

Wis. Hwy. 13
Bayfield, Wis.   *(715) 779-5023*

Some of the finest smoked fish to be found anywhere on the lake comes out of this unassuming fishery, where second-, third- and fourth-generation descendents of Ojibwe-Norwegian fishermen pick nets and fillet, smoke and sell their haul. The patriarch of the family, Wilfred, lives next door to the fish house and little retail shop and will regale you with fishing stories and history as he wraps up your purchase. Peterson's is open all year round — anytime.

Exploring the Gunflint Trail and Boundary Waters Canoe Area Wilderness

The **Gunflint Trail**, the **Boundary Waters Canoe Area Wilderness** (both in Minnesota) and **Quetico Provincial Park** (in Ontario) comprise a world of remote, abundant fishing. This densely wooded, watery vastness drains into Hudson Bay and the Arctic as well as Lake Superior; the lakes are cold and clear, and trout and walleye are prevalent. Smallmouth bass are common, northerns less so, and panfish are few.

You can drive up the Gunflint, hauling your motorized craft or snowmobile behind. But if you plan on going further inland into the Boundary Waters Canoe Area Wilderness, you'll have to forget the motors — they're not allowed in most places. In the summertime, people travel by canoe and foot; in the winter, by ski, snowshoe and dog sled. Outfitters can help you with all of these modes of transportation. There's nothing stopping you from grabbing a canoe (or skis or snowshoes), packing up your own gear and heading into the bush. Many people use these areas as a place for solitary wandering.

If you want someone else to do the work, however, there are two approaches for you: Stay at one of the many rustic secluded resorts along the Gunflint or get an outfitter to take you deep into the wilderness. Both operate year round; ice fishing and winter camping are popular. The resorts offer cabins, boats, motors, fishing advice and some recreational activities — and relief from the insects in the summer and the cold in the winter, either of which can be malevolent. Stays range from $75 to $250 a day for two people, depending on the season and cabin size. If you want meals included, add another $80 to $100. A fishing guide, who can take you to where trophy fish are biting, will cost another $100 to $150 a day. The guides will fix you up a hot shore lunch that is the hallmark of the northwoods resort experience: fresh fish, potatoes, bacon, beans and coffee, all cooked over an open fire.

In the BWCA and Quetico, where no motors are allowed, a person could paddle for months without seeing civilization, portaging between lakes with names such as Bearskin, Angleworm and Big Moose, dining on trout all the way. Unfortunately, permits don't allow you to stay that long. The areas would be loved to death, were it not for the permit system that dribbles people through them. It's best to reserve a permit three to five months in advance. You can get them from the forest services or through outfitters. Outfitters supply guides, food, tents, sleeping bags and canoes, skis or snowshoes for about $50 to $60 a day per person. Most trips are three to six days. You can go to fish, or view or photograph wildlife — moose is a big favorite. Make reservations with the outfitter.

Everyone strives for low-impact visits to this beloved area. No cans or bottles are allowed in the BWCA (except for insect repellant, medicines and toiletries), and you must haul all trash out with you.

Gunflint Trail and BWCA Outfitters

BEAR TRACK OUTFITTERS

Minn. Hwy. 61
Grand Marais, Minn.   *(218) 387-1162*

You can get outfitted for a fishing trip into the BWCA here. Bear Track arranges special flyfishing trips and provides fishing guides, licenses, fishing gear, boats, kayaks and canoes.

Hours are 8 AM to 8 PM seven days a week from May through the fall.

GUNFLINT LODGE AND
NORTHWOODS OUTFITTERS

Gunflint Lake, Gunflint Tr.
Grand Marais, Minn.   *(800) 328-3325*

The Kerfoot family is legendary here for their knowledge and love of this backwoods country. The attractive lodge can accommodate 75 to 100 guests, and both management and staff are happy to give you generous servings of fishing tips and the area's history.

HUNGRY JACK
LODGE AND CAMPGROUND

Gunflint Tr.
Grand Marais, Minn.   *(800) 338-1566*

Smallmouth bass and walleye await you in Hungry Jack Lake, where lodge owners can house up to 20 people in the cabins and more in the campground. The lodge is open year round; in the wintertime, it caters to snowmobilers, ice anglers and cross-country skiers. Boats, meals and fishing guides are available.

LITTLE VINCE'S GUIDE SERVICE

HC 86, Box 338
Grand Marais, Minn. 55604   *(218) 387-2168*

Vince Ekroot's dad was 6'7", so that settles the obvious question. The younger Ekroot has been guiding for most of the past 25 years in the area where he grew up. He'll take you after trout or walleye or whatever is biting best, 30 miles up the Gunflint. He'll fully equip you if you need it and even arrange your licenses. Call or write for reservations.

ROCKWOOD LODGE & OUTFITTERS

Gunflint Tr.
Grand Marais, Minn.   *(800) 942-BWCA*

On Poplar Lake, 32 miles from Grand Marais, Rockwood is open May through September. Each cabin has individual docks; if you want still more seclusion, rent a cabin out on an island in Poplar Lake. Rockwood Lodge will accommodate up to 40 guests overnight for scheduled canoe trips, and up to 50 in the cabins. Meals, guides and boats are available.

SAWBILL CANOE OUTFITTERS

Minn. Hwy. 61
Tofte, Minn. (218) 387-1360

Partial and complete outfitting for the BWCA is available here: camping equipment, fishing licenses, advice on canoe routes and good fishing spots, dried food, maps.

Sawbill is open 7 AM to 9 PM seven days a week from early May through October.

SAWTOOTH OUTFITTERS

Minn. Hwy. 61
Tofte, Minn. (218) 663-7643

Bring only yourself and your fishing rod and let Sawtooth handle the rest: canoes, bait, fishing advice, food, camping gear. You can get partial outfitting here too. Sawtooth also has books on the BWCA and the North Shore.

Hours are 7 AM to 7 PM daily from early May through September.

Odds and Ends

Private Fishing Holes

Several places on the South Shore offer sure-thing fishing in private holes. You bring nothing but your enthusiasm. You don't even need a license.

SPORTS HOLLOW

U.S. Hwy. 2 W.
Ashland, Wis. (715) 682-3838

Spring-fed ponds yield brown trout and rainbow trout at Sports Hollow. The business includes a picnic area, refreshments, a heated shelter, handicap accessibility, bait and tackle and fish-cleaning service. Call for a reservation.

IRON RIVER TROUT HAUS

205 W. Drummond Rd.
Iron River, Wis. (800) 262-1453

This spring-fed trout pond is open for fishing all year long. Brown and rainbow trout are just waiting for you. Gear is supplied, as is a fish-cleaning service. Call ahead for reservations.

The Trout Haus is also a bed and breakfast inn, and if you stay two nights you'll get your catch cooked for breakfast. From U.S. Highway 2, take Lea Street north for 2½ blocks, pass over the Tri-County Corridor and turn left on Drummond.

Smelting

Silvery little smelts flow from the Lake and up the streams in early spring to spawn, and smelters flow in similar numbers to the streams to harvest them. It's more like a holiday than like fishing.

The smelt come at night, so you'll see flashlights bobbing along the streams and bonfires by the Lake, as warmly dressed people wearing boots and carrying long-handled nets try to dip them out. The nets are sold at hardware stores and service stations throughout the area as smelt season approaches — around the time the ice leaves the streams, usually in April.

People bring home buckets or trash barrels full of smelt. Beheaded and snipped open with scissors and cleaned with a backward flip of the thumb, they're deep-fried and eaten whole, bones and all; or frozen whole for use as bait throughout the year.

The mouth of any river or creek that feeds into Lake Superior is likely to have smelt. A favorite gathering place is the Lester River at the eastern edge of Duluth — in a heavy smelt year, pedestrians looking for smelt, smelters and all-night parties keep traffic at a crawl.

Fish Hatcheries

Michigan, Minnesota, Wisconsin, Ontario and several tribes hatch and plant fish in Lake Superior. Here are two of the most visited hatcheries:

BRULE RIVER FISH HATCHERY
Off U.S. Hwy. 2
Brule, Wis.   *(715) 372-4820*
Lake Superior fish (trout and walleye) are bred here, and you can see the state operation informally or in guided tours. The kids will be allowed to feed the fish too. The hatchery is open 8 AM to 4 PM weekdays all year long. It's also open weekends June through September. The hatchery is off U.S. Highway 2.

FRENCH RIVER FISH HATCHERY
5351 North Shore Dr. (Scenic Hwy. 61)
Duluth, Minn.   *(218) 723-4785*
Bubbling jars at the lower hatchery keep walleye eggs moving, and breeding trout swim in open ponds at the upper, coldwater hatchery. The public is invited to take a look at the state operation from 8 AM to 4 PM weekdays. The fish are planted in Lake Superior and at inland lakes.

Hunting

"Ya been huntin'?"
"Yah. Already got mine."

To Insiders, such an exchange has nothing to do with squirrel, turkey or pheasant. It means deer meat (a.k.a. venison) is in the freezer. The whitetails are commonplace in our region, except after unusually snowy winters when they have a harder time finding food and escaping timber wolves. Even then, they have a way of bouncing back. Oh, that doesn't mean people don't pursue other game. There are plenty of ruffed grouse hunters and a few bear hunters. Black bear are at home here, even entering residential neighborhoods to help themselves to late summer food. If you're after ducks, geese, wild turkey or squirrels, however, you're better off going west toward the prairie flyways, or south to oak tree country.

It's true we have moose in Minnesota and Ontario, and nonresidents can hunt them in Ontario under certain conditions. But only residents can go after moose in Minnesota — and then only if they are lucky enough to get picked in the lottery. Four-hunter teams drop their names into a DNR hat in June, and approximately 380 licenses for 1,520 hunters are drawn for the fall hunt.

It's also true there are elk in Wisconsin and Michigan; but they recently were reintroduced and are still protected in Wisconsin, and only state residents can hunt them in Michigan. So deer remains the primary target for hunters in this region.

Most hunters head for state and national forests, especially recently logged areas. Jurisdictions (states, provinces and tribes) have varying rules about deer stands, baiting, length of season, how to register your harvest, hours and other regulations, so check the appropriate jurisdiction. Most have archery, firearms and muzzle loader seasons. You can get good hunting tips along with your ammunition and license at hunting supply shops and local natural resource offices.

Hunting Supply Shops

Twin Ports Area

CHALSTROM BAIT & TACKLE
5067 Rudy Perpich Memorial Dr.
Duluth, Minn.   *(218) 726-0094*

Archery equipment, an archery range, deer and bear registration and a gathering of local hunters defines Chalstrom's. The shop is open seven days a week all year long. In summer, hours are 5 AM to 10 PM; in winter, 6 AM to 8 PM.

From Central Entrance in Duluth, take Arlington Avenue (County Road 4) north. In 1995, the extension of Arlington formerly known as Rice Lake Road was given a new name in honor of the late Gov. Rudy Perpich.

GANDER MOUNTAIN
1307 Miller Trunk Hwy.
Duluth, Minn.   *(218) 726-1100*

Gander Mountain can fit you out with everything from a rifle to the latest product for keeping your hands warm while waiting in a deer stand. It also offers seminars on firearms safety, firearms certification, gun loading and more.

Hours are 9 AM to 9 PM Monday through Friday; 9 AM to 6 PM Saturday; and 10 AM to 5 PM Sunday.

NORTHWEST OUTLET
1814 Belknap
Superior, Wis.   *(715) 392-9838*

Most outdoors-minded insiders on this side of the lake have visited this landmark at some time. It's chock-full of canoes, guns, bows, cold-weather clothing, blaze orange outfits — just about everything you need for a hunting trip, including licenses. The salespeople are knowledgeable and can give you some local hunting tips.

The doors are open from 9 AM to 6:30 PM weekdays, except Thursdays when they close at 8 PM, and Saturday mornings.

SPORTSMAN'S CHOICE ARCHERY & FISHING
721 Belknap
Superior, Wis.   *(715) 394-6077*

Archery and fishing are the specialties here. You can get fitted out for bow hunting and pick up some hunting tips too. Summer hours are 7 AM to 6 PM every day. Winter hours are 8 AM to 5 PM Monday through Saturday and 8 AM to 1 PM Sunday.

Along the North Shore

BUCK'S HARDWARE HANK
First Ave. W. and First St.
Grand Marais, Minn.   *(218) 387-2280*

It looks like a gas station and hardware store, but Buck's is the place to come

Are You Hungry Jack?

Hungry Jack Lake, up the Gunflint Trail, doesn't have anything to do with pancakes.

A surveyor named Jack Scott was up there with his crew in 1884, and they were running low on food. Jack stayed while the rest of the men went back 40 miles to Grand Marais for supplies. A blizzard swept through the area, blanketing everything with snow and impassable drifts. It took the crew two weeks to get back to Jack. They found him — gaunt, but alive.

"Are you hungry, Jack?" a rescuer asked him.

"I'm Hungry Jack!" he responded.

for licenses, maps, hunting information and equipment (except for guns). Buck's will give you tips on where to get bear, deer and grouse, and aim you at a bow hunting guide.

The store is open 6 AM to 8 PM in the winter and until 9 PM in the summer, every day.

Along the South Shore

ANGLERS ALL
2803 E. Lakeshore Dr. (U.S. Hwy. 2)
Ashland, Wis. **(715) 682-5754**

Despite the name, Anglers All caters to hunters too. You can pick up what you need for archery and firearms, along with licenses and advice. Anglers All can aim you at a deer hunting guide too.

Hours are 6 AM to 6 PM Monday to Saturday and 6 AM to 4 PM Sunday.

FLAG RIVER OUTFITTERS
(FORMERLY FISHERMAN'S COVE)
500 Washington Ave.
Port Wing, Wis. **(715) 774-3886**

Because the Hanson family is into archery and hunting almost as much as fishing (they have a charter service and bait and tackle shop), they've changed the name of the business. Two family

members teach archery, and son Josh will guide your bow hunting trips (for deer and bear) and firearms hunting trips (for bear). Prices vary, depending on the hunter's success.

From Wis. Highway 13 in Port Wing, turn toward the lake at Don's service station; the shop is three blocks up on the right.

The shop opens March 15 to get ready for steelhead season in nearby streams and closes in late November so the family can go hunting. Hours are 9 AM to 5 PM Monday through Friday; 7 AM to 5 PM Saturday; and 7 AM to noon Sunday.

Thunder Bay Area

DOG LAKE RESORT
Dog Lake Rd. (Hwy. 589)
R.R. 14, Box 30, Site 12
Thunder Bay, Ont.
Summer **(807) 933-4407**
Winter **(807) 767-1809**

Hunt for bear or moose within a 100-mile radius with Brian Cashman as your guide. Brian and Susan also run a lodge at Dog Lake, with cabins, a bar, restaurant and camping facilities — you can get licenses here too.

The breakwall in Two Harbor's Agate Bay is ideal for casting or trolling for salmon.

W.F.O. BEARHUNT INC.

c/o Robert Kotanen
Hilldale Rd.   *(807) 767-5628*
Thunder Bay, Ont.   *cellular: (807) 624-8208*

Rob Kotanen's specialty is hunting bear and moose (archery, muzzle loader and rifle), but if you'd rather use a camera, he can handle that too.

About $1,100 (U.S.) gets you six bear hunting days, including accommodations and processing the bear (excluding the bear tag and your food). About $2,500 gets you 10 moose hunting days.

If a member of your party would rather go fishing, Kotanen has boats and tips available.

WFO Bearhunt's hunting success rate has been 90 to 100 percent over the past 10 years. Many hunters wind up with a wolf in addition to the big game (wolves are legal to hunt in Ontario).

Kotanen is a member of the North American Hunt Club.

WILD WATERS
EXPEDITIONS AND NATURE TOURS

R.R. 14, Dog Lake Rd.
Thunder Bay, Ont.   *(807) 767-2022*

Wild Waters arranges fly-in moose tours as part of its adventure- and eco-tourism and canoeing services.

Resource Commissions

1854 TREATY COMMISSION

1908½ W. Superior St.
Duluth, Minn.   (218) 722-8907

This commission handles natural resources issues — enforcement, licensing, resource management — in Minnesota's Arrowhead country for the Bois Forte and Grand Portage Ojibwe bands, which hold treaty rights in territory ceded in 1854. It also distributes frozen packaged fish and game to elderly tribal members living in the Duluth area and has literature on treaty history.

FOND DU LAC RESERVATION BUSINESS COMMITTEE

105 University Rd.
Cloquet, Minn.   (218) 879-4593

The committee handles enforcement, licensing and resource management in Minnesota's Arrowhead country for the Fond du Lac Ojibwe band, which with the Bois Forte and Grand Portage bands holds hunting, fishing and gathering rights on territory ceded in 1854.

GREAT LAKES INDIAN FISH & WILDLIFE COMMISSION

Maple Ln.
Odanah, Wis.   (715) 682-6619

This 11-tribe commission co-manages (with the state) natural resources in the northern third of Wisconsin, Michigan's Upper Peninsula and a big portion of Lake Superior. The Lake Superior Ojibwe bands ceded the land to the United States by treaty in 1836, 1837 and 1842 but specifically reserved their right to hunt, fish and gather there.

The commission employs biologists, wildlife managers and enforcement officers. You can get more information about the commission and treaty history at the office.

UNIVERSITY OF WISCONSIN SEA GRANT INSTITUTE

Communications Office
1800 University Ave.
Madison, Wis. 53705   (608) 263-3259

Sea Grant has a 20-page illustrated booklet on ice fishing. Send $1 for postage and handling.

On a summer day, water temperatures throughout Lake Superior can range from 45 to more than 70 degrees.

Inside
Watersports

Our inland sea is watery enough for millions of water skiers, skinny-dippers, wind surfers and rubber mat-paddlers. Lake Superior's hundreds of miles of public shoreline have plenty of room for sun bathers, barefoot waders and half-naked Frisbee throwers.

So where are they?

The first-time visitor to Lake Superior will probably be surprised at the scarcity of watersports activity (aside from fishing) in and along the Lake. In most places, most of the year, for most folk, the water is just too cold.

However, there are some exceptions — places where, if you hit it right, you can have a wonderfully refreshing swim, and activities (sailing, kayaking, canoeing) that let you be involved with the Lake without getting too wet. And then, of course, there are the rivers that feed into Lake Superior and offer wonderful places to jump in with or without a watercraft.

Water skiing, which originated in Minnesota, is not a Lake Superior sport and, while practiced at some nearby inland lakes, is not popular here as it is farther south.

Swimming

There are few experiences more overwhelming than swimming out into the clear, cold, empty waters of Lake Superior. You get the same sense of insignificance that an ocean gives you, augmented by a feeling that you are alone; looking down

through the clear water, you can see the rocks and sand several fathoms below and nothing moving except yourself. You feel like a single tiny star bobbing in the pure cold universe.

But you can't stay out long, even on a very warm day, or hypothermia — loss of body heat — will overcome you. When swimming in Lake Superior in the summertime, it's best to stay fairly close to shore and come in every 10 to 15 minutes to warm up — even if you're not aware that you're becoming numb — before the cold begins to affect your judgment.

When and where are the best swimming opportunities? They can be found all around the Lake, but they depend on water depth, the previous days' weather and direction of the wind and whether a rocky cove is situated to absorb the sun. The shallow waters of Wisconsin's South Shore are the warmest, but they also can be frigid if the wind is blowing from the land, sending the warmer surface water away from the shore. On the other hand, if the wind has been blowing from the Lake, the water near shore can become relatively warm. Summertime temperatures can range from 45 to more than 70 degrees.

Pollution has done its dirty work here, collapsing some once-popular swimming spots, such as Chippewa Park in Thunder Bay, Twin Ponds in Duluth and the St. Louis River below Cloquet, Minnesota.

Accessibility to Lake Superior is good

everywhere in our region. Public land is abundant, and every little roadside rest area seems to have a path or steps down to the Lake where you can test the waters. If they're too cold for swimming, no great loss; you can skip stones, let the kids work off some energy, hunt agates or beautiful pieces of driftwood, build a little fire and cook lunch, climb rocks or just watch the water.

Twin Ports Area

Duluth's **Park Point** is probably the most frequented swimming area in the region. The water is shallow here, and the long sandy beach and dunes make for ideal beach lounging (watch out for poison ivy). A hot summer's day draws crowds here to swim, picnic, play Frisbee and splash in the shallows. This is a good place for very young children on a windless day; the water remains shallow for a long way out, and the small swells gently washing toward the shore are captivating. On days when the waves are high, it's an exciting place to swim for adults — but beware an undertow, the fast deep current that can pull you away from shore. If you can't easily step or swim out of it, it's best to relax and swim with the current — but at an angle, until you're out of it without expending too much energy. Then you can turn and get back to shore. You'll lose both energy and body heat if you swim too hard or flail around in a panic. Cross the Aerial Bridge and head to the end of the point where there are lifeguards, a municipal beach house and plenty of parking. If you prefer a less crowded area, you can access the beach closer to the bridge at Lafayette Square. Please use only the public accesses; Park Point residents, particularly those whose homes border the public beach, get weary of people invading their privacy.

Another spot is **Barkers Island** in Superior, off U.S. Highways 2 and 53. Like Park Point, it's on the flat land and offers easy accessibility to the water. Follow the yellow signs to the swimming beach.

South of Superior on Wis. Highway 35 is **Pattison State Park**, home of Wisconsin's highest waterfall (165 feet), Big Manitou Falls (see our Waterfalls chapter), and a 300-foot sandy beach where there's excellent warm (!) swimming. A daily vehicle permit is $7.

A stony and colder swimming place is at Duluth's **Brighton Beach**, just northeast of the Lester River off London Road.

It's mostly used as a picnic spot, but people like to swim here too. Nearby, the Lester River has a couple of good swimming holes above Superior Street; just drive into the park and follow the crowd. Lester River is a place of boulders and cliffs, too rugged for small children and elderly people.

Along the North Shore

All along the shore you can find secluded places to swim — even secluded enough for skinny-dipping. At the **French River**, 7 miles from Duluth, you'll find three good swimming holes between the fish hatchery and the Expressway; one, above a small dam, is deep enough for diving, and another has a small waterfall that's fun to slide over or hide behind (this hole is a good spot for children, if parents are along). The third is a deep shady hole just below the Expressway, but wear footgear — there's sometimes glass around. A few miles farther northeast is **Stony Point**, a place strewn with boulders from which you can drop into small, usually very cold, pools and count the seconds until your toes go numb.

In **Two Harbors**, along Minn. Highway 61 at **Burlington Bay**, you'll find a campground, park and beach. **Grand Marais** has a municipal swimming pool in **Tourist Park**, (218) 387-1275, which is open year round. It's at the bottom of the hill on the southwestern end of town on Minn. Highway 61. Still farther northeast, on the **Grand Portage Reservation**, is Hat Point, from which some hardy locals like to swim out to a little island 300 yards away, warm up on the rocks and then swim back. Take Minn. Highway 61 just past the Grand Portage Lodge and Casino; turn toward the Lake on the next road. At the Lake, turn left and follow the road to its end.

Along the South Shore

Here, too, are plenty of places to turn off the road and hike down to the shore for a swim, and you'll find more people actually in the water here than on the North Shore where waters are deeper and consequently colder. You first might take a jog inland to **Amnicon Falls State Park** and some river-and-waterfall splash-swimming. Go south on County Road U from Wis. Highway 13; you have to pay the $7 daily use fee, unless you want to pay $3 for an hourly sticker (or $18 for an annual one). Farther east on Wis. Highway 13 are three villages with public swimming areas on Lake Superior: **Port Wing** (go all the winding way to the end of the marina); **Herbster**, where a campground and beach is maintained on Bark Point Road along the Lake, and where you can swim at no cost; and **Cornucopia**, with a sandy rest stop where you can swim. (One hardy young woman, well-greased against the cold, swam 26 miles from Port Wing across Lake Superior to Two Harbors, Minnesota, in the 1980s. The city of **Bayfield**, also on Wis. Highway 13, has a public sandy beach near the ferry dock that gets busy with local kids in hot weather. Instead of turning right to the ferry boat dock at the foot of Washington Avenue, continue straight a half-block. The **Bayfield Pool and Recreational Facility**, (715) 779-5408, on Broad Street and Wilson Avenue, has an indoor pool and is open year round. You can swim many places at **Madeline Island** (a ferry boat ride gets you there), especially at **Big Bay State Park**, LaPointe, Wisconsin, (715) 779-3346, where you can jump from high boulders into the clear icy water.

The city of **Washburn**, south of Bayfield, has two public beaches: one at

Thompson's West End Park and the other at Memorial Park. Both just off Wis. Highway 13 in Washburn and are well marked, and both are accessible for elderly people.

Ashland, on U.S. Highway 2, has three municipal beaches on the Lake. Maslowski Beach, at the west end of town near Fish Creek, is a sloping beach with a playground and lifeguard. Sunset Park is along Lake Superior in the center of town; turn toward the Lake from Ellis Avenue onto Marina Drive. On the east is Bayview Park, which is accessible from U.S. Highway 2 on 21st Avenue E.

Farther east on U.S. Highway 2, Iron County Road 122 goes toward the Lake to Saxon Harbor where swimming is available at a county park for a $1 single-day fee. It becomes Gogebic (Mich.) County Road 505, taking you to Little Girl's Point where you can picnic, swim and hunt agates on the sandy beach. Watch your little ones; the point is named for an Ojibwe child who drowned here in the early 1900s. The Ottawa National Forest, which takes up much of the eastern Upper Peninsula, has a few swimming places, among them Black River Harbor Campground on Lake Superior, (906) 667-0261. It's north of Bessemer on County Road 513, and the sandy beach here is accessible from a picturesque suspension bridge. You can swim here even if you're not staying at the campground. Inland, Ramsay Memorial Park, just south of U.S. Highway 2 between

Bessemer and Wakefield, has a swimming beach near the Keystone Bridge.

Thunder Bay Area

The Canada Games Complex, 420 Winnipeg Avenue, (807) 625-3311, has one of North America's largest swimming pools, built for the 1981 Canada Summer Games. It's 77 meters long, 21 meters wide and is divided into three sections: one for recreational swimming, one for diving and another for the Thunderslide, a 73-meter spiraling slide that ends up in the pool. The complex is open every day except Canada Day (July 1). Churchill Pool, 130 Churchill Drive, (807) 577-2538, and Volunteer Pool, 180 Martha Street, (807) 345-5143, both smaller indoor pools, have public swimming year round on Friday, Saturday and Sunday. Call for hours and fees.

Outdoors, the large and beautiful Boulevard Lake Park, accessible from N. Algoma or N. Cumberland streets near the Current River Dam, is the most frequented swimming spot in Thunder Bay. It has a sandy beach where swimming is supervised by lifeguards. Upstream, the Current River runs through Trowbridge Falls municipal park (off Trans-Canada Highway 11/17 on Copenhagen Road) where only strong swimmers can negotiate the river's fast current. There's a beach at Kakabeka Falls Provincial Park,

Insiders' Tips

If you're visiting our region in the fall, be sure to take a look at the Lake on a sunny morning after a frosty night. The will-o'-the-wisps rise gracefully from the cooling water as far as you can see, sometimes forming a dense fog bank that remains until the warming sun "burns" it away. The view is best from a high hill. Even crusty old-timers here stop to gaze at the beautiful seasonal sight.

Photo: Whitewater Challenge

The action is intense — even for onlookers — at the whitewater slalom challenges near Carlton, Minnesota.

Trans-Canada Highway 11/17, 18 miles west of Thunder Bay, where you can swim along the Kaministiquia River. Swimming is also available at **Hazelwood Lake**, the "jewel" of the Lakehead Region Conservation Authority areas. It includes a peaceful lake and beach and 25 square miles of forest and lake habitat. Follow Dawson Road to Hazelwood Drive and follow it until its end.

Kayaking and Whitewater Rafting

Kayaking is a burgeoning sport here, with the larger, more stable sea kayaks used on Lake Superior and smaller, more maneuverable kayaks on the rivers. Most rivers here, however, are too tumultuous for any but the most expert kayakers. The whitewater simply roils in the spring, and rapids range from Class III (difficult) to Class V (practically impossible). Nearly all the rivers on the North Shore, Thunder Bay and in Michigan's Upper Peninsula have rapids. Easier water is available on the lower Kaministiquia at Thunder Bay, the lower St. Louis at Duluth and the upper Brule on the South Shore.

Some outfitters will give you a course in kayaking when you rent a kayak, or the Canoe and Kayak Institute of the University of Minnesota-Duluth teaches sea and whitewater kayaking, mostly at the St. Louis River. Call (218) 726-6533 for more information. The Minnesota Department of Natural Resources in 1996 was planning a sea kayak "trail" along the North Shore that will feature campsites along the way.

Twin Ports Area

SUPERIOR WHITEWATER
950 Chestnut Ave.
Carlton, Minn. (218) 384-4637

A do-it-yourself rafting trip down the St. Louis River is available through Superior Whitewater. Four to six people per raft are coached down 4 miles of water by guides in kayaks. Trips are two to three hours long, and the occupants on each raft (from one to 10 rafts) handle the craft themselves. The $33 fee includes a paddle, raft, life jacket, guide and return shuttle. No one younger than 12 can ride. Call for reservations. For $49 per day, the company also guides folks who would rather use an inflatable kayak, which is fine for assertive novices.

TREK & TRAIL
824 Minnesota Ave.
Duluth, Minn. (218) 722-1027

This Trek & Trail (also see the "South Shore" entry) offers kayak rentals ($40 for a one-person craft; $50 for a double) and instruction, and its guided sea kayak tours take you along Park Point for short trips ($72 per person for a day) or up the North Shore for longer trips. Everything except personal gear and sleeping bags is included for $290 per person.

Along the North Shore

BEAR TRACK OUTFITTERS
Minn. Hwy. 61
Grand Marais, Minn. (218) 387-1162

Bear Track will rent or outfit sea kayak trips. It focuses on specialty trips — some for women only — both in the Boundary Waters Canoe Area Wilderness and at Isle Royale in Lake Superior. A solo sea kayak is available for $30 a day; a double, $38. Bear Track also carries maps and outfits for fishing, camping and canoeing. It's just south of Grand Marais.

CASCADE KAYAK
Minn. Hwy. 61, Milepost 98
Grand Marais, Minn. (218) 387-2360

Expert kayakers John Amren and Jennifer Stoltz will guide you on day tours of Lake Superior or multi-day trips into Canada. They also provide instruction or simply can rent you a kayak. Prices range from $22 for a kayak to $90 a day for guided tours, which include the guide, food, equipment and transportation.

Along the South Shore

BRULE RIVER CANOE RENTAL INC.
U.S. Hwy. 2 (715) 392-3132
Brule, Wis. (715) 392-4983

Possibly the most popular kayaking/canoeing/fishing river in the area, the lovely Brule (about 35 miles east of Superior) flows north into Lake Superior from Wisconsin. It's a pristine, wild river, and the state of Wisconsin allows no rubber rafts, inner tubes or rubber duckies on it. The upper part of the river is more scenic and quiet, thus better for inexperienced paddlers, with Class I and II rapids. Most kayaking is done on 12 miles of the lower river where in the spring the rapids are Class II to IV.

Insiders' Tips

In Minnesota, Wisconsin, Michigan and Ontario, each person in a watercraft must have a life jacket.

Brule River Canoe Rental can outfit you for just about any type of kayaking you'd like, including half-day guided sea kayak tours to explore caves on Lake Superior for $50 per person. You can rent kayaks and haul them yourself, get shuttled to a kayak drop-off and get training in how to kayak — all from this company. Renting a solo kayak for three days costs $63.

SAIL & DIVE
511 W. Lake Shore Dr.
Ashland, Wis.   (715) 682-9505

Kayaks, canoes, inflatable tubes and inflatable rafts are all available for rent at Sail & Dive. Most people use inflatable craft to paddle inland lakes to which it's hard to carry a boat. Customers tend to take the kayaks and canoes in their cars to places like Little Sand Bay Campground north of Bayfield on Lake Superior and paddle out to see the sea caves. Rentals are around $16 a day or $3 an hour.

TREK & TRAIL
222 Rittenhouse Ave.
Bayfield, Wis.   (800) 354-TREK

Trek and Trail will rent you a sea kayak after you've taken a safety course, which they provide. The company also offers a five-day guided tour of the Apostle Islands in double sea kayaks with sails. Double sea kayaks rent for $50 a day; singles are $40. Make reservations.

Thunder Bay Area

SUPERIOR WILDERNESS ADVENTURE TOURS
140 Chercover Dr.
Thunder Bay, Ont.   (807) 768-4343

Call in advance to arrange kayaking and canoeing tours in northwestern Ontario through this company, which will match your trip to your skill level and provide a

shuttle. Choices range from one-day river trips to two-week sea kayaking trips from Thunder Bay to Rossport, Ontario. Kayaks rent from $35 to $50 a day; guided trips are $75 per day per person.

WILD WATERS NATURE TOURS AND EXPEDITIONS LTD.
Dog Lake Rd.
Lappe, Ont.   (807) 767-2022

There's a lot of whitewater in the Thunder Bay area, and Wild Waters owner Bruce Hyer will outfit you for or guide you to it — or to whitewater and flatwater routes in the huge Wabamiki Provincial Park wilderness 100 miles north. Hyer helped convince provincial officials to make a park of the 2.5 million acres where half of the area is water and makes for some great paddling — the "best in the world," Hyer believes. You can rent kayaks here from $15 to $45 a person per day, or Hyer can get you up to the wilderness and outfit you from his outpost there. Wild Waters is about 15 miles from Thunder Bay off Dawson Road. Call first.

Canoeing

Canoeing possibilities are endless in our neck of the world. You can drop a canoe into Lake Superior just about anywhere and safely hug the shore, take a trip from river to river along the North Shore or visit the sea caves of the Apostle Islands National Lakeshore. You can head into the deep watery canoe country of the Boundary Waters Canoe Area Wilderness or nearby Quetico Provincial Park. You can drop your canoe in any one of dozens of rivers that feed into Lake Superior. You can bring it inland to a placid lake. You won't have any trouble finding good paddling water on your own, or the outfitters and rental companies listed subsequently can help you.

If you've never paddled a canoe, the best way to learn is to get in and go. Canoes aren't particularly expensive to rent, and water is never far away here. Choose a quiet, relatively shallow body of water until you get the hang of counterbalancing the tendency to tip and master paddling turns. It won't take long. If you prefer to be taught, however, the Canoe and Kayak Institute of the University of Minnesota-Duluth teaches canoeing, sea kayaking and whitewater kayaking, mostly at the St. Louis River. Call (218) 726-6533 for more information.

Canoe rentals include life jackets, paddles and often car racks on which to haul the canoe. Prices are lowest for aluminum canoes and highest for Kevlar lightweights.

Twin Ports Area

TREK & TRAIL
824 Minnesota Ave.
Duluth, Minn.   *(218) 722-1027*
Trek & Trail rents lightweight kevlar Wenonah canoes for $32 a day. Canoes are not rented for Lake Superior; most customers take them to the Boundary Waters Canoe Area.

WILLARD MUNGER INN
7408 Grand Ave.
Duluth, Minn.   *(218) 624-4814*
This motel in West Duluth is on a road that leads to the St. Louis River, and some folks like to rent a canoe and explore the large-river quietude of the broad lower St. Louis, which has islands and secluded places. You can rent a canoe at the inn for $14.95 for four hours or less, $21.95 for a full day. You don't have to be a motel guest. If you don't see a canoe out front amongst the rental bicycles, don't worry; you rent a canoe here but pick it up at a site closer to the water.

Along the North Shore

BEAR TRACK OUTFITTERS
Minn. Hwy. 61
Grand Marais, Minn.   *(218) 387-1162*
Bear Track sets people up for canoe trips into the Boundary Waters Canoe Area Wilderness and Isle Royale in Lake Superior but does not offer guide services. It stocks a range of canoes, from standard aluminum craft for $18 a day to Mad River and Wenonah canoes made of Kevlar for $34 a day. The price includes yoke and car-top carrier.

Insiders' Tips

It's an inland sea, right? Why aren't people surfing? What look like surfable waves, small (2 to 6 feet) but regular and perfectly formed, do roll into Lake Superior's shore once in a while — for a few hours after storms — and one would think a wetsuit-clad surfer could catch a ride. The problem is, you can't anticipate and catch these waves; the "hump" out on the horizon usually dissolves, and the surfable curl arises unpredictably where you and your board are not. During the rest of the year, Lake Superior makes irregular chop rather than regular waves.

Kayakers cruise among the Apostle Islands on Wisconsin's South Shore.

Photo: Wisconsin Tourism Development

SAWBILL CANOE OUTFITTERS

Sawbill Lake, Tofte, Minn.   (218) 387-1360

Canoes, advice on canoe routes and complete trip packages are available at Sawbill. Canoes are $18 to $28 a day, depending on the make. Although Sawbill doesn't guide trips, it will outfit you completely for a trip into the Boundary Waters Canoe Area Wilderness. Complete packages are $40 to $65 a person per day, depending on the type of equipment. Send an e-mail if you'd like: sawbill@boreal.org

SAWTOOTH OUTFITTERS

Minn. Hwy. 61
Tofte, Minn.   (218) 663-7643

Sawtooth rents canoes and outfits canoe trips for the Boundary Waters but also sets up people for trips into Quetico Provincial Park or to Isle Royale. Canoe rentals range from $15 to $28 a day, depending on the make of canoe. A three-day, two-night trip that includes all equipment except your toothbrush is $155 to $170 per person, depending on the make of canoe. Sawtooth does not arrange guided trips but can point you in the right direction.

VOYAGEUR CANOE OUTFITTERS

900 Gunflint Tr.   (218) CANOE IT
Grand Marais, Minn.   (800) 777-7215

Tips on where to go and canoes for $16 to $35 a day are available at Voyageur. The company's primary business, however, is outfitting for day and overnight trips. The average five-day package is $200 per person and includes food, equipment, tents and sleeping bags as well as a free overnight in the bunkhouse, so you can come the previous afternoon and get a quick course on your trip, the terrain and map-reading. Voyageur is at the end of the Gunflint Trail.

WILDERNESS WATERS OUTFITTERS

W. Minn. Hwy. 61
Grand Marais, Minn.   (800) 325-5842

Wilderness focuses on the area from Kawishiwi to the eastern end of the Boundary Waters at the Arrowhead Trail, and up the Gunflint Trail. Three-day packages are $120 to $190 per person and include canoes, sleeping bags, tents, food and other equipment. Your hosts will walk you through your trip before you leave. If you just want to rent a canoe and head out on your own, price ranges from $18 to $33; the daily rate is less for more days.

Along the South Shore

BIG SNO OUTFITTERS
U.S. Hwy. 2, Bessemer, Mich. (906) 663-4646

Big Sno rents 17-foot classic Old Towne canoes for $16 a day. All the rivers in the area, such as the Black, the Montreal and the Presque Isle, have easy water, and Big Sno can aim you in the right direction.

BRULE RIVER CANOE RENTAL INC.
U.S. Hwy. 2   (715) 392-3132
Brule, Wis.   (715) 392-4983

Possibly the most popular canoeing/ kayaking/fishing river in the area, the lovely Brule (about 35 miles east of Superior) flows north into Lake Superior from Wisconsin. The state of Wisconsin does not allow rubber rafts, inner tubes or rubber duckies on this wild, pristine river. The upper part of the river is more scenic and quiet — appropriate for inexperienced paddlers. However, some canoeists enjoy the tumultuous lower river, which runs right into Lake Superior. A 50-mile stretch takes about three days to paddle, with overnights at two state campgrounds along the way (you must stay at designated campgrounds). You can take guided tours or rent a canoe for $80 for three days, which includes shuttle, canoe, paddles and life vests.

SAIL & DIVE
511 W. Lake Shore Dr.
Ashland, Wis.   (715) 682-9505

Canoes, inflatable tubes and inflatable rafts are all available for rent at Sail & Dive. Most people use inflatable craft at inland lakes where it's hard to carry a boat. Customers tend to take the canoes in their cars to places like Little Sand Bay Campground north of Bayfield on Lake Superior and paddle out to the sea caves. It costs around $16 a day or $3 an hour for rentals.

Thunder Bay Area

SUPERIOR WILDERNESS ADVENTURE TOURS
140 Chercover Dr.
Thunder Bay, Ont.   (807) 768-4343

Call in advance to arrange canoeing tours in northwestern Ontario through this company, which will match your trip to your skill level and provide a shuttle. Choices range from one-day river trips to longer guided trips, which are $75 per day per person. Rentals range from $35 to $50 per day.

WILD WATERS NATURE TOURS AND EXPEDITIONS LTD.
Dog Lake Rd., Lappe, Ont.   (807) 767-2022

Bruce and Margaret Hyer will outfit your canoe trip in the Thunder Bay area or from their outpost in Armstrong, accessing the huge, watery Wabakimi Provincial Park (Ontario's newest). The company will outfit trips from three days to three months in length; each is custom-designed, so call for exact prices. You can rent a canoe and go on your own for $20 to $35 a day. Lappe is 15 miles from Thunder Bay off Dawson Road. Call first.

Sailing

Want to go sailing? If possible, we suggest you head for Wisconsin. What Wisconsinites like to call the nation's largest fleet of chartered and rental sailboats is centered in the Bayfield area. Here, sailing among the glorious Apostle Islands is a divine experience — the area is justifiably called the "Caribbean of the North." You can rent a sailboat and captain it yourself — assuming you can prove competency — or hire a captain to take you and your party sailing. If you don't know enough about sailing to take a craft out, hands-on classes are offered. The boats are fully equipped, but you should bring your own food and sleeping bags. Be sure to call first for reservations.

Twin Ports Area

SAILBOATS INC.
250 Marina Dr., Superior, Wis.   *(715) 392-7131*
The main office of this company is here in Superior, although most of its boats are in the Bayfield area (see the subsequent "South Shore" entry). It keeps five boats, from 29 to 32 feet in length, at Barkers Island Marina off U.S. Highway 2. You can rent a bare boat if you can show proof of sailing experience; if not, Sailboats Inc. will find a captain. Rentals cost $350 to $875 for two days, depending on length of boat, plus $300 for the captain.

SYNERGY FOR SAIL
3229 Minnesota Ave.
Duluth, Minn.   *(218) 348-3048*
"It's not the destination — it's the journey," says John Pegg, captain of the *Synergy*, a 30-foot sloop available for charter at Park Point. Up to four passengers can take the $120 two-hour trip, rent the boat for four hours for $200 or sail all day

for $350. A complimentary picnic is included in the all-day trip. Go across the Aerial Bridge to 11th Street and turn right to Harbor Cove Marina.

Along the North Shore

So you want to sail the North Shore? You'd better bring your own boat, and a whole lot of sailing experience. The violent waves on Minnesota's North Shore, where northeast storms are frequent and come unimpeded down the length of the Lake, can destroy breakwaters and hurl trees across the highway. The waves once smashed the cliff below Split Rock Lighthouse with such fury that they flung a rock-missile through a lighthouse window almost 200 feet above the water. All this has convinced local entrepreneurs that renting sailboats is just too risky in an area that is short on safe harbors. And don't think that because you can sail saltwater, you can handle the North Shore. The Greek captain of a saltwater cargo ship told reporters in Duluth after his maiden voyage on Lake Superior that he had never encountered such frightening seas in his 12 years' ocean-going experience, and would never return.

There are few manufactured works more graceful, balanced and perfectly fit for service than the birchbark canoe; you'll see them in museums everywhere in our region, and you can even buy them at The **Duluth Pack Store**, 359 Canal Park Drive, Duluth, (218) 722-1707. The thick birchbark ("wigwaas" in Ojibwe) is cut in the warm early summer when it pops off the tree. Thwarts and ribs are carved from cedar, and everything is sewn with split roots of tamarack or spruce. In the past, seams were made watertight with a pitch made of evergreen gum and powdered cedar charcoal; nowadays, people use tar.

Insiders' Tips

Along the South Shore

APOSTLE ISLANDS CRUISE SERVICE

City Dock   (715) 779-3925
Bayfield, Wis.   (800) 323-7619

You can't rent the *ZEETO*, a 54-foot masted schooner, but you can help sail it; or just sit back and let the captain do the sailing through the Apostles. Tours leave the dock every morning and again in the early afternoon and last three to four hours. The charge is $45 per person.

APOSTLE ISLANDS YACHT CHARTER ASSOCIATION

Madeline Island Yacht
Club Marina   (715) 747-2983
LaPointe, Wis.   (800) 821-3480

You can rent a sailboat or charter a captained boat here. The fleet includes 17 boats ranging from 25 to 45 feet in length. You must be able to prove that you can sail a boat; the charter master will go along at first for an on-the-water check of your docking, anchoring, sail-lifting and compass-setting abilities. The "bareboat" charge is $390 for the first two days; less for subsequent days. Add $125 for a captain. Bring food and bedding. If you'd just like to take a ride, you can hire a captained boat for $260 for a party of six.

CATCHUN-SUN CHARTER CO.

City Dock, Bayfield, Wis.   (715) 779-3111

This company has been giving sail-boat rides since 1982 in the 38-square-mile area of the Apostles. You can learn how to sail the 30-foot sloop as you go on twice-daily rides leaving from City Dock. Prices range from $40 per person for a half-day ride to $300 for full-day rides for just your party for the whole boat. It's best to reserve a spot a month in advance on weekends and two weeks in advance for weekdays.

SAILBOATS INC.

100 Manypenny Ctr.
Bayfield, Wis.   (715) 779-3269

You can rent a bare or captained boat for a two-day minimum here. If you don't have strong sailing experience but want to sail your own craft, you can take the four-day sailing school course (two days in class, two on the water) for $450; an advanced sailing course, in which you learn as you go to distant Isle Royale, is also available. Boats are $350 to $875 for two days plus $300 for the captain. Sailboats Inc. has 35 boats at marinas around Bayfield, ranging in length from 25 to 45 feet.

SUPERIOR CHARTERS

Wis. Hwy. 13, Bayfield, Wis. (715) 779-5124

Fifty-eight sailboats ranging in length from 27 to 45 feet are part of this fleet, and you can charter a bare boat or one with a captain. The two-day minimum trip costs from $260 to $510 a day, de-

Insiders' Tips

Here are two tips from a local Insider — Esther Nahgahnub of the Fond du Lac Reservation — who we suspect is simply trying to keep tourists away. 1) Take note of the increasing number of turkey vultures circling in the sky — "they're scoping tourists who didn't make it through the winter." 2) If you're on or in the big lake (Lake Superior), you should be on guard for "large dark things moving around down there that aren't fish."

Photo: Duluth News-Tribune

Winds off the shore of Grand Marais breathe life into a boat's sails while the Sawtooth Mountains rest peacefully in the distance.

pending on the boat, plus $300 for the captain. You can sail the boat yourself if you can prove experience, or individualized on-water instruction is available (figure on two to three days for rank amateurs). All the boats are at Port Superior, just south of Bayfield.

Thunder Bay Area

SAILBOATS ONTARIO
108 Robinson Dr.
Thunder Bay, Ont.   *(807) 767-1972*
You can travel for days to Rossport, Ontario, or to Isle Royale, Michigan; or go out on the Lake for a few hours near with this company, which is affiliated with Sailboats Inc. of Superior, Wisconsin. You can choose between a bareboat (sail yourself) or captained charter. Most people take bareboats out from four to seven days; the four-day rate ranges from $975 to $1,800, depending on the length of boat (27 to 33 feet, which will carry four to six people). The boats are fully equipped, with berths and galleys, and sailors bring only personal gear, food and bedding. You must prove sailing competency. If you'd rather have Capt. Rich Clarke and his son David take you around the bay from two to eight hours, the cost ranges from $150 to $550, depending on the length of boat — up to 37 feet long. Four to eight people can ride for that price. Sailboats Ontario will cater food — steaks, barbecues, hamburgers, snacks — for the charters.

The snowfall that shut down New York City during the winter of 1995-96 is a normal, business-as-usual winter event in the Lake Superior region.

Inside
Winter Sports

When the days grow short and the hardwoods lose their leaves, our thoughts turn to snow. For many Insiders, the thought is a very happy one. It means fresh, brisk air and a clean white blanket. It means racing downhill on Alpine skis, cutting through silent forests on Nordic skis, flying across snowy expanses on a snowmobile. It means spending some time alone in the woods, looking for animal tracks and peeking into nature-rooms formed by snow-laden spruce branches. It means cocoa and wood fires and long cozy evenings.

It means no mosquitoes.

When that first flake falls, there probably isn't one of us that doesn't feel at least a momentary bubble of happiness, a physical reminder of the rib-tickling delight we had as children during the year's first snowfall. As adults, when a blizzard approaches, we rush to grocery stores to "stock up." We look serious and hurried, as though we're under threat, but don't be misled (remember, we're very much like those solemn-faced New Englanders Mark Twain overheard saying, "That fella sure was funny. It was all I could do to keep from laughing"). Our shopping carts should clue you in about how serious we are. They're full of chips, doughnuts and pop, and the next stop for many of us is the video rental store. After an evening of hunkering down and a night of listening to the wind shriek and batter our homes, we awaken hopeful and

switch on the radio. Ahhh, the school is closed. The government center is shut down. The office or shop won't open. What happiness! Now we can go outside! And before long we're shoveling, digging caves into snowdrifts, clamping on skis, revving the snowmobile and feeling utterly joyful and free.

But it has to really snow first, you understand. The snowfall that shut down New York City during the winter of 1995-96 is a normal winter event for us, and business goes on as usual.

Snow falls everywhere and plentifully in the region, but nowhere so plentifully as on Michigan's Upper Peninsula and in nearby Wisconsin. A 20-mile radius here is known as "Big Snow Country," and for good reason. The usual annual snowfall is 17 feet — often much more — and some houses have snow decks (high platforms like boat docks, from which to emerge from homes when the snow is deep). Snow accumulates here because north winds blowing across the widest, unfrozen part of Lake Superior drop moisture against the mountain ranges. A similar phenomenon happens along Minnesota's North Shore, where snowfalls of 10 to 12 feet are common.

A good share of the switch to a tourist economy here has to do with snow, which usually blankets our region from late November into April. During that period, our area is literally crisscrossed with winter fun opportunities — thousands of miles of them.

Snowmobiling

Racing around on a snow machine is probably the most popular winter activity here — it's also probably the most unpopular winter activity here. Detractors see the sport as an invasion of noise, gas fumes and Darth Vader look-alikes into a snowy world that's supposed to be clean, silent and sleeping. But even the detractors can't ignore the happy faces behind the snowmobile masks — and the fact that snow machines have played important roles during blizzards. In one monster snowstorm in the mid-1980s, snowmobiles, driven by volunteers, were the only way to get doctors and nurses back and forth to Duluth hospitals during a three-day shutdown.

Minnesota and Wisconsin are national snowmobile hotspots. State agencies and dozens of snowmobile clubs are actively involved in trail-making and grooming. Besides the fact we have lots of snow, there's good reason for this development. Minnesota is the home of two major snowmobile manufacturers — Polaris in Roseau, and Arctic Cat in Thief River falls. They were established by competing brothers who together had designed one of the earliest snowmobiles. But it was a Wisconsin man, Carl Eliason, who in 1924 built what is believed to be the first machine-powered sled — a snowmobile. He manufactured 40 of them a few years later, and today Eliason's home state has 20,000 miles of trails, about 350 of them built along former railroad beds. Throughout North America, about 10 million people are involved in the sport, and 2.6 million snowmobiles are zooming around snow country.

Little public money goes into maintaining trails in Ontario, so the member-groups of the Ontario Federation of Snowmobile Clubs are especially busy with fund-raising and the actual work of building and maintaining the province's 27,000 miles of trails. To use these trails (and help maintain them in the absence of public dollars), you'll need a TOPT pass (Trans-Ontario Provincial Trail). They're available from **Thunder Bay Adventure Trails** (the local OSFC affiliate, which maintains 710 kilometers), (807) 473-8228, and from any of the many snowmobile dealers in the city. Passes cost $20 for one day, $40 for seven days and $100 for the year.

Snowmobiles cost around $100 to $125 a day to rent and about half that for half-days; some places charge extra for helmets. Package deals for longer use are available. You must be a licensed automobile driver to rent or use a snow machine. Most rental companies will show you how to use the machine. These firms also can supply you with detailed county and state snowmobile maps. You won't have any problem finding the main trails mentioned here; you'll be crossing these clearly marked trails as you drive into any of our towns. And most entrepreneurs at restaurants, gas stations, taverns and motels can give you directions.

Speaking of gasoline, snowmobiles run about 100 miles on a tank of gas, and if you stay to the trails you'll pass regular directions to fueling places — or the fueling places themselves.

Detailed trail maps are widely available at businesses — snowmobile shops, taverns, motels — and at chambers of commerce, visitors centers and state parks. You can access snowmobile trails virtually anywhere in our region, whether for an hour-long spin or for the 2,400-mile Lake Superior Circle Tour (see our Circle Tour chapter).

You'll need a trail-use permit in Michigan ($10 annually) and in Ontario

— the TOPT pass ($100 annually or $20 for a week). No fee is required in Minnesota and Wisconsin. Rentals average $100 per day for a weekday and $120 for a weekend day. Needless to say, the trails run through some very beautiful country — remote enough to feel wild, but rarely too far from fueling stations for both vehicle and rider. Enjoy yourself, but keep in mind this tip from the Bayfield (Wisconsin) snowmobile clubs: "When you ride and caution ceases/then you're apt to rest in pieces." We've included some of the main corridors, which connect with hundreds of miles of club trails.

Twin Ports Area

DULUTH CROSS CITY TRAIL

This 45-mile-long split trail goes along the mountain range in Duluth. The western section, 33 miles long, reaches from Hutchinson Road in Piedmont Heights to the village of Fond du Lac but passes over the Willard Munger State Trail, which connects with other state trails. The eastern section, 12 miles long, goes inland from the Lester River to a connection with the North Shore State Trail.

GANDY DANCER TRAIL
Superior-Dresser, Wis.

This major trail leaves south Superior and goes south 150 miles through both Minnesota and Wisconsin, along an old railroad grade. It connects with hundreds of miles of county, club and state trails.

NORTH SHORE STATE TRAIL
Duluth-Grand Marais, Minn.

This 154-mile trail, all groomed for snowmobiles, begins at the edge of northeastern Duluth, at Eagle Lake and Martin roads. It runs up the shore to the Gunflint Trail, and is the route used for the annual Beargrease Sled Dog Marathon.

TRI-COUNTY CORRIDOR
Superior-Ashland-Hurley, Wis.

A major multi-use recreational trail that goes from Allouez in east Superior through Iron River and Ashland, the 60-mile corridor connects with hundreds of miles of club trails to towns along the lakeshore and into Hurley, Wisconsin, and the Upper Peninsula. It passes through some of the area's premier scenic attractions, including Brule River State Forest and the Chequamegon National Forest (see our Parks and Forests chapter for details). (Bayfield County has 600 miles of well-groomed wide corridor trails, and Douglas County has another 350 miles.)

WILLARD MUNGER STATE TRAIL
Duluth-Carlton-Hinckley, Minn.

This multiple-use trail begins with a beautiful 7-mile ride into Carlton, and from there either continues south to the Twin Cities or hooks up with a vast network of trails in Carlton, Pine and Aitkin counties. (Carlton County alone has 500 miles of groomed trails.) It's accessible off Grand Avenue near the Lake Superior Zoo.

If you're planning a snowmobile trip in Ontario, call (800) 263-SLED first. You'll be mailed booklets, maps and a video showing snowmobiling regions of Ontario — all for free.

Insiders' Tips

Along the North Shore

NORTH SHORE STATE TRAIL
Grand Marais-Duluth, Minn.

The 154-mile North Shore State Trail runs parallel to Lake Superior about 5 miles inland from the shore and is the trail on which the annual Beargrease Sled Dog Marathon is held. You can access it from eight feeder trails that go to the shore. It also connects to the Tomahawk Trail that runs west to the Iron Range via the Yukon Trail (accessible near Two Harbors).

GUNFLINT TRAIL
Grand Marais, Minn.

The Gunflint provides nearly 100 miles of looping trails along and near the "real" Gunflint Trail (see the related sidebar in our Fishing and Hunting chapter) — the road that takes wilderness-seekers year round into the Boundary Waters Canoe Area Wilderness. The marked snowmobile trail connects with hundreds of miles of other trails in Cook County and with the North Shore State Trail.

Along the South Shore

IRON HORSE TRAIL
Hurley, Wis.

Fifty miles of fine express riding are groomed from Hurley to other points in Iron County, which has about 450 miles of trails in all. Hurley has consistently been voted one of the Top-25 Snowmobile Vacationing Areas by *SnowGoer Magazine*.

TRAIL 2
Ironwood-Bessemer, Mich.

More than 50 miles of this trail begins at the Wisconsin border, goes through Ironwood and on to Wakefield and Watersmeet. This trail and the following two trails (8

and 100) connect with 2,000 miles of trail in the Upper Peninsula and northwestern Wisconsin.

TRAIL 8
Wakefield, Mich.

This 65-mile trail goes northeast from Wakefield to Ontonagan.

TRAIL 100
Ironwood, Mich.

From Ironwood, Trail 100 goes north to Lake Superior and doubles back in a loop. The round trip is about 30 miles.

TRI-COUNTY CORRIDOR
Hurley-Ashland-Superior, Wis.

A major multi-use recreational trail that goes from Allouez in east Superior through Iron River and Ashland, the 60-mile corridor connects with hundreds of miles of club trails to towns along the lakeshore and into Hurley, Wisconsin, and the Upper Peninsula. It passes through some of the area's primary scenic attractions, including Brule River State Forest and the Chequamegon National Forest.

Thunder Bay Area

NIPIGON TRAIL

This trail joins the Thunder Bay Trail just west of the city, and continues at the edge of Thunder Bay northeast more than 100 miles.

THUNDER BAY TRAIL

This trail goes from the intercity area through Fort William and west about 100 miles. It hooks up with the Nipigon Trail near Thunder Bay.

TRANS-ONTARIO PROVINCIAL TRAIL
Across Ontario (through Thunder Bay)

Branches of this trail go through Thunder Bay. The wild Trans-Ontario extends

Wintertime treks on snowshoes reward you with beautiful views and access to just about anywhere.

from Quebec to Manitoba, with the main corridor beginning near Toronto and branching in a "Y" to Kenora (west of Thunder Bay at the Manitoba border) and near the Moose River at James Bay. The TOPT permit allows you to use all 27,000 miles of groomed trails. In 1994, a final, $30 million link was finished north of Lake Superior, meaning snowmobilers now can take a 2,400-mile trip all around the Lake.

Snowmobile Rentals

We recommend the following places for snowmobile rentals (and more):

TWIN PORTS AREA

Willard Munger Inn, 7408 Grand Avenue, Duluth, Minnesota, (218) 624-4814; **Allouez Snowmobile Rentals**, 4003 E. Second Street, Superior, Wisconsin, (715) 398-6631.

ALONG THE NORTH SHORE

Beaver Bay Sports Shop, Minn. Highway 61, Beaver Bay, Minnesota, (218) 626-4666; **Castle Danger Sports**, Minn.

Highway 61, Castle Danger, Minnesota, (218) 834-4646; **Superior Lumber & Sports**, Minn. Highway 61, Grand Marais, Minnesota, (218) 387-1771.

ALONG THE SOUTH SHORE

In Washburn, Wisconsin: **Redwood Motel & Chalets**, (715) 373-5512;

In Hurley, Wisconsin: **L & M Snowmobile Rental**, 2635 Margaret Street, (715) 476-2602; **A-1 Rentals**, Wis. Highway 77, (715) 561-4300 or (800) 483-3838; **Ave's Sports Center**, 701 Wis. Highway 51 N., (715) 561-2720, also guided tours and overnight trips;

And in Bessemer, Michigan: **Chuck's Cycle Chop**, 900 W. Lead Street, (906) 663-4415; **Superior Snowmobile Rental Inc.**, 75 W. Lead Street, (906) 663-6080.

THUNDER BAY AREA

In Thunder Bay, Ontario: **Bayway Transit & Tours**, 918 Cobalt Crescent, (807) 345-3673; **Thunder Bay Outdoors Adventures**, 3086 Oliver Road, (807) 683-5556, also guided tours of a few hours or a few days.

Downhill (Alpine) Skiing

Skiing is for everyone. You don't have to look like someone from a hot-dogging video to participate. You don't have to be single, athletic, 20-something and dressed for a ski poster. Many ski hills are geared to families — little kids, grandparents, couch potatoes and all. If you've never skied, give it a try at one of the ski hills listed subsequently. It's exhilaratingly great fun, certain to make you sparkle with delight. Just bring yourself in winter clothing. Ski hill employees are knowledgeable — they'll fit you with the right size ski and help you with the chairlift; and at many hills you can get lessons for free or for a small fee. Don't worry about the cold — you'll be surprised how hot you can get out there, and anyway there are heated chalets nearby.

You expert skiers can find challenging runs here too. A couple of ski hills in our region have double black diamonds that might make you feel like you're out West.

Ski hills are within an hour's drive from anywhere in our area. Snowboards have won acceptance at most. Some places have special snowboard hills and pipes; others allow them on the regular ski runs. Ski and snowboarding equipment can be rented at most ski hills.

Twin Ports Area

MONT DU LAC
Minn. Hwy. 23
Duluth, Minn.   *(218) 626-3797*

This family ski hill is actually in Wisconsin, but since it's surrounded by Minnesota has been granted a phone number that fits its neighbors'. From Duluth, the hill is off Minn. Highway 23 southwest of the St. Louis River, just beyond the village of Fond du Lac. It has a chairlift, rope tow, three runs, rentals (skis and snowboards), food and a lounge. The vertical drop is 310 feet, and the longest run is 1,500 feet.

Lift tickets are $6 to $15, depending on the day. Packages (full rental and lift ticket) are $8 to $20. Children 5 and younger ski for free with a paying adult.

SPIRIT MOUNTAIN
9500 Spirit Mountain Pl.   628-2891
Duluth, Minn.   (800) 642-6377

This city-owned hill has a new tubing park and an expanded snowboard park, 22 runs, and five lifts (one double, two triple and one quad); also three handle tows. This mountain has 700 feet of vertical and a longest run of 5,400 feet.

Eight-hour lift tickets are $32 for adults, $27 for teenagers, $22 for children ages 7 to 12 and people older than 65. The fee is $5 less during the week. Rental ski equipment costs $17. You can rent a big inner tube (they're a lot of fun for sliding!) and use the handle tow for $5 for two hours.

The hill is open from Thanksgiving to early April, and is right in Duluth; take Exit 249 from I-35.

Along the North Shore

LUTSEN MOUNTAINS SKI AREA
Minn. Hwy. 61
Lutsen, Minn.   *(218) 663-7281*

Moose Mountain is the most challenging hill of the three interconnecting mountains that make up Lutsen. The longest run is 1.6 miles, and the most difficult run is a double black diamond called The Plunge. Lutsen has 41 runs, a gondola and five double chairlifts. It boasts 1,088 feet of vertical. Amenities include rentals, a lounge, entertainment, dining and lodging.

Lift tickets are $35 for adults and $25 for children. Rentals are $22 for adults and $15 for children.

Along the South Shore

BIG POWDERHORN MOUNTAIN
Bessemer, Mich.   **(906) 932-4838**

This hill is the largest ski lodging area in the Midwest. Its focus is family skiing. About 30 percent of the 24 trails are for experts; Cannonball and Vertical Drop are extremely challenging. About 35 percent are for beginners. Nine double chairlifts carry 10,800 skiers an hour to the hilltop where they find a vertical drop of 600 feet and the longest run a mile. Snowboards are allowed on all runs, but there's a half-pipe available too. One-day lift tickets on weekends are $27 for adults, $21 for kids ages 13 to 17, and $16 for kids ages 7 to 12. Prices are about $5 less on weekdays and half-price for seniors. Equipment rental is $18 for adults and $13 for children 12 and younger. Powderhorn has three restaurants and lounges, a pool and saunas. Kids 6 and younger ski and stay free. From U.S. Highway 2 east of Ironwood, turn north at the fiberglass skier.

BLACKJACK SKI AREA
Blackjack Rd.
Bessemer, Mich.   **(906) 229-5115**

Blackjack serves everyone but especially focuses on kids, with classes and clubs. Four double chairlifts and two rope tows provide access to 20 runs. A park and half-pipe are available for snowboarders. The longest run here is 5,300 feet (Horseshoe), and the vertical drop is 465 feet. The most difficult run is Spillway. Amenities include a restaurant, cafeteria and lodging.

Lift tickets for adults are $26 on weekends and $22 on weekdays. For youngsters ages 9 to 15, tickets cost $20 on weekends and $18 on weekdays. Children 8 and younger ski free with a paying adult. Ski rentals are $18 a day for adults; $9 for children.

INDIANHEAD SKI AREA
500 Indianhead Rd.
Wakefield, Mich.   **(906) 229-5181**

Indianhead is especially busy as a racing slope, with the largest NASTAR program in the Midwest, and is the training site of the U.S. Ski Team. Nineteen runs are served by three double chairlifts, a triple and a quad; two T-bars and two beginner lifts. Indianhead has a mile-long run and a vertical drop of 638 feet. This resort also has restaurants, lounges, an indoor pool and spa, fitness and racquetball areas, game rooms and a ski/racing school.

Lift tickets for adults on weekends are $30; for juniors ages 13 to 17, they're $24; and for kids 12 and younger, $19. On weekdays, tickets cost $27 for adults, $22 for juniors and $17 for kids 12 and younger. Kids 6 and younger ski and lodge free with parents.

A single cross-country ski pass in Thunder Bay is good for Big Thunder, Lappe, Lakehead, Sleeping Giant, Kakabeka Falls and Kamview trails. (These trails are maintained by Thunder Bay Nordic Trails.) The weekday pass is $6.50 for adults and $3.50 for children; on weekends, the daily pass is $8.25 for adults and $4 for children. They're available at local sports shops or by calling Big Thunder, (807) 623-3735.

Insiders' Tips

MOUNT ASHWABAY SKI HILL
Ski Hill Rd.
Bayfield, Wis. **(715) 779-3227**

Although it's outside the snow belt, this hill still has plenty of snow to keep skiers happy. The hill has 13 runs, including Hemlock (the most difficult), which passes through some of the last hemlock trees in the region. Mount Ashwabay has a 317-foot vertical drop, and the longest run is 3,000 feet. You get uphill on a T-bar and four rope tows, and rest in the lounge and cafeteria.

All-day lift tickets on weekends, holidays and during the Christmas vacation cost $11 for adults, $8.75 for folks ages 12 through 18 and $6.30 for kids 11 and younger. The ski hill opens on Wednesdays after Christmas vacation, and tickets cost $7.50 for adults, $5.75 for kids ages 12 through 18 and $4 for children 11 and younger.

MOUNT ZION
Gogebic Community College
Ironwood, Mich. **(906) 932-4231**

The college teaches ski hill management, and the smallish hill is a snowball's throw from classrooms, right in back of the school. Ten slopes are accessible from a double chairlift and two rope tows. The longest run is a quarter-mile, and the vertical drop is 300 feet.

Lift tickets are $8.50 for a full day; another $8.50 gets you rental skis or a snowboard. The hill is open from mid-December to mid-March but closes from time to time; call first.

WHITECAP MOUNTAINS
Montreal, Wis. **(715) 561-2227**

The biggest ski area in Big Snow Country, Whitecap sits on three hills and has 35 runs. Four of them are double black diamonds (experts-only, almost ungroomable, with granite bluffs and cliffs): Val D'Isere,

St. George, Southern Cross and The Dragon. Kilimanjaro is the mogul field, for experts. The longest run, 1.4 miles, is Chourcheval, for novices. About one-third of the runs are for novices and a third for experts. Chair lifts include one quad, one triple and four doubles. The vertical is 400 feet.

Weekend lift tickets are $29 for adults, $23 for kids ages 12 to 17 and $18 for children ages 6 to 11. Weekday tickets are $23, $20 and $14, respectively. Rentals are $20 a day. There's a dining room and cafeteria in the main lodge, which is a Swiss inn-style motel. Snowboarding is allowed on all hills.

From U.S. Highway 2, go into Hurley and take Wis. Highway 77 west 11 miles. Turn right on County Road 3.

Thunder Bay Area

CANDY MOUNTAIN AND LOCH LOMOND
1800 Loch Lomond Rd.
Thunder Bay, Ont. **(807) 475-7787**

These two hills are several miles apart but owned by the same company. Loch Lomond opens first and has more racing than Candy, which has longer, flatter terrain that's better for cruising. A single lift ticket is good at both hills. Candy's 1.5-mile run is the longest run in the area, and Loch Lomond's Devil's Dive run is the steepest in Ontario. Loch Lomond's longest run is 1.25 miles. Both hills have vertical drops of more than 800 feet. More stats: Loch Lomond has 15 runs, rentals, one quad chairlift and two double chairlifts, a full-service lodge and instructors. Candy Mountain has 13 runs, food, a lounge, rentals, two double chairlifts, a T-bar and a rope tow. Snowboards are welcome at both hills.

Weekday lift tickets are $27 for adults and $18.50 for juniors; add $5 for weekend rates. Rentals are $17.39 for a full day and $13.91 for a half-day.

Who's Willard Munger?

Willard Munger Trail, Willard Munger Inn . . . who's Willard Munger?

He's the scrappiest environmentalist in the Minnesota State Legislature, an octogenarian who has chaired the House Environment and Natural Resources Committee for all but two of the past 23 years. During his 40-year legislative career, he has led battles to protect wetlands, clean up the St. Louis and other rivers, ban plastic containers, halt heavy logging practices and protect threatened species. He was honored by the Izaak Walton League with its prestigious Founders Award (the same award author Rachel Carlson was given for her *Silent Spring*). At age 85, he's the oldest legislator in Minnesota history, having been a political activist before any of the 200 current legislators were born.

He's also the fellow who until recently whipped up pancakes and served them to locals who gathered weekend mornings in his inn to berate or encourage him about his previous week's political activities in St. Paul. Although Munger has since turned the business over to his son and grandson, he continues to hang out at the inn on weekend mornings, so his constituents can drop in for coffee and conversation. They do. You can, too, if you want an Insider's look at state politics. The Willard Munger Inn is at 7408 Grand Avenue near the Lake Superior Zoo. (See our Accommodations chapter for details.)

MOUNT BALDY

322 Hartviksen St.
Thunder Bay, Ont.   *(807) 683-8441*

This family ski hill is just east of Thunder Bay. The longest run here is the Gold Run, a mile-long beginners slope. Expert skiers go to Main and Hornet, which are among 10 runs accessible by two double chairlifts, a T-bar and a rope tow. The vertical drop is 650 feet. The chalet has hot food, a lounge, equipment rentals, a ski academy and a 400-foot half-pipe for snowboarders.

On weekends, lift tickets are $28 for a full day and $24 for a half-day. On Monday and Tuesday, lifts are $12; and Wednesday through Friday, $21. Rentals are $23 for a full day and $20 for a half-day. The hill is 8 kilometers past the Terry Fox Lookout.

Cross-country (Nordic) Skiing

It used to be that cross-country skiing was a way to get across deep snow without sinking. Many people in our region still use their long skinny skis for just that, eschewing the groomed areas (where snow has been smoothed and packed) in favor of breaking a solitary trail over frozen lakes and rivers, old logging roads, fields and even highway medians.

Both the North and South shores are wealthy in ski trails. (Bayfield County, Wisconsin, alone has 160 miles.) That doesn't mean you have to stick to the trails; you can visit Madeline Island on skis, for example, leaving your car on the shore at Bayfield. You can ski along the shore, both on land and on ice, in the Apostle Islands National Lakeshore, in search of interesting caves and ice formations. You can head up iced, snow-covered rivers on both shores.

There are plenty of groomed trails, though, and we've included some of our favorites. For many of those in Minnesota, you'll need a Great Minnesota Ski Pass. It costs $5.50 for a season or $1.50 for a day and is available at Department of Natural Resources offices, ski shops, outfitters and courthouses.

Maps of trails are available at tourist centers, ski shops and motels.

Twin Ports Area

DULUTH CITY TRAILS

Five trails, ranging from 3 to 18 kilometers (remember, 1 km = .625 mi.), adorn the eastern part of Duluth. They're wooded with evergreens and aspen, winding through parks and wild areas and past creeks; you'll need a Great Minnesota Ski Pass to use them. They're kept in good condition by the city's **Parks and Recreation Department**, (218) 723-3337. For condition update, call the **Duluth Cross-Country Ski Trail Hotline**, (218) 624-3062.

JAY COOKE STATE PARK
Carlton, Minn. (218) 384-4610

More than 50 kilometers of groomed trails for all abilities are available in this lovely park near Duluth. You'll need the Great Minnesota Ski Pass and, if you park there, a vehicle sticker ($4 for the day; $18 for the year). Incidentally, outside the park in Carlton County are another 90 kilometers of groomed trails for all levels, which require a ski pass.

PATTISON STATE PARK
Wis. Hwy. 35, Superior, Wis. (715) 399-8073

A park sticker ($7 for the day, $25 for the year) is required to use the 4.3 miles of groomed trails here. The park is hilly, forested with hardwoods and evergreens and is quite wild even though it's close to an urban center. It's home to Wisconsin's highest waterfall — the 165-foot Big Manitou Falls on the Black River, which is lovely when frozen.

SNOWFLAKE NORDIC SKI CENTER
4402 Rice Lake Rd.
Duluth, Minn. (218) 726-1550

This private trail system has about 20 kilometers of rolling terrain that's perfect for intermediate skiers, although there are some beginner loops too. Some loops are lighted for nighttime skiing, and season tickets are available. Call for up-to-date fees, which were not set for the upcoming season as this book went to press.

SPIRIT MOUNTAIN
9500 Spirit Mountain Pl. (218) 628-2891
Duluth, Minn. (800) 642-6377

This city-owned complex has a Cross-Country Ski Center, where instructors will help you learn either traditional or ski-skating (a method that has mostly replaced traditional skating in races; skiers use their skis like racing skates). More than 20 kilometers of groomed trails for both types of skiing are available, as are indoor restrooms, a snack bar and a Nordic chalet. The fee is $7 per adult for a full day and $4 for a half-day. Kids are $2 less. Rentals are available.

SUPERIOR MUNICIPAL FOREST
28th St. and Wyoming Ave., Superior, Wis.

This beautiful forest right in the city of Superior and edging the St. Louis River has 25 miles of groomed trails, including some for ski-skating. Varied terrain — some flat and open, some wooded and hilly — make it good for all levels. All told, Douglas County has more than 50 miles of cross-country trails. Daily passes are $3 and are available at the trail; a season pass for Superior Municipal Forest costs $15.

Along the North Shore

CASCADE RIVER STATE PARK
Minn. Hwy. 61
Cascade River, Minn.   *(218) 387-1543*

A popular place for skiers, with trails along the edge of Lake Superior, Cascade has 18 miles, five shelters with picnic tables and toilets, and another shelter with a wood-burning stove and trail maps. Water and firewood are available.

GRAND PORTAGE SKI TRAILS
Grand Portage Lodge, Minn. Hwy. 61
Grand Portage, Minn.   *(218) 475-2401*

Secluded beaver ponds, frozen waterfalls and vistas high over Lake Superior are accessible by 91 kilometers of groomed trails here. The trails accommodate all levels of skiers. Most trails pass through a busy site known as Trail Center, which is next to the Grand Portage Lodge.

GUNFLINT TRAIL
Gunflint Trail Association   (800) 338-6932
Tip of the Arrowhead
Information Center   (800) 622-4014

An extensive cross-country ski system is laid out along the Gunflint Trail, from Minn. Highway 61 on Lake Superior inland to Lake Saganaga in the Boundary Waters Canoe Area Wilderness. The looping trail heads over the Sawtooth Mountains; it's mostly an uphill journey. Some people like to start at Bally Creek and come back toward Lake Superior — increasing speed as you cross ridges, open areas, rivers and switchbacks.

For maps and information, call one of the above-listed numbers or one of the North Shore outfitters listed subsequently. (See the Gunflint Trail sidebar in our Fishing and Hunting chapter.)

JUDGE MAGNEY STATE PARK
Minn. Hwy. 61, Hovland, Minn. (218) 387-2929

Intermediate skiers can enjoy this 8-kilometer groomed trail, which climbs and then loops back for a downhill run.

Skiers of all levels will enjoy the amenities at Indianhead Mountain in Michigan.

Photo: Duluth News-Tribune

NORTH SHORE MOUNTAINS
SKI TRAIL SYSTEM

This 212-kilometer system stretches along much of the North Shore, which loops inland, and includes Superior National Forest, Cascade River and Temperance state parks and private land. A new section of 30 kilometers has been added at Lutsen Nordic Center, which is accessible from chairlifts at Lutsen Ski Area. Except for the Lutsen section, there is no fee, but you do need a Great Minnesota Ski Pass. The terrain is suitable for all levels of traditional skiers and takes you through forests, over mountains and along Lake Superior vistas. Ski-skating areas are at Bally Creek, between the Caribou Trail and Solbakken, and above the Oberg Mountain parking lot at County Road 336.

Along the South Shore

APOSTLE HIGHLANDS SKI TRAILS
1414 Manypenny Ave.
Bayfield, Wis. *(715) 779-5960*
About 6 kilometers of groomed trails are perfect for the beginning and intermediate skier here. The view is spectacular, overlooking Chequamegon Bay.

BLACK RIVER HARBOR
CROSS-COUNTRY TRAILS
Bear Track Inn, N15325 Black River Rd.
Ironwood, Mich. *(906) 932-2144*
Fifteen kilometers on 10 groomed trails for all levels of skier include night skiing, trail maps, lodging and instruction. Snowshoers are welcome.

BLACK RIVER TRAILS
N12390 Black River Rd.
Ironwood, Mich. *(906) 932-3857*
Seven groomed trails encompassing 14 kilometers are good for novice and intermediate skiers. Snowshoers are also welcome. Services include maps, lodging and an eatery.

MOUNT ASHWABAY SKI HILL
Ski Hill Rd., Bayfield, Wis. *(715) 779-3227*
Forty kilometers of cross-country trails take you through hardwoods and hemlocks, accessible by four rope tows and a T-bar for $6.50. Equipment rentals are $8. A cafeteria and lounge are available.

MOUNT ZION
Gogebic Community College
Ironwood, Mich. *(906) 932-4231*
A groomed 3-kilometer novice trail is part of this downhill complex. You can also rent skis and use the warming shelter. The hill is open from mid-December to mid-March, but is closed for school holidays; call first.

RIVER FALLS TRAILS
River Falls Outdoors, N10675 Junet Rd.
Ironwood, Mich. *(906) 932-5638*
Five groomed trails covering 10 kilometers are good for all levels of skier. Instruction, a warming shelter, lodging and rentals are available. You can snowshoe and toboggan here too.

SKI BRULE
397 Brule Mountain Rd.
Iron River, Wis. *(715) 265-4957*
Groomed trails for novice through expert are available here for a $5 trail fee. The 23 kilometers go along the Brule River and through wooded country. Rentals are $15 for adults and $10 for children.

Thunder Bay Area

BIG THUNDER
NATIONAL SKI TRAINING CENTER
Ont. Hwy. 61 (south of Thunder Bay Airport)
Thunder Bay, Ont. *(807) 475-4402*
Fifty kilometers of trails take you

through maple and birch woods on groomed trails, for all levels of experience. Five miles are lighted. Amenities include rentals and a chalet with food. Expect to pay a daily fee; call in season for specifics.

CASCADES CONSERVATION AREA

Balsam St., Thunder Bay, Ont.   (906) 344-5857

Cascades offers advanced skiers a link to trails from Centennial Park. Intermediate and novice skiers can enjoy 6 kilometers of groomed trails.

CENTENNIAL PARK

Arundel St. at Boulevard Lk., Thunder Bay, Ont.

Cross-country trails of varying lengths and difficulties are available at this city-owned park in Port Arthur near Boulevard Lake off Arundel Street. Services include a heated chalet.

HAZELWOOD LAKE CONSERVATION AREA

Hazelwood Dr.
Thunder Bay, Ont.   (807) 344-5857

One of 10 Lakehead Region Conservation Areas, Hazelwood is open to the public for cross-country skiing. Follow Ont. Highway 102 past County Fair Plaza to Hazelwood Drive. Turn right and continue to the end.

KAKABEKA FALLS PROVINCIAL PARK

Harstone Rd.
Thunder Bay, Ont.   (807) 625-5075

Beginners and intermediates can try traditional or ski-skate on 15 kilometers. A daily fee can be paid at the fee box at the trailhead. Take Trans-Canada Highway 11/17 west past Kakabeka Falls to Ont. Highway 590; then go left on Harstone Road.

KAMVIEW NORDIC CENTRE

20th Side Rd. off Ont. Hwy. 61
Thunder Bay, Ont.   (807) 625-5075

Beginners and intermediates will find Kamview's 24 kilometers (five lighted) to their liking — there are some great views of the Norwester Mountains. A warm chalet, day care, a snack bar, rentals and lessons are available. From Ont. Highway 61 south of Thunder Bay Airport, turn right on 20th Side Road.

LAPPE NORDIC SKI CENTER

Concession 4 Rd. off Dog Lake Rd.
Thunder Bay, Ont.   (807) 623-3735

Five of the 11 kilometers of groomed trails here are lighted. Levels are from beginner through expert. Pay a daily fee at the box in the chalet. Changing and wax rooms (to re-tune skis), a sauna and canteen are available. Take Dawson Road west to Dog Lake Road, and go 3 kilometers west on Concession 4 Road.

SLEEPING GIANT PROVINCIAL PARK

Pass Lake, Thunder Bay, Ont.   (807) 625-5075

Fifty kilometers of trails are perfect for intermediate to advanced skiers. A chalet is open on weekends. Pay at the fee box at the trailhead. Take Trans-Canada Highway 11/17 east to Ont. Highway 587, then right 6 kilometers to Pass Lake.

Duluth's city officials won't direct you to the best sledding hills in town — which for generations have been great favorites for sledding and tubing — because of liability concerns. For the same reason, you won't see any teeter-totters in city parks, and slides are being removed too.

Insiders' Tips

WISHART CONSERVATION AREA
Onion Lake Rd.
Thunder Bay, Ont.   *(807) 344-5857*

Groomed trails through spruce and jackpine, over tough hills, include an "orange trail" for experts and "yellow" for novices. This is one of 10 Lakehead Region Conservation Areas. From Trans-Canada Highway 11/17, turn north on Balsam Street, go west on Wardrope Avenue until Onion Lake Road — then turn right.

Cross-country Ski Rentals

Cross-country skis can be rented for from $10 to $20 a day; the package includes bindings, boots and poles. We recommend the following places for rentals:

TWIN PORTS AREA
In Duluth, Minnesota: **Ski Hut**, 1022 E. Fourth Street, (218) 724-8525; **Continental Ski Shop**, 1305 E. First Street, (218) 728-4466. (Both shops also sell the Great Minnesota Trail Pass and have trail maps.)

ALONG THE NORTH SHORE
In Little Marais, Minnesota: **Fenstad's Resort**, 1190 Minn. Highway 61, (218) 226-4724;

In Tofte, Minnesota: **Sawtooth Outfitters**, (218) 663-7643;

In Lutsen, Minnesota: **Lutsen Resort**, Minn. Highway 61, (800) 258-8736; **Solbakken Resort**, (800) 435-3950;

In Cascade River, Minnesota: **Cascade**

Lodge, Minn. Highway 61, (218) 387-1112;

In Grand Marais, Minnesota: **Bear Track Outfitters**, 2011 W. Minn. Highway 61, (218) 387-1162.

ALONG THE SOUTH SHORE
In Ashland, Wisconsin: **Bodin's On The Lake**, Lake Shore Drive W., (715) 682-6441;

In Ironwood, Michigan: **Bear Track Inn**, N15325 Black River Road, (906) 932-2144; **Trek & Trail**, 174 E. Michigan Avenue, (906) 932-5858.

THUNDER BAY AREA
In Thunder Bay, Ontario: **Fresh Air Experience**, 311 Victoria Avenue E., (807) 623-9393.

Other Snow Sports

There are plenty of unorganized — sometimes disorganized — winter fun options in our region. Bring out the auger, jig pole, wax worms and skimmers, hike out on a lake — Island Lake near Duluth; Lake Superior at Chequamegon Bay or near the Twin Ports — and catch one of those winter fish, which taste especially good. Or hike out on Lake Superior along the shore to see the beautiful ice formations. Sometimes the skim ice floats in and piles up, and it looks like sheets of broken blue glass. You can skate just about anywhere. Every community has outdoor rinks — usually in parks and at

Insiders' Tips

How about traveling for days near the North Shore, either by cross-country skis or snowmobile — but spending your nights in comfortable lodges along the trail? **Boundary Country Water Trekking**, (800) 322-8327, does "lodge-to-lodge coordinating," planning your route and arranging reservations at 31 accommodations along the way.

Miles and miles of groomed and well-marked snowmobile trails traverse the shores of Lake Superior.

Photo: Duluth News-Tribune

schools. Thunder Bay, for example, has more than 100 outdoor sheets of ice. These sheets get flooded every so often to remove the nicks and potholes from overuse or intermittent thaws, and many have warming houses. You can call the local city parks department to get directions to the nearest rink, but they're ubiquitous, and you can probably find one in less time than it takes to make a phone call. Sledding is OK anywhere there's a hill on public land. Likewise, snowshoeing is done anywhere there's snow on public land — whether on city golf courses or in national forests or provincial parks.

Twin Ports Area

SLEDDING

Particularly good hills are at Pinehurst Park in Cloquet, off Minn. Highway 33 near Carlton Avenue; and, in Duluth, at Lincoln Park on W. Third Street and 26th Avenue, and at the hill at the end of Seven Bridges Road, which is accessible at Lester River on E. Superior Street. Sometimes the hills are so slick all you need is a slippery-

clothed bottom, but most people use plastic sleds or a flattened cardboard box.

SLEIGHING

At **Carol's Horse Drawn Hay & Sleigh Rides**, Wrenshall, Minnesota, (218) 384-4825, Belgian draft horses will take you through wooded trails and back to a log cabin warming house. Wrenshall is southwest of Duluth. Call for directions and reservations. On the other side of Duluth is **Kellerhuis' Stables**, Jean Duluth Road, (218) 525-2666, where Percherons and Clydesdales will take you on an hour-long sleigh ride through the woods of Normanna Township. The price is $75 for a wagonload of 10 people and $7 per person above that. Kellerhuis has a clubhouse with fireplace and hookups to heat up the food you bring; guests have use of the house for an hour after the ride. Kellerhuis is 12 miles from Duluth's Glenwood Avenue on Jean Duluth Road.

TUBING

Sliding down a hill on a big inner tube is enormous fun. You go fast, you can't control your direction and when you collide with someone it doesn't hurt. You can bring your own tubes and find your own hill, but renting them is handy because they're larger than car tubes and made of real rubber — more slippery. They're available at **Spirit Mountain Ski Hill**, 9500 Spirit Hill Place, Duluth, (218) 628-2891; $5 for the tube and two hours on the handle tow.

Along the North Shore

SNOWSHOEING

Snowshoeing is an honored tradition around Lake Superior where the snow gets so deep you can sink to your chest — if it weren't for snowshoes, that is. That's why the original people here invented them: to stay near the top of the snow. Snowshoes are great for getting from maple tree to maple tree at the beginning of the syrup season when the snow is still deep; they're great for moving through quiet snowy woods in a similarly quiet way. Bishop Frederic Baraga, "The Snowshoe Priest," used them; John Beargrease, the intrepid North Shore mail carrier, used them. Some people still use them for actual work, but more are turning the handy footgear into a recreational mode — a quiet mode. Wading or skimming the snow on snowshoes gives the hiker time to listen to birds, squirrels and other wildlife and to notice the tracks and play of sunlight around. Snowshoes can be bought at many outfitters in the region, and some shops rent them for about $10 a day. They come in various styles (bearclaw, Ojibwa, plainsman and Alaskan — some are long and narrow, others shorter and rounder), in kits or already assembled, and are made of traditional materials (wood and rawhide) or neoprene and aluminum. Prices range from $60 to $150.

You can rent snowshoes at **Sawtooth Outfitters**, Tofte, Minnesota, (218) 663-7643; **Fenstad's Resort**, 1190 Minn. Highway 61, Little Marais, Minnesota, (218) 226-4724; **Solbakken Resort**, Lutsen, Minnesota, (800) 435-3950; **Cascade Kayaks**, Cascade Lodge, Minn. Highway 61, Cascade River, Minnesota, (218) 387-2360; and **Bear Track's Bally Creek Camp**, (800) 795-8068.

Along the South Shore

SLEIGHING

Royal Palm Ranch, N12345 Black River Road, Ironwood, Michigan, (906) 932-0770, offers sleighing opportunities. Tuesday through Sunday, while the big snow of the Upper Peninsula lasts, you can travel on a one-horse open sleigh; a Clydesdale-pulled big sleigh; or a sleigh fitted with fur robes, hot cider, champagne, hot chocolate and beer. Go in the daytime or

Insiders' Tips

Much of Thunder Bay is off-limits to snowmobiles, including the built-up area east of the Thunder Bay Expressway and north of (and including) the Kaministiquia River, the County Park and Jumbo Gardens neighborhoods, the cross-country ski area in Trowbridge Falls Park, the Cascades Conservation Area, all city golf courses and the harbour. For details and other information on enforcement, call Thunder Bay Police, (807) 625-1260.

go by moonlight; the fee is $6 each, and the setting is woods, snow, rustic lodges and hay-bale sofas near open fires.

Winterwind Sleigh Rides, E4048 Airport Road, Ironwood, Michigan, (906) 932-0156, offers rides through forested trails in Big Snow Country. Winterwind is 5 miles from Big Powderhorn Ski Area.

SNOWSHOEING

Snowshoeing is allowed throughout the 2,500 miles of mainland shoreline of **Apostle Islands National Lakeshore**, 415 Washburn Avenue, Bayfield, Wisconsin, (715) 779-3397. You can rent snowshoes at **Apostle Island Outfitters**, Bayfield, (715) 779-3411, for $10 for a day. Other options include **Bear Track Inn**, N15325 Black River Road, Ironwood, Michigan, (906) 932-2144; and **Trek & Trail**, 174 E. Michigan Avenue, Ironwood, Michigan, (906) 932-5858.

On the **Black River Trails**, Bessemer, Michigan, (906) 932-2144, 15 kilometers on 10 cross-country trails are available for snowshoeing.

Thunder Bay Area

ICE CLIMBING

Get outfitted and prepared for climbing frozen waterfalls through **Alpamayo Exploration & Adventure Services** in Thunder Bay, (807) 344-9636. Courses range from a one-day introduction to extended guided wilderness expeditions, along 160 ice routes with heights up to 800 feet.

DOG SLEDDING

Take a look at our region from dog sled, as friendly huskies pull you (sometimes with thrilling speed) along the North Shore where there are spectacular views of the lake. At **Norwest Sled Dog Adventures**, 7 Jarvis Bay Road, Thunder Bay, Ontario, (807) 964-2070, one choice is the two-hour trip ($20 for adults and $12 for children), when you sit in the sled as you fly toward a destination of hot chocolate and a campfire. Another is a four-hour trip ($84 each), in which you help hook up and drive a team. The two-day trip costs $235 per person and includes hot meals and overnight accommodations.

SLEDDING

You can buy a plastic toboggan or saucer or dig out your grandparents' Flexible Flyer — but why bother? Do it like the pros in Thunder Bay.

Give people younger than 14 a snowy hill and you can be sure they'll find something slippery upon which to get down it. Here's the recipe of Thunder Bay youngsters: Tuck a piece of cardboard in a big garbage bag, head for Balsam Pit or one of the other hills at a city park and get on — or in. Or you could try the Thunder Bay alternative — a cookie sheet.

Balsam Pit is along Balsam Street in the north end of town, across from the school. Other good sledding places are **Chippewa Park**, in Thunder Bay South along City Road off Ont. Highway 61B, and **Centennial Park**, in Thunder Bay North near Boulevard Lake, off Arundel Street.

Although Isle Royale lies 22 miles from Grand Portage on Minnesota's North Shore, this wilderness archipelago is part of the state of Michigan — approximately twice that distance at its nearest point as the crow flies.

Inside
Parks and Forests

The range of choices for your playground is vast. From city parks and promenades along Lake Superior to pristine, densely wooded wilderness areas and islands where you can leave behind the sounds of so-called progress, you'll find literally millions of acres of parks and forests blanketing the Twin Ports, Minnesota's North Shore, Canada's Thunder Bay and the South Shore of Wisconsin and Michigan.

Besides reveling in the sheer quantity of natural areas (Insiders are admittedly smug since we have so much to choose from), we are equally spoiled by easy access. Many locals routinely enjoy frequent sailing excursions to the Apostle Islands in summer. Weekend trips to the Boundary Waters Canoe Area Wilderness are not uncommon. And skiing, biking and hiking opportunities amid incredible scenery abound — often just outside our back doors.

Expect to pay a day-use entry fee at state and some provincial parks as well as camping fees (if you plan to stay in the park overnight). See this chapter's "State and Provincial Parks" section for permit costs. See our Camping and Campgrounds chapter for details on camping fees.

The following selection of parks and forests in the western Lake Superior region is simply that: a selection of favorite places we've been . . . places we return to on a regular basis . . . places we want to share with you.

Municipal Parks

Twin Ports Area

Duluth

Duluth has more than 100 parks, trails and open spaces. Many are defined by the 22 or so creeks and rivers that run through the city en route to the Lake. These greenways are favorite getaways for Duluthians who have their pick of urban wildness in virtually every neighborhood.

Many of the parks are home to long-running annual events such as the Chester Bowl Fall Festival, the Bayfront Blues Festival in Canal Park and Viking Fest in Leif Erikson Park (see our Annual Events chapter). Enger Tower, with its extensive perennial gardens and picnic grounds, and the Rose Gardens, overlooking Lake Superior, are traditional locations for family reunions, weddings and company picnics.

THE LAKEWALK AND LAKE PLACE PARK
Downtown Duluth
Ask Duluthians to meet you at the Lakewalk, and they'll know instantly where to go. The Lakewalk has become the defining element of the renaissance of downtown Duluth and an integral part of the Canal Park waterfront.

Nationally recognized for its design, the

Lakewalk is a landscaped boardwalk and bike path winding up the shore from Canal Park for about 3 miles to 26th Avenue E. With expansive views of the Lake, the Aerial Lift Bridge and the ships and boats in the bay, Lakewalk is a favorite meeting spot for a leisurely stroll or a good run — and it's lighted at night. Benches with great views; small, secluded beaches reached by paths and stone steps; overlooks; and picnic tables dot the Lakewalk. The Lakewalk takes you by the Northland Vietnam Veterans' Memorial, the Fitger's Brewery Complex — which includes a hotel, restaurants and shops — Leif Erikson Park and the Rose Gardens.

You also can access the Lakewalk in Canal Park at spots near the Comfort Suites Motel and the Marine Museum as well as at the Duluth Convention & Visitors Bureau, Duluth Entertainment Convention Center, Fitger's Brewery and Second Avenue E. There's a public parking lot next to the Comfort Suites Motel and a trailhead — complete with complimentary doggy-doo-doo bags. Another less-crowded access point is at 21st Avenue E. off I-35; you'll find a small parking lot.

Lake Place Park is an urban park in the best sense of the word. The park was a result of freeway construction when Interstate 35 was routed partly underground through downtown Duluth, a rare but practical road development. The park sits atop the I-35 tunnel that funnels travelers up the North Shore. Access Lake Place via the lighted, wooden plank skywalks, bringing the foot traveler over from Duluth's main drag, Superior Street, to the park. Make a quick diversion to check out the sculptures, a wonderful series of waterfront public art beginning in Canal Park, featuring local, regional and international artists. Works include the delightful *Green Bear* bronze, a gift from Duluth's sister city,

Petrozavodsk, Russia, and the massive red granite *Stenen*, a gift from Sweden.

This well-designed park has wind shelters from which to watch the big rollers pound the shore on stormy days, plenty of benches and small private picnic areas — all accented by generous landscaping, including native birch, spruce and shrubs. The park is handicapped-accessible from Superior Street and the Lakewalk.

LEIF ERIKSON PARK
11th Ave. E. and London Rd.

Walk the Lakewalk east from either Canal Park or west from the trailhead at 21st Avenue E. and you'll pass through Leif Erikson Park, a slightly wooded space with an amphitheater facing the Lake and a handsome granite open stage with towers.

This is the home of the Viking Ship, a wooden replica from 1920s that is currently undergoing restoration through the dedication of a nonprofit group. You can view the restoration in process through the open sides of the building on the west end of the park. There's a public parking lot across London Road.

ROSE GARDEN
11th Ave. E. and London Rd.

"Roses grow here?" is frequently overhead at the Rose Garden, usually uttered from someone bent over, sniffing a Barbara Bush hybrid tea. The summer of 1995 was the first full season of bloom for the hundreds of hybrid tea roses, tree roses and floribunda roses grouped by color and landscaped with complementary shrubs and trees. This elegant garden, a favorite place for many Duluthians, was removed for more than two years while Interstate 35 was being constructed. Mulched by leaves brought by the bagful from the community for winter protection, the

40,000 or so roses are thriving and don't seem to mind the constant sniffing.

A popular spot for weddings, the gardens are formally laid out with the original fountain, statues, a faux-marble gazebo, Empire-style benches and shimmering views of Lake Superior — all residing atop the completely disguised tunnels of I-35.

LESTER RIVER PARK
Superior St. and Lester River Rd.

Lester River Park is in east Duluth at the confluence of the Lester River and Amity Creek. Occasional sightings of moose and black bear are not uncommon in this neck of the woods. Handsome white pines line the river banks, and a series of connecting trails lead park visitors along Amity Creek in the summer and the Lester-Amity Ski Trail in the winter. There's a picnic area and a often-used but unsupervised swimming area in the river. The Seven Bridges Road meanders over narrow stone bridges to connect Hawk Ridge and Skyline Parkway with the park on Superior Street.

BRIGHTON BEACH
Congdon Blvd. and 63rd Ave. E.

At the edge of east Duluth where Scenic Highway 61 begins, you'll find a sliver-size park, with a smooth rock- and driftwood-filled beach, hugging the shore of Lake Superior. This is a perfect spot to bring take-out food for a lunch at one of the many picnic tables or to sit in your car if it's cool outside and watch the surf, ships and other picnickers.

ENGER TOWER
Skyline Pkwy. and 16th Ave. W.

One of Duluth's foremost landmarks is Enger Tower, a five-story, native stone octagonal structure built in 1939. Like an inland lighthouse, the tower stands atop the Northern Highlands, up the hill from downtown Duluth. Green art deco-style neon decorates the top of the tower and is visible for miles. During a nighttime snowfall, the neon glow is strange and wonderful. Make the climb up the stairs to the top; it's worth the effort. The views of Duluth and Superior, the St. Louis River and the Lake are some of the best in town, especially on clear, sunny days, when you can see as far as 30 miles.

Extensive rock and shade gardens have been established in the last 10 years through the vision of former city gardener Helen Lind, drawing admirers who return again and again during the spring, summer and early fall to see the changing blooms and colors.

A simply styled shrine surrounded by gardens houses a huge bronze bell, a gift from Duluth's sister city of Ohara, Japan. The park's picnic grounds are filled with red oak trees and a granite and bluestone pavilion.

Enger Tower is a frequented but never crowded place. Trails run throughout the park, including a short path to a gazebo overlooking the city. There are plenty of places to find a private overlook of Duluth and the Lake.

LINCOLN PARK

25th Ave. W. and Third St.

Lincoln Park is a classic neighborhood park, rimmed with historic turn-of-the-century houses overlooking the park and decorated with the native bluestone and granite bridges and stone walls you'll find in many of Duluth's parks.

At the turn of the century, Lincoln Park was the site of concerts and elegant picnics in the style of Scandinavian aristocracy. Today, neighborhood kids use it for some thrilling sledding, both on the steep hills and on the frozen creek cascades.

This park is tucked away in the Miller Creek ravine, where the creek breaks free from upstream culverts and twists and turns on its way to Lake Superior. After a downpour, the creek can be a dangerous force; recent tragic drownings serve as a warning to be careful here. Upstream and over the hill, Miller Creek is a designated trout stream that has been (and remains) impacted by the expanding commercial development in the wetlands where it meanders. There's a picnic area, pavilion and children's area with hiking trails running up and down the creek. A parkway drive follows the creek up to Skyline Parkway.

PARK POINT RECREATION AREA AND NATURE PRESERVE

Minnesota Ave.

Near the end of Park Point lies the Park Point Recreation Area. Softball and volleyball areas and supervised swimming and picnic areas make this a popular summer hangout and a destination for in-line skaters starting at the Aerial Lift Bridge. The recreation area is the gathering place for windsurfers on the protected harbor side and a fine put-in spot for canoers looking for an evening paddle in the summer. Birders flock here in the spring and fall,

hoping to see the many songbirds, waterfowl, raptors and shorebirds that seasonally frequent this natural rest stop along the Lake.

The nature preserve trail starts just past the Sky Harbor Airport. Go past the gate. There's a sign for the nature trail on public property. Follow the gravel road to the woods or walk along the beach to reach the end of Park Point. The 2-mile trail runs through the middle of tall white and red pine forests past the historic Minnesota Point lighthouse to the Superior entry shipping canal (also the natural mouth of the St. Louis River). This is another birding hot spot during the fall and spring migrations.

CHESTER BOWL AND CHESTER CREEK

Skyline Pkwy. and 16th Ave. E.

Chester Bowl is one of Duluth's most loved parks, with baseball and soccer fields, a playground, a picnic area and a recreation center. The fall colors in the bowl, with its mix of maple, birch, aspen and fir trees, are stunning. Chester Bowl is home to Big Chester, a historic wooden ski jump used for many years to host championship competitions. A trail meanders through red and white pines and hardwoods that border Chester Creek down to Fourth Street and around the Bowl.

HARTLEY FIELD

Hartley Rd.

Don't let the name fool you into thinking that Hartley is only a baseball field. From about 1890 to 1941, this land was a dairy and produce farm run by the Hartley family. In 1929, Cavour Hartley donated 10 acres to Duluth for a recreation area. Today, the Fryberger Arena, the Woodland Community Center and a sports field occupy that 10 acres. But the adjacent property of approximately 640 acres is a signifi-

Skin and sand fill Duluth's Park Point Beach area.

cant wildlife area now used by the non-profit Hartley Nature Center to present environmental education programs to school children and families.

This park includes a conifer forest of mature red and white pine, balsam, jack pine, spruce and cedar; marshes; and hardwood forests of aspen, birch, red oak and maple. The park is ribboned with hiking and cross-country skiing trails and filled with wildlife. Two branches of Tischer Creek run through Hartley Field on their way to Lake Superior. Because of the large acreage and absence of roads running through the land, Hartley Field offers fairly intact wildlife habitats and great recreational trails — right in the city.

To access the hiking and skiing trails, take Woodland Avenue to Arrowhead Road. Go west to the first stop sign. Take a right to Hartley Road and follow it to the trailhead.

Superior

While Duluth perches on the steep slopes of North Shore, the city of Superior lies on flat, wide expanses of land border-ing the estuaries and wetlands of the St. Louis River and the Nemadji and Pokegama rivers. Though lacking the rugged geography of the North Shore, Superior offers a number of city parks with wild expanses, including the second-largest municipal forest in the country.

BILLINGS PARK
At the end of Royalton

Billings Park, tucked along the undulating coast of the St. Louis River, is Superior's largest city park. The 56 wooded acres lie along a mini-peninsula, including two points that extend into the harbor. Considered Superior's showpiece park, Billings includes a pavilion, a play area, a boat launch and hiking trails along the river.

From Tower Avenue, take N. 21st Street west until it ends. Go left to Royalton and follow it until it dead-ends. The park lies just north of the Superior Municipal Forest.

SUPERIOR MUNICIPAL FOREST
Near 28th St.

Many Duluthians pop for the $15 winter ski pass to use the well-groomed trails in this wooded and gently undulating

Isle Royale
National Park

Go figure. Even though Isle Royale lies 22 miles from Grand Portage on Minnesota's North Shore, this wilderness archipelago is "located" in Michigan. Designated in 1931 as a national park "to conserve a prime example of Northwoods wilderness," Isle Royale is made up of more than 200 islands stretching about 45 miles from northeast to southwest, and is about 8.5 miles at its widest point. Greenstone Ridge, the spine of the island, has several points reaching 1,300 feet above sea level, with Mount Desor (1,394 feet) the highest point on the island. In 1981, Isle Royale was designated an "International Biosphere Reserve" by the United Nations, recognizing its international scientific and educational significance.

Although there is a lodge, store and marina at Rock Harbor at its northeast end, Isle Royale is essentially an undeveloped wilderness with no roads or motorized vehicles. A well-studied pack of wolves lives on the main island, and moose are everywhere. What you won't see are whitetail deer, black bears, porcupine or raccoon.

More than 170 miles of hiking trails provide for a range of adventure from day hikes to week-long challenges on the rocky, wooded terrain. About a dozen inland lakes, nine of them connected by canoe portages, offer fishing for northern pike, trout, walleye and panfish, and true wilderness solitude.

How to Get There

Isle Royale is reached by ferry from Grand Portage, Minnesota, during the summer months, approximately mid-May through September. Where you're going and how you're exploring the island determines what ferry to take, where you get on or off and how much your excursion will cost. The *Voyageur II*, a 63-foot diesel cruiser, combines mail and passenger service between Grand Portage and various stopping points on the island, traveling clockwise around the island and spending the night at Rock Harbor. It's $40 for a one-way ride between Grand Portage and Windigo Harbor for an adult, and $25 for children younger than 12. Rates vary for other stops. The *Wenonah*, a 65-foot diesel-powered steel boat, makes two round trips a day from Grand Portage to Windigo. Cost is $30 (one way) for adults and $15 for children ages 3 through 12; kids younger than 3 travel for free. Group discounts are available. Sightseeing excursions are also offered. For a schedule and current prices, contact the **Grand Portage-Isle Royale Transportation Line**, (715) 392-2100.

Where to Stay

You can explore the islands by sailboat, sea kayak, canoe or on foot (backpack). There are 36 different campgrounds, many on bays or islands with docks. Eighty-eight three-sided sleeping shelters with screened-in fronts are scattered throughout the park and available on a first-come, first-served basis.

Isle Royale's coastline is indented by numerous, deep, fjord-like channels and inlets formed by ancient erosion of the parallel rock layers. This view is of McCargoe Cove, a fault trench that cuts diagonally across the island.

The park is officially open from April 15 through October, but consider weather when planning your trip. Mid-July to mid-August is generally the most temperate time, but not always. Because of the Lake's effect on the island's climate, nothing is ever totally predictable, except black flies and mosquitoes in June and July.

For a more luxurious approach, consider the **Rock Harbor Lodge**, (906) 337-4993 (May through September), and (502) 773-2191 (October through April). On the shores of Rock Harbor, the four lodges house 60 rooms, each with a private shower, bath and steam heat. All rooms have picture windows of the harbor and modern furnishings. The housekeeping cottages include an electric stove, refrigerator, utensils and china, and a private bath with dressing room. Cottage sleeping quarters have one double bed and two bunk beds with linens, blankets and electric heat. Lodge rooms are on the American Plan, which includes breakfast, lunch and dinner at the Rock Harbor Lodge dining room. The dining room is open to island visitors too. Lodge accommodations, including room and meals for double occupancy, cost $91.50 per day plus 4 percent sales tax. Housekeeping cottages (meals not included) for double occupancy cost $59.50 a day plus tax.

A marina store sells groceries and freeze-dried food for backpacking. Camping and hiking accessories, fishing tackle, camping fuel, photographic supplies and other sundries are stocked here. A gift shop sells handcrafted gifts, postcards, T-shirts and other souvenirs.

For park information, trail maps and a camping guide, write or call: **Isle Royale National Park**, 800 E. Lakeshore Drive, Houghton, Michigan, (906) 482-0984.

Reference Materials

We recommend the following books on Isle Royale:

Once Upon an Isle, by Howard Sivertson, published by Wisconsin Folk Museum, is the story of growing up on Isle Royale when it was home to

Scandinavian fishing families, with original paintings and reminiscences by the author.

The Superior Way, by Bonnie Dahl, published by Lake Superior Port Cities, is a sailing guide to Lake Superior, with in-depth cruising information on Isle Royale.

Isle Royale National Park: Foot Trails and Water Routes, by Jim DuFresne, published by The Mountaineers, is a backcountry guide to trails, campgrounds, portage systems and fishing spots on Isle Royale.

4,500-acre forest at the southern edge of Superior. It's only a 15-minute drive over either of the two bridges connecting the two cities.

The Superior Municipal Forest lies along the Pokegama and Kimball bays of the St. Louis River. These deep, fingerlike bays host a great blue heron rookery and pines tall enough for nesting bald eagles. Recent residential development has nibbled at the edges of this recreational treasure. But it's still a beautiful place, particularly for cross-country skiing in winter (when merlin falcons and bald eagles occasionally soar overhead) as well as for canoeing the quiet back bays and the slow-moving Pokegama River in summer.

WISCONSIN POINT
Wisconsin Point Rd.

Wisconsin Point is a wild and mysterious place, distinct in character from Park Point. The natural habitat is a combination of marsh near the Allouez Bay (named by Belgian settlers but pronounced "Eloise" by everyone) and woodlands of white and red pine and assorted hardwoods on the long Superior Bay sandbar. At the sandbar's end is the 1913 Wisconsin Point lighthouse, two light-keeper houses and the breakwater for the Superior Entry shipping channel. The lighthouse is not open for tours, but you can walk on the concrete walkway if you're willing to duck and dodge the hundreds of gulls and the bird droppings.

If you are looking for windswept, sandy beaches — filled with driftwood but lacking people — this is the place to go. The Point is a great spot for birding during spring and fall migrations and during winter when you might see snowy owls sitting on the ice in Allouez Bay. This area also attracts people looking for privacy for reasons adolescent to criminal, so be alert and lock your doors.

Take U.S. Highway 2 to Moccasin Mike Road east of Superior. Turn north on Moccasin Mike Road and drive until the road forks. Bear left on Wisconsin Point Road. (If you go right, you'll end up at the landfill.)

Thunder Bay Area

Thunder Bay

Thunder Bay, in its spectacular waterfront setting on Ontario's North Shore of Lake Superior flanked by flat-topped and steep-sided granite cliffs, was originally two cities called Port Arthur and Fort William. They combined as one city in 1970.

The city of Thunder Bay offers 4,000 acres of parkland in the city. The Lakehead Conservation Authority, a community-based environmental agency, and the Ontario Provincial Park System provide many parks and forests for recreation.

It is heartening to see Thunder Bay recognize the beauty of its waterfront and take steps to reclaim it, both as habitat for wildlife — evidenced by the wetland restoration of the Mission Marsh Conservation Area — and in the development of urban waterfront parks, such as the Prince Arthur Park and Marina downtown.

PRINCE ARTHUR PARK AND MARINA
Red River Rd.   *(807) 345-2741*

Smack dab on the waterfront in downtown Thunder Bay, Prince Arthur Park takes advantage of the spectacular scenery looking out at the Lake and the bustle of this international working harbor. There's a playground, pedestrian pathways, a winter skating rink, a picnic and recreation area near the historic depot, an art gallery, a restaurant and a full-service marina.

CENTENNIAL PARK
Arundel and Hudson Sts.   *(807) 625-2351*

This wonderful 147-acre forested park on Thunder Bay's north side flanks the Current River. It's a great place to bring kids. You can visit a 1910 replica of a bush logging camp built by Finnish carpenters. Children enjoy the playground and the animals at the farm. The Muskeg (Ojibwe for "marsh") Express train ride, another "for-kids" attraction, runs along the Current River (see our Kidstuff chapter for details). The park also features a network of recreation trails for walking and, in the winter, cross-country skiing and tobogganing. A heated chalet with bathrooms is open year round.

BOULEVARD LAKE PARK
At the end of N. Algoma St.

This spacious park, adjacent to Centennial Park in northern Thunder Bay, is comprised of 650 acres surrounding Boulevard Lake and extending down as far as the dam on the lower Current River. Facilities include two swimming beaches with dressing and wash rooms, tennis courts, miniature golf, a children's play area, concessions and a picnicking area.

This is a popular place for runners, in-line skaters and walkers, all of whom enjoy the twisting paved path that follows the Lake's perimeter and twists in and out of spruce forest and well-maintained parkland.

CHIPPEWA PARK AND WILDLIFE EXHIBIT
City Rd.   *(807) 622-9777*

Set along the shores of Lake Superior, Chippewa Park stretches across 270 acres and includes a sandy beach, recreation fields, a playground, amusement park, picnic area, modern camping facilities, historic tourist cabins and a concessions area.

A special feature of the park is the 10-acre wildlife exhibit where many animals indigenous to northwestern Ontario live in their natural habitats. An elevated walkway encircles the spacious exhibit, which is open from 11 AM to 8 PM during the summer season and costs $1 for adults; children 12 and younger are free.

To reach the park, take Ont. Highway 61 B to City Road south of Thunder Bay.

When berry-picking in the wild, remember to keep an eye out for black bears. While berries are a mainstay of their diets, bears are generally willing to share.

Insiders' Tips

State and Provincial Parks

All Minnesota state parks charge a vehicle entry fee: $4 daily and $18 annually for residents and nonresidents alike.

Wisconsin state parks also require vehicle permits for entry. Residents pay $5 daily or $18 for an annual pass. Nonresidents pay $7 daily or $25 annually. Both residents and nonresidents pay $3 for an hour's access.

In Michigan, all visitors should expect to pay $4 daily or $20 annually for a state park vehicle entry permit.

And, except as noted, Ontario's provincial parks require a day-use fee of all visitors — $7 daily or $40 annually.

Twin Ports Area

JAY COOKE STATE PARK
500 Minn. Hwy. 210 E.
Carlton, Minn.   *(218) 384-4610*

Jay Cooke State Park is about 20 minutes south of Duluth. The rugged St. Louis River gorge, its whitewater spectacle (when the dam is releasing water) and colorful human history are the foci of the park. Whitewater slalom races are held in the summer in the river gorge below the Thomson Dam Reservoir, attracting paddlers from around the world and drawing hundreds of spectators.

Oldenberg Point is a lush green picnic area with expansive overlooks of the St. Louis River valley. Miles of hiking trails snake along the St. Louis River and up the ridges above. A must-do for hikers includes crossing the wild gorge of the St. Louis River on the hanging foot bridge to access the web of hiking and cross-country skiing trails. (The steel suspension bridge sways and creaks with every step you take!)

Mountain biking and horseback riding are allowed on some park trails. Check in at the visitor center and pick up a trail map.

AMNICON FALLS STATE PARK
County Rd. U   *Summer (715) 398-3000*
Superior, Wis.   *Winter (715) 399-8073*

Amnicon is derived from the Ojibwe words "where the fish spawn." The Amnicon River is one of the major spawning grounds on the South Shore for Lake Superior's fish population. It also hosts a native species of muskellunge, a fish that's been around since the glaciers melted.

Pick up the "Geology Walk" handout at the park. It'll lead you past the Upper Falls, the Lower Falls and the Now and Then Falls and help you decipher the rock formations that give clues to the volcanic eruptions, earthquakes and oceans that produced the present-day scenery.

While Amnicon has no designated beaches and no lifeguards, you can wade and swim in the pools below the waterfalls — a delightful thing to do in the summer.

Check out the 55-foot covered bridge that spans the river at the Lower Falls. It was originally constructed at the turn of the century. A roof was added later and features a bowstring design with arched beams. Primitive camping and picnic grounds are available.

Amnicon Falls State Park is closed in the winter, but you may park at the gate and walk, ski or snowshoe your way to the falls if you wish.

Take U.S. Highway 2 east from Superior for 12 miles or U.S Highway 2 west from Ashland, Wisconsin, for 55 miles to County Road U. Drive a quarter-mile north to the park entrance. If you're on Wis. Highway 13 following the Lake Superior Circle Tour, turn south on County Road U and drive 4 miles to the park entrance.

PATTISON STATE PARK
6294 S.R. 35 S.
Superior, Wis. (715) 399-8073

Home to Wisconsin's highest waterfall — the 165-foot Big Manitou Falls on the Black River — Pattison State Park is open year round and offers cross-country skiing in the winter. In the summer, picnic areas and campgrounds, hiking trails, a 100-yard sand swimming beach at Interfalls Lake and a nature center offering exhibits and naturalist-led interpretative programs make this a popular park.

Pattison State Park is 10 miles south of Superior's city limit on Wis. Highway 35.

Along the North Shore

GOOSEBERRY FALLS STATE PARK
Minn. Hwy. 61 (218) 834-3855

Gooseberry Falls is one of Minnesota's most-visited state parks. It is the first in a series of eight state parks you reach driving from Duluth on Minn. Highway 61 up the North Shore. For this reason, it crawls with sightseers in July, August and September. The park attracts Gooseberry groupies to its series of five dramatic waterfalls in the Gooseberry River gorge, the hiking and skiing trails along the river, the lovely beaches at the mouth of the river and its rugged cliffs and shoreline.

The rustic rough-hewn log and native stone buildings that dot the picnic area and campgrounds (constructed in the 1930s by the Civilian Conservation Corps) are part of the park's charm too. A new visitors center with interpretative programs is accessible without having to pay to enter the park. Reservations are essential for the campground.

SPLIT ROCK LIGHTHOUSE STATE PARK
Minn. Hwy. 61 (218) 226-3065

Nearly 2,000 acres, Split Rock perches on the cliffs above Lake Superior and offers hiking, cross-country skiing, camping and picnicking. The cart-in campground (you park your car and haul your gear in provided carts) has 21 standard sites and four backpack sites, many of them overlooking the lake or tucked into the mountainside.

The Superior Hiking Trail runs through the park. The Day Hill Trail is a short hike that leads to sweeping views of the Lake, Split Rock Lighthouse and the distant Apostle Islands. Shoreline picnic sites are on the Little Two Harbors Bay, a short walk from the parking lot. Camping reservations are essential on peak summer weekends for the cart-in sites.

TETTEGOUCHE STATE PARK
Minn. Hwy. 61 (218) 226-3539

Tettegouche is one of the newer state parks on the North Shore. It was established in 1979, with the help of the Nature Conservancy, to preserve an important example of the North Shore highlands. Stunning natural features include rugged, semi-mountainous terrain; the Lake Superior shoreline; inland lakes; tumbling rivers and waterfalls, including the Baptism River; and pristine northern hardwood forests.

If you're looking for challenging hiking in varied terrain with panoramic overlooks, Tettegouche offers 17 miles of trails, including a self-guided interpretive trail to Shovel Point (overlooking Lake Superior) as well as paths to the 200-foot steep cliffs of Palisade Head — a hot spot for rock climbing and a vital nesting area for peregrine falcons. There are also 11 miles of skiing trails as well as camping and picnic areas.

A historically romantic feature in the park is the Tettegouche Camp, nestled on the shores of Mic Mac Lake. The camp includes a set of rustic Adirondack-style log buildings that date back to the final days of the logging era (around 1910). These dwellings were later used as a fishing camp by Duluth businessmen. The four log cabins are available for rental year round through the park but are only accessible by foot, on skis or snowshoes.

Traveler's note: The handsome, cedar-shake Tettegouche State Park headquarters and the Baptism River Wayside rest area, on the lakeside of Minn. Highway 61, are open 24 hours a day, seven days a week, year round.

GEORGE H. CROSBY-MANITOU STATE PARK
Lake County Rd. 7   *(218) 226-3539*

If you're looking for solitude and a chance to see wildlife, Crosby-Manitou is the most remote of the state parks along the North Shore. Moose are frequently spotted here, and there's ample evidence (tracks, seat, et al.) of black bears and timber wolves. Rugged and challenging hiking trails follow the Manitou River, revealing surprising waterfalls and overlooks. A primitive park with no running water, Crosby-Manitou has 16 backpack sites along the river, five walk-in sites and a picnic area on Bensen Lake.

To access the park from Minn. Highway 61, take Lake County Highway 1 to Finland. Then take Lake County Road 7 for 8 miles to the park entrance.

TEMPERANCE RIVER STATE PARK
Minn. Hwy. 61   *(218) 663-7476*

Temperance River and the Cross River State Wayside are just northeast of Schroeder. The 200 acres of Temperance and the 2,520 acres of the Cross River encompass an area known for its bare rock cliffs along the Lake Superior shore. The narrow Temperance River gorge is a must-hike. You'll discover deep potholes created by the rapidly falling current of the Temperance River. Both the Temperance and the Cross rivers are designated trout streams for brook, brown and rainbow trout. Steelhead salmon fishing is also good here.

There are two campgrounds on each side of the Baptism River. Temperance is the only Minnesota state park with campsites right on the Lakeshore. However, the campgrounds are fairly close to the highway — and the constant hum of traffic. But you can always find a little solitude in the picnic grounds or along the 8 miles of hiking trails and 12 miles of cross-country skiing trails.

CASCADE RIVER STATE PARK
Minn. Hwy. 61   *(218) 387-1543*

Cascade River State Park is known for its challenging cross-country skiing trails and the series of waterfalls on the Cascade

River. The hike to Lookout Mountain — 600 feet above Lake Superior — is a worthwhile trek. Enjoy trout fishing in the park, a year-round shelter, backpack sites, a campground and picnic sites along the Lake.

JUDGE C.R. MAGNEY STATE PARK

Minn. Hwy. 61   *(218) 387-2929*

The Brule River forms a wild, natural centerpiece of whitewater rapids and waterfalls in this state park 14 miles northeast of Grand Marais. The Brule attracts curiosity seekers to the famous Devil's Kettle Falls, where the river splits and drops, disappearing into a huge pothole (see our Waterfalls chapter). Hiking trails run throughout the Brule River valley, picnic grounds grace the banks of the river, and a rustic campground is nearby.

GRAND PORTAGE STATE PARK

Minn. Hwy. 61   *(218) 475-2360*

This is Minnesota's newest state park — a joint venture between the Grand Portage Ojibwe band and the Minnesota Department of Natural Resources. The park lies in the Grand Portage Indian Reservation and is one of the first state parks in the country to be managed in cooperation with a local Indian band. The park staff is composed of DNR personnel who are members of the Grand Portage band.

The 300-acre park, with 13,000 feet of Pigeon River frontage, is for day use only and includes hiking trails and a picnic area. The jewel of the park is the High Falls on the Pigeon River, a 120-foot waterfall that 17th-century fur traders were forced to detour en route to and from Lake Superior (see our Waterfalls chapter). The short hike to view the falls follows a wide gravel path and boardwalk that climbs up to several overlooks directly below the falls. Another natural wonder you can glimpse along the

Photo: Duluth News-Tribune

Bears are often seen scouring for food in springtime.

trail to the falls is the 10-foot-wide, 68-foot-tall Wolf Birch, considered Minnesota's biggest paper birch tree.

Along the South Shore

BIG BAY STATE PARK

Take the ferry from Bayfield to La Pointe
Madeline Island   *(715) 747-6425*
                Summer (715) 779-3346

Big Bay State Park on Madeline Island in the Apostle Islands is known for its 1.5 miles of fine white sand beach, sandstone bluffs and sea caves. This recreation area offers camping, hiking, biking, picnicking, fishing, swimming and naturalist-led programs. Campground reservations are essential for the summer months.

COPPER FALLS STATE PARK

Wis. Hwy. 169
Mellen, Wis.   *(715) 274-5123*

The cascades of Brownstone Falls, Copper Falls and Tyler's Fork are the "wow" attractions in Copper Falls State

Park — all reachable by hiking the short, well-marked trails. Founded in 1929, the park was named after the 29-foot falls that marks the first drop of the Bad River as it flows through about 2 miles of steep-walled, rugged canyons. Besides the river canyons, the 2,483 acres of parkland include a mixed hardwood and conifer forest.

Near Copper Falls is a picnic area, a log shelter, a concession stand and a play area. The campground is secluded from the picnic area. Swimmers will enjoy the sand beach at Loon Lake. For cross-country skiers, 22 kilometers of trails should fit the bill.

From U.S. Highway 2 in Ashland, turn south on Wis. Highway 13 and proceed for 24 miles to Mellen. From Mellen, drive 2 miles on Wis. Highway 169 to the park entrance.

PORCUPINE MOUNTAINS WILDERNESS STATE PARK
412 S. Boundary Rd.
West of Ontonagon, Mich.   *(906) 885-5275*

The 60,000 acres of the "Porkies," established in 1945, are one of the few substantial wilderness areas left in the Midwest. The interior of the park, with untouched stands of old-growth forest, is best accessed by more than 90 miles of foot trails and 16 rustic trailside cabins. This is a backpacker's heaven, but it's rugged country with steep grades and frequent stream crossings. For an introduction to the Porkies, stop at the visitors center. Two campgrounds — Presque Isle and Union Bay

— are part of the park. (See our Camping and Campgrounds chapter for details.)

From Ontonagon, take Mich. Highway 107 for 17 miles west to S. Boundary Road. Take a left and proceed south for a quarter-mile to the visitors center.

Thunder Bay Area

OUIMET CANYON PROVINCIAL PARK
Off Trans-Canada Hwy. 11/17
Northwest of Ouimet   *(807) 475-1531*

Ouimet Canyon is a day-use park featuring a massive canyon created by ancient volcanic fires. The canyon is an incredible 2-mile-long gorge, 350 feet deep and 500 feet wide. Hiking trails run along the perimeter. This is a free day-use only park.

The park is 7 miles northwest of Ouimet, 40 miles northeast of Thunder Bay.

SLEEPING GIANT PROVINCIAL PARK
Ont. Hwy. 587   *(807) 977-2526*
Near Pass Lake, Ont. Off-season (807) 475-1506

You could spend weeks in this stunning setting, amid some of the highest cliffs in Ontario, where miles of hiking and backpacking trails wind by alpine lakes, amazing bluffs and shoreline.

The Sleeping Giant rests here in what was formerly called Sibley Peninsula Provincial Park. The park blankets the 25-mile Sibley Peninsula, with lowlands to the east and high cliffs to the west.

The Thunder Cape Bird Observatory, which is open to the public, is on the point of the peninsula but is accessible only by

Insiders' Tips

Duluthians don't directly see the sunset because of the city's east-west slant below the rugged cliffs of the Northern Highlands. The sunset is reflected off the grain elevators across the harbor in Superior, Wisconsin, and on the salties (foreign ships) sitting in the harbor.

a tough hike or by boat. Staff at this important research station conduct spring and fall migration banding and count song birds, owls and raptors.

Camping, hiking, mountain biking and birding are popular pastimes here. Picnic grounds, campgrounds, hiking trails and backpack sites round out the facilities at this full-service park.

Take Trans-Canada Highway 11/17 north from Thunder Bay for 25 miles. Turn east on Ont. Highway 587 and follow it into the park.

KAKABEKA FALLS PROVINCIAL PARK
Trans-Canada Hwy. 11/17
Near Kakabeka Falls, Ont.   (807) 473-9231

Just 18 miles west of Thunder Bay near the little village of Kakabeka Falls is Kakabeka Falls Provincial Park. The park is easily accessible (it's right off the highway) and offers ample parking in the lot next to the falls. Boardwalks with railings cross above the falls, and viewing platforms are provided on both sides of the cascading water. The waterfall is a major attraction for visitors, plummeting 163 feet into a rugged gorge. (See our Waterfalls chapter.) Two campgrounds, picnic grounds and hiking trails are offered as well as a naturalist program for children.

MIDDLE FALLS PROVINCIAL PARK
Canada Hwy. 593   (807) 964-2097

On the Ontario side of the Pigeon River, which forms the international border, is the small but charming Middle Falls Provincial Park. It's near the Middle Falls (see our Waterfalls chapter), historically an obstacle for the 17th-century fur traders en route to and from Lake Superior. A picnic area and hiking trails are near the falls, and the campground is along the river.

National Forests

Twin Ports Area

SUPERIOR NATIONAL FOREST
District Headquarters
515 W. First St., Rm. 354
Duluth, Minn.   (218) 720-5324

Look at a map of Minnesota and consider the northeastern tip, called the Arrowhead. If you draw a line from Duluth to International Falls, three-fourths of the land to the east of that imaginary line is public land (state and national forests). This undeveloped, wild, remote land is home to the biggest concentration of timber wolves in the lower 48 states.

Superior National Forest's 3.8 million acres make it the largest U.S. Forest east of the Rocky Mountains. The pristine Boundary Waters Canoe Area Wilderness accounts for about a million acres of the Superior National Forest.

Established in 1909, the Superior National Forest is known for its northern boreal forests and thousands of lakes. It also provides critical habitat for many endangered and threatened species, including the timber wolf, bald eagle and peregrine falcon. Typical of national forests' multiuse recreation approach, the Superior National Forest provides trails and facilities for silent sports such as canoeing, camping, skiing, hiking, hunting, fishing and horseback riding as well as for motorized recreation by snowmobilers, ATVers and motorboat users.

Since the Superior National Forest is so immense, we suggest you contact the individual ranger station in the area where you'll be for up-to-date information on trails and conditions. Superior National Forest Offices include the following:

LaCroix Ranger District, Cook, (218) 666-5251; Laurentian Ranger District, Aurora, (218) 229-3371; Kawishiwi Ranger District, Ely, (218) 365-7600; Tofte Ranger District, Tofte, (218) 663-7280; and Gunflint Ranger District, Grand Marais, (218) 387-1750. You can also stop by the district headquarters in downtown Duluth for information. Hours are 8 AM to 4:30 PM Monday through Friday.

Along the South Shore

APOSTLE ISLANDS
NATIONAL LAKESHORE
National Park Service
Bayfield, Wis. **(715) 779-3397**

Called the "crown jewels of Wisconsin," the Apostle Islands are a designated wilderness area including an archipelago of 22 islands clustered at the tip of the Bayfield Peninsula in northern Wisconsin.

Part of the national park system, the Apostle Islands National Lakeshore was created in 1970 to safeguard the natural and cultural resources of 21 of these islands and 12 miles of shoreline, including the lighthouses on Sand Island, Devils Island, Michigan Island, Outer Island, Raspberry Island and Long Island, the historic fish camps, sandy beaches, sea caves, and hardwood and conifer forests. Madeline Island — with the resort town of LaPointe, a fur-trading past and its distinction as the historic home of the Ojibwe people — is the only island not included in the wilderness designation.

To explore the islands and historic lighthouses by day, take an excursion cruise from the Bayfield city dock or from Little Sand Bay, the official entry point for the National Lakeshore west of Bayfield; call Apostle Islands Cruise Service, (715) 779-3925, for details. For overnight adventure, there is wilderness camping on five of the islands. The Apostles are a premier sailing and sea kayaking area in the summer. A number of marinas in Bayfield and Washburn charter sailboats, and several outfitters offer sea kayaking trips in the islands. (See our Watersports chapter.)

For trip information, including nautical maps and camping permits as well as interpretative programs on the natural and cultural history of the islands, check out the Apostle Islands National Lakeshore Visitor Center in the former Bayfield County Courthouse on Washington Avenue in Bayfield.

CHEQUAMEGON NATIONAL FOREST
District Headquarters
113. E. Bayfield St.
Washburn, Wis. **(715) 373-2667**
Glidden Ranger District
Glidden, Wis. **(715) 264-2511**
Hayward Range District
604 Nyman Ave.
Hayward, Wis. **(715) 634-4821**
Medford Ranger District
850 N. Eighth St. (Wis. Hwy. 13)
Medford, Wis. **(715) 748-4875**
Park Falls Ranger District
1170 Fourth Ave. S.
Park Falls, Wis. **(715) 762-2461**

Encompassing 860,000 acres interspersed in separate tracts throughout

> **Insiders' Tips**
>
> Minnesota Point is one of the world's longest freshwater sand bars. Known locally as Park Point, the 7-mile-long strip extends from the Aerial Lift Bridge to the Superior entry shipping canal.

northern Wisconsin, the Chequamegon National Forest is filled with lakes, rivers and streams in diverse habitat. Northern hardwoods, pines and meadowlands blanket the region, and a restored brush prairie — the Moquah Barrens Wildlife Area in the Bayfield Peninsula — and the Penokee Range, a highland area with rock bluffs, are natural attractions.

Activities abound. You'll find great cross-country skiing in the Bayfield Peninsula and at Rock Lake near Cable; a variety of campgrounds; snowmobile and ATV trails; hiking and mountain biking trails; and excellent fishing. If you're seeking peace and quiet, the Rainbow Lake Wilderness Area is managed for non-motorized use only.

OTTAWA NATIONAL FOREST

District Headquarters
2100 E. Cloverland Dr.
Ironwood, Mich. (906) 932-1330
Bessemer Ranger District
500 N. Moore St.
Bessemer, Mich. (906) 667-0261
Iron River Ranger District
990 Lalley Rd.
Iron River, Mich. (906) 265-5139
Kenton Ranger District
Mich. Hwy. 28 (M-28)
Kenton, Mich. (906) 852-3501
Ontonagon Ranger District
1209 Rockland Rd.
Ontonogan, Mich. (906) 884-2411
Watersmeet Ranger District
Old U.S. Hwy. 2
Watersmeet, Mich. (906) 358-4551

The Ottawa National Forest is on the western end of Michigan's Upper Peninsula. It contains nearly a million acres of rugged, mountainous terrain in the north and west — unexpected geography for the Midwest — changing to nearly flat terrain in the east and south. Elevations range from 600 feet at the Lake Superior shoreline to more than 1,800 feet in the Sylvania Wilderness Area.

Ottawa boasts more than 400 lakes within its boundaries and 76 waterfalls on or near forest land, and it's the only National Forest on the Great Lakes with a marina. Three designated National Wilderness areas include Sylvania, Sturgeon River Gorge and McCormick. You'll also find nearly 200 miles of hiking and backpacking trails, including the beautiful Black River Harbor trail system that highlights the waterfalls of the Black River. Cross-country skiers, rejoice: This is big snow country; the average annual snowfall is 200 inches. Ottawa has 30 groomed cross-country ski trails and 1,000 miles of snowmobile trails.

If you know what area of the national forest you're interested in, contact the local ranger office for camping permits, maps and other information. Otherwise, start with the district headquarters in Ironwood.

Canada's Conservation Areas

Thunder Bay Area

Despite its rather bureaucratic name, the **Lakehead Region Conservation Au-**

Photo: Duluth News-Tribune

Moose are sometimes glimpsed in the Lake Superior region.

thority, 130 Conservation Road, Thunder Bay, Ontario, (807) 344-5857, a community-based environmental protection organization, works with cities and provincial government to restore, conserve and manage natural areas delineated by watersheds.

The Lakehead Authority areas cover 1,400 squares miles and 118 miles of Lake Superior Shoreline in the Thunder Bay region. We've highlighted some of our favorite conservation areas, but we suggest you contact the conservation authority for an illustrated guide.

LITTLE TROUT BAY
CONSERVATION AREA
Little Trout Bay Rd., south of Thunder Bay, Ont.

This is a lovely remote spot south of Thunder Bay off Ont. Highway 61 sev-

eral miles on a gravel road. The topography is similar to that of the rugged Pacific Coast along the San Juan Islands north of Seattle, Washington.

Little Trout Bay, a protected inland harbor on Lake Superior, offers a boat launch and some excellent fishing for salmon, pickerel, whitefish, rainbow trout and lake trout. Onshore activities include picnic facilities and hiking trails with spectacular views.

MISSION ISLAND
MARSH CONSERVATION AREA
106th St. on Mission Is., Thunder Bay, Ont.

Rusting railroad bridges, coal docks, abandoned factories and old marine repair shops — mixed in with an occasional neatly kept, modest wood-frame house — are the visual precursors to this restored wetland. On the site of a former garbage dump, Mission Island Marsh gives you an inkling of what the Mission Islands and adjacent McKellar Island must have looked like before the industrial boom of the early 1900s. A short boardwalk leads you to several views of the harbor and marshes.

From the corner of Walsh Street and Syndicate Avenue, cross the Jacknife Bridge and follow 106th Street to the park lot.

CEDAR FALLS CONSERVATION AREA
Concession Rd. V, near Kakabeka Falls, Ont.

Locals visit this lovely area in late spring to watch the trout jump up the falls. A cascading waterfall, lush evergreen forest and thick moss add a sprinkle of northern delight to Cedar Falls Conservation Area. A pleasant walk along a well-marked trail leads you to Cedar Creek and the falls. Fishing is allowed, and birding is good here.

Cedar Falls Conservation Area is in O'Connor Township just past Kakabeka Falls on Trans-Canada Highway 11/17. Turn left on Ont. Highway 590 and left again on the O'Connor Second Sideroad. Proceed along this road for about 2 miles and turn left (east) on Concession Road V. Follow this road for about a mile to its end.

HAZELWOOD LAKE CONSERVATION AREA
Hazelwood Dr., near Thunder Bay, Ont.

Hazelwood Lake is one of the closest inland lakes to Thunder Bay. Just a 25-minute drive from the city, this large, semi-wild area is perfect for family outings. You'll find a swimming beach, fishing opportunities, a picnic area and hiking trails.

Follow Ont. Highway 102 past County Fair Plaza to Hazelwood Drive. Turn right on Hazelwood Drive and follow it for 8 miles to its end.

With light-reflecting and fast-moving water, waterfalls can be difficult to photograph. To avoid glare, try taking pictures in the early morning or late afternoon, when the daylight is more subdued, or on a cloudy day.

Inside
Waterfalls

The beauty and power of waterfalls have captivated people for centuries. The enduring popularity of Niagara Falls as a major attraction attests to that. Waterfalls ring Lake Superior and make for great scenery. Many North Shore and South Shore cities and counties promote area waterfalls with special guides and maps. Local folks have their favorite spots, usually away from the roar of the crowd at the major falls.

Before the advent of pleasure travel, the waterfalls and whitewater rapids of Lake Superior's North and South shores were considered challenging obstacles to either detour or cross over by voyageurs carrying 400-pound packs of furs. The impressive series of waterfalls and rapids on the St. Louis River, which flows into Lake Superior, waylaid the fur-trading Frenchmen in their canoes. With the guidance and knowledge of Native Americans, the Grand Portage was developed to detour this unrunnable stretch and connect the Mississippi River with Lake Superior. Today, you can hike the historic Grand Portage Trail in Jay Cooke State Park south of Duluth and view the rapids from the swinging foot bridge.

Many state park facilities on the North Shore and South Shore have been built around the natural features of rivers and waterfalls. Grand Portage, Minnesota's newest state park on the Minnesota-Ontario border, is one example. Through this park winds an ancient trail created by

Native Americans and fur traders to circumvent the High Falls on the Pigeon River. It's now a hiking trail that leads to spectacular vistas.

Unlike the steep gradient of the North Shore's Sawtooth Mountains and Northern Highlands that formed waterfalls close to Lake Superior, the geology and geography of Wisconsin's South Shore is relatively flat. Many of the area's waterfalls, including Big Manitou Falls (Wisconsin's tallest) on the Black River, are farther inland from Lake Superior than their North Shore counterparts.

Geographically, Wisconsin's South Shore region is mainly lowlands with protective bays and broad, marshy estuaries. The geology is partly soft sandstone, which eventually becomes the fine sand beaches on the South Shore. In the western Upper Peninsula of Michigan, the land begins to rise toward the Porcupine Mountains. Cliffs and deep river gorges, such as the Black River Gorge and its series of stunning falls, appear.

It's hard not to be impressed by a thundering, record-breaking waterfall, but if you're looking for more humble cascades, we've got plenty of those too. In this chapter we'll lead you to our biggest falls as well as some intimate cascades you can probably have to yourself for awhile. The falls described in this chapter are all accessible by car or foot. We haven't included waterfalls on private property or those requiring a long hike through rugged country to catch a glimpse. Fortunately, you'll find fairly easy hiking trails along most North and South Shore rivers. And, in many places, folks can set up camp near the tumbling water; the rush and sigh of the falls can lull a camper into a state of peaceful slumber.

A Word to the Wise...

To all waterfall viewers, a few words of caution are in order: Play it safe around these natural areas. The rocks above and below waterfalls can be extremely slippery, and serious accidents occur each year when people fall from the tops of these falls or slip on the adjacent slick, moss-covered rocks and steps.

Use common sense to avoid tragedy: Keep an eye on children, stay well away from the edges of the falls and never try to walk across them.

Also, please stay on the trails. Scrambling around on the banks will loosen soil and harm vegetation. Such impact as well as carelessness with litter — including cigarette butts and discarded fishing line — hurts fish, wildlife and rare plants and hastens the destruction of many of these exquisite places.

Captivating Cascades

Twin Ports Area

THE RIVERS AND CREEKS OF DULUTH

Duluth has nearly two dozen rivers and creeks that make their way to Lake Superior through miles of deep green gorges lined with giant red and white pine and hardwoods and filled with cascading waterfalls and pools. Well-used hiking paths run along many of these waters, including the Chester, Amity and Tischer creeks and the Lester River. See one of these wild and wonderful gorges for yourself and you'll understand why we Duluthians are so protective of our green spaces.

Try hiking up **Chester Creek** from Fourth Street and 14th Avenue E. near the Whole Foods Coop. Around every corner you'll discover little pools and drops occupied by a resident great blue heron and whatever else happens to be hanging out (including ardent couples). Numerous bridges crisscross the creek. Beware of faster-moving mountain bikers and runners. A dramatic waterfall lies just under the Ninth Street Bridge where you can sit on the rocks and watch people go by.

The trail head for **Amity Creek** is on Skyline Parkway near the Seven Bridges Road. It's muddy in the springtime, but this classic winding, narrow drop-pool tributary of the Lester River makes for a great hike or mountain-bike excursion. Whitewater paddlers run this stream in the spring.

The Congdon Park Trail along **Tischer Creek** can be accessed upstream of Superior Street and 32nd Avenue E. on the west side of the creek. The creek eventually ends up on the grounds of Glensheen, the former Congdon-family mansion, now a historic home open for tours. Hike upstream from

Insiders' Tips

Take advantage of the numerous wayside pullovers along the North Shore's Minn. Highway 61. If the weather is too crummy for hiking, you can still view many waterfalls from inside your car. A great spot for this is at the Cross River near Temperance River State Park.

Photo: Duluth News-Tribune

The High Falls on the Baptism River are about a mile above Minn. Highway 61 in Tettegouche State Park.

this access point to view a lovely series of waterfalls.

A favorite summer swimming spot, the **Lester River** runs through a narrow series of drops and pools in east Duluth. Upstream from the Lester River Park on the Seven Bridges Road are "The Deeps," a series of wide pools with small cascading waterfalls. You'll know you're there when you spot a few cars, a handful of people and, occasionally, a moose.

ST. LOUIS RIVER GORGE

Spring and fall are the best times to visit Jay Cooke State Park and marvel at the St. Louis River's powerful display of force during periods of high-water flow. The St. Louis River is dam-controlled, so the riverbed is nearly dry at times — its roar reduced to a whimper, particularly in midsummer.

You can view the St. Louis River gorge,

its waterfalls and its rapids from either of two bridges. Stake out a spot on the old railroad bridge that is now part of the Willard Munger State Trail, a recreation trail running from Carlton to Duluth. Parking is available on Minn. Highway 210 east of Carlton near the highway bridge. Follow the trail through the woods near the cliffs. Or walk out on the swinging bridge, a 221-foot cable steel suspension bridge that spans the river gorge near the Jay Cooke State Park headquarters. Cross the bridge, suspended above dangerous rapids and jagged rocks, and feel it vibrate and sway ever so slightly with each footstep!

Along the North Shore

GOOSEBERRY FALLS

Gooseberry Falls is a series of five major waterfalls on the Gooseberry River. Five miles of well-used hiking trails follow the

An arm-in-arm couple admire a cascade at Gooseberry Falls State Park.

Photo: Duluth News-Tribune

river upstream from the Minn. Highway 61 bridge and downstream to Lake Superior. A 90-foot steel bridge spans the "Fifth Falls" about a half-mile upstream from the main parking area. A popular destination, Gooseberry Falls State Park can be a hectic place in the summer.

Many people simply pull over to look at the upper falls and miss the major falls below. Try the lesser-used Falls View Trail on the east-side bluff above the Gooseberry River. You'll be rewarded with the best views of the spectacular Lower Falls and its two-tiered cascade (a 60-foot drop) as well as excellent trailside picture-taking opportunities.

HIGH FALLS AND TWO STEPS FALLS

A well-used and easy hiking trail starts at the Minn. Highway 61 pullover along the Baptism River in Tettegouche State Park. It brings you to a roaring, sparkling feast for the eyes: Two Steps Falls and High Falls, the second-tallest falls (behind High Falls on the Pigeon River) in Minnesota, with a total drop of 70 feet. High Falls drops into a deep, wide pool. (Whitewater-paddler legend has it that hair boaters — risk takers — made a successful run over the falls in fiberglass kayaks years ago.)

MANITOU RIVER FALLS

It's worth driving off the beaten path to revel in the solitude of Crosby-Manitou

State Park. Hike the River Trail up the Manitou River to observe an enchanting series of waterfalls. Some ardent admirers say that the higher in elevation you hike, the more beautiful these falls appear. This is remote country, so be prepared with food, water, warm clothing and a first-aid kit at all times and bug repellant as well in summer. From Minn. Highway 61, take Lake County Highway 1 to Finland. Then take Lake County Road 7 for 8 miles to the park entrance.

TEMPERANCE RIVER GORGE

From its broad upland headwaters the Temperance River, known as "kawimbash" or "deep hollow river" to the Ojibwe people, narrows into fantastic deep gorges filled with waterfalls that continue to cut deep potholes into the lava rock of the riverbed. The main trail of the Temperance River State Park follows the winding river gorge and is interspersed with wonderful overlooks along its length. Signs interpret river-bed geology and history along the trail, which is accessible from the parking lot on Minn. Highway 61 east of Schroeder.

CASCADE FALLS

View the five major stair-stepping waterfalls of the Cascade River from the extensive state park trail system, including a footbridge that crosses the river gorge. The Superior Hiking Trail, the 200-mile path running along the North Shore from Two Harbors, Minnesota, to Canada, winds through the park and shares the foot bridge and trail that cross the river. Try

cross-country skiing here in the winter when the landscape and waterfalls are absolutely stunning. Access the trail from the Minn. Highway 61 pullover.

DEVIL'S KETTLE FALLS

On the Brule River in Judge C.R. Magney State Park east of Grand Marais, you'll find the infamous Devil's Kettle Falls. Above the drop, a jutting rock divides the river into two falls. The eastern waterfall plummets 50 feet into a deep gorge and pool. The western cascade plunges into a huge pothole and, according to local legend, disappears. Folklore has it that gallons of colored ink were dropped into the western falls to see if the stained water would show up at the mouth of the river, but (*Twilight Zone* theme music) not a drop of ink flowed into Lake Superior.

HIGH FALLS

In Minnesota's Grand Portage State Park, High Falls — one of the Midwest's highest waterfalls — drops 120 feet into a deep gorge surrounded by steep bluffs. The views are simply breathtaking. High Falls is within the Grand Portage Indian Reservation on the international border of Canada and the United States. The short trail to the falls is handicapped-accessible. Since Grand Portage State Park opened in 1989, High Falls has replaced the High Falls on the Baptism River as Minnesota's highest falls.

MIDDLE FALLS

Across the Minnesota border in Ontario, Canada, is Middle Falls Provincial Park, situated on the Pigeon River. To enjoy the views of Middle Falls, take advantage of the protected picnic area in the park. You can also cop a Canadian view of the High Falls on the Pigeon River from this park. From Minn. Highway 61, cross the Canadian border and drive a few miles on Highway 593 to the provincial park.

Along the South Shore

BIG MANITOU FALLS
AND LITTLE MANITOU FALLS

The 165-foot Big Manitou Falls — the tallest waterfall in Wisconsin — and 30-foot Little Manitou Falls are approximately 13 miles south of Superior, Wisconsin, on Wis. Highway 35. In Pattison State Park on the Black River, these breathtakingly beautiful falls attract picnickers, campers and hikers to the spectacular scenic overlooks.

AMNICON FALLS

The Amnicon River runs through a lovely series of narrow drop-pools over sandstone shelves. Swimming is allowed in the pools below the falls, and kids have a ball here. Just remember: There are no lifeguards. You can sit beneath the falls and enjoy the gentle whirlpools. Check out the great handicapped-accessible picnic areas in the park and the historic covered bridge over the river.

From Superior, take U.S. Highway 2 E. for 12 miles to County Road U. Drive a quarter-mile north to the park entrance.

MORGAN FALLS

Morgan Falls is on the south fork of Morgan Creek in Wisconsin's Chequamegon National Forest. Off the beaten track, you will discover a 70-foot cataract falling over the face of an enormous rock surrounded by hardwood forests and a protected microclimate of lush ferns and mosses. The half-mile hike to the falls is on a well-worn, sometimes soggy, path.

From Mellen take Wis. Highway 13 to County Road GG and head south. Turn north on U.S. Forest Road 187 and proceed to U.S. Forest Road 199. Look for signs and a parking lot.

COPPER FALLS AND BROWNSTONE FALLS

The waterfalls and gorges on the Bad River and Tyler's Forks of the Bad River in Copper Falls State Park boast some of Wisconsin's highest drops and are a relatively short, worthwhile hike away. Walk the loop trail for 1.7 miles from the park's concessions stand to Copper Falls on the Bad River, Brownstone Falls on Tyler's Forks, Devil's Gate in the Bad River Gorge and the Tyler's Forks Cascade. The confluence of the Tyler's Forks with the Bad River creates the 30-foot Brownstone Falls that plunges through a spectacular canyon. The 40-foot Copper Falls on the Bad River are double falls split by a huge boulder.

BLACK RIVER FALLS

The Black River National Forest Scenic Byway is an area of great natural beauty,

Photo: Duluth News-Tribune

An overlook provides a slightly obstructed view of the Big Manitou Falls in Pattison Park, Wisconsin.

particularly during the fall colors season and in the spring when the river is high. From U.S. Highway 2 east of Ironwood, take the Powderhorn Road north to Black River Road. This scenic drive through the Ottawa National Forest takes you along the Black River to Lake Superior, with overlooks and hiking trails at Rainbow, Sandstone, Gorge, Potawatomi and Great Conglomerate falls. The overlook at Potawatomi Falls is handicapped-accessible.

SUPERIOR FALLS

One of the highest falls in the area, Superior Falls drops 90 feet into the Montreal River near its mouth on Lake Superior. The Montreal River separates extreme northeastern Wisconsin and western Upper Peninsula Michigan.

The viewing area for this falls is about a mile east of Saxon Harbor just across the Wisconsin-Michigan border. Start at the U.S. Highway 51 and U.S. Highway 2 overpass north of Hurley. Proceed west on U.S. Highway 2 for approximately 12 miles. Turn north (right) on Highway 122 and proceed 4.2 miles (you'll cross the Wisconsin-Michigan state line). Continue an additional half-mile then turn left on a gravel road. Park and follow the trail to the falls.

Thunder Bay Area

KAKABEKA FALLS

Kakabeka Falls, the "Niagara of the North," plunges 128 feet into the Kaministiquia River gorge. Local legend explains that the roar of the cataract echoes the cries of the vanquished Dakota people who, long ago, were led over the falls by the Ojibwe woman Green Mantle in an effort to save her people from the enemy Dakotas. You can observe this huge, thundering waterfall from viewing platforms on both sides of the river. From Thunder Bay, take Trans-Canada Highway 11/17 west for 18 miles to Kakabeka Falls Provincial Park.

Since about 1900, ski jumpers from Duluth, Minnesota, and Iron Mountain, Michigan, have been top competitors, taking 18 national junior championships and 15 national senior championships.

Inside
Spectator Sports

Sports are big all along the big lake, no matter what the season. In the wintertime, we pour out of our homes to stand shivering beside hockey boards, at the base of ski jumps and amidst the barking pandemonium at the start of a sled dog race. In the summertime, we scream ourselves hoarse at dusty car races, cheer on sailboat competitors and toss cups of soothing water on marathon runners as they puff by in their sweat-squishy running shoes. We love watching anything that involves two teams and a ball, whether it's high school football or a bocce ball tournament in the park.

Three professional teams — the Duluth-Superior Dukes and Thunder Bay Whiskey Jacks (minors baseball) and the Thunder Bay Senators (minors hockey) — call our region home. So do some major international competitions. So when you come back from your camping trip or wilderness sojourn hungering for the clamor of a big-city crowd, we can oblige you.

We've organized this chapter more or less by the popularity of each sport in this region. We've also included information about spectator sports at area colleges and universities as well as annual sporting events that draw significant crowds.

Hockey

If any sport defines the region, it's hockey. Most communities have plenty of outdoor rinks (Thunder Bay, for example, has more than 50) as well as one or more

indoor rinks, and they're always full. In many households, hockey directs the family's activities throughout the season. Besides outfitting and driving their kids, parents sponsor hockey fund-raisers and hockey clinics and cheer for/yell at their offspring during games. From 4-year-olds so thickly padded they can't make their skates turn or stop, through the bantam and peewee traveling teams — girls' and boys' — to the agile college teams, organized hockey here is intensely played and intensely followed. For schedules of amateur games, call the **Duluth Amateur Hockey Association**, (218) 722-3810; the **Superior Amateur Hockey Association**, (715) 394-7879; the **Ashland (Wis.) Amateur Hockey Association** c/o Ashland Civic Center, (715) 682-2221; and the **Thunder Bay Amateur Hockey Association**, (807) 623-1542. All the high schools have teams too. For college hockey, see the college listings below.

Thunder Bay Area

Thunder Bay has something extra in hockey: A pro team and a training-for-the-pros team.

THUNDER BAY FLYERS
Ft. William Gardens, 901 Miles St.
Thunder Bay, Ont.   **(807) 622-5111**
A team for promising young hockey players from all over Ontario, the Flyers get an opportunity to work with college

and professional coaches. They play teams from Wisconsin, the Dakotas and elsewhere.

For tickets and game information, call (807) 625-2929.

THUNDER BAY SENATORS
901 Miles St. E.
Thunder Bay, Ont. *(807) 623-7121*

The Senators won the Colonial Hockey League championship for three of the four years it has played since the 1991-92 season. The pro league includes nine teams from Detroit to Moline, Illinois, and elsewhere in Ontario. Home games of the 70 to 80 scheduled are played in Fort William Gardens, which draw about 2,300 fans per event. The season begins with training camp October 1 and lasts through March; playoffs continue another month.

Ticket prices are $10 for adults, $4 for children younger than 13 and $8 for seniors. For tickets call (807) 625-2929.

Baseball

Fans boast that our two pro teams play real old-time baseball (meaning low-key commercialism and salaries more in line with those of ordinary people) on real grass, under real skies, in real ballparks. You can sit up close to the players here, exchanging comments and begging autographs; or you can chase foul balls on the other side of the wall. Other Northern League teams are the Sioux City (Iowa) Explorers, the Sioux Falls (South Dakota) Canaries, the Madison (Wisconsin) Black Wolves, the Fargo-Moorhead (North Dakota-Minnesota) Red Hawks, the Winnipeg (Manitoba) Goldeyes and the St. Paul (Minnesota) Saints. Most high schools and a few colleges in the region have baseball programs (see subsequent listings).

DULUTH-SUPERIOR DUKES
Holiday Center (Dukes Office)
203 W. Superior St. *(218) 727-4525*
Wade Stadium
34th Ave. W.
Duluth, Minn. *(800) DS-DUKES*

The Dukes play their home games in Wade Stadium, which was built in 1941 (of bricks from nearby Grand Avenue when it was turned into asphalt) and renovated for the Dukes' resurrection in 1990. An 80-game season is split in half — home and away.

Tickets are $6 for box seats, $4.50 for reserved and $3.50 for bleachers. The season begins in early June.

Take I-35 to the 40th Avenue W. exit; go to Grand Avenue, turn right and continue to 34th Avenue W. Wade is the classic brick stadium on your right.

THUNDER BAY WHISKEY JACKS
425 Winnipeg Ave. *(807) 344-JACK*
Thunder Bay, Ont. *(807) 346-BALL*

When this pro ball club is at home, it plays its Northern League games at Port Arthur Stadium, an old-fashioned brick ball park.

Tickets are $7 for reserved seats, $6 for general admission and $4 for kids and seniors. The team draws 100,000 fans a season. The ballpark is handicapped-accessible.

Turn right on Harbor Expressway from Canadian Highway 61 N. and continue to Memorial Avenue. The whiskey jack is the local name for a jay.

Curling

Curling is big in Minnesota and Ontario, a century-old legacy of Scottish immigrants that long ago crossed ethnic lines. Bonspiels (tournaments) bring curlers from all over the world to the region, and some of our own world-class curlers have been instrumental in boosting the sport to Olympian status. (After 400 years, curling is finally slated to be a full-medal sport in 1998, at the Winter Olympics in Japan.)

Most curling clubs welcome you to come watch the games and even will give you an opportunity to try your own hand (and foot) at delivering a 42-pound stone down the sheet of ice. For practice and bonspiel information, call the local curling club: **Duluth**, (218) 727-1851; **Superior**, (715) 392-2022; **Two Harbors**, (218) 834-2664; **Cook County** (Grand Marais), (218) 387-9031; **Fort William** (Thunder Bay), (807) 622-5377; **Kakabeka Falls** (near Thunder Bay), (807) 939-1391; and **Port Arthur** (Thunder Bay), (807) 345-9552.

Sailing

The Duluth Yacht Club has races in Lake Superior off the harbor, weather permitting, every Wednesday evening from mid-May to mid-September, Tuesday evenings in June and August, and frequently Saturday mornings throughout the season. The Wednesday races usually include about 30 sailing vessels, and the Tuesday races about a dozen.

Yachts plan their departure from the harbor to coincide with the exit of the *Vista Queen* at 5:45 PM, so the Aerial Lift Bridge won't have to go up specially for them. The race begins shortly afterward, on a triangle marked by permanent buoys, and can be seen from anywhere along the Lakewalk, at the pier and on Park Point.

Saturday races begin about 10 AM. You can't miss the boats; they're the ones with the brightly colored sails.

Skiing

Every ski hill is the site of competitions — slalom, downhill, moguls — for just about every level of skier and often

snowboarders too. Call the individual ski hills for schedules. See our Winter Sports chapter for details about regional ski mountains for recreational skiers.

Exact dates for the 1996-97 and 1997-98 seasons were not available at press time.

Twin Ports Area

MONT DU LAC
Minn. Hwy. 23
Duluth, Minn.   *(218) 626-3797*

This family ski hill is actually in Wisconsin, but since it's surrounded by Minnesota, it has been granted a phone number that fits its neighbors'. On a Sunday in January or early February each year, the hill sponsors a United States Ski Association (USSA) junior race (18 and younger). The Mont du Lac Kids Club also competes two or three times a year here, on Saturdays, with the Spirit Mountain Kids Club. NASTAR (National Standard Racing) also happens here.

A double chair lift brings skiers to five runs, of which Main and Bowl are the most difficult. A chalet with rentals, a lounge and a fast-food area is at the foot of the hills.

From Duluth, take Minn. Highway 23 southwest over the St. Louis River, just beyond the village of Fond du Lac.

SPIRIT MOUNTAIN
9500 Spirit Mountain Pl.   *(218) 628-2891*
Duluth, Minn.   *(800) 642-6377*

The city-owned ski slope has freestyle and snowboard parks and sponsors a host of tournaments and races (USSA and NASTAR, including the Ski Challenge, a statewide adult racing league event), which vary from year to year. Every year there's a season's-end party — usually on a weekend in late March — that includes mountain-bike races in the snow, water skiing (snow to water), barrel jumping on skis and snowboards, and "cardboard boat" races (all-cardboard, painted creations in the shape of canoes, snowmobiles or racing cars).

The hill has a new tubing park and an expanded snowboard park, 22 runs and five lifts (one double, two triple and one quad); also three handle tows. It's open Thanksgiving to early April and is right in Duluth; take Exit 249 from I-35.

Along the North Shore

LUTSEN MOUNTAINS SKI AREA
Minn. Hwy. 61
Lutsen, Minn.   (218) 663-7281

NASTAR races every Saturday and a yearly USSA racing weekend (usually late in the season) make Lutsen a good place to watch skiers perform. The ski area also sponsors the annual Moose Mountain Downhill Race.

Moose is the most challenging hill of the three interconnecting mountains that make up Lutsen. The longest run is 1.6 miles, and the most difficult run is a double black diamond called The Plunge. Lutsen has 41 runs, a gondola and five double chairlifts.

Amenities include rentals, a lounge, entertainment, dining and lodging.

Along the South Shore

Michigan's Upper Peninsula and the nearby Wisconsin area are known as "Big Snow Country," which makes it ski country too. The north winds blow across the widest, unfrozen part of Lake Superior and drop moisture against the mountain ranges. An average of 200 inches of snow fall in one season in the 20-mile radius of the "snow belt." In fact, skiing and snow are the reason most chambers of commerce in

the area don't have toll-free numbers — the staffs couldn't keep up with callers asking, "How much did it snow last night?" and "How cold is it?"

BIG POWDERHORN MOUNTAIN
Bessemer, Mich.   (906) 932-4838

This hill is the largest ski lodging area in the Midwest. Its focus is family skiing, and that includes NASTAR racing, for which it trains young skiers from age 3 as well as their grandparents. NASTAR races are held Thursday through Sunday throughout the season.

There also are spectator events during Hawaiian Weekend, the second weekend in March: bikini races, obstacle races, and "penguin" races (competitors climb inside a big trash bag and fly down the hill head-first, then run back up in the trash bag). A bartenders' race (for barkeeps from the region) is held in late March.

About 30 percent of the 24 trails are for experts — Cannonball and Vertical Drop are extremely challenging. About 35 percent are for beginners. Nine double chairlifts carry 10,800 skiers an hour to the hilltop where they find a vertical drop of 600 feet and the longest run a mile.

Snowboards are allowed on all runs, but there's a half-pipe too. Powderhorn has three restaurants and lounges, a pool and saunas. Kids 6 and younger ski and stay free.

From U.S. Highway 2 east of Ironwood, turn north at the fiberglass skier.

BLACKJACK SKI AREA
Blackjack Rd.
Bessemer, Mich.   (906) 229-5115

Blackjack serves everyone but focuses on kids, offering classes and clubs. NASTAR racing is Friday through Monday every week in season. And the Paul Steiger Dual Giant Slalom is held in early March.

A park and half-pipe are available for snowboarders. The longest run here is 5,300 feet (Horseshoe), and the vertical drop is 465 feet. The most difficult run is Spillway.

Blackjack maintains 20 downhill trails, four chairlifts and two rope tows. Amenities include a restaurant, cafeteria and lodging.

INDIANHEAD SKI AREA
500 Indianhead Rd.
Wakefield, Mich. (906) 229-5181

Although most hills have racing programs, Indianhead is especially busy. It has the largest NASTAR program in the Midwest, is the training site of the U.S. Ski Team, and has a snowboard park for recreation and competitions.

Nineteen runs are served by three double chairlifts, a triple and a quad; two T-bars; and two beginner lifts. Indianhead has a mile-long run and a vertical drop of 638 feet.

This resort also has restaurants, lounges, an indoor pool and spa, fitness and racquetball areas, game rooms and a ski/racing school. Kids 12 and younger ski and lodge free with parents.

MOUNT ASHWABAY SKI HILL
Ski Hill Rd.
Bayfield, Wis. (715) 779-3227

Although it's outside the snow belt, this hill still has plenty of snow to keep skiers happy. It sponsors its own races, such as the annual Cup Race the first Saturday in March and the races surrounding the annual Spring Fling on the second weekend in March. The Cup Race is for four-person adult teams. Spring Fling's events include cardboard box races, relays, timed events, an obstacle course, a jumping contest and an uphill race (pull 'em on and struggle uphill as fast as you can!).

The hill has 13 runs, including Hemlock (the most difficult), which passes through some of the last hemlock trees in the region. Mount Ashwabay Ski Hill has a 317-foot vertical drop, and the longest run is 3,000 feet. You get uphill on a T-bar and four rope tows, and rest in the lounge and cafeteria.

Thunder Bay Area

CANDY MOUNTAIN AND LOCH LOMOND
1800 Loch Lomond Rd.
Thunder Bay, Ont. (807) 475-7787

These two hills are several miles apart but owned by the same company. Loch Lomond opens first each year and has more racing than Candy, which has a longer, flatter terrain that's better for cruising.

At Loch Lomond, you can see CSIA (Canadian Skiing Instructors Alliance) races; kids' league races every weekend; and senior circuit races on Thursday evenings. Other races are the Mountain Smoker, a yearly fast giant slalom; Bailey's Pro Dual Slalom, sponsored by a local ski shop; and the Over-the-Hill Downhill (for older skiers).

Should you decide to try skiing yourself, your lift ticket is good at both hills.

Candy's 1.5-mile run is the longest run in the area, and Loch Lomond's Devil's Dive is the steepest run in Ontario. Loch Lomond's longest run is 1.25 miles. Both hills have vertical drops of more than 800 feet.

More stats: Loch Lomond has 15 runs, rentals, one quad chairlift and two double chair lifts, a full-service lodge and instructors. Candy Mountain has 13 runs, food, a lounge, rentals, two double chairlifts, a T-bar and a rope tow. Snowboarders are welcome at both hills.

MOUNT BALDY

322 Hartviksen St.
Thunder Bay, Ont.   *(807) 683-8441*

This ski hill is just east of Thunder Bay. It, too, has CSIA races, and was the site of the Ontario Juvenile Championship in 1996. It sponsors the club's own racing team and races from the Lake Superior Ski Division, which includes club skiers who are aiming at provincial or national races. Other races at Mount Baldy are the Enterprise Cup Series and the Manitoba Cup Series.

The longest run here is the Gold Run, a mile-long beginners' slope. Expert skiers go to Main and Hornet, which are among 10 runs accessed by two double chairlifts, a T-bar and a rope tow.

The chalet has hot food, a lounge, equipment rentals, a ski academy and a 400-foot half-pipe for snowboarders. The hill is 8 kilometers past the Terry Fox Lookout.

Ski Jumping

The western Lake Superior region has always been an international leader in ski jumping, producing Olympic jumpers and involving hundreds of children in the sport. On the U.S. side, the jumping teams are members of the 16-team United States Ski Association Central Division, which includes Minnesota and Michigan's Upper Peninsula. They compete with one another and occasionally with teams from Thunder Bay and elsewhere. The best go on to compete with Eastern, Rocky Mountain and Alaskan divisions. All the teams prepare their jumpers for the Junior Olympics.

BIG THUNDER SPORTS PARK

Little Norway Rd.
Thunder Bay, Ont.   *(807) 475-4402*

For the 1995-96 season, the 90- and 120-meter jumps at Big Thunder were closed because of a lack of funding, and long-distance jumping in Canada moved west to Calgary — the only other ski-jump center in the country. At the time of this printing, there was a possibility the Thunder Bay jumps would open again for the following seasons and again draw world-class long-distance jumpers. Nevertheless, the smaller jumps — which don't look small at all to non-jumpers — get active use throughout the season. The Thunder Bay Ski Jumping Club and the Ontario Nordic Ski Club, which include jumpers age 5 and older, use the 5-, 10-, 20-, 30- and 64-meter jumps just about every weekend. Regional, national and international competitions are held regularly.

From Canadian Highway 61, about 10

Insiders' Tips

Although there hasn't been international ski flying at the Copper Peak near Ironwood, Michigan, for several years, you still can enjoy the place billed as the longest artificial ski slide in the world and the only ski flying hill in the Americas. The 469-foot slide rests on a 364-foot rock formation. From June 15 to Labor Day, you can ride the (scary) chair lift and elevator to the top and see the breathtaking view: Minnesota, Wisconsin, Michigan, Thunder Bay and Lake Superior. It's 10 miles northeast of Ironwood on Black River Drive (County Road 513).

kilometers south of Thunder Bay, turn onto the Little Norway Road and follow it to the gate. Someone there can give you directions to the jumps.

CHESTER BOWL
1800 E. Skyline Pkwy.
Duluth, Minn. (218) 724-9832

The Duluth Ski Club practices and competes here, where the four jumps are kept busy after school and on weekends. Like the other U.S. teams in the region, the club is part of the United States Ski Association Central Division and prepares jumpers for international competition. A comfortable city-owned chalet near the foot of the jumps takes the frost out of viewing.

PINE VALLEY SKI HILL
Pine Valley, Cloquet, Minn.
Contact: Gene Schilling (218) 879-7144

The Cloquet Ski Club (ages 4 to 18) practices jumping here on Tuesday and Thursday evenings. They compete in two USSA meets a season as well as local and regional meets — all on the weekends. Jumps at Pine Valley are 10, 20 and 40 meters long.

From Minn. Highway 33 in Cloquet, turn up the road by the Armory next to Lumberjack Mall; go two blocks and turn left.

PINE MOUNTAIN
Sunset Rd., Ironwood, Mich.
Contact: Rich Aho (906) 932-3299

The Wolverine Nordic Ski Club, with jumpers from ages 4 to 18, practices and has meets here on 5-, 10- and 65-meter jumps. The 4-year-olds begin on the 5-meter jump and, as they grow, work their way through the 10- and on to the 65-meter jump.

You can watch practices and meets December to March. To reach Pine Mountain, turn north on the Section 12 Road

from U.S. Highway 2, just east of Ironwood. Go 1.5 miles to Sunset Road; turn right and go another mile.

Auto Racing

PROCTOR SPEEDWAY
800 N. Boundary Ave.
Proctor, Minn. (218) 624-0606

Every Sunday evening from mid-May through August, this dirt track hums with races of stock, super and modified cars. Hot laps begin at 5:30 PM, and the main races begin at 6 PM. Admission is $7.

SUPERIOR SPEEDWAY
Head of the Lakes Fairgrounds, Tower Ave.
Superior, Wis. (715) 394-7848

Late-model, modified, superstock and superior stock cars race around a 3-furlong, high-banked clay oval. Races are at 7 PM every Friday, May through September. Tickets are $7 for adults, $5 for seniors and kids ages 13 through 17 and $2 for children ages 6 through 12; kids younger than 6 are free.

Polo

DULUTH POLO CLUB
Pine Brook Farm, Jean Duluth Rd.
Duluth, Minn. (218) 525-5470

Spectators are welcome to watch polo practices and meets during the summer at the polo grounds here. A member of the U.S. Polo Association since 1968, this club competes in Madison, Milwaukee, Minneapolis, Des Moines, Winnipeg and Sioux Falls. Tournaments are on Sunday; call to see whether the club will be home or away. Practices are Wednesday and Friday evenings.

League Sports

League and Youth League slowpitch,

fastpitch and youth soccer are played throughout the region. For scheduling, call a local American Legion, the Veterans of Foreign Wars or city parks department, or drop in at playing areas weekends and evenings.

Twin Ports Area

58TH STREET COMPLEX
58th St., Superior, Wis.

Three fields with lights and bleachers here are primarily used by adults — mostly for men's softball. Take Tower Avenue south to 58th Street; turn east and go eight blocks.

LIEBAERT FIELD COMPLEX
Hayes Ct., Superior, Wis.

Liebaert is a five-field complex where youth baseball (Little League, Babe Ruth) and women's softball are played during the summer. It has lights and bleachers, and is off Belknap Avenue just east of the University of Wisconsin-Superior.

PARK POINT RECREATION AREA
Park Point, Duluth, Minn.

If you head out to the end of Park Point any summer evening, you're likely to come across a lively game of softball, sand volleyball and sometimes rugby. Cross the Aerial Lift Bridge and keep going until the road runs out.

WHEELER FIELD COMPLEX
34th Ave. W., Duluth, Minn.

Probably the finest slowpitch and fastpitch fields in the region are here, where you'll pass outdoor bocce ball courts on your way to the five fields. It's a pretty area, bordered on one side by a cottonwood-lined creek and with the big hills of Duluth as a backdrop.

Take the 40th Avenue W. exit from I-35; turn right at the first stoplight, on Grand Avenue, and continue northeast to 34th Avenue W. Wheeler is on your left. On the right is Wade Stadium, which abuts Little League fields.

Along the South Shore

BEASER PARK
Beaser Ave. and Eighth St., Ashland, Wis.

T-ball and Little League majors and minors (ages 5 to 12) are played here most evenings from late May to mid-July, with some tournaments in August.

HODGKINS PARK
14th Ave. E. and Seventh St., Ashland, Wis.

Two softball fields and a big hardball field are the site of daily summertime games of men's and women's softball, senior hardball and high school hardball. The fields are lighted and have concessions, bleachers, parking and a playground for children.

PENN PARK
Seventh Ave. E. and Ninth St., Ashland, Wis.

Most weeknights in the summer, you can watch Babe Ruth (ages 13 to 15) baseball here.

Thunder Bay Area

CENTRAL BALL DIAMOND
Central Ave. and Balmoral St.
Thunder Bay, Ont.

One large ball diamond here is the site of junior and senior hardball during the summer. Bleachers are available for spectators.

CURRENT RIVER PLAYFIELD SITE
450 Dewe Ave., Thunder Bay, Ont.

Seven ball diamonds and a soccer field stay busy here with Little League, adult slowpitch and senior ball. The site also has an ice arena, community center, play equip-

Photo: Duluth News-Tribune

Hundreds of spectators turn out to support runners in Grandma's Marathon.

ment for children and tennis courts. There are no lights.

FORT WILLIAM STADIUM
200 Legion Park Dr., Thunder Bay, Ont.

This major recreation area is attached to Chapples Golf Course, the International Friendship Gardens and an arena. It has lights; football and soccer are played here. The Thunder Bay Giants, a post-high school football team, has just joined the Minnesota League (no other teams from our region are represented) and plays its home games here.

PORT ARTHUR STADIUM
425 Winnipeg Ave., Thunder Bay, Ont.

Another major recreation area, the stadium is in a block of buildings with the city-run Canada Games Complex, the community auditorium and a hockey arena. This is the field where the Thunder Bay Whiskey Jacks play baseball, but junior and senior league baseball can be seen here too from May 15 to October 15.

PRINCE ARTHUR PARK AND MARINA
Red River Rd., Thunder Bay, Ont.

Ball fields are kept busy here, as In-

siders come to picnic, recreate and enjoy the beautiful park and lively harbor views. Follow Red River Road to the Lake; the park is at the end of the road.

WEST FORT PLAYFIELD SITE
397 Empire Ave., Thunder Bay, Ont.

Five ball fields and a soccer field get a lot of use in the daytime. There are no lights, so no night games, but there are bleachers.

College Teams

Twin Ports Area

COLLEGE OF ST. SCHOLASTICA
1200 Kenwood Ave.
Duluth, Minn.   *(218) 723-6551*

The Saints' teams play soccer, volleyball, basketball, hockey, tennis, softball and baseball. In hockey, the team participates in the National Collegiate Athletic Association's Division III; otherwise they play independently or as part of the National Association of Intercollegiate Athletics.

UNIVERSITY OF MINNESOTA-DULUTH
10 University Dr.
Duluth, Minn.   (218) 726-8168

The UMD Bulldogs hockey team competes in NCAA Division I; the team won the Western Collegiate Hockey Association western division title in 1993 and finished second nationally nine years earlier. The Bulldogs' chief rival is the University of Minnesota Golden Gophers.

Bulldog teams also play basketball, tennis, track, baseball, softball, volleyball and football in the Northern Sun Intercollegiate Conference (NCAA Division II). For schedules and tickets, call (218) 726-8595.

UNIVERSITY OF WISCONSIN-SUPERIOR
1800 Grand Ave.
Superior, Wis.   (715) 394-8193

Hockey, basketball, softball, baseball, track, volleyball and soccer keep the UWS Yellowjackets busy. These teams play in NAIA Division III, and in NCHA Division III in hockey.

Along the South Shore

GOGEBIC COMMUNITY COLLEGE
E-4946 Jackson Rd.
Gogebic, Wis.   (906) 932-4231 Ext. 346

The Samsons and Lady Samsons play basketball only at this two-year college, as part of the National Junior College Athletic Association (JUCO); nevertheless, they sometimes compete with four-year schools.

NORTHLAND COLLEGE
1411 Ellis Ave.
Ashland, Wis.   (715) 682-1699

The Lumberjacks and Lumberjills compete in NAIA Division II. Teams include soccer, basketball and volleyball.

Thunder Bay Area

LAKEHEAD UNIVERSITY
955 Oliver Rd.
Thunder Bay, Ont.   (807) 343-8110

The Nor'Westers — volleyball, skiing, basketball, wrestling, hockey and track — compete at Delaney Arena or the Norwest Center when home during their Ontario University League schedule, from November to February. For ticket information, call (807) 343-8213.

Annual Sporting Events

Twin Ports Area

AMERICAN QUARTER HORSE
ASSOCIATION HORSE SHOW
South St. Louis County Fairgrounds
At the end of Boundary Rd.
Proctor, Minn.   (218) 628-2401

By far the biggest horse show in the area, the four-day event toward the end of July draws about 400 horse-and-rider pairs from all over the Midwest. They compete in western (team penning, barrel racing and pole weaving) and English events. Admission is free. Call the fairgrounds or St. Louis County Extension Service, (218) 726-7512, for details.

From I-35 south of Duluth, take the Proctor (U.S. Highway 2) exit; go to Boundary Avenue and turn right. Boundary ends at the fairgrounds.

BEARGREASE SLED DOG MARATHON
Beargrease 100, 190 and 500
All depart from Ordean Jr. High School Field
40th Ave. E. and Superior St.
Duluth, Minn.   (218) 722-7631

Named for John Beargrease, the musher who hauled mail up and down the North Shore before the road was built, this January marathon draws 20 to 30 mushing teams from snowy areas of North America and big crowds to Ordean Field in Duluth to watch them depart. Three races originate there: the Beargrease 100 ends in Beaver Bay; the Beargrease 190 ends in Grand Marais; and the "real" Beargrease — 500 miles long — goes to Grand Portage and back. Another excellent vantage point is at the Primetime Steak House north of Duluth at the intersection of Jean Duluth and N. Tischer roads. Some spectators prefer heading for Duluth's Lester Park a few days later to watch the tired teams and mushers cross the finish line.

CARLTON COUNTY HORSE RACES
Carlton County Fairgrounds, 217 S. Front St. Barnum, Minn. (218) 389-6737

Everything goes at these races, which are during fair week in August. You'll see kids wearing football helmets riding Arabians bareback; professional jockeys riding thoroughbreds or racing quarterhorses who otherwise compete at parimutuel tracks; farmers on their family pets. Expect the unexpected: One recent year, a newly broken mustang decided to beat the field by jumping the fence and cutting across the oval's center. Betting isn't legal here.

For details on race dates, call the Carlton County Extension Service at (218) 384-3511. From I-35, take the Barnum exit west into town. Turn left at the stop sign; the fairgrounds are two blocks south on the left.

GRANDMA'S MARATHON
Canal Park, Duluth, Minn. (218) 727-0947

Join the throngs at Canal Park to welcome the front runners of this world-class marathon, or find a good spot along London Road or Scenic Highway 61 east of town. Thousands of runners come from all over the world to compete in Grandma's, a favorite because of the level course and cool breezes from Lake Superior along the whole 26.2-mile course. A half-marathon begins 13 miles from the finish line on Scenic Highway 61, and also ends at Canal Park.

The race begins in Two Harbors on the North Shore at 7:30 AM on a Saturday in June; front runners collapse near the tent and concession stands a couple of hours later. This is one of the biggest events in the region.

GREAT NORTHERN CLASSIC RODEO
Head of the Lakes Fairgrounds, Tower Ave. Superior, Wis. (218) 726-1603

This International Professional Rodeo Association event takes place on Labor Day

---

It's not all fun and games at a Duluth-Superior Dukes baseball game — not if you're a neighbor of Wade Stadium, that is. Foul balls knock out windows and crack into people in the surrounding residential neighborhood, and fans tramp through yards and over gardens in their hurry to the stadium. (We've been guilty of such trespass ourselves — the yards are well kept, fenceless and pleasant to walk through.) The problem has been getting out of hand, however, so please use the sidewalks. Whether the city can do anything about blocking foul balls was uncertain at press time.

Insiders' Tips

weekend and draws close to 10,000 spectators. The full rodeo menu is served: bull riding, team roping, steer wrestling, bronco riding, barrel racing and others.

Reserved seats are $8 for adults and $6 for kids and seniors. General admission is $7 for adults and $5 for kids and seniors.

The fairgrounds is south of downtown Superior.

HORSE EXTRAVAGANZA
Head of the Lakes Fairgrounds, Tower Ave.
Superior, Wis. (715) 394-7848
More than 50 teams (each with three horses and riders) compete in team penning at this annual event, which begins at 8 AM on the Saturday before Mother's Day and ends about 5 PM. You'll also see demonstrations of horse jumping, dressage and horseshoeing; and more than 40 booths. For more information, call the fairgrounds or Douglas County Extension Service at (715) 394-0363.

The fairgrounds is south of downtown Superior.

NATIONAL SNOCROSS
Spirit Mountain Ski Hill
Duluth, Minn. (218) 628-2891
In late November, Spirit Mountain begins to buzz, then roar, as 500 snowmobiles maneuver jumps, moguls and tight turns along a 3-furlong course. Drivers from Canada, Sweden, Finland and elsewhere compete for a $25,000 purse. Call the ski hill for information. Parking is available at the South St. Louis County Fairgrounds in Proctor (take the Proctor exit from I-35, continue to Boundary Avenue and up Boundary to the fairgrounds); shuttle buses carry spectators to Spirit Mountain. For more information, call Spirit Mountain or the Duluth Convention and Visitors Bureau, (218) 722-4011, and check out the entry in our Annual Events chapter.

OUTLAW SNOWMOBILE RACES
Barkers Island
Superior, Wis. (800) 777-7183
Sanctioned by the International Series of Champions (ISOC, pronounced "eye-sock"), this race draws 500 contestants from all over the country — amateur and pro. Racing begins on a Friday in late winter and continues through Sunday, and includes sport, pro stock, juniors, women's and semipro classes. A .33-mile track makes it easy viewing for spectators. The race is the second of a triple crown: The first is at Canterbury Downs racetrack in Shakopee, Minnesota, and the third is at West Yellowstone, Montana. Pros compete for a $30,000 purse. An expo (booths and vendors) and live entertainment are part of the event.

Admission is $12 for one day or $30 for all three. From U.S. Highway 2 in Superior, turn toward the Lake at the Duluth Convention and Visitors Bureau.

SAN JUAN 24 NORTH AMERICAN CHAMPIONSHIP SAILING RACES
Outside Duluth-Superior Harbor
Duluth, Minn. (218) 722-4011
This race series, for 24-foot-long San Juan-brand sloops, comes to Duluth about every fourth summer, and 1996 is one of those years. (Other years, races are held in Seattle, Washington; Portland, Oregon; and Sheboygan, Wisconsin)

About 25 of the fixed-keel sloops compete during seven races in mid-July. Friday's events begin at noon; Saturday's and Sunday's begin at 10 AM. Good viewing spots are the Lakewalk, at Park Point and from the pier — especially during the hour prior to the race when the sloops, with their brightly colored sails, move out under the Aerial Bridge into the open water.

The winner is crowned North American champion of this fleet. For more information, call the Duluth Visitors and Convention Bureau at the listed number.

ST. LOUIS RIVER WHITEWATER RODEO AND KAYAK SLALOM

Minn. Hwy. 210
Thomson, Minn.   *(218) 726-6533*

Watch top paddlers from the Midwest maneuver the rocks and white water of the St. Louis River just below Thomson Dam. Preliminaries begin at 8 AM Saturday — August 24 in 1996 and August 23 in 1997. Finals continue through Sunday. In the rodeo, paddlers try to keep their crafts in one churning spot.

From I-35, take the Minn. Highway 210 exit east into Carlton. Continue straight ahead at the four-way stop and begin looking for a parking place. Good viewing spots are from the Highway 210 bridge and from the well-marked path on the other side that winds downriver.

TRANS-SUPERIOR YACHT RACE

Every two (odd) years, in July, about 20 yachts set sail from Sault Ste. Marie, Michigan, at the far end of Lake Superior to race 338 nautical miles to Duluth. The trip takes two to four days. Just keep an eye on the horizon; when you spot sails, join those gathered along Duluth's Lakewalk, the Ship Canal and Park Point Beach to watch the boats arrive. Call the Duluth Visitors and Convention Bureau, (218) 722-4011, for details.

WET AND WILD PADDLING EXPO

Minn. Hwy. 210
Thomson, Minn.   *(218) 726-6533*

You can watch flatwater and whitewater paddlers or participate yourself in kayaking and canoeing at this event, which is held on June 1 in 1996 and May 31 in 1997. You can watch it free, but for only $5 you can try out various watercraft — sea kayaks, sprint kayaks, whitewater

boats, canoes and others — that six different manufacturers will have at the site. You can also take a free beginners' course.

An outdoor equipment and clothing sale and auction are part of the expo. Register at the site. See the previous St. Louis River Whitewater Rodeo listing for directions and good viewing spots.

WHIPPERSNAPPER RACES

Park Point
2401 Minnesota Ave.
Duluth, Minn.   *(218) 723-5233*

On the Friday before Grandma's Marathon (the second Saturday in June), about 400 kids ages 4 to 14 turn out for these races: 50- and 100-yard dashes, a quarter-miler and a half-miler. Admission is free; runners are given numbered bibs and refreshments, and winners receive ribbons and medallions. Races are run from noon to 3:00 PM at Park Point.

Along the North Shore

BEARGREASE SLED DOG MARATHON

Beargrease 100
Finish: Beaver Bay, Minn.
Beargrease 190
Finish: Grand Marais, Minn.
Beargrease 500
Midpoint: Grand Portage, Minn.   *(218) 722-7631*

Named for John Beargrease, the musher who hauled mail up and down the North Shore before the road was built, this marathon draws 20 to 30 mushing teams from snowy areas of North America. Three races leave Duluth from Ordean Junior High School Field. The Beargrease 100 ends in Beaver Bay, and the Beargrease 190 ends in Grand Marais. The main race, 500 miles long, reaches its halfway point at Grand Portage (the Ojibwe band there, of which Beargrease was a member, is a major sponsor) and returns to Duluth. All three places are good viewing spots, as are the intersection with U.S. Highway 2, 5 miles north of Two Harbors; the Finland Recreation Building on Minn. Highway 6; and the Sawbill Trail, at the intersection with the North Shore state snowmobile trail. For more information call (218) 722-7631. (See the "Twin Ports" subsection of this "Annual Sporting Events" section for additional information.)

GRANDMA'S MARATHON
Two Harbors, Minn.   (218) 727-0947

Top long-distance runners from all over the world, accompanied by thousands of runners who just hope they can last the distance, take off at 7:30 AM on a Saturday in June for this 26-mile race that ends in Duluth. You won't have any problem finding the starting point — there are more racers than there are townspeople. Viewing places are everywhere along Scenic Highway 61, the lakeside highway the runners use. (See the entry in this chapter's "Twin Ports" section as well.)

LUTSEN MOUNTAIN BIKE RACES
Lutsen, Minn.   (218) 663-7281

The bikes are tearing downhill in June at the Lutsen Mountain Bike Park. Downhill slalom races, straight downhill races and a cross-country race are all sanctioned by the National Off Road Bike Associa-

tion. The bike park has 18 miles of trails; bikes are mounted on ski gondola cars and carried to the top of Moose Mountain.

Along the South Shore

BESSEMER USSA
SNOWMOBILE OLYMPUS
N. Moore St.
Bessemer, Mich.
Contact: Bob Parker   (906) 932-4080

This United States Snowmobile Association-sanctioned race draws 180 drivers and in the 1994-95 season was voted the USSA Race of the Year. Professional drivers compete for points and money during the first weekend in December. The oval is doused with a million gallons of water so these unusual snowmobiles (hot rods, stock machines) can have the icy track they need.

You can reserve a trackside spot for your car, so you can watch the race near a heater and listen to it on your car radio. Otherwise, a ticket is $5 and a two-day pass $9.

From Bessemer, go 2 miles north on N. Moore Street.

BIRKEBEINER
Hayward, Wis.   (715) 634-5025

We're fudging our "South Shore" definition here a bit to include this must-see event (it's actually 50 miles south of the Lake).

The "Birkie," as Insiders call it, is an amazing race if for no other reason that 6,500 people wearing 13,000 very long skis manage to stay untangled. The largest cross-country ski race in North America, it draws elite competitors from all over the world. The main 52-kilometer race begins at Telemark Lodge near Cable, Wisconsin, and ends on Main Street in Hayward. Competitors now use freestyle, in which skis are used like long racing skates.

There are several associate races on Birkie weekend, so call for details. Shuttle services are available.

Paavo Nurmi Marathon

Hurley, Wis.   *(715) 561-4334*

Named for the Finnish winner of nine Olympic gold medals in the 1920s, this demanding marathon (it's a hard course in August heat) draws about 300 participants. It starts at 7:30 AM the second Saturday in August, in Upson, Wisconsin, and ends in Hurley's downtown on Silver Street and Fourth Avenue.

A favorite spot for spectators to cheer on the tiring runners is on Cemetery Hill, which is the toughest part of the course. Afterwards, everyone gathers at Riccelli Park for music, food, refreshments, awards and drawings. The race is part of the two-week Iron County Heritage Festival (see our Annual Events chapter).

Run on Water

Bayfield, Wis.   *(800) 447-4094*

There's nothing miraculous about it, even though the water is many fathoms deep: The race takes place in February. And there's nothing to worry about, either. Lake Superior's frozen expanse here is used like a county road between Bayfield and Madeline Island, with Islanders simply driving over the bank and across to the mainland in place of summertime ferry transport.

Usually, the snow is packed down and running is easy, but in 1996 a thaw made the going wet and slick. The 5-mile foot race was canceled only once since its inception in 1987; during the 1995 event, a big wind on the Lake made a whiteout so blinding people couldn't tell what direction they were running.

The city docks at the foot of Washington Avenue are a good vantage point — or walk out on Lake Superior.

Thunder Bay Area

Winter Carnival

Every year in late January and early February, Thunder Bay strikes a blow against cabin fever with a bash that offers some delightful spectator opportunities. Broomball, boot hockey, volleyball, armwrestling, sled dog races, slowpitch in the snow and outdoor curling are only some of the activities. About 8,000 people emerge from their dens to join the fun.

One of the most popular is the "Snow Man" competition, Thunder Bay's equivalent of Hawaii's Iron Man contest (yah . . . sure). Competitors skate for 2 kilometers, ski for 2 kilometers and run for 2 kilometers.

Most activities are at the Canadian-Lakehead Exhibition Grounds in central Thunder Bay. For more information, call the Visitors and Convention Bureau at (807) 625-2149 or the grounds at (807) 622-6473.

Powwows in our region begin with the Grand Entry, followed by the Flag Song and a veterans dance. People remain standing during all of these. Anyone who is or has been in the Armed Forces (or who has a family member in the Armed Forces) can join the veterans dance.

Inside
Annual Events

There are annual rites of passage: spring, summer, autumn, winter. There are anticipated annual lifestyle activities: maple syruping, gardening, berrying, fishing, wild ricing, hunting, logging.

Then there are the annual events: festivals and parties, concerts and competitions, dances and games. Many of them are tied to those larger natural cycles, and many have no reason whatever for being — except to have fun. Here are some of them:

January

BEARGREASE SLED DOG MARATHON
Departs from Ordean Jr. High School Field
40th Ave. E. and Superior St.
Duluth, Minn. (218) 722-7631

Named for John Beargrease, the musher who hauled mail up and down the North Shore before the road was built, this late January marathon draws 20 to 30 mushing teams from snowy areas of North America and big crowds to Ordean Field to watch them depart. Three races originate there: the Beargrease 100 ends in Beaver Bay; the Beargrease 190 ends in Grand Marais; and the "real" Beargrease — 500 miles long — goes to Grand Portage and back. Another excellent vantage point is at the Primetime Steak House north of Duluth at the intersection of Jean Duluth and N. Tischer roads. Some spectators prefer heading for Duluth's Lester Park a few days later to watch the tired teams and mushers in the Beargrease 500 cross the finish line.

(See our Spectator Sports chapter for details.)

DULUTH WINTER SPORTS FESTIVAL
Various areas in Duluth, Minn. (218) 722-4011

This six-week festival beginning January 1 and ending in mid-February is Duluth's version of the St. Paul Winter Carnival. About 65 different outdoor events include the Northwoods Sleigh and Cutter Parade; strong dog pulls and sled dog rides (in conjunction with the Beargrease Marathon — see the previous listing); snow races; and hockey, curling and broomball meets.

Clues given daily in local media point festival medallion-hunters to the right outdoor hiding place; the finder gets a cash prize ($300 in the past). About 200 hunters in 1996 descended on the Duluth Visitors and Convention Bureau lot near the Lake, apparently convinced it was the right place; it wasn't, but the bureau is the right place to call for details of this festival. There is no admission fee.

SUPERIOR SKI CLASSIC
Superior Municipal Forest
28th St. and Wyoming Ave.
Superior, Wis. (715) 394-7716

About 500 cross-country skiers show up for this series every third weekend in January. Races include a 42-kilometer trek, 15-kilometer freestyle and 15-kilometer classic. If you want to participate, you can register at Wisconsin Indianhead

Technical College, (715) 394-6677. It's free to watch, but call for entry details (the entry fee was not determined as this book went to press).

NORTHERN LIGHTS WINTER CARNIVAL
Various locations city-wide
Thunder Bay, Ont. **(800) 667-8386**

Usually held the last weekend in January, this city-wide, four-day celebration aims to good-naturedly thumb its nose at winter. Each day has a different sponsor with a full roster of indoor and outdoor events that run into the evening. A snowman-building contest for kids, tubing, ice sculpture competitions, sleigh rides, ski races, snow golf, darts tournaments and sawing contests are part of the fun-filled activities. A nightly bonfire and a top-notch fireworks display on The Coliseum's grounds warm the coldest evenings, as do the dances at The Coliseum near Inter-City Mall on Red River Road. Dog-sledding demonstrations and the Northwestern Ontario Moose-calling Competition give this festival a decidedly Canadian feel.

Various institutions around town — including Old Fort William on Broadway, Lakehead University at 955 Oliver Road and Confederation College on Nakina Drive — and area businesses participate.

A $3 carnival button serves as your admission for most events. Some activities, such as the darts tournament and the dances, have additional entry fees. Others, such as the "Big Shiver," reward you for taking a dip (or being one!) by diving into frigid water; prizes are awarded the oldest dipper, the largest dipping group, the best costume and the dipper hailing from the greatest distance away. And let's not forget the snow-shoveling competition where contestants attack a pile of snow, working for the best time.

BIG SNO FEST
Hurley-Ironwood Area **(715) 561-4334**

A variety of outdoors events are scattered through the last two weeks in January during the twin towns' winter carnival. Ski hills and chambers of commerce organize something for every evening: outdoor skating parties, moonlight skiing, radar snowmobile races, fashion shows, Big Bands and snow sculpture contests; it all ends with a family fun day. For more information, call the Hurley Chamber of Commerce. Admission is free.

UNITED NORTHERN SPORTSMEN'S ICE FISHING CONTEST
Island Lake **(218) 721-4843**
Duluth, Minn. **(218) 624-2106**

This popular annual contest (a tradition since 1952) takes place on Island Lake west of Duluth. On contest weekend, either the last in January or the first in February, the large lake is covered with cars, snowmobiles and anglers — some standing, some sitting, some huddled in shelters. To sign up, call the club, stop in at a tackle shop or drive out to Island Lake. The entry fee is $5. First prize for the biggest gamefish — perch, crappie, northern pike and walleye — is about $500.

From Central Entrance in Duluth, take Arlington Avenue north (County Road 4); continue along the extension, Rudy Perpich Road (formerly Rice Lake Road), until you reach Island Lake.

February

SUPERIOR CIRCLE SLED DOG RACE
Madeline Island, Wis. **(715) 747-2801**

Three days of events in early February include mushing races, strong dog pulls, bonfires and food. Vet checks and awards ceremonies are at the Isle Vista Casino on the mainland. About a dozen teams participate. You can watch the race for free; if you'd like to participate, call for details — the entry fee was not set at press time.

RUN ON WATER

Bayfield, Wis.   *(800) 447-4094*

Lake Superior's frozen expanse here is used like a county road between Bayfield and Madeline Island, with Islanders simply driving over the bank and across the ice to the mainland in place of summertime ferry transport. The 5-mile foot race in early February was canceled only once between its inception in 1987 and 1995 when a big wind on the Lake made a whiteout so blinding people couldn't tell what direction they were running. Usually the snow is packed down and running is easy, but in 1996 a thaw made the going wet and slick. The city docks at the foot of Washington Avenue are a good vantage point — or walk out on the Lake. (See also our Spectator Sports chapter.)

LAKEHEAD MUSIC FESTIVAL

Lakehead University
955 Oliver Rd.   *(807) 577-5155*
Thunder Bay, Ont.   *(807) 345-6021*

This is a three-week event in which college students compete for scholarships in piano, dance, band, choir, flute, organ, woodwinds, brass, percussion and voice. Preliminary competitions are in the Music and Visual Arts Building and the Bora Laskin Building. Winning students have a one-night performance — the Pizazz Concert — with the symphony at the Thunder Bay Auditorium, 450 Beverly Street, (807) 343-2300. Admission is $1 for preliminaries and $12 at the auditorium.

BIRKEBEINER

Cable to Hayward, Wis.   *(715) 634-5025*

This must-see event takes place 50 miles south of the Lake in mid-February. The "Birkie," as Insiders call it, is an amazing race if for no other reason that 6,500 people wearing 13,000 very long skis manage to stay untangled. The largest cross-country ski race in North America, it draws elite competitors from all over the world. The main 52-kilometer race begins at Telemark Lodge near Cable, Wisconsin, and ends on Main Street in Hayward. Competitors now use freestyle, in which skis are used like long racing skates. There are several associate races on Birkie weekend, so call for details. Shuttle services are available. Admission is free.

DULUTH BOAT, SPORTS AND TRAVEL SHOW

Duluth Entertainment Convention Center
Duluth, Minn.   *(218) 727-4344*

Every year in mid-February, crowds (try 150,000 people, 40 busloads from Thunder Bay alone) of people gather at the DECC to see the latest in sporting goods: RVs to life vests, travel plans to Canadian hunting options, boats and camping equipment. There's always a big-name entertainer, fun for kids and food. It's a five-day event, and admission costs $6 daily for adults, $2.50 for children.

BLUE MOON BALL

Bates Bar
Bayfield, Wis.   *(715) 779-5010*

Maybe you shouldn't attend this one. . . . It's so much fun, Bates Bar is already jammed beyond capacity. On the third Saturday in February, everyone dresses up —as though for a high school prom for adults — and get their feet moving to the music of live big bands. If you decide to squeeze in too, admission is $10 each.

March

ISOC OUTLAW SNOWMOBILE RACES
Barkers Island
Superior, Wis.   *(800) 777-7183*

Sanctioned by the International Series of Champions, ISOC (pronounced "eye-sock"), this race draws 500 contestants from all over the country, amateur and pro. Racing begins the first Friday in March and continues through Sunday. It includes sport, pro stock, juniors, women's and semi-pro classes. A .33-mile track makes it easy viewing for spectators. The race is the second of a triple crown: The first is at Canterbury Downs racetrack in Shakopee, Minnesota, and the third is at West Yellowstone, Montana. Pros compete for a $30,000 purse. An expo (booths and vendors) and live entertainment are part of the event. Admission is $12 for one day or $30 for all three. (See our Spectator Sports chapter for other details.)

From U.S. Highway 2 in Superior, turn toward the Lake at the Visitors and Convention Bureau.

SPRING CARNIVAL
Mount Ashwabay Ski Hill
Ski Hill Rd.
Bayfield, Wis.   *(715) 779-3227*

During Spring Carnival (usually in early March), hill-goers dress up in costumes and play: cardboard box races, re-lays, timed events, an obstacle course, a jumping contest and an uphill race (pull on your skis and go up as fast as you can!). There is no entry fee.

HAWAIIAN WEEKEND
Big Powderhorn Mountain
Bessemer, Mich.   *(906) 932-4838*

During the second weekend in March, people pretend the snows of Powderhorn are the sands of Waikiki and ignore frostbite as, bikini-clad, they participate in downhill ski races. For other events, participants wear their Hawaiian duds over their ski togs. One is the penguin race, in which people don a big black plastic trash bag and fly down the hill headfirst, then — still in the trash bag — run back up. The weekend includes obstacle races and an outdoor barbecue. There is no admission fee. Prizes include season ski passes and ski gear.

ST. PATRICK'S DAY PARADE
Superior St.
Downtown Duluth   *(218) 728-6406*

There aren't a lot of people of Irish descent here, but who cares? Everybody is yearning for green and a reason to banish winter, and a couple of thousand people turn out to help turn the seasonal tide. (Some of us secretly are honoring the mythical St. Urho, St. Patrick's Finnish competitor hereabouts, who is said to have driven grasshoppers out of Finland.) The parade starts around dark on March 17, if St. Paddy's Day lands on a weekday;

Insiders' Tips

It can't be said often enough. Bring your sweaters and windbreakers when you go to any outdoors events in our area. The wind from the Lake is both capricious and cold. The thing that distinguishes Insiders from everyone else is that Insiders don't store their blankets and winter clothing when summer comes.

when it lands on a weekend, the parade begins in the afternoon. Dress warm! The event is sponsored by KZIO radio.

SPRING FLING

Spirit Mountain
9500 Spirit Mountain Pl.   (218) 628-2891
Duluth, Minn.   (800) 642-6377

Spirit Mountain has a season-end party, usually on a weekend in late March, that includes mountain-bike races in the snow, water skiing (snow to water), barrel jumping on skis and snowboards, and "cardboard boat" races (all-cardboard, painted creations in the shape of canoes, snowmobiles or racing cars). Watching is free; participating will cost you the price of a lift ticket ($17 to $32, depending on your age and the day of the week). The hill is right in Duluth; take Exit 249 from I-35.

April

ARROWHEAD BUILDERS EXPO

Duluth Entertainment Convention Center
Duluth, Minn.   (218) 727-4344

Every year in early April, more than 150,000 people gather at the DECC to see the newest in home-building, furnishing and decorating options. The event includes the appearance of a big-name entertainer, fun activities for kids and plenty of food. It's a five-day event. Daily admission is $6 for adults and $2.50 for kids.

May

ASHLAND FOLK FESTIVAL

Northland College
Ashland, Wis.   (715) 682-1289.

The longest-running folk festival in the state (since 1972), this gathering brings folk performers from around the country who entertain with dulcimer, banjo, drum, fiddle and flute. Past performers include Greg Brown, Cary Newcomer, Skip Jones and

L.J. Booth. It takes place the second weekend in May on the lovely campus of Northland College. In good weather, daytime activities are outside: the children's concert, workshops, arts and crafts and an open mike. Evening performances are in the Alvord Theater because May in our parts is still a bit chilly at night, so come prepared. Ticket prices in 1995 were $5.

From U.S. Highway 2 in Ashland, take Ellis Avenue south for a mile.

HORSE EXTRAVAGANZA

Head of the Lakes Fairground
Tower Ave.
Superior, Wis.   (715) 394-7848

More than 50 teams (each with three horses and riders) compete in team penning at this annual event, which begins at 8 AM on the Saturday before Mother's Day and ends about 5 PM. You'll also see more than 40 booths and demonstrations of horse jumping, dressage and horseshoing. For more information, call the fairground or Douglas County Extension Service, (715) 394-0363.

FOLKLORE FESTIVAL

Fort William Gardens and Curling Club
901 Miles St. E.
Thunder Bay, Ont.   (807) 345-0551

The folklore festival, organized by the Thunder Bay Multicultural Association since 1978, honors the various ethnic groups who live in the city. Held the first weekend in May, costumed participants representing East Indian, Pakistani, Ojibwe, Finnish, Italian, Scottish, German and Scandinavian cultures each have their own area in the garden. Each area is set up like a miniature country; activities and attractions include dancing, singing and lots of ethnic food.

Admission ranges from $1 to $5. We recommend this event for people with children. The kids can run around the park if they get too antsy while the adults admire the flowers and costumes and finish eating whatever it is their kids decided they didn't like.

WET AND WILD PADDLING EXPO
Minn. Hwy. 210
Thomson, Minn.   *(218) 726-6533*

You can watch flatwater and whitewater paddlers or participate yourself in kayaking and canoeing at this event in late May or early June. You can watch it free, but for only $5 you can try out various kinds of craft — sea kayaks, sprint kayaks, whitewater boats, canoes and others — that six different manufacturers will have at the site. You can also get a free beginners course. An outdoor equipment and clothing sale and auction is part of the expo. Register at the site. (See our Spectator Sports chapter for additional information).

From I-35, take the Highway 210 exit east into Carlton. Continue straight ahead at the four-way stop and begin looking for a parking place. Good viewing spots are from the Highway 210 bridge and from the well-marked path on the other side that winds downriver.

June

GRANDMA'S MARATHON
Canal Park
Duluth, Minn.   *(218) 727-0947*

Join the throngs at Canal Park to welcome the front runners of this world-class marathon, or find a good spot along London Road or Scenic Highway 61 east of town. Thousands of runners come from all over the world to compete in Grandma's, a favorite because of the level course and cool breezes from Lake Superior along the whole 26.2-mile course. The race begins in Two Harbors on the North Shore at 7:30 AM on a Saturday in June; front runners collapse near the tent and concession stands a couple of hours later. Call in mid-January for an entry form; the fee is $25. Novices can participate, but the field is full at 7,000 entrants. This is one of the biggest events in the region. (See Spectator Sports for viewing details.)

UNITED NORTHERN SPORTSMEN'S WALLEYE FISHING CONTEST
Island Lake, Rudy Perpich Rd.   *(218) 624-2106*
Duluth, Minn.   *(218) 721-4843*

Hundreds of people gather at Island Lake in mid-June to participate in a fishing contest that has been going on since 1980. A $5 entry fee qualifies you to win prizes, including $300 for first place. The prize here isn't for the biggest fish; instead, anglers register each fish they catch during the weekend; registrations go in a hat and the ones drawn are the prize winners.

From Central Entrance in Duluth, take Arlington Avenue north (Country Road 4); continue along the extension, Rudy Perpich Road (formerly Rice Lake Road), until you reach Island Lake.

THUNDER BAY CHILDREN'S FESTIVAL
Various locations city-wide
Thunder Bay, Ont.   *(807) 343-2300*

The Thunder Bay Children's Festival is held for three days every summer in mid-June. Free outdoor activities for toddlers to 8th graders are held at the Nor'wester Park on Beverly and High streets and the Port Arthur Stadium on 420 Lisgar Street. The festival highlights the visual and performing arts and hosts cultural presentations from heritage groups, including Old Fort William. The Main Stage at Thunder Bay Auditorium, 450 Beverly Street, features big-name performers from Canada and the United

States. General-admission concert tickets cost $10.

THUNDER BAY FISHING FESTIVAL
Thunder Bay Marina and Marina Park
Thunder Bay, Ont. (800) 667-8386

The Thunder Bay Fishing Festival is always held on Father's Day weekend. Started as a family event for the holiday, the festival bestows awards for the best catch in different categories for men, women and children. In past years, more than 70 crews of anglers have competed for about $25,000 in prizes in the salmon and lake trout categories. The entry fee is $5 plus a separate $100 per boat fee for the Pot 'O Gold Fishing Tournament, which includes additional prize money. Any child younger than 12 who enters the fishing derby receives a prize, regardless of the type or size of fish caught.

Colorful tents dot Marina Park on the downtown waterfront and draw thousands of people for the food and entertainment. A giant hot tub party, beach volleyball and a beer tent are part of the fun for adults as well as live music in the evening. The kids keep busy with an ongoing schedule of entertainment and activities, including fishing in their own rainbow trout-stocked pond, rides, races and relays and face painting.

Past events have drawn nearly 5,000 people, so be prepared to join lots of families for a good time.

PARK POINT
ART FAIR AND RUMMAGE SALE
Park Point neighborhood, Duluth, Minn.

Since 1971, during the last weekend in June, the spit of land that is reached by crossing the Aerial Bridge becomes the site of the biggest rummaging event in the region. Besides some wonderful flea market buys, arts and crafts — pottery,

woodworking, fabrics and paintings — are on exhibit and for sale. There is no admission fee to this neighborhood event.

July

FOURTH OF JULY
Along the waterfront
Duluth, Minn. and Superior, Wis.

Duluth has a huge fireworks display at the waterfront beginning at dark — if it's not foggy, that is. Rain and fog have been known to postpone it for a week. Superior's display is across the harbor at Connors Point, and you can see something of both displays by going to only one. Good viewing spots are close to the action (Duluth's Bayfront or Superior's Barkers Island and Connors Point), in which case you're likely to get tangled in big-time traffic on the way home; or up on Duluth's hills.

In the late 1980s, Duluth had an unexpectedly remarkable display — a fiery piece of spent fireworks shell fell back in the fireworks cache, setting off the whole batch at once. It was a wonderful if scary display, looking from a distance like a war zone, that sent screaming harborside viewers on the run. Except for minor burns, no one was hurt. Many Insiders have been awaiting another "rocket's red glare, bombs bursting in air" blast, but no luck so far.

FOURTH OF JULY POWWOW
Red Cliff Reservation
Wis. Hwy. 13, north of Bayfield
Red Cliff, Wis. (715) 779-3700

Few powwows in our region are held in a more spectacular setting than this — on a bluff over Lake Superior. And few powwows "feed" better than this, with heaps of Lake Superior fish, wild rice, venison, fry bread, fruit and other foods

Seasonal Activities

Here's a look at our region's seasonal activities, using Ojibwe names for the month.

MANIDOOGIIZIS, THE SPIRIT MOON
(JANUARY)

The coldest time of year, this is the time to hunker down with your families and tell stories, play games or read books. This is also the time most of our communities have winter festivals — to warm us up with color and laughter in the coldest, darkest period of the year. It's often too cold for outdoor activities for anyone but the very hardy.

NAMEBINI-GIIZIS, THE SUCKER MOON (FEBRUARY)

Our suckers actually don't run until April, but our cross-country skiers and snowmobilers are running all over the place. We usually get a slight thaw or two — honeybees get a respite from their indoor life and gardeners order their seeds. The inland lakes are dotted with ice anglers.

ONAABANI-GIIZIS,
THE CRUST-ON-THE-SNOW MOON
(MARCH)

There have been a few thaws and re-freezes, and it's easier to stay on top of the snow when you're moving through the woods. The weather is warmer but somehow feels colder, with higher humidity and hard winds. Ski hills prepare to shut down with a final spring fling. The hawks return to the North from their seasonal migration.

ISKIGAMIZIGE-GIIZIS,
THE SAP-BOILING MOON
(APRIL)

The month usually opens with a snow cover and closes with the first green shoots emerging from the ground. This is the month for tapping maple trees for syrup, for putting away cross-country skis and snowshoes and for planning the garden. Late in the month, the smelt run begins. If the ice has cleared, the salties (foreign ocean-going vessels) return to the Lake.

ZAAGIBAGAA-GIIZIS,
THE BUDDING FLOWER MOON
(MAY)

Tulips and daffodils begin blooming mid-month, and by the end of the month the air is filled with the fragrance of wild cherries in the woods and the first lilacs in our towns. Fiddlehead wood ferns and marsh marigolds are picked for fresh greens, anglers crowd onto our lakes and rivers for the fishing opener, bicyclists burst onto the scene, and in-line skaters hit the streets as soon as the motorized sweepers have removed the winter's litter of sand and gravel. Gardens are planted — often not until late in the month.

ODE'IMINI-GIIZIS,
THE STRAWBERRY MOON
(JUNE)

Yes, indeed. Strawberries are ready for picking in the wild and at fruit farms. This also is when birchbark craftspeople gather bark — when the sap is up and the days are warm, and it pops off the tree. Mushrooms, many of them edible, burst through the forest litter and from decaying logs.

MISKWIMINI-GIIZIS,
THE RASPBERRY MOON
(JULY)

Not only raspberries (wild and cultivated), but "Juneberries" (they're a month late here and also are called service berries and Saskatoon berries) are ripening for some good munching as you stroll along creeks and rivers.

MIINIKE-GIIZIS,
THE BLUEBERRY MOON
(AUGUST)

This is the time blueberries, chokecherries, pincherries and highbush cranberries are ripe. Gardens are producing, and lazy summer days give way to crisp evenings by late month. The hawks head south.

MANOMINIKE-GIIZIS,
THE WILD RICING MOON
(SEPTEMBER)

With push-pole, wooden "knockers," canoe and license, pairs of ricers disappear into the rice beds of our inland lakes to harvest wild rice. The

season usually begins in late August and extends through much of September. Grouse hunters joyfully begin their sojourns.

Photo: Sam Cook

BINAAKWE-GIIZIS,
THE MOON OF FALLING
LEAVES
(OCTOBER)

Aspen, maples and tamaracks drop their foliage, and people prepare for winter — whether with antifreeze in the car, a check of weather

Harvesting wild rice is a much anticipated seasonal event in the Lake Superior region.

stripping in the modern house or hay bales and storm windows around the old house. Bow-hunters head to the woods for deer.

GASHKADINO-GIIZIS, THE FREEZING-OVER MOON (NOVEMBER)

Freezing-over time is welcomed here by many people who, by November, begin yearning for the beauty and fun of snow. The first snowfall usually happens well before Thanksgiving, and holiday travelers might get snowed in at their hosts'. Ski hills open, children dig out their sleds, and bikes are put away. Loggers are at work after the ground freezes and before the heavy snow falls. Deer hunters pour into the woods.

MANIDOOGIIZISOONS, THE LITTLE SPIRIT MOON (DECEMBER)

Like everywhere, our communities move into Christmas frenzy. The lakes and rivers are frozen, and cross-country skiers and snowmobilers are busy. Many of our neighbors begin planning an escape to warmer climes. The salties leave the Great Lakes, and the Soo Locks close.

served up under a big tent. The feast is included with the price of the powwow button ($3). Dancers and drummers come from throughout the region for the three-day event (beginning July 3), and vendors sell beadwork, tapes of drum and flute music, books, clothing, leather, blankets, food and other goods. You can camp at the nearby Red Cliff Campground and spend some time at the tribe's Isle Vista Casino (see our Nightlife and Casinos chapter) just across the highway.

FOURTH OF JULY FESTIVAL
Throughout Bessemer, Mich. (800) 522-5657

People crowd into Bessemer for the Fourth — and the third — and the second, first, 30th and 29th. This is one big Fourth Festival, which usually begins on June 29 and culminates with an impressive fireworks show at Massie Field, three blocks north of U.S. Highway 2 at Bessemer. Among the all-day events are riding lawn-mower races, sports tournaments, carni-

val rides, food booths and a big attraction — the yearly domino fall. In 1995, it involved carefully setting up 4,500 dominoes along two city blocks, winding like a figure 8 around a replica of the Mackinac Bridge. Unfortunately, during the night a passing skunk . . . just kidding. They went over as planned, on time, just like dominoes.

FOURTH OF JULY
Ashland, Wis. (800) 284-9484

A parade of old and new fire engines down the main street of town — with kids riding along — precedes the fireworks display on the bay. Vendors have booths out to celebrate the day.

FOURTH OF JULY
Bayfield and Madeline Island, Wis. (800) 447-4094

The fireworks on both sides of the water are a treat to watch from either vantage point. Bayfield fills up for the Fourth, and families bring their blankets and ice cream cones to the waterside park and stretch out in the grass (in Bayfield) or on the pier (on Madeline Island). Often the display is augmented with a parade of brightly lit sailboats. Many people come here for fireworks after enjoying the Red Cliff powwow (see the listing in this section).

TOFTE FOURTH OF JULY PICNIC AND CELEBRATION
Tofte Park, Minn. Hwy. 61
Tofte, Minn.   (218) 663-7804

A family tradition organized by the Lutsen/Tofte Tourism Association, this event welcomes both new visitors and old-timers to this former fishing village, now a growing resort town. (Tofte is a village in Norway and the last name of many old-time residents.) Food, music, dance and fireworks (of course!) are all part of the festivities.

In the morning, a kids' race and the Tofte Trek, a 10-kilometer run, are featured (there's a $10 entry fee for the adult run). A cannon shoot from boats on the Lake in mid-morning gets people psyched for the fireworks later in the evening. A late-morning parade is open to public participation and always includes lots of kids on bicycles and a few floats. There's food for sale at the park and firehall. Games with prizes and a square dance, with live music and a caller, happen at dusk before the fireworks; it all makes for a full day. Admission is free.

CORNUCOPIA COMMUNITY FISH FRY
Wis. Hwy. 13
Throughout Cornucopia, Wis.

Fried whitefish, a white elephant sale and specials at Cornucopia's charming waterfront shops are part of this holiday. Since "Corny" is worth a visit even when the fish isn't frying, the first Sunday in July is a good time to go. The former fishing village is on the flats along Lake Superior, and old fishing boats are interspersed among the fish houses-turned-shops.

OLD FORT WILLIAM GREAT RENDEZVOUS
Old Fort William, Broadway Ave.
Thunder Bay, Ont.   (807) 577-8461

The Great Rendezvous is held mid-July. It is a re-enactment of a traditional 1830s business meeting held every summer by fur traders, voyageurs, Indians and other players. It draws folks for demonstrations of historic crafts and games, storytelling of voyageur legends and Ojibwe tales and various competitions by costumed fort inhabitants. Admission is $7.25; for folks 60 and older and kids ages 6 through 18, it's $4.50.

TWO HARBORS FOLK FESTIVAL
PAP Acres   (218) 834-2600
Two Harbors, Minn.   (800) 777-7384

This weekend folk festival in early July features blues, folk and old-time bluegrass music. The laid-back, well-organized event is put together by a volunteer group of North Shore folks (many of them musicians) who simply love good music. The festival brings in big-name folk performers, and artists such as Greg Brown, Claudia Schmidt, Prudence Johnson and Pop Wagner appear regularly. There's a well-developed children's area with special music and activities for different ages.

For the past several years, the folk festival has been held at PAP Acres, a campground area near Two Harbors. Friday evenings usually kick off with a bonfire, a family dance and a jam session.

To get to PAP Acres, follow Minn. Highway 61 to 15th Street in Two Harbors. Head north and follow the signs to the festival. Tickets are available at the gate and range from $3 for a single event to $25 for the entire weekend.

TRANS-SUPERIOR YACHT RACE
Points along Lake Superior's shoreline
Duluth, Minn. (218) 722-4011

Every two (off) years in mid-July, about 20 yachts set sail from Sault Ste. Marie, Michigan, at the far end of Lake Superior to race 338 nautical miles to Duluth. The trip takes two to four days, although in one recent year an imbibing sailor showed up several days behind the others. Just keep an eye on the horizon; when you spot sails, join the crowds gathered along Duluth's Lakewalk, the Ship Canal and Park Point Beach to watch the boats arrive. Call the Duluth Visitors and Convention Center and check out our Spectator Sports chapter for details.

SAN JUAN 24
NORTH AMERICAN CHAMPIONSHIP
Points along Lake Superior's shoreline
Duluth, Minn. (218) 722-4011

This sailing race series, for San Juan-brand sloops that are 24 feet long, comes to Duluth about every fourth summer, and 1996 is one of those years. (Other years' races are in Seattle, Washington; Portland, Oregon; and Sheboygan, Wisconsin.) About 25 of the fixed-keel sloops will compete during seven races over a three-day weekend in mid-July outside the Duluth-Superior Harbor. Friday's races begin at noon; Saturday's and Sunday's begin at 10 AM. Good viewing spots are the Lakewalk, at Park Point, and off the pier — especially during the hour prior to the race when the sloops with brightly colored sails move out under the Aerial Bridge into the open water. The winner will be the North American champion of this fleet. For more information, call the Duluth Visitors and Convention Bureau or see our Spectator Sports chapter.

BIG BIKE & TRIKE
INTERNATIONAL GATHERING
Hurley, Wis. (715) 561-4562

Every July since 1990, touring motorcycles and three-wheel motorcycles leave Texas, Manitoba and other North American points to head for Hurley. About 200 of these unusual bikes and their riders arrive the third Thursday in July and stay around for a week, finishing up with a Saturday evening parade that's accompanied by 60 classic cars and fire engines. Spectators can get involved by casting ballots for their favorite machines, after looking them over during an all-afternoon show during which Silver Street is cordoned off. The event was dreamed up by the owner of the Branding Iron Steak House in Hurley (a trike rider) and the owner of the Blue Cloud Motel in Ironwood (a Gold Wing touring bike rider).

CONNORS ROCK FEST
Connors Point
Superior, Wis. (218) 723-1136

This fledgling rock 'n' roll festival happens the second Saturday in July. Performers include John Kay and Steppenwolf. Tickets are $12.50. This outdoor event also includes local bands.

VIKING FEST
Leif Erikson Park
Duluth, Minn. (218) 722-4011

During the third week in July, three days are devoted to the area's Scandinavian heritage. Descendants of people who plied the Atlantic in Viking ships offer ethnic music, games, foods and crafts. A replica of a Viking ship is nearby in this lovely lakeside park. If you're a stranger to traditional Scandinavian ways, this is an especially good place to get acquainted with their bright-colored clothing and crafts, tasty sweets and homespun music. Admission is free.

Photo: Duluth News-Tribune

The nation's largest cross-country ski race, the Birkebeiner, is held between Cable and Hayward, Wisconsin.

IRON COUNTY HERITAGE FESTIVAL
Throughout Iron County

Beginning the last weekend in July, this county-wide festival is a substantial celebration. It includes Old Hurley Casino Night (with a roulette wheel and other gambling events), a parade and tours of the historic districts led by residents in period dress. A popular activity is a trek along the historic Flambeau Trail (used by Ojibwe trappers and French voyageurs) that reaches from Lake Superior to Springstead, Wisconsin, 250 miles away. Participants go by foot, by bicycle or by canoe along any part of the trail or cover the whole thing in about seven days. Four August events (listed subsequently) are part of this festival.

AMERICAN QUARTER HORSE ASSOCIATION HORSE SHOW
South St. Louis County Fairgrounds
End of Boundary Ave.
Proctor, Minn.   *(218) 628-2401*

By far the biggest horse show in the area, this four-day event in late July draws about 400 horse-and-rider pairs from all over the Midwest. They compete in western (team penning, barrel racing and pole weaving) and English events. Admission is free. Call the fairgrounds or St. Louis County Extension Service, (218) 726-7512, for details.

From I-35 south of Duluth, take the Proctor (U.S. Highway 2) exit; go to Boundary Avenue and turn right. Boundary ends at the fairgrounds.

BAY DAYS
Between Main St. and Lake Superior
Downtown Ashland, Wis.   (800) 284-9494

This late-July event is divided between a cordoned-off Main Street and Lake Superior. Over several days, it includes 30 different events (sailboat races, broomball and other competitions), food booths and music. Call the Ashland Chamber of Commerce for updates.

HEAD OF THE LAKES FAIR
Head of the Lakes Fairground
Tower Ave.
Superior, Wis.   (715) 394-7716

Farm livestock, produce and judging all happen at this fair, but the main focus is entertainment, with headliner grandstand shows and a carnival on the midway. Opening day is a Tuesday in late July, which is free. After opening day, admission is $5. Past performers are country-western singer Pam Tillis and the rock band Firehouse. Other shows include stock car races and a demolition derby, which winds up the fair on Sunday. The fairground is south of the city.

August

IRON COUNTY FAIR

Iron County Fairgrounds   *(715) 561-2695*
Saxon, Wis.   *(715) 561-4334*

Here's another old-fashioned rural fair, with lots of livestock, music and exhibits. The fairgrounds are right on the hill in town. The fair is usually in the beginning of August. Admission is $4.

LOON DAYS

Throughout Mercer, Wis.   *(715) 561-4334*

The first Wednesday in August draws about 5,000 people into Mercer. Partly, they come to look over the woodwork, quilts, ornaments and other crafts at more than 300 booths. Mostly, they come to listen to people imitating loons as they compete in loon-calling events.

INTERNATIONAL FOLK FESTIVAL

Leif Erikson Park
Duluth, Minn.   *(218) 722-4011*

This festival has been happening since the turn of the century and now unfolds on the first Saturday in August. It's a gathering of the area's ethnic groups — Greek, Finnish, Ojibwe, Chinese, Italian and more — in a celebration that includes traditional dancing, food, music and crafts. Both vendors and visitors are in high good humor as the aromas of ethnic foods intertwine and weave an international spell. Admission is free.

GRAND PORTAGE RENDEZVOUS

Northwoods Shooting Range
Mercer, Wis.   *(715) 561-4334*

People dressed like voyageurs and mountaineers gather on the first weekend in August to compete in hatchet- and knife-throwing, black powder shoots and traditional archery. Call the Iron County Tourism Council, (800) 225-3620, to confirm the event location, which is subject to change.

PAAVO NURMI MARATHON AND RELAY

Upson to Hurley, Wis.   *(715) 561-4334*

Named for the Finnish winner of nine Olympic gold medals in the 1920s, this demanding marathon (it's a hard course in August heat) draws about 300 participants. It starts at 7:30 AM the second Saturday in August, in Upson, Wisconsin, and ends in Hurley's downtown on Silver Street and Fourth Avenue. The entry fee is $25; stop by the Hurley Chamber of Commerce the day before the race between 9 AM and 9 PM to register. A favorite spot for spectators to cheer on the tiring runners is on Cemetery Hill, which is the toughest part of the course. Afterward, everyone gathers at Riccelli Park for music, food, refreshments and awards and drawings.

THE FISHERMAN'S PICNIC

Various locations city-wide
Grand Marais, Minn.   *(800) 622-4014*

Called the "granddaddy of North Shore celebrations," the Grand Marais' Lions Club instituted the Fisherman's Picnic 58 years ago. A tradition for locals and summer visitors is the famous fish burger stand, selling delectable "fresh fried herring on a bun" sandwiches. Street dances, raffles for big-time prizes (somebody won a truck in 1995!), fireworks, fishing and golf tournaments, slow-pitch softball and diverse musical entertainment, including bluegrass and jazz, fill four days during the first weekend in August with fun and entertainment.

Make your motel or campground reservations well in advance. Many folks book accommodations a year out for this city-wide party.

Call the Grand Marais Chamber of Commerce at the listed number for further details about The Fisherman's Picnic.

RENDEZVOUS DAYS POWWOW

Grand Portage Reservation Powwow Grounds/
Grand Portage National Monument
Minn. Hwy. 61
Grand Portage, Minn.
Tribal Headquarters   (218) 475-2277
National Monument   (218) 475-2202

Held the second weekend in August, the Rendezvous Days Powwow is the event of the summer for folks at the tip of the Arrowhead on the North Shore.

Hosted by the Grand Portage Band of the Chippewa Tribe and the Grand Portage National Monument, the traditional (meaning non-competitive) dancing with drum groups takes place on the outdoor powwow grounds. Bleachers are provided, so spectators can sit and watch the action.

The event draws Indian people from around Minnesota and Ontario. Dancing begins at 1 PM each day and goes until about 9 PM or later. You'll find plenty of stands serving a taste of American Indian food, such as fry bread and "Indian tacos" — made with fry bread instead of corn shells.

The powwow is open to the public, and admission is free. You can also join in the dancing if the spirit moves you, because this is a celebration.

VOYAGEUR RENDEZVOUS FESTIVAL

Grand Portage National Monument
Minn. Hwy. 61
Grand Portage, Minn.   (218) 475-2202

This festival, held jointly with the Rendezvous Days Powwow, is in a reconstructed 17th-century fur-trading post on the shores of Lake Superior. The fort was the midpoint along the trading route between Montreal and the Northwest Territories. This event includes plenty of singing, dancing, trading, food and other fun-filled activities on the grounds of the fort and in the Great Hall where costumed voyageurs, trappers, traders and Indian guides come together.

The various styles of powwow dance outfits are directly related to the style of dance. Aside from men and women traditional dancers, whose outfits and dance steps are self-evident, there are grass dancers (usually young men) whose outfits flow with colorful yarn and who dance in a flowing fashion while appearing to pound down the grass with their feet; male fancy dancers (they wear two bustles, bright — sometimes neon — colors, and fur leggings), whose dancing is spectacularly acrobatic; female fancy dancers (usually very young) who wear bright outfits and hold shawls like wings as they twirl neatly; and shawl dancers, usually older women who dance sedately.

Insiders' Tips

Although August is the height of summer on the North Shore, bring rain gear and a jacket to stave off the cool Lake Superior winds. The Rendezvous Festival is free, but there is a modest admission fee to Grand Portage National Monument of $2 per adult or $5 per family. Seniors and children 16 and younger get in free. Regular hours are 8 AM to 5 PM daily.

GOGEBIC COUNTY FAIR
648 W. Cloverland Dr.
Ironwood, Mich. (906) 932-2700

Here's a real old-fashioned county fair, complete with harness horse racing. Horses and sulkies circle the track during both days of this fair, which is held the second weekend in August. Livestock shows, produce displays, auctions, a demolition derby, food booths and a midway are all part of the event.

WILD RICE FEST AND POWWOW
Bad River Reservation
New Odanah, Wis. (715) 682-7111

The late August powwow in Old Odanah hasn't regained its strength since moving a few years ago to New Odanah, probably because the new grounds still have a raw, invaded look from having been carved out of the forest. Nevertheless, the powwow draws some fine dancers and drummers, and vendors sell wild rice soup, fry bread, beadwork and other goods.

From U.S. Highway 2, turn north into New Odanah and follow the signs. You can't get on the grounds without a powwow button, which is sold at the entry gate. Admission is $5.

OJIBWE KEESHIGUN
Old Fort William, Broadway Ave.
Thunder Bay, Ont. (807) 577-8461

The Ojibwe Keeshigun is a Native American celebration held in mid- to late August, with hands-on crafts, demonstrations and traditional entertainment at Old Fort William.

The celebration is designed to pay tribute to the roles native peoples played in the development and expansion of Canada. You can view traditional moose, bear and beaver hide preparation and tanning. Cree, Oji-Cree and Ojibwe Indians perform traditional dancing and drumming. You may sample foods prepared in a historic way, including rabbit stew, bakwezhigan (bread), a maple drink, smoked fish, wild rice and Indian cake made of corn. Native crafts made in both traditional and contemporary techniques are displayed with demonstrations of moccasin-making, beadwork and makuks (birchbark baskets). Historic displays of beadwork and other items from the Thunder Bay Museum are on site as well as contemporary Indian art from the Thunder Bay Art Gallery. Admission is $7.25; for folks 60 and older and children ages 6 to 18, admission is $4.50.

CARLTON COUNTY FAIR
Barnum, Minn. (218) 389-6737

This charming fair, held the third weekend in August, features white clapboard buildings (holding Guernseys, Percherons, goats, produce and other farm life), a midway, people shearing sheep and spinning yarn, animal judging and other lively displays. A high point of the fair is the horse races where everything goes: kids wearing football helmets riding Arabians bareback, professional jockeys riding thoroughbreds or racing quarter horses who otherwise compete at parimutuel tracks or farmers on their family pets. Expect the unexpected. One recent year, a newly broken mustang decided to beat the field by jumping the fence and cutting across the oval's center. Betting isn't legal here. Admission is $1. For details, call the fairgrounds or Carlton County Extension Service, (218) 384-3511.

From I-35, take the Barnum exit west into town. Turn left at the stop sign; the fairgrounds are two blocks south on the left.

BAYFRONT BLUES FESTIVAL

Bayfront Park
Duluth, Minn.   *(218) 722-4011*

B.B. King, Koko Taylor and Percy Sledge all have performed at this festival, which is one of the biggest events in the entire region. (Sledge fell victim to an environmental-beat reporter during his 1995 visit, when he repeatedly was identified on television as "Percy Sludge.") Usually for three days the second weekend in August, the gathering attracts 40,000 spectators to enjoy 20 blues groups that perform nonstop on two stages. Rain or shine, both crowd and performers are anything but blue — this is an upbeat happening too joyful to be subdued by winds off the Lake. But bring warm clothing just in case. John Mayall, the father of British blues, was scheduled to perform in 1996. Admission is $15.

NORTHLAND
INVITATIONAL GOLF TOURNAMENT

Northland Country Club
3901 E. Superior St.
Duluth, Minn.   *(218) 525-1970*

More than 200 of Minnesota's finest amateur golfers descend on this private golf course the second weekend in August to participate in this well-attended event. Matches begin about 7:30 AM and continue all day on Friday, Saturday and Sunday. The public is welcome to watch the tournament; there is no charge.

SOUTH ST. LOUIS COUNTY FAIR

End of Boundary Ave.   *(218) 628-2401*
Proctor, Minn.   *(218) 723-4938*

A small, intimate fairground, with an old-fashioned farm fair flavor, the fair at Proctor has always emphasized horses and 4-H events at this mid-August happening. Other attractions are food booths, a midway, crafts booths and stock car races. St. Louis County is the largest county in the state — so large that many public offices, including the sheriff's office and the county fair, are divided into northern and southern branches. Admission is free.

From I-35 south of Duluth, take the Proctor (U.S. Highway 2) exit; go to Boundary Avenue and turn right. Boundary Avenue ends at the fairground.

MASH-KA-WISEN SOBRIETY POWWOW

Fond du Lac Reservation, Mission Rd.
Sawyer, Minn.   *(218) 879-6731*

The "Mash" powwow is the second weekend in August. On the shores of Big Lake, it's rimmed by a maple forest and next to the Mash-Ka-Wisen Treatment Center, which sponsors the event. Powwow buttons sometimes are sold for $3, entitling you to a feast on Saturday that includes wild rice, fry bread, venison and chicken. The powwow circle has branch-shaded bleachers, but they're often full; in any event, if you want a backrest, bring your lawn chair.

LAKE, RATTLE & ROLL MUSIC FEST

Connors Point
Superior, Wis.   *(218) 723-1136*

This festival brings in some big-name groups to shake up spectators with music from the 1950s and '60s. It's a two-day gathering the third week in August, and the Connors Point site on Lake Superior makes for a wide-open atmosphere. Performers include Gary Puckett, the Grass Roots,

Guess Who, Peter Noone, The Associates and Bobby Vee. Tickets are $20.

WOODEN BOAT
& MARITIME HERITAGE FESTIVAL
Chequamegon Boat Works
Second St. and Wilson Ave.
Bayfield, Wis. (715) 779-5995

People bring their beloved boats — whether little wooden rowboat, motorized skiff or big sailing schooner — to Bayfield on the third weekend in August for a get-together that makes for some good watercraft viewing. You can watch this boat show on Saturday from many points in Bayfield. If you'd like to be part of the event, bring your craft to Chequamegon Boat Works and enjoy a barbecue on Friday, glide around in the water on Saturday and join other boaters on Sunday for a trip to Long Island and a picnic. Anyone with a boat can join the picnic for free, but to participate in the show, the fee is $20 and includes docking and a T-shirt — unless you're a professional boatworker showing your wares, in which case it's $40.

ST. LOUIS RIVER WHITEWATER
RODEO AND KAYAK SLALOM
Minn. Hwy. 210
Thomson, Minn. (218) 726-6533

Watch top paddlers from the Midwest maneuver the rocks and white water of the St. Louis River just below Thomson Dam. Preliminaries begin at 8 AM on the fourth Saturday in August. Finals continue through Sunday. In the rodeo, paddlers try to keep their crafts in one churning spot.

From I-35, take the Minn. Highway 210 exit east into Carlton. Continue straight ahead at the four-way stop and begin looking for a parking place. Good viewing spots are from the Highway 210 bridge and from the well-marked path on the other side that winds downriver. (See our Spectator Sports chapter for additional information.)

September

PORT WING ANNUAL
FISH BOIL AND FALL FESTIVAL
Wis. Hwy. 13
Port Wing, Wis. (715) 774-3511

If you drive through Port Wing the Saturday of Labor Day weekend, you'll pass by a crowd of people standing around a steaming cauldron. Join them. It's fish boil they're after — a delightful bowlful of trout, potatoes and onions, cooked together in time-honored fashion. A meal with cole-slaw and bread is $8. If you stay until Sunday, you'll get brats (sausages, not unruly kids) and burgers and enjoy the arts and crafts exhibits.

GREAT NORTHERN CLASSIC RODEO
Head of the Lakes Fairground, Tower Ave.
Superior, Wis. (218) 726-1603

This International Professional Rodeo Association event takes place on Labor Day weekend and draws close to 10,000 spectators. The full rodeo menu is served: bull riding, team roping, steer wrestling, bronco riding, barrel racing and more. Reserved seats are $8 for adults and $6 for kids and seniors. General admission is $7 for adults

Insiders' Tips

Fresh raspberries in December? Put up your own home-made raspberry liquor and enjoy the perfume of summer all winter long.

Photo:Duluth News-Tribune

*Canines star in the John Beargrease Sled Dog Marathon along Minnesota's
North Shore in January.*

and $5 for kids and seniors. The fairground is south of downtown Superior.

SPIRIT OF THE LAKE FALL FEST
East End neighborhood
Superior, Wis. (715) 394-7716

A parade of fire engines and tours of the Old Fire House and Police Museum are the highlights of this neighborhood party. Expect the East End to be crowded with people, food booths, yard sales and vendors of arts and crafts. The bonus: a sailing regatta at Barkers Island. It happens on the second weekend in September.

October

BAYFIELD APPLE FESTIVAL
Downtown Bayfield, Wis. (800) 447-4094

Probably the biggest event on the South Shore, beloved by people within a 100-mile radius, this festival draws about 50,000 people a year. It's always the first weekend in October. The main ingredient is apples: cider, pies, peeling contests (can you believe 172 inches of peeling from one apple?), fritters, jams, sauces, jellies — and bags and bags of whole Wealthies, Duchesses, Macouns, Cortland Reds, Wolf Rivers, Firesides, Humes, Dudleys and Jonathans. Even if you're not an apple enthusiast, you'll enjoy this festival for its live bands, ethnic foods, street sales booths and great scenery, including a parade of decorated boats gliding through the silvery water of Lake Superior. The festival is on Bayfield's main street, which fronts the big lake. Bring a jacket; early October here can be as sweetly crisp as any apple.

BESSEMER PUMPKIN FEST
Throughout Bessemer, Mich. (800) 522-5657

When you're filled up with apples from Bayfield (see previous entry), head to Bessemer the second Saturday of the month for pumpkins. This small community expands by 6,000 to celebrate pumpkins, harvest and Halloween. The

• 315

main street is busy with seed-spitting and pie-eating contests; continuous live music; a children's parade with kids in Halloween costumes; hayrides; a pumpkin totem pole (erected by the Boy Scouts); a bake-off of breads, pies and cookies; a scavenger hunt; and an antique car show. The day winds up with a harvest dinner and dance. You won't have any trouble finding Bessemer; it's the town underneath the big orange balloons.

SHIP OF GHOULS

Aboard the SS William A. Irvin
Adjacent to Duluth Entertainment Convention Center
Duluth, Minn. (218) 722-4011

For the 10 days before Halloween, the retired laker *Irvin* (see our Attractions chapter for details) becomes a carrier of fear. Theater students from the University of Minnesota-Duluth do their best to make your journey through the ship memorable, beginning with a descent into chaos and winding through the ship's transformed and ghastly rooms. This spook house is aimed primarily at adults and is too spooky for many children, even those accompanied by parents; sturdy adolescents have been known to burst into terrified tears.

The *Irvin* is docked next to the Duluth Entertainment Convention Center. Admission is $5 for adults and $3 for children, with 50¢ off for a Food Shelf donation.

SPOOK SHIP

Aboard the SS Meteor
Barkers Island
Superior, Wis. (715) 394-7716

Like the *Irvin*, the retired ship *Meteor* (also see our Attractions chapter) becomes a house of horrors at Halloween time, thanks to some creative Superior high school drama students. Although it's appropriately scary, it's not as terrifying as the *Irvin*, making it a better choice for

children. Nevertheless, there are some children for whom this grizzly place is a bit too real.

The *Meteor* is docked at Barkers Island. Spook Ship days are the week before Halloween. Admission is $5; $1 off with a Food Shelf donation.

November

NATIONAL SNOCROSS

Spirit Mountain Ski Hill
9500 Spirit Mountain Pl.
Duluth, Minn. (218) 628-2891

The biggest snowmobile race in the country takes place here in late November. Spirit Mountain begins to buzz, then roar, as 500 snowmobiles maneuver jumps, moguls and tight turns along a 3-furlong course. Drivers from around the world compete for a $25,000 purse. Admission is $10. Call the ski hill for more information.

Parking is available at the South St. Louis County Fairground in Proctor (take the Proctor exit from I-35, continue to Boundary Avenue and proceed to the fairground); shuttle buses carry spectators to Spirit Mountain.

CHRISTMAS CITY OF THE NORTH PARADE

Along Superior St.
Duluth, Minn. (218) 727-8484

Thanksgiving gets bumped for commercialism with this parade on the Saturday evening before that holiday. Its widely advertised purpose is to kick off the Christmas shopping season; aside from that arguably dubious mission, it's one heck of a parade, with lots of floats, clowns and marching bands. The bundled-up spectators crowded along blocks of Superior Street watch in awe as scantly clothed baton twirlers manage to keep their limbs limber, and trumpet players manage to keep their lips separate from their frosty instruments. The event is sponsored by KBJR-TV.

JACK FROST FESTIVAL
Downtown Ironwood, Mich. (906) 932-1122

Events begin the weekend after Thanksgiving, with a downtown open house of merchants and taste tests of gourmet products; it ends with the Jack Frost Parade the first Friday in December. In between are live holiday music, a pasty bake-off and other holiday attractions.

December

BESSEMER USSA
SNOWMOBILE OLYMPUS
N. Moore St.
Bessemer, Mich. (906) 663-4542

This United States Snowmobile Association-sanctioned race draws 180 drivers and, in the 1994-95 season, was voted the USSA Race of the Year. Professional drivers compete for points and money during the first weekend in December. The oval is doused with 1 million gallons of water so these unusual snowmobiles (hot rods and stock machines) can have the icy track they need. You can reserve a trackside spot for your car, so you can watch the race near a heater and listen to it on your car radio. Otherwise, a ticket is $5, and a two-day pass is $9. From Bessemer, go 2 miles north on N. Moore Street. For more information, call the listed number or Bob Parker at (906) 932-4080.

RED LIGHT SNOWMOBILE RALLY
Hurley, Wis. (715) 561-4334

Wouldn't you know it? Hurley's second-biggest annual affair involves people who don't want to be tied down to a schedule of events. You just can't make those snowmobilers do anything but ride snowmobiles. The rally, then, is a big reunion of drivers from the three Lake Superior states, Iowa, Illinois and elsewhere. Thousands of snowmobilers pull into the Hurley area during the second weekend in December, kicking off the snowmobile season; about 200 participate in timed events and a poker run (you drive from one remote tavern to another, playing a continuous poker game).

WINTERWALK
Downtown Ironwood, Mich. (906) 932-1122

You're welcome to join this mid-December outdoor Christmas party. Ice-block luminaries (gallon-size ice blocks with votive candles in the middle) light the downtown sidewalks, and carolers stroll and sing. Santa visits the Senior Center where hot apple cider and cookies are served; all the while, people come and go as they please.

American humorist/ writer Mark Twain once said, "The coldest winter I ever spent was a summer in San Francisco." Visitors to the Twin Ports often say the same about Duluth.

Inside
Arts and Culture

Twin Ports Area

For a town its size — 85,000 people — Duluth hosts a vibrant and growing arts community. It offers a mix of fledgling arts organizations, such as the Dark Horse Theater and the Northern Women's Art Collective; a handful of small presses; a substantial number of literary workshops and readings; an expanding collection of coffeehouses and pubs presenting folk and blues music; and well-established, traditional performing- and visual-arts organizations, such as the Duluth-Superior Symphony Orchestra, the Arrowhead Chorale, the Duluth Art Institute and the Minnesota Ballet. And one of the oldest community theaters in the country, the Duluth Playhouse, is here.

In Superior, population 26,000, the center of the performing and visual arts action is found in the Holden Fine Arts Center, the Sky Lounge at Rothwell Student Center, Thorpe Langley Auditorium and the Web Recital Hall — all on the campus of the University of Wisconsin-Superior. Students and faculty art shows, recitals and theater productions take place in these facilities. Thirty miles south of Superior, in Solon Springs, the Lucius Woods Performing Arts Center is a summer concert venue set in a pine-filled park on Lake St. Croix. Lucius Woods is the summer home for the Duluth-Superior Symphony Orchestra as well as a concert series.

Not only do presenter organizations bring in talent for musical performances as well as literary and visual arts workshops, the area is replete with venues that host productions of original work by resident artists through its galleries, performance halls and theaters. What we do miss in the Twin Ports arts scene is an avant-garde and classic film presenter and a movie house that shows non-mainstream American films. You'll have to go to the Twin Cities (Minneapolis and St. Paul) for that; try the University Film Society, the Walker Art Center, the Uptown Theater and Suburban World Theater. To be fair, the College of St. Scholastica in Duluth as well as the universities of Wisconsin-Superior and Minnesota-Duluth occasionally present art films, but there's nothing steady to count on.

You certainly will find plenty of things happening in the Twin Ports' arts universe to keep you busy. But if you're seeking a weekend trip, the Twin Cities are an easy three-hour drive away on well-groomed interstate highway. Minneapolis and St. Paul are home to nationally recognized arts organizations, such as the Guthrie Theater, the Walker Art Center, the Minneapolis Institute of Arts, Theatre de la Jeune Leune, the Minnesota Orchestra and the St. Paul Chamber Orchestra. (Check out *The Insiders' Guide® to the Twin Cities* for details.)

The Performing Arts

Dance

MINNESOTA BALLET
506 W. Michigan St.
Duluth, Minn.   (218) 733-7570

Founded in 1965, the Minnesota Ballet is a school and performance organization housed in the St. Louis County Heritage and Arts Center. The School of the Minnesota Ballet offers classes to students age 3 to adult, with an annual enrollment of more than 200 students. Most of the children participate in the annual holiday presentation of the *Nutcracker Suite*, produced with the Duluth-Superior Symphony Orchestra. The school also holds spring and fall student performances. Artistic Director Allen Fields leads this professional company of eight dancers, which integrates classical tradition with modern and jazz dance. The company performs at the Duluth Entertainment Convention Center and tours regionally, nationally and internationally (most recently in Central America).

TAMARACK DANCE ASSOCIATION
2613 W. Fifth St.   (218) 723-1088
Duluth, Minn.   (218) 728-1438

The Tamarack Dance Association is a member-supported group that organizes contra and folk dances in the Twin Ports and occasionally brings in guest teachers for workshops in clogging, Scandinavian dances and other specialties. The association also features an Irish ceili dance in the fall and spring and presents Wild Thyme family dances. All performances are open to the public and feature instruction, live music and callers.

BLUE WATER DANCE GROUP
16½ First Ave. W.
Duluth, Minn.   (218) 722-6983

The Blue Water Dance Group both

teaches and performs modern dance. Performances are held throughout the year. Class offerings include composition, scoring and spatial and movement approaches.

Music

DULUTH-SUPERIOR SYMPHONY ORCHESTRA
506 W. Michigan St.
Duluth, Minn.   (218) 733-7575

The Duluth-Superior Symphony Orchestra (D-SSO), founded in 1932 as the Duluth Civic Orchestra, is the second-largest orchestra in Minnesota. It serves the communities of Duluth, Superior and the rural regions of Minnesota, Wisconsin and upper peninsula Michigan through tours, outreach programs and a series of outdoor summer festival concerts at the Lucius Woods Performing Arts Center in Solon Springs, Wisconsin. The orchestra, conducted by maestro Yong-Yan Hu, also performs a subscription series of concerts in the Duluth Entertainment Convention Center auditorium.

The D-SSO features a youth orchestra as well as an honors string ensemble for students around the region. An annual Young People's Concert is presented each February by the D-SSO adult orchestra, and the Chamber Ensembles in the Schools outreach program showcases the youth orchestra members to elementary school students.

LAKE SUPERIOR CHAMBER ORCHESTRA
P.O. Box 434
Duluth, Minn. 55801   (218) 724-5231

This professionally staffed ensemble makes its performance home in the Mitchell Auditorium at the College of St. Scholastica. Founded in 1987, the chamber orchestra, under the purview of artistic director and conductor Warren Friesen, features a summer series with

guest artists. In addition to its classical repertoire, the chamber orchestra continues to premiere work by regionally and nationally recognized composers.

UNIVERSITY OF MINNESOTA-DULUTH MUSIC DEPARTMENT

University of Minnesota-Duluth
10 University Dr.
Duluth, Minn. *(218) 726-8208*

The University of Minnesota-Duluth's music department features programs by students, teachers and guest artists, including the *Faculty Artist Series*, in Bohannon Hall 90 and the *Concerts in Tweed* at the university's Tweed Museum and concerts at the Marshall Performing Arts Center. Tickets are usually $5 or less — a real value, considering the caliber of performers.

UNIVERSITY OF WISCONSIN-SUPERIOR MUSIC DEPARTMENT

1800 Grand Ave.
Superior, Wis. *(715) 394-8115*

The nationally recognized music department at UWS presents a University Recital Series — eight performances during the academic year, featuring faculty and guest artists. Season passes are available — call for details. A variety of student performances happen during the year — orchestra, string ensembles, jazz band, choir and soloists.

COLLEGE OF ST. SCHOLASTICA DEPARTMENT OF MUSIC

College of St. Scholastica, Mitchell Auditorium
1200 Kenwood Ave.
Duluth, Minn. *(218) 723-6082*

The College of St. Scholastica's music department is known for its focus on music from Europe's medieval, Baroque and Renaissance periods, featuring voice and period instruments. Imbued with a notable faculty, the department presents an ambitious and sophisticated *Early Music Series* every year, starting in late fall and running through spring, in the college's Mitchell Auditorium. Faculty, students and guest artists are showcased. Ticket prices vary; call the Mitchell Auditorium box office, (218) 723-6700, for details.

ARROWHEAD CHORALE

506 W. Michigan St.
Duluth, Minn. *(218) 727-8025*

The Arrowhead Chorale, a 24-member select group, schedules fall, holiday and spring series. Concerts are held in different venues around the Twin Ports and along the North and South shores. The chorale's repertoire spans five centuries of western music traditions. Past programs have included Arvo Parts's *Berliner Messe*, Handel's *Messiah*, a production of *The Pirates of Penzance* and a series celebrating women composers.

This professional chorale is directed by Dr. Stanley Wold, professor of music at the University of Minnesota-Duluth. The Arrowhead Chorale's administrative home is at the Depot.

JOHN S. DUSS MEMORIAL MUSIC CONSERVATORY

2211 Greysolon Rd.
Duluth, Minn.   (218) 724-2052

The John S. Duss Memorial Music Conservatory exists to bring the pleasure of music to people. A rich musical community resource, the conservatory offers music training and theory, ensemble and chorale experience and individual lessons for pre-schoolers to senior citizens. Private lessons are available for every band and orchestral instrument, folk instruments and voice. Ensemble experience is offered as well, with youth choral groups, band ensembles and string ensembles.

Duss Music Conservatory has three non-auditioned adult choirs: the Twin Ports Women's Chorale, the Twin Port Troubadours and the John S. Duss Chorale Society, which presents two major performances a year. One is the renowned *Festival of Lessons and Carols* at St. Paul's Episcopal Church in December, which features the music and language of a different ethnic group each year. Past years have featured the Lessons and Carols sung in Polish, Finnish, Swedish and Russian. A spring sacred music concert is held at the Cathedral of Our Holy Rosary Church.

MATINEE MUSICALE

506 W. Michigan St.
Duluth, Minn.   (218) 727-8025

Matinee Musicale, with its charmingly curious name, has been bringing classical music to Duluth for nearly a century. Run entirely by volunteers, this organization presents a concert series of up-and-coming musicians and ensembles. Past performers include the Chicago Brass Quintet, baritone Kevin McMillan and pianist Jon Klibonoff. The organization also provides music scholarships to local university students as well as rating and recital experience through the Minnesota Federation of Music Clubs.

DULUTH COMMUNITY GOSPEL CHOIR

Various venues around Duluth, Minn.
Contact: Kathy Bergquist   (218) 525-6366

Founded in 1992, the 25-member Duluth Community Gospel Choir — an interfaith, multicultural group — recently performed at the 1995 National Association for the Advancement of Colored People (NAACP) Convention in Minneapolis. Rehearsals are held twice monthly and are open to anybody.

Theater

DULUTH PLAYHOUSE

506 W. Michigan St.
Duluth, Minn.   (218) 733-7550

One of the oldest community theaters in the country, the Duluth Playhouse (1914) was originally housed in the Lyceum Building, a much celebrated and missed downtown landmark. The theater is now in the Depot where you can view pieces of the old Lyceum building in the brownstone tragedy and comedy masks outside the new theater space. The playhouse hosts nine performances a year, sponsors new works by local playwrights and presents stage productions, such as

South Pacific and the community theater canon of Neil Simon and Noel Coward. The playhouse also features children's shows and workshops, providing a place for kids to learn and perform.

DARK HORSE THEATER

16½ First Ave. W.
Duluth, Minn. *(218) 722-6983*

This theater group was started by University of Minnesota Theater Department alumni who produce socially relevant and provocative theater, including Lee Blessing's *Patient A*, David Mamet's *Oleanna* and A.R. Gurney's *Love Letters*. Dark Horse is also home to the Acting Up drama school, which offers master classes in a variety of acting techniques.

RENEGADE THEATER

Various performance venues
Duluth, Minn. *(218) 624-7722*

A relatively new theater group, Renegade Theater concentrates on producing new comedic works by regional playwrights and presenting contemporary plays. Characterized as "comedy with bite," Renegade offers an annual Christmastime comedy holiday revue, a summer comedy revue and a Halloween spook show.

Lacking a permanent home, performances are held around Duluth at venues such as the funky Dreamland Ballroom, the Northshor Theater and the Star of the North Theater at Fitger's Brewery Complex. Past shows include *Laughing Wild* and *Beyond Therapy* by playwright Christopher Durang, Sam Shepard's *True West* and Arthur Kopit's *Road to Nirvana*.

Renegade Theater was chosen to host the Midwest premiere of *The Complete Works of William Shakespeare, Abridged,* a play featuring the canon of William Shakespeare in two hours(!).

COLDER BY THE LAKE

Various performance venues around town
Duluth, Minn. *(218) 626-3623*

This venerable comedic troupe is known for its satirical look at local politics in its sketches. Productions frequently include local luminaries from the political and artistic worlds as well as guest musical groups. Shows are broadcast live on KUMD-FM 103, the University of Minnesota community radio station. Colder by the Lake lacks a permanent performance space; the troupe most recently has appeared at UMD's Marshall Performing Arts Center.

CHANGE OF PACE PRODUCTIONS

Fitger's Brewery Complex
600 E. Superior St.
Duluth, Minn. *(218) 722-2787*

For light fare, Change of Pace Productions, in conjunction with Augustino's Restaurant, coordinates dinner theater productions at Star of the North Theater in the Fitger's Brewery Complex. This group features such classics as *I Do! I Do!* and *It Had to Be You*.

COLLEGE OF ST. SCHOLASTICA THEATER DEPARTMENT

Mitchell Auditorium, 1200 Kenwood Ave.
Duluth, Minn. *(218) 723-6133*
Box Office *(218) 723-6700*

St. Scholastica's drama department

For information about Thunder Bay's art and cultural activities, call the Arts Event Hotline, (807) 623-6544, sponsored by the Thunder Bay Regional Arts Council.

Insiders' Tips

presents three plays a year — professionally produced and performed by students. Past productions include Moliere's *The Miser*, *The Diary of Anne Frank* and several Greek tragedies.

UMD THEATRE
Marshall Performing Arts Center
University of Minnesota-Duluth
10 University Dr.
Duluth, Minn. (218) 726-8564

The UMD Theatre, run by the university's theater department, presents a variety of classic and contemporary works during the academic year, including Lanford Wilson's *Burn This*, Noel Coward's *Present Laughter*, Shakespeare's *The Tempest* and Alan Ayckbourn's *Mr. A's Amazing Maze Plays*. Ticket prices range from $6 to $10.

THE SHACK
SUPPER CLUB DINNER THEATER
3301 Belknap St.
Superior, Wis. (715) 392-9836

This Superior supper club features musical comedies by the Wine and Dine Players, such as *Tintypes* and *Same Time, Next Year*. Performances are held in February and October. Admission for the show and dinner is $25; the Sunday matinee is $20.

UNIVERSITY OF WISCONSIN-SUPERIOR
DEPARTMENT OF COMMUNICATING ARTS
1800 Grand Ave., Superior, Wis.
Box Office (715) 394-8380

During the academic year, the UWS theater department presents two national touring productions — for example, the San Francisco Mime Troupe and the Lovely Liebowitz Sisters — and three UWS-produced works, held in Manion Theater in the university's Holden Fine Arts Center. Auditions are open to community members. Ticket prices vary, so call the box office for details.

Literary Arts

LAKE SUPERIOR WRITERS' SERIES
506 W. Michigan St.
Duluth, Minn. (218) 727-8025

The Lake Superior Writers' Series is a sophisticated yet comfortable writers resource that provides contact with established authors. Workshops, held at the Depot, are well-organized and never crowded; cost varies, depending on the length of the workshop and the author leading it. Readings are held in an intimate setting where the audience and speaker can easily mingle and talk. The organization also sponsors a writers group (open to the public) and an advanced writers group (restricted by application review).

The *Writers' Series* began in 1978 to generate support and community for contemporary writers. Each season the *Writers' Series* brings nationally acclaimed authors to Duluth to share their work with area writers through public readings, performances, critiques and classes. Critical discussion and technical guidance are provided for both beginning and professional writers. Past guest authors include Edward Albee, Carol Bly, Anthony Bukoski, Patricia Hampl, Bill Holm, W. P. Kinsella, Mary Oliver, Linda Hogan, Roberta Hill Whiteman and Jim Northrup.

The Lake Superior Writers' Series also collaborates with the Duluth Public Library in presenting programs for readers as well as writers, including book discussion groups and "Writers Live at the Library" readings.

POETRY HARBOR
DeWitt-Seitz Bldg.
S. Lake Ave.
Duluth, Minn. (218) 728-3728

Poetry Harbor, a regional writer's organization, features Sunday night open

readings in the Dewitt-Seitz Building in Canal Park. This group sponsors various writing projects and publishes *North Coast*, a lively and fresh literary chapbook featuring regional writers.

THE LAKE SUPERIOR BOOK ARTS ASSOCIATION

P.O. Box 3645
Mount Royal Station
Duluth, Minn. 55803   *No phone listing*

A group of 20 to 25 people meet on an irregular basis to learn about letter press printing, hand-crafted bookbinding and papermaking through workshops and discussions. There is no fee for participants.

SPLIT ROCK ARTS PROGRAM

University of Minnesota
306 Westbrook Hall, 77 Pleasant St. S.E.
Minneapolis, Minn.   (612) 624-6800

The Split Rock Arts Program is a summer series of intensive, weeklong workshops in the literary and visual arts. The artists-in-residence are renowned practicing artists, craftspeople and writers from across the country and around the world. Workshops are held at the University of Minnesota-Duluth campus and the University of Minnesota's Cloquet Forestry Center. Past literary workshops include *Writing the Short Story* by Paulette Bates Alden; *American Families: A Reading and Writing Workshop* by Marisha Chamberlain; *The Remembered Earth: A Writing Workshop* by Roberta Hill Whiteman; *Mysterious Fiction: Elements of Suspense Writing* by Kate Green, *Journals and Diaries* by Phebe Hanson and *Writing a New Poetry* by Carolyn Forché. For non-credit students, weeklong workshops cost between $375 and $400.

Publishers

SAVAGE PRESS

P.O. Box 115
Superior, Wis. 54880   (715) 394-9513

Established in 1989 to support regional writers, Savage Press focuses on poetry, fiction, biography and regional history. It recently published its 18th book.

SPINSTERS INK

32 E. First St.
Duluth, Minn.   (218) 727-3222

Spinsters Ink is a small, award-winning press dedicated to publishing novels and nonfiction works that deal with significant women's issues from a feminist perspective. The press was founded in 1978 in upstate New York, moved to San Francisco, then Minneapolis and is now in Duluth. International in scope, Spinster's Ink has 37 books in print and produces four to six books a year.

HOLY COW! PRESS
P.O. Box 3170
Mount Royal Station
Duluth, Minn. 55803   (218) 724-1653

This small mobile press was founded in 1977 in Minneapolis, moved with its founder to Iowa, then Steven's Point, Wisconsin, and ended up in Duluth. Holy Cow! Press has published 45 books to date, primarily by Midwestern writers and artists. About half the works are by Minnesota writers. Poetry, short-story collections, children's books, anthologies and some nonfiction works are covered. Recent books include the award-winning book of poetry *Nice Fish* by Duluthian Louis Jenkins and *Witchtree: A Collaboration* by Joanne Hart and Hazel Belvo.

TIGHT SQUEAK PRESS
722 E. 12th St.
Duluth, Minn.   (218) 722-0919

Tight Squeak Press is devoted to the art and craft of producing limited-edition, letter press-set, hand-bound books.

WOLF HEAD QUARTERLY
University of Minnesota-Duluth
10 University Dr.
Duluth, Minn.   (218) 726-8228

Wolf Head Quarterly is a relatively new literary journal featuring poetry and fiction published through the English Department at the University of Minnesota. Anyone is welcome to submit work for publication. The journal is available in local bookstores.

Visual Arts

SPLIT ROCK ARTS PROGRAM
University of Minnesota
306 Westbrook Hall, 77 Pleasant St. S.E.
Minneapolis, Minn. 55455   (612) 624-6800

The Split Rock Arts Program's summer series of workshops in the literary and visual arts are taught by renowned practicing artists, craftspeople and writers at the University of Minnesota Duluth campus and the University of Minnesota's Cloquet Forestry Center. Past visual arts workshops include "Watercolors" by Cheng-Khee Chee; "Creating Ritual Art" by Ernest Whiteman; "Building Spirit Houses: A Sculpture Workshop" by Nancy Azara and "Nature Photography: Creating the Photographic Essay" by Craig and Nadine Blacklock.

TWEED MUSEUM OF ART
University of Minnesota-Duluth
10 University Dr.
Duluth, Minn.   (218) 726-8222

The Tweed Museum of Art at the University of Minnesota Duluth is a tremendous resource for area art lovers. In its traditional role, the museum has an extensive permanent collection of 19th- and 20th-century paintings by regional artists and a strong French Barbizon School and American Impressionist collection. The Tweed curates original contemporary exhibitions by local and national artists, promotes local collaborations and hosts traveling exhibits.

The Tweed hosts a lecture series by visiting artists and has initiated a new series called *Dialogues: Literary and Performing Arts*, which has featured notable writers such as poets Robert Bly and Louis Jenkins. *Concerts-in-Tweed*, a music series sponsored by the UMD Department of Music, is held in the galleries.

DULUTH ART INSTITUTE
506 W. Michigan St.
Duluth, Minn.   (218) 733-7560

The 100-year-old Duluth Art Institute, a member-based nonprofit organization, provides classes, exhibitions and other resources for regional artists and area residents throughout northeastern Minnesota and northwestern Wisconsin. The institute organizes classes for children and adults in painting, print-making, photography and ceramics and fibers. The Institute's galleries present more than 15 shows a year, including regional and national contemporary showings and the Arrowhead Biennial Exhibition, a juried competition.

NORTHERN WOMEN'S ART COLLECTIVE
c/o Duluth Art Institute
506 W. Michigan St.   (218) 733-7560
Duluth, Minn.   (218) 525-6224

The Northern Women's Art Collective was recently formed to support women artists in northeastern Minnesota and northwestern Wisconsin who work in various mediums. This member-based nonprofit group holds regular meetings, feature shows and workshops and is a great resource as well.

Retail Galleries

In addition to the major galleries at the Tweed Museum of Art and the Duluth Art Institute, Duluth has some commercial galleries. We've included a few of our favorites.

ART DOCK
394 Lake Ave., Duluth, Minn.(218) 722-1451

This gallery, in the DeWitt-Seitz building, sells the creations of more than 200 regional artists. There's a great selection of prints, paintings, photography, jewelry, music, books, textiles and pottery. Art Dock is open from 10 AM to 9 PM weekdays, 10 AM to 6 PM Saturdays and 11 AM to 5 PM on Sundays.

LIZZARDS ARTISTIC EXPRESSIONS
1101 E. Superior St.
Duluth, Minn.   (218) 728-1388

Lizzards features original artwork from 150 artists, including Richard Gruchalla's raku pottery, George Morrison's line drawings, Robinson Scott's hand-blown glass and Annie Labovitz's drawings and oil paintings. Hours are 10 AM to 5 PM Tuesday through Friday and 10 AM to 2 PM Saturdays.

LIZZARDS II
19 E. Superior St.
Duluth, Minn.   (218) 722-5814

Lizzards II features larger works — painting and sculpture — than those at the main gallery (see previous entry). Hours are 10 AM to 5 PM Tuesday through Friday and 10 AM to 2 PM on Saturday.

SIVERTSON'S GALLERY
361 Canal Park Dr.
Duluth, Minn.   (218) 723-7877

Sivertson's Gallery, and its counterpart in Grand Marais, are owned and operated by the Sivertson family whose paintings are featured in the galleries. Their work and the paintings, prints and sculpture of 15 regional artists and 30 artists from Alaska and Canada comprise "art of the North." Themes and motifs are earth-based, reflecting each artist's wild, natural surroundings.

Summer hours are 10 AM to 8 PM Monday through Saturday and 11 AM to 6 PM Sunday; winter hours are 10 AM to 5 PM Monday through Saturday and 11 AM to 4 PM Sunday.

Arts Presenters

DULUTH ENTERTAINMENT CONVENTION CENTER

350 Harbor Dr.
Duluth, Minn.   *(218) 727-4344*

The DECC presents a variety of popular music, including country music star Alan Jackson, folk duo Indigo Girls and child superstar performer Raffi. It also presents theatrical performances, such as a *Best of Broadway* series, with the shows *Cats*, *Gigi* and *The Will Rogers Follies*.

LUCIUS WOODS PERFORMING ARTS CENTER

Railroad St., Solon Springs, Wis.
Box Office   *(715) 378-4272*

This community-operated outdoor amphitheater is set on the shores of Lake St. Croix amid the pines and hardwoods of Lucius Woods County Park — an idyllic setting for some great summer concerts, including the Duluth-Superior Symphony Orchestra and various guest artists. The emphasis here is on family-oriented entertainment: in 1996, ragtime artist and musical historian Max Morath; Prairie Home Companion regular, ragtime artist Butch Thompson; and the 1950s/60s group White Sidewalls. The Labor Day festival features music, food booths, kids activities and a juried art show and sale. There's a swimming beach, play area, trails and camping in the park.

To get to Lucius Woods, take U.S. Highway 53 south from Superior 30 miles to Solon Springs. Take a left at the Dairy Queen and follow the signs.

SACRED HEART MUSIC CENTER

201 W. Fourth St.
Duluth, Minn.   *(218) 723-1895*

The Sacred Heart Music Center is in the beautiful, 100-year-old former Sacred Heart Cathedral, complete with two-story-high stained-glass windows, vaulted ceilings and marble altars. The arts organization is working to save and restore the building, a designated local landmark listed on the National Register of Historic Places, through a concert series and summer tours. Summer tours are free; concert tickets range in price from $4 to $10.

The center presents concerts designed to highlight one of the best acoustic spaces in town, particularly for voice, small ensemble, choral and organ recitals. The center also is home to a well-maintained, century-old Felgemaker tracker organ, considered one of the finest historic instruments in Minnesota and featured frequently in the concert series (see the related sidebar in our Places of Worship chapter).

MITCHELL AUDITORIUM PERFORMING ARTS SERIES

College of St. Scholastica
1200 Kenwood Ave., Duluth, Minn.
Box Office   *(218) 723-6700*

Held in the Mitchell Auditorium, a new, state-of-the-art performance space, the Performing Arts Series features concerts, dance and theater. Past performances include *In the Heart of the Beast* puppet theater, the Minnesota Opera, the Minneapolis Gospel Sound and the Ethnic Dance Theater. Ticket prices vary and are subject to change; please call the box office for details.

Along the North Shore

Up the North Shore from Duluth, Grand Marais has garnered a reputation as an artists colony. Its natural beauty has attracted writers, painters and musicians. Grand Marais' lighthouse and breakwater is a frequently painted scene. Farther up the shore, Grand Portage, with its rugged coastline, rocky cliffs and launch point for

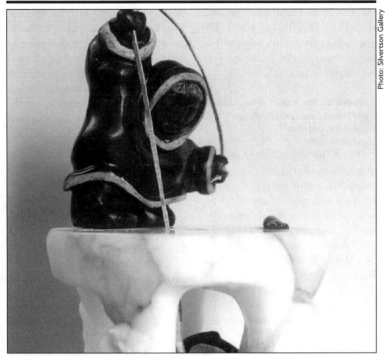

Hand-carved art such as this Inuit sculpture is displayed and sold at North Shore galleries.

ferries to Isle Royale, has also inspired many artists.

The Grand Marais Art Colony, founded in 1947, is the centrifugal force of the area's arts scene, carrying on the tradition of nurturing artists through classes and workshops. You'll find marvelous works — prints, paintings, ceramics and sculpture — in galleries in Grand Marais and along the shore.

The Johnson Heritage Post Art Gallery compliments the Grand Marais Art Colony with its permanent historic collection of regional artists' work and revolving exhibit program, housed in a handsome pine building in the center of town. Grand Marais has lively local folk and bluegrass music and folk dance scenes. Depending on the season, concerts and music festivals

are held either in Grand Marais Community Playhouse (housed in an old church), Schroeder Town Hall or outdoors near the town of Two Harbors. You can also catch live music at Sven and Ole's, a popular local pizza place in downtown Grand Marais on Wisconsin Street.

Performing Arts

TWO HARBORS FOLK FESTIVAL

PAP Acres   (218) 834-2600
Two Harbors, Minn.   (800) 777-7384

This annual July folk festival features blues, folk and old-time music. The festival brings in several notable folk performers, such as Greg Brown, Claudia Schmidt and Pop Wagner. Special music and activities are scheduled for kids of all ages. The folk festival is held at PAP Acres, a campground area near Two Harbors. (See our Annual Events and Festivals chapter for more information.)

NORTH SHORE MUSIC ASSOCIATION
Grand Marais Community Playhouse
First Ave. W. and Third St.
Grand Marais, Minn.   *(218) 387-1648*

The North Shore Music Association sponsors a number of concerts a year — mainly folk and bluegrass. These concerts are wonderful opportunities to see big-name artists in a small-scale setting. Past performers include Ann Reed, Greg Brown, Bill Staines and Randy Sabien. Concerts are held at a number of venues on the North Shore, including Schroeder Town Hall and Grand Marais Community Playhouse.

GRAND MARAIS COMMUNITY PLAYHOUSE
First Ave. W. and Third St.
Grand Marais, Minn.   *(218) 387-1648*

In addition to producing community theater, the Grand Marais Playhouse hosts a number of jazz, folk, Cajun and classical chamber music performances during the May through September concert season. Many talented musicians live in the Grand Marais area, and this is the place to see them perform. Tickets are reasonably priced (generally less than $10).

Visual Arts

GRAND MARAIS ART COLONY
Corner of Second St. and Third Ave. W.
Grand Marais, Minn.   *(218) 387-2737*

The nonprofit Grand Marais Art Colony, established in 1947, has a two-prong programming approach. One approach offers technical, media-oriented classes, such as watercolor painting, woodcut printing and fiber arts (the "how-to" part of the creation process);

the other approach includes mentor-based workshop opportunities for emerging writers and visual artists seeking to develop or re-energize their personal voices. Most of the workshops for visiting artists are held in summer from the end of June to mid-September, but the colony also offers classes and programs throughout the year. The weeklong classes are deliberately small — limited to 12 participants — to encourage openness. The cost of a weeklong workshop is $250.

JOHNSON HERITAGE POST ART GALLERY
115 W. Wisconsin St.
Grand Marais, Minn.   *(218) 387-2314*

The Johnson Heritage Post Art Gallery is named after the original trading post, built on the present site in 1906. The current building, a replica, was constructed of Montana lodgepole pine. It's a North Shore art museum and gallery that showcases area artists in an airy, well-lit and comfortable space.

The west wing of the gallery is dedicated to the work of Anna Carolina Johnson, a Swedish pioneer and a noted art teacher and painter. She also ran the trading post for many years. Her paintings and drawings depict what the area and its people looked like more than a half-century ago. Don't miss her exquisite painting of the Gunflint Wagon Road and the majestic white pines, a benchmark for local people traveling on this now-paved Gunflint Trail. (In 1995, two of these 200-year-old pines were cut down by vandals.)

The museum and gallery are open from May through October, Monday through Saturday from 10 AM to 5 PM and Sunday from 11 AM to 4 PM. From November through April, hours are 11 AM to 4 PM on Friday, Saturday and Sunday.

Retail Galleries

SIVERTSON GALLERY
6 Wisconsin St.
Grand Marais, Minn.   (218) 387-2491

The Sivertson Gallery is owned and operated by an artistically inclined family whose lineage traces to Isle Royale. Howard Sivertson is known for his highly detailed, colorful paintings that depict Isle Royale when it was a fishing village. His daughter, Liz Sivertson, presents large, abstract works inspired by outdoor motifs and symbols. The gallery features an extensive collection of regional artists, including Canadian Indians. Be sure to check out the woodcut prints by Betsy Bowen, who is known for her children's books.

Hours are generally 10 AM to 5 PM weekdays and 11 AM to 4 PM Sundays, but they may change monthly in summer and are restricted in winter; be sure to call ahead.

KAH-NEE-TAH GALLERY
Minn. Hwy. 61, Lutsen, Minn.   (218) 387-2585

Kah-Nee-Tah Gallery features the work of more than 75 regional artists, including original paintings, prints, photography and pottery. The gallery offers exquisite baskets and Norwegian-style covered wooden boxes made by a Two Harbors artist. Kah-Nee-Tah also has a great selection of jewelry, particularly earrings.

Summer hours are 10 AM to 5 PM daily; winter hours, 10 AM to 4 PM daily.

TIMES TWO DESIGN
813 W. Fifth St.
Grand Marais, Minn.   (218) 387-2234

Times Two Design offers original prints, paintings and photography by local and regional artists. The gallery also showcases oil, watercolor and acrylic paintings by owner/artist Jim Ringquist. Times Two is open 9 AM to 5 PM Monday through Friday year round.

Along the South Shore

On Wisconsin's South Shore, the Bayfield Peninsula, including Bayfield, Washburn and Ashland, is home to a number of art venues. In summer, the music and theater scene is dominated by the 60-night performance season at Lake Superior Big Top Chautauqua, a old-time tent show theater that hosts regional and national musicians and lively musicals inspired by the history of the surrounding area.

Northland College's *Arts and Letters* series brings music, theater and dance to the area. The college's Lifelong Learning Program also offers workshops in the literary and visual arts. The lively local community of visual artists, musicians, potters, weavers and writers on the peninsula bring their talents to area galleries and theaters. Check out the galleries in Port Wing, Cornucopia, Bayfield and Washburn for regional work.

Farther east in Ironwood, Michigan, just across the border from Hurley, Wisconsin, you'll find the Ironwood Theater. This lovingly restored former vaudeville house is the nucleus for year-round stage productions, music and the visual arts in Michigan's western Upper Peninsula.

Many presenter organizations on the South Shore not only host music, theater and lecture series but also offer classes in the visual and literary arts. Because of this extensive crossover, we've omitted the organizational headers that divide different disciplines (as in previous geographical sections), with the notable exception of "Retail Galleries."

NORTHLAND COLLEGE
ARTS AND LETTERS SERIES
Northland College, Alvord Theater
1411 Ellis Ave., Ashland, Wis. (715) 682-1307

The college's *Arts and Letters* series runs from September through May and includes five programs of dance, theater and classical music by artists and performing groups from outside the region. The St. Paul Chamber Orchestra appears regularly. Other past performers include the Minnesota Opera, the Juilliard Graduate School of Drama, the American Brass Quintet and the Ko-thi Dance Theater. The series is presented in the intimate, 250-seat Alvord Theater on the Northland College campus in Ashland. Tickets range from $8 to $10, and a season subscription costs around $40.

LAKE SUPERIOR BIG TOP CHAUTAUQUA
Mount Ashwabay Rd., Bayfield, Wis.
Tickets/reservations (715) 373-5552

Influenced by the early 20th-century Chautauqua movement, the nonprofit Lake Superior Big Top Chautauqua presents local, regional and national artists, such as humorist/writer Garrison Keillor, blues musician Taj Mahal, folk singers John Hartford and Richie Havens, country/folk musician Emmylou Harris and poet Robert Bly.

The 'centerpole' of this professional tent theater is its repertoire of original musicals, inspired by the history of the Bayfield Peninsula and illustrated on a big screen with hundreds of historic images. One of the most popular house musicals is *Riding the Wind*, the story of Bayfield and the Apostle Islands, set to original music and song. The house band accompanies the shows and brims with talent and energy. For many people, this show is a summer tradition. *Keeper of the Light* provides a compelling look at the lives of the Apostle Islands lighthouse keepers and their families, and *On the Velvet* takes you through the glory days of America's railroad history.

Reservations are advised for big-name shows and weekend performances of house musicals. Tickets are available on site before the shows, or you can stop by the administrative offices and box office in the brownstone Washburn Cultural Center on the main drag in Washburn.

The tent is set up on the grounds of Mount Ashwabay Ski Hill, 3 miles south of Bayfield on Wis. Highway 13 — watch for signs. And remember to applaud enthusiastically because, on many nights, the shows are taped for *Tent Show Radio,* a nationally distributed public radio broadcast sponsored by Wisconsin Public Radio.

NORTHLAND COLLEGE
LIFELONG LEARNING
1411 Ellis Ave., Ashland, Wis. (715) 682-1260

This outreach program through Northland College in Ashland offers workshops and classes in the visual arts — photography, textiles, mural painting and raku pottery (to name a few) — and the literary arts. Wordscapes, for example, is a 12-day nature writing workshop in the Apostle Islands. Since 1989, this annual midsummer event, which includes sailing, canoeing and kayaking, has attracted writers of all ages (14 to 70). Instructor come from as far away as Montana and Wyoming.

Many of the workshops and classes offered throughout the year are taught by area art and music professionals. Author/teacher Carol Bly has presented frequent summer workshops. Other notable professionals include Duluth artist Jan Hartley and Madison, Wisconsin, performance artist Bob Kann. Song-writing and performance workshops are offered as well.

Costs vary depending on length and associated credits. Non-credit classes range from $75 to $350; undergraduate workshops cost $220 per credit; and graduate workshops, $140 to $220 per credit.

IRONWOOD THEATRE
111 E. Aurora St.
Ironwood, Mich.   (906) 932-0618

The Ironwood Theatre, an elegant 1920s vaudeville house, has been restored to its former grandeur. A year-round series of programs, including musical theater, classical recitals, movies, organ concerts and children's events are offered. (Call for a schedule.) Past performers include the Duluth-Superior Symphony Orches-tra, the Guy Lombardo Orchestra and the Minneapolis Gospel Sound. The theater is also a venue for professional and community theater efforts and art exhibits.

OPEN MOUTH POETRY
P.O. Box 656
Washburn, Wis. 54891   (715) 373-2289

Open Mouth is a writers resource organization that features regular readings and open mikes in Hayward, Ashland and Bayfield. WOJB-FM 88.9, the tribal community radio station from the Lac Courte d'Oreilles reservation near Hayward, features the *Radio Poets* show in conjunction with Open Mouth. Open Mouth also publishes *Open Water,* an anthology of South Shore-area poets and writers that's available in local bookstores.

WASHBURN HISTORICAL
MUSEUM AND CULTURAL CENTER
1 E. Bayfield St. (Wis. Hwy. 13)
Washburn, Wis.   (715) 373-5591

Listed on the National Register of Historic Places, the restored brownstone Washburn Bank building now houses two floors of Washburn area history and exhibits by area artists. The building is open every Saturday year round; in July and August, it's open seven days a week from 10 AM to 4 PM. Admission is free.

Retail Galleries

Following is a sample of the many commercial galleries you'll discover on the Bayfield Peninsula. Check out our Shopping chapter for additional ideas.

KARLYN'S GALLERY
318 W. Bayfield (Wis. Hwy. 13)
Washburn, Wis.   (715) 373-2922

Gallery owner Karlyn Holmgren is a recognized painter and teacher who presents watercolor workshops internationally. Her spacious, well-lit gallery, built by her carpenter husband, Gary, and managed by her daughter, Renee, features area artists' work, including watercolors, prints, photography, stoneware, raku (lead-glazed Japanese earthenware), porcelain and jewelry.

BAYFIELD ARTISTS GUILD
104 Rittenhouse Ave.
Bayfield, Wis.   *(715) 779-5781*
Fourteen regional artists are represented here in the mediums of watercolor, acrylic and oil painting; basketry; woodworking; fiber; and pottery. The guild is open daily 10 AM to 6 PM from May through October.

FIRST STREET GALLERY
21 N. First St.
Bayfield, Wis.   *(715) 779-5101*
Housed in an historic downtown building, this gallery features paintings by area artists, including some particularly intense landscapes, as well as glass, jewelry and ceramics. First Street Gallery is open 9 AM to 5 PM seven days a week from mid-May through mid-October.

AUSTIN MILLER STUDIO
Ski Hill Rd.
South of Bayfield, Wis.   *(715) 779-5336*
You'll find a selection of original watercolors by noted painter France Austin Miller. The studio is open 10 AM to 4 PM Thursday through Monday from May 15 to October 15.

PORT WING POTTERY
Wis. Hwy. 13
Port Wing, Wis.   *(715) 774-3227*
Port Wing Pottery's home is the former St. Mary's Catholic Church. You can't miss this charming 1896 white,

steepled landmark as you round the bend in Port Wing. The gallery includes two floors of regional artwork — hand-blown glass, ironwork by a local blacksmith, wood carvings, pottery and paintings.

Summer hours (Memorial Day to Labor Day) are 10 AM to 5 PM Monday through Saturday and noon to 4 PM Sunday. Winter hours vary; call first.

Thunder Bay Area

Thunder Bay, has a number of performing-, literary- and visual-arts organizations. We chose to highlight some of the more outstanding artistic resources in the community. For example, the Magnus Theater is known for its professional productions; the Thunder Bay Art Gallery at Confederation College, for its permanent collection of Canadian Indian art; and the Thunder Bay Symphony Orchestra, for its six-month classical performance season at the Thunder Bay Community Auditorium. Old Fort William produces many art and cultural events during its summer season. Check out Lakehead University and Confederation College for arts activities in Thunder Bay. Both schools feature exhibits, stage productions and music programs.

Performing Arts

THUNDER BAY COMMUNITY AUDITORIUM
450 Beverly St.
Thunder Bay, Ont.   *(807) 343-2300*
This 1,500-seat performing-arts facility, built in 1985, is an acoustically exceptional hall. The auditorium presents a series of musical theater, popular music concerts and family-oriented entertainment. Recent shows include *Forever Plaid*, *The Will Rogers Follies*, the Vienna

Boys Choir and magician David Copperfield.

THE THUNDER BAY
SYMPHONY ORCHESTRA
Thunder Bay Community Auditorium
450 Beverly St.
Thunder Bay, Ont.   *(807) 345-4331*

The Symphony Orchestra makes its home at the Thunder Bay Community Auditorium for its regular-season (October to May) *Masterworks* and *Pops* programs. The auditorium also has hosted visiting symphonies, including the Toronto Symphony and the Moscow Philharmonic.

OLD FORT WILLIAM
Broadway Ave.
Thunder Bay, Ont.   *(807) 577-8461*

Old Fort William hosts a variety of performing-arts and cultural events during the summer months. The Thunder Bay Symphony Orchestra holds its summer season (July and August) at the Great Hall in the fort. The annual Great Rendezvous in mid-July features traditional music (see our Annual Events and Festivals chapter for details).

CORNWALL CONCERT SERIES
Lakehead University
Music and Visual Arts Building
Jean McNulty Recital Hall
955 Oliver Rd.
Thunder Bay, Ont.   *(807) 343-8787*

Faculty, staff, students and alumni perform every second Tuesday of the month from mid-September to March at 12:30 PM. Faculty and guest artists perform mostly classical music. Tickets range from $5 to $7. (Student performances are free.) This series makes for a nice midday break.

THE MAGNUS THEATER
639 McLaughlin St.
Thunder Bay, Ont.   *(807) 623-5818*

Magnus' professional theater company produces and presents musicals, comedies and dramas from September to April. The 1995-96 season included David Mamet's *Oleanna*, A.R. Gurney's *Love Letters* and Elliot Hayes' *Homeward Bound*. Tickets range from $13 to $23.50.

Visual Arts

THE THUNDER BAY ART GALLERY
1080 Kewatin St.
Thunder Bay, Ont.   *(807) 577-6427*

Thunder Bay Art Gallery, on the campus of Lakehead University, is a must-see if you're intrigued by Native American art. You'll find an outstanding permanent collection, including beadwork, quillwork, masks, baskets, paintings and sculpture. This public gallery, also a national exhibition center, hosts rotating exhibits of contemporary artists and produces major original exhibitions as well. It focuses on historical and contemporary art, craftwork and photography.

Admission is free. Hours are noon to 8 PM Tuesday through Thursday and noon to 5 PM Friday through Sunday. The gallery is closed on Mondays.

American writer Sinclair Lewis, famed for his indictment of small-town America in his novel *Main Street*, lived briefly in East Duluth in the 1940s in the mansion at 2601 E. Second Street.

Insiders' Tips

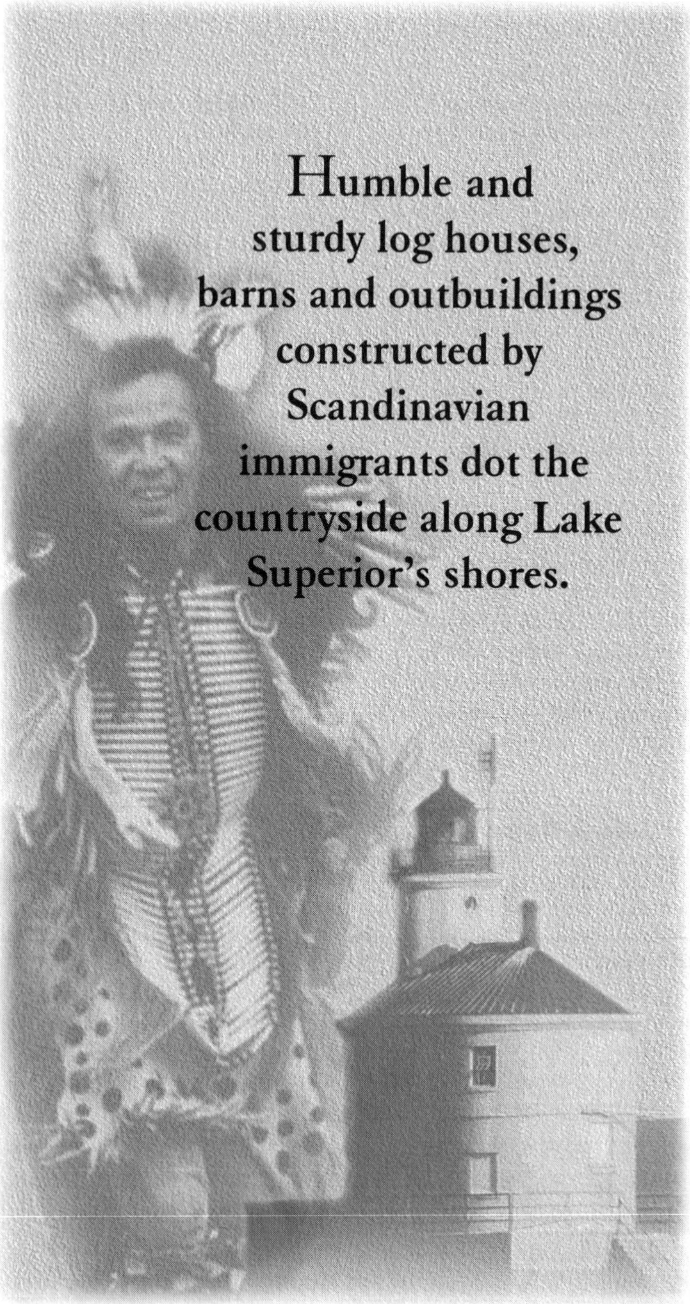

Humble and
sturdy log houses,
barns and outbuildings
constructed by
Scandinavian
immigrants dot the
countryside along Lake
Superior's shores.

Inside
Architecture and Historic Places

You can discover, in many towns and cities along Lake Superior's North and South shores, honest working architecture intact from around the turn of the century. These buildings and other structures are remnants of the mining, shipping and logging industries that influenced the boom-and-bust economies and development of many of the cities and towns in the western Lake Superior region.

We've picked some of our favorites as well as some of the most historically significant landmarks. Our self-titled genre of honest working architecture includes the handsome railroad depots, the impressive ore docks and grain elevators, the sturdy, picturesque lighthouses and the immigrant houses of Lake Superior. You may notice a lack of historic churches in this chapter; we've written about them in our Places of Worship chapter.

Some historic structures, such as the Aerial Lift Bridge and the ore docks on the St. Louis River in the Duluth harbor and in Two Harbors on the North Shore still accomplish the tasks for which they were originally designed. For that matter, some of the lakers you see hauling ore and grain are more than a half-century old. Other structures, such as the railroad depots, have survived demolition by making career changes to new roles as museums, antiques malls, restaurants and cultural centers.

Lake Superior has many working lighthouses as well as decommissioned light-houses saved for history. Some of our favorites, such as Split Rock Lighthouse on the North Shore and Minnesota Point Lighthouse at the end of Park Point, are easily accessible. Others, such as the Apostle Islands' six lights, require planning and a boat ride to reach the island-bound treasures.

As a result of the wealth generated by logging, mining and other industries, many mansions were built in Duluth and Superior from the 1890s to the 1920s. On Wisconsin's South Shore, the cities of Ashland and Bayfield claim some splendid turn-of-the-century houses in fine condition. In Thunder Bay, if you search in the Vickers Park area in Fort William and the area near downtown Port Arthur, you'll discover a few scattered head-turning houses, but not to the extent of Duluth's mansion district.

In contrast to the mansions of the port cities, humble and sturdy log houses, barns and outbuildings constructed by Scandinavian immigrants dot the countryside. Many of these hand-hewn log structures are still used today, particularly those on Wisconsin's South Shore dairy farms. The Wirtanen Finnish farm in St. Louis County, for example, is a designated historic area and worth a drive to the country to see. You'll also find immigrant housing in the towns and cities, some built by the mining and steel companies for their workers.

Tourism has always been part of the economic mix, particularly on Minnesota's North Shore. The North Shore Scenic Highway was completed in 1925 and spurred the construction of small tourist camps and family cabins. Many commercial fishermen and their families were the first to provide lodging for visitors along the North Shore.

We're intrigued by the historic lodges and the classic mom-and-pop tourist cabins that dot the North Shore, particularly so as the ubiquitous chain motels start to get a foothold in the area. The renowned **Lutsen Resort**, on the North Shore of Lake Superior, was Minnesota's first resort and the original site of a Swedish immigrant home and fishing business. The **Cascade Lodge** up the shore between Lutsen and Grand Marais features beam and boulder construction from the 1930s. Recently, the owners of Solbakken Resort painstakingly restored the 1934 **Sawbill Lodge**, which was relocated from the Boundary Waters. And, of course, there is the landmark 1929 **Naniboujou Lodge** near Hovland — built as a private club for the wealthy and famous.

Remnants of the mining and logging booms in the Upper Peninsula of Michigan, on the North Shore and the South Shore and in Thunder Bay can be found in the waterfront towns. The once-bustling industrial waterfront of Ashland, Wisconsin, is now filled with sailboats and fishing boats. The horizon is still dominated by the **Soo Line** ore dock, one of the largest structures of its kind in the world, last in service in 1965. Evidence of the iron ore industry, currently on the upswing (taconite production on the North Shore and the Iron Range is booming), can be seen in the train yards and ore docks busily loading ships in Duluth, Superior, Silver Bay, Taconite Harbor and Two Harbors

where the first load of iron ore was shipped from Minnesota in 1884. In Thunder Bay, the shoreline is dominated by the rows of colorful, modern grain elevators, holding wheat and other grains from the western provinces to be shipped eastward. A rustic 150-year-old mining village on the shores of the Sibley Peninsula (east of Thunder Bay) is evidence of the precious metals mining boom that continues today in Ontario.

Twin Ports Area

Duluth

Duluth runs long and skinny for 30 miles, nestled along the shores of Lake Superior and the bays of the St. Louis River. The city hosts distinctive neighborhoods, still referred to by their historic names. Many of them, like Fond du Lac, Morgan Park, West Duluth and Park Point were originally independent from Duluth. Starting in east Duluth, you have Lester Park near the waterfalls of the Lester River and Amity Creek; Lakeside, where the train continues to run; Hunters Park, Woodland, Kenwood and Congdon (all great neighborhoods for mansion-seekers); Chester Park, East End, Central Hillside, Duluth Heights, Park Point, West End, Piedmont, West Duluth, Bayview Heights, Riverside, Smithville, Morgan Park, Gary-New Duluth and Fond du Lac at the far west end of town.

Fond du Lac, the westernmost neighborhood, is close to Jay Cooke State Park and the St. Louis River. Grand Avenue/Minn. Highway 23 takes you to this sleepy neighborhood that once was an Ojibwe village. This is the oldest part of Duluth and the area where financier John Jacob Astor's fur-trading post operated in 1817. Though in rough shape, the relocated depot for the Lake Superior and Mississippi Railway, established in 1870 as the first railroad link from St. Paul, still stands. Also notable here is the 1867 **Peter J. Peterson house**, 13328 W. Third Street, the oldest house in Duluth, a simple two-story frame house with a porch.

Drive to the dead-end of 131st Avenue W. Today the trailhead for the Mission Creek Hiking Trail, this is the point where Skyline Parkway, the 30-mile scenic drive through Duluth, was designed to end. The rustic stone bridges remain but are now used by hikers.

Not to be missed is the company-built town of **Morgan Park** in western Duluth. Take Grand Avenue to 155th Street and follow its curve into this quiet, tree-lined neighborhood. Talk about a place with its own look! When US Steel built the town in 1913 to house workers from its now-defunct plant, Morgan Park was considered a model city. It had its own schools, two churches, a community center, a hospital and separately designed housing for bachelors. The company handled utilities and maintenance. The buildings are constructed of cinder block, and the interiors reflect the simple Mission-style influence of the time. As a Morgan Park resident, you were expected to keep your yard presentable. If you didn't, the company would cut your grass and send you a bill.

Morgan Park became part of Duluth in 1942. The homes are now privately owned, but a sense of continuity remains. If you talk to a resident, you're bound to learn that he or she is from many generations of family living in the neighborhood. Morgan Park retains a feel of cozy self-sufficiency with a new community center, active churches, a junior high school, ball fields, a bank, gas station and post office.

The neighborhoods of western Duluth, built along the wide bays and estuaries of the St. Louis River, sprang up to house the workers (and their families) who ran the factories, ironworks and shipbuilding industries that once dominated Duluth's economy. More than a dozen ore docks originally flanked the waterfront of the St. Louis River. Today, five remain and are used by the **Duluth Missabe & Iron Range Railroad** to ship taconite and the **Hallet Dock** to ship coal. You can watch from an observation platform as the train unloads open cars of taconite on the 1917 DM & IR dock 6. Take the 40th Avenue W. Exit from Interstate 35 and follow the frontage road to the DM & IR parking lot.

With the advent of the railroad, grain elevators were developed to store the wheat and grains coming into Duluth and Superior from the northern Great Plains and western Minnesota. These tall — sometimes tubular, sometimes square — structures are called elevators because the grain is off-loaded from railcars at the bottom then elevated to the top of these huge storage bins. The grain elevators of **Rice's Point** are visible from Garfield Avenue. The overlook on Skyline Parkway near Enger Tower is another great spot to enjoy harbor action. Rice's Point was the site for early grain elevators, now home to Cargill's and General Mill's elevators. The early elevators benefited from a new type of concrete construction that allowed for taller, stronger structures than earlier wooden counterparts.

Railroads were the dominant mode of transportation for people until after World War II. The logging and mining industries relied on the railroad lines to move their products to ships, rivers or to major markets. Duluth once had 15 depots, including the three main depots downtown: the Soo Line Depot, the

Union Depot and the Chicago Northwestern Depot.

The magnificent 1892 **Union Depot**, 506 W. Michigan Street, (218) 727-8025, is the only one left standing. But the Union Depot is now one of Duluth's major arts and cultural centers, saved and restored in the mid-1970s to house the Duluth-Superior Symphony Orchestra, the Minnesota Ballet, the Arrowhead Chorale, Matinee Musicale, the Duluth Playhouse and several cultural and historical organizations, including the Lake Superior Museum of Transportation, the Children's Museum, the Duluth Art Institute and the St. Louis County Historical Society. (Check out the Attractions and Arts and Culture chapters for more information.)

The 1899 **Endion Passenger Depot**, originally at 15th Avenue E. below London Road, was moved to the "corner of the Lake" near the Lakewalk where the charming red sandstone, gabled structure is home to the Duluth Convention and Visitors Bureau.

Duluth's mansion district, in East End, Congdon Park or eastern Duluth, is roughly bounded as the area between 21st and 26th avenues E. and Superior and Sixth streets. The area is loaded with period architecture, revealing various styles and surprises. It's great fun to drive up and down these blocks and admire the stately homes, which are not limited to the official mansion district area. For instance, there are terrifically impressive and delightful homes in the Woodland neighborhood. Just drive along Woodland Avenue, starting on Arrowhead Road and heading north. Check out the former Glen Avon streetcar station, 2102 Woodland Avenue, now a private residence. And London Road, from the end of the commercial district at 26th Avenue E.

northeastward up the shore, is a head-turning drive for "big house" seekers.

Some of our favorite historic homes in Duluth are:

•The 1900 **Arthur P. Cook House**, 501 W. Skyline Parkway. Called the House of Rocks, the building's lower half is constructed of rough native gabbro stone and features a steep, curving staircase that climbs up to an outstanding view of the harbor;

•The 1892 **John Smith House**, 218 94th Avenue W., with its Victorian tower overlooking the St. Louis River;

•The 1894 **Victorian House,** 520 N. Lake Avenue, also with a wonderful observation tower;

•The 1882 **Luke A. Marvin House**, 123 W. Third Street, with fantastic gingerbread porches;

•The 1902 **George Crosby House**, 2029 E. Superior Street, a handsome brownstone featuring a 80-ton entry piece with a carving of lion's head by George Thrana, a master stone carver, whose work also graces the former Central High School and Denfeld High School;

•The 1955 **Robert J. Starkey House**, 2620 Greysolon Road, designed in International style by Marcel Breuer, a Hungarian architect who studied at the renowned German Bauhaus School;

•The 1892 **Ronald M. Hunter House**, 2317 Woodland Avenue, with its Gothic gables and peaks;

•The 1892 **Oliver Traphagen House**, 1511 E. Superior Street (a.k.a. the "redstone"), with striking tower and porch, currently an advertising agency;

•And the 1891 **Munger Terrace**, 405 Mesaba Avenue, built of brick and brownstone in Châteauesque style, originally eight large residences of 16 rooms each, and currently divided into about 30 apartments.

The definitive mansion in Duluth that

A ship heads into the fog of Lake Superior as it leaves the Superior entry.

you can (and should) tour is **Glensheen**, 3300 London Road, (218) 724-8864. Built for Chester Adgate Congdon and Clara Bannister Congdon in 1908, this 22-acre property resembles an early 17th-century English country estate. Besides the 39-room Jacobean-style manor house are a carriage house, a bowling green, a boat house, a clay tennis court, formal gardens and a gardener's cottage. Now owned by the University of Minnesota, the mansion brims with original furnishings, light fixtures and art. (For more information, see our Attractions chapter.)

Downtown Duluth and the Central Hillside neighborhood right above downtown on the hillside hold many fine historic buildings. Look up the hill from Canal Park; the recently restored clock on the 1891 **Central High School** will catch your eye. Between Lake Avenue and First Avenue E., above Second Avenue, this outstanding example of Richardsonian Romanesque architecture survived a close call with the demolition ball. Today, its classrooms house the school district's administrative offices and programs. George Thrana's fantastic stone carvings of gar-

goyles and cherubs merit a close look. In **West Duluth Denfeld High School,** 44th Avenue W. and Fourth Street, built in 1925, also features Thrana's fantastic medieval symbols carved in limestone. The 1902 **Carnegie Library**, on First Avenue W. and Second Street, has a beautiful domed central court. Although the library is now an office building, it has retained its historic feel. It originally held two Tiffany windows, which are now exhibited at the Depot. The **Civic Center Historic District**, First Street and Fifth Avenue W., includes the 1909 **courthouse**, the 1928 **city hall**, the 1930 **Federal Building** the and the 1929 jail (on Second Street) — all designed in the Classical Revival style of the "City Beautiful Movement," inspired by the 1893 Columbian Exposition in Chicago.

You'll find other significant historic buildings by simply driving or walking east on Superior Street, starting at Fourth Avenue W. in downtown Duluth. Highlights include the 1910 **Alworth Building**, 306 W. Superior Street, once the tallest building in Duluth; the neat brownstone of the 1886 **Wirth Building**, 13 W.

The Gales of November Came Early . . .

So goes the song by modern-day troubadour Gordon Lightfoot that immortalized the wreck of the *Edmund Fitzgerald*.

Shipwrecks are everywhere in Lake Superior, many of them uncharted and waiting for discovery by curious divers. The Lake's cold, fresh water has preserved many of these wrecks. Most of them date from the 1870s or later, since Lake Superior was the last of the Great Lakes open to large ship navigation.

One of the Lake's most famous shipwrecks, the *Edmund Fitzgerald*, which rests off Whitefish Point near U.P. Michigan, is also one of the more recent wrecks; it sank on November 10, 1975, taking all 29 hands with it.

The 180-foot U.S. Coast Guard cutter *Mesquite* was the latest victim of Lake Superior's fury — run aground on Michigan's Keeweenaw Point on December 4, 1989. The *Mesquite's* crew was rescued, but the ship was battered beyond repair. The cutter was deliberately sunk and is a diving attraction today.

Photo: File Photo

A National Park Service diver approaches a segment of a paddlewheel of the Cumberland, *a wooden sidewheeler that ran aground on Isle Royale's Rock of Ages reef. The underwater archaeologists are methodically identifying the remains of the shipwreck.*

It's estimated that Lake Superior holds about 350 shipwrecks. The Minnesota Historical Society has published a guide to shipwrecks near Duluth and along the North Shore, many of which are accessible to divers. For the landlubber, the remains of the 1876 USS *Essex* can be seen in the shallow, clear waters at the end of Park Point in Duluth, on the bay side from the beach. The *Essex*, a 200-foot Navy auxiliary sailing warship, was retired in 1905 and deliberately burned and sunk in 1931. Sailing warships were obsolete by the 20th century, so the vessel was decommissioned — its scrap iron salvaged then sent to rest on the bottom of Lake Superior.

For more information on Lake Superior's shipwrecks, we recommend *Lake Superior Shipwrecks* by Julius Wolff Jr. and *Shipwrecks of the Lake Superior* by James R. Marshall — both published by Lake Superior Port Cities Inc.

Superior Street; the wonderfully carved fronts of the 1889 **Old City Hall and Jail**, 132 and 126 E. Superior Street; the 1925 **Hotel Duluth** (now the Greysolon Plaza), 227 E. Superior, whose elegant ballroom was used in the movie *Iron Will*; the 1890 **August J. Fitger's Brewery**, 600 E. Superior Street, now reincarnated as a hotel, restaurant and shopping complex; and the 1912 **Kitchi Gammi Club**, 831 E. Superior Street, designed by noted New York architect Bertram Goodhue.

To get a feel for Duluth's colorful history and architecture, we recommend the free summer walking tours of the Old Downtown District (from Lake Avenue to Fourth Avenue E.) that are led by costumed characters from Duluth's history. Interpreters portraying land speculator and railroad builder Jay Cooke, and Dr. Thomas Preston Foster, founder of Duluth's first newspaper in 1869, guide people through Duluth's **Old Downtown District**, now home to artist studios and thriving gallery and antiques shops that occupy Victorian- and Romanesque-style buildings from the late 1890s. Tours are offered every Saturday morning at 10 AM from Memorial Day to Labor Day; simply show up at the Lake Superior Fountain at Lake Avenue and Superior Street on the southeast corner. Parking is available across the street.

Down at the waterfront at Canal Park, the **Aerial Lift Bridge**, the city's major visual icon, dominates the setting. Constructed in 1905 and designed after a simi-

lar bridge in Rouen, France, the Lift Bridge first had a suspended gondola car that carried vehicles and people back and forth. In 1929, its 900-ton lift span was installed.

There's something romantic and courageous about a lighthouse. Lightkeepers kept the Fresnel lens clean, the oil burning and the fog horns bellowing. They also kept watch around the clock during the pre-radar days when the ships navigating Lake Superior depended on these beacons for safety and guidance through tumultuous waters and stormy nights. The waters of Lake Superior can turn deadly very quickly; gale force winds and storm-size waves of 20 feet or more are not uncommon. An estimated 350 shipwrecks rest silently in the watery graveyard that is Lake Superior.

There are three working lighthouses on the Duluth shipping canal: two south breakwater lights, built in 1901, and the north breakwater light, built in 1910. You can walk around these lighthouses along the shipping channel piers.

The crumbling remains of the 1859 **Minnesota Point Lighthouse** are hidden in the grassy dunes at the end of Park Point. Minnesota Point Lighthouse was once the most important light in the area and the center for navigational maps of Lake Superior. This original light was replaced in 1913 by the **Wisconsin Point Lighthouse**. You can hike to the lighthouse on the Park Point Nature Trail, which starts where the road ends at Park Point to the left of the Sky Harbor Airport.

Called "the boulevard" by Duluth old-timers, the historic **Skyline Parkway** stretches for 30 miles from one end of Duluth to the other and offers stunning views of the city, the harbor and the Lake from 400 to 600 feet above Lake Superior. The construction of Skyline Parkway began in 1889, and the route was first traveled by people in horse-drawn buggies. The drive was completed in 1939. Its eastern section starts at the Seven Bridges Road, a narrow road that winds along Amity Creek and the Lester River and is decorated by stone-arch bridges. Skyline Parkway becomes mostly a gravel road after Spirit Mountain — offering spectacular views of the St. Louis River Valley and wooded sections ending at Beck's Road above Gary-New Duluth.

Duluth is a treasure house of urban residential and industrial architecture. But to really get a feel for the immigrants who came to farm and to work in the mines and on the railroads, you need to check out the 1904 **Eli Wirtanen Finnish Farmstead**, maintained by the St. Louis County Historical Society. This property boasts a collection of hand-built log farm buildings, most of them original to the property. The place is usually empty (it's in the middle of nowhere). Wander the cut-grass paths that lead you through the meadows to the horse barn, the hay shed, the sauna and the root cellar. There's a main house and guest house with some furnishings, the original privy and a replica of the pig pen. The St. Louis Historical Society holds a Heritage Festival here each summer. Call (218) 733-7580 for more information. The Eli Wirtanen homestead is about 40 miles north of Duluth, 20 miles south of Biwabik. It's a half-mile west of St. Louis County Road No. 4. The turn is marked by a sign.

RECOMMENDED REFERENCES

For more in-depth information on Duluth's architectural treasures, we suggest *Boomtown Landmarks* by Laurie Hertzel, published by Pfeifer-Hamilton. The classic reference book for Duluth's architecture, *Duluth's Legacy, Volume 1*, published by the city of Duluth, is out of print, but copies can be found in used bookstores and at the Duluth Public Library.

Superior

In Superior, you'll find three remaining historic depots: The 1910-15 **Union Depot** (a.k.a. Lake Superior Terminal and Transfer Railway), a brownstone at 933 Oakes and Broadway, is now an antiques mall; the early 1900s **Soo Line Depot**, Winter Street and Ogden Avenue, was a passenger depot; and the turn-of-the-century former **Northern Pacific East End Depot**, E. Fifth Street, today is a senior citizens center.

Fairlawn Mansion and Museum, U.S. Highway 2/53, (715) 394-5712, is a commanding four-story Queen Anne Victorian — an abrupt and elegant contrast to the neighboring 1950s and '60s ranch homes along busy U.S. Highway 2 that border Superior's waterfront. On the historic former Bay Street, once the fashionable East End neighborhood for the well-to-do, Fairlawn is one of the few remaining mansions that used to line this street. (Duluth's equivalent is London Road.)

The restored 42-room mansion, built in 1890 for lumber and mining baron Martin Pattison and his wife, Grace Emma Pattison, is now a museum and cultural center housing the collections of the Douglas County Historical Society. Permanent and touring exhibits are on the second and third floors, including the important collection of nationally recognized photographer David F. Barry, who extensively documented Indian tribes, particularly Dakota tribes, in the early 1900s. Another permanent collection, *Ojibwe of Lake Superior,* consists of original portraits and biographies of these Native Americans. Fairlawn also hosts concerts, readings, a Sunday lecture series, a summer ice cream social and a fall murder mystery.

If you're a ship buff, get a good look at the **Fraser Shipyards**, visible from U.S. Highway 2 or Main Street off Fifth Avenue. This 65-acre working shipyard dates to 1891; it's the birthplace for dozens of Great Lakes ships and was a major building site for U.S. vessels during World War II. Work here also includes repairs and overhauls on the current Great Lakes fleet of lakers and thousand-footers. You can get a close-up look at the century-old timber construction of an ore dock at **Loons Foot Landing**. This public boat launch is near the intersection of 30th Avenue E. and U.S. Highway 2.

At the end of Wisconsin Point off Moccasin Mike Road is the 1913 **Wisconsin Point Lighthouse**. You can walk out on the breakwater to look at the lighthouse from the outside, but it's not open for inside tours. Note the two lighthouse-keeper houses nearby on the Allouez Bay side, complete with real keepers (today, the U.S. Coast Guard).

Along the North Shore

Two Harbors

The waterfront in Two Harbors is where you'll find the honest working architecture of this town. The 1907 depot, last used for passengers in 1961, now houses the **Lake County Historical Society**. It was once the headquarters for the Duluth & Iron Range Railway. Walk down to the waterfront and admire the newly refurbished *Edna G.* tugboat. She retired in 1981 as the last steam-powered tug operating on the Great Lakes. Two of three iron docks built in 1907 are used today to ship taconite on the Lake. These steel structures replaced timber docks built in 1884; they were the first steel docks in the country. The 1892 **Two Harbors Light Station** is a working lighthouse, run by the Coast Guard to assist the ore ships in and out of the harbor. As seen in the design of many historic lighthouses, the red-brick light tower and keeper's house are attached. Guided tours are available through the Lake County Historical Society, (218) 834-4898.

Completed by the U.S Lighthouse Service in 1910, the **Split Rock Light Station** has been restored to its 1920s appearance. Split Rock is considered one of the most spectacular lighthouses in the country and was featured in 1995 on a first-class U.S. postage stamp. You can tour the lighthouse, the fog-signal building and the keeper's house. In the interpretive center, history exhibits and a surprisingly entertaining film about the light-

The clock tower of the old 1891-1892 Central High School at Lake Avenue and Second Street in Duluth is a skyline fixture. Recently renovated, the clock chimes on the quarter hour.

house and the people who kept it going are part of the admission package. The lighthouse and its grounds are kept through a collaborative effort between the Minnesota Historical Society and the Minnesota Department of Natural Resources. Admission from Memorial Day to Labor Day is $4 for adults, $2 for kids ages 6 through 15 and $3 for senior citizens; children younger than 6 are free. A state park sticker is not required. In winter, there is no admission fee, but you must purchase a state park sticker ($4). The interpretive center is open in winter (except December), but the lighthouse and other historic buildings are closed; you can walk the grounds, however. For more information, call (218) 226-6372. (See the Attractions chapter for more information.)

Four North Shore historic lodges —

the old Sawbill Lodge at Solbakkens Resort, Lutsen Lodge, Cascade Lodge and Naniboujou Lodge — are all worth a visit. Except at Solbakken, you can enjoy lunch or dinner in each of the lodges' wonderful dining rooms. All of these lodges are along Minn. Highway 61.

Lutsen Lodge is the oldest resort in Minnesota, carrying on the Nelson homestead name, chosen by Swedish emigrant Charles Axel Nelson to commemorate the Battle of Lutzen in Germany, in which the Swedish King Gustav Adolph II was killed.

The first lodge, built in 1898, was destroyed by fire. The present lodge, built in 1952, was designed by Twin Cities architect Edwin Lundie, who created the Swedish-style, barn-red and white, wood-clad structure with gabled windows. The pine beams were logged and hand-hewn by the late George Nelson Sr. and his brother, Oscar, from a lumber mill they operated on the property.

Farther up the Minn. Highway 61, near Cascade River State Park (see our Parks and Forests chapter), **Cascade Lodge** faces the Lake. The dining room has great views and is particularly cozy on a rainy afternoon. The original resort was constructed in the 1920s but was torn down to build the current lodge in 1939.

In 1986, the owners of Solbakken Resort moved the 1934 **Sawbill Lodge** to their property from 40 miles away on Sawbill Lake. The lodge houses an office, a big lounge with a stone fireplace, a gift shop, a ski shop and a sauna. For practical reasons, the original lodge was expanded to make room for three suites with fireplaces on a walkout level.

Sawbill Lodge was famous in the 1940s and '50s for its year-round weather reports, which were sent via ham radio to WCCO, a Twin Cities AM radio station. The Sawbill Lodge was also renowned for the moose that literally dropped in one winter; the snow was so high, the beast walked onto the roof and *crunch!* . . . (If you can't guess what happened, you haven't been paying attention!)

Grand Marais doesn't have many significant historic buildings, but the downtown area, bounded by Minn. Highway 61, Broadway Avenue and Wisconsin Street, is filled with wonderful storefronts (c.1920 to the 1940s). Two buildings particularly worth checking out are the former lighthouse keeper's residence, 4 Broadway Avenue, today the home of the **Cook County Historical Society**, and the **Birch Terrace Supper Club**, Minn. Highway 61, built of pine logs in 1898 as a family home.

The famous 1929 **Naniboujou Lodge**, near Hovland, on the Brule River, is known for its celebrated history, its strik-ing original architecture and its original dining room interior, decorated with colorful Cree Indian designs and reeking of glamour from its role as a private club during Prohibition.

Grand Portage, 7 miles south of the Minnesota/Ontario border, is home to the reconstructed fur-trade stockade, the **Grand Portage National Monument**. It is built on the site of the original 1784 stockade. (For more information, see the Attractions and Annual Events chapter.)

Along the South Shore

Bayfield and the Apostle Islands

Practically the entire town of **Bayfield** is recognized as historically significant, according to the National Register of Historic Places. Bayfield's wooded hillside setting, on the tip of the Bayfield Peninsula and overlooking the Apostle Islands, its Victorian houses, lush flower gardens and brownstone buildings qualify it as potential subject matter for one of those idyllic pictures found on an insurance calendar. Once a center for fishing and logging, Bayfield now flourishes as the quintessential quaint summer-tourist town. It's popular with the sailing and sea-kayaking crowd. Many summertime residents have been coming here to family vacation homes for years. (The winter population is about 800; that figure more than doubles in summer.)

You can tour Bayfield and its historic buildings on foot, but be prepared for the hills; bring good walking shoes and drinking water. The brownstone on some of the buildings was quarried from Stockton and Bass islands, two of the Apostle Islands. The handsome stone was used to construct the former courthouse on

Washington Avenue between Fourth and Fifth Streets, which now serves as the visitors center for the Apostle Islands National Lakeshore. The 1904-05 **R.D. Pike Building** 201 Rittenhouse Avenue, was constructed of brownstone. It was the town's only bank until 1980. The 1903 brick and brownstone **Carnegie Library**, 37 N. Broad Street, is still used as a public library. Complete with wonderful high ceilings and oak furniture, the library's steep front steps create a grand entrance.

Mansion-seekers and admirers of Victorian architecture will find quite a few head-turning homes in Bayfield; some are bed and breakfast inns, but many remain private homes. A landmark building is the former 1890 **Allen C. Fuller House** at 301 Rittenhouse Avenue, known as the resplendent **Old Rittenhouse Inn**, (715) 779-5111, a bed and breakfast inn for the past 22 years. Proprietors Jerry and Mary Phillips are avid supporters of historic preservation and don't mind if you take a peak inside. The acclaimed Rittenhouse Inn restaurant is open to the public for dinner too.

The 1892 **William Knight House**, now a private residence on 108 N. Third Street, is an imposing Queen Anne Victorian with a brownstone base. The 1908 **Frank Boutin Jr. House**, 7 Rice Avenue, a handsome brick mansion with wraparound porch, is now an inn named **Chateau Boutin**. The 1885 **Theodore Ernst House**, a private residence on 17 N. Fourth Street, has some of the most ornate and detailed lace trim carpentry in town.

In the historic downtown district along Rittenhouse Avenue and First Street, check out the buildings that reflect Bayfield's shipping past.

The 1900 **Booth Cooperage**, Washington Avenue and Front Street near the Madeline Island ferry landing, (715) 779-3400, is now a museum that celebrates the art of barrel-making. Commerce relied on barrels for transporting fish as well as other staples and building supplies. The museum is open daily from Memorial Day to October from 9:30 AM to 5:30 PM. Admission is free.

Farther up Washington Street, the historic 1926 **city jail** is a 25-foot by 25-foot structure with thick fieldstone walls and iron gratings over the door and windows. This was the village jail for years — the repository of many unruly citizens. A little off the beaten path is the 1912 **bridge over Ravine Park** at the west end of town on Rice Avenue between Second and Third streets. Once used by horse-and-buggy travelers, it's now a charming pedestrian crossing used by local folk to walk through the neighborhood. The recently restored 230-foot wood-plank and wrought-iron bridge spans a deep ravine laced with hiking trails along a creek and lined with ferns and wild flowers. The ravine splits a quiet Bayfield neighborhood of well-kept old houses; Rice Street crosses the bridge as a thoroughfare. This tucked-away park and bridge have a timeless quality that is the essence of Bayfield.

RECOMMENDED REFERENCE

The definitive guide to Bayfield's charming architecture is *Brownstone and Bargeboards*, published by the University of Wisconsin. It's available through the Bayfield Heritage Association, P.O. Box 137, Bayfield, Wisconsin 54814, (715) 779-5958.

LaPointe and Madeline Island

Take the 20-minute ferry ride over to Madeline Island from Bayfield. You don't need your car if you want to save on the

Restoration and Preservation

Have you bought an old house and committed yourself to restoring it? Are you interested in the local history of an old storefront?

Duluth's **Preservation Alliance** is an active, dedicated member-based group that works to save significant buildings and record their histories (between fixing up members' own historic homes). The alliance holds monthly meetings to share restoration stories and tour different historic buildings. A popular annual tour of Duluth's historic private homes is an early fall tradition for old-house enthusiasts as well as the snoopy and the curious. Tickets are available to the general public. For more information, write: Preservation Alliance, P.O. Box 252, Duluth, Minnesota 55801.

Other regional organizations that either support preservation of historic sites and buildings or preserve regional history include:

Bayfield Heritage Association, P.O. Box 137, Bayfield, Wisconsin 54814, (715) 779-5958;

Cook County Historical Society, 4 S. Broadway Avenue, Grand Marais, Minnesota, (218) 387-2883;

Ironwood Area Historical Society, P.O. Box 553, Ironwood, Michigan 59338, (906) 932-0287;

Iron County Historical Society, 202 Iron Street, Hurley, Wisconsin, (715) 561-2244;

Lake County Historical Society, Depot Building (on the waterfront), Two Harbors, Minnesota, (218) 834-4898;

St. Louis County Historical Society, 506 W. Michigan Street, Duluth, Minnesota, (218) 733-7580;

Thunder Bay Historical Museum, 425 Donald Street E., Thunder Bay, Ontario, (807) 623-0801.

ferry fee; you can walk or rent bicycles or mopeds on the island.

LaPointe, with a year-round population of 125, is the oldest town in Wisconsin. Founded in 1835, its fur-trading history dates back to the 1700s; later, it became a center for Protestant and Catholic missionary activities, logging and fishing and, later still, a summer resort town (which it remains). It is the spiritual home of the Ojibwe, whose town here is said to have numbered 6,000 in the late 16th and early 17th centuries. Little remains of that settlement, because building materials were wood and bark.

Walk around the town. Check out the historic schoolhouse. Tour the historic fort (now, a museum). Walk down Nebraska Row and admire the historic houses owned by many generations of Nebraska families seeking relief from the Great Plains heat. Check out the cemetery by the little white frame church where many of the original settlers and Indians are buried. Peek into the old white frame library. The roads of the island are dusty and narrow. As you walk these quiet lanes, notice the hand-hewn log barns built by early farmers. The island has a sleepy feel. Enjoy an iced tea or a beer at one of the dockside restaurants and watch the ferry come across. You'll feel centuries of history here.

Lighthouses of the Apostle Islands

The largest intact collection of lighthouses in the country are on the Apostle Islands. The six Apostle Islands lighthouses are considered the finest collection of such structures in the country. Each is unique in appearance and history; several are pre-Civil War vintage. During the summer months, tours are available through the National Park Service at the 1901 **Devils Island Lighthouse**, the 1874 **Outer Island Lighthouse**, the 1863 **Raspberry Lighthouse**, the 1857 **Michigan Island Lighthouse** and the 1881 **Sand Island Lighthouse**. No formal tours are available at the 1858 **LaPointe Light** on Long Island, but volunteers at the site can answer questions. Contact the National Park Service at (715) 779-3397 for details.

Washburn

As in Bayfield, many buildings in Washburn were constructed of locally quarried brownstone. Highlights in Washburn include the restored 1890 **Washburn Bank** building on the main drag (Wis. Highway 13) in Washburn is now a cultural center and museum. (See our Attractions chapter for more information.) Washburn also has a 1904 **Carnegie Library** and a 1892 historic county courthouse built of brownstone. To view several Victorian mansions of note, simply get off of Wis. Highway 13 and drive around the residential areas.

Ashland

Don't miss Ashland's lively main street. It's still the working main drag and shopping district for the town — and it's an architectural delight. Listed on the National Register of Historic Districts, the six-block stretch, starting in the middle of town at Ellis Avenue and running east to Chapple Avenue, has a array of architectural styles, ranging from the handsome brownstone front of the former courthouse to the art deco working post office. This is a main street that still works for local people; there's a bakery, movie theater, several florists, a crafts center, secondhand shops, cafes, bars and clothing stores.

The mansion district in Ashland is on Chapple Avenue from U.S. Highway 2 to 11th Street just south of Main Street, starting with the **Wilmarth Museum**. The **Ashland Historical Society Museum** is housed in the 23-room Wilmarth Museum; exhibits tell the story of Ashland's first 100 years. Continue south on Chapple Avenue; quite a few of the privately owned Victorian homes here have been restored.

Ashland was once a thriving hub for railroads. Two train depots remain in Ashland, the 1889 **Soo Line Depot**, 400

Third Avenue W., (715) 682-4200, which houses two restaurants and a micro-brewery, and the 1884 **Chicago and Northwestern Depot**, which houses a health club.

You can start walking on Ashland's newly developed waterfront trail near the marina by the Hotel Chequamegon. Take a peek inside. Although a new building, the hotel's design, decor and spirit honor the memory of the original 1877 **Hotel Chequamegon**. If you walk east down the waterfront trail, you'll get a terrific view of the Soo Line ore dock. At 90 feet tall and 1,888 feet long, this concrete structure is one of the largest ore docks in the world. It was first built in 1916 and, in 1924, doubled in length to its current size. It was shut down in 1965.

Ironwood and Hurley

Ironwood, Michigan, was born as a result of the iron ore discovered in the Gogebic Range in 1872 and, at the end of the 19th century, played into wealth by steel magnate Andrew Carnegie. It's not a big town; you can drive up and down Aurora Street, the main drag, and see it all pretty quickly. We've chosen five historic buildings in Ironwood that came into being as a result of the mining and shipping industries. Sadly, a few of Ironwood's oldest buildings, the 1890 Davis & Fehr brownstone and the 1891 city hall, were recently demolished. But those that remain are noteworthy.

The 1893 Chicago and Northwestern Railway Depot, now called **Old Depot Park**, is between Lowell and Suffolk streets behind the post office. This building, listed on National Register of Historic Places, currently is home to the Ironwood Historical Society and a regional museum of mining and railroading ex-

hibits. The depot hosts band concerts, festivals and other events on the surrounding landscaped grounds. The depot is open daily Memorial Day to Labor Day from noon to 4 PM. Call (906) 932-0287 or 932-4142 for more information.

Ironwood is working diligently to save and restore some of its fine historic buildings. Most recently undergoing enlightened modernization efforts is the 1921 **Memorial Building** at the corner of McLeod and Marquette. It's a fine example of Second Renaissance Revival architecture. Built to honor the soldiers of World War I, the building houses city offices and courts, a swimming pool, gymnasium and auditorium. Wander through the elaborate foyer (notice the terrazzo) to the auditorium and inspect the mural paintings that depict the history of Gogebic County.

The **Ironwood Theater**, 111 E. Aurora Street, (906) 932-0618, also on the National Register of Historic Places, is the heart of cultural activities for the western Upper Peninsula. A dedicated group of volunteers has been working to restore the interior and exterior of the theater while promoting the it as a regional arts center. A year-round series of programs, including musical theater, classical music, movies, organ concerts and children's events are offered. Call for a schedule.

This 1928 vaudeville theater, built during the mining boom of the 1920s, was one of the first air-conditioned buildings in the country. Its elaborate interior is Venetian-style, with stunning restored murals, and features a Barton organ to accompany silent movies. On the building's exterior, the classic vertical neon-lighted marquee, canopy, stained glass and entry with bronze doors have been restored to their former elegance.

The original Renaissance-style theater seats, a style popular in 1920s and '30s vaudeville and movie palaces, have been reproduced. The Ironwood Theater seats also served as the model for reproductions for numerous theaters around the country, including the Lincoln Theater in Washington, D.C., and the City Center, home of the Joffrey Ballet, in New York City.

The **Curry House**, on the corner of Day Street and McLeod Avenue, is a private residence listed on the National Register of Historic Places. Originally built for Solomon Curry, a mining superintendent who helped build Ironwood, the house has been totally restored to its original condition by the present owners. The 18-room house features original stained-glass Tiffany windows, a ballroom and a wraparound porch.

The 1901 brownstone and brick **Carnegie Library**, 235 E. Aurora Avenue in downtown Ironwood, (906) 932-0203, was the first Carnegie Library built in Michigan. This well-loved, working library still uses its original circulation desk, chairs and tables. It was built from funds donated by philanthropist Andrew Carnegie, who, from 1881 to 1918, contributed $56 million to create some 2,800 libraries.

Hurley, Wisconsin, lies on the west side of the Montreal River across from Ironwood, Michigan. The town's been cleaned up a bit since its rabble-rousing days of saloons, brothels, bootlegging and general rowdiness. During the mining boom around the turn of the century, Hurley was a favorite spot for loggers, miners and unsavory characters to spend money. Nowadays, the historic saloons, called taverns in Wisconsin, welcome the snowmobile crowd in winter and the cabin crowd in summer.

To get a look at Hurley's wild past, take the historic walking tour of downtown that's offered in summer by the Hurley Chamber of Commerce, (715) 561-4334.

During Hurley's Heritage Festival in midsummer, the walking tour is augmented by costumed characters, including a miner's widow accepting a ham from the mining company as a death benefit for her late husband, the Silver Street Preservation Band playing ragtime and Dixieland, a period burlesque show and a raid on a bootlegger's joint.

Each of the saloons represents a different piece of history as you stroll from bar to bar. The **Iron Nugget** has mining paraphernalia; **Freddy's Old Time Saloon** and the **Iron Horse** have railroad history; the **Bank Club** has logging history; **Nora's Red Carpet Lounge** has the **Silver Street Preservation Band**; the **Mahogany Ridge** is a candy-store front for bootleggers; and the **Silver Dollar** is the former site of many a burlesque show.

Thunder Bay Area

Thunder Bay was originally two sister cities: Port Arthur on the north end and the older Fort William on the south end. They combined in 1970 to become Thunder Bay.

The name Thunder Bay is derived from centuries earlier when the local Native Americans called the area Animikii, which translates as "thunder." The first Europeans arrived in the 17th century, and the name was changed by the French-speaking explorers to Baie de Tonnerre, or Thunder Bay.

To get a sense of the early days of fur-trading activity, plan a full day to visit **Old Fort William**, Broadway Avenue, (807) 577-8461, the largest reconstruction of a fur-trade post in the world. Interpreters in the authentic costumes of craftsmen, voyageurs, farmers, Indians, soldiers and traders wander around the fort, playing

Photo: Duluth News-Tribune

The Aerial Lift Bridge is a main attraction in Duluth.

their parts in the daily life of the post as it was around 1815.

The fort offers a full calendar of events, including concerts, walking tours, living-history programs, banquets and arts and crafts fairs. Not to be missed are two traditional summer events: the **Great Rendezvous**, 10 days of festival entertainment on the second weekend in July, and the **Ojibwe Keeshigun**, a festival held in August to honor Old Fort William's Native American culture.

The fort is open daily from 10 AM to 5 PM from April to early October. Admission fees vary with the season; inquire about student and senior rates. Season passes are also available. Children younger than 6 are admitted free. Hours of operation and admission fees may change, so call the fort or Thunder Bay Tourism, (800) 667-8386, for specifics.

To get to Old Fort William, take Highway 61 south from Thunder Bay to Broadway Avenue. (The fort is southwest of Thunder Bay.) You can also write for information: Old Fort William, Vickers Heights Post Office, Thunder Bay, Ontario, Canada, POT 2ZO.

Thunder Bay's development, like Duluth's, changed significantly with the coming of the railroad in the 1870s and '80s. Thunder Bay became the chief port on Lake Superior, linking Canada's rich agricultural west with the rest of the world. By the early 1900s, Thunder Bay ranked as the world's No. 1 grain-handling port.

One of the few historic remaining depots in Thunder Bay is the 1906 **Canada National Railway Station** in Prince Arthur Landing Marina Park east of Cumberland Street. The former Northern Pacific depot now is home to a yacht club, the Long Tails Restaurant and a toy-train club. In the 1930s, an addition (which is quite apparent) was tacked onto the end of the depot. The good news is that the city has approved architectural plans to modify the addition to make it blend as much as possible with the original depot.

The small but lovely waterfront park near the depot has walking paths, a picnic area and playgrounds and represents the beginning of Thunder Bay's waterfront revitalization efforts. From here, you can view the dozens of gaily painted grain elevators that dominate the shoreline, defining the visual edge of the Thunder Bay harbor. Though many of the historic grain elevators have been razed, you can still find some — as well as historic railroad bridges — in old Fort William where the Kaministiquia River meets Lake Superior and splits into the McKellar and Mission rivers. A grain elevator resembling a medieval castle flanks the river at the end of Isabella Street. The bridge to Mission Island was considered an engineering feat 80 years ago.

The Local Architectural Conservation Advisory Committee (LACAC) in Thunder Bay is a citizen advisory group that works with the city council to protect landmark buildings through its Heritage designation program. The committee has put together two architectural walking-tour maps of Thunder Bay north (old Port Arthur) and Thunder Bay south (old Fort William). These tours includes contemporary architecture as well as historically significant buildings.

Much of Thunder Bay's truly interesting historic architecture is interspersed between unremarkable structures over a wide area, so expect a hearty walking tour — or take your car. You can pick up tour maps at the Thunder Bay City Hall, 500 Donald Street E., or the kiosk at the Thunder Bay Mall at the intersection of Trans-Canada Highway 11/17 and Ont. Highway 61.

The architectural walking tour maps are also available at the **Pagoda** between Cumberland Street and Red River Road near Prince Arthur Landing Marina Park and the Prince Arthur Hotel. This delightful octagonal structure, which looks like someone lopped off the top of a chubby Queen Anne Victorian tower and planted it near the harbor, was recently renovated. It opened in 1909 with pomp and circum-

stance and served as Port Arthur's publicity office and tourist information bureau. The open cupola was designed to accommodate a band to welcome visitors arriving by train or boat to the city. Today, it has resumed the role of tourist information center on its original site.

One of our favorite Thunder Bay neighborhoods is the old Finnish section, which encompasses a four-block area bordered by Bay and Algoma streets, just southwest of downtown old Port Arthur. The center of the neighborhood was and is the 1910 **Finnish Labour Temple** building, 314 Bay Street, now called the **Finlandia Club** or the **Hoito**. A locally designated Heritage building, the brick two-story structure, with a central tower over the front steps, is a distinctive landmark that still bustles with activity.

The last time we stopped by to eat Finnish pancakes at the basement-level **Hoito Restaurant** (see our Restaurants chapter), (807) 345-6323, the women of the club were holding a fashion show and bake sale on the main floor, while on the second floor the buzz of men's voices floated out from Finlandia Club bar. The building is a little tattered, but it stands as a reminder that the largest population of Finns outside of Finland — about 13,000 to 14,000 — live in Thunder Bay.

Walk around this neighborhood. There are dozens of shops and businesses, including Finnish restaurants, a Finnish bakery, delis and a grocery store or two, imported gifts and crafts shops and a landmark Finnish bookstore. Many of them occupy historic storefronts. When you're paying for your purchases, more than likely, you'll hear locals chatting in their mother tongue.

If you're interested in mansion-gawking in Thunder Bay, you definitely need to go by car. The mansions and Victorian houses — with carpenter's lace, towers and porches we like to admire — are scattered around town.

In the old Fort William area near Vickers Park on Selkirk Street and McGregor Avenue, you'll find a number of big homes, including the Heritage-designated Murphy house. Drive down Isabella Street toward the river to view more homes.

In old Port Arthur, drive up Algoma Street toward Boulevard Lake. Up on High Street near Hillcrest Park, there are some lovely old homes interspersed with newer houses; the same is true on Summit Avenue and Winnipeg Street. From High Street, take the Red River Road toward downtown; there are a few striking old houses along this route.

We suggest you get off the main drag and drive around the residential areas in the old parts of town. In the old Italian neighborhood below Hillcrest Park, there are some charming little Victorian houses tucked next to the hillside, which are rewarding discoveries to stumble upon. If you want enjoy the inside of a finely renovated and furnished turn-of-the-century mansion-turned-gourmet restaurant, we recommend lunch or dinner at **Harrington Court**, 170 N. Algoma Street, (807) 345-2600. (See our Restaurants chapter.)

If you're intrigued by tucked-away little villages, complete with legends and the ghosts of miners, it's worth the trip out of town to visit **Silver Islet**, a historic mining town nestled against the cliffs at the end of the Sibley Peninsula. Off shore about 2 miles from the town is the tiny rocky island Silver Islet — site of one of the richest veins of silver in Canada and a deserted mine shaft. This area was mined in the mid 1800s, with cribs built out into the water to extend the shores of the 90-foot-wide is-

land. Once a thriving mining town, Silver Islet is now a summer retreat comprised of cottages and cabins, built next to the cliffs along the lakeshore, without power or running water. (The last year-round resident has been gone for awhile.) Most of the log structures date from the 1850s. These were built using rare French log-construction techniques; some are marked with historic plaques. A tea room in the old general store is open in the summer months and is definitely worth a stop to learn more about this fascinating area. To get to Silver Islet, take Trans-Canada Highway 11/17 east from Thunder Bay for 25 miles. Turn south on Canada Highway 587 and follow it for approximately 20 miles through Sleeping Giant Provincial Park; the road ends at the Silver Islet dock.

RECOMMENDED REFERENCE

For an additional historical perspective on Thunder Bay's architecture, we recommend *Into the New Century: Thunder Bay 1900-1914*, published by the Thunder Bay Historical Museum Society. This book is filled with photographs of ships, trains and railroads, factories, harbors, schools, marching bands, drama clubs, sporting events, main streets, houses and disasters in early Fort William and Port Arthur — all from the museum's extensive collection. Photos were selected to give a sense of what life was like during this boom time.

Books on Silver Islet include Bill MacDonald's *Emanations* and *Further Emanations, Vol. II,* published by Porphry Press, and Elinor Barr's *Silver Islet: Striking It Rich in Lake Superior*, published by Mothersill Printing.

This **Season** it's the **Bay** to **Watch!**

In Thunder Bay, we do every season like nowhere else! Adjust the heat and max up the action - we've got endless days packed with fun for all ages no matter what the season. Time travel through Old Fort William, go shopping in little Finland, enjoy our fine dining, fairs, festivals and fantastic winter sports. It all takes place on the scenic shores of Lake Superior.
Watch us now! Thunder Bay is set to surprise you any time of the year!

Enjoy the best exchange rate in years.

Call toll free:
1-800-667-8386

Or write:
Tourism Thunder Bay
500 E. Donald St., 1st Floor
Thunder Bay, Ontario P7E5V3

TOURISM
Thunder Bay
Superior by Nature

Inside
Attractions

All right. We've made some decisions about including certain attractions in this chapter that might seem arbitrary choices. Sure, we've highlighted some genuine historical attractions such as Old Fort William in Thunder Bay, the *William A. Irvin* in Duluth, the Fairlawn Museum in Superior and significant natural attractions such as the Apostle Islands National Lakeshore near Bayfield. We've provided a bit more than the standard information about some of these places, based on our own experiences as well as conversations with others. Many of the attractions you'll read about in this chapter, especially ships, lighthouses and forts, are discussed in our Architecture and Historic Places chapter as well; check it out for additional perspectives.

Twin Ports Area

Duluth

SKYLINE PARKWAY

Called "The Boulevard" by old-timers, this 30-mile drive stretches from one end of Duluth to the other and offers stunning views of the city, the harbor and the Lake from 400 to 600 feet above Lake Superior. The parkway is marked by green trees painted on the asphalt and special signs, and granite and bluestone boulders flank its shoulders. Overlooks capture views of the city. The construction of Skyline Park-

way began in 1889, and it was first used by people in horse-drawn buggies. The drive was completed in 1939.

The eastern section of the parkway starts at the Seven Bridges Road. It's a narrow route that winds along Amity Creek and the Lester River, and the stone-arch bridges crossing these waters are a tight squeeze. Following the Seven Bridges Road from Superior Street brings you to Hawk Ridge, a nature preserve with a series of overlooks along the road where birders congregate every fall to watch thousands of hawks and eagles pass on their annual migration. (See the related sidebar in our Recreation chapter.) This section of the parkway is closed in the winter.

Skyline Parkway was originally designed to end in the Fond du Lac neighborhood in western Duluth near Jay Cooke State Park. The road and bridges still exist but are now used as the Mission Creek Hiking Trail. Skyline Parkway now terminates at Beck's Road near Gary/New Duluth, becoming a gravel road after Spirit Mountain and offering more spectacular views of the St. Louis River Valley.

NORTH SHORE SCENIC DRIVE

Unless you're in a big hurry to get up the North Shore, ignore the expressway to Two Harbors and opt for the North Shore Scenic Drive. Most people maintain the 55 mph speed limit or less on this serene two-lane road, which, at points, literally hugs the Lake. Skinny-tire cyclists love this route.

There are plenty of roomy waysides from which to view the Lake. And some of our favorite eateries — the Scenic Cafe and Emily's in Knife River, in particular — are along this route. The North Shore Scenic Drive begins at Brighton Beach on Minn. Highway 61 and continues for 26 miles to Two Harbors.

GLENSHEEN

3300 London Rd.   *(218) 724-8864*

Newcomers to Duluth are surprised by the quantity and quality of turn-of-the-century mansions here, many of them in eastern Duluth. The iron mining and logging industries helped transform Duluth into a prosperous city, and stately, sometimes grandiose, homes were built for the families who reaped the benefits of this new wealth.

Glensheen is one of the more outstanding residences from this period. Built for Chester Adgate Congdon and Clara Bannister Congdon in 1908, this 22-acre property resembles an early 17th-century English country estate. In addition to the 39-room Jacobean-style manor house, you'll find a carriage house, bowling green, boat house, clay tennis court, formal gardens and a gardener's cottage.

Although spacious, Glensheen doesn't have the drafty, formal feel typical of many mansions of similar scale. The rich, hand-carved woodwork throughout the house, the plush carpeting, the leaded-art glass windows and exquisite Arts & Crafts-influenced lighting fixtures create a warm ambiance. Many of the original paintings and custom-designed furnishings are still in place.

Glensheen was one of the first mansions to be built on the lakeshore. Prior to its construction, it wasn't considered fashionable to live "on the Lake," and most mansions were built up the hill.

Depending on your interest, time and budget, you can choose from several tour options to see Glensheen. The Living Museum Tour is self-guided and features University of Minnesota theater students and volunteers wearing period costumes and playing the roles of the butler, maid, housekeeper, maintenance man and friends of the Congdon family. You'll encounter these characters throughout the house, and they'll chat with you about life with the Congdon family. These Living Museum tours cost $8 for adults; $7 for kids ages 12 to 15 and seniors 62 and older; and $4 for children ages 6 to 11. A family rate of $25 covers parents or guardians and children 17 and younger.

Another option is the guided tour, led by a trained docent, which covers all areas of the house except the third floor and the attic. A self-guided tour of the carriage house and grounds follows. Admission is the same as for the Living Museum Tour.

If you like to snoop, make a reservation for the special tours of the third floor and attic. There you'll find the infirmary, the three boys' rooms, two guest rooms and beautiful paintings in the hallway. The attic is the storage area for the original Oriental rugs once found throughout the house

Call today for your 4 Season Adventure Guide
to North of Superior Tourism
1-800-265-3951
wwwnosta@lakeheadu.ca
1119 E. Victoria Ave., Thunder Bay, Ontario, Canada

— now stored to protect them from the wear and tear of the public. Glensheen is open year round. Admission is $10 for adults and $5 for children 11 and younger.

If you want to see the entire house from top to bottom, admission is $17 for adults; $16 for kids ages 7 to 17 and seniors 62 and older, and $8 for children 6 and younger. Or, wander the grounds and admire the extensive flower and vegetable gardens (Glensheen employs a full-time gardener and seasonal staff) for $4. Summer-season hours are 10 AM to 4 PM daily except Wednesday from May through June and September through October; 9 AM to 4 PM daily from July through August. Daily tours are offered in winter at 11 AM and noon weekdays except Wednesday and 11 AM through 2 PM weekends from November through December and in April; tours are offered 11 AM to 2 PM weekends only from January through February.

TWEED MUSEUM OF ART
University of Minnesota
10 University Dr. *(218) 726-8222*

The Tweed presents more than 40 exhibitions each year, hosting both contemporary and historical displays in five of its nine galleries. Its permanent collection includes works by 19th- and 20th-century American painters, with a recent focus on artists who have taught and produced art in Duluth. Prominent in the Tweed's European collection are the 19th-century French paintings of the Barbizon School and several old master works.

Museum hours are 9 AM to 8 PM Tuesday, 9 AM to 4:30 PM Wednesday through Friday and 1 to 5 PM Saturday and Sunday. The museum is closed on Monday.

The Tweed Museum is off Ordean Court at the end of Stadium Drive near the Jacques Lipchitz sculpture of Sieur du Lhut.

KARPELES MANUSCRIPT LIBRARY MUSEUM
902 E. First St. *(218) 728-0630*

Former Duluthian David Karpeles is a successful businessman who made his fortune in real estate. He has created seven Karpeles Manuscript Library Museums around the country that, in total, display one of the world's largest private collections of significant original documents, including letters, speeches and manuscripts from the fields of history, literature, science, art and music.

In the past year, the Karpeles Manuscript Library Museum has displayed letters written by Mark Twain discussing his book *Tom Sawyer*, correspondence from aviator Charles Lindberg, letters and notes by writer Rudyard Kipling and letters and documents from Louisa May Alcott, Dorothy Sayer, Susan B. Anthony and Elizabeth Barrett Browning. Drafts of important historical documents such as the *U.S. Bill of Rights*, the *Emancipation Proclamation*, Handel's *Messiah* and more have been displayed.

The museum is housed in the architecturally commanding former First Church of Christ Scientist building—built in 1912. The main room, with exhibits, is gently lighted by tall stained-glass windows and a magnificent domed ceiling. Classical music wafts through the exhibit area, creating a tranquil atmosphere. Admission is free. Summer hours are noon to 4 PM, seven days a week from Memorial Day to Labor Day; for the remainder of the year, the museum is open Tuesday through Sunday from noon to 4 PM. Call ahead to find out about the current exhibit.

CANAL PARK
AND DULUTH'S WATERFRONT
Canal Park Dr.

In another life, Canal Park was a gritty industrial area by day and a red-light district by night.

Today the brick warehouses, bordello and mattress factory are part of Duluth's renovated waterfront, housing restaurants, galleries, bookstores, shops and other businesses. You'll still find a strip joint and a few manufacturing businesses, but by and large Canal Park has been reincarnated.

The **Aerial Lift Bridge** anchors the Canal Park area, a reminder that Duluth is a working international port. The bridge rises to a full height of 138 feet in 55 seconds to allow the giant lake carriers (lakers) and

foreign ocean-going ships (salties) to enter and depart the harbor through the ship canal.

One of the best things to do in Duluth (and it's free) is to watch the ships come in. You can stand on the protected piers as the ships glide through the canal — less than 25 feet from where you stand. The gargantuan scale of these ships gives you a temporary perspective on your importance in the world.

Next to the Lift Bridge, the **Central Park Marine Museum**, (218) 727-2497, is one of the most visited museums in Minnesota. Exhibits focus on commercial shipping in Lake Superior and the Duluth-Superior Harbor and include intricate ship models and historic displays of Great Lakes shipping artifacts. Operated by the U.S. Army Corps of Engineers – Detroit District, the museum is open year round, and admission is free; just be sure to call ahead about seasonal hours. Even if the museum is closed, you can check the television screen next to the museum entrance for a current listing of ship arrivals and departures. The shipping season runs approximately from March through December.

After ship-watching on the piers, take a stroll on the **Lakewalk** to see more of the waterfront. It connects with the canal pier. The Lakewalk is to Duluth's waterfront what the boardwalk used to be to Atlantic City, New Jersey: a gathering place for people to take in the fresh air and admire the scenery. This award-winning, landscaped boardwalk and bike path winds 3 miles up the lakeshore from Canal Park to 26th Avenue E. The Lakewalk takes you by colorful murals, the **Northland Vietnam Veterans' Memorial**; the **Fitger's Brewery Complex**, which includes a hotel, restaurants and shops (see our Accommodations, Restaurants and Shopping chapters for details); and **Leif Erikson Park** and

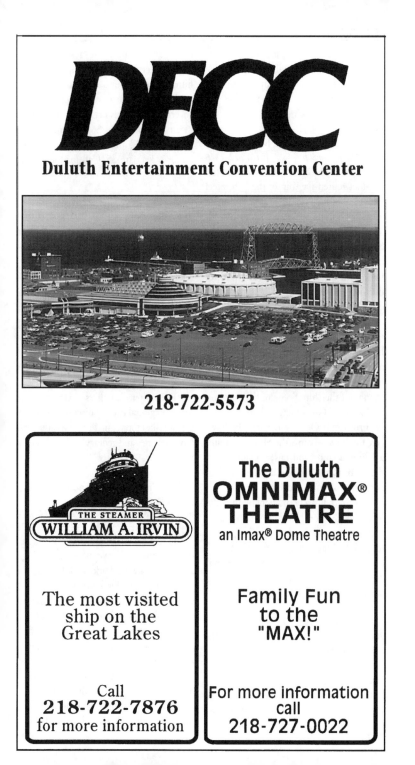

the **Rose Garden** (see our Parks and Forests chapter). Lakewalk also is a great place to view folks taking part in other recreational activities, such as windsurfing, sailboat racing and rowing.

SS WILLIAM A. IRVIN

In the Minnesota Slip   *(218) 722-7876*

A tour of the SS *William A. Irvin*, the 610-foot retired flagship of the U.S. Steel Great Lakes Fleet, is the next best thing to actually hopping aboard a laker in Duluth and heading down-bound through Lake Superior. Called the "Queen of the Lakes" by Capt. John J. McDonough, who piloted her for the last time in 1986, the *Irvin* retired after 40 years of carrying iron ore and coal.

A regular 60-minute tour takes you from bow to stern, with stops at the pilot house, lounges, staterooms, guest galley and dining room. A 90-minute hard-hat tour takes a more in-depth look at the mechanics of the ship. Some of the tours are led by retired Great Lakes sailors.

From mid-October through Halloween, the *Irvin* becomes the Ship of Ghouls, a haunted ship fund-raiser organized by the University of Minnesota Theater Department to benefit local food banks.

The *Irvin* has a permanent berth in the Minnesota Slip near the Duluth Entertainment Convention Center and is open for tours from May through October. Admission is $5 for adults and $3 for children ages 3 through 12; children 2 and younger are admitted free.

DULUTH OMNIMAX THEATRE

301 Harbor Dr.   *(218) 727-0022*

The new Omnimax Theatre, connected to the Duluth Entertainment Convention Center (DECC), is a 270-seat state-of-the-art facility that opened in April 1996. Omnimax films, 10 times larger than conventional movies, are projected on a large

dome and incorporate a sophisticated sound system. You don't simply watch the film; you're surrounded by it.

Films involve family-oriented topics covering natural history, travel and human history. Admission is $6 for adults and $4 for children 12 and younger; student and senior tickets are $5. Call for the current showing.

LAKE SUPERIOR CENTER

353 Harbor Dr.   *(218) 720-3033*

The Lake Superior Center's current, albeit temporary, facilities offer an introductory set of exhibits on the world's largest freshwater lakes: Lake Superior and Lake Baikal in Russia. A ground-breaking is planned for late 1996 on this site for a freshwater aquarium and environmental learning center.

The center is open 11 AM to 5 PM Wednesday through Sunday from May through Labor Day. Admission is free.

The center also offers a winter lecture series. Regional experts discuss a variety of Great Lakes topics, including weather systems, fisheries and geology. Call for a schedule.

THE VISTA FLEET HARBOR CRUISES

Harbor Dr.
Information   *(218) 722-6218*
Reservations   *(218) 722-1728*

To get a thumbnail sketch of Duluth on a summer's day, we suggest two things: Drive the Skyline Parkway following the length of the city for a bird's-eye view and take a cruise on the Vista Fleet for an intimate look at the goings-on in the harbor.

The Vista Fleet excursion service offers daily sightseeing cruises from mid-May to mid-October. The fully narrated cruise takes you under the Aerial Lift Bridge, along the shore and to the harbor for a close-up view of the grain elevators, ore docks and the lakers and salties loading

and unloading their cargo. There's also a lunch cruise, several variations of evening dinner cruises and late-evening moonlight cruises. Call for reservations and prices.

ST. LOUIS COUNTY
HERITAGE AND ARTS CENTER

506 W. Michigan St.   *(218) 727-8025*

Thank goodness local people rallied in the mid-1970s to save and restore the historic former Union Depot, an architectural treasure, from being demolished. Today's St. Louis County Heritage and Arts Center once was the main debarking point for the thousands of immigrants who settled and worked in northern Minnesota. Built in 1892 and currently listed on the National Register of Historic Places, the Depot, as it is commonly called, is considered to be one of the country's finest remaining examples of Châteauesque, French Norman-style architecture.

In its new role, the Depot is home to five performing arts organizations: the Minnesota Ballet, the Duluth Playhouse, the Duluth-Superior Symphony Orchestra, Matinee Musicale and the Arrowhead Chorale. It also houses three museums: the Duluth Children's Museum, the Lake Superior Museum of Transportation and the

St. Louis County Historical Society. The Duluth Art Institute, a visual arts organization, is also under the Depot's roof.

The **Duluth Art Institute**, (218) 733-7560, offers contemporary art exhibits by local, regional and international artists in the Theater Hall and Balcony galleries. Classes and workshops for photography, ceramics and mixed media arts are taught in the art studios.

Exhibits, events and programs at the **Duluth Children's Museum**, (218) 733-7543, are designed for children and families to celebrate world cultures as well as local cultures.

The **St. Louis County Historical Society**, (218) 733-7580, maintains an extensive collection of information and artifacts covering the region's immigrant and Native American heritage. Significant works in the collection are the Eastman Johnson paintings and drawings of the local Ojibwe people from the 1850s, Herman Melheim's fantastic hand-carved furniture and Tiffany stained-glass windows.

The **Lake Superior Museum of Transportation**, (218) 733-7590, draws train lovers from around the country. The museum is home to Minnesota's largest (60 pieces) and most varied collection of antique locomotives and railroad rolling stock. The dining car china exhibit includes china services with their distinctive logos from more than 20 different railroad lines.

Our favorite train in the collection is the 1913 Duluth & Northern Minnesota Railroad Locomotive No. 14, a former logging camp locomotive lovingly restored by a group of railroad fans in 1992. This classic locomotive, which looks like it came from the pages of *The Little Engine That Could*, starred in the 1993 movie *Iron Will*. During the summer, No. 14 is a working engine that chugs its way up the North Shore to Two Harbors. You can hear its distinctive whistle as it departs from the Depot and see its clouds of steam and gray smoke from miles away. Passenger rides are available in summer on Engine No. 14 along the North Shore Scenic Railroad line. Call the museum for departure times and ticket fees.

The depot is open 10 AM to 5 PM daily. Admission is $5 for adults, $3 for children ages 3 through 11; families — parents and children 11 and younger — are $15. The general admission fee includes access to the three museums and exhibits at the Duluth Art Institute.

Lake Superior Zoological Gardens
Grand Ave. and 72nd Ave. W. (218) 723-3747

The huge polar bears are the big draw here. You can watch them swimming underwater; occasionally, they'll bang against the viewing wall, causing crowds to shriek and scatter. The bears are part of the Polar Shores exhibit that also feature penguins, harbor seals and other Arctic animals.

Another big attraction is the Children's Zoo, where kids can touch and hold animals, and the Animal Interaction Area (remember petting zoos?) where kids can walk among pygmy goats, Vietnamese pot-bellied pigs and sheep. There's also an Australian Outback exhibit with kangaroos, a

nocturnal creatures exhibit and an Asian exhibit with Siberian tigers and snow leopards.

From April 1 to October 31, the zoo is open from 9 AM to 6 PM. Admission is $4 for adults and $2 for children ages 4 to 11; children ages 3 and younger are free. From November 1 to March 31, hours are from 10 AM to 4 PM. Admission is $2 for adults; $1 for children ages 4 to 11; and children ages 3 and younger are free.

Foster Aviation
Sky Harbor Airport
5000 Minnesota Ave.　　　　(218) 722-6410

Take a bird's-eye look at Duluth's harbor (including the downtown skyline and Aerial Lift Bridge) and Lake Superior from a single-engine airplane. The 20-minute scenic flights offered here cost $20 per person and are available year round, weather permitting. Call for tour schedules and to reserve a seat.

Tom's Logging Camp
5797 North Shore Dr.
Duluth, Minn.　　　　(218) 525-4120

Tom's Logging Camp, a tourist fixture for nearly 40 years, is 10 miles northeast of Duluth on Scenic Highway 61. You'll notice the larger-than-life fiberglass horses pulling an antique logging wagon near the entrance. Don't expect Paul Bunyan to greet you here, but do expect a delightful tour of a replica logging camp: a harness shop with a shoeing stall, a barn, a blacksmith's shed, a bunk house and a cook's shack. Historical photos of life in the camp and many authentic tools, hardware and other items fill the buildings. Mannequins dressed like lumbermen fill the bunk beds and sit at the dining room tables. Kids are always impressed by the huge, gnarled hands on the dummies.

there's a gift shop filled with Minnetonka moccasins, Wisconsin cedar

boxes, pottery, jewelry, original hand-carved oak mirrors, jellies, syrups, wild rice and T-shirts, sweatshirts, belts and more.

A circle trail takes you through the logging camp past deer, goats and rainbow trout in a pond and a North Shore and Lake Superior fishing museum with commercial fishing equipment, including a skiff, gear, netwinders, motors and a large, specially designed boat used in Lake Superior by a Norwegian commercial fisherman.

Admission to tour the camp and museum is $2 for adults and $1 for children ages 6 through 15; kids 5 and younger are free. Tom's Logging Camp is open 8 AM to 8 PM daily from May 1 through the first weekend in October.

Superior

BARKERS ISLAND
Marina Dr.   *(715) 392-7131*

Barkers Island is the focal point for Superior's waterfront on Superior Bay. It bustles in the summer with sailboats, windsurfers, motorboats and big ship traffic; in the winter, snowmobile races are held on the ice. This man-made island has walking paths, a children's playground, a full-

service 420-slip marina, a hotel, restaurant and shops. At the west end of the island is the SS *Meteor* Maritime Museum.

SS METEOR AND THE GALLIARD
Whaleback Wharf at Barkers Island
U.S. Hwys. 2 and 53   *(715) 392-5742*

The SS *Meteor* is the sole remaining whaleback ship in the world. Affectionately called "pigboats" because of their snout-like bow and awkward silhouette, 43 of these oddly shaped ships were built in Superior in an attempt to improve on Great Lakes ship design. The SS *Meteor* was the last one built (in 1896) and is now listed on the National Register of Historic Sites. Next to the SS *Meteor* is the *Galliard*, the last steam-powered dredge on the Great Lakes, now preserved in this waterfront collection.

Touring the SS *Meteor* is a worthwhile experience — although we feel the ship's dignity is somewhat insulted by its resting place on a bed of cement adjacent to a miniature golf course, a string of souvenir shops and a hot dog stand.

Guided tours of the SS *Meteor's* operational sections are available daily from 10 AM to 5 PM from mid-May to the end of September and 10 AM to 5 PM on weekends for the first two weeks in October.

Admission is $5 for adults, $4 for students and seniors and $15 for families.

FAIRLAWN MANSION AND MUSEUM
U.S. Hwys. 2 and 53   *(715) 394-5712*

Stand on Duluth's Park Point and look south across the bay to Superior. The distinctive four-story Victorian tower of the Fairlawn Mansion will immediately catch your eye. This 42-room mansion was built in 1890 on the city's waterfront for lumber and mining baron Martin Thayer Pattison and his wife, Grace Emma Pattison. Today it's a museum housing the collections of the Douglas County Historical Society, with permanent and touring exhibits on the second and third floors. All of the rooms on the main floor are restored and decorated with turn-of-century Victorian furnishings.

Fairlawn is a lively community space, hosting concerts, literary events, lectures, an ice cream social in the summer and a murder mystery evening on Halloween. It's open daily from 9 AM to 5 PM. Admission is $5 for adults; $4 for seniors and students; $3 for children ages 6 through 12; and free for children 5 and younger.

THE OLD FIRE HOUSE
AND POLICE MUSEUM
U.S. Hwys. 2 and 53 and
23rd Ave. E.   *(715) 398-7558*

This 1898 brick hall is the last of Superior's old fire houses. Known as the East End Fire Hall, it now houses a museum collection of fire-fighting and po-

lice memorabilia, including a restored horse-drawn 1906 steam pumper, a restored 1929 Model-A Ford fire truck and a 1944 "Old Mack" pumper truck. Tours are available from 10 AM to 5 PM daily from June through August. A $3 general admission fee is charged.

Along the North Shore

THE DEPOT MUSEUM
Depot Building, 520 South Ave.
Two Harbors, Minn.   *(218) 834-4898*

Housed in the 1907 headquarters of the Duluth & Iron Range Railroad, this museum's collection highlights the history of Lake County: from the geology of the area to the first shipment of iron ore from Minnesota and the logging companies from the turn of the century. Outside, under the shelter of the Depot's train shed, are several historic railroad locomotives, the *Malley* and *Three-Spot*.

Admission to the Depot Museum is $2 for adults; $1 for children ages 9 through 17; and children 8 and younger are free. It's open daily from late April through October and on weekends during the winter months. Hours are 9 AM to 6 PM (or later, depending on business) from Memorial Day through mid-October (summer season) and 9 AM to 4 PM in winter. The depot museum is open year round, but be sure to call ahead in winter.

Insiders' Tips

Ever wonder if there's a relationship between the 22 Apostle Islands and Jesus Christ's 12 Apostles? As the story goes, early European settlers incorrectly counted only 12 islands and named them accordingly. (Of course, the Ojibwe people who lived here for hundreds of years already had names for the islands.)

"Show me your garden, and I shall tell you what you are."

— Alfred Austin

Do you enjoy walking through formal gardens or studying somebody's sidewalk perennial plot?

We do.

Duluth calls itself the "Garden City of the North" and employs a head city gardener to maintain this distinction. For public gardens in Duluth, check out **Enger Tower** on Skyline Parkway and the **Rose Garden** on 12th Avenue E. and London Road. The flower and vegetable gardens at the historic, 22-acre **Glensheen** estate, 3300 London Road,

Photo: Duluth News-Tribune

Duluth's Rose Garden is located near the Lakewalk.

are worth the $4 grounds pass to stroll through. The Park Point Garden Club is known for its community effort along **Minnesota Avenue**.

Many people grow their own fruits and vegetables for fresh eating, canning and preserves. The vegetable and flower gardens in eastern Duluth's Lakeside and Lester Park neighborhoods and in Gary-New Duluth are attractions all their own in these residential areas.

In Thunder Bay, visit the **International Friendship Gardens** at Victoria Avenue between Tarbutt and Waterloo streets, featuring 18 sections by different countries; the free **Centennial Conservatory** on Dease Street off Balmoral Avenue, with its tropical house and changing displays; and the formal sunken gardens at **Hillcrest Park** on High Street, with great views of the harbor.

Bayfield, on Wisconsin's South Shore, is known for its protected microclimate, and family-run orchards just outside of town grow lush fruits and berries. Check out the perennial bed by the stop sign at the intersection of Sixth Street and Rittenhouse Avenue, then drive around the neighborhoods of Bayfield to view the delightful gardens that decorate many of the historic homes. A few of the Bayfield orchards grow and sell hardy perennials and dried flowers, including Hauser's Superior View Farm on County Road J, Good Earth Gardens on County Road J and the Blue Vista Farm on Fish Hatchery Road.

THE EDNA G.

Agate Bay, Paul Van Hoven Park
Waterfront Dr.
Two Harbors, Minn.   **No phone**

After strolling through the Depot Museum (see preceding listing), walk down to the waterfront for a guided tour of this historic 1896 tugboat. She's the last remaining coal-fed, steam-powered tugboat on the Great Lakes — retired in 1981 and recently refurbished at the Fraser Shipyards in Superior. While you're admiring the *Edna G.*, lakers may be loading and unloading at the ore docks just beyond the tug.

LIGHTHOUSE POINT
AND HARBOR MUSEUM

Lighthouse Point   **(218) 834-4898**

You can follow the quarter-mile path to Lighthouse Point and Harbor Museum or you can drive; ample parking is available. The museum is housed in the Agate Bay Lighthouse Station (built in 1892), and guided tours of the working light tower and the restored assistant keeper's house are offered.

Lighthouse Point tours are $2.50 for adults and $1 for children ages 9 to 17; children 8 and younger are free. The museum is open daily from late April through October and on weekends during the winter months. The lighthouse is open for guided tours 9 AM to 5 PM from Memorial Day through mid-October.

SPLIT ROCK LIGHTHOUSE

Minn. Hwy. 61
South of Beaver Bay, Minn.   **(218) 226-6372**

Recently featured on a U.S. postage stamp, the 1910 Split Rock Lighthouse is one of Minnesota's most-loved landmarks on the North Shore. It became part of the Minnesota park system in 1971 and since has been restored by the Minnesota Historical Society to its pre-1924 appearance. One of the keeper houses has also been restored. You'll find Split Rock Lighthouse and the History Center within Split Rock lighthouse State Park.

The lighthouse and grounds are open from May 15 through October 15 from 9 AM to 5 PM daily. In the winter, only the History Center is open (October 16 to May 14) Friday, Saturday and Sunday from noon to 4 PM except in December when it's closed. Summer admission is $4 for adults, $3 for seniors and $2 for children ages 6 to 15; children 5 and younger are free. During the winter, admission is free, but you must purchase a state park sticker ($4 daily).

THE NORTH SHORE FISHING MUSEUM

Minn. Hwy. 61
Tofte, Minn.   **(218) 663-7804**

The North Shore Fishing Museum, scheduled to open as this book goes to press, honors the stories of the Scandinavian immigrants who settled the North Shore and made a sometimes harsh living by fishing the big Lake. The village of Tofte itself is named after a village in Norway. Descendants of many of the area's original settlers still live nearby. On display, you'll find an original Mackinaw sailboat used for fishing Lake Superior, net winders, splitting

Two of Sinclair Lewis' novels — *Babbitt* and *Kingsblood Royal* — are believed to have been inspired by his sojourn in Duluth where he lived in the early 1940s. Since they're both scathing commentaries on small-mindedness (the first relating to status-seeking and the second to racism), Duluth has never attempted to claim them.

Insiders' Tips

Photo: Duluth News-Tribune

Polar bears are a big draw at the Lake Superior Zoological Gardens in Duluth.

tables to clean fish, shipping boxes and other commercial fishing artifacts.

The museum will be open daily year round; hours will vary, so call first. A nominal admission fee is expected.

LUTSEN RESORT

Minn. Hwy. 61	(218) 663-7212
Lutsen, Minn.	(800) 258-8736

Established in 1898, the famous Lutsen Resort was the first resort in Minnesota. It's tucked down on the shore of the Lake amid fine pebble beaches next to the Poplar River. Lutsen is worth a stop to admire the award-winning Swedish-style structure, built in 1953 after a fire destroyed the previous lodge.

The site was originally a home and fish and logging camp for the Nelson family, the resort's founders. Resourceful Swedish immigrants as they were, the late George Nelson Sr. and his brother Oscar logged and milled the lumber used to build the current lodge. Its design, reminiscent of Scandinavian homes — sporting a dark red painted exterior with white trim, detailed gabled windows and fanciful wood carvings — was designed by noted Twin Cities architect Edwin Lundie.

Go inside to admire the huge stone fire-place in the lobby, the hand-hewn logs and the low-ceilinged, cozy dining room with views of the Lake. People at Lutsen treasure the lodge and don't mind sightseers. Newspaper clippings about the history of the place are displayed near the lobby. We like to stop here to enjoy views of the Lake and to grab a bite to eat; the pie of the day is posted on a sign hung along Minn. Highway 61, and the fresh pan-fried herring — a mild-tasting native Lake Superior fish — makes a delicious sandwich.

LAKE REGION AVIATION INC.

Two Harbors Airport	(218) 834-2162
Two Harbors, Minn.	(800) 955-3900

Take a 15-minute spin for $20 per person over the Agate and Burlington bays and watch the ships loading at the ore docks. Or, gaze downward at Gooseberry Falls, Split Rock Lighthouse and the ore docks during a 45-minute trip ($45 per person). The Duluth Harbor Trip (50 to 55 minutes) costs $55 and features the Aerial Lift Bridge, the downtown skyline and Hawk Ridge. Or, for $75 per person, take a 70-minute aero-tour that combines attractions from the Duluth Harbor Trip with the ore docks, Agate Bay Light, Gooseberry Falls and Split Rock Lighthouse.

Trips in a single-engine aircraft are available seven days a week year round — weather permitting, of course. Reservations are recommended, but walk-ins are welcome. General daily hours are 8 AM to 6 PM, but call in advance to make sure tours are running that day.

NANIBOUJOU LODGE
Minn. Hwy. 61
North of Grand Marais, Minn. (218) 387-2688

A stone's throw from the mouth of the Brule River, Naniboujou is a handsome historic lodge with a glamorous past. It's renowned fine restaurant in the spacious central dining room is warmed by the original designs of brightly colored, Cree Indian-influenced designs on the walls and ceiling, and stone fireplaces. Naniboujou was originally a private club during Prohibition and hosted celebrities including baseball star Babe Ruth, boxer Jack Dempsey and writer Ring Lardner. The lodge is named for the legendary Ojibwe "first man," a trickster who in other regional dialects is known as Maniboujou and Wainiboujou.

Naniboujou Lodge is 14 miles north of Grand Marais on the National Lakeshore.

SAWTOOTH AIR
Cock City Airport
Devil's Track Lake   *(218) 387-2721*
Grand Marais, Minn.   *(218) 307-2008*

How about an aerial view of the North Shore? Scenic rides along the Lake or into the Boundary Waters Canoe Area Wilderness cost $25 per person for a 20-minute ride, either by wheel plane or sea plane.

GRAND PORTAGE
NATIONAL MONUMENT
Off Minn. Hwy. 61
Grand Portage Reservation
Grand Portage, Minn.   *(218) 475-2202*

Grand Portage is a reconstructed, late 1700s fur-trading post and stockade. A base for the North West Company from 1784 to 1803, the palisade surrounds the Great Hall — site of the Rendezvous, an annual company celebration — a canoe warehouse, fur press, kitchen and lookout tower.

Start with the exhibits and audiovisual presentation in the Great Hall to get a sense of place. Then wander around and drink in the atmosphere. The Grand Portage Ojibwe band donated the land for the monument in 1958.

Grand Portage National Monument is 7 miles south of the United States-Canada border. The park entrance is a mile from Minn. Highway 61.

The historic buildings are open from mid-May to mid-October. Hours are 8 AM to 5 PM daily. A admission fee is charged: $2 for adults and $5 for families; but seniors and children 16 and younger get in free.

MOUNT ROSE TRAIL AND OVERLOOK
Grand Portage National Monument
Off Minn. Hwy. 61
Grand Portage Reservation
Grand Portage, Minn.   *(218) 475-2202*

The Mount Rose Trail is a half-mile climb upward 300 feet via a series of steps and a paved walkway to the summit of Mount Rose. The round-trip hike takes about an hour. A trail map and natural features guide is available from the National Park Service at the monument. The view of Grand Portage Bay features Hat Point, Grand Portage Island and Raspberry Point.

Along the South Shore

APOSTLE ISLAND NATIONAL
LAKESHORE VISITOR CENTER
415 Washington Ave.
Bayfield, Wis.   *(715) 779-3397*

This visitors center is housed in an old brownstone county courthouse where you

The Haunted and Holiday Ships of Lake Superior

The laker *William A. Irvin*, and the SS *Meteor* whaleback, Duluth's and Superior's two historic ships become haunted ships during the Halloween season. The University of Minnesota Theater Department takes over the *Irvin* and treats it like a giant set for a horror movie. It's first-rate scary — even for adults. The Superior Jaycees haunt the SS *Meteor* with similar effect. (Families with young children are advised to come to the toned-down daytime tours.) Ticket sales benefit local charities.

For the December holidays, some of the working ships decorate their bows with lights and Christmas trees, and the grain and cement elevators in Duluth and Superior glow with festive lights. Look for the Christmas tree at the top of the Harvest States grain elevator in Superior and watch the ship listings in the *Duluth News-Tribune* for the upbound *Charles M. Beeghley*, a laker that usually has a lit Christmas tree on its bow, and the *Adam E. Cornelius*, with lights in the shape of a Christmas tree on its pilot house.

Photo: Duluth News-Tribune

A haunted gorilla head with artificial steam is part of the decorations that would turn the William A. Irvin *into a haunted ship this year for the Halloween feature "600 feet of terror."*

can learn about the history of the Apostle Islands through exhibits and a film. A lecture series is offered in the summer as well. Pick up camping permits, park information and nautical maps for the islands here.

The center is open year round, but hours and days vary depending on the season. From November 1 to Memorial Day the Center is open Monday through Friday from 8 AM to 4:30 PM; Memorial Day through Labor Day, 8 AM to 6 PM seven days a week; and Labor Day to mid-October, 8 AM to 5 PM daily.

LITTLE SAND BAY VISITOR CENTER
Apostle Island National Lakeshore
County Rd. K, Little Sand Bay, Wis.
Visitor Center (715) 779-7007
Western District Ranger Office (715) 779-3459

Little Sand Bay Visitor Center, west of Bayfield, is at the official entry point to the Apostle Islands National Lakeshore. Lakeshore exhibits, park information and camping permits are available here. Little Sand Bay is a primary launch site for sea kayakers, and you'll find a great sand beach and a small municipal campground here.

In the summer from Memorial Day to Labor Day, the center is open daily from 9 AM to 5 PM. After Labor Day until September 30, the center is open from 9 AM to 5 PM Wednesday through Sunday.

Take Wis. Highway 13 west for 5 miles from Bayfield to County Road K. Turn north and drive 13 miles to Little Sand Bay.

LIGHTHOUSES OF THE APOSTLE ISLANDS

The Apostle Islands are the site of the largest intact collection of lighthouses in the country, some of them dating to before the Civil War. Tours are available through the National Park Service at the **Devils Island Lighthouse** (erected in 1901), the **Outer Island Lighthouse** (1874), the **Raspberry Lighthouse** (1863), the **Michigan Island Lighthouse** (1857) and the **Sand Island Lighthouse** (1881). Nok formal hours are available at **La Pointe Light** (1858) on Long Island, but volunteers on site can answer questions. Contact the National Park Service at (715) 779-3397 for tour details.

MADELINE ISLAND

Madeline Island, the largest of the Apostle Islands, lies just offshore from the northeastern tip of the Bayfield Peninsula. It's a 20-minute ferry ride from Bayfield to this history-steeped island and the town of LaPointe. Madeline Island is home to about 180 year-round residents.

The westernmost spiritual center of the Ojibwe Indians, following their great migration from the East Coast, "Moningwunakauning" ("place of the golden-breasted woodpecker") remains the site of yearly Ojibwe ceremonies; its easternmost end is owned by the Bad River band.

The island became an important center for the fur trade in the 17th century; later, logging and fishing dominated the island. By the early 20th century, the island began its transformation to its present role as a summer destination and resort community. **Nebraska Row**, a street of historic summer homes, was established by well-to-do Nebraskans seeking to escape the summer heat of the plains.

The **Madeline Island Historical Museum**, operated by the State Historical Society of Wisconsin, (715) 747-2415, has extensive collections and displays of artifacts and memorabilia that illustrate three centuries of the island's colorful history.

The museum is one block east of the ferry landing. It's open 10 AM to 4 PM from late May to early October. Admission is $3 for adults, $2.70 for seniors and $1.25 for children 6 and older.

Insiders' Tips

While some locals call them "flying rats," and mutter, "it's like that Alfred Hitchcock movie *The Birds*," glossy tourist literature suggests you "sit back and enjoy the beautiful gulls" in Canal Park. We advise that you check your seat first. Like the hand-fed pigeons in New Orleans' French Quarter, these aggressive, french fry-seeking gulls can be obnoxious to the point that one Duluth city council member attempted to pass an ordinance making it illegal to feed them.

IRONWOOD THEATRE
111 E. Aurora St.
Ironwood, Mich.   (906) 932-0618

The Ironwood Theatre, an elegant 1920s vaudeville house, has been restored to its former grandeur. It presents a summer program of theater, concerts and classic movies. Past performers include the Duluth-Superior Symphony, the Guy Lombardo Orchestra and the Minneapolis Gospel Sound. Ironwood Theatre is home to professional and community stage productions.

Thunder Bay Area

OLD FORT WILLIAM
Broadway Ave.   (807) 577-8461

Old Fort William is one of Thunder Bay's most distinctive attractions, featuring the world's largest reconstructed fur trading post. Forty-two historic buildings sprawl in the curve of an oxbow near the Kaministiquia River on 10 acres, including a huge wharf and canoe landing, working farm and Native American encampment. The fort recreates the peak years of the fur-trade era, around 1815, when the North West Company gathered tons of beaver, fox and otter pelts from the Canadian wilderness for sale in the European market.

Much of the history of the fort is presented in the visitors center, called "Rendezvous Place," with a multimedia video exhibit and huge murals. Costumed interpreters are stationed around the fort, demonstrating every aspect of daily life during the fur-trading days. Craftsmen, voyageurs, farmers, Native Americans, businessmen and military officers play their respective roles in the fur-trade business as you wander around.

Special events are offered throughout the season to focus attention on particular

Photo: Duluth News-Tribune

The Squaw Bay ice caves draw admirers to Wisconsin's South Shore.

aspects of the fur trade, including the annual Great Rendezvous, 10 days of festival entertainment on the second weekend in July, and Ojibwe Keeshigun, an August weekend honoring Old Fort William's Native American culture. (See our Annual Events chapters for more information.)

McGillivray's Landing and the Cantine, both on-site informal eateries, serve food catered by the award-winning Airlane Hotel. At McGillivray's Landing offers sandwiches and light lunches indoors and out (weather permitting). The Cantine features 1830s-inspired cooking — stews, soups, biscuits and homemade bread — served cafeteria style. The servers and cooks wear period costumes.

For information on fees and event schedules, call the fort or Thunder Bay Tourism toll-free at (800) 667-8386. To get to Old Fort William, take Ont. Highway 61 south to Broadway Avenue. The

Rock Me on the Water

Peek inside any cabin near Lake Superior, and we bet you'll see a favorite Lake Superior rock or two sitting on a window ledge or piled in a jar or basket. You don't have to be an official rock hound to enjoy Lake Superior's geology.

The stone and pebble beaches, many of them found at the mouths of rivers from Duluth up the North Shore are known for their wonderful striped agates and wave-smoothed bluestone and granite. Try your luck at **Knife River**, **Flood Bay**, **Gooseberry River** and the **Baptism River**.

Some people scour the shores looking for beach glass — small, smooth pieces of blue, green, white, brown and clear bottles and jars worn down by the water and abrasive sediment. Duluth's **Park Point** is a good place to look for these simple treasures. (We toss half-done pieces back in the Lake for another smoothing cycle.)

Thomsonite is a North Shore gemstone, characterized by its "eyes" surrounded by bands of red and green. Stop by the **Thomsonite Beach Resort**, near Lutsen, Minnesota, on Minn. Highway 61, (218) 387-1832, to visit with jeweler Tania Feigal who mines and polishes rough Thomsonite, then crafts the gemstone into exquisitely designed pieces.

Thunder Bay is known for its amethyst gemstone. This dark-purple crystallized quartz is Ontario's official mineral. It's mined near Thunder Bay at a number of sites where you can pick out your own rocks or purchase them as jewelry from gift shops.

The **Thunder Bay Mine Panorama**, 35 miles northeast of Thunder Bay off Trans-Canada Highway 11/17 on E. Loon Road, is the oldest and largest mine in the area. Tours take place four times daily; there's also a gift shop. The **Ontario Gem Mining Company** is 45 miles east of Thunder Bay on Highway 11/17, then 2 miles south on Dorion Amethyst Mine Road. The **Pearl Lake Amethyst Mines** have pick-your-own sites, a picnic area, scenic lookout and a gift shop. To reach Pearl Lake, drive 40 miles east of Thunder Bay on Highway 11/17 to Pearl, then head 2 miles north on Number 5 Road and turn on the Pearl Lake Amethyst Mine Road.

Photo: Duluth News-Tribune

Many treasures await rock collectors and beach combers on Lake Superior's shores.

fort is southwest of Thunder Bay. It's open daily 10 AM to 5 PM from mid-May through mid-October.

THE TERRY FOX MONUMENT
Trans-Canada Hwy. 11/17
A half-mile east of Hodder Ave.

The late Terry Fox was the courageous Canadian man who attempted to run across Canada to raise money for cancer research, after losing one of his legs to the disease. He made it halfway across the country but was forced to stop, ending his journey very close to this spot. The nine-foot-tall bronze statue of Fox rests on a 45-ton granite base with a foundation of local amethyst. You'll also find a new visitor information center here. This is a fine spot to take in the top-notch views of the Sleeping Giant rock formation.

THE SLEEPING GIANT
AND MOUNT MCKAY

The city of Thunder Bay is set on a natural harbor of Lake Superior, with the Sleeping Giant dominating the view to the northeast and Mount McKay protecting it to the south, rising more than 1,000 feet above the city.

Both stunning rock formations have their own legends to explain their presence. The Sleeping Giant is the Ojibwe Indian spirit Nanabijou who turned to stone when the secret of the silver mines at the point of the Sibley Peninsula was discovered by white men. Some of the best viewing spots are Hillcrest Park on High Street and the Prince Arthur Park and Marina in downtown Thunder Bay. The Sleeping Giant is part of the Sleeping Giant Provincial Park

where you can hike to the rock formation. Purchase of a provincial park day pass ($7) is required.

Mount McKay, originally called Thunder Mountain, is sacred ground to the Ojibwe people. The mountain is believed to be the breeding grounds and nesting area for Anikem, the Thunderbird. The Mount McKay scenic lookout is at 500 feet and features a snack bar, picnic tables and an easy hiking trail to the mountain top. Take Ont. Highway 61B south across the Kam Bridge, turn left and follow the signs through the reservation. A nominal fee is charged to access the lookout point.

THUNDER BAY FLYING CLUB
Ont. Hwy. 61 and Neebing Ave.
Thunder Bay, Ont. **(807) 577-1118**

Sure, you can hike the Sleeping Giant. But why not fly over it instead? Thunder Bay Flying Club provides charters, sightseeing flights and flying lessons. Charters cost $138 (Canadian) per hour. Half-hour sightseeing tours in a four-seat, single-engine plane cost $45 per person.

KAKABEKA FALLS
Trans-Canada Hwy. 11/17
18 miles west of Thunder Bay

Kakabeka Falls in Kakabeka Provincial Park are a big tourist draw in Thunder Bay. The falls are a short drive from town and are easily accessible. Boardwalks and viewing platforms flank both sides of the mist-filled gorge where the falls drops 28 feet into the Kaministiquia River, which feeds Lake Superior. (Check the Waterfalls chapter for more details.)

Kids love Park Point's beach, with its fine, creamy-white sand, rolling dunes covered with native grasses and wild roses and constantly changing shoreline decorated with driftwood, agates and smooth skipping stones.

Inside
Kidstuff

Whatever happened to making your own fun? Well, for better or worse, most kids nowadays, particularly those age 5 and older, expect to be entertained with bells and whistles. The port cities and towns of Lake Superior have a lot of kid-oriented goings-on, ranging from zoos and children's museums to special events and festivals to elaborate outdoor playgrounds. And many seemingly timeless attractions and activities, such as old trains, big boats, rock-skipping, picnics and beach-walking, continue to hold their own, engaging children of all ages as they have for decades. Tourism development on the North and South shores has (so far) avoided theme parks and kid-sucking attractions like Mystery Spots and giant water slides.

Public libraries (see this chapter's sidebar), resources rich in children's books and programs, can be found in most of the small towns along the North and South shores, thanks in good part to the turn-of-the-century philanthropy of steel magnate Andrew Carnegie. Carnegie provided money to build libraries. Between 1881 and 1918, he contributed $56 million to create some 2,800 libraries in the United States. Duluth, Superior and Thunder Bay have large libraries. In fact, Duluth's library system, which includes a main library and three branches, is considered one of the finest of its size in the country.

In this chapter, we've considered two criteria that affect what kids and parents

do: weather and money. We've provided an assortment of indoor and outdoor activities, and many of the latter are free for the taking. For the indoor activities, we've tried to provide a range of things to do at different costs. Don't forget to check the Annual Events, Parks and Forests, and Attractions chapters for more kid-oriented ideas and details.

Twin Ports Area

The Twin Ports are replete with things for kids to do, both indoors and out. You'll find some great kid-oriented museums and activities as well as plenty of parks and beaches to satisfy any young person's urge to run and play.

Duluth

The Depot, 506 W. Michigan Street, (218) 727-8025, is home to a number of wonderful, kid-oriented arts and cultural activities and, as such, is a popular place for families. One entry fee for adults and one for children cover admission to all of the participating organizations' current exhibits. Officially named the St. Louis County Heritage and Arts Center, it's home to nine nonprofit arts and cultural organizations, including the Duluth Children's Museum, the Lake Superior Museum of Transportation and the St. Louis County Historical Society.

The **Duluth Children's Museum**,

Public Libraries for the Kids

Libraries are treasure houses for kids. Many parents enjoy regular visits with their kids to the local library, and we heartily endorse establishing this kind of family tradition.

We've included a smattering of libraries — main locations and branches where applicable. Please call for specific hours, as they vary daily, seasonally and by location.

Happy reading!

Illustration: Courtesy Bayfield Heritage Assoc.

Twin Ports Area

The main **Duluth Public Library**, 520 W. Superior Street, is designed to look like a Great Lakes ore carrier. Nooks and crannies abound, and the second-story windows overlook the harbor. There's a substantial children's book section, complete with computers, games, puppets and other learning toys, and an indoor play area for little ones; call (218) 723-3818 for information. Amazing Library Kids is a popular family read-aloud program held every winter. Call (218) 723-3839 for hours and event details, including librarian-led story times.

The Duluth Public Library's three branches also maintain children's book sections: **Lester Park Branch**, 54th Avenue E. and Tioga Street, (218) 525-3746; **West Duluth Branch**, 5830 Grand Avenue, (218) 723-3801; and **Woodland Branch**, 3723 Woodland Avenue, (218) 724-1268.

The newly expanded **Superior Public Library**, 1530 Tower Avenue, (715) 394-8860, in downtown Superior, offers children's story times with the children's librarian, summer reading programs, computer games and a parent's quiet room with puzzles and toys.

Along the North Shore

The **Two Harbors Public Library**, Fourth Avenue and Sixth Street, (218) 834-3148, was originally a 1909 Carnegie Library. It received an addition in 1983 and currently maintains a children's book section. Its summer program (mid-June through August) includes entertainers/storytellers, story hours, and summer reading programs in which prizes are awarded for every five books read.

The **Grand Marais Public Library**, First Street and W. Second Avenue, (218) 387-1140, is another children's resource. The summer program, held mid-June through July, features performers (jugglers, comedians, storytellers), story hours for younger kids and a thematic reading program for older kids that's designed to keep their skills sharp.

Along the South Shore

Many South Shore libraries offer video and cassette rentals as well as children's books.

Ashland's **Vaughn Public Library** is downtown at 502 W. Main Street, (715) 682-7060, offers a summer reading program (mid-June through mid-August) for both kids who read and kids who don't, story hours and, occasionally, entertainers, such as storytellers.

The following libraries are housed in early 1900s era, brownstone and brick Carnegie Library buildings: **Washburn Public Library**, 307 Wash Avenue, (715) 373-6172, with a weekly summer reading program (mid-June through August), craft projects, occasional entertainers (such as clowns) and numerous sections for children and young adults; **Bayfield Public Library**, 37 N. Broad Street, (715) 779-3953, featuring occasional entertainers, such as clowns, and a weekly Carnegie Kids story hour with activities on Wednesdays from mid-June through the first week in August; and **Ironwood Public Library**, 235 E. Aurora Avenue, (906) 932-0203, with a formidable children's book section and plans in the works for a July kids program.

Thunder Bay Area

The **Waverly Resource Library**, 285 Red River Road, (807) 344-3585, is the main library for old Port Arthur (a.k.a. Thunder Bay North). It maintains a separate and extensive children's "department."

The **Brodie Resource Library**, 216 Brodie Street S., (807) 623-0925, is the old 1912 Carnegie Library. It's become quite popular with the kids following the recent installation of a CD-ROM multimedia station in the children's section.

The **County Park Mall Library**, County Fair Plaza on Red River Road, (807) 768-9151, is a branch library with a children's section.

Mary J.L. Black Library, 151 Brock Street W., (807) 475-5906, a branch library in the West Fort neighborhood, has an excellent children's section, with cassettes, videos and compact discs.

(218) 733-7543, hosts permanent and changing exhibits that focus on world cultures and natural history. Past exhibits include a kid's-eye view of the St. Louis River ecosystems and a traveling show of mechanical dinosaurs. The museum's outreach program includes exhibits in Superior.

"Can we go see the trains?"

Glad you asked.

Kids are fascinated by the extensive collection of antique trains and rolling stock in the **Lake Superior Museum of Trans**portation, (218) 733-7590. They can crawl on the trains and take a streetcar ride. In the same area as the trains is a scaled-down, turn-of-the-century storefront village. Kids like to peek into the windows. The Depot is the arrival and departure site for the North Shore Scenic Railroad passenger service and for limited summer runs of the museum's restored steam engine No. 14. Call for ticket prices and schedules.

Some of the arts organizations headquartered at the Depot schedule children's classes and programs. The **Duluth Art Institute**, (218) 733-7560, offers children's classes in painting, drawing and other mediums. The **Minnesota Ballet**, (218) 733-7570, offers extensive dance classes for kids. And the **Duluth-Superior Symphony Orchestra**, (218) 733-7575, performs special Lollipops Concerts for children.

The **Lake Superior Zoo**, Grand Avenue and 72nd Avenue W., (218) 723-3747, is an great place for a family outing. The zoo is open year round. From April 1 through October 31, admission is $4 for adults, $2 for kids ages 4 through 11 and free for kids 3 and younger. From November 1 through March 31, admission is $2 for adults, $1 for children ages 4 through 11 and free for kids 3 and younger. The zoo's afternoon New Year's Eve Party, with free admission, cookies, hot cocoa, face-painting and fireworks, is an annual tradition for hearty northern families.

Permanent zoo exhibits include Polar Shores, featuring the celebrity polar bears; Australian Outback; Northern Exposure; a children's petting zoo with pygmy goats, sheep and Vietnamese potbelly pigs; an Asian animal exhibit; and a nocturnal exhibit. (See our Attractions chapter for more details.)

Duluth boasts a myriad of lush parks, most of them near streams and rivers that cascade down to Lake Superior. (See our Parks and Forests chapter for details.) Every elementary school in town has a playground with equipment, and dozens of recreation and community centers maintain skating rinks and sports fields. You can also find a league for just about every sport and every age. For more specifics, call **Duluth Parks and Recreation** at (218) 723-3337 and check out our Recreation chapter.

Some of our favorite Duluth parks and playgrounds for kids and adults include the community-built **Playfront Park**, in downtown Duluth near Bayfront Park. This multilevel wooden structure is a kid's delight, filled with tunnels, swings, slides, ropewalks and handy benches on which parents can relax while keeping an eye out.

Another equally elaborate but lesser-used play structure, also community-built, can be found in the little town of Esko, about 20 miles southwest of Duluth. Take Interstate 35 to the Thomson/Esko exit. The playground is at the intersection of Minn. Highway 61 and Thomson Road. Bridgeman's Ice Cream Parlor (next door) is operated by Esko High School students.

"Let's go to the beach!"

Yes, the Twin Ports are well more than a thousand miles from any ocean. Nevertheless, we have our share of beaches. Our Parks and Forests and Watersports chapters provide details not found in this chapter, so be sure to check them out as well.

The beach in Duluth is at **Park Point Recreation Area and Nature Preserve**. Although the annual water temperature of Lake Superior averages 38 degrees, there are usually several days during the summer when you can actually swim in the Lake without wearing a wet suit. But chilly water doesn't stop Duluthians from going to the beach.

The entire 7-mile Park Point beach amazes newcomers with its fine, creamy-white sand, rolling dunes covered with native grasses and wild roses and constantly changing shoreline decorated with driftwood, agates and smooth skipping stones — all wonderful pickup toys for children and dogs. You can get on the beach at the **Tot Lot** public parking area about two blocks after crossing the Aerial Lift Bridge on Minnesota Avenue; at the **Lafayette Recreation Center**, 3026 Minnesota Avenue, where you'll find a public parking lot and a landscaped trail to the beach; or at the end of Park Point where there's plenty of parking, and you'll have an easy walk to the beach.

The beach at the Park Point Recreation Area has lifeguards on duty from June to late August and a public beach house with restrooms and concessions. (Keep in mind there are no bathrooms or drinking water on the beach.) At the Park Point Recreation Area, you'll find a sandbox area with a wooden replicas of the Aerial Lift Bridge and an ore ship. Although these structures are a little worse for wear, kids still enjoy playing captain on the boat.

If the kids are set on swimming, try the **Pike Lake** AAA picnic area and beach on 4895 E. Pike Lake Road (off U.S. Highway 53), (218) 729-8160. This is a private beach, so you must be a AAA member or a member's guest to gain access. It's often crowded here, but there's a lifeguard on duty when the weather is pleasant and the swimmers are many, a roped swimming area and lots of boating action on the Lake.

Another park with running room, hiking paths and rocky, hidden overlooks is the **Enger Tower**, off Skyline Parkway and 18th Avenue W. Cries of "Come on, Dad!" are heard frequently, as kids scramble up the steps of the five-story stone tower to admire the views of Lake Superior. (This is an excellent strategy to wear down the kids' battery levels a bit.) Enger Tower has a picnic area and a handsome stone shelter set among oak trees, well-kept perennial gardens, hiking trails and a cliffside gazebo.

For stone-skipping and picnicking, try **Brighton Beach** on Scenic Highway 61 just past the Lester River on the far east end of Duluth. This public park has picnic sites facing the Lake and a rugged, stone- and driftwood-filled beach. **Chester Bowl**, at Skyline Parkway 1800 E., is another favorite wooded park for hiking along Chester Creek. It also has a playground, picnic area and sports fields.

Of course, the **Lakewalk** is always engaging, whether for the people-watching or Lake-gazing. This landscaped boardwalk and bike path winds up the shore from Canal Park in downtown Duluth for about 3 miles to 26th Avenue E. The Lakewalk is replete with picnic tables, secret spots, private overlooks, stone steps and rocks for kids to climb and explore. Little stone beaches offer toe-dipping and rock-skipping possibilities. It's a wonderful walk for parents who have babies in strollers. You can also get on the Lakewalk at the Fitger's Brewery Complex, 600 E. Superior Street (see our Attractions chapter). (Look for the line of people snaking out from the Portland Malt Shop, a tiny brick building east of Fitger's, and follow the trail of lost ice cream-cone tops on the steps down to the Lakewalk.) Another Lakewalk access is available at 21st Avenue E. off I-35.

The easiest way to see the big boats up close is to visit **Canal Park** in downtown Duluth where the lakers and the salties glide through the shipping channel under the Aerial Lift Bridge. Protected

The sun sets on a budding ice skater.

walkways along each side of the channel bring you within greeting distance of the gargantuan ships.

The **Canal Park Marine Museum**, (218) 727-2497, next to the shipping canal, is free and open year round. It posts the current boat schedule of arrivals and departures on a computer screen near the front door. You can also call the museum's **Boatwatcher's Hotline**, (218) 722-6489, for a listing. There's an extensive collection of ship memorabilia, model ships and exhibits inside. On the second floor, a captain's pilot house looks out over the lake. Kids love to play with the hands-on navigation equipment.

The *William A. Irvin*, the retired flagship of the USS Great Lakes fleet, is open for summer tours in the Minnesota Slip; call (218) 722-5573 for tour and general information and check out the listing in our Attractions chapter. Another boat to admire is the recently retired tugboat *Essayons,* which is tied up in the Minnesota Slip near the Minnesota Slip Bridge.

For an up-close look at the ships loading at the ore and coal docks in summer, the narrated harbor tour on the excursion boats of the Vista Star Fleet, (218) 722-6218, is a kid-pleaser. To see the upper stretches of the St. Louis River, take the 12-mile train ride on the **Lake Superior and Mississippi Railroad**; call (218) 624-7549 weekends or 727-0687 weekdays. The excursion train, sporting vintage open-window coaches, follows the original tracks of the first railway into Duluth, starting at the Western Waterfront Trail parking lot at Grand Avenue and 71st Street. Rides are available on summer weekends from July to early September.

The **Grand Slam Adventure World**, 395 Lake Avenue, (218) 722-5667, is a 30,000-square-foot, high-tech amusement center in Canal Park, offering activities for toddlers to teenagers. The center is smoke- and alcohol-free and features an 18-hole miniature golf course, a video arcade, Laser Tag, Adventure Playland, basketball, baseball and a fast-food restaurant. Admission is free, but you must buy tokens for the different games. Don't count on ambiance here; plan on being overstimulated. We found the noise from the video shoot-outs and car-racing and the screams bouncing off the cement floors and metal walls, as well as the glare of the fluorescent lights, overwhelming enough to send us crawling into the toddler tunnel with our 3-year-old friend. The kids, however, don't seem to mind.

The **Omnimax Theatre**, 301 Harbor Drive, (218) 727-0022, shows family-oriented films, 10 times larger than conventional movies, projected on a large dome and enhanced by a sophisticated sound system. Admission is $6 for adults and $4 for children 12 and younger.

On snowy winter days, Duluth kids, blessed with steep hills in their own neighborhoods, will make or find a spot to sled, slip or slide. (Old-timers talk about horse-drawn coal wagons spilling on Duluth's steep hills in the winter. Youngsters were sent out by penny-pinching families to gather the scattered coal before the driver returned with help.) You might check out the **Ridgeview Golf Course** on W. Redwing Street in east Duluth for a not-too-steep sliding hill; or, for an inexpensive option, try tubing at **Spirit Mountain**, 9500 Spirit Mountain Place, (218) 628-2891, Duluth's main ski hill in west Duluth.

There's always wiggling and twirling going on at the **Wild Thyme** family dances, (218) 728-1438. Held throughout the year in Trepanier Hall at the YWCA, 202 W. Second Street, kids are taught simple circle and square dances, with live music and a caller. Refreshments are available, and tickets are reasonably priced.

Superior

In Superior, you'll find plenty of parks for picnicking, playing and running. The **Superior Park and Recreation Department**, (715) 394-0270, can provide a list of facilities and programs. Also check out our Parks and Forests chapter for information about some of our favorites.

Barkers Island on the lakeshore, next to U.S. Highway 2/53, is one of most popular areas, with a children's playground, walking paths and a beach. The 56-acre **Billings Park**, tucked along the coast of the St. Louis River, is Superior's largest city park. It includes a pavilion, play area, boat launch and hiking trails along the river. To get there, take N. 21st Street until it ends; go left toward Royalton and proceed until the road dead-ends. The secluded **Wisconsin Point** area on the shore of Lake Superior is filled with kid's building materials: sand, water, rocks and piles of driftwood. Take U.S. Highway 2 to Moccasin Mike Road east of Superior. Turn north on Moccasin Mike Road and drive until the road splits; stay left on Wisconsin Point Road.

Let's turn indoors for a moment.

Open in summer only, the **Old Firehouse and Police Museum**, U.S. Highway 2/53 and 23rd Avenue E., (715) 398-7558, is filled with old fire trucks and pumpers.

The **Fairlawn Mansion and Museum**, 906 Harbor View Parkway E. (U.S. Highway 2), (715) 394-5712, offers children's programs, including a popular summer ice cream social.

The **SS *Meteor* Maritime Museum**, (715) 392-2773, on Barkers Island, is open for summer tours; a miniature golf course is nearby. You can also catch harbor cruises here at the dock in the summer on the **Vista Fleet**, (218) 722-6218.

Along the North Shore

Minnesota's North Shore is a kid's paradise for outdoor play, with hiking trails, miles of waterfront, and rocks — big and small — to climb, collect and skip across the Lake's surface. But don't overlook the historic and educational attractions, including a tugboat, lighthouses and environmental programs for the young and young-at-heart.

Two Harbors

Big ships. Old trains. Storybook tugboats. A pretty red-brick lighthouse. Take the kids to the downtown waterfront in Two Harbors. Check in at the depot, operated by the **Lake County Historical Society**, (218) 834-4898, for information on tours of the *Edna G.* (the last remaining steam-powered tugboat of the Great Lakes, moored in the harbor), tours of the lighthouse and wonderful exhibits on the area's logging and mining history in the depot building. Gift and candy shops round out the attractions in the depot, and you'll find several locomotive engines and rolling stock outside.

Two Harbors is a working port from which taconite mined on the Iron Range is shipped. The waterfront is an ideal place to watch the ships come and go. You can walk out on the long harbor breakwater for ship-watching, but use caution here with kids. A safe bet is to hunker down at one of the picnic tables at Lighthouse Point to check out the harbor activities.

Two Harbors has a half-dozen parks, each adopted by recreation groups. One of these is **Lakeview Park** near Burlington Bay, in the square block between First and Second streets on Second Avenue. It's a popular park for family reunions, with a pavilion overlooking the lake.

A traditional mid-July event with lots of stuff for kids is the **Two Harbors Folk Festival**, (218) 834-2600 or (800) 777-7384. This three-day festival, featuring nationally known folk acts, includes a children's tent where storytelling, face-painting, dancing and music are the standard activities fare. Day or weekend passes are available, and children younger than 11 get in for free.

Beaver Bay

Up Minn. Highway 61, about 20 miles northeast of Two Harbors and 8 miles south of Beaver Bay, is the beloved **Split Rock Lighthouse**, (218) 226-6372, operated by the Minnesota Historical Society on the grounds of Split Rock Lighthouse State Park. Plan to spend a morning or afternoon here; enjoy a picnic and a hike. Admission to the lighthouse is $4 for adults, $2 for children ages 7 through 15 and free for kids 6 and younger. Seniors get in for $3, and the family rate is $10. From May 15 through October 15, visitors do not need to purchase a state park sticker. From October 16 through May 14 only the History Center is open (except in December when its closed), and you must purchase a state park sticker ($4 daily).

There's plenty to see, indoors and out, and plenty to engage kids of different ages. Start with the history center; check out the award-winning introductory film as well as the exhibits on Lake Superior navigation, shipwrecks, commercial fishing and North Shore tourism. (Beware the museum store: The charming light-up, scaled-down models of the lighthouse and lots of books are sure to tempt anyone's penchant to purchase.) Tours of the grounds include the lighthouse tower, the foghorn building and the keeper's houses with costumed

We All Scream for Ice Cream

As a result of our nonscientific survey, done entirely via random sample, we recommend the following ice cream places (particularly in the warmer months, of course).

Twin Ports Area

DULUTH
Dairy Queen, Canal Park Drive, in Canal Park (we got free samples during our last visit, and there's a place to sit down); **Portland Malt Shop** near the Fitger's Brewery Complex on Superior Street; and **Bridgeman's Ice Cream Parlor** near the Miller Hill Mall on 2202 Mountain Shadow Drive.

Be sure and grab lots of napkins for the inevitable ice cream spill disaster.

SUPERIOR
Bridgeman's Ice Cream Parlor on 1106 Belknap Street.

Along the North Shore

Dairy Queen on Minn. Highway 61 in Two Harbors; and **Sven and Ole's Restaurant**, 9 W. Wisconsin Street, in Grand Marais (*the* place for frozen yogurt with all the trimmings).

Along the South Shore

Dairy Queen on Wis. Highway 13 in Washburn (the first underground Dairy Queen in the country; the ice cream stays frozen longer!) and **La Bontes**, the little ice cream stand near Greunke's Inn on Rittenhouse Avenue in downtown Bayfield.

Thunder Bay Area

Calabria Restaurant on 287 Bay Street in the old Italian neighborhood near downtown Port Arthur, has delicious gelato (an intensely flavored Italian ice cream.)

interpreters on site who talk about "life back then" as lighthouse keepers. **Split Rock Lighthouse State Park** has a beachside picnic area and challenging hiking trails that are easily accessible on foot or by car from the lighthouse grounds. (See our Parks and Forests chapter for more information.)

If the kids are clamoring to get their sea legs, **Kollar's Lake Superior Excursions**, Minn. Highway 61, Milepost 52, in eastern Beaver Bay, (218) 226-4100, will take you along the stunning high cliffs and sea caves of the North Shore on the 150-person, 110-foot-long excursion boat *Grampa Woo*. Cruises are scheduled from May to early October. Keep in mind that you won't be in the calm Duluth harbor anymore, and if the seas are rolling, you may turn a little green around the gills.

Finland

The **Wolf Ridge Environmental Learning Center**, 230 Cranberry Road, (218) 353-7414 or (800) 523-2733, is a nonprofit outdoor residential school set on 1,400 acres overlooking Lake Superior. Summer and winter programs include family vacations and family weekends as well as special weeklong Elderhostels for grandparents and grandchildren.

Lutsen

The closest thing to an amusement park on the North Shore is at **Lutsen Ski Area**, Lutsen Mountain Road, (218) 663-7281; it's a distant relative at best. In the summer, a giant alpine slide shoots screaming kids and adults down a mountain. Half the fun is getting to the slide by riding the chairlift up the mountain. Another thrill for kids is a trip on the **Gondola Skyride**, which takes passengers above the Poplar River Valley to the top of Moose Mountain for views of the Lake and the mountains. The **Lutsen Mountain Bike Park**, accessed by the Gondola Skyride, is a pay-to-ride, 18-mile set of rugged trails along the mountain ridges (see our General Recreation chapter for details). In winter, this area is the premier downhill skiing area for northern Minnesota. Ski lessons for children are available.

The **Village Homestead Stables** at Lutsen, (218) 663-7241 or (800) 642-6036, are open year round for guided trail rides and pony rides for children. In summer, take a hay ride; in winter, sleigh rides are offered, complete with bonfires and hot chocolate.

The **Superior National Forest** people and the Lutsen-Tofte tourism people have joined resources to offer naturalist-led and summer and winter programs,

Scooping for prize catches entertains kids.

including snowshoe hikes, wilderness daytrips and fireside programs, many of which are appropriate for children. Call (218) 663-7280 for a schedule of events.

Grand Marais

The **Grand Marais Municipal Indoor Pool**, Eighth Avenue W., (218) 387-1275, is open year round and has a wading pool for children. Admission is $3.17 for ages 2 through 15 and $4.03 for folks 16 and older; you can stay all day until you're pruned.

Open year round, the **Grand Marais Art Colony**, on the corner of Second Street and Third Avenue W., (218) 387-2737, offers workshops for young adults. Author and illustrator Betsy Bowen, whose striking woodcuts grace several nationally recognized children's books, includ-

ing *Antler, Bear, Canoe*, is a resident of the area and teaches adult classes here.

Along the South Shore

For inexpensive summer fun, the South Shore's main outdoor attractions are its fine white sand beaches. Depending on which way the wind is blowing, the water is usually warm and sometimes swimmable in many of the protected bays. If not, there are scads of driftwood to examine and miles of beach-walking to be had.

Bayfield Peninsula

We'll start on the Bayfield Peninsula, which juts off the South Shore of Wisconsin, with the Apostle Islands strewn at its tip. Here you'll find some of our favorite beaches just off Wis. Highway 13 — also the route for the Lake Superior Circle Tour (see our Circle Tour chapter). Some are officially named beaches; others are unnamed or locally named. These beaches are well-loved and have become annual summer destinations for several generations of families and local people who are somewhat protective of them. So, please carry out your trash, leash your dogs and leave the driftwood to drift some more.

Brule River Beach: Follow Wis. Highway 13 to the turnoff (marked by signs) toward the mouth of the Brule River. Drive several miles to a parking area with picnic tables and bathrooms.

Herbster City Beach: This beach near the city campground has running water and restrooms. Take Bark Point Road off Wis. Highway 13 towards the lake and follow the shore.

Cornucopia Beach: Heading east from Duluth/Superior on Wis. Highway 13, you'll come across the tiny town of Cornucopia — a sailing mecca in summer. A row of stores includes a sweet shop with ice cream, popcorn and other goodies. Public restrooms and running water are available nearby. The beach here borders a natural, warm-water harbor with a gradual drop-off.

Big Bay Beach: Out on Madeline Island, the beaches at Big Bay State Park are known for their beauty. Catch (and pay for) the 20-minute ferry ride from the dock in Bayfield. Follow the signs to the state park. You'll need to pay for a day pass.

Little Sand Bay: The official Apostle Islands National Lakeshore entrance has an accessible beach and campgrounds nearby. Take Wis. Highway 13 west for 5 miles from Bayfield to County Road K. Turn north and drive 13 miles to Little Sand Bay.

Memorial Park Beach: The town of Washburn has a public swimming beach on the Chequamegon Bay side. From Wis. Highway 13, turn into the Memorial Park Campground to reach the beach. Facilities here include showers, restrooms and a playground.

For winter swimming, try the **Bayfield Pool and Recreation Facility**, Broad and Wilson, (715) 779-3201. It's open year round, and the admission fee covers an all-day stay.

Thunder Bay Area

The shores of Lake Superior near Thunder Bay are too rocky and rough for swimming, but there are plenty of public parks for an outdoor dip (see our Parks and Forests chapter for details about Thunder Bay parks and conservation areas). You'll find a roped-off beach, picnic area and playground upstream of the falls at **Kakabeka Falls Provincial Park**, Trans-Canada Highway 11/17, (807) 473-9231. **Marie Louise Lake** at **Sleeping Giant Provincial Park**, Highway 587, (807) 977-2526, has a swimming beach; take Trans-Canada Highway 11/17 north from

Thunder Bay for 25 miles, turn east on Highway 587 and proceed into the park.

In town, there are supervised swimming beaches at **Boulevard Lake Park**, at the end of N. Algoma Street in north Thunder Bay. The **Hazelwood Lake Conservation Area**, Hazelwood Drive, (807) 344-5857, has swimming and picnic grounds; follow Highway 102 past County Fair Plaza to Hazelwood Drive, turn right on Hazelwood Drive and follow it to its end.

Thunder Bay also has a number of outdoor, city-run swimming pools. Call **Thunder Bay Community Services**, (807) 625-2351 for information about schedules, fees and locations. For indoor swimming, the **Canada Games Complex**, 420 Winnipeg Avenue, (807) 625-3311, is one of your best bets. Facilities include an Olympic-size swimming pool, a swirlpool and a giant waterslide. The complex offers child care and a number of recreational programs for kids.

Boulevard Lake Park; **Centennial Park**, Arundel and Hudson streets, (807) 625-2351; **Chippewa Park**, Highway 61B, (807) 683-3912; and **Marina Park**, Red River Road (on the downtown waterfront), have walking paths and outdoor playgrounds. Chippewa Park, south of town and close to Old Fort William, has rides for young kids, including a merry-go-round, Tilt-a-whirl, roller coaster and bumper cars.

At Boulevard Lake you can rent canoes and paddle boats and play mini-golf. Centennial Park has a replica of a logging camp, train rides and a petting zoo.

Until 1970, Thunder Bay was divided into two cities: Port Arthur and Fort William. Because of this history, Thunder Bay boasts two large central public libraries with extensive children's sections and programs. The children's programs at these full-service libraries bring in storytellers, puppet shows, local writers and performers; provide toys and puzzles; offer an ongoing literacy program; and maintain an extensive French collection (many children in Thunder Bay are bilingual). Children's videos and cassettes are also available. Call the Hours and Activities line, (807) 623-1004, for program information. Nonresidents can purchase a temporary summer library card for $3 per month. Storytelling programs cost $1 for tourists and visitors. See this chapter's related sidebar for locations and hours.

The children's bookstore, **Elfabets Books**, 197 Algoma Street S., (807) 344-0083, specializes in Canadian children's books. Browsing is encouraged in this shop, which maintains an extensive selection of new releases, classics, books in French, audio and video cassettes and interactive storybooks on CD-ROM. The **Sweet Thursday Bookshop**, 30 St. Paul Street, (807) 344-2866, in downtown Port Arthur near the harbor, is another recommended source for children's books.

The **Children's Museum**, Broadway Avenue, (807) 345-0338, in Old Fort William, offers hands-on activities and programs for kids and parents. Housed in Old Fort William's library, it's open daily (in summer only) from 11 AM to 4 PM.

The **Thunder Bay Children's Festival**, (807) 343-2300, is held annually for three days in mid-June. Free indoor and outdoor activities, for babies to 8th graders, are held at the Thunder Bay Community Auditorium, the Norwester Baseball Diamonds and the Port Arthur Stadium. The festival highlights the visual and performing arts and hosts cultural presentations from many heritage groups and Old Fort William.

Inside
Shopping

Ours is for the most part a wild, unspoiled area populated with relatively few people. But we do shop, and shopping here isn't much different from elsewhere on the continent. The main cities of Duluth, Superior, Thunder Bay and Ashland have their malls and Wal-Marts, their commercial strips and supermarkets and convenience stores, their local specialty shops in restored historic areas, their antiques shops and bookstores. In the long expanses in between the cities, gift shops with a regional flavor dot the byways and smaller communities. You don't have to shop to enjoy our region. But if shopping is your thing, you don't have to forego it either. Besides, we're only a few hours' drive away from the place the whole world, it seems, likes to shop: The **Mall of America**, (612) 883-8800, the largest enclosed retail/entertainment complex in the United States. It has 400 specialty stores, in addition to services, amusement, theater and restaurants. Take I-35 south from Duluth and connect with I-494 in the Twin Cities; take the Cedar Avenue exit (technically, the Mall sits at the intersection of I-494 and Minn. Highway 77 in Bloomington, Minnesota).

Malls and General Shopping

Twin Ports Area

Duluth

THE MILLER HILL CORRIDOR

By far the biggest mall area in our region, this commercial corridor on U.S. Highway 53 has been transformed in the past 25 years from a forested road and farmsteads to a blur of nonstop signs, lights and eager shoppers. It stretches from Duluth into Hermantown. The first mall leg on the corridor is **Stone Ridge Plaza** (which was a considerably higher ridge until the solid rock was reduced to rubble in the early 1990s to make way for stores). Here you'll find a **Barnes & Noble** bookstore, **ShopKo** (a discount store), **Cub Foods**, **Toys R Us**, **Payless** shoes and **Office Max**. Closer to the highway are two freestanding buildings; one contains a complementary package of bridal, floral and tuxedo shops; the other, **Red Wing Shoes**, **Scandinavian**

Insiders' Tips

Designs and the **Big and Tall** clothing store. Just beyond (northwest) is the impressive **Gander Mountain**, 1307 Miller Trunk, where you can buy tents, snowshoes, hunting and fishing equipment and outdoor clothing. Nearby is the **Duluth Camera Exchange**, 1405 Miller Trunk, for everything in photographic equipment and film processing.

Also along U.S. Highway 53, on the other side of Trinity Road, is **Miller Hill Mall**, one of a 90-member nationwide family of malls (including the Mall of America) owned by Simon Property Group. Miller Hill Mall's 110 stores attracted 10 million shoppers in 1995, who bought $62 million worth of goods. Anchor stores include **Sears**, **JCPenney**, **Glassblock** (a local quality department store) and **Montgomery Ward**. This mall has 17 apparel shops (including the newly opened **Victoria's Secret**), eight jewelry stores, two bookstores (**Waldenbooks** and **B. Dalton Bookseller**), 10 shoe stores, a three-screen cinema and dozens of specialty shops. The skylight-domed food court features rows of tables surrounded by fast-food booths selling Chinese, Italian, Greek, Mexican and American foods. Four restaurants in the mall offer conventional seating and wait staffs. The mall is scheduled for an expansion in late 1996, which could include a popular Dayton's department store. Mall hours are 10 AM to 9 PM Monday through Friday; 10 AM to 6 PM Saturday; and noon to 6 PM Sunday. For mall information, call (218) 727-8301.

Just beyond the northern boundary of the mall's parking lot is the **Village Mall**, a string of attached shops that open to the outdoors. You can park close to your store here. Stores include the locally owned **Cimarron**, one of the few truly cosmopolitan clothing shops in the area; **Minnesota Fabrics**, a favorite for folks who like to sew their own sew their own clothing, do their own upholstery and make their own draperies; **Village Pet Shoppe**; and **Betty Lou's Health Foods** (opened by a former local employee of a chain health store here after it changed its emphasis to bodybuilding). The downtown **European Bakery** also has an outlet here. Nearby is **Wild Birds Unlimited Nature Store**, selling bulk seeds, feeders and other bird attractions. Continuing north a block are **Kmart**; and **Michael's**, a large and densely packed showcase of arts and crafts supplies.

Around back is **Village Mall II**, with a skateboard and snowboard shop, a uniform store, **Twin Ports Bible & Book** and **Sylvester's Bargain Emporium** (up to 85 percent off on brand-name designer clothing).

Cross Maple Grove Road and you're in **Burning Tree Plaza**, whose hottest spot is **Best Buy**, for just about anything new that uses microchips, digital dials or remotes. There's also a **TJ Maxx**, an **Eddie Bauer Outlet**, **Northwest Fabrics & Crafts**, **Leathers Galore**, **Nevada Bob's Golf** (golfing equipment and accessories) and **Super One** grocery store.

Continuing up the Miller Trunk Corridor are discount stores (**Target, Kohl's** and **Wal-Mart**); building-supply plantations (**Menard's, Knox**); car lots and auto parts stores and the **Harley-Davidson Sport Center**, 4355 Stebner Road. Several bright shopping spots on the northern end of the corridor are locally owned: **Energy Plus**, 4811 Miller Trunk, selling upscale woodstoves, fireplaces, spas, saunas and accessories; **Gordy's Farm Market & Garden Center**, 4897 Miller Trunk, an old reliable that has expanded with the corridor; and **Wood Magic**, 5105 Miller Trunk, with Fenton handmade blown

Duluth's Downtown
West Superior Street
300
BLOCK

Stroll the charming cobblestone walkways
or enjoy the indoor comfort of the skywalk system
where you will find unique shops and
services catering to your every need...
on the
300 Block of Downtown Duluth's West Superior Street.

Anne Childs • 722-4731
Bagley & Company Jewelers • 727-2991
Barbo's Columbia Clothing • 722-3339
The Frame Corner & Gallery • 722-7174
J.S. Meier Women's Apparel • 727-1449
John Marxhausen Jewelry Designer & Goldsmith • 727-1625
Paper Unlimited • 727-4011
Peterson Anderson Flowers, Inc • 722-0888
Toys for Keeps • 720-3568
Union Optical • 722-0721

Over 20 specialty shops to discover

glass, Heritage lace, ceramics and kitchen cupboards.

DOWNTOWN

Downtown shopping is primarily on Superior Street and the parallel First Street, one block up the hill. We'll begin at the west end of Superior Street and work eastward.

The lavender-colored **Palladio**, 401 W. Superior Street, is the sister store of the Village Mall's Cimarron. Like Cimarron, it features elegant cosmopolitan clothing and footwear. In the next few blocks are **Duluth Camera Exchange**, **The Frame Corner & Gallery**, **Paper Unlimited**, **Ann Childs** clothing, **Peterson Anderson Flowers**, **Union Optical**, **Barbo's Columbia Clothing**, **Toys for Keeps** (upstairs along the skywalk), **Allenfall's** fine apparel for both genders, **Sylvester's Bargain Emporium**, **J.S. Meier** clothing, **John Marxhausen** jewelry (custom, goldsmithing and original designs, housed upstairs as part of the skywalk system), **Bagley and Company Jewelers**, **Security Jewelers**, **A & E Supply** (office/art/stationery), **Minnesota Surplus** (boots and shoes, outdoors wear, camping accessories), **Austin-Jarrow** (sports shoes and clothing; partner "Jarrow" used to have a different last name — plus a first name — but switched to a one-word moniker early in his long-distance racing career), **Sawmill Unpainted Furniture** (lots of clean-lined wooden furniture awaiting your paintbrush), **Ace Hardware**, **Mainstream Fashions for Men** and **Snyder's** drugstore.

The intersection of Second Avenue W. and Superior Street is the busy hub of downtown, and the **Holiday Center**, 727-7765, is probably the reason (although some chocolate lovers might credit the **Fanny Farmer** candy store on the other corner). The two-story Holiday mall is packed at lunchtime when office workers descend for food (at the half-dozen food establishments) and quick shopping for jewelry, greeting cards and gifts. **General Nutrition Center**, three women's clothing stores (**Goldie's Too**, **L. Marie's** and **Vanity**), **Explorations** (educational toys for children), **McGregor-Soderstrom** men's wear, **Watches International** and **Waldenbooks** offer a variety of shopping options. You can take a breather and catch up on news at the **Christian Science Reading Room**, and get the best French bread in the Twin Ports at **The Greenery**. The second floor of the Holiday Center continues west along the Skywalk system, with two blocks of store accesses and a notable shop right on the skywalk near Lake Avenue: **Kelly's**, whose artist-owner sells his portraits of the Duluth area along with coffee beans, coffee and kitchen accessories, and some fresh brew to keep you going.

Down on Superior Street, just below Kelly's, are **USA Foxx & Furs**, with the largest selection of furs in the area; **Global Village**, a two-story collection of affordable but classy imports, including India beads and cotton clothing as well as futons and wicker; and **Ragstock**, with funky vintage secondhand clothing. And you'll find even funkier items next door at the **Trading Post**; the half shop, half museum is packed full of military goods, clothing, bones, feathers, furs, leathers, stone-tipped arrows, antlers and stuffed animals. Next door, on the corner of Superior Street and Lake Avenue, you can get jewelry ready-made or to order at **Eslabon's**.

The Electric Fetus, 12 E. Superior, sells tapes, CDs and some records (alternative, New Age, pop, rock, international, folk, country, local, classical, rap, jazz), clothing, funky jewelry, therapeutic aromas,

The Harmony of Fine Material & Creative Thought

- Department
- Steinback Nutcrackers
- Buyer's Choice Carolers
- Specialty Gifts

inc.

Cat's Meow Village
including Aerial Bridge
& Enger Tower

"Exclusively" at...

mainstreet
4433 E. Superior Street, Duluth   525-3755

massage oils, candles and incense. Across the street, **The Music Center** sells a full line of dancing shoes and clothing as well as musical instruments and sheet music. **The Last Place on Earth**, 33 E. Superior, sells what the police call "drug paraphernalia" and what the owners call "tobacco accessories"; also T-shirts, tapestries, posters, head-banger tapes and "adult novelties." A **Tandy** shop (leather, beads, crafts), a futon store and the **Collection Connection** (comics, sports cards, Dungeons & Dragons) are between Lake Avenue and First Avenue E.

At 206 E. Superior Street is **Carlson Book**, a cavernous place with a huge selection of magazines, records, tapes, CDs and the largest selection of used books in the region. The **Duluth Oriental Grocery**, 323 E. Superior Street, has a rich supply of quality Asian foods, including bulk rice, dry and frozen fish and homemade kimchee. The family-run store offers personalized service and sells kitchen goods, such as woks, tea pots and bamboo ware.

A favorite for the shopper on the lookout for quality gifts and unusual items is the tasteful 11-building complex of **Fitger's Brewery Complex**, 600 E. Supe-

rior Street, (218) 722-8826. It was a brewery, renovated in the mid-1980s, and a huge copper vat and copper vents still shine against whitewashed rock walls. The cornerstone of the complex is the highly acclaimed **Fitger's Inn** (see our Accommodations chapter). Fitger's includes four restaurants and a coffee shop, and two dozen specialty shops, including **Catherine Imports** (imported jewelry, art, home dexor, stained glass items, flowers and more), **Benetton-on-the-Lake** (clothing), **Made in the Shade** (beautiful handmade pottery, jewelry, glasssware and woodcraft), **Endion Station Crafts & Pleiades Jewelry** (natural fiber yarns, stone, metals, basketry, jewelry and art), **Snow Goose** (Minnesota mementos, candles, books, games and collectibles), **Sandpiper** (clothing for women), **Holidays at the Lake** (Christmas ornaments as well as gifts and decor for almost any holiday), the **Outdoor Company** (fishing equipment, soft cotton shirts and sweaters, Rainforest and Outback labels) and **Lake Superior Brewing Company** (home-brew supplies, glassware, clothing and collectibles). Fitger's shops are open 10 AM to 9 PM Monday through Saturday and 11 AM to 5 PM Sunday. You can park free in the ramp.

Just east of Fitger's is **Superior Lake Gifts**, 716 E. Superior Street, with gifts representative of Duluth and Lake Superior.

One block up from Superior Street is First Street, a one-way heading west. Most commerce here is west of Lake Avenue, the dividing line between eastern and western street addresses. First Street boasts four food stores that somehow have survived the vagaries of progress — probably because they've been loved for several generations. At **European Bakery**, 109 W. First Street, you can get the only Jewish pumpernickel and best medium rye in the region; also challah, bagels (their new health bagel is a meal in itself), sweet baked goods, gefilte fish, halvah and other Jewish goodies. Across the street is **Ideal Market**, an old-fashioned downtown market that carries a full line of items and still makes deliveries; and **Fichtner's Sausage & Meats**, 134 W. First, a popular butcher shop that's surprisingly small for its formidable quantity of butchers and meats.

Farther east on First Street is a kosher butcher shop, but you'd never know it from the beat-up, unsigned exterior. Nevertheless, the meat inside **Sher Brothers & Co.**, 25 E. First Street, 722-5563, is fresh and strictly kosher, and the owners are friendly and talkative. Other First Street shops include **Arthur's Men's Formal Wear**, 25 W. First Street; **Collectible Treasures**, with carousels, elephants, music boxes, at the corner of First Street and Second Avenue W.; and **Picchu Alpaca**, 211½ W. First Street, with alpaca wool sweaters and sheepskin rugs. **Duluth Tobacco & Gifts**, 25 N. First Avenue W. (on the hill between Superior and First streets), has a broad selection of tobaccos and pipes.

CANAL PARK DISTRICT

Canal Park is a big favorite for visitors because of the scenery (the Lake, the Aerial Bridge and the park along the shipping canal), the relaxed atmosphere, pedestrian and (in summer time) horse traffic, and the attractive commercial settings.

The **DeWitt-Seitz Marketplace**, 394 Lake Avenue S., (218) 722-0047, is at the center of Canal Park. It's a beautiful renovated warehouse that's on the National Register of Historic Places. A dozen shops and restaurants circle the wide old pine center stairway, including **Hepzibah's** (confectionery). **Tales to Tell Bookstore** (regional and children's books), **The Blue Heron** (cooking, kitchen and other food-related items), **Torke Weihnachten** (Christmas shop), **J. Skylark** (toys and gifts), The **Art Dock** (pottery, glassware and fabric art), **Window Works** (window treatments and home accessories)and **Cruisin'** (postcards and gifts). **The House of Note** on the third floor features violins, violas and cellos, new and used. In the basement is **Amazing Grace Bakery**, which features not only baked goods but also live entertainment.

Most other shops in Canal Park are in the one-story string of shops along Canal Park Drive. **The Flying Fish** and **Spirit of the Lake** sell gifts, and **Northern Lights Bookstore** has a particularly nice selection of children's books and photography books, many oriented toward our region. Continuing toward the Aerial Bridge is the **Blue Note**, a coffee shop where you can buy dry coffee and accessories (see our Nightlife and Casinos chapter for details). Next door is the **Duluth Pack Store**, which began generations ago as a canvas tent-and-pack manufacturer (the factory, Duluth Tent and Awning, continues in operation at Garfield Avenue and W. Superior Street) and now

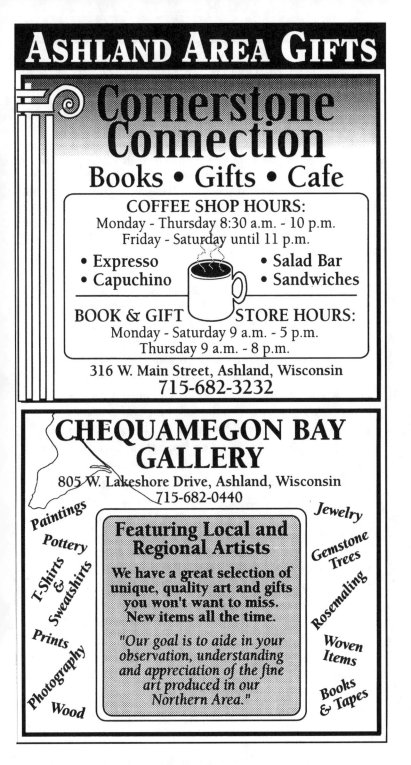

has expanded its line to include Kevlar and birchbark canoes, beaded leather tobacco pouches and wool socks, camp cookwear, Pendleton blankets and a large selection of canoe paddles and snowshoes. Walk between the two shops to the back of the building to find **The Cottage**, with quality gifts — fabrics, glass and a large selection of handwork.

Back on the street, **Twin Ports Cyclery** is another Duluth standby for bicycles and bicycle repair and now also sells cross-country skis, accessories and clothing. **Inland Coast Traders Ltd.** has Duluth- and

Minnesota-insignia T-shirts and sweatshirts and features Helly Hansen extreme-weather gear; and other shops in this row sell home furnishings, antiques (see our "Antiques" section in this chapter) and sports memorabilia.

You'll have to go up to the sixth floor of the **Meierhoff Building**, 325 Lake Avenue S., for the gift shop of **Lake Superior Magazine**, 722-5002. It's worth a trip, because the shop sells wonderful maps of Lake Superior as well as Lake-oriented books, postcards, gifts and back issues of the magazine.

Insiders' Tips

If you'd like to make a daytrip going after Scandinavian and Finnish gifts, here are some places to go: **Bergquist Scandinavian Gift Shop**, 1412 Minn. Highway 33 S. (take the Highway 33 exit from I-35 into Cloquet and continue until you see the big red horse on your right), was founded in 1948 by the Bergquists. They have custom-designed presents and many imports and wholesale items. The addresses or directions to the following stores are listed in our Shopping chapter: **Scandinavian Designs Unlimited** and **Norwegian and Swedish Imports** in Duluth, **Rustic Inn Gifts** in Two Harbors, **Antilla's Gallery and Handcrafted Gifts** in Little Marais, the **Viking Hus** and **Lake Superior Trading Post** in Grand Marais and the **Finnish Bookstore** in Thunder Bay. On the South Shore, visit **Joanne's Scandinavian Gifts**, 223 Rittenhouse Avenue, in Bayfield; and the **Little Finland Gift Shop**, Wis. Highway 13 just east of Hurley. **Irma's Finland House**, (218) 741-0204, is 85 miles from Duluth in Virginia, Minnesota, but worth a trip if you're after imports from the European countries of the northern lights. It's big — 6,300 square feet — and features Finnish, Norwegian, Swedish and German gifts and food as well as sauna supplies. Take Minn. Highway 53 north from Duluth, and at the third stoplight in Virginia, turn right; the shop is in the Northgate Plaza about six blocks down.

PLAZA/LONDON ROAD AREA

Duluth's other commercial corridor begins near **The Plaza** shopping area at 10th Avenue E. and Superior Street. The Plaza has a **Jubilee** food store, a **Mister Movies** that has plenty of foreign films for rent, **Winslow's Hallmark** (a huge selection of greeting cards), **Alternatives** (incense, herbs, massage oil, jewelry, books) and **Walgreen's**.

Nearby The Plaza is a Duluth landmark: **Silver's Dress Shop**, 1123 E. Superior Street, a quality women's clothing shop specializing in sportswear, formal wear, outfits for the working woman and bridalwear (see this chapter's Insiders' Tip for details). Farther east is the **Patty Cake Shop**, 1434 E. Superior, a local favorite for sweet baked goods (try the bear claws!) and crusty breads. Next door, across the avenue, is **Stewart's Wheel Goods**, with bicycles, ice and in-line skates, hockey equipment, bicycle gear and a repair shop. This long-time favorite is also a busy skate exchange. Two big ski shops can be found in this neighborhood: **Continental**, 1305 E. First Street, and the **Ski Hut**, up the hill a few blocks at 1032 E. Fourth Street. Both feature rentals, full-service ski tuning and repair, and a full line of downhill and cross-

country skiing and snowboarding equipment. Continental also sells in-line skates, water skis, climbing and tennis equipment, and beachwear.

Moving down the hill to London Road, the lakeside avenue that carries traffic east out of town, we come to a commercial corridor that runs to 26th Avenue E. Gas stations and fast-food restaurants are interspersed with several locally owned stores of interest. **Norwegian & Swedish Imports**, 2014 London Road, is a modest shop that contains a wealth of gifts (dried Scandinavian fruit soup, carvings, pewter, crystal), and you can learn a lot about Scandinavian history and culture from the owners. They were considering retirement in mid-1996 but were planning to sell to someone who would continue the shop's business. **Marine General Sports**, 1501 London Road, has the largest selection of fishing tackle, life jackets, rain gear and boat accessories in the region.

Farther east on London Road, at 24th Avenue E. in the **Edgewater Plaza**, is the **Kitchen Cupboard**, a small shop packed with gifts, handcrafts and kitchen ware. The **Lake Aire Bottle Shop**, 2416 London Road, boasts it has the largest collection of wine, beer and liquor in the upper Midwest. The organic-minded food shopper will want to shop at the **Whole Foods Co-op**, 1332 E. Fourth Street, and **Positively Third Street Bakery**, another cooperative at 1202 E. Third Street. Both places are full of delectable foodstuffs, and you can get a line on alternative concerts, groups and events from their bulletin boards. An old dependable music store, **Hawley Music Co.**, recently moved from its longtime downtown location to this neighborhood. You'll find instruments for sale and rent at 1131 E. Fourth Street.

The **Lakeside** neighborhood in eastern Duluth has several shops, including **Mainstreet**, 4433 E. Superior Street, with stained glass items, pottery, stitchery and exquisite Christmas collectibles.

WEST DULUTH

Valley Center, at I-35 and Central Avenue, is the hub of the West Duluth shopping. The center has a **Kmart, Walgreen's, Fashion Bug** clothing store, rental shop, **Duluth Camera Exchange, Radio Shack** and a secondhand paperback store. A **Super One** supermarket is nearby.

At the fragrant **Italian Village**, 301 N. Central Avenue, sausage is homemade, olives come in a barrel and olive oil by the gallon, salamis and cheeses are bulk imported, and the Italian-descent proprietor will serve you cappuccino, smiles and lore of the neighborhood's Italian community.

While you're in the neighborhood, check out **Central Sales** across the street at 314 N. Central Avenue. This cavernous, densely-stocked place has everything from tools to computer fans, used bicycles to remaindered house paint. You can get a great buy here, and it's always packed with talkative customers.

The main street of the area is Grand Avenue, with shops, services and a post office. A landmark is **West Duluth News**, 5628 Grand Avenue, with a wide selection of magazines and newspapers. It also sells tobacco, paperbacks and gifts.

Although residents of Cloquet, about 25 miles southwest of Duluth, have plenty of stores of their own — mainly in the strip area along Minn. Highway 33 — many do their heavy shopping in Duluth. But the reverse movement happens, too, at specialty shops like **Bergquist Scandinavian Gift Shop** (see our Insiders' Tip) and **Maxi's Fashions**, 917 Cloquet Avenue, where you'll find clothing size 14 and up as well as gifts.

Superior

Superior's shopping is spread out along two long streets and a mall. Tower Avenue, which runs north and south, was once the main street of downtown. But most commerce has moved south on Tower to a commercial corridor, leaving behind restaurants, bars, services, a few shops and empty storefronts. The city has tried mightily to reinvigorate the once-bustling downtown, but not even the two lovely old movie houses found a viable new place in the scheme of things. Nevertheless, a few old favorites remain, drawing people from far away: **Berger Hardware**, 525 Tower Avenue, has a huge assortment of every imaginable item you could use in hardware, including parts so long outdated that it's impossible to buy them elsewhere. The place is great fun to browse; some items that could be in a blacksmithing or farm museum are on the walls, as though displayed there and then forgotten until they went out of use, and some items for sale are hard to find elsewhere, such as maple sap spigots and decorative rings for your woodstove pipe. Farther south,

Bear Shoe Works, 801 Tower Street, sells Red Wing shoes and men's boots. Common Health Foods, 1019 Tower Street, sells whole and organic foods, while Lignell Drugs across the street is an old standby, with gifts and sundries. Superior Sports, at 1210 Tower, has sporting goods and bicycles and also rents ski equipment. Ritsa's Tailoring and Formal Wear is at 1313 Tower.

The corner of Tower and Belknap remains the city center hub to some extent, mostly because of the traffic flow but also because the new library is on one corner and an old favorite, Globe News, is on the other. Globe sells a variety of newspapers, magazines and tobacco. One block west on Belknap, on the corner of Banks, is another old favorite, Northwest Outlet, selling virtually everything in outdoor and sporting goods and wear. A Super One supermarket is nearby, as are two large liquor stores.

The brightly painted Upper Lakes Foods wholesale and frozen outlet is a couple of blocks north on 1228 Banks Avenue. Continuing south on Tower, the Finnish American Bookstore, 1720 Tower Avenue, has Finland-oriented and Finnish-language books; Superior Design & Coffees, 1828 Tower Avenue, sells dry coffee and gifts alongside its sandwich-desert shop. A Walgreen's variety store and pharmacy is at 2015 Tower Avenue.

Another commercial crossroads is farther south at 28th Street, which begins a newer commercial corridor on Tower. Midtown Plaza has a Jubilee Foods, Hardware Hank and Kmart near this corner. Fast foods and gas stations dot the area, and farther south are Target and Wal-Mart discount stores, Campbell's Building Materials Center, Payless shoes, and auto parts and car sales dealerships.

About 1.25 miles east of Tower on 28th Street, at Hill Avenue, is the Mariner Mall, (715) 392-7117, where you can get your teeth fixed and a doctor's opinion along with your new shoes. The mall has about two dozen shops anchored by JCPenney. Other shops include B. Dalton Bookseller, Younkers Department Store, Walgreen Drug Store, General Nutrition Store, Athlete's Foot, Radio Shack, On Cue book shop, id Boutique and Braun's clothing store and several jewelry and accessory shops. You'll also find a four-screen movie theater and the Mariner Medical Clinic Ltd.

In back of the mall you might notice a series of greenhouses; they belong to Bay Produce Company, a not-for-profit hydroponic (grown in water) tomato producer that employs people with disabilities. Bay Produce tomatoes are sold in most Twin Ports stores and have a ripened-on-the-vine flavor that is a wintertime treat.

Belknap Street goes east to the bay, past restaurants, government buildings, churches, the University of Wisconsin-Superior, office buildings and service shops. Along the way is Daugherty Appliances, 1705 Belknap Street, the People's Drug Store, on a corner at 1124 Belknap Street, and the Belknap Plaza, 114 Belknap Street. The plaza has a Ben Franklin, Jubilee supermarket, Play-It-Again sports (second-hand sporting goods) and a drugstore.

Going out of town on U.S. Highway 2, you'll pass through the Allouez neighborhood, which looks more like a little village. It has bars, liquor stores, bait shops and, in the summer, fireworks and paddy "wild" rice stands (see our wild rice sidebar in this chapter). It's not illegal in Wisconsin to sell firecrackers and other fireworks, and Minnesotans flock across the bridges before the Fourth of July to stock up.

Along the North Shore

A drive up Scenic Highway 61 out of Duluth will bring you to a couple of shopping spots before the scenic part of the highway rejoins the main road at Two Harbors. The **Corner Cupboard**, 5283 North Shore Drive (another name for Scenic Highway 61), sells Amish quilts, handcrafted items and books from the region, collectibles and Borkholder furniture. **Candletiques**, 5746 North Shore Drive, has handmade blown hummingbird feeders, hand-braided wheat, homemade jams and jellies and handmade candles patterned after turn-of-the-century glassware. **Tom's Logging Camp**, 5797 North Shore Drive, sells factory-made moccasins, jewelry, gifts and souvenirs. You can take a break from shopping to see the authentic tools and buildings of a Northwoods logging camp.

Two Harbors Area

Four miles southwest of Two Harbors, on Scenic Highway 61, is **Loon Landing**; you can't miss the big carved loon out front. The shop has Minnesota-made arts and crafts, stained glass and other gift items. Another big-bird gift shop greets you as you enter Two Harbors — this one is a big rooster, advertising **Weldon's Gifts**, which has a lot of floor space filled with gifts and souvenirs.

The highway goes through **Two Harbors** as Seventh Avenue; it passes shops, restaurants, fast foods, Laundromats, mo-

tels, gas stations and grocery stores before leaving town a mile to the northeast. **The Oldest Sister**, 830 Seventh Avenue, is a gift shop in an old-time setting in two buildings (one is the original log cabin). Victorian items, ceramics, chocolates, candles, books and statues are some of the upscale gifts here, and you can get ice cream too. In the summer time, visitors are welcome to relax and enjoy the sounds of a player piano on the deck. Nearby is the **Blueberry House**, 826 Seventh, with wonderful baked goods. **Shari's Kitchen**, a restaurant at 812 Seventh Avenue, has gifts and antiques too. A couple doors down is **The Old Gas Station Gift House**, with pricey Victorian gifts, dry flower arrangements, handmade cards and other items. And its sister-store, **Seventh Heaven Restaurant**, sells local crafts along with coffee, bagels and cookies. **Mimi's**, in a restored home at 731 Seventh Avenue, has women's wear. You'll find gifts and jewelry at **Agate City/Robert's Jewelry** and **Country Crafts**, both at 728 Seventh Avenue in a renovated body shop.

The town's **Minimall**, at Seventh Avenue and Seventh Street, has a bridal shop and **Victoria's House**, which sells chocolates, wrapping paper, cards and jewelry. Gifts and blankets with a northern woodsy flavor are featured at the **Elusive Moose**, 625 Seventh Avenue, where a whole stuffed moose greets you.

To get to downtown Two Harbors, turn toward the lake on Waterfront Street; it will bring you to Lake Avenue, the

---

Insiders' Tips

Here's something handy for the Thunder Bay shopping traveler who has young children in tow: You can rent car seats, cribs, high chairs and strollers at the **Gingerbread House**, 207 Simpson Street. The shop also has high-quality used children's clothing and toys.

town's main street. Although Lake Avenue is losing business to the Seventh Avenue corridor, you'll find a few busy shops here, clustered within two blocks: **Lauralee Department Store**; **Ben Franklin** (a big old-fashioned version, with serviceable china, goldfish, some hardware, fabrics, office supplies and gifts); **Falk's Pharmacy**, with a large assortment of gifts and sundries; **Ray's Shoe Store**; and a **True Value** hardware store.

Continuing out of Two Harbors on Highway 61, we near Silver Creek Cliff and two shops: **Silver Creek Gifts**, 363 Highway 61, with birch basketry, agates, nature art, wild rice, candles, cedar products, bird feeders and Indian pottery. Closer to the cliff is the **Pioneer Crafts Co-op**, which stocks wood and fiber work, pottery and folk art, all from northeastern Minnesota.

Farther north, in the town of **Castle Danger**, **Rustic Inn Gift Shop** features Mikasa crystal, apparel, Christmas items and other gifts.

Beaver Bay Area

The little town of **Beaver Bay** is in two parts, west and east, divided by a bay and forest, and you can see the whole of both towns from Minn. Highway 61. In West Beaver Bay, the **Beaver Bay Agate Shop and Museum** sells rocks, minerals and fossils from around the world. Admission to the museum is free. You can also get gas, sundries and liquor in the village.

Head inland on Minn. Highway 1 to the town of **Finland** where you'll find the **Little Finn Shop**, with gifts, imports and handcrafts and candy for sale in an historical one-room schoolhouse. You can also get groceries, gas, hardware and maps at the **Finland Co-op** there.

In East Beaver Bay is **Beaver Bay Sport Shop**, a snowmobile dealer that also sells live bait, fishing tackle, fishing and hunting licenses, snow boots and camping equipment.

Silver Bay is easily recognizable by the enormous taconite plant along the Lake. Its shopping area is not, however. Turn inland, up the hill at the semaphore and follow the road to the **Silver Bay Shopping Center**, which includes **Julie's Variety & Hardware**, **Dianna's Hallmark Shop** (cards and gifts), **Zupancich Brothers Big Dollar Store** (groceries) and **Zup's Kozy Korner Bakery**.

About 8 miles north of Silver Bay on Minn. Highway 61 is **Little Marais** where **Antilla's Gallery and Handcrafts** sells items from a patio (planters and window boxes, birdhouses and feeders, silk flowers and chain saw art), a two-floor Scandinavian barn (brass and copper weather vanes, sauna stoves, wooden pails and other supplies, nautical items, homemade quilts and books) and the original shop (with Scandinavian gifts: fine jewelry, glassware, linens, rosemaling, sweaters, wood carvings and electric music boxes).

In **Schroeder**, the **Cross River General Store and Bottle Shop** features homemade sausage; **Superior Bakery** handles the staff-of-life and sweet-tooth departments; the **Schroeder Short Stop** has licenses, baits and tackle along with convenience items; and **Dillon's Scrimshaw Jewelry** has offbeat carvings from deer antlers and other items. **Grandpa's Bait**, a mile up County Road 1, has a full line of bait and tackle.

Continuing up Minn. Highway 61 into **Tofte**, **Waters Edge Trading Company** sells outdoor clothing, books, gifts, food and camp items; **North Shore Market & Bottle Shop** has groceries and liquor; **Surf Side Resort** has antiques and

Wear Your Tartan

If you're from Thunder Bay, there's a way to show it to the world. Wear a piece of clothing made with the city's official tartan. A tartan is a plaid-like pattern whose colors and layout show what Scottish clan you belong to. But it also can show what geographical area you come from, regardless of your ethnic background.

Each of the provinces and territories of Canada and many Canadian cities have a distinct "district tartan," duly approved by and registered with the Scottish Tartans Society in Pitlochry, Perthshire, Scotland. The **Head of the Lakes Tartan**© was developed by locals Joan Forrester Troniak and Fiona Irwin for the city's 25th anniversary in 1995. (Thunder Bay is the ancient name for the area occupied by Port Arthur and Fort William, which joined into one city in 1970.) Troniak, who with her husband owns a gift shop that sells many different tartans, planned the colors for the Thunder Bay tartan.

"The background is dark blue, for Lake Superior," Troniak said. "There's a small line of lighter blue for the rivers leading into the Lake; a really dark green for the northern forests and a lighter green for our city parks; a bit of white for our northern climate; and purple for the amethyst that is found here."

Irwin wove the fabric, using the traditional "sett" that is required for tartans (traditional colors, identical warp and weft so the weave comes out in a square and weaving in a twill at a 45-degree angle from the bottom right to the top left). The pair kept rearranging the colors according to Irwin's strict guidelines until they had a pattern that seemed just right. They sent a swatch of the finished cloth to Scotland with an application; approval came soon after. The Thunder Bay City Council accepted it as the official tartan on February 6, 1995.

Troniak said she has been surprised by the way the community has embraced the tartan. It seems to touch something deep in people, she said.

"You know, in our troubled times, people are so scared; we're worried about our jobs, our future — and this seems to be something that can bring us together and make us feel like we belong. This is the tartan of all the people who are in the area, whether they're Scottish or not.

"People send tartans to children who have moved away from the city, to remind them of where they're from. It gives a warm feeling; it says, 'This is yours, because you are part of Thunder Bay.'"

The tartan has found acceptance in formal activities too.

At the national women's curling championship in Thunder Bay in early 1996, the master of ceremonies wore the Head of the Lakes tartan kilt and sash for the opening ceremonies. And it's found among the clan tartans, haggis and bagpipes of annual revelers on "Robbie Burns Day" in February (for Scottish poet Robert Burns).

Now, you can buy scarves, men's ties, women's shawls, handwoven throws and wool worsted fabric, all in the Head of the Lakes Tartan, at Conn's

Head of the Lakes© *is the official tartan of the City of Thunder Bay, Ontario, Canada.*

Mill, the Troniaks' shop (you can also order the items in a particular clan tartan). The shop also sells and mail-orders lace and linens, Celtic jewelry and some kilts and fabrics, including 100 percent cottons and 100 percent wool worsteds.

Troniak can wear either the Head of the Lakes Tartan or the McDonald Tartan, because her father's family – the Forresters — are from a small clan that came under the protection of the larger McDonald clan.

Conn's Mills has a related history. Troniak's great-grandfather was a Scot named Conn who immigrated from Ayrshire and settled in Nova Scotia (Latin for "New Scotland") in early 1800s. He set up a grist mill for wheat flour and corn meal, and a lumber mill. A village grew around the mills and was called Conn's Mills.

gifts; and **Sawtooth Outfitters** handles outdoors equipment, food and clothing.

Clearview General Store at **Lutsen** has groceries, clothing and some gifts and outdoors items. (You can get gas in Schroeder, Tofte and Lutsen, and all stations are on Minn. Highway 61.) **Solbakken Resort** at Lutsen has a book shop with regional books and field guides and a new gift shop with Minnesota and Scandinavian crafts and gifts.

As you approach **Grand Marais**, you'll pass several outfitters and outdoors shops that hug Minn. Highway 61, such as **Bear Track Outfitting Co.** Park and get out

for a stroll around downtown Grand Marais — it's a lovely town, and most shops are near one another. Drop in at **Joynes Department & Ben Franklin Store** for foot gear, clothing, Norwegian sweaters, fine woolens, jams and teas, Hudson Bay blankets and odds 'n' ends. **Lake Superior Trading Post**, down at the harbor, is a must-visit, with name-brand outdoors clothing, elegant gifts, books, maps, snowshoes, jewelry and collectibles. Next, drop by **Beth's Fudge & Gifts** (on the bay; turn right at the end of Main Street) to satiate your sweet tooth.

Buck's Hardware Hank, First Avenue

W. and First Street, has fly-fishing gear, licenses, maps and outdoors equipment. The **Yarn Junction**, 20 First Avenue W., has yarn and knitting supplies; and the **Book Station**, 12 First Avenue W., has a good selection of regional books.

Stephan Hoglund Fine Jewelry Design, 107 W. Wisconsin Street, specializes in Lake Superior designs, lake gemstone jewelry and diamond and gold wedding bands. Next door is the **Waltzing Bear Bookstore & Coffee Brewers**, with literature, nonfiction and poetry. **White Pine North**, 15 W. Wisconsin Street, has specialty coffee, gourmet foods, chocolates, sport clothing and fine gifts.

The **Viking Hus**, right on Minn. Highway 61, has Scandinavian gifts: Carl Larsson books and prints, Lisi cards, jewelry, ethnic foods and coffee, Norwegian sweaters, Danish iron and candles, linens, porcelain and crystal. **Johnson's Big Dollar Store** (groceries and meats) also is on the highway.

Continuing up Minn. Highway 61 toward the United States-Canada border, stop at the **Grand Portage Lodge Gift Shop** for Ojibwe-made deerskin moccasins, beaded chokers and jewelry, porcupine quill work, cards and other gifts. It's easily visible from the highway in **Grand Portage**.

Just a half-mile on the U.S. side of customs, **Ryden's Border Store** along the highway bulges with 10,000 U.S. and Canadian gifts and souvenirs, cowboy boots, Carhart heavy-duty winter wear and duty-free liquor and cigarettes. You can get gas and your money exchanged here too. Winter hours are 7 AM to 8 PM daily; May through October, hours are 5 AM to 10 PM daily.

A few minutes north of the border into Ontario is the **Middle Falls Gift Shop**, just off Minn./Ont. Highway 61 on Ont. Highway 593, with fine bone china, T-shirts and sweatshirts, Canadian crafts and local pottery.

Insiders' Tips

Sick of the mob at the mall? The self service and fast service at most clothing stores? Looking for a sanctuary to relax in while a knowledgeable professional helps you choose clothing? **Silver's Dress Shop**, 724-8897, 1123 E. Superior Street in Duluth, is the place to go. Lean back on a sofa and drink coffee while the gracious staff selects or helps you select clothing and accessories (sportswear, formal wear, working outfits and bridalwear). Silver's opened in the early 1930s, with a few unique designer dresses catering to a few friends. Those were the days when the job of a wealthy woman was to look good at social functions. These days, that woman is probably working and hasn't as much time to spend on shopping — and that means Silver's continues its specialty of coaching the client in coordinating outfits, spending plenty of time with each one, and in general providing quality goods with quality service.

Along the South Shore

The South Shore is a relatively quiet place commercially in the wintertime, but most communities do a bustling summer time business in gifts and crafts. East of Ashland, the South Shore is accessed by U.S. Highway 2. From Ashland to near Superior, Wis. Highway 13 takes you along the South Shore.

Beginning from the west on Wis. Highway 13, in the village of **Port Wing**, you'll find two shopping choices: groceries and smoked fish at **Johnson's** store and pottery and handcrafted wooden chests at **Port Wing Pottery**. Both hug the highway, and you can't miss them. The pottery is in a green-trimmed white clapboard church, which still has the bell intact in the belfry. Owner Shane Upthegrove throws pots in half the church and sells wares in an artistic setting in the other half. You're welcome to watch her work at the wheel and at the firing shed out back. The shop is open 10 AM to 5 PM seven days a week in the summer, and she's often there during the winter too.

Continuing east on Wis. Highway 13, the **Cabin Fever Quilt Co.** is just east of **Herbster**. Turn left at the Cardinal Lumber Co. onto Old School Road and drive down to the Lake. Turn right; the shop is the fourth place on the right on Bark Point Road. It's an attractive wooden cabin; from May to October, you can buy artistic handmade picture quilts and other handcrafts from local people, such as rugs and apple dolls. Quiltmaker Connie Daniels lives next door, so there are no special hours.

East of Herbster lies **Cornucopia**, a tiny fishing village that now has more shops than fish houses and more sailboats than fishing boats. The Siskuit River splits the marina into two parts: **Siskiwit Bay Marina** (the newcomer marina owner has declared the river is misspelled, but people here ignore him — Siskiwit is spelled about six different ways along the Lake, and all are correct) on the west side serves the sailboat crowd and has a gift shop featuring stained glass.

Cornucopia Public Harbor has a string of shops, all in old fishing buildings: **The Good Earth**, with books, cards and gifts; **What Goes 'Round**, with used quality books, furniture and tools; **River's End**, with gifts, gallery antiques and organic produce; **Cornucopia Gift Shop**, with teas, jewelry, souvenirs, baskets, glassware and handcrafts; and **Hart's Handweaving**, with handwoven woolens and cotton clothing. These places are open in summer only.

A half-block inland is "Corny's" year-round business district, with a post office, restaurant and **Ehler's** general store, which has been selling fresh meat, groceries and hardware for eight decades.

Bayfield Area

Wis. Highway 13 rounds a bend and turns south at the Red Cliff Reservation; **Buffalo Bay Store** is just before the bend, a geodesic dome quick mart that sells discount cigarettes and liquor, gas, wild rice, clothing and some Ojibwe crafts. **Peterson's Foods** around the bend has a full line of meats, fresh produce and smoked fish. (For other smoked fish retailers, see our Fishing and Hunting chapter.)

Nearing **Bayfield** on Wis. Highway 13 is **Ahnen's** roadside stand, an old favorite where, in the summer time, you can get excellent homemade jams and jellies. For that matter, you can get jams and jellies just about anywhere in the Bayfield area, which because of peculiarities of weather

Wild About Rice

If you buy "wild rice" at $1 to $4 a pound, you should know that you're probably not experiencing "real" wild rice — the mahnomen that grows naturally in the shallow lakes and rivers of northern Minnesota, Wisconsin and Ontario. Wild rice was always cultivated in a modest way by Indian people of the past, but recent rapid developments are fast-forwarding the transition from wild to domestic grain. Nowadays, paddy growers (mostly in California, where it's not native, but also in Minnesota) do high-tech experiments with various hybrids, grow the rice in controlled environments and harvest it with machines. This cheaper product is often sold as "cultivated wild rice."

Photo: Duluth News-Tribune

Making a big business of mahnomen ("real" wild rice) is something akin to sacrilege for many Indian people, to whom wild rice has been a Creator-given staff of life. On the other hand, some tribes are getting in on the action of raising the more market-stable paddy rice. Unlike real wild rice, the cultivated version takes a long time to cook and won't fluff up unless you use a pressure cooker. But even then, it lacks the rich, nutty flavor of mahnomen. (So what mass-produced food does have that good old-fashioned flavor?)

Natural wild rice is a genuine delicacy costing $5 to $12 a pound (depending on the year's harvest). You

Jim Northrup harvested a load of rice from a reservation lake.

can buy it at many food stores, some gift shops, most reservations and at all whole foods stores. It has a lighter color than the almost-black paddy rice and will be marked "hand-harvested natural lake wild rice." It takes only 10 to 20 minutes to cook.

If you've already bought commercial rice, don't dismay; Insiders know two ways of using it. One is with a special cooking technique: Get a nice smooth basalt rock from Lake Superior, a little larger than a baseball; wash it well and place it in the kettle with the washed rice and water. Bring the water to a boil and simmer; when the rock is soft, the rice is done. The other use is suggested by Jim Northrup, a lifelong ricer and award-winning writer from the Fond du Lac Reservation near Duluth. He spreads it under his car's spinning wheels in the wintertime, and it gives some traction — not as good as sand, but really good sand is scarcer here than fake wild rice.

and soil is a regular northern fruit bowl. To get to the bowl's center, take Washington Avenue up the hill from the ferry dock about 1.5 miles to Betzold Road. You'll see a "sign mall" there directing you to different apple orchards and berry fields. **James Erickson Orchard & County Store** is to the right on Betzold Road, a half-mile down. There, you can pick your own apples and strawberries or buy apples, wild rice, maple syrup, cheeses, pottery and wood crafts — and look over the antiques and collectibles shed. **Bayfield Apple Company** is another mile down at the intersection of County Road J. It has the biggest raspberry orchard in the Midwest, selling fresh fruit, apple and mixed berry ciders and jams and jellies. You're welcome to watch the crew make ciders and jams.

Aside from fruit and fish, Bayfield's specialty is gifts. There are no fast-food franchises or discount stores in or near Bayfield, and all the shops — those catering to tourists as well as those serving the practical daily needs of residents — are small, one-story, locally owned outlets all within easy walking distance of one another. On Rittenhouse Avenue, the main street that descends to the city park and waterfront, is a grocery store, **Trek & Trail** (outdoor gear), two candy shops, **The Yulery** (Christmas gifts and decorations), clothing shops, a hardware store, **Donalee Designs** (silversmithing) and **Joanne's Scandinavian Gifts**, 223 Rittenhouse Avenue. **Granny's and Gramp's** bakery features various heavy breads baked in a special steam machine and apple pie that won a first place at the Bayfield Apple Festival. Granny and Gramps couldn't enter other years because they were too busy making apple fritters!

Manypenny, S. Second and S. Broad streets, which lead from Rittenhouse to-

ward the bay, have several galleries and a few other shops: **Stone's Throw**, selling stoneware, jewelry and some Native Americana; **Superior Sail Loft**, with sails, totes and duffel bags; the **Sea Store**, selling rubber boots and shoes, maps, lamps and other seafaring equipment and clothing; and **Apostle Island Outfitters**, with outdoor gear, gifts, clothing and Minnetonka brand moccasins. The city's big pharmacy also is in this section of town.

A couple of streets that head north from Rittenhouse in the city dock area also have shops. On N. Front Street you'll find antiques shops, galleries, the **Dock Shop** and **Monkey Business** T-shirts. On N. First Street is **Antiques at Twenty North First**, a used book shop that also sells antiques. (See this chapter's "Antiques and Thrifts" section for details.) **Call of the Wild**, featuring gifts of the Apostle Islands, and another outlet of **Trek & Trail** are on nearby Washington Avenue, at the entrance to city dock and city beach. Also on N. First, open year round, is the **Viking Mall**, with a grocery store and liquor store.

Don't forget the shopping on **Madeline Island**. If you enjoy strolling, park your car at Bayfield's ferry dock and ride over on the ferry boat (see our Getting Around chapter for details); it's a lot cheaper as a walk-on, and the shops on the island are all in walking distance from the dock. Like many of the gift shops in Bayfield, these shops are closed in the winter. **Dockside Gifts** sells souvenir clothing, nautical, wildlife and wildflower gift items, jewelry and dolls. **Go Waterfront Gallery** sells fine quality regional and worldwide crafts as well as local and regional art. **Vi's Lighthouse Gifts** features Apostle Islands photographs and art, lead crystal cut glassware, miniatures, children's items and nature collectibles. **Woods Hall Craft Shop** has original design handwoven rugs, scarves, table runners, handcrafted jewelry and pottery. Souvenir clothing and gift items are featured at the **Rendezvous Center**, between the Pub and the Madeline Island Yacht Club.

Back on the mainland, heading south from Bayfield on Wis. Highway 13, you'll see the renowned **Eckels Pottery Shop** on the right. It's open year round, seven days a week. Visitors are welcome to watch the entire process of making handcrafted stoneware and handpainted fine porcelain, made with lead-free glazes and fired so they're ovenproof, waterproof and usable in microwave ovens. Nearby is another branch of County Road J (remember the one in Bayfield?); turn right and go a mile west to **Blue Vista Farm** where you'll see 2 acres of flowers, about 1,000 apple trees and several acres of blueberries and raspberries. You can buy them picked, packaged, squeezed (cider) and dried (flowers), or you can stroll through the orchards and pick them yourself in season. Blue Vista is open May to November.

Washburn, 12 miles south of Bayfield, is the governmental center of the county and not a big draw for tourist shopping. Nevertheless, it does have a few shops of interest and is a good place for ordinary needs: groceries, hardware and drugstore items. **The Floral Gallery** has both flowers and gifts, and **Therene's Boutique and Hair Salon** has an unusual selection of jewelry, gifts and cards. You can also buy AVEDA natural products here.

At **Washburn Produce and Liquor** on the western edge of town on Wis. Highway 13, you can buy cheese, maple syrup, wild rice, liquor and, in season, produce. The mounds of pumpkins outside in the fall are a joy to behold.

Ashland Area

With a population of 8,600, **Ashland** is the largest of South Shore communities and has a reputation for protecting the environment and community life while trying to maintain a healthy economy. That attitude may have contributed to the fact that this is one of the rare cities whose downtown is still fairly intact.

About four blocks along Main Street — parallel with Lake Shore Drive (U.S. Highway 2) just a block away — is where you'll find this downtown, a delight for those who yearn for "real" downtowns. **JCPenney** still anchors a corner, and there's still a downtown movie house here. Many of town's professionals work in offices on this street near the city and county buildings and the beautiful Vaughan Library. Consequently, the downtown bustles during the day, although most shops shut down in the evening.

On Main, between Sixth and Second avenues W., you'll find three jewelry stores (including fine china, clocks and glassware); **Primarily Plants** (greenery); a bakery; **Inner Light** (candles, pottery, incense and other gifts relating to angels); **Bay City Cycles**, selling bicycles; two bridal shops; an unpainted furniture store; **Designers' Outlet** (fine carpets, wicker, furniture and lamps); **EC Crafts & Ceramics** (stained glass, brushes, paints, cross-stitch, bisque and greenware); the **Army Navy Store** ("the workingman's friend"), selling choppers (roomy, unadorned buckskin mitts with woolen mittens inside), snowshoes, jackets, snow pants and safety equipment; **The Hub** (men's wear and tuxedos); **Designs** (fine clothing for women); **Maurice's** men's and women's clothing; **Sports Stuff**, selling boxing and exercise equipment, hats and clothing; **Happy Hallmark Shop**, with cards and gifts; the **Athletic Shop** (team clothing); and the **New England Store**, with figurines and knickknacks.

On the cross-street is **Chequamegon Food Co-op**, 215 Chapple Avenue, with natural and health foods. Up two blocks at 216 Fourth Avenue W. is **C.M.N. Doll Shop**, with a wide selection of handpainted porcelain dolls and doll clothing. Back down on Main but farther west is the **Craft Connection**, 911 W. Main Street, with art and craft supplies and contemporary beadwork.

Lake Shore Drive (U.S. Highway 2 in town) is a combination of a strip, heavy industry and a Lake view. It's about 2 miles long, with fast-food eateries, gas stations, quick marts, liquor stores, motels, restaurants and local shops. At the western end of the strip is **Bodin's**, which sells skis, bikes, camping equipment, paddles and other outdoors and sports equipment. Moving east, you'll find **Waterfront Antique and Gift** at the corner of Beaser, which, besides antiques, also carries used books; fruits and vegetables at **Ashland Produce**; two supermarkets; and **Chequamegon Bay Gallery**, with the double draw of arts and gifts from the region plus fudge and Wisconsin cheese. Nearby, also on Lakeshore Drive, is a **Medicine Shoppe Pharmacy**, **Sail 'N' Dive** (cross-country skis, snowshoes, snowboards and snowboard rentals), **Coast-to-Coast Hardware** and **Anglers All** sporting goods shop.

Still farther east, on the way out of town, is the **Plaza Shopping Center**, with a **Pamida** discount store, a drugstore, the **Economart Grocery** (which collapsed in early 1996 under the weight of unusually heavy snowfalls but was able to re-open within days) and **Ashland Northern Merchandise**, with gadgets, crystal, porcelain dolls and toys. Last on the strip are a **Wal-Mart** and **Payless** shoe store.

It's a short distance down U.S. Highway 2 to the **Bad River Reservation**. Several smoke shops dot U.S. 2 on the reservation where you can buy discount tobaccos and, at some shops, discount liquors too. **Bear Trap Trading Post** has no liquor, but it does have beautifully decorated white buckskin fringed bags, deerskin pouches, beadwork, porcupine quill work, birchbark basketry and beading supplies. The nearby **Three Eagles** shop also features Ojibwe handcrafts, including a large selection of beaded deerskin moccasins, moose hide moccasin boots and turquoise-silver jewelry.

Hurley/Ironwood Area

Just before you reach **Hurley**, look for **Little Finland Gifts** on the left along U.S. Highway 2. It's a log cabin built in the traditional Finnish "fish tail" log construction, and it includes both gifts and a museum. It's open 10 AM to 2 PM Wednesdays and Saturdays.

At the turn of the century, Hurley

How do you say "apple pie" in Ojibwe? "Batemishiminebaashkiminasiganibiitooyingwesijigani-bakwezhigan." (It is linguistically acceptable to wrestle this word into manageable sections by putting hyphens between word clusters, but Ojibwe writers think it's more fun to leave it be and watch your reaction.)

Insiders' Tips

was the R and R center where loggers and miners were relieved of their paychecks, and that legacy is still evident. In six blocks along the town's main street, Silver Street, you'll find 19 saloons. You can also find a drugstore, grocery store and hardware store and a logfront building with a big sign hanging out in front: **The Iguana Factory**. Rene, who is 4.5 feet long, lives here, along with tropical fish, exotic birds and pet supplies. You can't buy Rene, but the other items are for sale.

Silver Street dips down to a little bridge crossing the Montreal River, putting you into Michigan and onto Ironwood's main street, Aurora. Except for a **Pamida** discount store, **Radio Shack**, **Ben Franklin** and a remarkable gift shop — **Wildernest** — the downtown along Aurora Street is mostly services, restaurants, furniture stores, bars, banks and bakeries. You'll find pasties at all bakeries (try the **Famous CAP Pastry Kitchen & Pasty**, 127 W. Aurora Street) and many cafes in this area. A pasty is a meat- or vegetable-filled pastry that was introduced by Cornish miners. Pasties consequently are common fare both here and on Minnesota's Iron Range.

Wildernest, 111 E. Aurora Street, is a large, roomy store, very tastefully arranged, that sells unusual gifts: three-dimensional puzzles, odd-shaped kites, Raintree wooden puzzles and games, books by local authors, coffeetable and children's books, Sheila's Collectibles (wooden Victorian homes and lighthouses), birdhouses, nature tapes, photographs of native plants and animals by local people and fine woven fabrics. **Elle Stevens Jewelers**, 135 E. Aurora Street, has collectibles, gifts and fine jewelry. A variety of watches can be found at **Ives Watch**, 107 E. Aurora Street, where you can also get your watch repaired. **J.R. Warren** sells fine jewelry at 110 E. Aurora Street.

Suffolk Street intersects Aurora downtown. Near the intersection is **Northwind Natural Foods Co-op**, 210 S. Suffolk Street, with whole and organic foods and nutritional supplements. Across the street is **Hulstrom's City News & Agate Shop** where you can get a variety of newspapers and magazines — and gemstones. On the other side of Aurora is **The Sporting Look**, 119 S. Suffolk Street, with Russell athletic wear, sports novelties and sports medicine products. **The Diamond Shop**, 125 S. Suffolk Street, sells fine jewelry.

Nearby, at 505 McLeod Avenue, is the **Equestrian Connection**, with saddlery and supplies for both English and western. Besides feed, the **Range Flour & Feed Store**, 301 E. Frederick Street, sells tropical fish, hamsters, gerbils, reptiles, birds and aquariums. **The Fabric Patch**, 121 N. Lowell Street, has a large selection of quilting books, craft patterns and quilting fabrics. **Gloria's Boutique**, 323 Douglas Boulevard, specializes in dolls, stuffed animals, wigs, toupees and gifts from around the world.

Most serious day-to-day shopping in the twin towns has moved out to U.S. Highway 2 in Ironwood. Amongst the motels, quick marts and gas stations are a **Super One** supermarket; the **Hobby Wheel**, with bikes, skis and rentals; the **Family Dollar** variety store; and **Trek & Trail**, with mountain bikes, skis and fly-fishing equipment. The nearby Ironwood strip mall is anchored by **Kmart** and **JCPenney**. It also has a **Hallmark** card shop, **Dunham's Discount Sports** (toboggans, sleds, basketballs, clothing), **On Cue** (books, movies and music), **Carlson's County Market** (24-hour discount foods), **Fashion Bug** clothing, **Michael's Shoes** and **Maurice's** men's clothing.

It All Comes Out in the Wash

Anyone who is forced to spend several hours a week in a Laundromat knows they can be some of the most miserable places on earth, with dirty floors, broken machines and unwashed dented aluminum ashtrays that fly off the folding table scattering ashes whenever the door swings open.

That's why two Laundromats in Duluth warrant a visit — especially if you have clothes that need washing.

Photo: Duluth News-Tribune
Taco is the guy who escaped his Chester Park Laundromat home.

One is the cleanest, greenest Laundromat in the area — maybe in the world! **Spirit Valley Laundromat**, 628-3147, is at 232 N. Central Avenue, a block from the I-35 Central exit south of downtown. The green-thumb owner lives upstairs, keeping a close watch over equipment and more than 150 hanging baskets, as her employees polish and scrub and vacuum nonstop. The plants are healthy, there's no smoking inside, you'll find fairly recent magazines to peruse while you wait, and the carpeted floor is clean enough for your toddler to roll about. And the machines all work!

The other is the **Chester Park Laundromat**, 724-5025, at 1328 E. Fourth Street (from Superior Street, drive up 14th Avenue E. five blocks until it dead-ends, turn left and park by the wooded ravine). This place is a bit tattered, but that's not why you're here. Look up over the machines; hanging from the ceiling, running the length of the Laundromat, is a wire mesh-enclosed aviary. Parrots cavort and finches sing here while you wash your clothes. In the mid-1980s, one of the parrots flew down to the waterfront for a little holiday in a fruit warehouse. The alarm was sounded, he was discovered and returned home to the Laundromat, safe and sound and satiated.

He could have gone to the Whole Foods Coop next door, where there are mounds of organically-grown fruits, a deli that sells healthy lunches, and coolers filled with juices, rice and soy drinks and kefir. That's the other reason for hanging around this neighborhood while waiting for your clothes to dry!

Thunder Bay Area

Although Thunder Bay has been a united city since 1970, the former city centers of Port Arthur and Fort William remain evident. Shopping here tends to cluster in those two areas, which are now called Thunder Bay North and Thunder Bay South, and in a third, intercity area.

South-side merchants say there's "more in store in the south core," and it's a good place for a visitor to start. **Victoriaville Centre**, in the heart of the Fort William District at 500 Donald Street E., 623-4944, is primarily an office mall, with about 100 offices. But it also has lots of food outlets and shops in its indoor pedestrian promenade. Among them are **Gift Avenue**, one of the city's largest gift stores (crystal, artwork, toys, souvenirs, Canadian products and free gift wrapping); **Decorators Corner**, everything for the home; **B.J.'s Den** (men's items, such as shaving brushes, belts and gifts); **Churchley's Jewelers**; **This, That and Almost Everything** (knickknacks, souvenirs, yarn); **The Kitchen Store** (you can fill up your kitchen from its selection); **Hallmark** card store; **Coles, The Book People**; **Accents**, with women's clothing and special-order accessories and lingerie; and a **Saan's** discount store.

For the shopper who would rather visit attractive, independent shops, visit the nearby cluster known as the **May Street Merchants**: **Eagle Feather**, 126 N. May Street, sells carvings, dream-catchers, paintings, prints, posters, wind chimes, batik and handwoven clothing. **Grandma's Natural Foods**, 119 N. May Street, has whole and health foods. **Victoria's Cupboard**, 111 N. May Street, features dried florals and antiques. **Conn's Mills**, 109 N. May Street, stocks Celtic jewelry, kilts, Victorian prints, fine laces and linens, afghans and quilts (see this chapter's sidebar). **Yesterday's**

Treasures, 107 N. May Street, is an outlet for sports cards, coins, comics and other memorabilia, while **Marj 'n' Millie's Country Crafts & Supplies** is at 129 S. May Street. **Karen Fron Crafts & Gifts for Gracious Living**, 113 S. May Street, sells linens, laces, fabric, gourmet oils and crafts.

Global Experiences, 510 E. Victoria Avenue, has environmental and cultural gifts (cleansers, clothing, children's gifts and specialty foods). **The Little Mermaid**, with upscale bridal and evening wear for women, is at 429 E. Victoria. Nearby is **Hull's Family Bookstore**, 127 S. Brodie Street, with evangelical Christian- and family-oriented books, gifts and videos.

A few blocks west is **Sincerely Yours Porcelain Dolls**, 214 S. Norah Street, where the owner makes the figures by hand. In the same neighborhood is **Thunder Books**, 809 Miles Street E., which has a large selection of sci-fi new releases, fantasy and horror books, and Dungeons & Dragons games.

West on Arthur Street, just west of Highway 61, is **Thunder Bay Mall**, 1101 W. Arthur Street, with 20 stores and services anchored by **Kmart** and **A&P Grocery**.

Northeast is the **Northwood Park Plaza**, 425 N. Edward Street, 577-7933, a neighborhood mall anchored by **Zellers** discount store, **Northwood Foods** and **Shoppers Drug Mart**.

Moving back toward the Lake, we come to the **Intercity Shopping Centre**, 1000 Fort William Road, 623-6646. Anchored by **Sears** and **Zellers**, this is the largest center in northwestern Ontario, with a food court and about 75 stores. Among them: **Classic Bookshop**, a general bookstore; **Silk & Satin** lingerie; **Lewiscraft**, selling gifts and crafts; **The Mighty Dollar**, a chain discount store; **Athlete's Foot** shoe store; **Pantorama**, with a large and varied selection of jeans, pants, slacks and some sporty tops; **Suzy Shier**, with clothing for teenagers; **Radio Shack**; **Coles, The Book People**, a general bookstore; **Amos & Andes Imports**, with wool/cotton sweaters, rainsticks and jackets; **Music City**, with CDs, cassettes and videos of great performances; and **Japan Camera**, where you can get your film processed in an hour.

About two blocks north of Intercity is **Wal-Mart**, at Memorial and 10th avenues. Just south of that is the **Great Canadian Super Store**, 600 Harbor Expressway, with groceries, clothing, furniture and more. At the **McIntyre Center** on nearby Memorial Avenue, 622-5731, is **Native Arts and Crafts**, with Ojibwe and Inuit creations such as moccasins, beadwork, porcupine quill work, pipes, gauntlets, tamarack carvings, soapstone carvings, blankets and parkas. A few blocks west is **Gear Up For Outdoors**, 894 Alloy Place, with cold-weather clothing, footwear and accessories, snowshoes, arctic sleeping bags and vehicle survival kits.

Up at the **Heart of the Harbor**, the **Thunder Mountain Store**, 28 S. Cumberland Street, also sells sleeping bags and outer wear: Gore-Tex and Polartec fleece from Sierra Designs. Also in the neighborhood is **Northern Woman's Bookstore**, 65 S. Court Street, and **Sweet Thursday**, 30 St. Paul Street, with a quality selection of books.

Nearing the Keskus Harbour Mall, you'll find **Mystic**, 291 Park Avenue, with natural products for the mind, body and spirit. **Keskus Harbour Mall**, 230 Park Avenue, 345-5335, has its main entrance off Red River Road. Anchored by **Eaton's** clothing store, this mall has a food court with a view of the Lake and 50 other shops. **Collector's Companion**, just across from Eaton's, sells Drake porcelain dolls as well as products from Boyd's Bears, Sandicast, Krystonia and Pendelfin. **Kitty Cucumber Children's Boutique** is next door to the mall entrance, 38 S. Cumberland Street, and sells boys' and girls' designer clothing.

A short trip west on Oliver Road will bring you to Lakehead University where you can visit the **Intersection Gift Stop** (clothing, candles, stuffed animals, cards) and the **Alumni Bookstore**, which carries a fair selection of books along with textbooks. Both are in the **University Center**, the main building.

North of the university, the **Catholic Truth Society of Canada**, 705 Red River Road, sells religious articles, books, gifts, CDs and videos. A few blocks west of Keskus Harbour Mall is **Farrant & Gordon Ltd.**, 234 Pearl Street, with men's wear, formal rentals and a tailor shop.

A few blocks farther west is the **Bay Street** area, with many interesting shops. Here, you'll find the **Finnish Book Store**, on the corner of Bay and Algoma, specializing in European imports, ethnic books and Canadian gifts; **Fireweed**, 182 S. Algoma Street, selling upscale contemporary crafts of clay, fiber, wood, metal and stained glass; and **Elfabets Books & More for Kids**, 197 S. Algoma Street, with quality books for kids of all ages: classics and new releases, Canadian regional and French-language. **The Harri Bakery**, 223 S. Algoma Street, is a great favorite in Thunder Bay, specializing in Finnish breads, cakes, pastry and fruit tarts. **Global Experiences**, 41 S. Algoma Street, has environmental and cultural gifts (cleansers, clothing, children's gifts and specialty foods).

County Fair Plaza, 767-8758, is in the northwest section of town at 1020 Dawson Road, just west of the Thunder Bay Expressway. With **Zellers** as an anchor, the plaza has a grocery and 35 shops and services, including a **Classic Bookshop** and a huge **Beaver** lumber and building supplies store.

Folks in Thunder Bay like gift baskets, whether loaded with gourmet foods, cheese, fruit, dried floral arrangements or everything; and there are plenty of shops to supply them. Here are a few: **A Tisket, A Tasket**, 38 S. Cumberland Street; **Kelly's Nutrition Center**, 640 River Street (all-natural-foods get-well baskets, and specialty baskets for celiacs and diabetics); **George's Market**, at the corner of River and Balsam streets; **Petals 'N' Pots**, 1000 Russell Street; **Baskets by Marie**, 510 Thorndale Crescent; and **Hello Dolly**, 240A Red River Road.

Antiques and Thrifts

For the true bargain hunter as well as the serious collector, we suggest our tried and true four-part formula. First, haunt your local antique shops and let the dealers know what you are collecting. A good dealer will keep a card of your desires and call you when he or she finds something up your alley. Our second strategy is to work the estate sales and get a number for the first rush, the first day. You'll be rubbing and bumping elbows with the frenzied dealers, but that's just fine. Our third strategy is to attend auctions, but make sure you have plenty of time to look over the stuff. A hairline crack on a Roseville vase makes it less than a bargain.

Estate auctions are held either on-site

or at another announced location. Pick up a copy of the Sunday *Duluth News-Tribune* for classified ad listings. For auction action in Duluth and Superior, the main auctioneers are Seller's Auction, which holds auctions every Monday at 4:30 PM at 2103½ W. Third Street, Duluth; Nordic Auction, 3932 Grand Avenue, Duluth, and Oulu, Wisconsin; Crescent Auctioneering, 124 W. Winona Street, Duluth; and Campbell Company, 1628 London Road, Duluth.

And, finally, make the rounds of the local thrift shops regularly; new merchandise is always coming in.

Antiques Shops

Twin Ports Area

DULUTH

In the Twin Ports, the antique scene has boomed in the last couple of years. **Brass Bed Antiques**, 329 Canal Park Drive, was the original waterfront antique shop, started in 1972 when Canal Park was still an industrial area. It's crammed full of stuff, ranging from Stickley armchairs and art to pottery, rugs and glassware, in an old storefront with antique hardware a specialty. Stroll from Brass Bed Antiques down to the **Antique Centre Duluth**, 335 Canal Park Drive, a one-story mall; dealers specialize in everything from painted china, linens and primitives to toys, pottery and art glass. Cross over to the **Canal Park Antique Center**, 310 Lake Avenue S. This extensive, two-story mall can take more than an hour to go through. It's filled with oak, walnut and pine furniture, prints, kitchen collectibles, fine porcelain, outdoor collectibles, pottery and clocks. Walk from Canal Park to Superior Street where you'll find several antiques and collectibles shops, including **Retro Americana**, 38 E. Superior Street, with lots of kitschy, dig-through stuff, and **Antiques on Superior Street**, 11 W. Superior Street, in the brownstone storefront. Consignment antiques and collectibles, ranging from fine jewelry to bedroom sets, are tastefully displayed.

Woodland Antiques, 1535 Woodland Avenue, near the University of Minnesota, is a house with the first floor and porch chock-full of nicely displayed merchandise. The collection includes quality glassware, advertising items, dolls and toys, seasonal decorations, jewelry, prints, Indian collectibles and textiles.

D.B. Enterprises Antiques, in Twig, about 20 miles northwest of Duluth on the Miller Trunk Highway (U.S. Highway 53) is worth the drive. The shop specializes in lighting, Victorian and primitive furniture, crockery, art pottery and pictures.

Main Street Antiques, 612 Cloquet Avenue, Cloquet, about 25 miles from Duluth, is also worth the drive for the many rooms of antiques and collectible furniture, pottery, glassware, prints, toys and linens.

SUPERIOR

If you cross the river to Superior, budget a chunk of time and energy for the two-story **Superior Antique Depot** on Oakes and Broadway. This renovated depot has dozens of dealers with lots to look at in a sunny, pleasant setting. The Depot carries a full line of antiques, including glassware, pottery, seasonal decorations, lots

You can't miss the huge fish hanging out of the Beaver House bait shop in Grand Marais.

of Red Wing, wicker, oak, quilts, kitchen collectibles, lamps, tools and toys.

The **Port of Call Marketplace**, at E. Second Street and U.S. Highway 2, is an antiques and collectible consignment shop. Although modest in size, the store is packed with lots of glassware, linens, jewelry, toys, vases, pictures and lamps. Check out the bargain room in the basement.

Along the North Shore

On the North Shore, we always stop at **Carousel Antiques** in Two Harbors on Minn. Highway 61. This large, jam-packed store, with a little attic of furniture, has an extensive selection of antiques and collectible pottery and glassware, including Red Wing, Roseville, McCoy, Weller, Hull, Hall, Noritake, Nippon and Carnival as well as Depression glass and Fiesta ware. Toys, prints and railroad items are other popular inventory.

Second Chance Antiques, 127 Seventh Street, Two Harbors, occupies a huge space that was formerly a fire hall. Goods, which are on consignment, include furniture, china, crockery, glassware, tools and prints.

In Beaver Bay, stop by **Bay Antiques**, Minn. Highway 61. The antiques and collectibles are nicely displayed. Here you'll find flow blue, painted china, cut and pressed glass, textiles, oak and wicker, pictures and kitchen items.

In Grand Marais, there are two stores in which we like to poke around. **Lake Superior Collectibles**, on First Avenue W., is a big old storefront filled with a jumble of good stuff. (Wear a sweater; it can be damp in the store.) The front rooms are stuffed with old magazines, jewelry, buttons, glassware, linens and pottery. The back rooms hold lots of tables, chairs, trunks and odds and ends. **Magpie Antiques**, 110 Second Avenue, on the Lake next to Best Western, is a well-organized shop with a range of kitchen items, glassware, linens and toys. The last time we visited, a mint-condition red and white quilt caught our eye.

Along the South Shore

On the South Shore, you can make the rounds in Bayfield, Washburn and Ashland for some fine antiquing. In Bayfield, our favorite place is **Antiques at Twenty North First** at (surprise!) 20 N. First Street. This handsome cottage, with antiques and collectibles displayed lovingly in every room and on the porch,

is a treat to browse. The proprietors specialize in estate jewelry and books, but you can always find wonderful advertising graphics, primitives, glassware and vintage clothing. And there's a big bargain basement. If you like a dig-through challenge, don't miss **Sally's** open-air shop, a quarter-mile north of Bayfield on Wis. Highway 13.

When in Washburn, check out **Wooden Sailor Antiques**, 18 W. Bayfield Street, for advertising collectibles, linens, pottery and furniture. Across the Chequamegon Bay in Ashland, try the **Antique Inn**, 2016 E. Lake Shore Drive. This spacious, well-organized shop has cases of pottery, china, toys and postcards, a room of kitchen collectibles and a room dedicated to furniture.

Also in Washburn, at the west end of town, look for **Waterfront Antique and Gift** at the corner of Beaser and U.S. Highway 2. Spacious rooms are filled with antique tables and cupboards displaying collectible glassware and pottery. The porch is now a library with collectible and used books.

Eight miles west of Ashland on U.S. Highway 2, make a stop at **Over the Hill Antiques**, a tiny storybook cottage near the highway. We've found some wonderful things tucked in this shop, including a great tramp-art corner stand and McCoy vases, and the proprietors are always friendly.

In Ironwood, two stores worth a browse are the **Depot Antique Shop**, 318 N. Lake Street, and **Carriage House Antiques**, 303 S. Lowell Street, which sells glassware, furniture, coins, guns and linens.

Thunder Bay Area

In Thunder Bay, expect value for your dollar and lots of fun tea pots, cheese covers, lovely plates and tea sets. We like to stroll through old downtown Port Arthur and browse several shops, including **Linda and Norm's Antiques and Collectibles**, 18 Cumberland Street S., where we've seen and bought some wonderful lamps; **Northern Light Antiques**, 20 Cumberland Street N., a shop with Canadian quilts, furniture, pottery and glass; and **Jennifer's Antiques**, 19 Cumberland Street S., a mix of new and old fine china, glassware and vintage jewelry. Another shop with a mix of nice-quality furniture, pottery, vases, kitchen collectibles and tins is **Sunshine Antiques**, 1120 Lithium Drive.

Thrift Shops

Thrifts, also known as secondhand shops, come and go in many of the small towns along the shore. We've mentioned the classic thrifts — the Salvation Army and Goodwill — which have regular hours and organized merchandise, and several independent shops.

Twin Ports Area

DULUTH

For secondhand shops, try the mothership **Goodwill Store**, 700 Garfield Avenue. You can sometimes come across nice vintage furniture, but don't expect any "finds." The **Salvation Army Shop**, 5614 Grand Avenue, is clean and well-organized. It carries mainly clothing, but the last time we were in, there was a Victorian pump organ for sale. The **St. Vincent de Paul Thrift Stores**, 109 W. Fourth Street and 1923 W. Superior Street, can be claustrophobic, with their cluttered and usually overheated atmosphere. But you never know what you might find. We have a friend who bought a used upright piano for a song. The piano, covered with layers of old paint, turned out to be a Steinway.

SUPERIOR

You'll find some of the same secondhand shops in Superior as in Duluth, including the **Goodwill Store**, 1719 Belknap Street, and the **St. Vincent de Paul Thrift Store**, 1217 John Avenue. Both stores carry mostly men's, women's and children's clothing and household items. We've found some nice hammered-aluminum pieces at these shops. In addition, check out the **Superior Flea Market**, Tower Avenue & Broadway Street.

Along the North Shore

The **Second Hand Rose**, on Minn. Highway 61, is in the basement of Bay Antiques. The shop features clean used home furnishings and clothing.

Along the South Shore

In Ashland, check out the **Senior Center Bargain Hut**, 420 Chapple Avenue, and **The Thrift Shop**, 202 Main Street, run by volunteers from Memorial Medical Center. In Washburn, there is the **ABC Thrift Shop**, 118 W. Bayfield Street. These stores have clothing, kitchen items and sometimes furniture.

In Duluth's real estate market, a full view of Lake Superior will add $10,000 to $15,000 to a property's value.

Inside
Real Estate

Whether your dream home is a rustic log cabin complete with Finnish sauna, a Queen Anne Victorian, a mansion with servants quarters and a carriage house or a sleek, contemporary Lake home, the choice of housing stock, particularly in Duluth and Superior, is quite diverse. Pricing is wide-ranging, with many factors to consider: view, schools, lot size and neighborhood property values, among others. However, relatively inflated price tags on housing located in the "hot" vacation/retirement property areas, such as Grand Marais, Minnesota, and Bayfield, Wisconsin, reflect the strong buyer demand in those markets.

Twin Ports Area

Duluth and Superior each are made of distinctive neighborhoods, many of which were independent villages and townships before they joined the larger cities.

In each of these neighborhoods, residential real estate prices generally are guided by the assets of the specific location. Home values increase with the influx of new assets or the improvement of existing ones, whether it's the prestige of an old-money neighborhood, an incredible view of Lake Superior, schools, proximity to amenities such as parks and trails or clusters of upscale new housing in previously undeveloped areas.

Duluth

In Duluth, the neighborhoods and the buildings that comprise them reflect the influence of both ethnic and class distinctions that were much more apparent at the turn of the century and into the early 1900s.

In eastern Duluth, the blocks of well-kept mansions as well as the well-designed neighborhoods of Congdon, Hunters Park, Glen Avon, Marley Heights and Woodland are reminders of the vast logging, mining and railroad wealth and employment generated by this area's natural resources. At one time, all heavy industry — ironworks, shipbuilding, factories, the huge U.S. Steel plant — was located in western Duluth. Several neighborhoods, including Morgan Park and Riverside, were built as company towns to house workers. The far-west Fond du Lac neighborhood once was home to several brownstone quarries. Today, food-processing plants, a postal service encoding center and several paper- and wood-product mills are chief employers in western Duluth.

Comparatively speaking, Duluth currently enjoys some of the most affordable real estate in the country. The 1993 *Places Rated Almanac* listed Duluth/Superior as 6th of 343 metro areas in terms of affordable housing. And while that standing may have changed slightly, one thing about the Twin Ports' housing market hasn't: Real estate buyers still get a lot of bang for there buck here. According to the Duluth Area Realtors Association, average housing costs for 1995 were $53,987 for a house with two or fewer bedrooms, $81,890 for a three-bedroom house, $110,878 for a four-bedroom house and $160,022 for a five-bedroom-plus house.

Feeling a little cramped in your present home? A mansion in Duluth is a bargain compared with a similar property in Minneapolis/St. Paul. The days of incredible real estate deals have changed from the early to mid-1980s when the recession hit. The taconite industry went bust, and Duluth's population dropped as people left the city seeking jobs; nevertheless, you can buy a bona fide mansion with carriage house and servant's quarters for less than $400,000. For a mansion (without carriage house) that needs work, prices of $200,000 are not uncommon.

Following a market adjustment in 1993, residential real estate generally has increased in value each year. In 1994, an average price listing for a home in Duluth was $74,266; in 1995, $81,167 (approximately an 8 percent increase in value). In addition to conventional house-shopping factors such as schools, parks and neighbors, there are a couple of things particular to Duluth to consider: the weather and the Lake.

LAKE SUPERIOR AND THE LAKE EFFECT

Lake Superior dominates the Twin Ports with its sheer physical beauty, its stunning changes of scenery and the always engaging port traffic of lakers, salties and sailboats. The Lake exerts its ability to control and change the weather on a daily basis. It's called the "Lake Effect."

The close proximity of Lake Superior, the largest of the Great Lakes, affects the local weather, causing cooler summer temperatures and warmer winter temperatures near the Lake. Watch or listen to a local weather forecast; meteorologists consistently give three temperatures: downtown Duluth, downtown Superior and over the hill at the airport.

The Lake Effect diminishes as you go "over the hill." That is to say, the weather changes with the increase in elevation as you head south from Duluth on Interstate 35 or northwest on U.S. Highway 53 toward the Iron Range. Not in a day but in a matter of minutes, weather and climate can change from foggy and cool 70s near the Lake to sunny skies and 80-degree temperatures over the hill.

Remember, when deciding where to live in Duluth or Superior, you have a choice in weather. Near the Lake in Duluth, it's cool and often foggy — even in summer; expect cold days in the spring from the Lake effect but warmer winters.

Insiders' Tips

Most people think the best time to sell a house is in July and August. Not true, according to Realtor Dan Byrnes. He says that, in the Twin Ports area, buying interest picks up in February following the holiday lull, climbs through June, then levels off. Buyers want to be in their new homes before summer, and many potential buyers are out of town on vacation in July and August. After Labor Day, house sales pick up again and then slow down during December and January.

Or enjoy pleasant springs but hotter summers and colder winters over the hill. In Superior, the Lake effect alters weather in the east and north parts of town, but the farther away from the Lake you go, the warmer it gets.

A ROOM WITH A VIEW

Another real estate factor particular to Duluth (and the North and South shores, for that matter) is a view of the Lake. It's common knowledge in Duluth's real estate market that a full Lake view will add $10,000 to $15,000 to the property value.

In Duluth, the best full views of the Lake, the Aerial Lift Bridge and Park Point (we're not just talking about a glimpse of a corner of the lake from a bathroom window or a panorama of the industrial harbor) can be had from the following neighborhoods: Central Hillside, upper Piedmont, Kenwood above the University of Minnesota, sections of Hunters Park off Glenwood Avenue, parts of Congdon above the Northland Country Club and, of course, Skyline Parkway, the 30-mile boulevard that skirts the edge of the hilltop running from the Lester River in eastern Duluth to Spirit Mountain in western Duluth. Homes along the Skyline Parkway have protected views because of the no-build city zoning in that area.

If you desire lakefront property in Duluth proper, you're limited to the stretch of diverse housing along London Road in East Duluth. Many mansions, including the historic Glensheen (see our Attractions chapter), are located lakeside on London Road and range in price from $120,000 to $400,000.

Superior

In contrast to hilly, narrow Duluth, Superior sprawls out flat and is hemmed in by water. The South Shore of Lake Superior rims the east side of town. The deep bays of the St. Louis and Pokegama rivers flank the north and west edges of the city. And the Nemadji River and acres of vital wetlands border the south. Superior was platted in the 1870s to be the "Chicago of the North," and small lots of 25 feet by 120 to 140 feet are common.

Many of the older neighborhoods reflect the boom economy of Superior in the late 1800s. Starting in the North End, you'll find spectacular mansions tucked between 1950s ramblers, especially along U.S. Highway 2 (a.k.a. Harbor Drive) running east/west through the north part of town. Immigrant row houses and simple, lap-sided pine dwellings still stand adjacent to the immense railroad yards that dominate the landscape throughout Superior. In the East End, the original downtown, a number of historic buildings remain. The current downtown area at Tower Avenue and Belknap Street, with shops, restaurants and the public library, is the site of much daily activity.

Generally, Superior's residential real estate is less expensive than Duluth's. The price of a three-bedroom house in Superior ranges from $40,000 to $60,000. On the other hand, there's a spate of new, upscale 3,000- to 4,000-square-foot homes being built near the Superior municipal golf course and the Nemadji River for $100,000 to $200,000. Other new areas of development are behind Memorial Hospital on Tower Avenue and near the Superior Municipal Forest in Billings Park.

Superior's real estate market also includes many desirable older neighborhoods, including the Central Park area near Hill Avenue and 21st Street and Harbor Drive, featuring many 1920s and '30s brick colonial homes, some Victorians, English Tudors and French Colonials, ranging in price from $100,000 to $150,000. The closer the property to this neighborhood's city park, the more expensive the house on it.

In Superior, the Billings Park area, from Arrowhead Pier to 28th Street, was developed between about 1910 through the 1950s. This prestigious residential area features many English Tudor and other Revival-style homes. In the last 12 years, new homes have sprung up on the peninsula along the St. Louis River from 28th Street to Billings Drive. In general, housing prices in Billings Park start at about $140,000.

Resources

GREATER NORTHWEST
ASSOCIATION OF REALTORS INC.
1406 Belknap St.
Superior, Wis.   *(715) 392-7798*

This association offers the Multiple Listing Service for properties in Superior, Douglas County and parts of Bayfield County. Buyers guides, maps and information on licensed Realtors are available.

DULUTH AREA
ASSOCIATION OF REALTORS
1209 E. Fourth St.
Duluth, Minn.   *(218) 728-5676*

This association offers the Multiple Listing Service and can furnish a list of licensed Realtors upon request.

ARROWHEAD BUILDERS ASSOCIATION
802 Garfield Ave.
Duluth, Minn.   *(218) 722-5707*

You'll find a list of members, builders and remodelers, including addresses and phone numbers; however, the association

will not recommend a particular builder. This group also organizes the annual Home Show held each April at the Duluth Entertainment Convention Center, which includes hundreds of exhibits and seminars (see our Annual Events & Festivals chapter for details).

DULUTH AREA CHAMBER OF COMMERCE
118 E. Superior St.
Duluth, Minn.   *(218) 722-5501*
The Duluth Chamber of Commerce offers a relocation package, which includes information on clubs and organizations, the Top-5 employers, a Realtor guide, a map and tour guide and medical and dental information. You can pick up a package at the COC's offices or, for a $5 fee, have one mailed to you.

SUPERIOR CHAMBER OF COMMERCE
305 E. Second St.
Superior, Wis.   *(715) 394-7716*
The Superior Chamber of Commerce can provide a listing of licensed Realtors as well as general information about the city.

Along the North Shore

In Cook County, home of Grand Marais, the residential real estate market is strongly driven by the demand for summer homes. Some of these properties are current or future retirement places for people who spend summers on the North Shore and winter in the southwestern United States.

In the summer, Cook County's population swells from about 4,500 people to between 10,000 and 15,000 residents. The majority of these folks are from the Twin Cities, but some also come from Wisconsin, Iowa, Kansas and Nebraska. Cook County covers 930,000 acres, less than 10 percent of which is privately owned. Superior National Forest, the Boundary Waters Canoe Area Wilderness, several state forests, county land and the Grand Portage Indian Reservation make up the bulk of the county's acreage. So, the amount of land that can be developed and built upon is scarce.

Actual lakeshore property where you can easily walk down to Lake Superior is dwindling and, as a result, has risen in value in the last few years. In Cook County, only four unimproved (in its natural state, uncleared and without utilities installed) shoreline lots on Lake Superior were sold in 1995.

According to Marlin Hansen of

Detrick Realty in Grand Marais, the average cost of Lake Superior shoreline is about $500 per lot-width foot. To own a home in this area is a challenge for local people making $20,000 to $30,000 a year. Housing costs have jumped in the past several years. For example, in the city of Grand Marais, $55,000 was the average home price between 1992 to 1994; in 1995, the average price jumped to $67,000. In the rural residential category, houses range in price from $50,000 to $60,000. In contrast, the top sale in 1995 for a Lake Superior home with shoreline was $450,000.

Resources

GRAND MARAIS
CHAMBER OF COMMERCE
15 N. Broadway St.
Grand Marais, Minn.   (800) 622-4014

The Grand Marais Chamber of Commerce can provide a listing of Realtors in Cook County and other general information about the area.

DULUTH AREA
ASSOCIATION OF REALTORS
1209 E. Fourth St.
Duluth, Minn.   (218) 728-5676

In addition to maintaining information about the Twin Ports area, the Duluth Area Association of Realtors can also provide a list of licensed Realtors along the North Shore.

ARROWHEAD BUILDERS ASSOCIATION
802 Garfield Ave.
Duluth, Minn.   (218) 722-5707

The association can provide a list of members as well as North Shore builders and remodelers, including addresses and phone numbers. (See the previous listing in this chapter's "Twin Ports Real Estate Resources" section for more information.)

Along the South Shore

Like the North Shore, the South Shore has attracted heavy interest from out-of-towners who love the scenery and the serenity and are looking to buy vacation and retirement properties. The South Shore's clay soil results in constantly eroding cliffs along the Lake but formidable growing conditions away from the shoreline. Most of the western Bayfield Peninsula is dotted with Finnish farms.

Wis. Scenic Highway 13, part of the Lake Superior Circle Tour (see our Circle Tour chapter), runs along the Lake at times, but much of its route on the peninsula is several miles away from the shore. Because of unstable soil conditions and limited road access, the amount of residential building along the Bayfield Peninsula to the west is sparse. However, on the east side of the peninsula near Chequamegon Bay, you will find limited lakeshore lots, many of which have been developed.

Another factor in limited residential development is the Apostle Islands National Lakeshore, which protects 21 of the 22 Apostle Islands, and the Red Cliff band

Duluth's real estate taxes are based on estimated market value (EMV), as is the case throughout Minnesota. In Superior, Wisconsin, real estate taxes are generally higher than in Duluth, as there is no homestead credit; however, unlike Duluth, utilities such as trash pickup are included in city services.

There are many new developments in the Twin Ports area, most of which offer interested buyers a model-home tour.

of Ojibwe who control some of this area. Also, the interior of the peninsula is dominated by the Chequamegon National Forest. For many people seeking vacation property, Madeline Island in the Apostle Islands is highly desirable. It's also highly exclusive and expensive.

Madeline Island and its small town of LaPointe have been a summer resort mecca since the turn of the century. You're more likely to find a weekly summer rental than something to buy, since many cabins and homes here pass along through generations of family. Limited new development has been in the premier range of custom-built estates.

Bayfield and Washburn, on the beautiful Bayfield Peninsula, have long been popular tourist destinations, with many family vacation homes in the area. The majority of new building in the area has focused around construction of vacation properties. According to local Realtors, quite a few nice lots remain for sale, many with Lake views. Many people are buying land now with the intention of retiring to the area later.

In the town of Bayfield, residential real estate prices have skyrocketed within the past five years. For example, a modest Victorian home (nearly the entire town is a designated historic district) that sold in the mid-$30,000s at the start of the decade would command more than double that price today.

Many homeowners chose to restore and renovate their homes, although limited new-home construction has occurred just outside the historic district. In 1995, home prices in Bayfield ranged from $50,000 to $100,000.

You'll find some condominiums available too: **Bayfield on the Lake**, First Street, (715) 779-3621, offers individually owned units, and **Reitan Boatyard Condominiums**, Broad Street, (715) 779-5807, offered by Apostle Islands Realty, include studios and one-bedrooms with or without a loft, ranging from $50,000 to $65,000. City homes range from $50,000 to $80,000, and a few unimproved city lots are still available. Two city lots are required to build in Bayfield. Lots of 4,800 square feet (40 feet by 120 feet) generally sell for $4,000 to $5,000 each. At the Apostle Highlands (18-hole golf course), 1433 Apostle Highlands Boulevard, (715) 779-5960, 1.5-acre homesites are available. Lot prices range from $8,900 to $69,000. Prices are affected by Lake view and access to the golf course.

Washburn is much more a year-round locals town than it's more picturesque and expensive northern neighbor, Bayfield, which is more a tourist town. Houses in Washburn range from $35,000 to $300,000, and prices are affected by the availability of public water and sewer. Many people have built just outside of Washburn on the hills overlooking Chequamegon Bay. One particular point of note: The school system here is considered one of the best in the area.

The town of Ashland is on the cusp of Chequamegon Bay near lush wetlands. Its industrial roots remain today on the waterfront: Note the operating power plant and the wood products business. But industry has not depleted some wonderful real estate. You'll find blocks of intact historic Victorians in Ashland at great prices. Recently, an ornate five-bedroom Victorian sold for $129,900 — a real bargain.

Resources

BAYFIELD CHAMBER OF COMMERCE
P.O. Box 138
Bayfield, Wis. 54814   (800) 447-4094
The Chamber maintains a list of licensed area Realtors.

ASHLAND CHAMBER OF COMMERCE
320 Fourth Ave. W.   (715) 682-2500
Ashland, Wis.   (800) 284-9484
The Ashland Chamber of Commerce can provide a relocation package and a listing of licensed area Realtors.

WASHBURN AREA CHAMBER OF COMMERCE
204 W. Bayfield
Washburn, Wis.   (715) 373-5017
The Washburn Chamber of Com-

merce offers a relocation package and a listing of licensed area Realtors.

MADELINE ISLAND CHAMBER OF COMMERCE
LaPointe, Wis.   (715) 747-2801
The Madeline Island Chamber of Commerce can provide listings of summer properties and licensed Realtors.

A Sense of Community

The following newcomer resources and volunteer organizations can help you get involved in community services and activities. Contact the agency nearest you for details.

GENERAL COMMUNITY INFORMATION
Duluth Information
and Referral Service   (218) 726-2222
Thunder Bay Community
Information Center   (807) 626-9626

VOLUNTEER CONNECTION
Red Cross
Ashland, Wis., area   (800) 244-9522
Duluth, Minn.   (218) 722-0071
Ironwood, Mich.   (906) 932-2525
Thunder Bay, Ont.   (807) 623-3073

United Way
Greater Duluth, Minn.   (218) 726-4770
Superior-Douglas County, Wis. (715) 394-2733
Thunder Bay, Ont.   (807) 623-6420

Voluntary Action Center
Duluth, Minn.   (218) 726-4776

Volunteer Attorney Program
Duluth, Minn.   (218) 723-4003

The Volunteer Centre
Thunder Bay, Ont.   (807) 623-8272

WELCOME WAGON
Duluth, Minn.   (218) 727-8697
Thunder Bay, Ont.   (807) 344-3418

Realtors

In this section, we've included a sampling of real estate agencies that serve the Twin Ports area, including a few companies from the North or South shores. Some are local, family-run companies; others are affiliates or franchise members of regional or national companies. If a Duluth realty company doesn't have a Superior office, many times it has an affiliation with a company that has Realtors licensed to do business in Wisconsin. Most realty companies provide newcomer relocation services in addition to helping you find a place to live.

We've noted the number of full-time Realtors (meaning registered professionals who make a living selling real estate) at the companies we've included in this chapter. This is by no means a comprehensive listing. Besides referencing this guide, we also suggest you talk to friends about referrals and call the professional Realtor association for a listing (see this chapter's association listings, mentioned previously).

APOSTLE ISLANDS REALTY

117 S. First St.   (715) 779-5807
Bayfield, Wis.   (800) 514-6700

Locally owned and operated Apostle Islands Realty specializes in vacation (especially lakeshore) as well as residential and commercial properties. The company employs five full-time Realtors. Apostle Islands recently merged with Trudeau Realty, making it the major local real estate company in the area. The company's Apostle Island Rentals division, (715) 779-3621 or (800) 842-1199, deals with short-term rental properties.

BOWMAN REALTORS

2 E. First St.
Duluth, Minn.   (218) 727-8001

Bowman is the oldest continually operating residential real estate firm in Duluth. Locally owned and operated since 1910, Bowman employs seven full-time Realtors who deal in residential, commercial and corporate properties. The company works with a Wisconsin-licensed Realtor.

CENTURY 21
NORTHERN STATES REALTY

1309 Belknap St., Superior, Wis. (715) 394-6671

This realty, with 15 full-time Realtors, specializes in lakeshore recreational as well as residential and commercial properties in Superior and in Douglas and Bayfield counties. Northern States is the local Century 21 affiliate, providing access to relocation services and the national VIP Referral Network for buyers and sellers.

DETRICK REALTY

Minn. Hwy. 61 W.
Grand Marais, Minn.   (218) 387-2131

This North Shore company is owned and operated by licensed Realtor Virginia Detrick. The company specializes in residential real estate as well as vacation properties in this burgeoning travel destination. Detrick employs four full-time Realtors.

EAST WEST REALTY

1732 London Rd.
Duluth, Minn.   (218) 728-5161

Locally owned and operated since

Money magazine rated Duluth 14th out of 300 U.S. metropolitan areas for overall livability in 1992. Duluth ranked high in clean air and water, safety, medical care, education, the arts and recreation.

Insiders' Tips

1964, East West Realty is one of the larger companies in town. Century 21 in Superior is East West's affiliate. This company staffs 60 full-time Realtors.

EDINA REALTY
31 W. Superior St.
Duluth, Minn.   (218) 727-1900
1423 Belknap St.
Superior, Wis.   (715) 394-5585

Edina Realty was founded in 1955 in the Twin Cities and today is one of the biggest players in that market. The Duluth office has 24 full-time Realtors, and Superior's has seven. The company specializes in residential and commercial properties. Lil Stocke, a longtime family-owned and operated real estate company in Duluth, recently became part of Edina Realty.

EDMUNDS REALTY
2200 Water St.
Duluth, Minn.   (218) 724-7900

This family-owned company has been in business since 1952. It currently staffs 15 full-time Realtors. This company's staff members consider themselves senior specialists, with expertise in helping people to decide whether or not they're ready to change housing and providing options for seniors. The company has a broker licensed in Wisconsin. Edmunds also handles commercial properties.

HERITAGE REALTY
1716 W. Lakeshore Dr.
Ashland, Wis.   (715) 682-9528

Nine full-time Realtors service residential, vacation and commercial properties.

Heritage maintains a branch in Iron River, Wisconsin, on U.S. Highway 2, (715) 372-8144.

KSA REALTORS
Alworth Bldg., Ste. 204
306 W. Superior St.
Duluth, Minn.   (218) 727-7496

Locally owned KSA Realtors has been serving the Twin Ports area since 1962. The company staffs 10 full-time Realtors who focus on residential real estate. (KSA stands for Kohlbry, Swenson and Associates.)

LYNN BEECHLER REALTY
509 Lonsdale Bldg.
Duluth, Minn.   (218) 723-8101

Locally owned by Lynn Beechler, this realty company, with four full-time agents, has been in business more than 15 years. It focuses on Duluth's residential real estate market.

MESSINA-ZUNICH REALTY, INC.
1512 E. Superior St.   (218) 728-4436
Duluth, Minn.   (800) 385-8842

Messina-Zunich has 16 full-time Realtors. The company is affiliated with Better Homes and Gardens, a national brokerage firm, and has been in business about 12 years. Messina-Zunich specializes in residential listings.

RE/MAX TWIN PORTS
600 E. Superior
Duluth, Minn.   (218) 722-1701
Mariner Mall, N. 28th St.
Superior, Wis.   (715) 392-8700

RE/MAX is a national chain with locally owned franchises. The Duluth office has 18 full-time Realtors; the Superior office has 11. RE/MAX specializes in residential and commercial properties.

SUPERIOR 'N' FOREST REAL ESTATE
1219 Seventh Ave.
Two Harbors, Minn.   *(218) 834-5050*

This company specializes in land for recreational use as well as lakeshore vacation and residential properties in Lake and St. Louis counties. Two full-time Realtors are on staff.

SUPERIOR PROPERTIES INC.
Clearview Store
Minn. Hwy. 61   *(218) 663-7971*
Lutsen, Minn.   *(800) 950-4361*
Branch office
Minn. Hwy. 61   *(218) 387-1657*
Grand Marais, Minn.   *(800) 950-4360*

A privately owned firm with five full-time Realtors, Superior Properties'

strength is vacation and residential listings in Cook County. This company also handles vacation rental properties.

WOODLAND REALTY
229 W. Bayfield
Washburn, Wis.   *(715) 373-5030*

This locally owned real estate company of three full-time Realtors deals with properties throughout the Washburn area. Its emphasis is on residential and commercial listings on the Chequamegon Peninsula.

The St. Louis County Social Services Department offers the *Community Resource Guide* for older adults. Call (218) 726-2222.

Inside
Retirement

We're living longer, and with medical advances and better awareness about nutrition and exercise, enjoying healthy later years. This new-found longevity is increasing the nation's older-adult population. According to a U.S. Census Bureau study, America's 65-and-older population will grow from one in eight to one in five people by 2050.

Twin Ports Area

The Twin Ports have a significant older-adult population. Some folks attribute this to the hardy Scandinavian immigrant base and the toughening Lake effect, which causes long, cold winters. Typically, people don't move to this area to retire. Retirees stay here if they can't afford to move or have grown so accustomed to life here that they don't want to move somewhere else.

According to the Arrowhead Area Agency on Aging, 25 percent of Duluth's population will be older than 65 by the year 2000. St. Louis County was ranked 178th out of 500 counties nationally for people older than 65. People older than 65 account for nearly 17 percent of St. Louis County's population — more than 4 percent higher than the national average of 12.8 percent.

The Douglas County and Superior population of 42,007 is noticeably older than the rest of Wisconsin. According to the Wisconsin Bureau of Aging, 24.5 percent of the state's population is age 65 and older; but in Douglas County, that same group represents 28.3 percent of the population. Both St. Louis and Douglas county's social services encourage independent living for seniors through a well-developed network of programs and services. Many home-owning seniors are longtime residents. But if staying at home is impossible because of daily living needs or a senior wants to move to more communal living, a number of options are available.

For the fragile elderly, Duluth has eight nursing homes — two public and six private; Superior has seven — all privately operated. We've organized housing services into several categories, including independent living, individual apartments in a multi-unit building and, in some cases, services or amenities catering to the older adult; assisted living, a broad category requiring a precise definition of levels of care and services provided; and apartment and condominium complexes — some are specifically designed and marketed to a 55-and-older or 62-and-older age bracket. We've also provided a selection of senior centers in Duluth and Superior.

Resource Organizations

The **Arrowhead Area Agency on Aging**, 330 Canal Park Drive, Duluth, (218) 722-5545, and the **Douglas County Commission on Aging**, 1718 N. 13th, Superior, (715) 394-3611, are the best places to start if you're researching housing options and other older-adult services. Both these nonprofit umbrella organizations maintain a list of housing options and can direct you to other pertinent services.

Housing Terms

Following are some brief definitions of all the acronyms and section codes associated with housing options:

HUD Section 8 housing is rental housing that is privately owned, built and managed but receives federal subsidies for renters. Rent is based on 30 percent of a person's income.

HUD Section 236 housing includes privately managed properties that set a low- and high-end rental costs, so the rent is based on 30 percent of a person's income plus the rent baseline set for that specific property.

Public housing properties are developed, built and managed by a public housing authority, such as the Duluth Commnity Development and Housing Authority. These properties receive federal subsidies for rent, and rental fees are based on total income.

Independent-living Options

CLIFFORD LUND RESIDENCE
914 Tower Ave.
Superior, Wis.   (715) 392-3722

This public housing high-rise in downtown Superior offers different levels of assisted living for adults 62 and older and people with disabilities. There are 91 units in the building, all of which are one-bedroom apartments. Rent is based on income. Services include a community room with weekly bingo, free lunches once a month and weekly bus service to the grocery store.

SUPERIOR GOLDEN APARTMENTS
2315 Banks Ave.
Superior, Wis.   (715) 394-9468

Apartments for folks 62 and older are priced according to income. There are 84 one-bedroom units and four two-bedroom units in this section 8 building. Services include a community room with planned activities such as a sewing club, exercise classes, bingo and a card club. Bus service is available for grocery shopping.

ROYALTON MANOR APARTMENTS
1900 New York Ave.
Superior, Wis.   (715) 392-1014

Managed by Catholic Charities, Royalton Manor Apartments has cafeteria service and is the only senior living facility in Superior with this service. Royalton Manor subsidized public housing with 157 units, one-bedroom with or without kitchenettes, for people 62 and older or handicapped folks. Royalton Manor has a tenant service coordinator, a social worker on staff and a full 40-person dietary department. Healthcare services through a contracted agency are available. A monthly activity calendar and a small library with book service through the Superior Public Library are offered.

PHOENIX VILLA
1001 Clough Ave.
Superior, Wis.   (715) 392-3447

Managed by Catholic Charities, Phoenix Villa apartments include 81 one-bedroom units for independent living. Rents are based on income. This section 8 housing is open to adults age 62 and older. Laundry facilities are available on each floor and there's a community room for bingo and cards. A bus takes people shopping for groceries every week.

LENOX PLACE

701 W. Superior St.
Duluth, Minn.   *(218) 722-0739*

Lenox Place, a high-rise apartment building in downtown Duluth with great views of the Lake, is managed by Bowman Properties. It's open to adults 62 and older or handicapped folks. It has no market-rate apartments — only Section 8 housing — so rents are based on income. There are 152 units, most of which have one bedroom; but a few two-bedroom apartments are available. Amenities include a library room, a community room, a laundry room, emergency pull-cords in the bedroom and bathroom, and walk-in showers.

Lenox Place has an active building club that meets monthly and organizes dinners and other social and leisure activities. Staff from the Benedictine Health Center organize social activities. Controlled-entry security and 10 carports plus 20 headbolt heaters are available.

FAITH HAVEN APARTMENTS

4901 Grand Ave.
Duluth, Minn.   *(218) 628-2602*

Faith Haven, for residents 62 and older, is self-managed by a nonprofit organization and board of directors. Rates for each of the 125 one-bedroom units range from $260 a month for qualifying moderate senior income to a market rate of $367 a month. Amenities include an in-house grocery store and beauty parlor. There are no social programs or healthcare services, but there is a public community room and coffee shop. The building has a security entry system and is on a main bus line.

WOODLAND GARDEN APARTMENTS

127 Calvary Rd.
Duluth, Minn.   *(218) 724-2989*

This three-story, 60-unit building has spacious one-bedroom and a few two-bedroom apartments. Managed by the Edmunds Company, Woodland Garden Apartments is a Section 8 housing option for adults age 62 and older or handicapped individuals. Rents are based on income.

The building has an active residents club that takes trips, plays cards, gardens and organizes ice cream socials in summer and lunches on stormy days in winter. Residents receive a noontime meal, courtesy of Duluth Parks and Recreation services. The community room has hosted wedding and funeral receptions, mature flower gardens (they'll plow up a spot if a resident wants one) and a sunny library with large-print books. The back of the property includes a woodsy setting with two duck ponds.

Controlled-access security and off-street parking with headbolt heaters are available. Emergency pull-cords are provided in bathrooms and bedrooms.

GATEWAY TOWER

600 W. Superior St.
Duluth, Minn.   *(218) 727-0929*

Managed by Bowman Properties, Gateway Tower in downtown Duluth offers 153 units, including efficiencies and one-bedroom apartments. Rent costs are based on Section 236 housing income levels for folks 62 and older or handicapped persons. Gateway Tower is across the street from the public library and close to the Depot cultural center. Two community rooms are available and an active social club organizes bingo, card nights and coffee parties.

GREYSOLON PLAZA

231 E. Superior St.
Duluth, Minn.   *(218) 722-7523*

In the heart of downtown on the main drag through the old part of the city, you'll find the Hotel Duluth (c.1925), now an apartment complex for older adults. Managed by Bowman Realty, the former hotel maintains its elegant front entrance, lobby and ballroom. The 151 one-bedroom units have variable rents based on income. There's a small grocery store in the building as well as a restaurant, a beauty shop and a community room. Apartments start on the fourth floor, and laundry service is available on each floor. Units are equipped with emergency pull-cords, and an elevator key provides controlled-access security. This complex is on a bus line and close to medical services. The staff from Benedictine Health Center organizes social activities.

Assisted-living Options

ST. ANN'S RESIDENCE
330 E. Third St.
Duluth, Minn.   (218) 727-8831

St. Ann's Residence is near three main hospitals and The Duluth Clinic in downtown as well as several bus route stops. This privately run assisted-living complex has 102 rooms, mostly one-room suites with private bath but no kitchen; some two-room suites are available. All suites are furnished, but you can bring your own furniture if you wish. Monthly rates range from $700 to $1,500 a month and include three meals a day. Resident care is available with a registered nurse Monday through Friday from 7 AM to 4 PM, and aides are available seven days a week until 9 PM. The front desk is staffed 24 hours a day, and a security entrance is provided. On-site security service is provided from 4 PM until 8 AM. Amenities include a game room, an extensive library with a selection of large-print books and magazines, and a chapel.

ARTHUR E. KING MANOR
222 E. Second St.
Duluth, Minn.   (218) 726-2800
MIDTOWNE MANOR I
2021 W. Second St.
Duluth, Minn.   (218) 726-2800
MIDTOWNE MANOR II
2011 W. Second St.
Duluth, Minn.   (218) 726-2800
TRI-TOWERS
222-228 E. Second St.
Duluth, Minn.   (218) 726-2800

In 1979, a new service program — the first of its kind in the nation — was created at King Manor, a public-housing building, to help older adults continue to live in apartments on their own. Meals, nursing services, housekeeping, personal care and activities are provided in partnership with the St. Louis County Social Service Department and the Housing Redevelopment Authority of Duluth, which manages the four buildings' apartments, including King Manor's 98 units, Midtowne Manor I's 102, Midtowne II's 102 and Tri-Towers's 290.

Rent is 30 percent of a resident's income. The cost of services is based on 20 percent of a resident's income and the level of service required. All apartments have emergency pull-cords in the bedroom and bathroom.

From one to three levels of services — assisted living, congregate housing and general congregate dining — are available to residents based on health and other needs at each of the centers. King Manor and Midtowne II feature all three levels of service; Midtowne I and Tri-Towers are both based on the congregate housing service.

The Assisted Living Program includes medication assistance; three meals a day; an emergency call system; health status checks; nursing services; social worker services; personal-care services, such as bathing and nail care; laundry and linen changes; light housekeeping; transportation to in-town medical appointments; and activities. This program is available at King Manor and Midtowne Manor II.

The Congregate Housing Service Program, available at King Manor, Tri-Towers and Midtowne Manors I and II, includes two meals a day served in the dining room, light housekeeping, laundry and linen changes, personal-care assistance, rides to medical appointments and social worker services.

The General Congregate Dining Program at King Manor and Midtowne Manor II includes one meal a day.

MOUNT ROYAL MANOR
100 Elizabeth St.
Duluth, Minn. *(218) 728-4264*

Mount Royal Manor, a privately managed apartment building, houses residents of mixed age including working adults as well as retired people. It has 114 units, including efficiencies and one- and two-bedrooms, that range in price from $550 to $675 per month. Four levels of assisted living are available, with a nurse on call 24 hours and a home healthcare worker and healthcare aides available on-site 24 hours a day. Meals are available through the assisted-living program.

Mount Royal Manor, in the Woodland neighborhood near the University of Minnesota, is close by many services and a bus line. A cluster of shops and the Mount Royal post office are within easy walking distance. The nearby supermarket will deliver groceries. Features include a community room with library, a security system, two elevators, a maintenance person on the premises and an outdoor screenhouse that residents enjoy, particularly in summer.

Apartment and Condominium Complexes

MOUNT ROYAL PINES
66 and 70 E. St. Marie St. *(218) 724-7900*
Duluth, Minn. *(800) 777-4571*

Managed by the Duluth-based Edmunds Realty, Mount Royal Pines consists of two buildings with 81 total units. Rental rates for one- and two-bedroom apartments range from $671 to $1,306 a month; rates varying according to apartment location and design. All units have Urgency Call cords. Geared toward active seniors 62 and older, the two buildings are in the Woodland neighborhood in eastern Duluth, near the Mount Royal shopping center and the University of Minnesota. Shopping opportunities and a post office are within easy walking distance, and the local grocery store will deliver.

The complex is on a major bus line. The buildings afford great views of the Lake from the hillside, wooded location. Walking paths on the well-landscaped grounds and award-winning flower gardens are notable attractions.

This luxurious complex has plenty of amenities, including a tastefully decorated dining club with a chef and a fitness center with trainers who cater to older-adult needs. Other social areas include a billiards room, a fireside room and a library. Several sun lounges and a spa area with

Jacuzzi round out the recreation and leisure options. For visitors, the complex offers a guest motel suite. Heated indoor parking is available.

MILLER CREEK CLUBHOUSE COMMUNITY
Sundby and Haines Rds.
Duluth, Minn.   *(218) 722- 2990*

Called a clubhouse community and geared for buyers 55 and older, this new-for-1996 condominium development features 60 condo-cottages — four in each of 15 buildings. All condominiums have two-bedrooms, and fireplaces and patios are available. Four floor plans range from 970 to 1,650 square feet in size and $85,000 to $140,000 in price. These maintenance-free units have private entrances and attached garages with available RV and boat parking. Near the Miller Hill Mall, Miller Creek Clubhouse Community is in a wooded area and is a short drive from the airport.

CHATEAU APARTMENT HOMES
3800 London Rd.
Duluth, Minn.   *(218) 525-6002*

In eastern Duluth's Congdon neighborhood on the mansion-lined London Road, you'll find Chateau Apartment Homes. Half the residents in these general-housing units are retired adults, and the others are working professionals. Three buildings house a total of 141 one-, two- and three-bedroom apartments. Rents range from $580 to $1,450 a month. This quiet, well-kept development has off-street parking with separate garages, free laundry, community gardens and a security system.

ASPENWOOD CONDOMINIUMS
Arrowhead and Rice Lake Rds.
Duluth, Minn.   *(218) 726-1992*

Managed by East West Realty, the multi-unit Aspenwood Condominiums are popular with snowbirds — people who spend summers in Duluth but flee south in winter. These condos, remodeled housing from a now-closed Air Force base, are spacious two- and three-bedroom units, each with full basement, designer kitchen and garage. The grounds are professionally maintained, and for the snowbirds who leave, an alarm system notifies the caretaker if any utilities malfunction during the winter. Costs start around $50,000.

BARKERS ISLAND TOWNHOMES
Barkers Island Dr.
Superior, Wis.   *(715) 392-7131*

Barkers Island Townhomes are at the far end of Barkers Island, past the marina and the hotel/restaurant complex. A planned community of 30 units, eight of which are currently complete, these townhomes have been a hit with Superior's snowbird retirement crowd. The location offers privacy and great views of Superior Bay and Park Point. Marketed to a general audience, the latest phase of townhomes — two- or three-bedroom, 1,200-square-foot, two-level units — start at $120,000 and include a dock.

Senior Centers

The following select senior centers in the Twin Ports provide social activities,

Photo: Duluth News-Tribune

A lone figure fishes along Lake Superior's shore.

regularly scheduled bingo and card games, and special events, such as birthday celebrations and pancake breakfasts. Each center has a changing roster of events, and most serve a hot meal Monday through Friday at noon — call the day before for a reservation.

Several centers serve as host stations for the Retired Senior Volunteer Program (RSVP), a federally funded, locally managed program using seniors to volunteer in the community.

GARY-NEW DULUTH SENIOR CITIZENS CENTER

1104 Commonwealth Ave.
Duluth, Minn.   *(218) 626-3376*

This senior center offers a senior dining program, local van service and health education. Recreation activities include cards, arts and crafts, ceramics, field trips, picnics and bingo. A RSVP volunteer station is here.

RAINBOW SENIOR CENTER

211 N. Third Ave. E.
Duluth, Minn.   *(218) 727-8147*

The Rainbow Senior Center is a lively downtown spot. It has a cafeteria, mini-bus transportation, a health unit with a healthcare access worker, and financial and insurance assistance. Recreational activities include crafts, painting, quilting, billiards, cards, woodworking, dances, an exercise class and special events.

WEST END SENIOR CENTER

2014 W. Third St.
Duluth, Minn.   *(218) 722-4107*

The West End Senior Center offers senior dining, Sunday and evening meals, healthcare, local van transportation, and legal and tax assistance. Recreation activities include arts and crafts, cards, three popular pool tables, exercise classes, dances and a Grandma's and Grandpa's Band. The center hosts an RSVP volunteer station.

SUPERIOR/DOUGLAS COUNTY SENIOR CENTER

1527 Tower Ave.
Superior, Wis.   *(715) 394-3644*

At the Superior/Douglas County Senior Center, there are healthcare services, including blood pressure checks, and a hot lunch program. Van transportation is available for trips, dances, bingo, a twice-weekly exercise classes and cribbage. The Kazoo Band keeps things lively.

EVERGREEN SENIOR CENTER
5380 Grand Ave.
Superior, Wis.   *(218) 723-3663*

This center offers dining, health education, local van service and a RSVP volunteer station. Recreational fun includes cards, cribbage, bingo, bridge, arts and crafts, field trips, picnics, the Hillbilly Band and a walking club.

EAST END SENIOR CITIZENS CENTER
2431 E. Fifth St.
Superior, Wis.   *(715) 398-9922*

Cards and bingo are the big activity at this center. A monthly Smear tournament offers cash prizes and booby prize. There's a weekly painting class offered in the morning, and once a month, the members have a lunch catered by various local restaurants. Monthly group birthday parties are part of the schedule. There is no regular hot lunch program here.

Along the North Shore

Several of the larger towns along the North Shore have significant retirement populations. When the taconite-processing industry in Silver Bay, Minnesota, went into a slump around 1990, the blocks of ranch-style homes built during the 1950s boom days went on the market for bargain prices. These homes were purchased by retirement-age individuals who now enjoy greatly increasing property values due to a tight housing market and the again-booming taconite industry. In Cook County around Grand Marais and in Lake County, many upscale single-family retirement/vacation homes have been built in the past 10 years.

Two Harbors

Two Harbors has a two types of senior housing options — independent living at Bayview Terrace and Harbor Point Apartments and assisted living at Barros House and The Cottages. Two Harbors is a fairly compact town, with many services, restaurants and shops within walking distance from these places.

BAYVIEW TERRACE
505 First Ave.
Two Harbors, Minn.   *(218) 834-2728*

Bayview Terrace is a 59-unit high-rise with 36 one-person, one-bedroom units, 23 two-person, one-bedroom units and three two bedroom units. Near old downtown Two Harbors, Bayview is public housing so rent is based on income. Stores and services, such as the post office, are within walking distance, and a bus is available. The Senior Citizens Council, a support and advisory group, meets at Bayview Terrace. There's a small library, a community room and a lounge.

HARBOR POINT APARTMENTS
101 Third Ave.
Two Harbors, Minn.   *(218) 834-5441*

Harbor Point Apartments offer 40 one-bedroom units. The building is across the street from Lake View Park and near the Lake. There's a daily coffee hour, a monthly birthday club and a bus for shopping and other trips. For security, there's a manager on duty 24 hours a day and a buzzer system. Harbor Point is section 8 housing — rent is based on income.

BARROS HOUSE
414 First Ave.
Two Harbors, Minn.   *(218) 834-6174*

The privately run Barros House is a small-scale, family-style, assisted-living facility. It has 10 rooms for residents and provides on-site meals in a small dining room. The staff provides regular activities for the residents, including trips around town. A favorite trip is a visit to the greenhouse.

THE COTTAGES
325 11th Ave.
Two Harbors, Minn. **(218) 834-7300**
Operated by Lake View Memorial Hospital, The Cottages is another small-scale, assisted-living facility. There are two side-by-side double duplexes and five units for a total capacity of 30 residences. Each resident has a private bedroom. A staff member is available 24 hours a day, meals are provided, and social outings are held on a regular basis.

Grand Marais

Grand Marais is another compact town, based on a waterfront boundary to the south and the Superior National Forest to the north. The market is booming for sales of private retirement and vacation homes, and land for new development is currently on the market — a rare occurrence, since only 10 percent of the land in Cook County is privately owned.

HOMESTEAD COOPERATIVE
11th Ave. W. and Second St.
Grand Marais, Minn. **(218) 387-1358**
This 26-unit building is managed by the Ebeneezer Society and affiliated with Fairview Health Systems. The property features one- and two-bedroom apartments

for sale, ranging in price from $81,400 to $115,900 and in size from 760 to 1,092 square feet. The cooperative is being marketed to retirees. Amenities include a community room, guest rooms, enclosed garages with plug-ins, transportation services, craft and exercise rooms, a library and reading area, a three-season porch and a workshop.

SAWTOOTH RIDGES
701 W. Fifth St.
Grand Marais, Minn. **(218) 387-9247**
This facility offers 24 one-bedroom units, with caretakers who live on-site. The building is managed by the Ebeneezer Society and affiliated with Fairview Health Systems. There are woods and gardens with great views of the Lake. Sawtooth Ridges residents are an active bunch who plan meals and activities together.

HARBORVIEW APARTMENTS
11 E. Third St.
Grand Marais, Minn. **(218) 387-2163**
HarborView is an independent-living facility housed in a 31-unit building a block off Minn. Highway 61. One- and two-bedroom apartments are available. You'll find live-in managers and a community room with some social programs. This is section 8 housing with rents based on income.

GRAND MARAIS APARTMENTS
First Ave. and Fourth St.
Grand Marais, Minn. **(218) 387-1227**
This 16-unit building has no managers on site. There are four one-bedroom units and 12 two-bedroom units avail-

able. The apartments on the second story have great views of the Lake. A common laundry facility is provided. The building is section 8 housing with rents based on income.

Along the South Shore

Bayfield and Washburn, Wisconsin, on the beautiful Bayfield Peninsula, have long been tourist destinations. Many family vacation homes dot the area, and vacation properties comprise the majority of new construction here. According to local Realtors, quite a few lots are still available — many with Lake views. Many people are buying land now with the intention of retiring to the area

For public housing in Bayfield County, the Housing Authorities of the city of Washburn and Bayfield County have rental units in the town of **Bayfield** and the town of **Washburn**. The rental units are not specifically designed or managed for seniors, and they are open to anyone who qualifies for public housing. For more information, contact the housing authority at 420 E. Third Street, Washburn, Wisconsin, (715) 373-2653.

City homes range from $50,000 to $80,000; a few city lots are also available. Lots of 40 by 120 feet generally sell for $4,000 to $5,000 each. Two city lots are required to build in Bayfield.

Homesites are available at the Apostle Highlands 18-hole golf course, 1433 Apostle Highlands Boulevard, (715) 779-5960. Half-acre and full acre lots range

from $8,900 to $69,000, depending on view and proximity to the golf course.

In **Ashland**, there's a number of public housing retirement options for seniors seeking independent living. The three buildings managed by the city of Ashland are all clustered together. Near these buildings, the **Senior Center**, 600 Fourth Street W., (715) 682-6502, offers social and recreational activities including arts and crafts, cards, bingo and planned outings. It's also the office for Ashland's **RSVP** (Retired Senior Volunteer Program) and provides a hot lunch Monday through Friday as well as Meals on Wheels service.

ASHLAND ARMS
716 Fourth St. W.
Ashland, Wis.   *(715) 682-8412*

Ashland Arms, an independent-living facility, is privately managed by Theis and Talley Management to provide senior housing. The two-level, 36-unit building features one-bedroom apartments. Some units have views of the Chequamegon Bay. Two units are fully handicapped-accessible, including wheelchair-accessible showers. Rents are based on Section 8 income guidelines. The community room with a small library is an active place for birthday parties, baby showers and church group meetings. The lobbies on Events are organized throughout the year, including rummage and bake sales, a holiday cookie exchange, card games and crafts. The Ashland senior citizen center is across the street.

BAYFIELD ON THE LAKE
First St. at the City Marina
Bayfield, Wis.   *(800) 842-1199*

These 12 individually owned units consist of one, two or four bedrooms with views of the Lake, fire places and decks. They range is size from 1,000 to 2,000 square feet. None of the condos are currently for sale; rents range from $130 and higher per night in summer and $75 to $95 in winter.

BAY RIDGE
409 Vaughn Ave.
Ashland, Wis.   *(715) 682-7066*

Bay Ridge is a small-scale building with 11 apartments, 10 of which are one-bedroom units (one is a two-bedroom apartment). One unit is completely handicapped-accessible. There's a large community space for residents, with a community kitchen, and landscaped grounds with gardening space.

BAY TERRACE
600 Fourth St. W.
Ashland, Wis.   *(715) 682-7066*

Bay Terrace, another public housing project for seniors seeking independent living, has a two-year waiting list. It's a desirable location because half of the 30 units are two-bedroom apartments; the other 15 are one-bedroom units. The building is single-story, making it easily accessible. Rents are based on income. There is no community space here.

BAY TOWER
319 Chapple Ave.
Ashland, Wis.   *(715) 682-7066*

It's the tallest building in Ashland. Bay Tower has 85 one-bedroom units in an eight-story building. There are two community rooms, a garden, patio and laundry facilities. Rents are based on income. Residents cross the street for recreational and social activities at the Senior Center.

REITAN BOATYARD CONDOMINIUMS
Broad St.
Bayfield, Wis.   *(715) 779-5807*

These units are available for sale or rent through Apostle Islands Realty, with studios and one-bedrooms (with and without loft), ranging from $50,000 to $65,000. Rents are $75-plus in summer and $55-plus in winter. The units are 600 to 700 square feet with kitchenettes and decks.

24 Hour Emergency Care

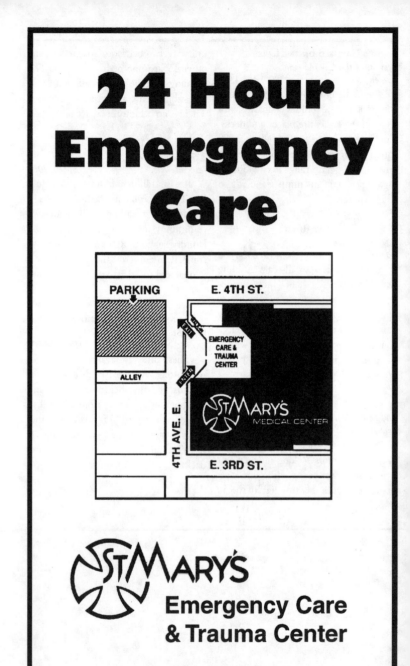

St Mary's

**Emergency Care
& Trauma Center**

726-4357

Inside
Hospitals and Healthcare

Perhaps it's the purifying winter cold or air-freshening forests; maybe it's the orderly lifestyle; possibly it's just the way the genes have shaken out.

Or it could be the healthcare.

Whatever the reasons, people in our region are a healthy lot. We value that health — an attitude that has resulted in an abundance of conventional medical services as well as an assortment of alternative therapies.

Duluth is the hub of healthcare in western Lake Superior, where hospitals have state-of-the-art equipment and about 375 physicians practice. Most doctors are specialists: urologists, neurosurgeons, cardiologists, psychiatrists and others. More than 100 are primary-care physicians, a scarce commodity nationwide that in Duluth is encouraged through the combined efforts of the medical community and the local university medical school. (During her healthcare reform initiative of 1993, First Lady Hillary Clinton cited Duluth as the nation's leader in turning out family-practice doctors.)

Counseling for mental health and chemical dependency likewise is widely available in the area. So-called "alternative" health practitioners — herbalists, aroma/touch therapists, acupuncturists, kinesiologists — also practice, as do about 75 chiropractors. Some physicians and chiropractors pursue holistic approaches to health. Some medical doctors work with traditional American Indian doctors and methods.

The intellectual life of the medical community is vibrant. Research, ongoing training and involvement in the education of others — both in the community and at the university — are all strongly encouraged and supported.

Trauma care here is thorough and dependable, even in remote areas. The emergency response coordinates deep-woods rescue teams with smaller local hospitals, highly trained ground and air ambulance responders and the Duluth medical center. It's virtually seamless, a remarkable achievement in so large an area. The system reflects more than 20 years of very hard work by otherwise competing medical providers who saw the importance of a unified regional view of healthcare. Using some high antennas to reach over the Sawtooth Mountains and past the magnetism of the iron-rich soil, the providers were among the first in the country to develop an online emergency communication system. Doctors in Duluth can guide emergency workers on an ambulance 100 miles away or monitor a patient's body responses online at half that distance.

Since the crime rate here is relatively low, emergency-care resources are expended primarily on non-intentional mishaps: heart attacks, strokes and snowmobile, auto and chain saw accidents.

We hope your stay in our area is accident-free; but should you run into a problem, fast emergency aid is just a phone call away (see our subsequent Emergency Numbers gray box).

Emergency Numbers

FIRE, POLICE, AMBULANCE

In Minnesota, Wisconsin and Ontario	911
In Michigan	0 (Operator)
Michigan State Police	(906) 224-9691
Minnesota State Patrol	911
Ontario Provincial Police	(800) 465-6777
Wisconsin State Patrol	(715) 635-2141

POISON CRISIS LINES

Ashland, Wis.	(800) 815-8855
Duluth, Minn.	(800) 222-1222
Ironwood, Mich.	(800) 562-9721
Superior, Wis.	(608) 262-3702
Thunder Bay, Ont.	(800) 268-9017

Twin Ports Area

Hospitals

COMMUNITY MEMORIAL HOSPITAL
512 Skyline Blvd.
Cloquet, Minn.   (218) 879-4641

High on a wooded hill overlooking the St. Louis River, this 36-bed community-built hospital offers 24-hour emergency service and general acute care as well as extended care in an attached, 88-bed nursing home. In 1996, it announced it will allow new mothers to stay an extra day at the hospital, even if the patient's insurance plan doesn't pay for it. The state's "Liberalis" chemical dependency program for women is housed on the third floor of the hospital.

MILLER-DWAN MEDICAL CENTER
502 E. Second St.
Duluth, Minn.   (218) 727-8762

The city-owned hospital began as a general acute-care public hospital in 1934, but over the years developed into a specialty complex. Patients with serious burns, frostbite and other soft-tissue wounds are received on a 24-hour basis and treated in the hospital's Regional Burn Center. With two linear accelerators and a cobalt machine, Miller-Dwan is also the area's main cancer treatment center. A dialysis center serves outpatients on the premises and also offers dialysis treatment in homes and at three satellites in the area. Other specialties are surgery (reconstructive, eye, plastic and general surgery); chemical dependency and mental health services for all ages; and assisted living for adults.

Most patients are admitted only on referral, but mental health and burn patients are also received on an emergency basis. The emergency mental health crisis line is (218) 723-0099; the burn center number is (218) 720-1215 or (800) 766-8762.

ST. LUKE'S HOSPITAL
915 E. First St.
Duluth, Minn.   (218) 726-5555

Founded by Episcopalians in 1881, St. Luke's is the oldest hospital in Duluth and the only hospital in the region to be designated a Level II Regional Trauma Center. It has a 24-hour emergency room and an able, committed staff for general acute care. About 1,260 employees work at the 267-bed, not-for-profit hospital.

St. Luke's specialties are trauma, hospice, neurosurgery, mental health, cardiac care, obstetrics, home care and occupational medicine. Physicians who practice here tend to come from Northland Medical Associates.

ST. MARY'S MEDICAL CENTER
407 E. Third St.
Duluth, Minn.   (218) 726-4000

Founded by the Benedictine Order in 1888, St. Mary's remains a Benedictine-

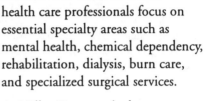

owned-and-operated hospital. It has a 24-hour emergency room and an able, committed staff for general acute care. Specialties at the 324-bed hospital are cardiology, high-risk obstetrics, cancer, orthopedics and neurosurgery. Most of the region's premature or seriously ailing infants are nursed in St. Mary's neonatal intensive care unit. The hospital has about 2,200 employees. Physicians who practice here tend to come from the Duluth Clinic.

As of this printing, St. Mary's was considering a merger with the Duluth Clinic, to which it is already joined by a skywalk and cooperative programs.

St. Mary's Hospital-Superior
3500 Tower Ave.
Superior, Wis. **(715) 392-8281**
The former Superior Memorial Hospital merged with Duluth's St. Mary's Medical Center in 1995, after 32 years as a community-supported and run hospital. Superior's only hospital has 42 beds and offers general acute-care services, outpatient clinics and a 24-hour emergency room.

In cooperation with the Douglas County Health Department, it will begin in 1996 a community-wide health assessment so as to differentiate its local focus from that of the metro medical complex across the bridge. Also in late 1996, this hospital will add an eight-bay dialysis unit (in conjunction with Duluth's Miller-Dwan Medical Center) and inpatient hospice beds.

Specialty Clinics

Duluth Clinic Ltd.
400 E. Third St.
Duluth, Minn. **(218) 722-8364**
The third-largest medical specialty clinic in Minnesota (the renowned Mayo Clinic is the first), the fast-growing Duluth Clinic comprises 280 physicians in 42 specialties and sub-specialties, supported by almost 1,500 paramedics. Partly because of the sheer number of doctors, it's the primary force driving the direction of medical care in the region. Clinic physicians also are involved in basic research (more than 100 projects at any one time).

The Duluth Clinic has come a long way since it was established as a family practice in 1915. The familiar blue-on-white butterfly logo now identifies 22 small local clinics throughout the region. They were absorbed rapidly — mostly in the past five years — in competition with the mushrooming systems in the Twin Cities and elsewhere. The number of physicians in the clinic organization has doubled in that time — not only through the mergers, but also due to heavy recruitment from outside the region.

The clinic logo also appears on various office doors at the St. Mary's and Miller-Dwan medical centers, which flank the clinic and share some programs with it. At the time of this printing, the clinic and St. Mary's were considering a merger.

The neighborhood clinics — Hermantown, West Duluth, Lakeside, East Superior and South Superior — handle their own appointments, but you can call the main clinic for numbers. The main clinic is open 8 AM to 5:30 PM; West Duluth is open 8 AM to 5 PM; and the others are open 8:30 AM to 5 PM.

Duluth Community Health Center
2 E. Fifth St.
Duluth, Minn. **(218) 722-1497**
Most Insiders call it the "Free Clinic," because that's what this intimate, attractive little building on the hillside offers. Supported by volunteer doctors, donations and a sliding-fee scale depending on your income (they take your word for it), the

St. Luke's
Urgent Care

Hours:
10:00 a.m. - 8:00 p.m.
7 days a week

No Appointment Needed

Two Convenient Locations

SLH Clinic Building
1011 E. First St.
725-6095

4886 Miller Trunk Hwy
Hermantown, MN 55811
733-5700

St. Luke's
Hospital & Regional Trauma Center

clinic is open to anyone. AIDS testing and counseling, pap smears, child health, immunizations and general care are offered here.

Hours are 9 AM to 5 PM Monday, Tuesday and Thursday, and 9 AM to noon Friday. Call for appointments. The clinic is open on occasional Tuesday evenings; just when depends on when the availability of volunteer doctors, so call first.

HUMAN DEVELOPMENT CENTER
1401 E. First St.
Duluth, Minn.   *(218) 728-4491*
24-hour crisis line   *(800) 634-8775*

An attractive brick building under spreading trees houses the area's mental health center, where the dedicated staff of 120 is quick to recognize someone in need. The nonprofit center serves St. Louis, Carlton and Lake counties.

Included in its menu of offerings are individual counseling; group therapy; support group facilitating; helping people with mental illness find jobs and housing; social activities; and managing a building where participants learn independent living. No one in crisis is turned away.

The center opens at 8 AM and closes at 5 PM Monday, Thursday and Friday; at 6 PM Tuesday; and at 7:30 PM Wednesday.

MARINER CLINIC
69 N. 28th St.
Superior, Wis.   *(715) 392-2273*

Three family practitioners, an ophthalmologist and a podiatrist work at this clinic, which St. Luke's Hospital bought in January 1996. You'll find it in the Mariner Mall next to JCPenney. Hours are 8 AM to 5 PM weekdays.

MEMORIAL MEDICAL TREATMENT CENTER-TWIN PORTS
Board of Trade Building, Ste. 407
1507 Tower Ave.
Superior, Wis.   *(715) 392-9300*

A branch of the Ashland hospital's Alcohol and Drug Treatment Center, this satellite works with chemical dependency issues on an outpatient basis. Call for an appointment.

NORTHLAND MEDICAL ASSOCIATES
1000 E. First St.
Duluth, Minn.   *(218) 726-5114*

The fast growth of the Duluth Clinic spawned this protective affiliation of physicians who wanted to maintain their independence — from the Clinic and from one another. It has the advantage of size for cooperative buying power, but each doctor or physician-group has the flexibility of independence to maintain an individual relationship with patients.

The Northland group includes 61 physicians in 18 independent groups. Of those, 17 doctors are primary care physicians; the rest cover most of the sub-specialties. Most are housed in the main building; a few have offices in other neighborhoods. The group is associated primarily with St. Luke's Hospital.

Hours are 8 AM to 5 PM weekdays.

RAITER CLINIC
417 Skyline Blvd.
Cloquet, Minn.   *(218) 879-1271*

Cloquet has managed to maintain its

independence during the health-system repositioning of recent years — neither the three clinics nor the hospital have lost their autonomy. The Raiter Clinic is the largest of the three in town, with nine family practitioners, an internist and two general surgeons. It was established in the 1930s, when three Raiter brothers — two physicians and a pharmacist — opened a clinic and hospital.

The clinic will accommodate walk-in patients, and is open 8 AM to 5 PM weekdays.

TWIN PORTS VETERANS ADMINISTRATION OUTPATIENT CLINIC
3520 Tower Ave.
Superior, Wis. **(715) 392-9711**

The only such service in several states, this clinic has been busy since it was built in 1989. It's a satellite of the Minneapolis Veterans Administration Medical Center and offers general medical and psychiatric care to eligible veterans. Walk-ins are accommodated, but it's better to call for an appointment and the government's latest eligibility requirements. Hours are 8 AM to 4:30 PM weekdays.

Tribal Clinics

CENTER FOR AMERICAN INDIAN RESOURCES
215 W. Fourth St.
Duluth, Minn. **(218) 726-1370**

"CARE" is a downtown clinic, pharmacy and general social services one-stop for urban Indian people. It's owned and operated by the Fond du Lac Ojibwe band, which remodeled the former Duluth Catholic Diocese headquarters into an attractive, accessible service center. Three physicians and a nurse practitioner work under the press of an always-full waiting room, and other professionals help clients with a wide range of issues, among them family-building and healing; chemical dependency; child welfare; and finding solutions to employment and housing troubles. Public health and maternal-child health nurses provide outreach and immunizations.

Traditional Indian practitioners are welcome to doctor at CARE. Alternatively, the staff will refer patients who request it to traditional practitioners who will doctor them at home with herbs or ceremonies or both. "It is important to remember that traditional medicine is not for everyone," the clinic brochure cautions.

CARE is supported with funds from Fond du Lac, U.S. Indian Health Service, conventional insurance and direct billing. Any member of a federally recognized tribe is eligible for service. Bring your enrollment card. Hours are 8 AM to 4:30 PM every weekday but Wednesday, when CARE is open 1 to 4:30 PM.

MASH-KA-WISEN TREATMENT CENTER
Fond du Lac Reservation
Sawyer, Minn. **(218) 879-6731**

Ojibwe for "strength," Mash-ka-wisen is an inpatient chemical dependency treatment center that serves primarily American Indians and takes a traditional approach to healing. "Mash" is owned and operated by the 11 Ojibwe and Dakota tribal governments in Minnesota, although its clients include people from other tribes and states. Admission is by referral. See our Annual Events chapter for details on the center's annual sobriety powwow, a favorite on the traditional powwow circuit.

MIN-NO-AYA-WIN HUMAN SERVICES CENTER
Fond du Lac Reservation
Cloquet, Minn. **(218) 879-1227**

Ojibwe for "good health," the tribally-run Min-no-aya-win center uses both Indian Health Service and tribal funds to provide medical services, dentistry, counseling, support group facilitation and other social and wellness services. The staff includes four physicians, three dentists, a pharmacist, lab and X-ray technicians, three nurse practitioners and a physician's assistant. Outpatient medical services and referrals are also offered.

The clinic is for any enrolled member of a federally recognized tribe. Walk-ins are accommodated, although appointments are preferred. Hours are 8 AM to 4:30 PM Monday through Friday.

Walk-in Facilities

DULUTH CLINIC WALK-IN CARE
407 E. Third St.
Duluth, Minn.   (218) 725-3292

Housed next to St. Mary's Medical Center's emergency room, this clinic makes seeing a doctor simple. The service is for those who are ailing and have no physician; or who are too pressed to await an appointment with their usual doctor but are not sick enough to justify using the emergency room. The long hours are handy too. It's open 7 AM to 10 PM seven days a week.

ST. LUKE'S URGENT CARE
1011 E. First St.
Duluth, Minn.   (218) 725-6095

Use this pleasant office as you would a doctor in the simple old days. The service is for people who are ailing and have no physician; or who are too pressed to await an appointment with their usual doctor, but are not sick enough to justify using the emergency room. Just walk in; the doc will ask you some questions, poke you a few times and maybe write you a prescription, give you advice or reassurance, or refer you to a specialist. The evening and weekend hours are handy too.

The clinic is opened from 10 AM to 8 PM seven days a week.

ST. LUKE'S URGENT CARE-HERMANTOWN
4886 Miller Trunk Hwy.
Hermantown, Minn.   (218) 733-5700

The demand over the hill for urgent-care services convinced St. Luke's to open a similar clinic in the Duluth suburb in early 1996. Its hours are 10 AM to 8 PM.

Family-practice Clinics

DULUTH FAMILY PRACTICE CENTER
330 N. Eighth Ave. E.
Duluth, Minn.   (218) 723-1112

Graduates of family practice programs all over the country compete to get into this unassuming but fast-growing center to fulfill their residencies. It's also a good place for the patient, offering a relaxed atmosphere where rules can be flexed to accommodate a walk-in from out of town. While the 30 young doctors might not have a wealth of experience, they are dedicated and personable and are supervised closely by experienced professionals. The center has a fine track record for putting physicians into small and rural communities and for working closely with American Indian traditional practitioners and practices.

PUUMALA CLINIC
40 12th St.
Cloquet, Minn.   (218) 879-7923

Here's a family practice clinic in the fullest sense of the phrase — it's run by a family of family practitioners. Founded in 1936 by Drs. Reino and Marie Bepko Puumala, the descendants now continue the tradition: their son, Dr. Ricard; his wife, Dr. Barbara; and that couple's daughter, Dr. Victoria Puumala. A fourth, non-family family practitioner also is on staff. Dr. Barbara is the physician for the state's Liberalis chemical-dependency program for women, which is housed in the Cloquet hospital. Dr. Ricard, like his father before him, is the Carlton County Coroner.

The clinic is open 8:30 AM to 5:30 PM, but patients aren't seen until around 10, when the docs get back from hospital rounds. It will accommodate walk-in patients.

Along the North Shore

Hospitals

GRAND MARAIS HOSPITAL
Gunflint Tr. and Fifth St.
Grand Marais, Minn.   *(218) 387-1500*

A new emergency room and expanded inpatient services have settled this 16-bed hospital even more firmly as an essential part of the scenic Grand Marais landscape. Four family-practice doctors are on staff; a radiologist, pathologist and chiropractor are consultants. Services include a 24-hour emergency room, laboratory, X-rays, cardiac care, ambulance service and home care. A 47-bed nursing home is attached.

LAKE VIEW MEMORIAL HOSPITAL
325 11th Ave.
Two Harbors, Minn.   *(218) 834-7300*

Sitting on a rise near Lake Superior at the edge of town, Lake View is a general acute-care hospital (30 beds) and nursing home (15 beds) that originally was established in 1957. The emergency room is open 24 hours. It also runs two cottages for foster care for adults with impaired memories.

Tribal Clinics

GRAND PORTAGE HEALTH SERVICES
Grand Portage Reservation
Grand Portage, Minn.   *(218) 475-2235*

Community health is stressed at this tribally-run Indian Health Services clinic. Three registered nurses and two community health workers have achieved a 100-percent immunization rate in the service population: American Indians and non-Indians on the reservation. Other health professionals at the clinic include a chiropractor, a certified massage therapist and a licensed nutritionist. A physician holds office hours Tuesday and Thursday from 9 AM until noon. The clinic is open from 8:30 AM to 4:30 PM weekdays and staffs a 13-member volunteer ambulance crew.

St. Mary's Medical Center in early 1996 became the first Duluth hospital to allow a chiropractor staff privileges. (A hospital at Moose Lake, 45 miles away, in 1992 became the first in the state to put a chiropractor on staff.) The medical establishment here and nationwide has long disdained chiropractic, but several pressures have brought about gradual change. One is a combination of lawsuits, lobbyists and changes in insurance coverage. Another is that younger doctors tend to be more comfortable working with chiropractors (or even use them themselves); a third is that physicians' patients are requesting the combined care.

Insiders' Tips

Although it exists primarily for on-reservation residents, it will serve anyone.

The clinic is next to the elementary school, across from the new community center. It's open 8 AM to 4:30 PM Monday through Friday.

Family-practice Clinics

BAY AREA HEALTH CENTER
50 Outer Dr.
Silver Bay, Minn.   (218) 226-4431

Feeling poorly? Just call Dr. Sarah or Dr. Deb. These two family practitioners — Drs. Nelson and King, respectively — have resurrected the comforting institution of the house call when it's just too hard for a patient to leave home. Strengthened by a nurse practitioner and two physician's assistants, Bay Area focuses on keeping this community healthy through preventive medicine, education and promoting lifestyle changes.

Along the South Shore

Hospitals

GRAND VIEW HOSPITAL
N10561 Grand View Ln.
Ironwood, Mich.   (906) 932-2525

A general acute-care hospital with 54 beds, Grand View has branched out with its Grand View Health System into other businesses: home health, equipment, a pharmacy and clinics. A physician is on duty 24 hours a day at the hospital, which

offers obstetrics, chemotherapy, surgery, orthopedics and urology on its menu of services.

MEMORIAL MEDICAL CENTER
1615 Maple Ln.
Ashland, Wis.   (715) 682-4563

This 161-bed community hospital opened in 1972 on the day two other Ashland hospitals agreed to close. Besides general acute-care and hospice care, its 360 employees run the Comprehensive Community Mental Health Center and the Alcohol and Drug Treatment Center, both on the hospital campus. Ashland Memorial also offers dialysis through an arrangement with Miller-Dwan Medical Center in Duluth. The 24-hour crisis line for mental health services is (715) 682-8678.

The hospital is a mile south of U.S. Highway 2 off Beaser Avenue.

Specialty Clinics

DULUTH CLINIC-ASHLAND
1625 Maple Ln.
Ashland, Wis.   (715) 682-2358

Formerly Medical Associates North, this large clinic joined the Duluth Clinic in early 1995. It includes nine family practitioners, a general surgeon, four internists, two pediatricians, three OB-GYN specialists, a dermatologist, a gastroenterologist and three emergency physicians.

The clinic has its own four satellites: in Ironwood, Michigan; and in Iron River, Washburn and Hayward, Wiscon-

St. Mary's Medical Center, The Duluth Clinic and Miller-Dwan Medical Center in Duluth are connected via a skywalk as well as cooperative programs.

Photo: Duluth News-Tribune

sin. Doctors from Ashland rotate to the satellites (call the Ashland clinic for satellite hours). The Ashland clinic is open 8:30 AM to 5 PM weekdays.

GRAND VIEW CLINIC-IRONWOOD
N10565 Grand View Ln.
Ironwood, Mich.   *(906) 932-1500*
Part of the Grand View Health System, the Ironwood clinic includes two obstetricians, an orthopedist and 10 family-practice doctors. Clinic hours are 8 AM to 5 PM weekdays.

GRAND VIEW CLINIC-HURLEY
501 Granite Ave.
Hurley, Wis.   *(715) 561-2255*
Formerly the Iron County Clinic, these physicians joined the Grand View Health System in the early 1990s. One pediatrician and one internist, a husband-and-wife team, see patients here. Clinic hours are 8 AM to 5 PM weekdays.

REGIONAL HOSPICE SERVICE
1615 Maple Ln.
Ashland, Wis.   *(715) 682-8677.*
Four hospitals in the region — in Ashland, Hayward and Spooner, Wisconsin, and in Ironwood, Michigan — cooperatively operate this outpatient hospice service.

Tribal Clinics

BAD RIVER HEALTH CLINIC
Bad River Reservation
New Odanah, Wis.   *(715) 682-7133*
Bad River's new clinic was opened in late 1995 and is in the process of expanding. As of this printing, it was offering the services of family nurse practitioners five days a week; a physician sees patients four hours a week. The clinic's hours are 8:30 AM to 3:30 PM weekdays, except Wednesday afternoons.

The clinic serves Bad River tribal members but will offer limited services to members of other federally recognized tribes.

RED CLIFF COMMUNITY HEALTH CENTER
Red Cliff Reservation
Bayfield, Wis.   *(715) 779-3707*
Since the tribally owned and operated Red Cliff clinic was opened in 1992, it quickly outgrew its quarters; the grand opening of a new clinic was slated for October 1996.

As of this printing, an osteopath sees patients Monday through Thursday, a family-practice doctor sees patients on Friday, and nurses and health representatives see to home-health visits, immunizations, prenatal-care classes and other services. Hours are 7 AM to 5 PM weekdays.

The new clinic will include two laboratories, X-ray services, a dental clinic and another doctor or physician's assistant. Only tribal members are served in the older clinic, but the new one will be open to everyone in the area.

Family-practice Clinics

CHEQUAMEGON CLINIC
206 Sixth Ave. W.
Ashland, Wis.   (715) 682-6622
Six family practitioners and a general surgeon operate out of this clinic, which also has a satellite in nearby Washburn. Hours are 8 AM to 5 PM Monday, Tuesday, Wednesday and Friday; 8 AM to 9 PM Thursday; and 9 AM to noon Saturday. Walk-ins are accommodated.

CHEQUAMEGON CLINIC-WASHBURN
320 Superior Ave.
Washburn, Wis.   (715) 373-2216
A satellite of the clinic in Ashland, family-practice doctors from that clinic rotate here to hold office hours 9 AM to noon Monday, Tuesday and Thursday, and 9 AM to 4 PM Wednesday.

HEALTH CENTERS OF BAYFIELD COUNTY
20 S. Broad St.
Bayfield, Wis.   (715) 779-4000
A community effort produced this new clinic of nurse practitioners, where basic primary care is offered on a sliding-fee scale. Physicians from regional clinics back up the nurses. This clinic opened in early 1996 and has a satellite

in the minimall in Iron River, Wisconsin, and a mobile unit. Call for more information.

The nurses are on call 24 hours; the clinic's hours are 9 AM to 3 PM weekdays. Occasionally it will be open evenings and weekends, but call first.

Thunder Bay Area

Like in the United States, Canadian healthcare is feeling the economic pinch of higher expectations, inflation and ever-increasing costs of highly specialized equipment. In Canada, the medical system is run by the provinces, which put a stronger emphasis on prevention and basic care than their neighbors to the south. That means there are more family doctors to go around (family doctors make up the vast majority of the city's 250 physicians), but sub-specialists are scarce.

Thunder Bay's three hospitals have been in the process of merger. McKellar General Hospital in Old Fort William combined in 1995 with the General Hospital of Port Arthur, and the two are slated to absorb the acute care of St. Joseph's Hospital (also in Port Arthur) sometime in 1996. St. Joe's will continue to offer extended long-term care, and one of the three emergency rooms likely will be turned into an urgent-care clinic.

Thunder Bay has a children's hospital, psychiatric hospital and nursing home hospital that have not been listed here because they require referrals. Crisis care, whether for children or for mental health issues, is directed first to the general hospital emergency rooms.

The usual patient flow is from Thunder Bay to Duluth, where there are more available specialists with more high-tech equipment. But it isn't uncommon for a U.S. visitor (or other foreigner) to use the Ontario health system, particularly for

There is an abundance of conventional medical services in communities of the Lake Superior region.

Photo: Duluth News-Tribune

emergency reasons. No one is turned away at Thunder Bay hospitals, although you'll probably find a bill awaiting you when you get home.

Hudson Bay to White River. Services include two emergency rooms, neurosurgery, obstetrics, oncology and general surgery.

HOSPITALS

ST. JOSEPH'S GENERAL HOSPITAL
35 N. Algoma St.
Thunder Bay, Ont.   (807) 343-2431
"St. Joe's" is gradually relinquishing its acute-care services to Thunder Bay Regional and taking more chronic, long-term patients. Completion of the process is expected in mid-1996.

THUNDER BAY REGIONAL HOSPITAL
McKellar General Hospital
325 S. Archibald St.
Thunder Bay, Ont.   (807) 343-7123
The General Hospital of Port Arthur
460 N. Court St.
Thunder Bay, Ont.   (807) 343-6621
With a total of 460 beds and 2,000 employees, these merged hospitals handle most of the acute care in a large area: from near the Manitoba border to

Walk-in Clinics

PORT ARTHUR CLINIC
194 N. Court St.
Thunder Bay, Ont.   (807) 345-2332
The only clinic in Thunder Bay that takes walk-in patients, Port Arthur was established to relieve the pressure on the city's emergency rooms. If you have a health problem that isn't serious enough for the ER but is too pressing to await an appointment with a doctor, Port Arthur Clinic is a good place to go.

The clinic is open 9 AM to 9 PM weekdays and 11 AM to 4 PM on weekends.

Nonmedical Wellness Services

Alternative healthcare is something more than acupuncture needles and chiropractic adjustments.

Among the other treatments is **Reiki**

(pronounced ray-KEE), which in Japanese means "universal energy." In therapy, it's a healing system whereby a practitioner uses laying-on of hands to help the body gather its own natural energies to heal itself. Patients say it relieves pain and acute conditions very quickly.

Ortho-bionomy is similar, in that it enhances the natural ability to release pain, tension and stress. A therapist positions and moves the body into "release positions," which are intended to result in a deep, integrated self-release that allows healing to happen naturally.

Herbal therapy is the use of traditional plants and medicines, usually Asian, to cure disease.

Aroma therapy is based on the idea that the sense of smell triggers powerfully healing ideas, memories and reactions. Scented oils (floral, herbal and spicy) are used in massage in various combinations, depending on the effect desired. For example, a combination of lavender and tangerine is said to help in relaxation; and a combination of ginger and peppermint aids in clearing the mind.

CHRISTAL CENTER
394 Lake Ave. S.
Duluth, Minn. *(218) 722-2411*
Housed in the DeWitt-Seitz Marketplace in Canal Park, this small sunlit suite of rooms is the site of on-site therapeutic massage; Reiki; acupuncture; aroma, herbal and water therapy; ortho-bionomy; sauna and skin care. A certified, licensed staff is available.

DULUTH FAMILY SAUNA
18 N. First Ave. E.
Duluth, Minn. *(218) 726-1388*
A public sauna under a health heading? Yah, sure: This is country where Suomis (Finns) have left their cultural mark. To many Insiders, a sauna calls up a simple image of a rustic outbuilding, with a woodpile alongside, where the whole family gets clean together — to keep bodies strong and obliterate infections — and babies used to be born.

The Duluth Family Sauna is heir to that legacy. It's seen a lot of bodies and has a worn look that puts off some people; but there's no better spot in the area to relax when the cold has settled deep in your bones and you're certain you'll never be warm again. The six private rooms include both a changing area and two-tiered sauna that will easily accommodate a family of four, although more can fit.

The hours are noon to 10 PM Sunday through Thursday and noon to midnight Friday and Saturday. The cost is $7.95 for one person and $11.50 for a couple. Children younger than 12 are admitted free with their parents. Towels are provided at no charge. The time limit is two hours unless the place isn't busy. Most weekdays you can just walk in, but on weekends a reservation is advisable.

EAGLE'S NEST INSTITUTE
5096 Arnold Rd.
Duluth, Minn. *(218) 724-8233*
Massage therapy, aroma therapy, childbirth education, meditation, t'ai chi chih and yoga are offered at this attractive "nest" in rural Duluth. All therapists are certified, and the institute also offers courses in massage and yoga.

Resources and Referrals

Medical Societies

LAKE SUPERIOR MEDICAL SOCIETY
918 Medical Arts Bldg.
Duluth, Minn. 55802 *(218) 727-3325*
This is a professional association of physicians where you can get referrals and

information about whether a particular doctor has ever been admonished or suspended for irregular conduct.

INDIAN HEALTH SERVICE
Federal Bldg.
Bemidji, Minn. 56601   *(218) 759-3412*
This is the regional, three-state office (Michigan, Wisconsin and Minnesota) of the U.S. Public Health Service's division. It has information about IHS clinics, health workers, programs and eligibility.

Public Health

The following agencies track and can give you information about communicable diseases (whooping cough, AIDS, influenza, etc.), immunizations, environmental health (Lyme disease, mercury toxicity, etc.) and other public health issues. They work closely with state health departments. These include:

Ashland County Nurse, 301 Ellis Avenue, Ashland, Wisconsin, (715) 682-7028;

Bayfield County Nurse, 117 E. Fifth Street, Washburn, Wisconsin, (715) 373-6109;

Cook County Public Health, Grand Marais, Minnesota, (218) 387-2282;

Douglas County Health Department, City-County Complex, Hammond Avenue and Belknap Street, Superior, Wisconsin, (715) 394-0404;

Gogebic County Public Health, West Upper Peninsula District, 210 N. Moore, Bessemer, Michigan, (906) 667-0200;

Iron County Nurse, 300 Taconite Street, Hurley, Wisconsin, (715) 561-2191;

Lake County Health Department, County Building, 601 Third Avenue, Two Harbors, Minnesota, (218) 834-8325;

St. Louis County Health Department, 222 E. Superior Street, Duluth, Minnesota, (218) 725-5200.

"Open enrollments" are allowed in Minnesota; students can attend public school in any district statewide, at no charge.

Inside
Child Care and Education

Child Care

Finding trustworthy child care is a continuing challenge and an emotionally charged process for working parents. In many instances, the choice boils down to a word-of-mouth referral from a neighbor, friend or colleague as a starting point for the critical process of checking out prospective providers.

In some of the sparsely populated rural areas along Lake Superior's North Shore in Minnesota and its South Shore in the western Upper Peninsula of Michigan, choices in child-care facilities are limited. Fortunately, a number of reputable referral services are now available to parents. Some resorts on Minnesota's North Shore, including Lutsen Lodge and Bluefin Bay (see our Accommodations chapter), and ski resorts in Michigan's western Upper Peninsula, including Powderhorn (see our Winter Sports chapter), provide child-care services for guests.

Types of Services

Child-care services are organized into several categories and age groups. Child-care providers are licensed to take care of children of different ages. These age groups include infant/toddler, preschool and school age to 11 years old.

Licensed family child care is a home-based service, many times provided by parents who have children of their own.

Child-care centers are generally larger operations, run many times out of a church basement or their own building, with a licensed staff and the ability to accept kids of a wider age range. Because of their capacity, the centers generally offer more structured activities for children.

Licensing Requirements

Depending on the number of children, home-based family child care in Minnesota and Wisconsin is a county-licensed enterprise. In Minnesota and Wisconsin, child-care centers, preschools and nursery schools are state-licensed. In Ontario, there are strict licensing requirements — outlined in the Day Nursery Act — to protect the welfare of children. This particular provincial law sets minimum ratios of children to child-care providers; fire, health and safety standards; inspection criteria for proper facility exits and general cleanliness; and accredited early-childhood training for care providers.

However, licensing by a county or state is neither a stamp of approval nor a recommendation. State licensing requirements merely satisfy a minimum set of standards, covering life-safety issues, such as accident prevention and fire-safety planning, and provider training in first-aid skills and nutrition. In Minnesota, a criminal background check is completed on everyone 13 years and older in the home of a family child-care provider. Checks are also run on child-care center staff as part of their licensing application in Minnesota.

Parents must do the legwork to assure the proper care for their child. In Minnesota parents can check with the county licensing board for complaints against a family child-care provider, determination of complaints and substantiation of abuse or neglect by a family child-care provider — all public information. For child-care centers, preschools and nursery schools licensed by the state, parents can check with the state for similar information: **Department of Human Services Licenses Center**, 444 Lafayette Road, St. Paul, Minnesota, (612) 296-3971.

Note: It is critical for parents to know that a complaint under investigation but not yet substantiated is *not* public information.

Salient Questions

The Arrowhead Child Care Resource and Referral, a St. Louis County Social Service-based child-care referral service, suggests that parents take at least two steps after the initial referral: a phone interview and an on-site visit for further evaluation. Listen to your gut feelings and use common sense. Ask for at least three references. Here are some of the questions to ask a prospective provider:

• How are the children disciplined?

• Is the environment smoke-free? In Minnesota, all licensed child-care facilities are required to be smoke-free. The law stipulates that as long as there are children on site, the facility must be smoke-free.

• Who are the other children? How many are there, and what are their ages?

How many of their own children are involved?

• Are there pets?

• What kind of training does the provider have? The state of Minnesota requires infant/toddler CPR training, first-aid training and six hours a year minimum life-safety training, with fire safety a key part. What educational background in child development does the provider have? Generally, more extensive education or training is an indication of commitment to care.

• Are the children allowed to watch television? If so, what and how much are they watching?

• Are the toys and activities age-appropriate?

• What happens when a child is sick or you are on vacation?

• How much time is planned vs. free time?

Resource and Referral Agencies

The **Arrowhead Child Care Resource and Referral** serves Aitkin, Carlton, Cook, Itasca, Koochiching, Lake and St. Louis counties in Minnesota. For help in finding child care in Duluth and St. Louis County, and on the North Shore, call (218) 726-2273 or (800) 450-0450. For information in the Iron Range area, call (218) 749-7188.

The Arrowhead referral service, staffed with counselors, offers a specialized data base program to match parental needs to licensed family child care, centers, preschools and nursery schools, sick care programs and after-school programs. The service lists more than 900 providers and offers, for a reasonable sliding scale fee, an individualized printout of detailed profiles of appropriate providers. You can do

this over the phone or drop by their offices at the Government Service Center, 320 W. Second Street in Duluth. Arrowhead also offers valuable support materials.

The **Bethany Crisis Nursery**, run by Lutheran Social Services, provides help for parents in crisis. The program offers free child care for up to three days in licensed host homes. The service is available 24 hours a day for parents in southern St. Louis County (including Duluth); call the hotline at (218) 626-3083.

Another Thunder Bay resource is **Communities Together for Children**, (807) 622-2435, 801 Victoria Avenue E. This agency maintains a list of all providers in Thunder Bay and offers support and training for child-care providers.

The **Northwest Wisconsin Child Care Resource and Referral**, based in Hayward, Wisconsin, serves Douglas, Bayfield, Ashland, Iron, Washburn, Sawyer, Price, Burnett, Rusk and Barron counties and the St. Croix, Bad River, Lac Courte Oreilles and Red Cliff Ojibwe bands. In addition to child-care referrals, this organization works with child-care providers to offer ongoing training and support services. For parents seeking child care in these areas, the referral service is free. In Wisconsin, call (800) 733-5437; outside Wisconsin, call (715) 634-2299.

The **Adults & Childrens Alliance**, 2885 Country Drive, Suite 165, St. Paul, Minnesota, is a well-established national child-care referral service. It offers support services for child-care providers in 37 states, including Minnesota, Wisconsin and Michigan, and referral services for parents seeking child care. This organization primarily works with child-care providers who are enrolled in a federal food program. For referral services, call (800) 247-1640.

For child care in Thunder Bay, start with the **Ministry of Community and Social Services**, (807) 622-2272, 710 Victoria Avenue E., for a list of licensed day-care providers and other resource material.

Education

Lake Superior has a humbling influence on the people who live around it, so we like to leave the bragging to others. We would be presumptuous to say that this is an area where people value education more than just about anywhere on the continent. But let us point out that there are only about 300,000 of us from Thunder Bay, Ontario, to Ironwood, Michigan, and we have five four-year colleges and universities, three community colleges and three technical schools, and relatively low high-school dropout rates (.5 to 3 percent).

In general, our public primary and secondary public schools are relatively safe, well-behaved places. There are no police needed in the schools, and students don't fear for their lives. Weapons and open fighting are unusual in the Twin Ports and almost nonexistent in Thunder Bay; in the smaller North and South shore schools, the major offenses are smoking on the school grounds and wearing inappropriate clothing. Only one college-prep school exists in our region, partly because so many of our public schools offer much the same environment: high academic standards; arts programs; safe, intimate, personalized learning environments; state-of-the art technology; and community partnerships. In Minnesota, "open enrollments" are allowed, meaning students can opt for a different school district anywhere in the state, at no charge.

The Minnesota Center for Arts Education near Minneapolis (listed subsequently under "Referrals") is a public high school where talented students from anywhere in the state can focus on art, dancing and music.

Virtually all schoolchildren in Thunder Bay attend either the Lakehead Public Schools or the Lakehead Roman Catholic Separate Schools. College preparatory work is done within the schools, in a (formerly) grade 13, now called Ontario Academic Courses. Junior and senior kindergarten, for 4- and 5-year-olds, is not compulsory. While sports are enormously popular in Thunder Bay, sports in schools are nowhere as extravagant or consuming as they are in the United States. The schools don't have stadiums, and the public turnout for games — even hockey — is not large. The study of the French language is emphasized at all schools, because Canada is officially a bilingual country.

A small percentage of primary students throughout our region receive their education at home. Contact the state departments of education (listed subsequently) for information about home schooling. The only city with a significant number of such students (about 150) is Duluth. For the most recent contact numbers for home school support groups, call Information & Referral, (218) 726-2222.

Primary and Secondary Schools

Public Schools

ASHLAND PUBLIC SCHOOLS
120 E. Main St., Ashland, Wis.   (715) 682-7080

The Ashland system includes 2,400 students. Senior high students attend an attractive single-story spread; about 920 K through 5 students are housed in a new pod-concept school; and about 550 middle-school kids are in a three-story school — one grade per story, so that the adolescents can get more individualized teaching and guidance. Another 420 youngsters attend a K through 6 school about 12 miles south of Ashland. The district encompasses 422 square miles. The typical class size in elementary school is in the low 20s; higher grades are in the high 20s. Strengths in this district include the gifted-and-talented program; drama program; a complete sports program and orchestra (both are uncommon in northern Wisconsin); and environmental studies, in which students (sometimes in kayaks) monitor Lake Superior's water quality.

"Village Partnership" is the framework for bringing the school and community closer together; through it, youngsters get work experience at local businesses; parents, teachers and administrators have "site councils" that act as governing bodies; and a committee made up mostly of band members from the nearby Bad River Reservation helps coordinate education for the school's 320 Indian students.

BAYFIELD PUBLIC SCHOOLS
315 Sweeny Ave., Bayfield, Wis. (715) 779-3201

With more than 500 K through 12 students, this school district is small enough to bring all its youngsters to one beautiful site — the historic old brownstone school and adjoining new building high on a hill overlooking Chequamegon Bay. The typical class size is 20. In a cooperative program with local resort owners, students get hands-on experience during a two-year hotel management apprenticeship program. Another community partner is the nearby Red Cliff Ojibwe band (more than half of Bayfield's students are Red Cliff members); half of the parent-teacher conferences are held on the reservation, and the band spon-sors the school's athletic and honors banquets. In both 1995 and 1996, Bayfield students won toothpick bridge-building contests sponsored by the Minnesota Department of Transportation, competing against the big schools in Duluth and the surrounding area. A Bayfield student took five top awards, including three from the Air Force, Navy and Army, at the National Native American Science and Engineering Fair in 1996 (for his physics project, a shortcut to making superconductors). An elementary school on nearby Madeline Island became part of this district in the 1980s, after parents there petitioned to join the district; formerly, high-school students were forced to commute to or find winter lodgings in distant Ashland.

COOK COUNTY PUBLIC SCHOOLS
Grand Marais, Minn.   (218) 387-2271

The arts colony of Grand Marais has influenced the local school district — partly from proximity and partly because of community partnering — so its arts curriculum is second to none in the region. It includes visual arts, music and performing arts. A point of district pride is the independence of the graduates; officials say these small-town 18- or 19-year-olds are able to adjust quickly to big-city universities, fine colleges and military academies and have a good survival rate, reflecting a school experience that nourishes self-confidence. Another strength is an internal mutual-support system the students — from varying ethnic and economic backgrounds — have established. Community partnerships include the Grand Portage Reservation Tribal Council, the arts colony and the Grand Marais Playhouse. About 730 students attend three elementary schools (one of them a historic log building at Grand Portage) and one secondary school.

DULUTH PUBLIC SCHOOLS
215 N. First Ave. E.
Duluth, Minn.   (218) 723-4150

The second-biggest district (13,700 students) in the region, it has a history of wranglings among school board members and superintendents that sometimes have trickled down to the school level. Nevertheless, the district boasts some excellent teachers and programs and maintains low dropout rates and good national test scores. Three magnet schools, open to any primary child in the district, offer language (Ojibwe and Spanish); music; and math/science. The district runs alternative centers for students who have been in trouble and two schools for youngsters who can't adjust to the normal school setting. The three high schools are located at each end and in the center of the long, narrow town; also in the district are 13 elementary schools and three middle schools. The Secondary Technical Center downtown provides high-schoolers with training in areas such as aviation. The district has latchkey and early childhood education programs and runs family centers at four sites in town.

FOND DU LAC OJIBWE SCHOOL
105 University Rd.
Cloquet, Minn.   (218) 879-0241

This school was established in 1980 by the Fond du Lac Ojibwe band on its reservation in Cloquet. Community leaders felt tribal children weren't flourishing in nearby schools; to save them and to survive as a people and culture, they opened a tribal school using traditional (outcome-based, results-oriented and community-focused) methods of education. A new school was being built in 1996. About half the 200 K through 12 students are in high school, and despite the small pool, the school generally fields a football team that competes

with public and private schools in the area. Ojibwe culture is woven into the curriculum; the typical classroom size is 15 students. The school is open to everyone, but tribal students are a priority. The school runs buses into Duluth and other surrounding areas to pick up youngsters from other districts. It operates as a tribal grant school and is accredited by the North Central Association.

HURLEY PUBLIC SCHOOLS
1-S-517 Range View Dr.
Hurley, Wis.   (715) 561-4900

About 800 youngsters, grades K through 12, attend the single school in Hurley. The student-staff ratio is 12-to-1, which doesn't reflect class size because some grades are combined. The $7 million school was built in 1991, following a referendum that surprised many in this economically depressed city by passing on the first round. New athletic fields — tennis, softball, football and baseball — were expected to be ready for the 1996-97 school year. The Hurley football team advanced to state competition in 1995.

IRONWOOD PUBLIC SCHOOLS
634-646 E. Ayer St.
Ironwood, Mich.   (906) 932-0200

On a rise a few blocks from downtown, in an attractive residential neighborhood graced by large trees, is the Ironwood central school building, which includes middle and high schools. This district is consistently among 10 districts in the state of Michigan with the lowest dropout rates and the greatest number of graduates opting for higher education. The district has a strong music program and full sports program, and a student-teacher ratio of 16-to-1. Three K through 8 schools are located throughout the city.

Brian Mattson perfects his finger painting at Early Years Child Care in Duluth.

LAKE SUPERIOR SCHOOL DISTRICT
405 Fourth Ave.
Two Harbors, Minn. *(218) 834-8216*

This widespread district encompasses Silver Bay, Minnesota, to the northeast and part of Duluth Township to the southwest and serves 2,220 students. High schools in Two Harbors and Silver Bay both have many extracurricular activities, including football, band, choir and junior band; active booster clubs help out with sports programs when money runs out. High schools house grades 7 through 12; in Two Harbors, one of the grade schools houses K through 3; the other, grades 4 through 6. The Two Harbors high school has a reputation for a strong French program and frequently sends students to regional and state competitions; in 1996 Silver Bay high school biology students headed to state competitions as well. The district regularly sends students on to U.S. military academies; in 1996 alone, three graduates were slated for

those prestigious schools. Strong PTAs exist in Two Harbors and at North Shore Elementary, closer to Duluth; Silver Bay has a strong PTO. "Peer helpers" are students who help other students, and the Youth Development Committee is a group of students who buy and run a business, then sell its products.

LAKEHEAD BOARD OF EDUCATION
2135 Sills St.
Thunder Bay, Ont. *(807) 625-5100*

With 16,600 students, Lakehead is the region's largest school district, educating its charges in six high schools and 37 elementary schools. There's an active Parent Council in each school, and schools and districts have more autonomy than in the United States; except for basic federal rules, such as human rights and safety, and basic provincial guidelines on curriculum, the district directs how its children will be educated. More than half the district's income is from local assessment, which the school district's Board of Trustees sets. If voters don't like the tax, the option is to vote the trustees out of office.

The Lakehead system has 22 programs for children with special needs distributed throughout the district. All public school children in grades 1 through 8 study French 40 minutes every day. Students whose parents wish them to be fully bilingual are enrolled in a French immersion program, in which the entire curriculum of senior kindergarten and 1st grade is taught entirely in French; the next four grades are 75 percent in French; the next three grades are half in French; and in high school, a student can pick and choose which classes will be entirely in French. Six of the 37 elementary schools are French-immersion schools, and one high school has a French immersion option. Most English-speaking students who go through this program are functionally bilingual by grade 4 and fully bilingual by grade 8. Schools are safe, relatively orderly places; there are few weapons in Thunder Bay in general, and none have been found in schools.

SOUTH SHORE SCHOOL DISTRICT
Port Wing, Wis.   *(715) 774-3361*

This district, which is big geographically (380 square miles) but small in number of students (350), has strong support from this mostly rural community. It has one of the highest per-student spending rates in the state ($9,400 yearly, compared with a state average of $5,400) as well as the state's second-highest tax rate. All but 50 of the K through 12 students attend the main school in Port Wing; rural Oulu, 17 miles away, keeps its K through 5 pupils close to home at a small school there. The attractive Port Wing site is near Lake Superior, making it easy for the school's excellent biology program to educate students hand-on in water quality and wildlife is-

sues. This school's state-of-the-art instructional media center has one CD-ROM computer for every three students; about half are on the Internet.

In addition to standard curriculum, South Shore also offers Spanish (students have gone to state competition in this subject); family and consumer education; every sport except football; and vocal and instrumental music classes, whose students also compete statewide. Classroom sizes are typically less than 20 students in the lower grades; upper grades vary from five (South Shore school offers advanced or elective courses if as few as five students sign up) to 22. Its School-to-Work program connects students with worksites in surrounding communities.

SUPERIOR PUBLIC SCHOOLS
3025 Tower Ave.
Superior, Wis.   *(715) 394-8710*

Since 1984, when the Wisconsin Bar Association began running mock trial competitions, Superior high school students have come in first in the state four times and placed second four times. When they've headed on to the national level — in open competition with public and private schools nationwide — they've taken a second and a fourth place; in 1994, they were the top public school trial team. Academics are strong in this 5,700-student district, but sports are too: High school teams won a state football championship in 1990 and state hockey championships in 1994, 1995 and 1996. Besides a high school, the district has two junior highs and seven elementary schools, with a student-teacher ratio of 15.5-1. Two of the elementary schools are new, as are a technology education wing and performing arts center at the high school. The high school has five Advanced Placement (college prep) courses, and a discipline-based art education program is used throughout K through 12. Superior is one of 30 original schools in Wisconsin's ongoing School Reform Program led by statewide business and education groups.

WASHBURN PUBLIC SCHOOLS
310 W. Fifth St.
Washburn, Wis. *(715) 373-6188*

This district's 850 students are divided between two buildings: a newer one for grades K through 5, and across the street, down the hill toward the Lake, the old school houses grades 6 through 12. It has a strong vocational program — a Washburn teacher recently was named Vocational-Technical Teacher of the Year in Wisconsin — and every year youngsters in this program qualify for national competitions of the Future Business Leaders of America, the Future Home Economists of America and the Vocational-Industrial Clubs of America. The music program also is strong, and the school is a fiber-optics site, exchanging coursework with other schools on the network, including the University of Wisconsin-Superior and Wisconsin Indianhead Technical College. The average class size is 21. About 63 percent of Washburn graduates go on to post-secondary education.

WRENSHALL PUBLIC SCHOOLS
207 Pioneer Dr.
Wrenshall, Minn. *(218) 384-4274*

The single school at rural Wrenshall is known for its warm, accepting atmosphere, which draws students from all over Duluth (Minnesota's open enrollment allows district crossovers). Although it's one of the smallest school districts in the state, with about 400 students (half of them high-schoolers), it enjoys big-school opportunities: an Olympic-size swimming pool, a band that garners state honors, a full sports program and two fully equipped, up-to-

date computer rooms. Youngsters grades K through 12 ride the bus together and are schooled in the same building complex; the atmosphere of the school is relaxed and well-mannered. Classroom sizes typically are 15 to 18 students. Its Kids Plus Program, developed with the help of a local philanthropic organization, is a wholistic approach to answering the needs of the community. Students participate with area adults on identifying local needs and working on a final project, such as a recreation center.

Private Schools

BEAVER RIVER CHRISTIAN SCHOOL
5095 Fish Lake Rd.
Duluth, Minn. *(218) 721-4515*

Christian scripture is the hallmark of this school of 120 students tucked into a woodsy setting in rural Duluth. The core academic curriculum is augmented with a satellite link (Linc Program), which provides upper-level math, science and other subjects for its older students. Civility is expected here; when a public school driver recently filled in for the school's regular driver, he remarked how surprisingly well behaved the students were. Beaver River serves preschoolers through 12th graders; class sizes vary according to enrollment and new combinations of grades. The school is a member of the Association of Christian Schools International.

CATHOLIC DIOCESE OF DULUTH
2830 E. Fourth St.
Duluth, Minn. *(218) 724-9111*

This diocese has 13 schools throughout northern Minnesota. In Duluth, about 750 children are given an almost-standard public education ("the main difference is God," a parish spokesman says) at four elementary schools — Holy Rosary, St. James, St. John's and St. Michael's. A family atmosphere and local parish governance make for an intimate learning environment that is another draw, for non-Catholics as well as Catholics. The pupil-teacher ratio is 15-to-1. There have been discussions about starting a Catholic high school in Duluth; there is no Catholic high school anywhere in the region outside of Thunder Bay.

CATHOLIC DIOCESE OF SUPERIOR
1201 Hughitt Ave.
Superior, Wis.   (715) 392-2937

This diocese operates 18 schools in a big section of northwestern and west-central Wisconsin, educating 3,160 pupils in preschool through 8th grade. Four schools are in our area. **Cathedral School**, 1419 Baxter Avenue, (715) 392-2976, serves 353 students in Superior; others are in Bayfield, Washburn and Ashland (listed subsequently). This diocese offers a standard Catholic education.

HOLY FAMILY SCHOOL
232 N. First St.
Bayfield, Wis.   (715) 779-3342

Holy Family has 52 pupils and is part of the Catholic Diocese of Superior (see previous entry).

IDA COOK HEBREW SCHOOL TEMPLE ISRAEL
1602 E. Second St.
Duluth, Minn.   (218) 724-8857

For grades 3 through 6, this school prepares youngsters for understanding and participating in Hebrew-language services in anticipation of bar and bat mitzvahs. Classes are held twice weekly for an hour and 45 minutes. The only Hebrew school in the entire region, it also offers classes twice monthly, on Sundays, to youngsters from outside the area. Adult Hebrew classes are also available here.

LAKE SUPERIOR SEVENTH-DAY ADVENTIST CHRISTIAN SCHOOL
1331 E. Superior St.
Duluth, Minn.   (218) 724-8561

A small school — 11 pupils in mid-1996 — that educates grades 1 through 8, Lake Superior's students come from the two Seventh-Day Adventist churches in the Twin Ports. The small building is attractive and has a pleasant outdoor play area. Core curriculum is tailored to biblical scripture; for example, biology includes Creation theory and history includes biblical prophecy. The school is accredited by the Minnesota Non-Public School Accreditation Association.

Insiders' Tips

The town of Port Wing on the South Shore has the distinction of being the first community in Wisconsin to provide free transportation for students. Until 1913, kids walked to an assortment of schools in log buildings and churches. But after a three-story white clapboard building went up in Port Wing, they were gathered in via canvas-covered horse-drawn wagons called "school rigs." The Port Wing school was torn down — despite considerable controversy — in the 1980s. You can still see the big bell tower, which has been preserved in the town park along Wis. Highway 13.

LAKEHEAD ROMAN CATHOLIC SEPARATE SCHOOL BOARD

212 Miles St. E.
Thunder Bay, Ont.   *(807) 625-1555*

One-third of Thunder Bay's students — 8,000 youngsters — attend Lakehead Catholic schools, which include two high schools and 22 elementary schools. The district offers a standard public-school curriculum, augmented with regular church attendance and classes about Catholic family living. You must be Catholic to attend these schools. The district has a French elementary school for children whose first language is French, as well as a French immersion school where English-speaking youngsters are taught primarily in French.

LAKEVIEW CHRISTIAN ACADEMY

155 W. Central Entrance
Duluth, Minn.   *(218) 723-8844*

"Training young champions for Christ: spiritually, educationally, socially, emotionally and physically" is the mission statement of this academy, which began in Duluth in 1979 as a church school and became independent, with an elected parent board, in 1991. Lakeview is situated in a former Duluth public school building, and uses it to good advantage — cafeteria, gymnasium (university students from the area lead gym classes), computer lab, band room, 2,500-volume library slated to grow to 8,000, and chapel at which pastors from more than 20 area churches lead services. The school has temporary accreditation through the Minnesota Non-Public School Accrediting Association; final approval was expected in mid-1996. Because this school has just entered a rapid growth period (with the new building and the addition of 9th grade to its preschool through 8th grade student body), it's expected that the student population will greatly increase beyond the 130 students in the 1995-96

school year. Typical class size is fewer than 15 students in lower grades and not more than 20 in higher grades. Only students from Christian homes are accepted.

MARANANTHA ACADEMY

4916 Wis. Hwy. 35
Superior, Wis.   *(715) 399-8757*

Maranantha's mission is to help Christian families and their churches raise and educate their children. Its scriptural focus is integrated into the core academic curriculum. For example, world history is related in the context of preparing for the Cross until the crucifixion of Christ and reacting to the Cross since that time. More than 120 youngsters grades K through 12 from 17 churches attend this independent, nondenominational school where a typical class size is 15. Transportation is available via the public school bus. Maranantha is a member of the Association of Christian Schools International.

THE MARSHALL SCHOOL

1215 Rice Lake Rd.
Duluth, Minn.   *(218) 727-7266*

High on a hill above Duluth, with a grand view of Lake Superior, is Marshall, known for its excellent academic program. It's the only college preparatory school (and oldest private school) in our region. Ninety-eight percent of its graduates go on to college, many to prestigious Ivy League schools and U.S. military academies. Its 55 1996 graduates were offered a total of more than $315,000 in academic scholarships, and 23 percent of the class of 1996 was commended by the National Merit Scholarship Program. The average national standardized (ACT) test score is 20.8, Minnesota's average is 21.8, and Marshall's is 26. Academics, however, isn't the only parameter that distinguishes this school. It has strong theater, arts and music programs.

In the required outdoor education program, students learn leadership and team building through Outward Bound and trips to the Boundary Waters Canoe Area Wilderness. Marshall's student-athletes regularly excel at tennis, golf and track and field and participate in team sports. Every student is required to do community service (helping elderly people with chores; volunteering in service agencies; participating in programs to help children, disabled people or people with literacy problems); most put in much more than the requisite hours.

It's an inclusive school ethnically and economically — scholarships and in-school work-for-tuition are available — but entering students must score above the 50th percentile in standardized testing and maintain at least an average academic record. Marshall began as a Catholic high school, and students still are encouraged to participate in nondenominational chapel activities. The school's interior is as tattered as a public school — Marshall sinks most of its money into academics — but is very attractive nonetheless, with many full-length windows along its single-level expanse and a student commons area that doubles as a student art gallery (worth a visit for art lovers). About 530 students grades 5 through 12 attend this school. The average class size is 19, with a student-teacher ratio of 14-to-1.

MONTESSORI SCHOOL
313 Mygatt Ave.
Duluth, Minn. (218) 728-4600

An educational experience for children ages 3 to 13, Montessori is probably the most popular form of alternative education in the nation. There has been a Montessori in Duluth since the 1960s; the current school was founded in 1981 and has 60 children. Like other Montessoris,

its focus is on fostering the child's natural drive to learn and guiding him or her appropriately through the stages of mental development, laying the groundwork for language, math and geometry, helping the child become an independent learner. For example, young children play with puzzles that are binomial and trinomial cubes. By 5th grade, they unconsciously have absorbed the concept of cube root, which prepares them for larger geometric and mathematical concepts. The result of this type of mental/neurological development is an adult who might not necessarily go on to higher education but has the capacity to be self-taught, takes charge and does what he or she most wants to do. Because the Montessori learning process is a continuum, Montessori does not allow children to start the program after age 5; the school is nearly always full.

NORTHWOODS CHRISTIAN ACADEMY
610 U.S. Hwy. 51
Hurley, Wis. (715) 561-4355

This interdenominational school emphasizes family values, teaching 115 youngsters (grades K through 5) a standard curriculum from a Christian perspective. It's a calm, secure setting — nourishing to pupils — and the school is open to students with special needs. Reading is phonics-based; family involvement is common. In 1996 the school was meeting in part of a church but had plans to add grade 6 and move into larger rooms on the same property during the 1996-1997 school year. The outdoor play area provides plenty of room to run. Teachers are licensed by the state of Wisconsin.

OUR LADY OF THE LAKE SCHOOL
215 Lake Shore Dr.
Ashland, Wis. (715) 682-7622

This grade school has nearly 200 students and is part of the Catholic Diocese of Superior (see previous entry).

OUR LADY OF PEACE CATHOLIC GRADE SCHOOL
108 S. Marquette St.
Ironwood, Mich.   (906) 932-3200

Little ones can learn Italian at this school of 155 students, set amid big trees in the older residential part of town. OLP offers an otherwise standard Catholic education to youngsters from preschool through 6th grade. Non-Catholics also are accepted. The learning environment is intimate — typically 15 pupils per class — and a bus is available. The school is part of the Catholic Diocese of Marquette, 347 Rock Street, (906) 228-8630.

ST. LOUIS SCHOOL
713 Washburn Ave.
Washburn, Wis.   (715) 373-5322

St. Louis has 86 grade-schoolers and is part of the Catholic Diocese of Superior (see previous entry).

SUMMIT SCHOOL
1600 N. Eighth Ave. E.
Duluth, Minn.   (218) 724-3133

This relatively new independent, locally run school emphasizes academic and social skills and offers a continuum of studies that can supplement The Marshall School (see previous entry), although the two are not affiliated. In the 1995-96 school year, Summit had 25 pupils in grades K through 4. While there are plans for growth, it will continue to limit its class size to 15. Summit also offers a preschool and day care and has an outdoor play area.

Referral Numbers

The following state departments and centers can answer many public education-related questions you might have. Call your respective state's department.

Michigan Department of Education, 608 W. Allegan Street, Lansing, Michigan 48933, (517) 373-0457;

Minnesota Center for Arts Education, 6125 Olson Memorial Highway, Golden Valley, Minnesota 55422, (612) 591-4700;

Minnesota Department of Children, Families and Learning (formerly Department of Education), Capitol Square Building, 550 Cedar Avenue, St. Paul, Minnesota 55101, (612) 296-6104;

Wisconsin Department of Public Instruction, 125 S. Webster, Madison, Wisconsin, (608) 266-3903.

Four-year Colleges and Universities

COLLEGE OF ST. SCHOLASTICA
1200 Kenwood Ave.   (218) 723-6046
Duluth, Minn.   (800) 447-5444

Ranked among the top 10 regional liberal arts colleges in the United States by *U.S. News & World Report* in 1994 and 1995, this Benedictine-run school offers a strong and highly respected curriculum (a professor who transferred to Scholastica from another four-year academy recently quipped that it was "like moving from Haiti to Switzerland" (meaning he appreciated Scholastica's abundant resources and greater academic freedom).

The college's stately buildings and 160-acre campus, established in 1908, have an aura more of an academic retreat than a hurried educational center. Its 1,850 students aim at bachelor's degrees in 30 majors, including natural sciences, music, literature, nursing, theological studies, math, family and consumer sciences, physical therapy, social sciences and dietetics.

Scholastica was the first college in the country to offer a major in medical records administration. It has pre-professional programs and a certificate program in gerontology and offers minors in peace and justice studies, arts, four European foreign languages, women's studies, gerontology, theater and philosophy. In addition, the school offers licensure in teacher education, coaching, early childhood family education, media generalist and nursing home administration programs.

Students can take some of their required courses at the University of Minnesota Duluth or the University of Wisconsin-Superior. Clinical experience in health science is available at St. Mary's Medical Center, also run by the Benedictines. Opportunities for studying in Costa Rica, Ireland and Russia (Scholastica has a "sister college" relationship with a college there) are available.

The college frequently sponsors symposiums on peace and justice issues. The new Mitchell Auditorium is the site of many concerts, including performances by members of student chamber ensembles, the choir and other musical groups. The Saints men and women compete in cross-country, soccer, volleyball, basketball, softball, baseball, hockey and tennis. On-campus housing is available.

LAKEHEAD UNIVERSITY
955 Oliver Rd.
Thunder Bay, Ont. *(807) 343-8110*

Established in 1965, Lakehead is now considered one of the top business schools in Canada and has the only forestry program in Ontario, of 18 universities in the province. The 150 scenic hectares are high on a hill overlooking the city and, across the water in the distance, the Sleeping Giant. On-campus housing hugs the banks of the McIntyre River, which flows through the campus, and most of the college buildings circle man-made Lake Tamblyn, named for the university's first president.

About 6,000 students — the vast majority from Ontario — work for bachelors degrees in such majors as nursing, visual arts, music and engineering. A popular program is the Outdoor Recreation, Parks and Tourism major, which results in a joint degree with geography or natural sciences. Lakehead also offers masters degrees in psychology, English, social work and natural sciences. In 1995 it began a new Ph.D. program in clinical psychology. Lakehead offers one of the largest choices of languages in the region: Cree, French, Finnish, German, Italian, Latin, Ojibwe and Spanish.

Lyn McLeod, a provincial MP (member of parliament) from Thunder Bay, recent candidate for Ontario premier and now leader of the opposition, graduated from Lakehead.

NORTHLAND COLLEGE
No street address
Ashland, Wis. *(715) 682-1224*

The focus of this liberal arts school is the environment; in the words of a longtime professor, the college uses "the tools of the liberal arts to understand the role of humans in nature . . . encouraging true scientists who are curious and humble and concerned about developing a depth of understanding." The school has three environmental programs and offers excursions to study wildlife in such far-flung places as Jamaica, East Africa, the Galapagos and Costa Rica.

The college's Sigurd Olson Environmental Institute, established in 1972, gives students a chance to work on environmental projects in the Lake Superior region. Students can earn credit, money or both in practical work experience with the U.S. Fish & Wildlife Service, National Park Service and other agencies.

Northland offers 23 majors and 30 minors, with strong programs in Native

Photo: College of St. Scholastica

The College of St. Scholastica is a private school in Duluth.

American studies, literature, philosophy and sciences. It also has pre-professional programs in dentistry, law, medicine, pharmacy and veterinary medicine.

Northland was founded in 1892 as a United Church of Christ school; now it's an ecumenical community where religious expression is welcomed but not required. About 800 students from 42 states and 12 countries attend Northland. On-campus housing is available. The student-teacher ratio is 16 to 1. It was named the best environmental college in the United States in 1994.

UNIVERSITY OF MINNESOTA DULUTH
10 University Dr.
Duluth, Minn.   *(218) 726-7171*

The largest school in the region, UMD sits high on a hill overlooking Lake Superior; its 7,500 students are schooled in a network of interconnected buildings (as a protection against the sometimes fierce winds that blow over the hill).

It has several claims to fame, other than the fact that in 1994 *U.S. News & World Report* identified UMD as the 10th-best regional university for the money. One is

the medical school, which brings students through their first two years before sending them on to the University of Minnesota in Minneapolis for the next two. UMD's program emphasizes family practice and rural medicine, an emphasis that was advertised nationally by First Lady Hillary Clinton during her healthcare-reform campaign. (Sixty percent of the medical school's former students now practice in small communities, and 73 percent are primary-care physicians.) A significant aspect of the medical school is its specialized program to train American Indian physicians.

Another UMD claim to fame is the hockey program; the Bulldogs won the WCHA regular-season title in 1993 and came in second nationally nine years earlier. And the third is its theater program, which has produced nationally acclaimed scripts and performances.

Altogether, UMD offers 11 bachelor degrees in 80 majors and has 17 graduate programs. Through the university, students can travel and study in Finland, France, England and Sweden or stay home and work with faculty members through the Undergraduate Research Opportunities

Program. The Natural Resources Research Institute is at UMD, as is Minnesota Sea Grant Program's central office. UMD's Large Lakes Observatory conducts research on freshwater resources.

Many of the most influential people in the city graduated from UMD: the mayor, the county sheriff, the city police chief, several city councilors, the public school superintendent, the local state senator, the head of the county social services department and influential business people. UMD took a hard hit during 1995 state funding cuts and was forced to cancel its language majors, but continues to offer four languages regularly and another half-dozen when teachers are available.

Several busy places on campus are the Planetarium, which offers regular star shows; the Tweed Museum of Art, with its continuing art openings and high-quality exhibits (a Jacques Lipschitz sculpture stands outdoors near the entrance); and the Marshall Theatre for Performing Arts, the site for UMD productions and other theater, ballet and music performances.

Student housing is available.

UMD is the heir of a normal school and teachers college that opened in 1895.

UNIVERSITY OF WISCONSIN-SUPERIOR
1800 Grand Ave.
Superior, Wis.   *(218) 394-8230*

This school has a reputation for lively inquiry and flexibility. One of 13 campuses in the University of Wisconsin system, UWS offers bachelor's degrees in 36 liberal arts majors. Through its Extended Degree Program, students can study independently and earn credits by being assessed for prior learning experiences. UWS also offers master's degrees in educational administration, counseling, speech and other fields.

Because it's a relatively small four-year school, it draws community college students who want to complete their four-year degrees in another small public school — particularly from the Lac Courte Oreilles Tribal College in Wisconsin and the Fond du Lac Tribal and Lake Superior community colleges in Minnesota.

The college has 2,000 full-time students, always with a generous sprinkling of foreign students — mostly from Sri Lanka, Japan and West Africa. About a quarter of the student body is older than 24. UWS canceled its football program in 1992, funneling that money into women's sports and already existing teams, which appears to have strengthened its intercollegiate sports profile. On-campus housing is available.

The school has a lively theater program and, as this book went to press, a state-of-the-art science building remained scheduled to open in 1996. The Lake Superior Research Center is housed on campus, and federally funded researchers there use UWS students to help look into eco-balance phenomena involving exotic species such as the zebra mussel and Eurasian ruffe.

UWS is heir of a normal school that opened in 1896.

Two-year Colleges

FOND DU LAC
TRIBAL & COMMUNITY COLLEGE
2101 14th St.
Cloquet, Minn.   *(218) 879-0800*

This state-tribal school opened its doors in 1987 and moved into its lovely new building in 1992. It offers associate's degrees in liberal arts and science; it has a strong arts curriculum, particularly for its size, with concentrations in literature, theater, music. Course offerings include pre-professional studies in law, medicine, nursing, occupational and physical therapy, pharmacy, dentistry and veterinary medicine; law enforcement; American Indian studies (law, current issues, history, culture, Ojibwe language); business; human resources and others.

About 800 students attend Fond du Lac. The circular college building, on a high hill in a grove of pines, is decorated in thunderbird and bear motifs. The Ruth Myers Library & Archives serves both as a college library and as an archive of Ojibwe works and videos.

This is one of 29 tribally controlled colleges in the United States and one of 62 college and university campuses that make up the Minnesota State College and University system. The college is accredited by the North Central Association of Colleges and Schools and is a member of the American Indian Higher Education Consortium.

GOGEBIC COMMUNITY COLLEGE
E4946 Jackson Rd.
Ironwood, Mich.   (906) 932-4231

This attractive college lies at the foot of Mount Zion, a ski hill operated as a training ground for students involved in the school's ski area management program. The college is in the heart of Big Snow Country, near a half-dozen ski hills, and attracts students who later will intern at ski hills throughout Colorado, Vermont and the Midwest.

The college offers associate's degrees in arts, science, and applied science, business and technology. Other programs offered

the 1,200 students include nursing, natural resources, natural sciences, arts, social work and corrections.

Condominium-style student apartments are on campus. Gogebic is accredited by the North Central Association of Colleges and Schools.

LAKE SUPERIOR COLLEGE
2101 Trinity Rd.   (218) 722-2801
Duluth, Minn.   (800) 432-2884

Another of the 62-campus system of Minnesota State Colleges and Universities, Lake Superior is a recent creation — a combination of the former Duluth Community College, the former Duluth Technical Institute and the new airplane fire-fighting school. It occupies several campuses in Duluth and offers associate's degrees and diplomas as well as more than 50 academic and occupational majors.

Occupational courses range from auto body repair and fashion to civil litigation and architectural drafting. A large percentage of the occupational courses are devoted to health professions and fire-fighting, reflecting the nursing focus of the former Duluth Community College and the inclusion of the national fire-fighting school.

Its liberal arts curriculum is relatively diverse, including visual arts, lively arts, languages, philosophy, and many literature, natural sciences and history courses. About 3,000 students attend this community college. A $10.8 million expansion planned for 1996-97 will consolidate most classes at the Trinity Road

For tuition purposes, Minnesota community colleges consider "residents" to include seasonal agricultural workers from other countries as well as any Canadians who have more than 50 percent Indian blood.

Insiders' Tips

campus in an attractive, airy building high on the hillside that's handy to the Miller Hill Mall, residential neighborhoods and downtown. However, the two fire-fighting training sites, a computer flex lab and off-campus diesel and truck driving programs will continue in their current venues throughout the city.

ESL (English as a Second Language) tutoring, student theater, student newspaper, services to Indian people and intramural sports are some of the extras here, and students may be able to advance their standing by testing for credits or garnering credits for experience.

Technical Schools

CONFEDERATION COLLEGE
1450 Nakina Dr.
Thunder Bay, Ont.   (807) 475-6110
Confederation is beautifully situated between Lakehead University and the International Friendship Gardens, along the McIntyre River. It's home to 3,500 students working toward diplomas and certificates in about 70 business and technical programs. Confederation's specialties are international business development, aviation (flight management, airplane engineering and maintenance) and entrepreneurship. Other offerings include Aboriginal studies, health sciences, applied arts and trades apprenticeships.

Because of its international business focus, the college offers a variety of cross-cultural communication courses as well as a surprising number of languages: Japanese, Swedish, Ojibwe, Polish, Ukrainian, Russian, Italian, Finnish, Chinese, German, Spanish, French and Portuguese.

On-campus housing is available. Confederation was established in 1967.

LAKE SUPERIOR COLLEGE
2101 Trinity Rd.   (218) 722-2801
Duluth, Minn.   (800) 432-2884
This combination liberal-arts college and technical school is a melding of the former Duluth Community College, the former Duluth Technical Institute and the new airplane fire-fighting school. Occupational courses range from auto body repair and fashion to civil litigation and architectural drafting. A large percentage of the occupational courses are devoted to health professions and fire-fighting, reflecting the nursing focus of the former Duluth Community College and the inclusion of the national fire-fighting school. (See the previous listing for additional information.)

WISCONSIN INDIANHEAD
TECHNICAL COLLEGE
2100 Beaser Ave.
Ashland, Wis.   (715) 582-4591
600 N. 21st St.
Superior, Wis.   (715) 394-6677
This college has four campuses in the so-called "Indianhead" area of the state — the northwestern section that is said to resemble a man's profile looking west. WITC is one of 16 colleges in the Wisconsin Technical College system. About 85 percent of the system's graduates are working in fields related to their education within six months of graduation, earning $1,400 to $2,300 a month. WITC is fully accredited by the North Central Association of Colleges and Secondary Schools.

Two WITC campuses are in our region, in Superior and Ashland. About 350 daytime students and thousands of evening adult students are served here. They study business, health, emergency services (paramedic, policing, emergency medical technician) and hospitality. The school has five associate degree programs and six one-year vocational programs.

Other Educational Opportunities

WOLF RIDGE
ENVIRONMENTAL LEARNING CENTER
230 Cranberry Rd.
Finland, Minn.   *(218) 353-7414*

An investigative serene retreat in the hills along Minnesota's North Shore, Wolf Ridge is primarily for school children who come during the school year to spend a few days learning about the environment. During winter weekends and in the summer, though, it provides a variety of programs (wetlands ecology, bird study, beaver ecology, orienteering, rock climbing and more) for individuals, families, teachers, ElderHostel, youth leaders and others. Eleven graduate students are accepted yearly into a nine-month naturalist training program, and four or more college students join a yearly three-month internship.

DULUTH BUSINESS UNIVERSITY
412 W. Superior St.   *(218) 722-4000*
Duluth, Minn.   *(800) 777-8406*

In downtown Duluth, DBU offers two-year associate in applied science degrees in accounting, hospitality management, medical assistant, medical office/health code specialist, veterinary clinic assistant, office administration, and sales and marketing management. It also offers diplomas in these specialties, which require 12 to 21 months of study.

DBU was founded in 1891 and currently enrolls approximately 200 students.

The Lake Superior
region is rich in
public-radio
programming.

Inside
Media

The media scene in our region is much the same as elsewhere in the United States and Canada: fragmented, competitive, ubiquitous. Daily newspapers and TV news vie for audience; TV news continues to compete with instant entertainment and Talk Radio; and both broadcast and print journalism balance the ability to reflect their local communities in the context of our-of-town ownership. Meanwhile, specialty periodicals, public radio and weeklies in county seats are adding community flavor.

Folks in our region tend to be better-than-average media consumers. Their keen interest in news has been attributed to the long winters. But, whatever the cause of this active consumption, we're fortunate to have a variety of news sources from which to choose.

Daily Newspapers

THE DAILY PRESS
122 Third Ave.
W. Ashland, Wis. *(715) 682-2313*

The Ashland paper has always been willing to jump into the local political fray and may be one of the reasons this town remains so interesting for its size (population 8,600). Believe it or not, this morning paper has almost the same circulation as there are people in Ashland: 8,200. *The Daily Press* also publishes a *Northwoods Travel Guide*, a seasonal tabloid that lets

you know what's going on in northwestern Wisconsin and the Upper Peninsula.

The *Press* is published Monday through Saturday and costs 50¢ at the newsstand. It's owned by Murphy-McGinnis Media Inc.

DULUTH NEWS-TRIBUNE
424 W. First St.
Duluth, Minn. *(218) 723-5281*

The region's largest newspaper, with a circulation of 68,000 daily and 86,000 on Sundays, the 127-year-old *News-Tribune* regularly takes statewide awards in both journalistic writing and photography. It's heir to papers of the mid-1800s, and for generations, until the early 1980s, it was two papers: The morning *News-Tribune* and the evening *Herald*. Owner Knight-Ridder Inc. is the nation's second-largest newspaper company and owns, among others, the *Miami Herald* and *St. Paul Dispatch-Pioneer Press*.

The *News-Tribune* has longtime-popular columnist Sam Cook, an outdoors writer whose work has also been published in book form. Cook's Sunday outdoors page also is a big favorite with readers. If you need a calendar or a look at local color, 12 of the paper's best season-oriented photos published during the previous year are put together in an annual calendar.

The *News-Tribune* also publishes thick summer and winter tabloids that let you know what's going on along the North and South shores and in the Twin Ports. The daily paper is 50¢; Sunday's is $1.50 at the rack and less expensive when home delivered. The *News-Tribune* sells retail tourist products at its Miller Hill Mall kiosk.

THE IRONWOOD DAILY GLOBE
118 E. McLeod Ave.
Ironwood, Mich.   (906) 932-2211

This paper publishes every day except Sunday and has a good reputation for investigative reporting. It has a circulation of 7,500 and is owned by Bliss Communications of Jayneswille, Wisconsin, which owns other newspapers and radio stations in the state. The price is 50¢.

THE SUPERIOR DAILY TELEGRAM
1226 Ogden Ave.
Superior, Wis.   (715) 394-4411

Established in 1890, the *Telegram* is a published five afternoons a week, with a Saturday morning "Weekender Edition." It has considerable civic-pride support in Superior, where the community will go out of its way to keep an evening news tip until the next morning, in time for the *Telegram's* midday deadline. The idea is to help the hometown paper scoop the *Duluth News-Tribune*, which has a late-night deadline. The circulation is 10,500, and the paper is owned by Murphy-McGinnis Media Inc., which owns a half-dozen other papers in the area. Copies are 50¢ for the daily and 75¢ for weekender.

THUNDER BAY CHRONICLE-JOURNAL
75 Cumberland St. S.
Thunder Bay, Ont.   (807) 343-6200

This paper is the result of a joining of two papers in early 1996. Back in the days when Port Arthur and Fort William were competing towns, there was the *Port Arthur News Chronicle* and the *Fort William Daily Times Journal*. The cities amalgamated in 1970, and so did the papers, into a morning *Times-News* and an evening *Chronicle-Journal*. In March 1996, the two combined into a daily morning paper. Circulation is about 40,000. It's owned by Thomson Newspaper Co. of Toronto.

A popular local column is "Howard Reid's People," a combination of community information, humor and light-hearted gossip. The Thunder Bay paper regularly grabs Ontario awards for journalistic excellence. For two years in a row, 1993 and 1994, it also won an annual national honor: the B'nai B'rith of Canada's Media Human Rights Award. (The paper stuck to its highroad guns, enduring flak and commercial pressure, about some tasteless jokes that had been made about Indians, blacks and women by a Chamber of Commerce speaker. The chamber eventually relented and pledged to be more sensitive.)

The *Thunder Bay Chronicle-Journal* costs 75¢.

Non-dailies

BUDGETEER PRESS
5807 Grand Ave.
Duluth, Minn.   (218) 624-3665

Most people call this free weekly the "budgeter," probably because it has a lot of ads and a TV schedule, and you don't have to pay for the paper or your own want ad. It also has news of the booster variety; the uncritical support of western Duluth businesses and activities makes it dear to the hearts of readers in the western part of town. It's owned by Murphy-McGinnis Media Inc.

BUSINESSNORTH
1718 N. 13th St., Ste. 206
Superior, Wis.   (715) 392-1141

BusinessNorth was established by a former *News-Tribune* business writer who thought the community needed a paper

Photo: Duluth News-Tribune

Students tour the Duluth News-Tribune *to see how a paper is published.*

that relays a sense of who the players are in the business community and what the connections are — putting a face on the industries and companies that drive the economy of the region. The idea caught on, and circulation of this monthly publication now is 6,100. It had been a free paper targeted to business people but in 1996 began a gradual change to paid subscriptions. Recent stories include in-depth reporting of a shake-up at a local long-distance carrier; the building and heavy construction industries in the region; and "Minnesota's fiscal time bomb" — the state budget.

CATHOLIC HERALD CITIZEN
1512 N. 12th St.
Superior, Wis. *(715) 392-8268*

The official paper of the Catholic Diocese of Superior, the weekly *Herald Citizen* has reported Catholic news about and for the 16 counties of northwestern Wisconsin since 1953. The paper is available by subscription only for $32 a year.

COOK COUNTY NEWS-HERALD
Grand Marais, Minn. *(218) 387-1025*

This delightful little rural weekly has a reputation for being willing to take on any issue, which is both a source of pride and a source of irritation for readers and advertisers. It's locally and independently owned, reports the county's legal news and has a circulation of 4,800. It's 75¢ at the newsstand.

THE COUNTY JOURNAL
324 W. Bayfield
Washburn, Wis. *(715) 373-5500*

With a circulation of 4,000, the *Journal* aims to cover all the communities of Bayfield County — Washburn (the county seat), Bayfield, Iron River and others. It reports on county government meetings and also does some investigative journalism. The weekly *Journal* costs 50¢.

DULUTH SKYWORLD NEWS
5807 Grand Ave.
Duluth, Minn. *(218) 624-3665*

Positive news about downtown Duluth

is the focus of this monthly tabloid, which is distributed free in various downtown locations. The paper includes announcements, events, profiles and business news.

THE DULUTHIAN MAGAZINE
118 E. Superior St.
Duluth, Minn.   (218) 722-5501

A bimonthly publication about and for local businesses, the *Duluthian* is published by the Duluth Chamber of Commerce and is free to members. Otherwise, it's available by subscription for $24.

FINNISH-AMERICAN REPORTER
1720 Tower Ave.
Superior, Wis.   (715) 394-4961

Finnish-American papers historically have been printed in Finnish and with a political slant. This monthly paper attempts to be non-political and reflect Finnish-American culture in the language most American Finns now speak — English. Readers contribute heavily to this paper, and it features poetry, humor, memoirs, writing competitions, history, sports news and a calendar of events that covers Finnish communities all over North America. It also prints hard news and obituaries. Its revenues come from the 3,000 subscriptions sold in every state and several countries. The subscription price is $18 a year in the United States and $24 abroad. For subscriptions, write P.O. Box 549, Superior, Wisconsin 54880.

HURLEY HERALD
129 S. Curry St.
Ironwood, Mich.   (906) 932-1299

This monthly magazine, published just across the state line from Hurley, Wisconsin, in Ironwood, Michigan, is full of offbeat tidbits: excerpts from diaries from Hurley's boom time, holidays of the month (King Kamehameha I Day, Robert E. Lee's birthday), jokes, reprints from old Hurley

newspapers ("Old Jim Smudge died last week. Jim was about as ornery a cuss as ever was born, and most people will be glad to learn of his demise"), quirky sections ("bartender of the month" and "tavern of the month") and long lists of league-play results. The price is 50¢.

IRON COUNTY MINER
216 Copper St.
Hurley, Wis.   (715) 561-3405

The official newspaper of Iron County, the *Miner* focuses on community news from both Hurley and nearby Mercer, Wisconsin. It was established in 1885 and has a circulation of 3,000. The price is 40¢.

LABOR WORLD
2002 London Rd.
Duluth, Minn.   (218) 728-4469

This newsy biweekly covers activities of local labor and industry and also prints national labor news. It's free of charge to working and retired union members. *Labor World's* home is the Labor Temple on London Road.

LAKE COUNTY NEWS-CHRONICLE
109 Waterfront Dr.
Two Harbors, Minn.   (218) 834-2141

The *News-Chronicle*, the official paper of Lake County, prints news of city council meetings, the school board and county government as well as reports on high school sports, tourism and community events. The weekly paper is owned by Two Harbors Printing Company Inc. and has a circulation of 3,200. The price is 75¢.

LAKE SUPERIOR MAGAZINE
325 Lake Ave. S.
Duluth, Minn.   (218) 722-5002

An upscale magazine that describes places, activities and people all around the Lake, this attractive full-color glossy is a

Tune-in Your Favorite Stations

Twin Ports Area

KDAL 610 AM — Talk and sports CBS news network

KDAL 95.7 FM — Light music

KDNW 97.3 FM — Christian contemporary music and talk

KDNI 90.5 FM — Christian contemporary music and talk

KKCB 105.1 FM — Country

KLXK 101.7 FM — Old rock

KQDS 94.9 FM — Classic rock and new rock

KQDS 1490 AM — Classic rock and new rock

KTCO 98.9 FM — Hot country

KUMD 103.3 FM — Public radio: Alternative, jazz, investigative news

KUWS 91.3 — Wisconsin Public Radio/University of Wisconsin-Superior, the "Ideas Network," local commentary

KZIO 102 FM — Top-40

WDSM 710 AM — Talk Radio and sports

WEBC 630 AM — Talk Radio and sports

WNCB 89.3 FM — Top-40 Christian

WNXR 107.3 FM — 24 hours of light music

WSCD 92.9 FM — Minnesota Public Radio, classical music

WSCN 100.5 FM — Minnesota Public Radio, news and information

WWJC 850 AM — Christian: talk, music, Bible teaching

Along the South Shore

WATW 1400 AM — "Memory station" (old songs)

WBSZ 93.3 FM — Hot country

WEGZ Eagle 106 FM — country

WHRY 1450 AM — Oldies from the 1950s through the '70s.

WHSA 89.9 FM — Wisconsin Public Radio, classical music and news

WJJH 96.7 FM — Easy and contemporary rock

WNCB 90.9 AM — Top-40 Christian

WOJB 88.9 FM — Lac Courte Oreilles Reservation/Wisconsin Public Radio: ethnic music (Ojibwe, Afro-Pop, folk), community news

WRSR Smooth 104.3 FM — Smooth jazz

WUPM 106.9 FM — Adult contemporary pop

Thunder Bay Area

CBON 89.3 FM — A CBC affiliate that broadcasts news and information in French.

CBQ 101.7 FM — CBC affiliate; classical music, drama.

CBQ 88.3 FM — CBC affiliate; information and local and national news.

CJLB AM — Country

CJSD 94 FM — Rock, Top-40

CKPR 580 AM — Rock, Top-40, news

KIKS 105.3 FM — Country

bimonthly that costs $3.95 for a single issue and $21 for a subscription. This is a great magazine for the newcomer to our region. The magazine also puts out the yearly *Lake Superior Travel Guide* for $4.95.

NEW MOON MAGAZINE

2127 Columbus Ave.
Duluth, Minn. (218) 728-5507

A truly unique and attractive magazine, *New Moon* is written entirely by and for girls. About 22,000 magazines, which are published every other month, are distributed in the United States and Canada. A year's (six-issue) subscription is $25; single issues are $4.95. *New Moon Network* is a new publication for parents, teachers and others who work with girls and is available by subscription for the same price. In 1995, *New Moon Magazine* was named the best magazine for grades 4 to 6 by the Parent's Choice Foundation.

NEW REVIEW
34 E. Superior St.
Duluth, Minn.   (218) 722-5987

The mission of this attractive monthly tabloid is "celebrating the arts of the Lake Superior region," and that it does. It's full of poetry, art, book reviews and commentary and has a large calendar of regional arts and activist events. It's free at various bookstores and coffeehouses throughout the region, from the Upper Peninsula to Thunder Bay. A one-year subscription is $15.

NEWS FROM THE SLOUGHS
Odanah, Wis.   (715) 682-7893

"Sloughs" rhymes with "news" and refers to the environmentally delicate (but still healthy) lowland area that defines the Bad River Reservation. This attractive, tribally owned monthly newspaper is a mix of community news and strong environmental and historical reporting. It also features fiction and poetry.

You can get the *News* at all tribal businesses along Minn. Highway 61 and at many outlets in other communities on the South Shore. There is no charge for the paper.

THE POST
1126 Roland St.
Thunder Bay, Ont.   (807) 622-8588

This large weekly tabloid contains community news and events, columns, stories and entertainment. The circulation is 48,000 on alternating weeks. Otherwise, it's 62,000, when the paper is distributed outside Thunder Bay. Algoma Publishers puts out *The Post* and the monthly *Thunder Bay Guest*, a handy free magazine for visitors. *The Post* is free at newsstands and available by mail through subscription for $170 a year in the United States, $40 in northern Ontario and $80 elsewhere in Canada. It's owned by Fraser Dougall Inc.

SENIOR REPORTER
5302 Ramsey St.
Duluth, Minn.   (218) 624-4949

This monthly magazine started in 1987, and it has grown to a circulation of 8,000 covering six counties in the region. The magazine focuses on activities and issues for senior citizens but is designed for readers 45 and older, so as to include people who need information to prepare for the golden years and people who have elderly parents. It includes solid news, community events, health news, advice and commentary. Slightly larger print makes for easy reading. Subscriptions are $15 a year.

Insiders' Tips

Folk-rocker Neil Young first met Stephen Stills in Thunder Bay (then Fort William) at the now-defunct Fourth Dimension coffeehouse. Both of these gifted musicians later performed and recorded with the influential group Buffalo Springfield and then with Crosby, Stills, Nash & Young.

THUNDER BAY MAGAZINE

1184 Roland St.
Thunder Bay, Ont.   *623-8545*

An upscale full-color glossy magazine, this bimonthly gives you an Insider's look at places and activities in Thunder Bay: forestry, food, homes, sports, health, fashion and communication. One recent issue featured the Canadian Women's Curling Championship (also known as Scott Tournament of the Hearts) and "Satisfying Soups" — recipes for hearty meals made from nutritious ingredients. The magazine is published by Thunder Bay's White Oaks Publishing. About 31,000 magazines are distributed by subscription only; they cost $16.95 annually. White Oaks also publishes the yearly *Lake Superior Circle Tour Travel Guide*, which sells for $2.

TWIN PORTS PEOPLE

2631 W. Superior St.
Duluth, Minn.   *(218) 726-1610*

Recently redesigned, this monthly paper was established in 1988 by a freelance journalist who felt local people would like some positive community news. It includes local medical community reports, two or three personal profiles and a section written entirely by Lake Superior College students. The latter articles are run exactly as received — typos, misspellings and all — so the students can learn from their mistakes. Its 8,000 papers are distributed free.

Television Stations

KBJR TV-6

230 E. Superior St.
Duluth, Minn.   *(218) 727-8484*

The NBC affiliate is found on channel 6 and serves the entire region from the Canadian border at Grand Portage to Michigan's Upper Peninsula. It's owned by Granite Broadcasting Corp., which has about nine similar-size stations all over the country.

KDLH TV-3

425 W. Superior St.
Duluth, Minn.   *(218) 733-0303*

"Channel 3" also broadcasts throughout the region, from the Canadian border to the UP. The CBS affiliate is part of the 15-station stable of Benedek Broadcasting Corp.

WDIO TV-10

10 Observation Rd.
Duluth, Minn.   *(218) 727-6864*

This ABC affiliate is part of the Hubbard Broadcasting Inc., which owns 11 radio and TV stations throughout the country. Channel 10 serves the region from Grand Marais in northeastern Minnesota to the Upper Peninsula.

WDSE TV-8

1202 University Cir.
Duluth, Minn.   *(218) 724-8567*

"Channel 8" is Duluth's public TV station, an affiliate of the Public Broadcasting System. It broadcasts through the whole region, from Grand Portage at the Canadian Border to Michigan's Upper Peninsula.

THUNDER BAY TELEVISION

87 N. Hill St.
Thunder Bay   *(807) 346-2600*

The only local television company, TBTV's Channel 2 is a Canadian Broadcasting Corporation (CBC) affiliate, and its Channel 4 is an affiliate of Canadian Television (CTV). You can watch national network and local news on these channels. It's owned by Fraser Dougall Inc.

Cable Companies

Bresnan Communications, (218) 722-2288, provides 56 cable stations to customers in the Twin Ports. **Northland Cablevision**, (218) 879-1511, serves Minnesota areas near Duluth: Carlton, Cloquet, Esko, Hermantown and Proctor. Two cable companies serve Minnesota's North Shore: **Regional Cable TV**, (800) 466-0800, is in Knife River and rural Two Harbors. **Northland Cablevision**, (800) 678-2792, serves Two Harbors, Silver Bay, Beaver Bay and Grand Marais. **Shaw Cable**, (807) 767-4422, makes 31 channels available in Thunder Bay. On Wisconsin's South Shore, **Marcus Cable**, (715) 682-2166, provides 31 channels to viewers in Ashland, Washburn and Bayfield. In addition to serving the Twin Ports area, **Bresnan Communications**, (906) 932-1831, provides cable service in Hurley, Wisconsin, and on Michigan's western Upper Peninsula, including Ironwood, Bessemer and Wakefield.

Radio

If you're driving into our region from the Twin Cities, you'll notice that you lose Twin Cities radio stations near Moose Lake at a high rise in the land and begin picking up Twin Ports stations. Not even the powerful WCCO of Minneapolis, which reaches listeners in other parts of northern Minnesota and even as far away as Colorado, can get past that hill. But we have our own old standby for school closings, disasters and terrible storms: KDAL. If a KDAL announcer isn't talking about emergencies, it means they aren't happening. And we're rich in public radio. Both Minnesota and Wisconsin were leaders in establishing the public service; from radios in the Twin Ports, you can tune in a half-dozen stations, and there is no community in our region that can't access at least one. In Thunder Bay, you have your choice of three public radio stations. (See this section's gray box for details.)

Inside
Places of Worship

The religious communities in Duluth and Superior are an active, vital and diverse part of the larger communities. For people moving to the area, we suggest you church-shop by attending services and programs at several churches. David Tryggestad, minister at Duluth's First Lutheran Church, commented that people look for different things in a church's programs and services. It could be a strong Sunday school program and good nursery care. Some people seek a traditional service; others prefer something more contemporary. Many people base their evaluation and choice on the strength of a church's music programs.

By and large, mainstream Protestant and Catholic churches dominate the Twin Ports. Many Bible-based churches are growing and as a result Christian schools are flourishing (see our Child Care and Education chapter).

But you'll also find communities of the Baha'i faith; full-gospel churches; congregations of Mormons, Serbians, Pentecostals, Quakers, Greek Orthodox, Orthodox Jewish, Christian Scientists and Unitarians; and unaffiliated community churches.

In this chapter, we've highlighted a few churches and synagogues based on their longevity and historic importance in the community as well as their architectural beauty. For a complete list of places of worship and their respective telephone numbers, we suggest you consult the Yellow Pages.

Twin Ports Area

The Twin Ports' immigrant history is made up of Scandinavians, Italians, Welsh, Scots, Slovenians, Poles, Germans, Serbs and Croats who came to farm and to work in the mining and logging industries. Not surprisingly, houses of worship in this area reflect the religious affiliations these immigrants maintained in their homelands.

Duluth

Today, Duluth is home to a significant Lutheran population, reflecting the area's Scandinavian and German immigrant influence. Many of the existing Lutheran parishes were originally founded to provide services in the language for one particular Scandinavian immigrant group.

First Lutheran, 1100 E. Superior, has a 125-year-old parish history and is one of the original Norwegian Lutheran churches in the Twin Ports area; **Gloria Dei**, 219 N. Sixth Avenue E., with its 1910 distinctive pitched, gabled front was one of the original Swedish Lutheran churches in town. Younger generations from these parishes, wanting to worship in English, branched off and formed new churches. Some of these thriving congregations today include the **Lutheran Church of the Good Shepherd**, 45th Avenue and Colorado, and **Lakeview Covenant**, 1001 Jean Duluth Road.

In the Central Hillside neighborhood, **St. Peter's Catholic Church**, 810 W. Third Street, was built in 1926 by Italian stone mason immigrants whose descendants still make up a good section of the parish; and **St. Mary's Star of the Sea**, 325 E. Third Street, is a lovingly tended 1905 Polish-based Catholic parish.

While most church congregations today are a homogeneous lot, you can still find Lutheran services held in Finnish at **Kenwood Lutheran**, 324 W. Cleveland. And in the West End, there are two active Serbian Orthodox churches: **Mala Gospodjna Serbian Orthodox Church**, 1129 101st Avenue W., and **St. George Serbian Orthodox Church**, 1216 104th Avenue W.

The Jewish community in Duluth has its immigrant roots in Hungary, Russia, Lithuania and Germany from the 1870s. There were originally five to six separate Jewish congregations in Duluth. Today, there are two synagogues: **Temple Israel**, 1602 E. Second Street, consists of merged reformed and conservative congregations; **Adas Israel**, an orthodox synagogue, is at 302 E. Third Street. Although Adas Israel, built in 1900, has been covered with modern siding, the beautiful stained-glass windows

still grace the exterior of this historic building.

St. Paul's Episcopal Church, 1710 E. Superior Street, was built in 1912. Its design, the brainchild of noted New York City architect Bertram Goodhue, was inspired by the Canterbury Cathedral in England. It's constructed of a soft blue-gray stone, with a slate roof and neo-Gothic stone carvings and trim. The Parish Wing was commissioned in 1928 and designed by Halstad and Sullivan of Duluth. The interior wood and stone craftsmanship and the lead and stained-glass windows are stunning. This structure is the third St. Paul's Episcopal Church in Duluth (the other two burned on the same site); the first services were held on Christmas Day 1869.

Another architecturally significant church is **First Presbyterian**, 300 E. Second Street. Designed by noted Duluth architects Traphagen and Fitzpatrick and built in 1891, this church epitomizes Duluth's age of brownstone when many fine buildings where constructed of the native brownstone mined from quarries on Lake Superior's South Shore and the Apostle Islands and from the village of Fond du Lac. The congregation here recently celebrated 125 years of fellowship. First Presbyterian's outstanding five-story corner tower is a much-loved part of Duluth's Central Hillside landscape.

Another distinctive (and more recent) addition to Duluth's skyline is the **First Methodist Church**, at Central Entrance

Pull Out
the Stops

For aficionados of pipe organ music, Duluth is considered a mecca for both new pipe organs and significant older instruments in their original acoustic environments. Dan Jaeckel, whose organ-building business, Jaeckel Inc., 1602 London Road, is based in a former Duluth elementary school, has earned an international reputation for his thoughtful design and meticulous craftsmanship of tracker pipe organs. You can hear the results of his handiwork in Duluth's churches: **First Lutheran**, 1100 E. Superior Street; **Pilgrim Congregational**, 2310 E. Fourth Street, which has a full-size Jaeckel tracker organ; **St. Joseph's Church**, 151 Linden Street W.; **Holy Cross Lutheran**, 8 E. Locust Street; and **First United Methodist**, Central Entrance and Skyline Parkway. An-

The historic 1898 Felgemaker tracker organ is located at Sacred Heart Music Center in Duluth.

other renowned organ builder, Robert Sipe, of Dallas, Texas, built the organ at **Cathedral of Our Lady of the Rosary**, 2801 E. Fourth Street.

You can also hear an unaltered and maintained 1898 Felgemaker tracker organ performed in its original, acoustically exquisite environment at the **Sacred Heart Music Center**, 201 W. Fourth Street. The former cathedral, now a designated local landmark and performing arts center, features an organ concert series with local, regional and international artists. Call (218) 723-1895 for more information.

and Skyline Parkway. Nicknamed the Copper Top, this 1965-66 era church was designed by noted architect Pietro Belluschi and can be seen from Canal Park, looking up the hillside. It is home to one of the largest Methodist congregations in Duluth.

Pilgrim Congregational Church, at 2310 E. Fourth Street, designed by German and Lief Jensen and built in 1916-17, is another classic stone structure in east Duluth. It displays 14 Tiffany art

glass windows, the first of which was installed in 1918, and the last, in 1954. It's home to an impressive tracker pipe organ, designed by master organ builder Dan Jaeckel, whose internationally recognized instrument-building business is headquartered in Duluth. Pilgrim's parish recently celebrated 125 years of fellowship.

The charming brownstone **Glen Avon Presbyterian Church** at 2105 Woodland Avenue was built in 1905 for the then-streetcar suburbs of Glen Avon and Hunter's Park, where Scottish people settled.

The **United Protestant Church**, 88th Avenue W. and Beverly Street, was one of two churches built in the steel company town of Morgan Park between 1915 and 1917. Morgan Park, built and operated by US Steel until 1933, was a self-contained community, with its own schools, hospital, community center and utilities. United Protestant was built with cement blocks, similar to those used to construct the neighborhood houses, but was designed to look like stone with a Gothic face. The other Morgan Park church is **St. Margaret Mary Catholic Church**, 1467 88th Avenue W. It was built between 1915 and 1917 at the entrance to the steel plant. It's design is Spanish Colonial, but it was constructed of cement block and stucco instead of adobe.

Finally, we feel compelled to close our Duluth section with **Sacred Heart Music Center**, (218) 723-1895, 201 W. Fourth Street. Formerly Sacred Heart Cathedral, the last Roman Catholic services here were held in 1985; the building is now a performing arts center. Listed on the National Register of Historic Places and recently designated a city landmark, this red brick and brownstone, triple-spired former cathedral has two-story stained-glass windows, Italian marble altars and a nationally significant pipe organ (see this chapter's sidebar). Tours are available in the summer and a concert series is held in the fall and spring.

Superior

St. Francis Xavier Catholic Church, 2316 E. Fourth Street, is a handsome red brick and brownstone church built in 1905. It's in Superior's East End neighborhood and has an active congregation. Because of the church's excellent acoustics, it's used frequently for concerts.

Cathedral of Christ the King, 1111 Belknap Street, has the largest Catholic congregation in Superior. Built in 1927, the church features Spanish-influenced architecture.

Hammond Avenue Presbyterian Church, 1401 Belknap Street, was constructed in 1911. The organ was partly funded by millionaire Andrew Carnegie.

Along the Shores

Some of our favorite churches are tucked away in small towns, off the main

Insiders' Tips

Many churches are known for their special banquets and meals that are open to the public. The Twelve Holy Apostles Greek Orthodox Church, 632 E. Second, (218) 722-5957, holds an annual Greek summer barbecue. First Lutheran Church, 1100 E. Superior Street, (218) 728-3668, is known for its Advent feast of lutefisk, lefse and meatballs in early December; and the Serbian churches hold feasts (of the gastronomic kind) on Vidovdan, June 26; on Serbian "slavas;" at Easter; and at Christmas (January 7 on the Julian calendar).

drag and waiting to be discovered and appreciated for their enduring presence. Following are some of them.

Along the North Shore

Two Harbor's 1906 **Presbyterian Church**, on the corner of Third Avenue and Waterfront Drive, was built from brownstone quarried in Port Wing, Wisconsin.

Grand Marais' historic first Catholic church, **St. John's**, was built in 1895. No longer in use except for a Fourth of July weekend service, this little white, wood-frame church, just east of Grand Marais on the lake side of Minn. Highway 61, is in the old settlement of Chippewa City. For information and tours, inquire at the Cook County Historical Society in the old Keeper's House, 4 Wisconsin Street, Grand Marais.

Grand Portage's **Holy Rosary Church**, constructed of logs in 1865, is still in use today. Contact the Grand Portage Lodge, (218) 475-2401 or (800) 543-1384, for details.

Along the South Shore

St. Mary's Orthodox Church in Cornucopia near Wis. Highway 13 is an exotic onion-dome treasure on Lake Superior's shore.

Bayfield's **Christ Episcopal Church**, 125 N. Third, is an 1870 gem, with a quaint, gingerbread exterior of carpenter gothic style.

Madeline Island's white, wood-frame **St. Joseph's Catholic Church**, built in 1901, offers summer services.

Ashland's **Our Lady of the Lake Church**, 201 Lakeshore Drive E., was built in 1886. This Catholic church, formerly St. Agnes, underwent a $2 million restoration in 1995 that included the installation of an elevator, renovations to the kitchen and social room, new pews and a new heating system. In 1991 St. Agnes merged with Holy Family Catholic Church to become Our Lady of the Lake.

Who drew the line here? The Great Divide watershed marker, designating the boundary between Wisconsin's two main drainage areas, can be found on County Road D in Grandview Township. Rain falling north of this point drains to Lake Superior and then flows 2,000 miles to the Atlantic Ocean; rain falling south of this line is destined to run 1,600 miles to the Gulf of Mexico.

Inside
Beyond the Ports and Shores

Two inland areas here exert such an influence on us Lake dwellers that we've included them in this book, even though they're not near Lake Superior. One is the Hayward-Cable area in Wisconsin, beautiful farming-logging country that was transformed into a major tourism region mainly through the efforts of one man — the late, colorful Tony Weiss of Hayward, whose sheer force of character over three decades brought high-profile skiing, musical events with big-name performers, festivals and resorts into existence here.

The other area is Minnesota's Iron Range, which supplied most of the steel that helped the Allies win World War II and whose people are as strong, unprepossessing and multi-veined as its raw iron.

For people living in the Twin Ports, a daytrip to the Cable-Hayward area — to fish, golf, visit friends or to spectate or participate in one of the world-class athletic festivals — is a pleasant jaunt.

Hayward is 60 miles (about an hour's drive) from Superior and about 70 miles from Duluth. It's a lovely drive. Take U.S. Highway 2 east from Duluth to Wis. Highway 27 and head south. If you want to go directly to Hayward, continue south on Wis. Highway 27. To reach Cable, turn east on County Road N; this route winds through red and white pine forest before emerging in Drummond at U.S. Highway 63, which leads south to Cable and Hayward. If you have time, you can veer off the main route and meander along the

back roads. (Be sure and pick up a detailed map.)

Cable, with a year-round population of 817, is about 17 miles north of Hayward on U.S. Highway 63. It's a quiet, unassuming town and doesn't have the hustle and bustle of the larger Hayward, population 1,900.

The Iron Range

To most of us, "The Range" has vague boundaries. On the western side, near Grand Rapids, it blends into a world of loggers and anglers. On its north side, at Ely, it blends into the tourism economy of the Boundary Waters Canoe Area Wilderness. It fades into the lowland region of Cotton to the south and reaches Lake Superior mainly as trainloads of ore or taconite pellets, coming in for shipping.

Technically, the Range is a much bigger area, encompassing the Mesabi and Cuyuna iron ranges and reaching from Grand Portage, in the far northeast corner of Minnesota, southwest to Crosby-Ironton. But however you define its boundaries, this mining region has an essential center — a place where mines, mind-sets and culture pulse together — and that will be our focus in this section. Insiders call it the "Iron Trail."

To reach this trail, drive north to the Range from Duluth on U.S. Highway 53. You'll soon notice you're passing through a lowland area of spruce, sphagnum moss and tamaracks, which lose their needles in the fall; this is an example of the muskeg-swampy northern Minnesota wetlands. Some people find it a dismal world, but it's a rich feeder system for our lakes and rivers; it's also a source of nutrients for moose, crayfish, wild tea, wild rice and thousands of other flora and fauna that support our existence.

The little town of **Cotton** on U.S. Highway 53 hosts a big event every year: the **Minnesota State Old Time Fiddle Championship and Festival**. The festival is usually in mid-August, and fiddlers come from across the United States and Canada. In 1996, eliminations begin at 7 PM August 16 in Cotton High School, and events continue the next day through the contest finals ($6 admission) that begin at 6 PM. For more information, call (218) 482-5549.

Farther up U.S. Highway 53, you'll reach the **Laurentian Ridge**. This is a continental divide from which waters flow in three directions: to Hudson Bay and the Arctic; to Lake Superior and on to the Atlantic; and toward the Mississippi and the Gulf of Mexico. At the Minn. Highway 37/Hibbing exit is a good old restaurant with a new look — **Brantz Food and Spirits**, (218) 744-3595, where barbecued ribs in a special sauce fall off the bone.

Back on U.S. Highway 53 is what Insiders call the "Eye-Triple-R-B," the **Iron Range Resources and Rehabilitation Board**. This is a unique state agency whose mission is to restore economic vitality to the Iron Range, which has been running out of iron for several decades and been forced to diversify. One of the thrusts of this agency is to develop "heritage tourism," celebrating the ethnicity of the area. Other achievements are helping (with money and expertise) small businesses and services, and large tourist attractions, such as a successful skiing resort at Biwabik, a growing tribal casino complex at Tower and a golf

range, not yet open, near the ski resort. The agency helped create more than 2,000 jobs in 1994 and 1995. On the other side of U.S. Highway 53 is the **K&B Drive-in** where carhops attend to customers in their vehicles and pasties are on the menu.

A short way beyond K&B is **Eveleth**, your true entree to the Iron Range. It's easy to spot as you approach because of the slag heaps in the distance and the two water towers, one labeled "hot" and one "cold." Eveleth is the home of the **U.S. Hockey Hall of Fame**, (218) 744-5167, which is open for touring every day, all year, and is a must-see for hockey fans. In the main part of town, you'll see a 10-story, 6.5-ton hockey stick and a 5-foot puck — reminders that, on the Range, hockey is a way of life. The Christian brothers of Warroad, Minnesota, made the stick just the way they make their award-winning real sticks — only bigger. Nearby is **Paul's Italian Market**, 623 Garfield Street, where you can get homemade porkettas (see our "Hibbing" section later in this chapter), sausages and other Italian specialty foods. If you're in town during the summer, drive through Eveleth's residential neighborhoods; this is one of the flower-growing-est towns in the area. West of Eveleth is the **Leonidas Overlook**, the highest man-made point on the Mesabi Iron Range. You'll get a large look at what some people see as devastation and others see as a glorious panorama — the heights and depths of the old iron digs. It's open year round from 7 AM to 6 PM. If you're in the mood for golf, try the nine-hole **Eveleth Municipal Golf Course**, 8554 Old Mesabe Road, Eveleth, (218) 744-5943, or the 18-hole **Virginia Municipal Golf Course**, Ninth Street N., Virginia, (218) 741-4366.

From Eveleth, head east to Gilbert and Biwabik. Even little **Gilbert** has a curling club; the sport is popular through-

out the area. Gilbert also is home to the **Iron Range Historical Society**, (218) 749-3150, which is in an attractive brick building that formerly served as the city hall. It has displays on mining and early immigration, and a research library. It's open Monday through Wednesday from May to September. And stop by **Koshar's Sausage Kitchen**, 101 S. Broadway Street, with homemade ethnic sausages.

You'll notice as you travel that the gravel of the railroad grades, the rocks along the way and the sides of the strangely shaped hills are red, orange or purple. That's from the iron that permeates this soil. The high-grade ore, which in some places here was so soft it could be taken out with a shovel, was mined from 1890 to the mid-1900s. Since then, the focus has been on using low-grade iron through the taconite process.

Most of the ore was mined in open pits, and townsites — "locations" — were forced to move as miners tunneled through them, following the veins. Some of the oddly shaped hills you'll see throughout this area are slag heaps, the refuse from mining; other odd-shape prominences are what remain of hills that were removed as ore.

Biwabik, where one of the earliest mines was opened, now looks like no Ranger ever dreamed possible. After Giant's Ridge ski resort opened just east of town, Biwabik merchants began changing their look; now stores on the two-block main street have a Bavarian or Swiss appearance. Most successful of all the changes is City Hall, a remarkable three-story Bavarian-style building that opened in 1995. It saved the town's grocery store — Jamboree IGA, which otherwise would have closed — by making store space available (there's little sign of the usual supermarket commercialism outside). Upstairs are airy city offices, the police department and several private offices.

Biwabik hosts an annual **Weinachtfest**, a well-attended one-day event the first Saturday in December that includes sleigh rides, children's events in the park and its two gazebos, candy, craft and ethnic food stands, fireworks and, at 6 PM, the turning on of park and town Christmas lights.

East of town on Minn. Highway 135 is the **Vermilion Trail Park and Campground**, a lovely park with big pines, a modern playground for young kids, a boat launch and fishing dock. Beyond the park is **Giants Ridge Recreation Area**, (218) 865-4143, nestled among 60 acres of Superior National Forest and overlooking two lakes. Nine ski runs here accommodate novice and experienced skiers. World-class cross-country ski trails serve as an official training center for the United States Ski Association. Giants Ridge has a lovely restaurant and lodge and mountain biking and hiking trails. The rental center has skis, canoes, bikes and in-line skates. Giants Ridge is open daily year round.

Head back to U.S. Highway 53; take the cutoff at Gilbert that goes right to Virginia. Even from Highway 53, you'll have a panoramic view of the city and, far in the distance, U.S. Steel's Minntac taconite mine and processing plant. **Minntac**, (218) 749-7300, is open for free tours at 10 AM and 1 PM Friday from Memorial Day through Labor Day; wear sturdy shoes.

But if you want a really spectacular view, take the well-marked turnoff to **Mineview in the Sky**, (218) 741-2717, open daily from late May to mid-September. This is a 20-story free overlook above the 690-acre, 3-mile-long Rouchleau Mine pit

and the city of Virginia. It features mining information, local crafts and souvenirs, restrooms, a playground and a picnic area. Hospitality hosts will answer questions. About 3 million tons of ore were removed from this mine between 1898 and 1977, when it closed, and almost an equal amount of waste.

Three taconite mine/plants are also visible from this overlook. To the north is Inland Steel's Minorca facility; to the west is Minntac; on the south is Eveleth Taconite. In addition, natural ore is being mined at the Auburn pit, alongside U.S. Highway 53 as it enters Virginia.

Virginia's malled strip on the highway has motels and plenty of shopping, including a **Herberger's** (quality department store) in the Thunderbird Mall. But the main city is worth seeing, even though the downtown is fading rapidly despite valiant attempts to keep it alive. Check out **Finntown/Kaleva Hall**, (218) 749-2497, an interpretive museum where walking tours of historical sites (**B'nai Abraham Synagogue**, the **Virginia Brewery**, a Finnish sauna and others) can be arranged. Near the hall is an impressive free mineview (an enclosed dock that stretches out over a pit-cliff that edges the east side of town) and picnic area.

Some beautiful neighborhoods grace this city of 9,000; you might appreciate the five-bulb street lights on Fifth Avenue W., attractive town parks, playgrounds, tennis courts and ball fields. A public swimming beach with lifeguards and a picnic area is right across the lake from downtown at Ninth Avenue W. Virginia is home to **Virginia Regional Medical Center**, the *Mesabi Daily News* and **Mesabi Community College**.

If anyone in your party has a sweet tooth, you simply must stop downtown at **Canelake's**, 414 Chestnut Street. This

shop has been making candy in Virginia since 1905, and wonderful candy it is — chocolates, fudges, nuts, cremes and others. (You also can buy toothbrushes here! The owner's brother is a dentist.) Another sweet you should try while you're on the Range — and Virginia is as good a place as any — is "potica" (pronounced "po-TEET-sa") a rich Balkan (Slovene, Croat, Serb) sweetbread, rolled around a crushed-walnut mixture and sliced. Most bakeries in the area carry potica.

The **Virginia Heritage Museum**, (218) 741-1136, is open year round from 11 AM to 3 PM Tuesday through Saturday. Its archives chronicle Virginia's history. The **Natural Harvest Food Co-op**, 119 Chestnut Street (on Bailey's Lake downtown), is known not only for excellent local and organic produce, but also for its socially conscious buying.

One of the big area festivals is the yearly **Land of the Loon Festival** in Olcott Park in Virginia. The mid-June party features ethnic arts, crafts, music, food and a 20-foot statue of the state bird.

Continuing north from Virginia on U.S. Highway 53, you'll come to a U.S. Highway 169 turnoff. If you continue on Highway 53, you'll arrive in **Cook**, where

the best malted milks in the region are served in a cowboy-style cafe — **The Montana** — on River Street. Cook is also an access to **Sturgeon River State Forest**, **Kabetogama State Forest** and the east side of sprawling, beautiful **Lake Vermilion**.

Taking U.S. Highway 169 (which becomes a state highway in this section), however, will bring you to the other side of this large lake, and the Bois Forte Ojibwe band's **Fortune Bay Casino**. This beautiful casino, amid pine woods and not far from the lake, has 20 blackjack tables and 364 video gambling machines. The 24-hour casino, (218) 753-6400, offers about the best buffet around, which includes salmon, lamb, wild rice and lovely fruits and vegetables.

One of the most prolific wild rice lakes in ricing country is managed by the Bois Forte band on its reservation at **Nett Lake**. The long-grained rice harvested here is available at many shops in the region.

At nearby **Soudan**, visit the **Underground Mine State Park**, just off Minn. Highway 169, open daily in the summertime. This park is the site of Minnesota's last operating underground iron ore mine (most iron was mined at open pits) and is a half-mile deep. Tours are offered regularly from Memorial Day through Labor Day, and group tours off-season can be arranged by calling (218) 753-2245.

East of here is the little town of **Embarrass**, which regularly registers the coldest temperature readings in the United States outside Alaska. In 1982, its official thermometer broke at -52 degrees Fahrenheit, and in early 1996 a new one registered -59° F (although nearby Tower, Minnesota, dipped to -60° F that unusually cold winter).

Now the Iron Trail will take you back east on Minn./U.S. Highway 169 past Virginia to **Mountain Iron**. The **Wacootah Overlook** here, on a high slag heap, and the **Mountain Iron Mineview** on the north end of Mountain Avenue both offer views of the Minntac plant. Also in Mountain Iron, on Main Street, is a statue of **Leonidas Merritt**, one of the seven Merritt brothers who developed mining in Minnesota.

Near Mountain Iron, about a mile north of Minn. Highway 169, is the town of **Kinney**, which attempted good-naturedly to secede from Minnesota in the 1980s. Next on Minn. Highway 169 is the little town of **Buhl**, which brags it has the best drinking water in the world (try it; it is good). Buhl also has a lovely airy park high on a hill, a pleasant diversion if you want a break from touring. **Burton Park** has a playground, basketball and tennis courts, small deciduous trees and a picnic area. It's on S. Memorial Drive.

As you approach **Chisholm** on Highway 169, you'll see an 85-foot "iron man" (he's actually bronze, but he's a miner) standing on a hill. He signals the approach to **Ironworld Discovery Center**, (800) 372-6437, a popular theme park that describes the iron industry in an interpretive center and open mine pit overlook; celebrates the ethnic variety of the area with foods, crafts and festivals; and offers fun, such as a 31-foot tubular slide and transportation on a vintage electric trolley. The trolley takes passengers along the historic Glen Mine and an outdoor museum of vintage mining equipment, and walking trails lead visitors to a restored miner's home. Probably the most well-attended event here is the **International Polkafest**, held in late June for 1996. Ironworld is open from the end of May to early October and costs $7 for adults and $5 for children; admission is free for very young kids. Next to Ironworld is the **Iron Range Research Center Library and Archives**, (218) 254-3325, open year round, where a knowledgeable staff can help you trace your roots. The Library is a division of the IRRRB.

Ironworld isn't all there is to Chisholm, however. Take a drive into the "downtown," approaching from the east across the **Longyear Lake Bridge of Peace** where flags from all nations of the world fly in summertime. There are a couple of wonderful little shops here — **Rolling Thunder**, for example, where "Jackhammer Jimmy" and "Lotta Thunder," a married couple, run their pretty motorcycle-stuff shop at 210 W. Lake Street. A "pretty" motorcycle shop? Yes indeed. It's white, with live plants, a newly sand-blasted brick wall, a great big squeaking screen door and a back deck for sipping coffee if you belong to the Handlebar Club ($2.50 for an annual membership, and you get a cup with your name on it to hang in the back club room where Lotta also keeps her Harley). No swastikas, skulls/crossbones, nudity, daggers or foul language are allowed here. But you can listen to the blues and Elvis on the jukebox (next to Jackhammer Jimmy's 1963 Harley) and get leather motorcycle togs and enough motorcycle parts to build one from the ground up.

Doc Graham, of baseball and *Field of*

Dreams fame (played by Burt Lancaster) was from Chisholm, and the scene where Kevin Costner and James Earl Jones talk to the woman newspaper owner and look over Doc's (real) obituary was filmed in the offices of the *Chisholm Free Press*. Veda Ponikvar — the woman who actually owned the paper, was a good friend of the doctor and wrote the obituary — retired in 1996, but the paper continues in publication.

You can see photos of old Chisholm in the **Spirit of Tibros Food and Drink** establishment, 222 W. Lake Street, a smoky but attractive place with wooden booths. Down the road and across the street is **Valentini's Supper Club**, 31 W. Lake Street, a third-generation family enterprise where excellent sausages and pasta are made on the premises (neighbors buy it wholesale), and the lasagna is the best to be found. Orthodox crosses rise over modest Byzantine churches on the south side of town — one Russian, one Serbian — and the Balkan Community Center and "Slovenski dom" (Slovenian Home) are gathering centers. All this reflects the variety of second-wave immigrants that settled all over the Iron Range. (The first wave was mostly Yankees who followed on the heels of loggers to develop the mines in the late 1800s.)

Also in Chisholm, at Memorial Park at the end of Main Street, is the **Minnesota Museum of Mining**, (218) 254-5543. Here, visitors can climb aboard mining trucks, a steam locomotive and a 1910 Atlantic steam shovel, or tour replicas of an underground mine and old mining town. It's open Memorial Day through Labor Day, and admission is $3 for adults, $2 for kids and nothing for young children.

Continuing on Highway 169, you might take a short detour on Minn. Route 5 to the **Side Lake** area where you'll find lodging (a motel, a country inn and a bed and breakfast inn), a Civilian Conservation Corps campground and **McCarthy Beach State Park**, with camping, hiking and riding trails, boat rentals and a swimming beach.

U.S. Highway 169 next brings you to **Hibbing**, population 18,000, a contained, personable city of considerable grace that has nevertheless turned out some colorful characters. Iron Rangers in general are known elsewhere in the state as independent, freewheeling, sometimes cantankerous folks, with a strong practical streak coupled bewilderingly with an ability to dream grand dreams. People in Hibbing seem to have distilled those qualities. Among Hibbing notables are **Bob Dylan** nee Zimmerman, who lived in Hibbing from age 7 (he was born and spent his early years in Duluth) until going off to college at the University of Minnesota where he dropped out because he liked singing better. The Zimmermans lived at 2425 Seventh Avenue E. Then there was the beloved and unpredictable late governor **Rudy Perpich**, born into a Croatian-speaking family at a "location" just west of town, who brought business and jobs to the Range, world trade to the state and Mikhail Gorbachev and the Super Bowl to the Twin Cities. And we can't forget **Jeno Paulucci**, the man Minnesotans hate to love or vice-versa — he still has that feisty Range quality of doing things his own way — and whom northern Minnesotans tend to love with no limitations. The colorful multimillionaire (named "Employer of the Year" by President Richard M. Nixon) grew up in Hibbing as a poor boy but made good with Chun King, Jeno's Pizza and other foods. Stop by the **Paulucci Space Theatre**, (218) 262-6720, U.S. Highway 169 and E. 23rd Street, a planetarium that has daily shows June to September and special seasonal shows. Admission is $3.

Jeno came by his food inclinations naturally. Another Hibbing Italian food family are the Frabonis, whose second generation makes what we're convinced is the best sausage in the world. Fraboni's fresh garlic and hot Italian sausage has no preservatives and along with home-done hams and other sausages are distributed throughout our region. Fraboni's also was the first company to commercialize the "porketta," an Italian-seasoned pork roast that has long been common in homes hereabouts. Porketta sandwiches are standard menu fare here.

Mmmm, that makes us hungry. That means heading downtown to the **Atrium and Zimmy's Bar**, 531 E. Howard Street (lots of windows, Bob Dylan memorabilia, salads and excellent lunches and dinners); **Sportsmen's Restaurant & Taverna** next door (roast turkey, pork and beef dinners; steaks, fish and Greek lamb; and weekend salad bars); or **Lybba's Sunrise Deli** in an old theater at 2135 First Avenue E., where you can get gyros, pasties, salads, Italian foods and quick lunches.

Did you know that Hibbing is the home of **Greyhound Bus Lines** since 1914? If you want to know more, visit the **G.B. Origin Center** in the Memorial Building at Fifth Avenue and 23rd Street. Pictorial displays, hundreds of artifacts, a video show and the 1914 Hupmobile and other historic buses are here to see. The center is open Monday through Saturday from mid-May to September. Also at the Memorial Building, and open the same days, is the **Hibbing Historical Museum**, with revolving displays, topic islands, models and audiovisual displays that depict the life of the town since it was established in 1893. Admission is $1.

Hibbing also is home for well-attended stock-car races every Saturday from Memorial Day weekend through Labor Day weekend on the Hibbing Raceway at the North St. Louis County Fairgrounds. The northern county fair (St. Louis County is so big, it has two fairs; the other is in Proctor near Duluth), in late July and early August, also is at the fairgrounds, on U.S. Highway 169 near Hibbing Community College.

And if you're in town after Labor Day, stay for the **Hibbing World Class Rodeo** where more than 200 competitors from all over North America compete. In 1996, it's scheduled for late September.

Hibbing has its share of motels, but **The Kahler**, 1402 E. Howard Street (off U.S. Highway 169), is probably the best known and finest. A room for two costs about $80 (in-season rate) and includes an indoor pool, whirlpool and sauna; the handicapped-accessible hotel also has a restaurant.

This city also is home to **Hibbing Community College**, the *Daily Tribune* and **University Medical Center – Mesabi**. It has an 18-hole, private golf course — the **Mesaba Country Club** — and a nine-hole, par 34, 2657-yard municipal course, (218) 263-4720. Swimming is available at indoor pools, (218) 263-8851, and at **Kelly Lake Beach** and **Carey Lake Park**, both with lifeguards from mid-June to mid-August.

A big tourist attraction is the **Hull Rust Mahoning Mineview**, Third Avenue E., which is a National Historic Site. The world's largest open-pit mine, it already includes 2,290 acres and is growing, because the **Hibbing Taconite Company** is still at work mining on the northern perimeter. Since ore-shipping began in 1895, 1.4 billion tons of earth have been removed from this site. The mineview is open May 15 through September 30 and has information guides, mine exhibits, scenic views, a walking trail, a BMX track (where competitions are held), a park and picnic area. Hull Rust, (218) 262-4900, is free.

The National Freshwater Hall of Fame is in Hayward, Wisconsin.

We saved the best for last — two buildings that visitors simply must see. The **Hibbing High School**, built in 1920, is at Eighth Avenue E. and 21st Street. It's a magnificent Bedford stone-and-red brick building that would cost $50 million today to build. Check out the auditorium, with a full Broadway-size stage, chandeliers of Czechoslovakian cut glass and a Barton vaudeville organ (one of two left in the country). The ceilings have moldings handmade of braided horsehair and bronze, an Irish technique that is all but obsolete. **Hibbing City Hall**, at Fourth Avenue E. and 21st Street, was built a year later and modeled after Faneuil Hall in Boston. The 20th-century Georgian building features a clock tower and four floors dominated by central staircases and decorated with beautiful murals. It was placed on the National Register of Historic Places in 1981. (Side exterior doors lead to bathrooms. Nothing is written over the men's side; over the women's is engraved: "Womens Comfort Station.")

If we were to leave Hibbing and continue west, we'd arrive in **Grand Rapids** on the Upper Mississippi, birthplace of Judy Garland and one of the more attractive towns of Minnesota. But that's another trip, and we're going in the other direction — to Wisconsin.

Cable

This is vacation land for many people who stay at the numerous area resorts, many of them family-run places going back several generations, or private family cabins. Two major lakes draw scores of vacationers: Lake Namakagon, a 3,300-acre inland lake dotted with cabins and resorts, and Lake Owen, covering 1,323-acres (the western half of which is under national forest jurisdiction). Both are excellent fishing lakes.

Cable started as a railroad center and logging town in the late 1800s. Acres of white pine forest were eventually logged out by the 1920s. Today, family-owned logging operations and lumber- and wood-products companies remain active in the area. Chequamegon National Forest, for example, is logged for red pine and aspen. A fair number of corporate-owned timber plantations also are in the region.

When in Cable, don't miss the **Cable Natural History Museum**, County Road M, two blocks east of U.S. Highway 63, (715) 798-3890. You'll find traveling exhibits and a permanent collection of wildlife exhibits, including birds of prey, songbirds and mammals. The museum is known for its lively summer lecture series, field trips and outdoor workshops for adults and children. A staff naturalist can answer

Antiques and Rummage Sales

If old-timey items tickle your fancy, you'll find plenty of antiques and collectible shops in the Hayward-Cable area. Stone Lake has a community rummage sale in June, and Hayward has an antiques show in July. About 16 shops offer a variety of goods. You can pick up a map of dealers at either Cable's or Hayward's chamber of commerce. Just be sure to pay attention to hours of operation; most shops are seasonal and offer either limited hours in the winter months or are closed completely.

Some of our favorite shops include the following:

Antiquity Square, U.S. Highway 63 S. and Florida Avenue, Hayward, (715) 634- 5155. This antiques mall, housed in a two-story brick building that's on the National Register of Historic Places, has an excellent, diverse selection of pottery, glassware, primitive smalls, linens and furniture. Seasonal hours are 10 AM to 5 PM daily from May through October, and 10 AM to 4 PM Thursday through Sunday from November through April.

Sebek Antiques, a mile south on Wis. Highway 27, (715) 634-3340, is a gingerbread cottage surrounded by tall pines. It's filled with primitives, fine ceramics from R.S. Prussia and others, lamps, wicker and political collectibles. Hours are 9:30 AM to 4:30 PM Monday through Saturday from May through October, and by chance or appointment from November through April.

Honeycreek Antiques is a 2.5 mile drive south of Cable on U.S. Highway 63, (715) 798-3958. The shop specializes in primitive country furnishings. It's open year round from 10 AM to 5 PM Thursday through Tuesday.

America's Heritage Antiques, (715) 798- 4464, is in downtown Cable next to the Gallery. This tidy, well-organized shop sells classic country furniture. The last time we were there, we admired an indigo-blue Norwegian trunk and an elegant gilt-framed painting of horses. Heritage Antiques is open from May 31 to October 15, Monday through Saturday from 10 AM to 4 PM and Sunday from 11 AM to 3 PM.

The **Annual Stone Lake Community Garage Sale**, (715) 865-2826, is held the first weekend in June and includes more than 50 participants. Check out the crafts and the flea market — and be sure to grab some refreshments. Stone Lake is 15 miles south of Hayward on Wis. Highway 70.

The **Hayward Antique Show and Sale**, is an extensive display and sale put on by the Hayward Antique Club in early July. Call (715) 634-8227 for details, as the location varies.

questions and help you decide, for instance, whether you saw a timber wolf or a coyote. Museum hours are 10 AM to 4 PM Tuesday through Saturday year round; in summer, the museum is also open Sunday from 10 AM to 2 PM.

Another worthwhile stop, particularly if you're staying in the area, is the **Forest Lodge Library**, County Road M (next to the museum), (715) 798-3189. Built in 1925, the oldest log library in Wisconsin is a full-service public facility, with 6,000 books in its collection. It's a cozy place, with a stone fireplace and hardwood floors. The library offers children's programs in summer. Open year round, hours are Tuesday and Thursday from 10 AM to 5 PM; Wednesday and Friday, 2 to 5 PM; and Saturday, 10 AM to 1 PM.

The **Chequamegon National Forest**, with a total of 850,000 acres, is parceled out in big chunks throughout northwestern Wisconsin. You'll find great hiking, biking, fishing, camping and hunting in these environs. The Hayward Ranger District, Route 10, Box 50, Hayward, Wisconsin 54843, (715) 634-4821, has maps and current information on recreation trails and conditions.

We enjoy the wooded, rolling terrain of the **Rock Lake Semi-primitive Area**, 8 miles east of Cable on County Road M, for challenging mountain biking in summer and early fall and excellent cross-country skiing in winter.

The 4,446-acre **Porcupine Lake Wilderness Area** south of Grandview on County Road D offers camping, fishing and hiking opportunities; it's open for non-motorized use only.

At the 6,583-acre **Rainbow Lakes Primitive Area** northwest of Drummond, camping, hiking, cross-country skiing and fishing abound; this area is also for non-motorized use only. (See our Camping and Campgrounds and Parks and Forests chapters for more details.)

The **Namekagon River**, part of the St. Croix Wild and Scenic Riverway system, loops through northwestern Wisconsin before joining up with the St. Croix River. It's a gentle river with many access points, campsites and wilderness scenery. Maps of the river system are available at the Cable Area Visitor Center, County Road M, (800) 533-7454.

Biking and skiing competitions have put the Cable-Hayward area in the limelight. "She's doing the Birkie this year" is heard frequently in local conversation. Cable is renowned for the **American Birkebeiner** cross-country ski race, which draws 6,500 competitors from around the world. It's the largest cross-country skiing race in the United States. The Birkie, which will turn 25 years old in 1997, is held on the last Saturday of February at the Telemark Resort, 3 miles east of Cable on County Road M. It covers 55 kilometers of hilly trails and offers cash prizes. For more information, contact the American Birkebeiner office, 107 Main Street, Hayward, (715) 634-5025.

The **Chequamegon Fat Tire Festival**, held the second weekend after Labor Day, brings 2,500 cyclists to the area and draws nearly 10,000 spectators. It's the biggest off-road bicycle race in the country. Competitors ride most of the same trails used by cross-country skiers. This is a family event that's chock-full of activities, including the Short and Fat Race, a half-version of the full 40-mile race. Orienteering races, lap races and spaghetti and pancake feeds round out the fun.

Because of the popularity of the fall fat-tire race, a new competition was organized for the third weekend in May 1996. The **Cable Area Off-Road Classic**, a 20-mile race, begins at the Lakewoods Resort and finishes in downtown Cable.

For more information about either event, call the Chequamegon Area Mountain Biking Association (CAMBA) at (800) 533-7454 or write P.O. Box 141, Cable, Wisconsin 54821.

Fore!

The Cable-Hayward area is turning into a golfer's paradise where you can play a different course every day of the week — each in a wooded setting. You'll find 11 golf courses within a 30-mile radius, all of which are no more than a 30-minute drive from one another. Pick your pleasure: executive par 3, nine- or 18-hole courses, including **Forest Ridges at Lakewoods Resort**, 8 miles east on County Road M, (715)

794-2561 or (800) 255-5937; the **Hayward Golf & Tennis Club**, three blocks north of Main Street on Wittwer Street, (715) 634-2760; and **Ross' Teal Lake Lodge and Teal Wing Golf Club**, 20 miles east of Hayward on Wis. Highway 77, (715) 462-3631 or (800) 323-8325.

Hayward

Like Cable, Hayward was a logging town from the 1880s to the 1920s. It earned a reputation as a wild saloon town (note the slogan "Hurley, Hayward and Hell"). In the 1930s, Chicago gangsters frequented the area, no doubt to cool down in the area's myriad lakes and streams.

Well, Hayward still has a significant wood-products industry. As for wild nightlife, check out the **LCO Casino**, run by the Lac Courte Oreille Ojibwe band, 4 miles east of Hayward on County Road B, (800) 526-2274.

The Hayward area is well-known regionally for its more than 200 great fishing lakes — and just about as many resorts.

Don't miss the chance to stand in the open jaws of the world's largest muskellunge, a kitschy attraction amid giant fiberglass bass and panfish in a landscaped park at the **National Freshwater Fishing Hall of Fame**, Wis. Highway 27 S., Hayward, (715) 634-4440. This premier fishing area hosts plenty of fishing tournaments and events, including **Fishing Has No Boundaries**, 321 Main Street, Hayward, (715) 634-3185, a ground-breaking educational fishing event for disabled persons held in late May.

Two walleye contests are held in September, one sponsored by the Walleyes for Northwest Wisconsin Club, (715) 634-2524, and the **Hall of Fame Walleye Tournament**, sponsored by the National Fresh Water Fishing Hall of Fame, (715) 634-4440. The **Muskies Inc. Chapter Chal-**

lenge Musky Tournament, P.O. Box 609, Hayward, Wisconsin 54843, (715) 462-3563, is held in early October. And in late June, Hayward holds its **Musky Festival** (nearly 50 years old), with a parade, a queen pageant, a 10K run and plenty of food and music. Lo, the royal musky! For more information, contact the Hayward Area Chamber of Commerce, P.O. Box 726, Hayward, Wisconsin 54843, (715) 634-8662 or (800) 724-2992.

Another must-attend is the two-day **Lumberjack World Championships**, County Highway B at the Lumberjack Bowl, (715) 634-2484. This televised international competition is held in late July. Events include log-rolling, chain-saw carving, chopping and sawing and tree-climbing. You can also watch a lumberjack exposition starting in early June at **Scheers Lumberjack Shows**, (715) 634-5010.

The largest traditional powwow in the region is hosted by the Lac Courte Oreilles Ojibwe Tribe at the Lac Courte Oreille Pow-Wow grounds on County Highway B. Held in late July, the **Honor the Earth Traditional Pow-Wow**, (715) 634-8934, is a celebration for many tribes and nations. The event includes speakers, sports, games, food, dancing and singing. The tribe also holds **Ojibwe School Dress-up Pow-wows** the first Friday of every month and other powwows throughout the year. The Lac Courte Oreilles Cultural Village is open for tours from May 1 to October 31, Tuesday through Saturday, from 1 to 5 PM. Call (715) 634-5806 for more information.

While many of the resorts in the Cable-Hayward area have fine restaurants, there are some good, reasonably priced independent establishments in and near Hayward where you'll find tempting and tasty things to eat.

Historyland's Cook Shanty, a mile east of Hayward on County Road B, (715) 634-2579, serves up lumberjack-style cooking family-style — in huge servings with tin plates and tin cups. It's known for homemade doughnuts, apple pie and potato bread.

For breakfast, check out the German apple pancakes at the **Pancake House**, (715) 634-5115, part of the Lumberjack Village on Lake Hayward, where you can dine outside (weather permitting, of course).

In town, try **Karibalis Restaurant**, 212 Main Street, (715) 634-2462, a popular lunch spot for locals, serving huge burgers and great salads; or the **Moose Cafe**, 106 N. Dakota, (715) 634-1337, a mom-and-pop diner with blue-plate specials, such as meat loaf and mashed potatoes. And for great ice cream made on the premises, don't miss **West's Hayward Dairy**, 124 W. Second, (715) 634-2244, a local institution.

Hayward Bakery & Cheese, 211 Main, (715) 634-2428, is known for its heavy, European-style rounds of homemade sourdough bread. Choose from country Italian, country French, Bohemian rye, cranberry and multi-grain. And **Backroads Coffee Shop**, 123 W. Second, (715) 634-4950, the retail outlet for a nearby coffee-bean business, is the place to get exotic java brewed from fresh-roasted beans.

For accommodations, the sky's the limit. Camping is available in the national forest at **Perch Lake Campground** near Drummond and **Two Lakes Campground** on Lake Owen. (See our Camping and Campgrounds chapter.) If you seek more traditional accommodations, literally hundreds of cabins and resorts dot the area. Call or write the Hayward Lakes Resort Association, P.O. Box 1055, Hayward, Wisconsin 54843, (715) 634-4801, for assistance in choosing a lodging.

Depending on your needs and desires — fishing, watersports, golf, family-based lodging or peace and quiet — we think you'll find a suitable resort. We're im-

pressed by the group of Quiet Lakes, including Lost Land Lake, Teal Lake and Ghost Lake. The 10-mph speed limit on these lakes means water-skiing and Jet-Skiing are logistically prohibitive activities — hence the quietude.

Teal Lake has six wilderness islands, and Ghost Lake is a fairly undeveloped flowage. The resort owners and families on these lakes have prevented overcrowding by supporting some of the tightest zoning and development codes in Wisconsin.

If bed and breakfast inns are what you prefer, you'll find a handful around the Cable-Hayward area, including a few in historic homes.

The **Mustard Seed Bed & Breakfast**, 10605 California Avenue, Hayward, (715) 634-2908, is in a 1894 home, close to skiing and biking trails and Hayward's Main Street.

The **Barker Lake Country Lodge and Golf Course**, Golf Course Road, near Winter, Wisconsin, (800) 373-0365, is housed in a 1920s private estate built by Chicago gangster Joe Saltis, who shared his home with Al Capone.

And the **Spider Lake Lodge Bed and Breakfast**, County Road M, 9 miles from Cable, (715) 462-3793 or (800) 653-9472, is in a handsome 1923 log lodge, with fieldstone fireplaces and a sand beach.

Basic Resources

The following chambers of commerce are staffed by friendly people who are willing to chat with you about your travel desires in a patient and helpful way:

Hayward Area Chamber of Commerce, P.O. Box 726, Hayward, Wisconsin 54843, (715) 634-8662 or (800) 724-2992;

Cable Area Chamber of Commerce, P.O. Box 217, Cable, Wisconsin 54821, (715) 798-3833 or (800) 533-7454.

Lake Superior is considerably higher than the other Great Lakes and empties over 22-foot falls into Sault Ste. Marie's St. Marys River, which carries Superior's water into Lake Huron.

Inside
The Circle Tour

Here you are near Lake Superior. How about a trip all the way around the Lake? This lovely if lengthy journey (1,300-plus miles), which Insiders call the Lake Superior Circle Tour, will give you a sense of the vastness of the largest freshwater body on the face of the Earth. It will take you past rugged rock cliffs, alongside rolling sand dunes, to panoramic overlooks and historic sites — and, in between, small communities and a few large ones. We trace the tour through the eastern and northern sections of Lake Superior we haven't discussed elsewhere, providing highlights of natural features to see along the way and information about the towns the route passes through. As for the areas we've already covered in other chapters, we briefly revisit them with respect to the route. We urge you to check additional resources for areas or subjects of particular interest to you *before* starting the Circle Tour. To help you prepare for your travels in Ontario and Michigan's Upper Peninsula, we've provided local tourism association addresses and phone numbers (see this chapter's gray box); we also mention the tourist information centers you can stop at along the way.

Tourism Associations and Visitors Centers

(In Ontario and Michigan's Upper Peninsula)

The following associations and centers can provide information for folks who plan to travel Lake Superior Circle Tour routes in Ontario and Michigan's Upper Peninsula.

North of Superior Tourism, 11190 Victoria Avenue E., Thunder Bay, Ontario P7C 1B7, (800) 265-3951;

Thunder Bay Tourism, Terry Fox Monument stop, Thunder Bay, Ontario, (800) 667-8386;

Township of Nipigon, 25 Second St., Box 160, Nipigon, Ontario P0T 2J0, (807) 887-3135;

Rossport Tourism Association, R.R. 1.6, Onion Lake Road, Thunder Bay, Ontario P7B 6B3, (807) 345-6595;

Schreiber Tourist Information, P.O. Box 40, Schreiber, Ontario P0T 2S0, (807) 824-2711;

Tourist Information Centre, Township of Terrace Bay, P.O. Box 1207, Terrace Bay, Ontario P0T 2W0, (807) 825-9721;

Algoma-Kinniwabi Tourism, 553 Queens Street E., Sault Ste. Marie, Ontario P6A 2A3, (800) 461-6020;

Sault Convention and Visitors Bureau, 2581 I-75 Business Spur,

Sault Ste. Marie, Michigan 49783, (800) MI-SAULT;

Marquette County Convention & Visitors Bureau, 2552 U.S. Highway 41 W., Suite 300, Marquette, Michigan 49855, (800) 544-4321;

Ishpeming-Negaunee Area Chamber of Commerce, 661 Palms Avenue, Ishpeming, Michigan 49849, (906) 486-4841;

Baraga County Tourism and Recreation Association, 775 E. Broad Street, L'Anse, Michigan 49946, (906) 524-7444;

Keweenaw Tourism Council, 1197 Calumet Avenue, Calumet, Michigan 49913, (800) 338-7982;

Ontonogan County Chamber, P.O. Box 226, Ontonogan, Michigan 49943, (906) 884-4735;

Lake Gogebic Area Chamber of Commerce, P.O. Box 114, Bergland, Michigan 49910, (906) 575-3265;

West Michigan Tourist Association, 156 Fulton E., Grand Rapids, Michigan 49503, (616) 456-8557 or (800) 543-2YES;

Upper Peninsula Travel and Recreation Association, P.O. Box 400, Iron Mountain, Michigan 49801, (800) 562-7134.

Our clockwise exploration of the Lake Superior Circle Tour starts in Duluth, Minnesota, and heads northeast toward Thunder Bay, Ontario.

The drive from Duluth to Thunder Bay is approximately 200 miles. You'll take the historic Lake Superior International Highway established in 1925. Today, it enjoys the mundane designation of Minn. Highway 61 until it reaches the border of Minnesota and Ontario. At that point, its the same road with a different name —

Ont. Highway 61, which proceeds to Thunder Bay. Between Duluth and Thunder Bay, you'll pass through many wonderful coastal Minnesota towns, including Two Harbors, Tofte, Grand Marais and Grand Portage, seven state parks in Minnesota and Middle Falls Provincial Park in Ontario. All of these parks have day-use facilities, including hiking trails along rivers, some with cobblestone beaches and picnic areas. (See our Parks and Forests, Camping and Campgrounds, Restaurants, Accommodations and Attractions chapters for in-depth information on the Minnesota, Thunder Bay, Upper Peninsula and Wisconsin Circle Tour towns.)

Minnesota's North Shore

Two Harbors (population 3,650), about 20 miles north of Duluth on the Circle Tour route, is a iron ore railroad and shipping port and a booming tourist gateway to Minnesota's North Shore. Plenty of gift shops with locally made items, antiques shops and a selection of good restaurants couple with the historic waterfront, including a train museum and depot, a restored tugboat and picturesque lighthouse and views of the ore docks and ships to make this town a worthwhile stop.

Thirty miles from Two Harbors, you'll pass through the edge of **Silver Bay** (population 1,895), another taconite mining-built town and inland port. In another 28 miles, you'll come to the historic Norwegian fishing village of **Tofte** (population 100), now a booming resort town. Don't miss the great homemade breads, soups and pastries at the **CoHo Cafe** (see our Restaurants chapter). Pick up a box lunch to take on the road. From Tofte, you'll pass by **Carlton Peak**, 927 feet above Lake Superior, the tallest peak on the North Shore.

Just north of Tofte is Lutsen, a tourist haven year round. An important logging center at the turn of the century, the Lutsen area is the site of the state's first resort begun by the pioneering Nelson Family. Other hostelries accommodate both summer tourists and winter skiers. Attractions include the Lutsen Mountain ski area, an 18-hole golf course, an alpine slide, a gondola ride to the top of Moose Mountain, biking trails, the Lake and a smattering of shops, lodging facilities and restaurants. The Caribou Trail begins here.

From Lutsen, it's about 20 miles into the charming harbor town of **Grand Marais** (population 1,175). Grand Marais is the social and artistic center for the tip of the Arrowhead region. It is home to galleries and gift shops, a theater, the **Grand Marais Art Colony** (see the Arts and Culture chapter) and a diverse selection of restaurants offering everything from home-cooking to Mexican dishes, pizza, pasta and nouvelle cuisine. The **Gunflint Trail** (see the Fishing and Hunting chapter) to the **Boundary Waters Canoe Area Wilderness** (see our Fishing and Hunting chapter), begins in Grand Marais.

From Grand Marais, it's about 44 miles to the international border. Don't miss a stop at **Grand Portage National Monument** (see Attractions), about 5 miles before the border crossing. It's a reconstructed trading post set on the beautiful harbor. This spot is also a jump point for ferry service to **Isle Royale National Park** (see our Parks and Forests chapter).

Thunder Bay Area

From the border, you'll drive approximately 55 miles to the working port city of **Thunder Bay**, Ontario, nestled in the shadows of the Nor'Wester Mountains.

At Thunder Bay (population 125,000), the route changes as you take Trans-Canada Highway 11/17. Known as the expressway in Thunder Bay, this route will whiz you along the western edge of town. For a splendid view of the harbor and friendly tourist information staff, stop at the **Visitor Information Center,** (807) 983-2041, at the **Terry Fox Monument** (see our Attractions chapter). Must-see attractions in Thunder Bay include **Old Fort William,** (807) 577-8461, the largest reconstructed fur-trading fort in the world.

Ontario's North Shore

From Thunder Bay heading northeast is where we begin our full narrative on the Lake Superior Circle Tour. This route through Ontario is known for its rugged, scenic beauty and series of wonderful provincial parks. We'll focus on the natural beauty of this route and highlight a few of the towns along the way. It's a fairly remote area but with excellent roads and communities with inexpensive motels not more than a few hours apart. (If you're looking for lots of shopping, upscale resorts and urban excitement, stick to the area we've already described or head straight for Sault Ste. Marie in Ontario.)

North of Thunder Bay 40 miles, turn off Trans-Canada Highway 11/17 onto Ont. Highway 587 to enter **Sleeping Giant Provincial Park,** (807) 977-2526 (see Parks and Forests). Located on the **Sibley Peninsula,** the park is filled with rugged landscapes of marshy lowlands, rocky highlands and interior alpine lakes. Camping, hiking, mountain biking, cross-country skiing, birding and wild flower-seeking are a few of the many things to do here. There's a remote bird observatory in the park, and the habitat is recognized for its many species of orchids and ferns. (See the Camping and Campgrounds, Parks and Forests and Recreation chapters for details.)

Don't miss **Silver Islet**, a tiny former mining village tucked at the end of the Sibley Peninsula. It's filled with a row of distinctive, historic log houses. A general store and tea room is open in the summer. (See the Architecture and Historic Places chapter for details.) **Pass Lake** (population 27), which you'll pass through on Ont. Highway 587 while driving into Sleeping Giant, was settled by Danes at the turn of the century. **Karen's Kitchen Restaurant** on the Lake features great pies and salads. It's only open in the summer.

The section of the Circle Tour from Thunder Bay to Nipigon runs through Ontario's amethyst region. A crystalline form of quartz, Ontario amethyst is considered some of the most beautiful in the world. There are mines and gemstone shops in the vicinity, many of them near the town of **Pearl**, about 12 miles from the turnoff to the Sibley Peninsula. Two of our favorites are **Castagne's Rock Shop**, (807) 983-2047, and the **Ontario Gem Company** (amethyst mine), Marino Mountain Showing, 4.7 kilometers south on Dorion Amethyst Road off Trans-Canada Highway 11/17. You can pick your own stones at the mines or visit a gem shop for raw stones and jewelry. (See the related sidebar in our Attractions chapter for more information.)

Ouimet Canyon Provincial Park, (807) 977-2526, is the next provincial park on the Circle Tour. Called Canada's miniature Grand Canyon, this park's canyon walls (350 feet high and 500 feet apart) stretch for 2 miles. Hiking trails with observation points rim the edge of the canyon. The park is open for day use only. Its geology and botany make it a worthwhile side trip (about 7 miles) from the main drag, Trans-Canada Highway 11/17. (See our Parks and Forests chapter for additional information.)

The drive from Thunder Bay to Nipigon is almost 100 miles. At Nipigon, drive to the end of Ont. Highway 628 to the town of **Red Rock**. This is where the Nipigon River empties into Lake Superior. The deep red cliffs here bare the rust-colored layers of rock that typify this region. Ancient pictographs found in this region along Nipigon River cliffs are painted with red ochre, made from the hematite found in these rocks. You can see them only from boats. Call the **Nipigon Tourism Center**, (807) 887-3188, for charter information. From **Nipigon** (population 2,500), the Circle Tour takes an easterly route. The town is at the junction of Can. Highways 11 and 17. From here, the route travels past some spectacular scenery. Be sure to take advantage of the many pullover overlooks, some with picnic tables. The chains of islands that differentiate Ontario's Lake Superior Shore from Minnesota's North Shore dot the Lake's horizon. Deep, cliff-lined harbors, rocky bluffs and outcrops, dense woods of conifers and hardwoods and the relatively undeveloped shoreline, much of it Crown Land, give the area a wild, raw character. But brace yourself for the starkly contrasting visual impact of the busy pulp mills and gold-mining industry near some of the Circle Tour towns.

Nipigon was historically a logging, mining and railroad town. Tourism is the most recent addition to the economic mix. This area, on the Nipigon River between Nipigon Bay and huge Lake Nipigon, 40 miles to the north, was the site of exploration and fur-trading activities in the mid-to late 1600s, including journeys by Sieur du Lhut (Duluth's namesake) and Fr. Claude Allouez, who made a trip up the river in 1678. During construction of the Canadian Pacific Railway between 1883 and 1885, the town and the Nipigon River became significant links for bringing in supplies.

Nipigon hosts a Visitor Information Centre, open from late May to early September, at the corner of Trans-Canada Highway 11/17 and Maats Road. The **Nipigon Marina**, (807) 887-3040, offers full-service facilities to outfit boaters. Camping is available at the **Stillwater Campground**, just west of Nipigon on Trans-Canada Highway 11/17, (807) 887-3701.

St. Ignace Island, named after the founder of an order of Jesuit priests, is the second-largest island in Lake Superior. (Access to the island is by boat or sea kayak.) Call Nirivian Island Expeditions, (807) 475-6390, for charter information. It is the largest of the Nirivian island chain in Nipigon Harbor, set in a cluster of about 60 surrounding islands. Considered a sacred place (hence the island chain's Nirvana-derived name), St. Ignace Island unofficially was declared an island nation in 1978 by citizens intent on protecting its natural beauty and abundant wildlife, including woodland caribou, wolves and black bear. Seventy-five miles of hiking trails wander among more than 50 lakes, rocky shores and high bluffs in spruce forests. Visitors permits are required through the **Nirivian Embassy**, P.O. Box 508, Nipigon, Ontario P0T 2JP, (807) 887-2438.

Rossport (population 113) is approximately 70 miles from Nipigon and about 187 miles from Thunder Bay. This tiny, unpretentious seaside village is a popular stopping point for recreational sailors who take advantage of the sheltered Schreiber Channel and the lovely chain of islands, the largest of which is Wilson Island. **Halcyon Harbor Bait and Tackle**, (807) 824-2561, One Dock Street, Rossport, is a major gathering spot for visiting boaters. Operated by friendly locals, this bait and tackle shop also offers snacks, ice, showers, laundry facilities and nautical charts and arranges fishing and diving charters. Rossport began as a fishing village. Every July, Rossport hosts North America's longest-running freshwater fishing tournament, **Rossport Fishing Derby**, started in 1937. Cash prizes are given for the biggest lake trout and salmon.

The village was a stop for the Canadian Pacific Railroad. The **Rossport Inn**, (807) 824-3213, 6 Bowman Street, overlooking the Rossport Harbor, was established in 1884. It was created to serve travelers on the railway line. With seven guest rooms and a Finnish log sauna, the Rossport Inn is said to be the oldest operating hotel on Lake Superior's North Shore. The inn's restaurant is known for its fresh whitefish and trout dinners and home-baked bread. The **Serendipity Gardens Cafe and Gallery**, (807) 824-2890, 8 Main Street, features outdoor patio dining in the warm weather months. The cafe is known for its lovely perennial and herb gardens and its cozy, informal atmosphere. Its menu features Mediterranean-inspired food such as Shrimp alla Grecque, fresh lake trout and wild blueberry shortcake.

Camping is available at **Rainbow Falls Provincial Park**, (807) 824-2298, which has two campgrounds — the **Rainbow Falls Campground** and the **Rossport Campground** (with more than 130 sites, some with electric hookup). Both campgrounds have showers. Four easy hiking trails offer views of the park and surrounding area. The beaches and warm waters of **Whitesand Lake** in the park offer summer swimming. The sparkling **Rainbow Falls** on the Whitesand River can be viewed from a bridge that spans the falls.

Continuing 20 miles farther on the

Circle Tour, **Schreiber** (population 2,000), is close to several provincial parks and offers a range of service for campers. A section of the **North Superior Hiking Trail**, part of the **Voyageur Trail**, is within walking distance of town.

The **One Stop Voyageur**, (807) 824-2501, offers a motel, gas station, groceries, laundry facilities, video rentals and gift shop in one retail complex. Schreiber is known as Little Italy because of its significant Italian population. Try the **Rosie and Josie Restaurant**, 99 Ontario Street and Trans-Canada Highway 17, (807) 824-2031, for pasta and pies.

Terrace Bay (population 2,700), is 15 miles down Trans-Canada Highway 17 from Schreiber. The town takes its name from the area's series of rocky glacial deposits that descend some 325 feet to Lake Superior like a giant set of steps. The nine-hole **Aguasabon Golf Course**, (807) 825-3844, attracts players with its Lake overlooks. The 100-foot **Aguasabon Falls** can be viewed by hiking a boardwalk through a deep gorge to an observation deck at the west end of the city.

Slate Islands Provincial Park near Terrace Bay is a 14-square-mile archipelago of eight islands. Preserved for wildlife, the islands are critical habitat for the elusive woodland caribou. Nearby is **Neys Provincial Park**, (807) 229-1624, on the Coldwell Peninsula. The area served as a German prisoner-of-war camp during World War II, but little of the camp remains today. The campground here has 117 basic sites and 27 additional sites with electricity. Services include swimming and picnic areas, a boat launch, a Laundromat and interpretive programs. The beaches at Neys are interspersed with sand, pebbles and wide, flat, smooth shelves of rock that make for great picnic

spots; you'll have a great view of **Pic Island** from the protected harbor.

Marathon (population 5,500) is a booming town, teeming with the prosperity of gold mining and pulp-making. From Trans-Canada Highway 17, take Ont. Highway 626 3 miles to get into town. This is the place to stock up on groceries, gas and other essentials. And check your tires and oil here, as the next significant town on the Circle Tour, **Wawa**, is several hundred miles away through remote wilderness.

An **Information Centre and Scenic Lookout**, (807) 229-0480, is 3 miles beyond the intersection to Marathon on Trans-Canada Highway 17. At this point, the Lake Superior Circle Tour route veers away from the Lake's shore, turning inland. But you can see the rugged coast by hiking or sea kayaking in **Pukaskwa National Park**, which covers 48 miles along the shore. From Marathon, follow Trans-Canada Highway 17 for about 7 miles to Ont. Highway 627, the turnoff to Pukaskwa National Park, (807) 229-0801. Then, it's a 7.5 mile drive to the **Hattie Cove Campground and Visitor Center** at the park, (807) 229-0801. Pronounced PUCK-a-saw, the park spreads between the Pic and Pukaskwa rivers along Lake Superior's shore. The park opened to the public in 1983. The campground has 47 basic sites, 29 sites with electricity and showers, and is near the protected waters of Hattie Cove where you'll find white sand beaches and safe inlets to explore by canoe. Several day-hiking trails offer a taste of the **Coastal Trail** and a picnic area near Hattie Cove.

Continuing back on the official Circle Tour route from Marathon, it's approximately 45 miles to **White Lake Provincial Park**, (807) 822-2447. The family campground at this park offers 163 campsites, 24

The Circle Tour

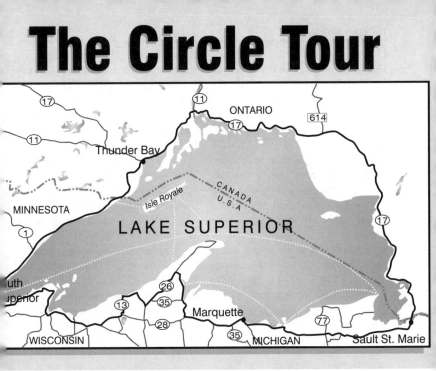

with electric hookup. Showers, a Laundromat and a boat launch and picnic area are some of the park's services. A playground for kids, interpretative services and self-guided trails are available, and swimming in the warm waters of White Lake is a popular activity. The park also is the put-in for paddlers running the White River to Lake Superior.

The next town on the route is **White River** (population 1,000). A Tourist Information Centre is at the corner of Trans-Canada Highway 17 and Elgin Street. White River is famous as the birthplace of Winnie the Pooh, the bear cub that inspired English author A.A. Milne to write his classic children's stories. As the story goes, Capt. Harry Colebourn, a Canadian soldier, bought an orphan black bear cub for $20 from a trapper in White River. He took the cub with him, naming her Winnie after his home town of Winnipeg, Ontario. When he was sent to England

to fight in World War I, Colebourn gave the cub to the London Zoo. Milne's son, Christopher Robin, became friends with the bear cub, and from that friendship came the delightful stories.

Obantanga Provincial Park, (807) 822-2592, is at the northeast cluster of a group of headwater lakes, approximately 40 miles from White River on Trans-Canada Highway 17. It has 112 regular camping sites, 20 with electricity. Backcountry campsites are available on the 32 lakes accessible by motorboat or canoe. The park services include showers, a Laundromat, picnic and swimming areas and a boat launch and boat rental.

Wawa (population 4,600), is approximately 50 miles from Obantanga Provincial Park. The town put itself on the map because of its mascot — a 28-foot-high, 4,400-pound Canada goose statue next to the **Travel Information Centre** at the intersection of Trans-Canada Highway

17 and Ont. Highway 101. Wawa is an Ojibwe term for a goose landing on water. Wawa is a major jumping-off point for hunters and anglers flying into the bush to access more than 12,000 inland wilderness lakes. Try the **Wawa Motor Inn**, 100 Mission Road, (800) 561-2278, for accommodations. The owners cater to the outdoors crowd, with 70 rooms and 18 log chalets, an indoor pool, Jacuzzi and sauna. A fun place to browse is **Young's General Store**, 111 Mission Road, (705) 856-2626. It's filled with antique general store merchandise, a famous stuffed moose and plenty of souvenirs, fresh fudge, maple syrup and Hudson Bay blankets for the shopping-starved in your group. Tackle and fishing licenses, groceries, propane and gasoline are available here.

From Wawa, the Lake Superior Circle Tour route swings back to the Lake, heading south into the immense **Lake Superior Provincial Park**. This park was founded in 1944 and features Lake Superior's wild shoreline. It is more than 900 square miles in size and covers the southern section of the **Canadian Shield**, the ancient volcanic rock of lava, basalt and granite. The park is a backpacker's paradise, with dozens of inland lakes, rivers and driftwood-strewn beaches. The park's habitat is a meeting of the transitional southern hardwood forest with the northern boreal forests. Indian pictographs at **Agawa Rock**, red ochre drawings made on the granite cliffs on Lake Superior, are a must-see. A park naturalist is on duty during summer months at the site. Hiking conditions here can be treacherous. Lake Superior Provincial Park offers three drive-in campgrounds and backcountry camping. **Agawa Bay Campground**, with showers, is right on the Lake on a driftwood beach.

Rabbit Blanket Lake Campground, with showers, has lakeside campsites, and the primitive **Crescent Lake Campground** only has hand-pumped water. All the campgrounds can be reached by calling Lake Superior Provincial Park, (705) 856-2284.

From Lake Superior Provincial Park, Trans-Canada Highway 17 continues to follow the curve of the Lake Superior Coast. The **Montreal River Harbor** (population 26), is worth a stop for its stunning canyon views where the Montreal River meets the Lake. From the Montreal River Harbor, the Circle Tour drops down to **Pancake Bay Provincial Park**, (705) 882-2209. The park is named after the voyageurs who would celebrate their proximity to fresh supplies at Sault Ste. Marie by cooking up the last of their flour in pancakes. The 2-mile white sand beach at Pancake Bay is one of the longest on Lake Superior and draws folks to dip their toes in the shallow, sun-warmed waters. Sunbathers enjoy its seclusion and warmth, protected from the lake's winds by the arms of the bay. Although small in acreage, Pancake Bay has a large campground with 338 sites, 69 with electric hookup. Showers are available.

The nearby **Batchawana Bay Provincial Park**, (807) 882-2021, set on a large lake bay, is a day-use park, perfect for swimming, sailing or sea kayaking from its sand beaches into some of the warmest water on the Lake. The **Batchawana Tourist Association**, (705) 882-2235, at the park, is a good resource for information about the area.

The town of **Batchawana Bay** (population 120), offers plenty of tourist services. Check out the **Salzburger Hof**, (705) 882-2323, a lakeshore restaurant specializing in German and Austrian food within a full resort compound. The **Whispering Pines**

Snowmobiling through Michigan yields beauty at every turn.

Photo: Michigan Travel Bureau

Resort, (705) 882-2197, at the mouth of the **Chippewa River,** has cottages and chalets and a Finnish sauna. From Batchawana, the Circle Tour route moves inland while heading southward to the **Goulais River Valley,** crossing the Goulais River into Sault Ste. Marie.

The Sault Ste. Maries

Politically and governmentally, **Sault Ste. Marie** is two cities — one in Canada, one in the United States — with the same name. Geographically and historically, this is one city that straddles the **St. Marys River,** with a foot in each country.

Either way this is a fascinating community. The **Canadian Sault Ste. Marie,** home of **Algoma Steel Corporation** and the state-of-the-art **Ontario Forestry Research Institute,** (705) 946-2981, is the larger city, the size of Duluth but on marshy flatland, and has an abundance of cultural and touring opportunities. The American Sault, population 16,000, has the locks.

The locks. They're what make Lake Superior an economic force in the world. Lake Superior is considerably higher than the other Great Lakes and empties over 22-foot falls into St. Marys River, which carries Superior's water into Lake Huron. The "Soo" locks raise and lower the ships from thaw to freeze-up. It wasn't until the first Soo locks were built in 1855 that shipping began in earnest on Lake Superior. Now, almost 100 million tons of cargo pass through the locks every year. The biggest lock, which can serve the "thousand-footer" lakers, is 1.4 miles long.

Currently, there are four busy locks on the American side and one inactive lock on the Canadian, which was damaged in the late 1980s and has yet to be repaired. The Soo Locks themselves are the main point of interest here, drawing big crowds all summer long. Along them, you can find 19th-century buildings as well as bird-watching, world-class fly fishing and picnicking opportunities. You can get a good look at them from viewing sites on either side, or ride through them aboard a tour boat which operates from June to mid-October. **Lock Tours Canada**, (705) 253-9850, and **Soo Locks Boat Tours**, (800) 432-6301, offer daytime sightseeing cruises and evening dinner cruises.

Attractions are many here: double-decker **English-style bus tours** of both towns with **Hiawathaland Tours**, (800) 387-6200; the **Spruce Haven Petting and Wildlife Zoo**, (705) 779-2423, with African pygmy goats and ibex mountain goats, ostriches and Vietnamese potbellied pigs; and many museums. **Algoma University College**, (705) 949-2301, features Old Shingwauk School, formerly a boarding school, as the centerpiece of a resource library. The campus also has a 150-year-old cemetery. The college's strengths are its music and arts programs. Tours are available by calling (705) 759-5443. **Sault College of Applied Arts and Technology**, (705) 759-2554, trains students as chefs and hotel managers, engineers and bush and commercial aviators.

Another attraction is the **Ermatinger Stone House**, 831 Queen Street E., (705) 759-5443, the oldest surviving stone house in Ontario. The home was built by a fur trader in 1814 for his Ojibwe wife and was the center of social life here. You'll find memorabilia from the fur trade inside. Tours are available.

The **Norgoma Museum Ship,** (705) 256-7447, is docked next to **Roberta Bondar Park** (named for the first woman astronaut from Canada) on Bay Street near Bruce

Street, and is open daily from June to October. This was the last cruise vessel built on the Great Lakes; it later served as an auto ferry. Marine exhibits and a snack bar are aboard.

The Canadian Sault has loads of shopping: the **Station Mall** on the waterfront, 239 Bay Street, (705) 949-7949, with 140 stores; the **Cambrian Mall**, 44 Great Northern Road, (705) 759-4900, with 70 shops; and the downtown **Queenstown** neighborhood — in the Queen, Wellington and Bruce streets area — with about 60 shops.

The 2-mile **International Bridge** carries traffic between countries and is administered by a joint **International Bridge Authority**, (906) 635-5255. Crossing the border is as simple as at Pigeon River (the Minnesota/Ontario border) — bring some ID and make sure your dog has proof of a rabies shot.

The **American Sault Ste. Marie** is the oldest town in Michigan and the third-oldest in the United States. Jacques Marquette and Claude Dablon, two French priests, built a mission here in 1668 and named it after the Virgin Mary. A walking tour of the city's five historic churches is offered on Sunday in the summertime. They're within a mile of each other, are more than 100 years old and have been restored; call (906) 632-3301. Bishop Frederic Baraga's home here was restored too, as was the oldest house in Michigan — the **John Johnston House**, built in 1793. You can see, but not tour, Baraga's home; Johnston's is open daily on July and August afternoons. At the **Tower of History**, 326 E. Portage Avenue, (906) 635-3050, visitors can go up 21 floors for a 20-mile view of the locks and two cities. It's open from mid-May to mid-October. The nearby **River of History Museum**, (906) 632-

1999, exhibits 8,000 years of the region's past. A favorite eating spot here is the **Antlers Bar**, 804 E. Portage Avenue, (906) 632-3571, where the food is good, sawdust covers the floors and voyageur gear and mounted animals decorate the walls. And a favorite lodging/dining spot is the **Ojibway Hotel**, 240 W. Portage Avenue, (800) 654-2929, a highly rated hotel with a view of the Soo Locks three blocks away. **Old Fort Brady**, which shares a site on Easter Day Avenue with **Lake Superior State University**, still has some intact buildings. The university has one of the top hockey programs in the United States and Canada.

Before you leave the Sault to head into the Upper Peninsula, pick up a free Michigan map at the **Sault Area Chamber of Commerce and Convention and Visitors Bureau**, (906) 632-3301, 2581 I-75 Business Spur (the chamber shares a parking lot with Marie's Pastries and the Skyline Motel). The **Can-Am RV Campground**, (906) 474-6122, is just off the I-75 business spur downtown.

Michigan's Upper Peninsula

The Upper Peninsula (UP) is a scenic, relatively wild area of long sandy beaches and dunes, huge rocky hills and sometimes challenging roads. It has an astounding amount of public land for an area that's half the size of Wisconsin: 24 state parks, three state forests, two national parks, three vast national forests, a national wildlife refuge and almost 100 county and local parks, many of them with camping facilities. The UP has 150 waterfalls, 4,300 inland lakes, more than 1,100 miles of Great Lakes shoreline and hundreds of miles of rivers and streams. Camping opportunities are everywhere, as are beautiful places to canoe, fish, ski, snowshoe, hike or just get out of your car

and stretch in solitude. The peninsula isn't so wild, however, that you can't find indoor lodging within an easy drive — there are cabins, bed and breakfast inns, upscale motels and budget motels (Super 8s, for example, are in Sault Ste. Marie, Munising, Marquette, Baraga, Houghton and Ironwood). If you were to drive directly from the Sault to the other end of the Upper Peninsula, you'd cover about 350 miles; the Circle Tour, however, is a meandering, mile-eating excursion.

This book is about Lake Superior, right? Does that mean you wouldn't go out of your way a bit to see lakes Michigan and Huron? We think you would; so our first off-Circle Tour jog in Michigan is a 45-minute trip south on I-75 to **St. Ignace** and the 5-mile-long **Mackinac Bridge**.

The Mackinac (pronounced MACK-i-naw) is the world's longest suspension bridge, and you can walk every foot of it on Labor Day, along with 70,000 other people. That's the only day the bridge is open to pedestrians. The other 364 days, it costs $1.50 for car and passengers to cross it to Michigan's Lower Peninsula.

There they are: **Lake Michigan** on your right and **Lake Huron** on your left. Now, let's turn around and get back to Lake Superior.

We could cut across on Mich. Highway 123 to **Paradise** on Whitefish Bay, but we'd be missing some very pretty scenery. If you want to take the longer lakeshore route, return on I-75 to Sault Ste. Marie and take the **Curley Lewis Memorial Highway** west to Brimley and around Whitefish Bay. At **Brimley**, right on the bay, is **King's Club Casino**, (906) 248-3241, run by the Bay Mills Ojibwe band and open every day. Just a mile east of Brimley, on Whitefish Bay, is **Brimley State Park**, (906) 248-3422, with fishing, swimming, a boat launch and plenty of campsites.

Nearby is the **Point Iroquois Light-house**, which since 1870 has marked the narrow channel between the shallow sandy beaches of the point and the rocky reefs of **Gros Cap** (on the Canadian side of Whitefish Bay). You can climb up into the lighthouse (72 steps) for a panoramic view of the bay and the ships passing by. The lighthouse, (906) 635-5311, is open Memorial Day through Labor Day.

Take the Lakeshore Drive around the bay to **Paradise**, a point of departure for scuba divers seeking shipwrecks to explore. Lake Superior has had more than 350 shipwrecks, many of them in this area (it's called the "Graveyard of the Great Lakes"). The *Edmund Fitzgerald*, which went down here in 1975 with all hands, was one. That wreck was immortalized in a ballad by modern-day troubadour Gordon Lightfoot. It was enormously popular in communities all around the Lake because most Great Lakes ships' hands are from our shores. If you want to know more about this and other wrecks, continue up the shore to **Whitefish Point** and the **Great Lakes Shipwreck Museum** at Whitefish Point, (906) 635-1742. It's open daily from Memorial Day to mid-October.

Another attraction here is the outdoor **Whitefish Point Bird Observatory**, (906) 492-3596, also at the end of Whitefish Point outside Paradise. You'll follow a series of boardwalks out onto delicate sand dunes near the Lake where birds linger or pass in migration. The annual hawk migration is dramatic here; every spring, they sweep up from Lower Michigan, cross White-fish Point and return in the fall.

Back at Paradise, take Mich. Highway 123 west to **Tahquamenon Falls State Park**, Michigan's largest, (906) 492-3415, with 319 campsites. Here, you'll find the magnificent **Tahquamenon Falls**, also known as "Little Niagara." The cliff over which the water drops is 48 feet high and 200 feet wide, and handi-capped-accessible overlooks are available from which to watch the plunge. Another set of falls 4 miles downriver also is part of the park.

A more touristy way to get to the falls is on the **Toonerville Trolley**, (906) 876-2311, an open narrow-gauge railway that leaves Soo Junction. Sandwiches and re-freshments can be bought on board, and the ride takes you to a riverboat that heads into the upper, more remote part of the river on a narrated cruise. Soo Junction is a few miles off Mich. Highway 28 east of Newberry.

Newberry is a good-size town with some attractions, such as the **Tahquamenon Logging Museum** on N. Mich. Highway 123, (800) 831-7292. The museum documents the rich logging his-tory of the region. The Newberry area has plenty of hotels (**Best Western**, 906-293-5114; **Comfort Inn**, 906-293-3218; **Days Inn**, 800-325-2525), bed and breakfast inns, cabins, lodges and restaurants. Try the **Two Hearted River Cafe**, by the mouth of the Two Hearted River and Lake Superior on County Road 423. A rustic camp-ground, a lodge and canoe rentals also are available here.

If you'd rather, turn west about 5 miles before Newberry on County Road 37 and follow it around northward to **Deer Park** on the wide-open Lake. Here, you'll find grand views, driftwood, agates, fishing and a year-round general store. A close look at the map might jog your literary memory: there's the village of **Two Heart**, the **Two Hearted Lakes**, the **Little Two Hearted Lakes** and the **Two Hearted River**. Yes, this the "Big Two-Hearted River" country, setting of Ernest Hemingway's freshwa-ter fishing tales. Follow unpaved County Road 58 to **Muskallonge Lake State Park**, (906) 658-3338, which has a boat launch, swimming, camping, hiking and fishing.

Continuing on County Road 58, still mostly unpaved but scenic, we come to **Grand Marais**. Michigan's Grand Marais and Minnesota's Grand Marais are like those twins raised far apart who never-theless live mirrored lives. This Grand Marais, like its counterpart far across Lake Superior, was a fishing village and has a lighthouse, docks, interesting shops and restaurants, a great pizza place and ab-sorbing places to visit. For example: the **Grand Marais Maritime Museum**, (906) 494-2669, and the **Grand Marais His-torical Museum**, alongside a bronze fish-erman that stands as a memorial to gill-net fishermen who died on the Lake. **Grand Sable Lake** and **Bayshore Park** are good spots for swimming and picnick-ing. The **Grand Sable Sand Dunes** stretch for 7 miles along the shore, and the **AuSable Point Lighthouse** is another at-traction.

If you're weary of unpaved roads, you should head down to Seney on Mich. High-way 77 from here, then pick up Mich. High-way 28 and take it into Munising. **Seney**

edges the biggest wildlife refuge east of the Mississippi — the 96,000-acre **Seney National Wildlife Refuge** in the **Great Manistique Swamp**. A visitors center here, (906) 586-9851, is open mid-May to mid-October, from which you can take guided (or unguided) walking tours and visit the displays and wildlife observation tower. Transplanted trumpeter swans have settled in this refuge.

If you're not tired of gravel roads, con-tinue on County Road 58 through the **Pictured Rocks National Lakeshore**, (906) 387-2607. It's a glorious 40 miles of sand dunes, waterfalls and sand beaches. You can get a good view of the naturally stained rocks (caused by water seeping through minerals in the high cliffs) on one of the two-hour **Pictured Rocks Boat Cruises**, (906) 387-2379, that leave from Munising between late May and mid-October. Peregrine falcons have been re-introduced in this area; watch for them while hiking or boating near the shore-line.

Munising is a lovely little city, with white birch forests, lots of sand dunes and, surrounded as it is by **Hiawatha National Forest**, with many hiking and camping opportunities. Also at Munising is the **Alger Underwater Preserve** where scuba divers can see five shipwrecks and natural un-derwater formations. For dive charters and narrated tours in a glass-bottomed boat, call **Grand Island Charters**, (906) 387-4477.

Continuing east on Mich. Highway 28 (this 40 miles has been rated one of Michigan's Top-10 scenic roads) we come to **Marquette** (population 21,000), the larg-est city on the UP and about halfway be-tween the Sault and Wisconsin. This is the home of **Northern Michigan Uni-versity**, where the Wildcats play football in the largest wooden dome in the United

States. It's also home to the **U.S. Olympic Education Center** and **Marquette General Hospital**. The city has four golf courses, 11 art galleries, three museums and plenty of antiques stores, gift shops and specialty book stores. The **Marquette Maritime Museum**, (906) 226-2006, next to the Coast Guard Station on Lakeshore Drive, has displays and exhibits of historic boats and maritime hardware, such as a Fresnel lighthouse lens. It's open daily from late May through September. The city-owned **Presque Isle Park** has the largest outdoor pool in the Midwest, a full-service marina, bicycle rentals and a 160-foot water slide; it also has great natural beauty with cliffs, sand and pebble beaches and forests.

A pleasant side trip is a visit to the little village of **Big Bay** on County Road 550 north of Marquette. The **Thunder Bay Inn** here in the Huron Mountains was owned by Henry Ford and used by his executives and was the set of the movie *Anatomy of a Murder*. The inn, (800) 732-0714, offers a shuttle service to town and is open year round. Another interesting inn here is the **Big Bay Point Lighthouse**, (906) 345-9957, the country's only bed and breakfast inn in a working lighthouse.

The first natural luge course in the United States is at **Negaunee**, west of Marquette on Mich. Highway 28. The 2,525-foot run drops 290 feet and has 29 curves (for the 29 iron ore mines that once were worked in Negaunee). National and international competitions are held here yearly from late December to early March, and spectators are welcome on weekends. Part of the run can be used by the public for practice. **Lucy Hill**, (906) 475-LUGE, is south of Negaunee on old Mich. Highway 35. If you're after trout or walleye, try **Teal Lake** in Negaunee; if you're after

iron-ore lore, visit the **Michigan Iron Industry Museum**, (906) 475-7857, 73 Forge Road, with displays, dioramas and hands-on exhibits. The museum is open daily May through October. West of **Negaunee** is **Suicide Bowl**, near **Ishpeming**, site of the International Ski Jumping competitions in February. You can climb up in the summertime for a grand view of the hills and trees below — especially fine during fall color.

The **U.S. National Ski Hall of Fame**, 610 Palms Avenue, (906) 485-6323, is in Ishpeming — skiing in the United States originated here. It honors almost 300 men and women who have enriched the sport of skiing and includes a ski library, displays of modern ski warfare, old-style and modern rope and gondola lifts, 4,000-year-old skis and other memorabilia and a gift shop. The hall is open seven days a week all year.

Going west on Mich. Highway 28, which becomes U.S. Highway 41, will bring you past three state parks and two state forests in about 75 miles, and to **Keweenaw Bay**.

The **L'Anse Indian Reservation**, at L'Anse and around the bay to Baraga, Assinins and the community of Keweenaw Bay, is home to the Keweenaw Bay Ojibwe band, (906) 353-6623, which has a casino on the west side of the bay and settlements all around it. On the east, along the Abbaye Peninsula at Pequaming, Henry Ford once had a summer home, the Bungalow, which is on the National Register of Historic Places.

West from L'Anse is the town of **Baraga**, named for the Slovenian priest who traveled widely around Lake Superior and developed an Ojibwe dictionary. A 35-foot copper statue of the "snowshoe priest" rises six stories above the **Red Rock Bluff**; it holds a 7-foot cross and 26-foot snowshoes. Motels and restaurants are available here.

Toward the end of July every year, the **Keweenaw Bay Indian Community** has its annual powwow in **Ojibwa Park**, featuring dancing and drumming, food and crafts. Call (906) 353-6623.

Baraga has several hotels, among them **Super 8**, (906) 353-7246; **Best Western**, (906) 353-7123; and **Ojibwa Resort**, 800-323-8045, which is part of the casino complex. The latter two have restaurants.

Remember that wolf-head shape of Lake Superior? Take a look at the map. The **Keweenaw Peninsula** is the wolf's mouth.

Traveling up the peninsula on U.S. Highway 41, you'll come to **Arnheim**. Turn left on the only road there, go inland 6 miles and you'll come to a National Historic Site — the **Hanka Homestead Museum**, (906) 353-7116. It's open every afternoon except Wednesday from Memorial Day to mid-October. This is a lively outdoor exhibit at a restored 1920 Finnish farm. The museum hosts a yearly "Juhannus" summer solstice celebration in June, which begins with the lighting of the Juhannus bonfire at 6 PM, followed by storytelling, a sing-along and homestead tours. Demonstrations of log cabin-building, rug-making, treadle machine work, blacksmithing and other crafts happen the next day.

This area is what Insiders call **Copper Country**, and it saw a lot of copper mining in the late 1800s and early 1900s. Continuing up the peninsula on U.S. Highway 41 will take you through mining towns and past many mine shafts, buildings and rock piles. The peninsula was the site of ancient copper digs and the first mineral rush in the United States. The last copper mine on the peninsula closed in 1968.

The city of **Houghton** (population 7,500) was born during the early mining boom. By 1865, it was a busy port and a business and cultural center. The historic downtown area has interconnected retail stores and a trolley replica that tours the streets, which are often festooned with flowers and flags. The city has boardwalks, fishing piers, a beach, a pavilion and docking as well as restaurants and motels. **Michigan Technological University** is here, whose mineralogical museum displays 30,000 rocks and gemstones from around the world. The museum is open weekdays year round. MTU was named by *U.S. News and World Report* as one of the country's top universities. During winter carnival in early February, the MTU engineering students build large snow and ice sculptures. Nearby **Hancock**, the state's northernmost city, is the home of **Suomi College**, the only Finnish college in the country. The two communities are joined

---

Point Iroquois in Michigan received its unlikely name as a result of a battle here in about 1780. A party of Iroquois fighters had come into Ojibwe country intending to hassle their enemies and camped here. But an Ojibwe war party, coincidentally passing on its way east to battle the Iroquois, discovered the intruders. The Iroquois lost the ensuing battle, and apparently that was the last time they ventured into Ojibwe territory.

Insiders' Tips

by a double-decker lift bridge that crosses the **Keweenaw Waterway**.

The **Coppertown USA Museum and Visitor Center** on Red Jacket Road in Calumet, (800) 338-7982, tells the story of copper mining, showing the tools and techniques people used in prehistory, the past century and modern times. Calumet is also home to the elegant **Calumet Theatre**, built in 1898. Douglas Fairbanks Sr., Sarah Bernhardt, Lillian Russell and John Philip Sousa all performed here. Calumet also hosts the **Calumet Copper Classic** sled-dog race (800) 338-6660 in early January.

In **Laurium**, a bed and breakfast inn is operated in the opulent Hoatson mansion. At a time when miners were making 25¢ an hour, the owner of the C & A Mining Co. built and furnished his 40-room home for $85,000. Guided tours direct you past the embossed, gilded elephant-hide wall coverings; stained glass; silver leaf ceilings; hand-carved oak grand triple staircase; 1,300-square-foot ballroom; two room-size cedar closets; and a turntable in the two-story carriage house. Tours happen daily from June to October. Call (906) 337-2549. The inn is open for lodging year round.

Copper Harbor, at the tip of the peninsula, is a quaint community in a picturesque area. If you're hungry, stop at the **Pines** on U.S. Highway 41, (906) 289-4222, for family-style cooking and famous cinnamon rolls, or the **Brockway Inn**, on Mich. Highway 26 at the base of **Brockway Mountain**, (906) 289-4588. Or take your sweet tooth to the **Last Frontier Gift Shop**, (906) 289-4212, where you can enjoy homemade fudge, fresh muffins or the cones and sundaes at the soda fountain (you can get gifts made of copper and agates here, too). Lodging is available at the **King Copper Motel**, a

mile from Fort Wilkins next to the Isle Royale boat dock, (906) 289-4214; **Fort William State Park**, which has 165 campsites with electric hookups and showers, (906) 289-4215; among others. You can take a boat tour to the **Lighthouse Point** to see the oldest operating fully restored lighthouse on the Lake. Or visit old **Fort Wilkins**, down along the water in town, where 12 original structures built in 1844 are still standing. The **Fort Wilkins Historic Complex**, (906) 289-4215, is open daily from mid-May to mid-October and features costumed employees acting the parts of soldiers, wives and officers of the period. The park has 165 modern campsites and a boat launch.

Isle Royale (see the related sidebar in our Parks and Forests chapter) — the wolf's eye in Lake Superior's wolf-head shape — is more than twice as far from Michigan than from Minnesota's shore, but you can get there from here too — on **Isle Royale Ferry Service**, (906) 289-4437, down at the dock.

Take Mich. Highway 26 toward **Eagle Harbor**, not forgetting to drive up **Brockway Mountain**. It has several scenic overlooks, but the one at the top, 700 feet above the Lake, is stupendous. You can see far along the Keweenaw Peninsula as well as the Lake and freighters in the distance; if the weather is right, you can see Isle Royale, 50 miles away. The 7-mile drive up the mountain was voted in 1980 the most scenic drive in the state — not just the UP — by MDOT engineers; it's the highest above-sea-level drive between the Rockies and the Alleghenies. This is another good lookout for migrating hawks as well as eagles. Back down at the harbor, do some beachcombing for greenstones, driftwood and agates.

Suicide Hill Ski Jump near Ishpeming, Michigan, is the site of the International Ski Jumping competitions in February.

Continue south on Mich. Highway 26; your destination is **Ontonagon** and Silver City on the Lake. Both are in Ontonagon County, which is home to the beautiful **Porcupine Mountains Wilderness State Park** — 92 square miles of virgin forest and rugged Lake Superior shoreline. The county **Historical Museum**, 422 River Street, (906) 884-6165, has a replica of the famous **Ontonagon Boulder** (a 6,000-pound chunk of copper that was removed from the area in 1843) and mining exhibits. Take Mich. Highway 64 to Silver City and then continue on Mich. Highway 107 into the Porcupine Mountains Wilderness. The park's visitors center, (906) 885-5275, is on S. Boundary Road, just off the highway. West of park headquarters is the **Porcupine Mountain Ski Area**, (906) 885-5275,

a big, popular complex of 14 ski runs overlooking Lake Superior. Take the park road to **Lake of the Clouds** for a panoramic view of the lake and forest.

Returning to **Silver City**, head south on Mich. Highway 64 to **White Pine**, where the only remaining copper mine on the Upper Peninsula is still in operation. This mine produces the purest copper in the world. **Copper Range Corp.**, which owns White Pine, was beginning an experiment in mid-1996 to extract ore by filling the underground mine cavities — about 6 square miles — with a sulfuric acid solution and leaching out the ore. The long-term (24-year) project would pour between 7 billion and 11 billion gallons of this acid solution into the cavity. Because the site is only a few miles from Lake Superior, and also because railroad carloads of 100 percent sulfuric acid would be hauled along the South Shore, the project is attracting the attention of citizens concerned about the environmental impact to the Lake and the region.

Continuing on Mich. Highway 64 to **Bergland**, you'll reach **Lake Gogebic**, the largest inland lake on the UP and a hotspot for fishing (northern pike, bass and jumbo perch), snowmobiling, skiing and hiking. The lake is tucked in the million-acre **Ottawa National Forest**, (906) 932-1330; **Lake Gogebic State Park**, (906) 842-3341, is on the west side. It's the best area on the UP to spot eagles and their nests. Fine dining and lodging are nearby. The **Lake Gogebic Motel**, (906) 575-3262, is along Mich. Highway 28 in **Bergland**, a block from the Lake. The **Gogebic Lodge**, along the west side of the Lake on Mich. Highway 64, (906) 842-3321, also has dining. The park itself has 165 camping sites with electric hookups and showers.

From Lake Gogebic, take Mich. Highway 28 to **Wakefield** where we'll pick up U.S. Highway 2 for the final leg of the tour. The highway travels right through Big Snow ski country: **Indianhead Ski Hill**, (906) 229-5181, in Wakefield; the **Blackjack**, (906) 229-5115, and **Big Powderhorn**, (906) 932-4838, ski hills between Bessemer and Ironwood; **Mt. Zion Ski Hill**, (906) 932-4231, in Ironwood; and **Whitecap**, (715) 561-2227, just across the state line in Montreal,

Wisconsin. All except Mt. Zion have food, lodging and high-gear skiing.

Wisconsin's South Shore

U.S. Highway 2 continues through Wisconsin along 30 miles of high farm country and down into the **Bad River Reservation** at **New Odanah**. The **Bad River Casino**, (715) 682-7121, here was being expanded in early 1996. The road continues into **Ashland**, Wisconsin, an attractive town with some good restaurants, among them **The Depot**, 400 Third Avenue W., (715) 682-4200; and two in the **Hotel Chequamegon**, 101 Lake Shore Drive, (715) 682-9095 — **Fifield's** and **Molly Cooper's**. (See our Restaurants chapter for details.) Ashland was established in the late 1800s as a major shipping port. Turn north on Wis. Highway 13 just east of Ashland to follow the Lake into Washburn and Bayfield. Everyone loves **Bayfield** for its beauty and charm, and it's a good place to stop for a bite to eat because the food is good everywhere. For a summer side trip, leave your car at **City Dock** and walk onto the **Madeline Island ferry** for a 20-minute trip to **LaPointe**. You can visit the excellent and recently remodeled **Madeline Island Museum**, (715) 747-2415, which faces the boat dock; some gift shops; and a lounge near the Lake before catching the ferry back to Bayfield.

Bayfield is the center of the **Apostle Islands National Lakeshore**, which includes most of the islands and a stretch of the mainland. Visit the lakeshore office, 415 Washburn Avenue, (715) 779-3397, for information on this beautiful park. Like other towns along Wis. Highway 13, Bayfield was a fishing village for decades and still has some working commercial fishermen, so fresh and smoked fish is easy to find here.

North of Bayfield 3 miles is the **Red Cliff Reservation**. Its **Isle Vista Casino**, (800) 226-8478, features video gambling, food and weekend entertainment, and the reservation has a popular Fourth of July powwow every year. Curving west on Wis. Highway 13, you'll pass through the little towns of **Cornucopia** (strengthening as a tourist town), **Herbster** (waning) and **Port Wing** (holding its own). "Corny's" public harbor has a string of shops, all in old fishing buildings: books, cards and gifts; furniture and tools; **River's End** gifts, gallery antiques and organic produce; teas, handwoven goods, baskets and souvenirs. **Port Wing Pottery**, (715) 774-3222, also right on Wis. Highway 13, is in an old church and is the site of the potter's workshop and pottery-wood-working gift shop. You can't see the sandy beach areas of Herbster and Port Wing from the highway, but they're worth the brief detour, with their settling old fishing boats and fish houses and easy access to the water.

Port Wing is about the halfway point between Bayfield and Superior, and the rest of the route takes you away from the Lake through relatively uneventful country — except for attractive dips past the Brule and Amnicon rivers and a surprising sight about a half-mile past the Amnicon, on the left: a northern European windmill. It's no longer in use, but the descendants of the man who built it in 1904 (to mill flour) are preserving it.

Back to the Twin Ports

At the junction Wis. Highway 13 and U.S. Highway 2, turn north on Highway 2. It will take you into flat **Superior** and hilly **Duluth** — and complete your Circle Tour.

Index of Advertisers

Index

Army Navy Store 412
Arrowhead Area Agency on Aging 435
Arrowhead Builders Association 426, 428
Arrowhead Builders Expo 301
Arrowhead Child Care Resource and
        Referral 464
Arrowhead Chorale 321
Art Dock 327, 396
Arthur E. King Manor 438
Arthur's Mens Formal Wear 396
Arthur's Nightclub 102
Arts and Culture 319
Ashland Airport 48
Ashland Arms 444
Ashland Chamber of Commerce 430
Ashland County Nurse 461
Ashland Folk Festival 301
Ashland Motel 136
Ashland Northern Merchandise 413
Ashland Produce 413
Ashland Public Schools 466
Aspenwood Condominiums 440
Athlete's Foot 402, 416
Athletic Shop 413
Atrium and Zimmy's Bar 504
Attractions 357
ATV Trails 147
Augustino's 58
Austin Miller Studio 334
Austin-Jarrow 394

B

B. Dalton Bookseller 392, 402
B.J.'s Den 416
Backroads Coffee Shop 509
Bad River Casino 106
Bad River Health Clinic 457
Bagley and Company Jewelers 394
Bait and Tackle Shops 200
Baraga County Tourism and Recreation
        Association 512
Barbo's Columbia Clothing 394
Barker Lake Country Lodge and Golf
        Course 509
Barkers Island 365, 383
Barkers Island Inn 64, 117
Barkers Island Townhomes 440
Barnes & Noble 391
Barros House 442
Baseball 282
Baskets by Marie 418
Bay Antiques 420
Bay Area Health Center 456
Bay Area Rural Transit 46
Bay City Cycles 412

Bay Days 309
Bay Front Inn 131
Bay Produce Company 402
Bay Ridge 445
Bay Terrace 445
Bay Theatre 102
Bay Tower 445
Bay Walk Inn Best Western 117
Bayfield Apple Company 411
Bayfield Apple Festival 315
Bayfield Artists Guild 334
Bayfield Chamber of Commerce 430
Bayfield County Nurse 461
Bayfield Inn 75, 132
Bayfield on the Lake 445
Bayfield Pool and Recreation
        Facility 159, 388
Bayfield Public Library 379
Bayfield Public Schools 467
Bayfield, Wis. 347
Bayfront Blues Festival 313
Bayview Terrace 442
Baywood Place Bed & Breakfast 132
Beach Resort 131
Bear Shoe Works 402
Bear Track Inn 251
Bear Track Outfitters
        202, 213, 226, 228, 407
Bear Track's Bally Creek Camp 250
Bear Trap Trading Post 413
Beargrease Sled Dog
        Marathon 290, 293, 297
Beaser Park 288
Beaver 418
Beaver Bay Agate Shop and Museum 405
Beaver Bay Sport Shop 405
Beaver River Christian School 471
Belknap Plaza 402
Bellows, The 58
Ben Franklin 402, 405, 414
Benetton-on-the-Lake 395
Bennett's Bar & Grill 59
Berger Hardware 400
Bergquist Scandinavian Gift Shop 398, 400
Bessemer Pumpkin Fest 315
Bessemer USSA Snowmobile
        Olympus 294, 317
Best Buy 392
Best Western Cliff Dweller Motel 125
Best Western Crossroads Motor Inn 143
Best Western Holiday House 136
Best Western NorWester Resort Hotel 144
Best Western Powdermill Inn 138
Bethany Crisis Nursery 465
Beth's Fudge & Gifts 407

INSIDERS' GUIDE ORDER FORM

Complete the form below and mail to: The Insiders' Guides Inc., P.O. Box 2057, Manteo, NC 27954 or call **(800) 765-2665** to charge to your VISA or MC.

Name: _____

Address: _____

_____

City: _____ State _____ Zip _____

Insiders' Guide® Titles

Qty.	The Insiders' Guide® to ...	$$$	Amount	Qty.	The Insiders' Guide® to ...	$$$	Amount
	Atlanta	$14.95			Richmond	$14.95	
	Boca Raton & The Palm Beaches	$14.95			Sarasota/Bradenton	$14.95	
	Boulder	$14.95			Tampa Bay	$14.95	
	Branson	$14.95			The Twin Cities	$14.95	
	Cape Cod	$14.95			Virginia's Blue Ridge	$17.95	
	Charleston, SC	$17.95			Virginia's Chesapeake Bay	$14.95	
	Cincinnati	$14.95			Washington, D.C.	$14.95	
	Civil War Sites in the Eastern Theater	$14.95			Wichita	$14.95	
	Denver	$14.95			Williamsburg	$14.95	
	Florida's Great Northwest	$14.95			Wilmington, NC	$14.95	
	The Florida Keys	$17.95					
	Golf in the Carolinas	$14.95					
	Indianapolis	$14.95					
	The Lake Superior Region	$14.95					
	Lexington	$14.95		Subtotal			
	Louisville	$14.95		Add $4 S&H per book			
	Mississippi	$14.95		NC residents +6% sales tax			
	Myrtle Beach	$14.95		**TOTAL**			
	North Carolina's Central Coast	$14.95					
	North Carolina's Mountains	$17.95					
	North Carolina's Outer Banks	$17.95		Payment in full (check or money order)			
	The Pocono Mountains	$14.95		must accompany this order form.			
	Relocation	$14.95		Please allow 2 weeks for delivery.			

Who you are and what you think are important to us.

Fill out this coupon and we'll give you an Insiders' Guide® for half price!

Which book(s) did you buy? _____

Where do you live? _____

In what city did you buy your book? _____

Did you find out about this book and the series through the World Wide Web? _____

Did you use any of our online services? _____

Where did you buy your book? ❑ catalog ❑ bookstore ❑ newspaper ad

❑ retail shop ❑ other _____

How often do you travel? ❑ yearly ❑ bi-annually ❑ quarterly ❑ quarterly +

Did you buy your book because you were ❑ moving ❑ vacationing

❑ wanted to know more about your home town ❑ other_____

_____

Will the book be used by ❑ family ❑ couple ❑ individual ❑ group

What is you annual household income? ❑ under $25,000 ❑ $25,000-$35,000

❑ $35,000-$50,000 ❑ $50,000-$75,000 ❑ over $75,000

How old are you? ❑ under 25 ❑ 25-35 ❑ 36-50 ❑ 51-65 ❑ over 65

Did you use the book before you left for your destination? ❑ yes ❑ no

Did you use the book while at your destination? ❑ yes ❑ no

On average per month, how many times do you refer to your book? ❑ 1-3 ❑ 4-7

❑ 8-11 ❑ 12-15 ❑ 16 and up

On average, how many other people use your book? ❑ no others ❑ 1 ❑ 2

❑ 3 ❑ 4 or more

Is there anything you would like to tell us about Insiders' Guides? _____

_____

_____

Name _____ Address_____

City _____ State_____ Zip_____

We'll send you a voucher for ½ off any Insiders' Guide© and a list of available titles as soon as we get this card from you. Thanks for being an Insider!

BUSINESS REPLY MAIL

FIRST-CLASS MAIL   PERMIT NO. 20   MANTEO, NC

POSTAGE WILL BE PAID BY ADDRESSEE

THE INSIDERS' GUIDES INC.
PO BOX 2057
MANTEO NC 27954-9906